# Brilliant
## Microsoft®
# Windows 8.1

## Steve Johnson

**Perspection, Inc.**

Brilliant Windows 8.1

0789752808                          -

Que Corporation              2014

**PEARSON**

Harlow, England • London • New York • Boston • San Francisco • Toronto • Sydney • Auckland • Singapore • Hong Kong
Tokyo • Seoul • Taipei • New Delhi • Cape Town • São Paulo • Mexico City • Madrid • Amsterdam • Munich • Paris • Milan

**Pearson E**
Edinburgh Gate
Harlow
Essex CM20 2JE
England

and Associated Companies throughout the world

*Visit us on the World Wide Web at:*
www.pearson.com/uk

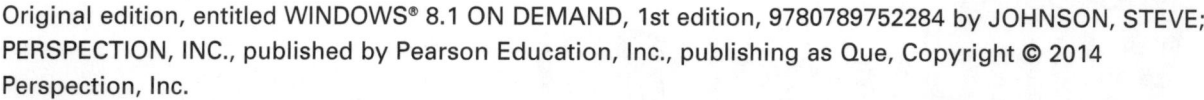

Original edition, entitled WINDOWS® 8.1 ON DEMAND, 1st edition, 9780789752284 by JOHNSON, STEVE; PERSPECTION, INC., published by Pearson Education, Inc., publishing as Que, Copyright © 2014 Perspection, Inc.

This UK edition published by PEARSON EDUCATION LTD, Copyright © 2014

This edition is manufactured in the USA and available for sale only in the United Kingdom, Europe, the Middle East, and Africa.

The right of Steve Johnson to be identified as the author of this work has been asserted by him in accordance with the Copyright, Designs and Patents Act 1988.

ISBN: 978-0-7897-5280-2

**British Library Cataloguing-in-Publication Data**
A catalogue record for this book is available from the British Library

10 9 8 7 6 5 4 3 2 1
17 16 15 14 13

Printed and bound in the United States of America

# Brilliant Guides

## What you need to know and how to do it

When you're working on your computer and come up against a problem that you're unsure how to solve, or want to accomplish something in an application that you aren't sure how to do, where do you look?? Manuals and traditional training guides are usually too big and unwieldy and are intended to be used as an end-to-end training resource, making it hard to get to the info you need right away without having to wade through pages of background information that you just don't need at that moment – and helplines are rarely that helpful!

*Brilliant* guides have been developed to allow you to find the info you need easily and without fuss and guide you through the task using a highly visual, step-by-step approach – providing exactly what you need to know when you need it!!

*Brilliant* guides provide the quick easy-to-access information that you need, using a detailed index and troubleshooting guide to help you find exactly what you need to know, and then presenting each task on one or two pages. Numbered steps then guide you through each task or problem, using numerous screenshots to illustrate each step. Added features include "See Also…" boxes that point you to related tasks and information in the book, whilst "Did you know?…" sections alert you to relevant expert tips, tricks and advice to further expand your skills and knowledge.

In addition to covering all major office applications, and related computing subjects, the *Brilliant* series also contains titles that will help you in every aspect of your working life, such as writing the perfect CV, answering the toughest interview questions and moving on in your career.

*Brilliant* guides are the light at the end of the tunnel when you are faced with any minor or major task!

# a

# Acknowledgments

## Perspection, Inc.

*Brilliant Microsoft Windows 8.1* has been created by the professional trainers and writers at Perspection, Inc. to the standards you've come to expect from Que publishing. Together, we are pleased to present this training book.

Perspection, Inc. is a software training company committed to providing information and training to help people use software more effectively in order to communicate, make decisions, and solve problems. Perspection writes and produces software training books, and develops multimedia and web-based training. Since 1991, we have written more than 150 computer books, with several bestsellers to our credit, and sold over 5 million books.

This book incorporates Perspection's training expertise to ensure that you'll receive the maximum return on your time. You'll focus on the tasks and skills that increase productivity while working at your own pace and convenience.

We invite you to visit the Perspection web site at:

*www.perspection.com*

## Acknowledgments

The task of creating any book requires the talents of many hard-working people pulling together to meet impossible deadlines and untold stresses. We'd like to thank the outstanding team responsible for making this book possible: the writer, Steve Johnson; the production editor, James Teyler; the proofreader, Beth Teyler; and the indexer, Kristina Zeller.

At Que publishing, we'd like to thank Greg Wiegand and Loretta Yates for the opportunity to undertake this project, Cindy Teeters for administrative support, and Sandra Schroeder for your production expertise and support.

*Perspection*

## About The Author

**Steve Johnson** has written more than 90 books on a variety of computer software, including Adobe Photoshop CC, Adobe InDesign CC, Adobe Illustrator CC, Adobe Dreamweaver CS6, Adobe Edge Animate, Adobe Flash Professional CS5, Microsoft Windows 8, Microsoft Office 2013 and 2010, Microsoft SharePoint 2013, Microsoft Office 2008 for the Macintosh, and Apple OS X Mavericks. In 1991, after working for Apple Computer and Microsoft, Steve founded Perspection, Inc., which writes and produces software training. When he is not staying up late writing, he enjoys coaching baseball, playing golf, gardening, and spending time with his wife, Holly, and three children, JP, Brett, and Hannah. Steve and his family live in Northern California, but can also be found visiting family all over the western United States.

# Contents

**5** **Working with Contacts and Calendars**        **135**

# Introduction

Welcome to *Brilliant Microsoft Windows 8.1*, a visual quick reference book that shows you how to work efficiently with Windows 8.1. This book provides complete coverage of basic to advanced Windows skills.

## How This Book Works

You don't have to read this book in any particular order. We've designed the book so that you can jump in, get the information you need, and jump out. However, the book does follow a logical progression from simple tasks to more complex ones. Each task is presented on no more than two facing pages, which lets you focus on a single task without having to turn the page. To find the information that you need, just look up the task in the table of contents or index, and turn to the page listed. Read the task introduction, follow the step-by-step instructions in the left column along with screen illustrations in the right column, and you're done.

## What's New

If you're searching for what's new in Windows 8.1, just look for the icon: **New!**. The new icon appears in the table of contents and throughout this book so you can quickly and easily identify a new or improved feature in Windows 8.1. A complete description of each new feature appears in the New Features guide in the back of this book.

## Keyboard Shortcuts

Most menu commands have a keyboard equivalent, such as Ctrl+P, as a quicker alternative to using the mouse. A complete list of keyboard shortcuts is available on the web at *www.perspection.com*.

## How You'll Learn

**How This Book Works**

**What's New**

**Keyboard Shortcuts**

**Step-by-Step Instructions**

**Real World Examples**

**Workshops**

**Get More on the Web**

# Step-by-Step Instructions

This book provides concise step-by-step instructions that show you "how" to accomplish a task. Each set of instructions includes illustrations that directly correspond to the easy-to-read steps. Also included in the text are time-savers, tables, and sidebars to help you work more efficiently or to teach you more in-depth information. A "Did You Know?" provides tips and techniques to help you work smarter, while a "See Also" leads you to other parts of the book containing related information about the task.

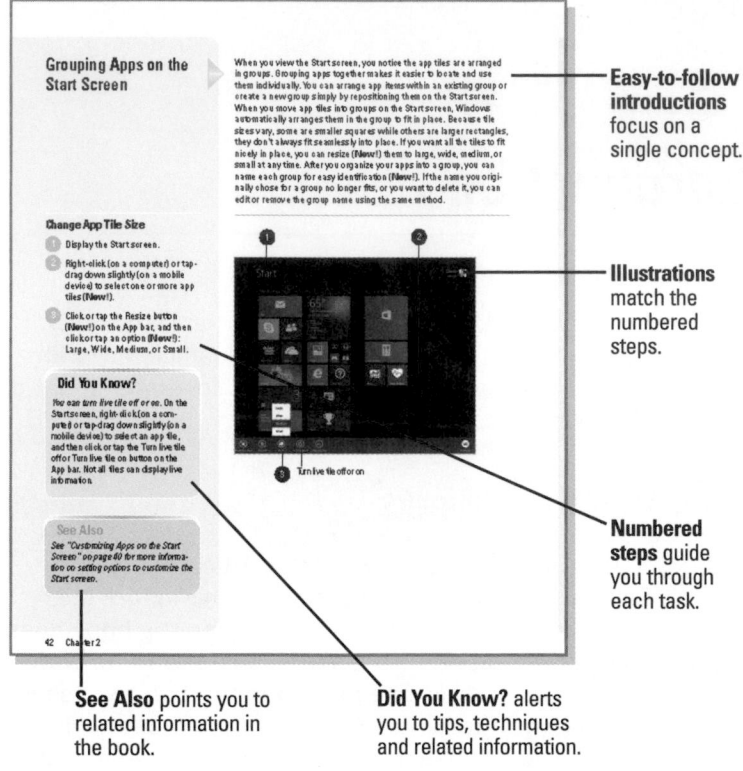

**Easy-to-follow introductions** focus on a single concept.

**Illustrations** match the numbered steps.

**Numbered steps** guide you through each task.

**See Also** points you to related information in the book.

**Did You Know?** alerts you to tips, techniques and related information.

# Real World Examples

This book uses real world examples files to give you a context in which to use the task. By using the example files, you won't waste time looking for or creating sample files. You get a start file and a result file, so you can compare your work. Not every topic needs an example file, such as changing options, so we provide a complete list of the example files used through out the book. The example files that you need for project tasks along with a complete file list are available on the web at *www.perspection.com*.

**Real world examples** help you apply what you've learned to other tasks.

## Workshops

This book shows you how to put together the individual step-by-step tasks into in-depth projects with the Workshop. You start each project with a sample file, work through the steps, and then compare your results with a project results file at the end. The Workshop projects and associated files are available on the web at *www.perspection.com.*

The **Workshops** walks you through in-depth projects to help you put Windows 8.1 to work.

## Get More on the Web

In addition to the information in this book, you can also get more information on the web to help you get up to speed faster with Windows 8.1. Some of the information includes:

### Transition Helpers

◆ **Only New Features.**
Download and print the new feature tasks as a quick and easy guide.

### Productivity Tools

◆ **Keyboard Shortcuts.**
Download a list of keyboard shortcuts to learn faster ways to get the job done.

**Additional content** is available on the web. You can download a document of keyboard shortcuts.

## More Content

◆ **Photographs.** Download photographs and other graphics to use in your Office documents.

◆ **More Content.** Download new content developed after publication.

You can access these additional resources on the web at *www.perspection.com.*

Download and use **Photographs** to help you add impact to your documents.

# Getting Started with Windows 8.1

## Introduction

Microsoft Windows 8.1 introduces a breakthrough user experience that is designed to help you intuitively view, find, and organize information on your PC whether it's a desktop computer, tablet, or mobile device. Windows 8.1 delivers better personal productivity and digital entertainment with a new touch-based interface to go along with the traditional Windows desktop. Before you get started with Windows 8.1, check out the new features, which includes a lock screen for security, home screen with tiles to display information and start apps, broad range of standard full-screen apps, the Windows Store to purchase and update apps, and the SkyDrive to sync data to the cloud, as well as improvements to the Desktop, File Explorer, Control Panel, and Task Manager. A complete description of each new feature appears in the New Features guide in the back of this book.

Microsoft Windows 8.1 is an **operating system**, a program that controls the basic operation of your PC and the programs you run. A **program**, also known as an **application** or **app** (for short), is task-oriented software you use to accomplish a specific task, such as word processing, performing calculations, or managing files on your device. Windows 8.1 displays programs on your device within windows (thus the name of the operating system). A **window** can contain an app, the contents of a file, or other usable data. A **file** is a collection of information (such as a letter or list of addresses) that has a unique name, distinguishing it from other files. Windows 8.1 uses tiles, icons, and thumbnails to provide information or meaningful symbols for the items they represent. This use of tiles, icons, thumbnails, and windows is called a **graphical user interface** (**GUI**, pronounced "gooey"), meaning that you ("user") interact ("interface") with your device through the use of graphics.

## What You'll Do

**Introduce Windows 8.1**

**Start Windows 8.1**

**Use the Mouse or Gestures**

**Explore the Start Screen**

**Use the Start Bar**

**Use the Charms Bar**

**Explore the Windows Desktop**

**Use the Desktop Taskbar**

**Manage Desktop Windows**

**Use Tabs, Menus, and Toolbars**

**Choose Dialog Box Options**

**Use Windows Help and Support**

**Switch Users**

**Power Down**

# Introducing Windows 8.1

## Windows 8.1 Editions

Windows 8.1 comes in four editions: the Windows 8.1 Edition for consumers; the Windows 8.1 Professional Edition for business and power users; the Windows 8.1 Enterprise Edition for corporations, and the Windows 8.1 RT Edition for touch-optimized devices.

The **Windows 8.1** Edition provides a basic secure entry point for using Windows 8.1 with PC computers and tablets powered by x86 processors (both 32 and 64 bit).

The **Windows 8.1 Professional** Edition adds to the basic Windows 8.1 experience by providing features for encryption, virtualization, PC computer management, and domain and remote desktop connectivity. Windows Media Center is also available as a media pack.

The **Windows 8.1 Enterprise** Edition is for large corporations with advanced data protection, compatibility, and international support needs.

The **Windows 8.1 RT** Edition provides an entry point for using Windows 8.1 on PC computers, tablets, and mobile phones with ARM (Advanced RISC Machines) or WOA (Windows on ARM) processors. Windows RT will include touch-optimized desktop version of Microsoft Word, Excel, PowerPoint, and OneNote.

If you live in an European Economic Area, the above editions have an N (**New!**), which doesn't include media apps—Windows Media Player, Camera, Music, and Video; you need to download them from the Microsoft web site or other ones from a third-party.

## Windows 8.1 User Experience

Windows 8.1 provides two distinct user interface experiences: one using touch gestures and the other using a keyboard and mouse. Both offer a new and intuitive navigation experience that help you more easily find, organize, and use your apps and files on PC computers, tablets, and mobile phones.

The touch gesture experience provides controls for touch screens or trackpads to work with and navigate within Windows and applications. For example, you can use a single-finger slide to move the mouse cursor or a single or two finder tap or double tap to click or double-click at the cursor location. You can also use a two finder slide to scroll horizontally or vertically, or a two finger pinch in or out or a three finder slide up or down to zoom in or out.

In addition to simulating mouse features, you can also use swipe gestures to navigate and display commands. For example, you can swipe in from the right edge to toggle the Charms bar, swipe down from the top edge to toggle the app commands, or swipe in from the left edge to switch to the last app.

The keyboard and mouse experience provides a traditional way to use Windows 8.1 on a PC computer. Windows 8.1 comes with keyboard shortcuts to help you navigate the operating system on a PC. For example, you can press Ctrl+Plus Sign to zoom in or Ctrl+Minus Sign to zoom out, or press Win+D to open the desktop. The Win key appears on most keyboards in the lower-left corner as ⊞.

The key to using a mouse with Windows 8.1 is to understand how to use the corners and edges of the screen. Pointing to a corner on a PC computer displays a bar, icon, button, or thumbnail that you can use to perform operations. For example, you can point to the upper- or lower-right corner to display the Charms bar, or point to the upper- or lower left corner to display the Start bar.

# Starting Windows 8.1

Windows 8.1 automatically starts when you turn on your PC computer or mobile device. When you first start Windows 8.1, you see a Lock screen, a full screen image with the time, date and notification icons (with app status), or the Sign in screen, a secure way to identify yourself on your device. With a simple drag of a mouse, press of a key, movement of your finger, you can dismiss the Lock screen to display the Sign in screen. After you sign in by selecting a user and entering a password or gesturing on a picture, you see the Start screen, which you can use to work with apps. If you sign in with a Microsoft account, such as hotmail.com or live.com, your device becomes connected to the SkyDrive cloud, which allows you to share information with others.

## Start Windows 8.1

1. Turn on your PC computer or mobile device, and wait for Windows 8.1 to start.

2. If the Lock screen appears, click anywhere on the screen or press and key or move your finger sideways from the edge.

3. Click or tap your username or picture. Click or tap **Sign-in options**, if available.

4. Type your password. Be sure to use the correct capitalization.

   ◆ **Picture password.** Click or tap icon; drag a  sequence of gestures. Click or tap **Switch to password** to type a password.

5. Click or tap the **Submit arrow**, or press Enter.

   The Windows 8.1 Start screen appears.

6. On first use, the following appears (depending on your installation):

   ◆ **On-screen help.** Follow the on-screen instructions to show you how to get started.

   ◆ **Help+Tips app.** The Help+Tips app opens to help you get started. You can also click or tap the Help+Tips tile to open it; see the topic on page 522 for more details on using the app.

Start screen — Username (account)

## For Your Information

### Activating or Displaying System Information

If you need to activate Windows or find out your Windows version, system details, or computer or workgroup name, you can quickly display System Information from any screen. Click or tap Settings on the Charms bar, and then click or tap Change PC settings. If needed, click or tap Activate Windows, and then click or tap Activate. Click or tap PC and devices, and then click or tap PC info. You can also right-click or tap-hold the lower-left corner of the screen, and then click or tap System or press Win+Pause/Break. In the System window, you can view information, change settings, or activate your Windows version.

# Using the Mouse or Gestures

The user interface for Windows 8.1 is designed to work on PC computer desktops and mobile devices, including smart phones and tablets. You can control Windows by using a pointing device on your PC computer or gestures with your finger on a mobile device. A **pointing device** is hardware connected to or built into the PC computer you use to position the **pointer**, the small symbol on the screen that indicates the pointer's position. The most common pointing devices are a **mouse** for desktop computers and a **touch pad** for laptop or notebook computers. When you move the mouse across a flat surface (such as a desk or a mouse pad), or place your finger on the touch pad and drag it across, the pointer on the screen moves in the same direction. The shape of the pointer changes to indicate different activities. Once you move the pointer to a desired position on the screen, you use the buttons on the mouse or touch pad to access the PC computer's functions, "tell" your system what you want it to do. Other available pointing devices include **trackballs**, which function similarly to the mouse, and stylus pens, which work with a tablet pad or mobile device to move the pointer and enter handwritten information. For a mobile device or PC computer touch screen or pad, all you need is your finger to make gestures. A **gesture** is the movement of one or more fingers on a touch screen or pad. For example, dragging your finger with a flicking motion at the end of the movement is called **swiping**. Some mobile devices also include a **stylus pen** which you can use like on a PC computer.

Positioning the mouse pointer over an item on the screen is called **pointing**. When you point to an item, Windows often displays a **ScreenTip**, identifying the item or displaying status information. A typical mouse has two mouse buttons, however, some models include a third button or wheel in the middle. The act of pressing the left mouse button once and releasing it is called **clicking**, also known as single-clicking, and the act of touching and removing your finger is called **tapping**. The act of clicking or tapping an item, such as a tile or icon, indicates that you have selected it. To perform an operation on a tile or icon, such as opening or moving it, you must first select it. In some instances, such as working with the desktop, you need to click the left mouse button twice in a row, known as **double-clicking** or tap twice, known as **double-tapping**, to open a window, program, or file. Holding down the left mouse and moving is known as **dragging**.

Clicking the right mouse button is known as **right-clicking**. Right-clicking an item displays a menu, either the App bar or shortcut menu in the desktop. When a step tells you to "click," it means to click the left mouse button. If you are supposed to click the right mouse button, the step will instruct you to "right-click." If you press and hold your finger on a mobile device it does the same thing as right-clicking an item. Anytime you click or tap anywhere outside a selected item, such as the commands bar, Windows automatically cancels the operation and deselects the item.

When you cannot see all of the items available on a screen, scroll bars appear (when you move your mouse) on the right and bottom edges of the screen or within a window. Scroll bars allow you to display the additional contents of the window by dragging or swiping left or right or up and down. If your mouse has a wheel between the two mouse buttons, you can roll it to quickly scroll a few lines or an entire screen at a time.

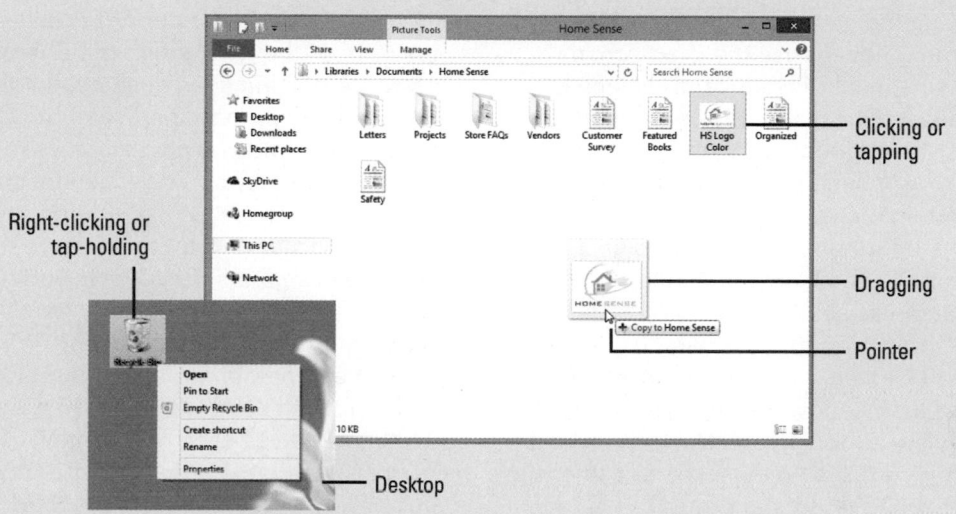

Right-clicking or tap-holding

Clicking or tapping

Dragging

Pointer

Desktop

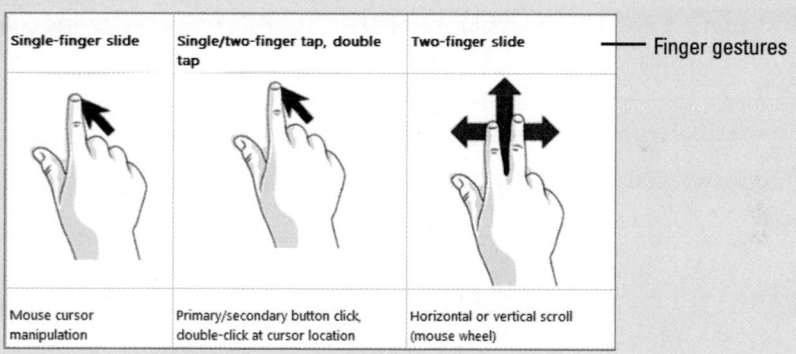

Finger gestures

| Single-finger slide | Single/two-finger tap, double tap | Two-finger slide |
|---|---|---|
| Mouse cursor manipulation | Primary/secondary button click; double-click at cursor location | Horizontal or vertical scroll (mouse wheel) |

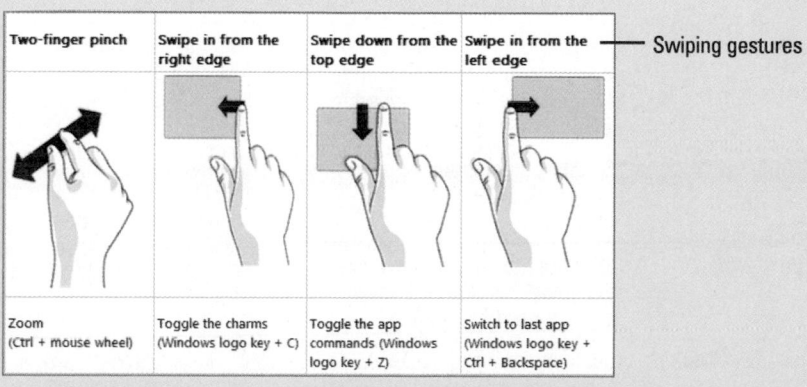

Swiping gestures

| Two-finger pinch | Swipe in from the right edge | Swipe down from the top edge | Swipe in from the left edge |
|---|---|---|---|
| Zoom (Ctrl + mouse wheel) | Toggle the charms (Windows logo key + C) | Toggle the app commands (Windows logo key + Z) | Switch to last app (Windows logo key + Ctrl + Backspace) |

# Exploring the Start Screen

The key to getting started with the Windows 8.1 is learning how to use the **Start screen**. The Start screen provides a central place to access apps, utilities, and device settings. When you start Windows 8.1 and sign in, the Start screen appears, displaying app tiles in groups with information. **Tiles** allow you to view status information for the specific app or open the app to work with it. Windows 8.1 comes with an array of standard apps, such as Mail, People, Music, Calendar, Weather, Photos, and Games, and you can download more from the Windows Store. You can use the **Apps view button** arrow (**New!**) to view all the apps on your system. The key to using the Start screen is to understand how to use corners and edges. Pointing to a corner on a PC computer or swiping an edge on a mobile device displays a bar, icon, or thumbnail that you can use to perform operations. When you point to the upper- or lower-right corner or swipe in from the right edge, the **Charms bar** appears, displaying search, share, start, device, and setting options. When the Charms bar is visible, Windows also displays the date, time, and system or app notification icons on the left of the window. When you point to the lower-right corner of the Start screen, the **Zoom button** appears that allows you to change the screen size to display items smaller or larger for better viewing. When you point to the upper- or lower-left corner or swipe in from the left edge, the **Start bar** appears. The Start bar, which contains thumbnails of currently opened apps, allows you to switch between open apps or the Start screen. The table lists the Start Screen features, and describes how to access them using either a PC computer or mobile device.

## Start Screen

| Feature | Description | On a PC computer | On a mobile device |
|---|---|---|---|
| Tiles | Displays program specific information or opens the app | Click to open the app | Tap to open the app |
| User account | Identifies the current user and opens a menu, where you can change account picture, lock, or sign out | Click to display a menu with options | Tap to display a menu with options |
| Charms bar | Provides options to search for and share information, switch to the Start screen, work with devices, and change settings | Point to the upper- or lower-right corner | Swipe in from the right edge |
| Start bar | Switches to an open app or the Start screen | Point to the upper- or lower left corner, and then move up or down | Swipe in from the left edge |
| Zoom | Changes the screen view size to display items smaller or larger for better viewing | Click to display a menu with options | Tap to display a menu with options |
| Apps view (**New!**) | Displays the Apps screen with all the installed apps | Click the Down arrow on the Start screen | Tap the Down arrow on the Start screen |

## Start Screen Options

You can customize the Start screen appears by changing options in the Taskbar and Navigation properties dialog box (**New!**). In the Desktop, right-click or tap-hold the taskbar, and then click Properties. On the Navigation tab (**New!**), you can set options to show the Apps view when you go to the Start screen or show the desktop when you sign in, close all apps. You can also set options to show the Start screen when you press the Windows logo or Win key (⊞). If you want a consistent look, you can set an option to use the same background for your Start and desktop screens.

## Corner Navigation Options

Pointing to a corner allows you to navigate in Windows. You can set options in PC settings to turn some features on or off. Point to the lower- or upper-right corner and move up or down (on a computer) or swipe left from the right edge of the screen (on a mobile device), click or tag Settings, click or tap Change PC settings, click or tap PC and devices, click or tap Corners and edges (**New!**), and then drag the slider on or off to enable or disable pointing to the upper-right corner to show charms (**New!**) or clicking the upper-left corner to switch between my recent apps (**New!**).

Start screen      Background      User account

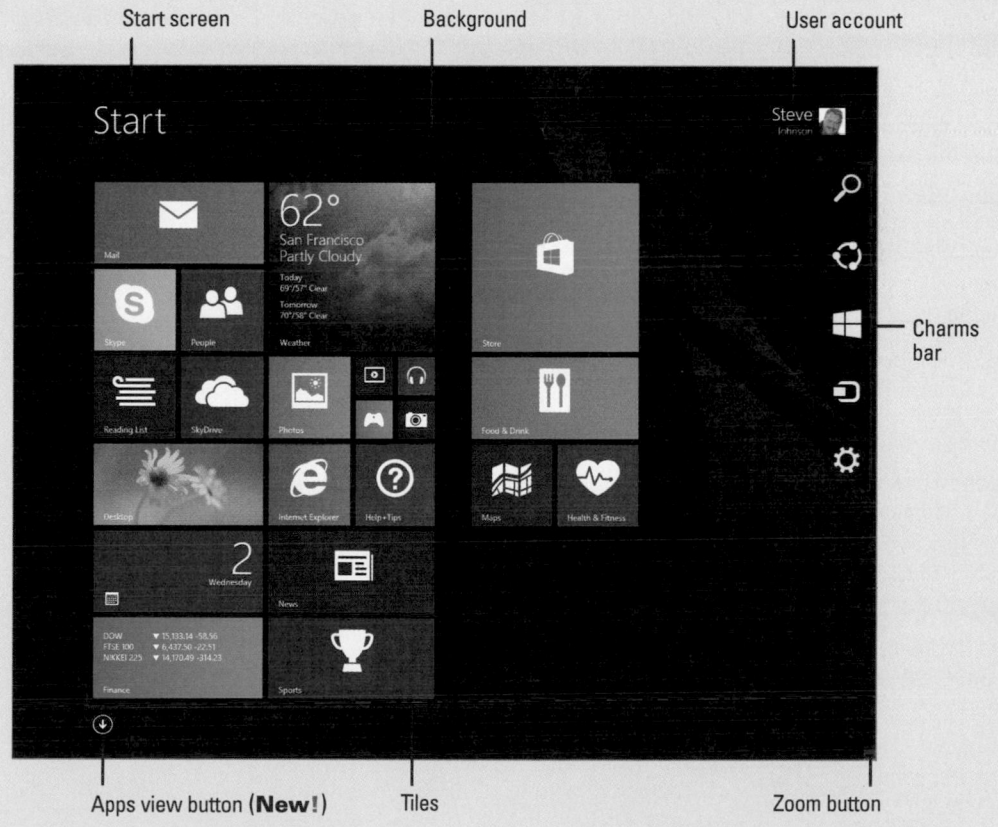

Charms bar

Apps view button (**New!**)      Tiles      Zoom button

# Using the Start Bar

The Start bar allows you to switch between or close currently open apps and the Start screen. When using Windows 8.1, the Start bar is not visibly noticeable on the screen. You access the Start bar by pointing to the upper- or lower-left corner on a PC computer or swiping in from the left edge on a mobile device. When you point to the upper- or lower-left corner, a thumbnail appears. If you have more than two apps open and move down from the upper-left corner or up from the lower-left corner, the Start bar appears with thumbnails for all open apps or the Start button (**New!**). When you click the lower-left corner on a PC computer, Windows switches between the most recently used app and the Start screen. When you click the upper-left corner on a PC computer, Window switches between all open apps.

## Use the Start Bar

◆ **Display Start bar.** Point to the upper- or lower-left corner (on a computer) or swipe in slightly from the left edge and then back quickly (on a mobile device).

   If you have more than two apps open, move down from the top or up from the bottom to display thumbnails.

   You can click or tap a thumbnail to display the app.

◆ **Switch between the Start screen and the most recently used apps.** Click the lower-left corner (on a computer) or swipe right from the left edge (on a mobile device).

   When you point to the lower-left corner, the **Start button** (**New!**) appears, which you can click or tap to display the Start screen.

◆ **Switch between all open apps.** Click the upper-left corner (on a computer) or swipe right from the left edge (on a mobile device).

   **TIMESAVER** *Press Alt+Tab to cycle through open apps or press Alt+Shift+Tab to reverse the cycle order.*

◆ **Close an app.** Right-click or tap-hold a thumbnail on the Start bar, and then click or tap Close.

App thumbnail

Start button (**New!**)          Start bar

# Using the Charms Bar

The Charms bar allows you to access search, share, start, device, and set options for Windows 8.1. When you point to the lower- or upper-right corner or swipe in from the right edge, the Charms bar appears, displaying Search, Share, Start, Devices, and Settings buttons. The Search button allows you to search for apps, settings, and files on your PC computer or mobile device. The Share button allows you to share an app or information between other users on different devices. The Start button displays the Start screen. The Devices button allows you to work with and send information or files to devices, such as a printer or second screen. The Settings button allows you to access Help information and display, set, or personalize PC computer or mobile device settings, including networks, volume, display, notifications, language, and power, for Windows 8.1. The Settings button is also allows you to set app-specific options. When you select a button on the Charms bar, a panel appears, displaying available options.

## Use the Charms Bar

**1** Point to the lower- or upper-right corner and move up or down (on a computer) or swipe left from the right edge of the screen (on a mobile device).

**TIMESAVER** *Press Win+C to display the Charms bar.*

**2** Click or tap a button from the Charms bar.

◆ **Search.** Search for information.

◆ **Share.** Share information.

◆ **Start.** Display the Start screen.

◆ **Devices.** Use devices, such as printers, and change options, such as a second screen.

◆ **Settings.** Access help and Windows options.

A panel appears, displaying available options. The options vary depending on the active window, such as the Start screen or an app.

**3** Click or tap an option from the panel.

**4** To go back to the previous panel, click or tap the **Back** button.

# Exploring the Windows Desktop

The traditional desktop available in Windows 7 is available in Windows 8.1 as an app you can open from the Start screen. Simply click or tap the Desktop tile on the Start screen to open it. You can also use a keyboard shortcut; press Win+D (desktop), Win+B (active app), or Win+M (minimize all apps). The **desktop** is an on-screen version of an actual desk, containing windows, icons, files, and programs. You can use the desktop to access, store, organize, modify, share, and explore information (such as a letter, the news, or a list of addresses),

whether it resides on your PC computer or mobile device, a network, a Homegroup (shared home network), or the Internet. The bar at the bottom of your screen is called the **taskbar**; it allows you to start programs and switch among currently running programs or to the Start screen (**New!**). The left side of the taskbar displays the **Start button** (**New!**) and pinned programs. The default programs pinned to the taskbar include Internet Explorer and File Explorer, however, you can customize it with other programs. The right

Desktop icon

Background picture on desktop

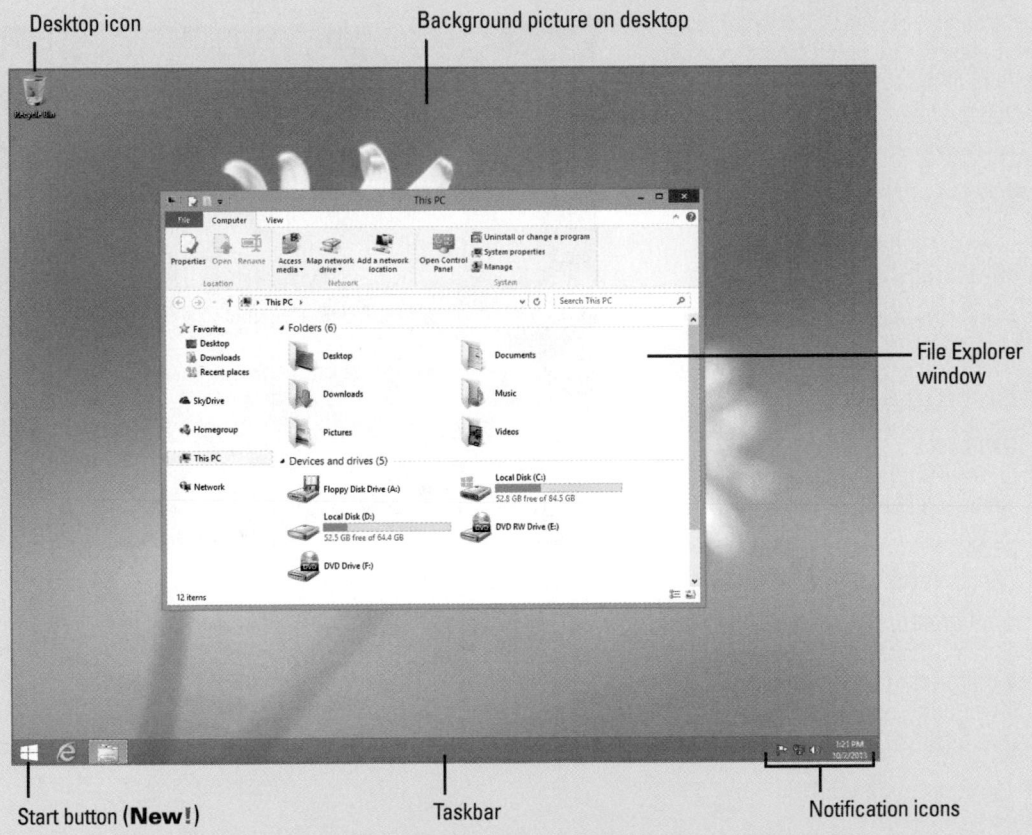

File Explorer window

Start button (**New!**)

Taskbar

Notification icons

side of the taskbar is the **notification area**, which displays the time, the date, and program related icons. You can click or tap an icon to display a window of options. For example, when you click or tap the Volume icon, a window appears where you can adjust or mute the volume. If icons in the notification area are not used for a while, an arrow appears to hide the icons and reduce clutter. You can click or tap the arrow to display hidden icons or click or tap a link to customize the notification area to select which icons and notifications appear on the taskbar. You can also quickly drag a hidden icon on or displayed icon off the notification area to add or remove it from the taskbar. Next to the notification area is the Show desktop button (the blank button at the right end of the taskbar), which allows you to quickly show the desktop. If you upgraded your PC computer to Windows 8.1 from a previous version of Windows, your desktop might contain additional desktop icons and toolbars.

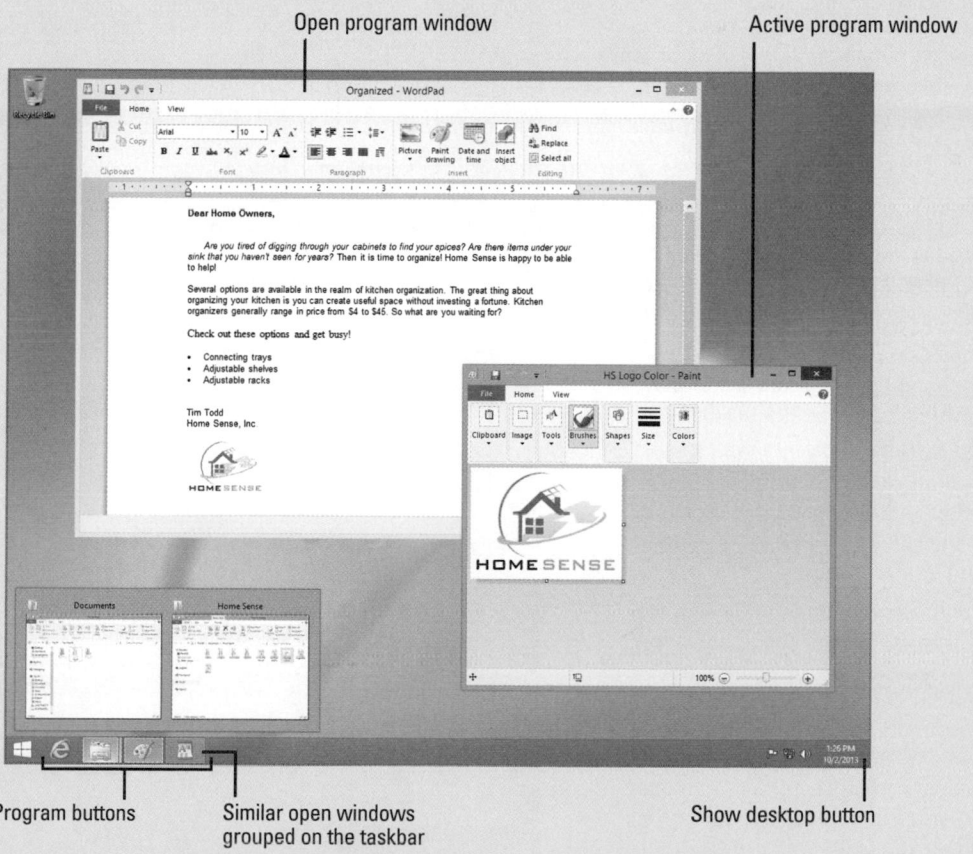

Open program window

Active program window

Program buttons

Similar open windows grouped on the taskbar

Show desktop button

# Using the Desktop Taskbar

The horizontal bar at the bottom of the desktop is called the taskbar; it contains several important items: Start button (**New!**), program and taskbar buttons, notification area, and Show desktop button. The taskbar allows you to start programs, files, and windows, as well as switch among currently running programs or open windows or to the Start screen (**New!**). For easy access, you can pin programs and windows to the taskbar. The default programs pinned to the taskbar include Internet Explorer and File Explorer, however, you can customize it. The Show desktop button minimizes all open windows to display the desktop. When you point to the Show desktop button, all open windows appear transparent, which allows you to peek at the desktop. In addition to tracking frequently used programs, Windows also tracks recently opened files, known as jump lists, which you can open from the taskbar. From the taskbar, you can also show or hide a touch screen keyboard for use on mobile devices.

## Use the Desktop Taskbar

◆ **Pin to the Taskbar.** Right-click or tap-hold an open program or taskbar button, and then click or tap **Pin this program to taskbar.**

◆ **Unpin from the Taskbar.** Right-click or tap-hold a pinned item on the taskbar, and then click or tap **Unpin this program from taskbar.**

◆ **Access a Jump List.** Right-click or tap-hold a taskbar button, and then click or tap a recently opened item.

◆ **Show desktop (minimize all windows).** Click or tap the **Show desktop** button on the taskbar.

◆ **Show desktop.** Point to the **Show desktop** button. Right-click or tap-hold the **Show desktop** button, and then click or tap **Peek at desktop** to turn it off and on.

◆ **Switch among open programs or windows.** Click or tap in a window to make it active, or point to a taskbar button for an open program or window, and then click or tap a name or icon. A live thumbnail appears when you point to an open program or window taskbar button. When you point to it, the program or window temporarily appears until you move the mouse.

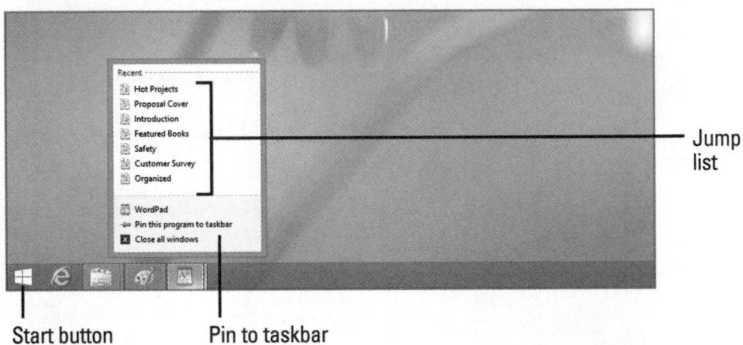

Start button    Pin to taskbar    Jump list

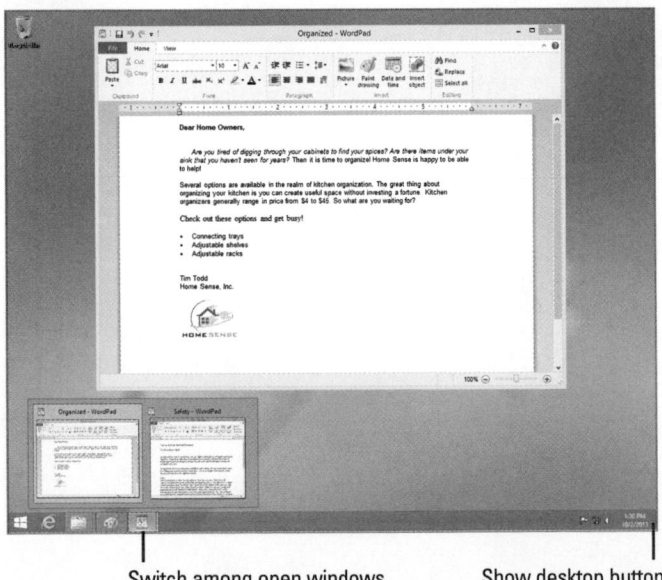

Switch among open windows    Show desktop button

- **Show or hide toolbars.** Right-click or tap-hold a blank area of the taskbar, point to **Toolbar**, and then click or tap a toolbar.
    - **Address.** Use an Address bar to access the Internet.
    - **Links.** Use to access Internet links.
    - **Touch Keyboard.** Use a touch screen keyboard.
    - **Desktop.** Use to access the desktop.
- **Arrange windows.** Open the windows you want to arrange, right-click or tap-hold a blank area of the taskbar, and then click or tap **Cascade windows**, **Show windows stacked**, or **Show windows side by side**.
- **Show Task Manager.** Right-click or tap-hold a blank area of the taskbar, and then click or tap **Task Manager**.
- **Lock or Unlock the Taskbar.** Right-click or tap-hold a blank area of the taskbar, and then click or tap **Lock the taskbar**.
- **Customize the Taskbar.** Right-click or tap-hold a blank area of the taskbar, and then click or tap **Properties**.
- **Keyboard Shortcuts to Open Apps on the Taskbar.** You can use keyboard shortcuts to open an app on the taskbar. Press Win+1 to open the first app on the taskbar. For a default setup, Internet Explorer opens. Press Win+2 to open the second app, and so on. You can rearrange the apps to customize which app opens.
- **Keyboard Shortcuts to Minimize or Restore All Windows.** Press Win+M to minimize all windows or Win+Shift+M to restore all windows. Press Win+Home to minimize all but the current window.

Touch keyboard

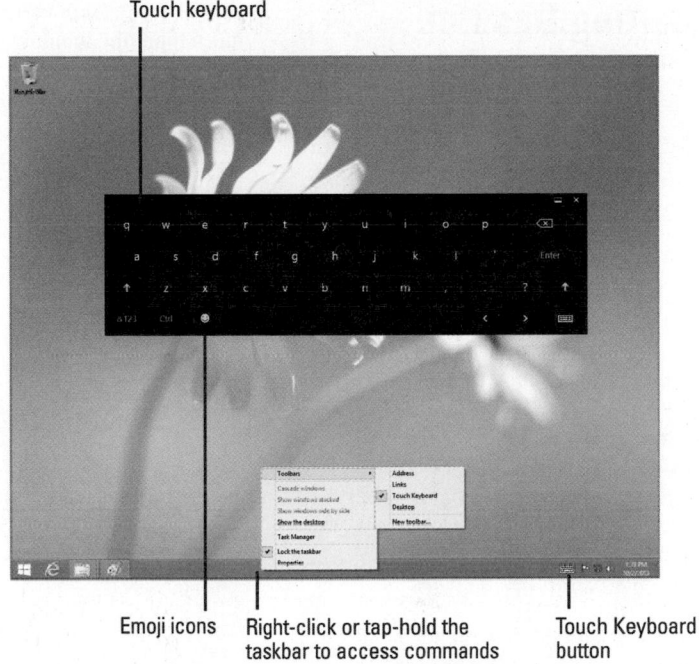

Emoji icons   Right-click or tap-hold the taskbar to access commands   Touch Keyboard button

## For Your Information

### Using to a Touch Keyboard

When you type on a touch keyboard on a touch-sensitive screen, the keyboard tries to learn and guess the current and next word you're typing, and shows suggestions above the keyboard (**New!**). You can choose a suggestion by tapping it, or using a gesture to slide your thumb left and right across the Spacebar to cycle through the them so you don't have to take your fingers off the keyboard. You can quickly insert numbers with a swipe on the top row of the touch keyboard (**New!**). In addition, emoji character symbols are in color for easier viewing (**New!**).

The touch keyboard supports long-press gestures, which allows you to access other keys on the keyboard. For example, you can long press the question mark key to reveal an exclamation mark. Once, you know a key is available under another one, you can perform a short swipe up on the question mark key to quickly use the exclamation mark key.

# Managing Desktop Windows

One of the most powerful things about Windows is that you can open more than one window or program at once. This means, however, that the desktop can get cluttered with many open windows for the various programs. The desktop groups similar types of windows under one button on the taskbar, which you can use to switch among open windows and programs. You can identify a window by its name on the title bar at the top of the window, which you can also use to move or resize it. Each window is also surrounded by a border and resize buttons in the upper-right corner that you can use to resize the window.

## Switch Among Open Windows

1. In the desktop, click or tap anywhere in a window to make it active, or point to a taskbar button for an open program or window, and then click or tap a name or icon. You can also press Alt-Tab to switch windows and other Windows apps.

   ◆ A live thumbnail appears when you point to an open program or window taskbar button. When you point to the thumbnail, the program or window temporally appears until you move the mouse.

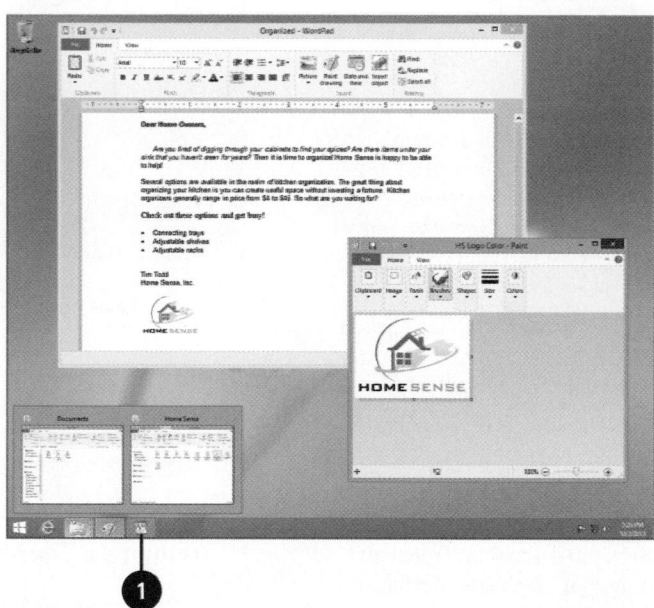

## Move or Resize a Window

1. In the desktop, point to the window's title bar.

2. Drag the window to a new location.

   ◆ **Maximize active window.** Drag the title bar to the top edge of the desktop or double-click or double-tap the title bar.

   ◆ **Resize active window for side by side use.** Drag the title bar to the left or right edge of the desktop.

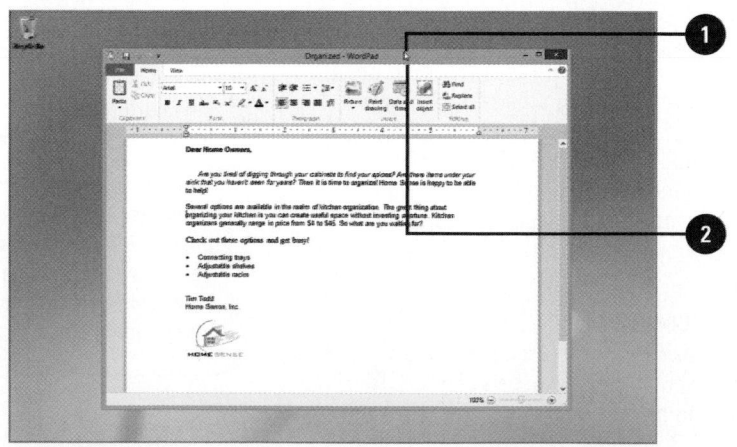

## Use Buttons to Resize and Close a Window

In the desktop, all windows contain the same sizing and close buttons:

◆ **Maximize button.** Click or tap to make a window fill the entire screen.

◆ **Restore Down button.** Click or tap to reduce a maximized window.

◆ **Minimize button.** Click or tap to shrink a window to a taskbar button.

◆ **Close button.** Click or tap to close the window.

◆ **Show desktop button.** Click or tap to minimize or restore all windows.

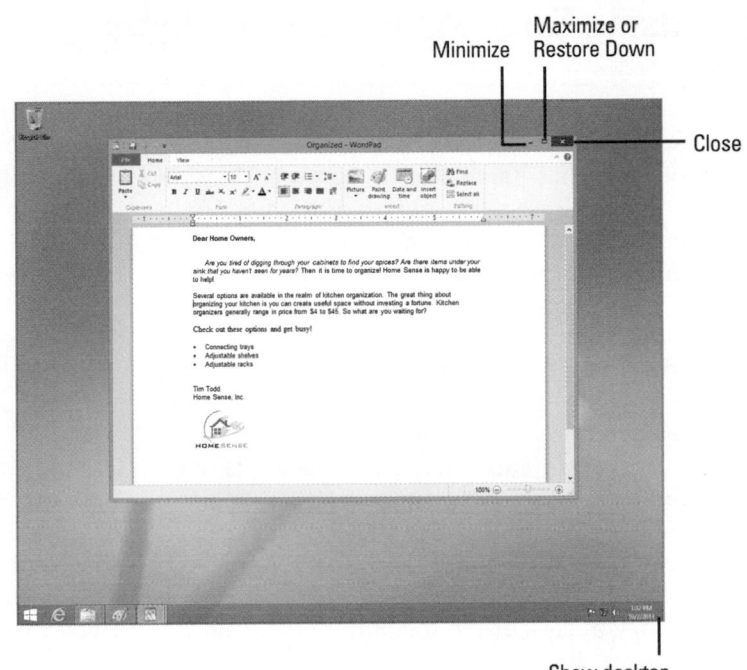

Minimize    Maximize or Restore Down

Close

Show desktop

## Use the Pointer to Resize a Window

◆ **Resize a window using a border.** Move the pointer over a border in a non-maximized window until the pointer changes into a two-headed arrow, and then drag to the size you want.

◆ **Resize all open windows on the desktop.** Right-click or tap-hold a blank area of the taskbar, and then click or tap a command:

  ◆ **Cascade windows.**

  ◆ **Show window stacked.**

  ◆ **Show windows side by side.**

◆ **Minimize or restore all open windows except active one.** Drag the title bar back and forth (shake) to minimize or restore all open windows except the active one.

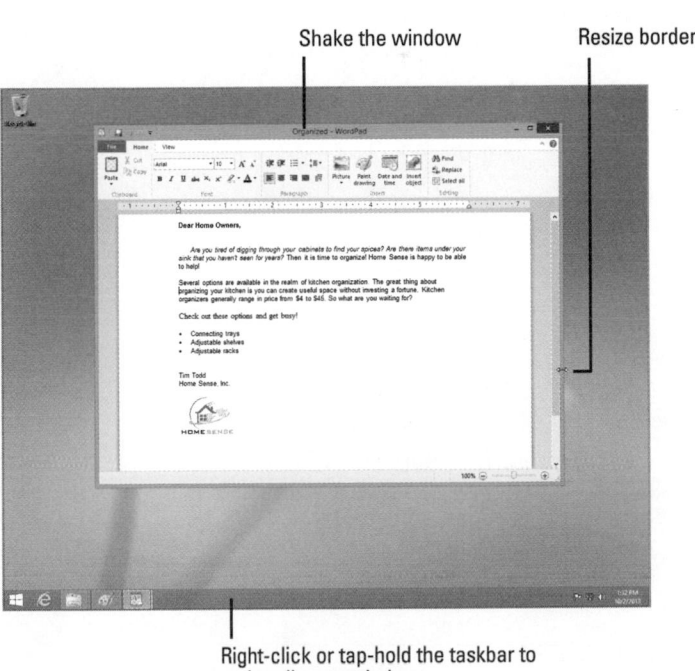

Shake the window      Resize border

Right-click or tap-hold the taskbar to resize all open windows

# Using Tabs, Menus, and Toolbars

A **command** is a directive that provides access to a program's features. Each Windows program has its own set of commands, which are located on a tab, menu, or toolbar. The use of tabs, menus, and toolbars vary depending on the program. A **tab** or **menu** organizes commands into groups of related operations. Each group is listed under the menu or tab name, such as File or Home. To access the commands, you click or tap the tab or menu name, and then click or tap the button or command. If a menu appears, click or tap a command. On a menu, a check mark or selected icons identifies a currently selected feature, meaning that the feature is enabled, or turned on. To disable, or turn off the feature, you click or tap the command again to remove the check mark. A bullet mark also indicates that an option is enabled. To disable

a command with a bullet mark next to it, however, you must select another command (within the menu section, separated by gray lines) in its place. If a command on a tab or menu includes a keyboard reference, known as a **keyboard shortcut**, you can perform the action by pressing the first key, then pressing the second key to perform the command quickly. You can also carry out some of the most frequently used commands by clicking or tapping a button on a toolbar. A **toolbar** contains buttons that are convenient shortcuts for commands. When you point to a button, a ScreenTip appears with a description and the keyboard shortcut, if available. A **pane** is a frame within a window where you can access commands and navigation controls, such as the Navigation pane in File Explorer.

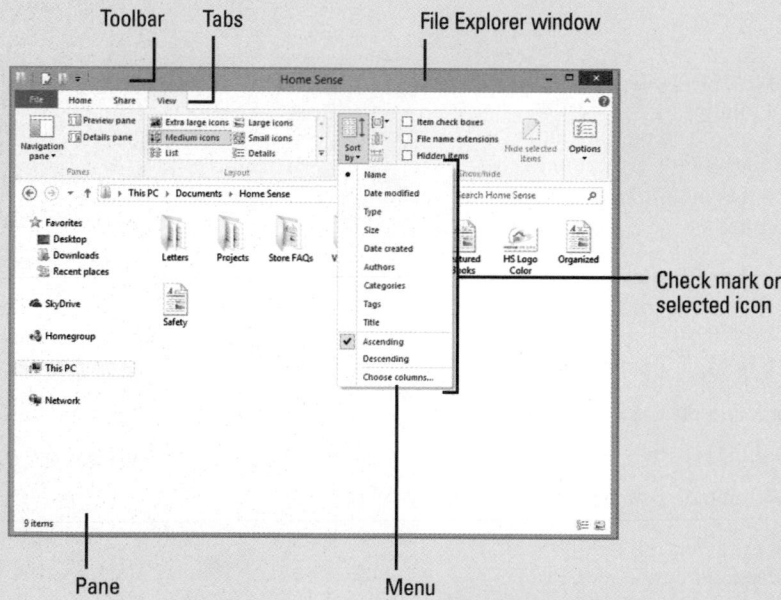

Toolbar   Tabs                    File Explorer window

Check mark or selected icon

Pane                    Menu

# Choosing Dialog Box Options

A **dialog box** is a window that opens when you choose a command followed by an ellipsis (. . .). The ellipsis indicates that you must supply more information before the program can carry out the command you selected. Dialog boxes open in other situations as well, such as when you open a program in the Control Panel. In a dialog box, you choose various options and provide information for completing the command.

## Choose Dialog Box Options

All dialog boxes contain the same types of options, including the following:

◆ **Tabs.** Click or tap a tab to display its options. Each tab groups a related set of options.

◆ **Option buttons.** Click or tap an option button to select it. You can usually select only one.

◆ **Up and down arrows.** Click or tap the up or down arrow to increase or decrease the number, or type a number in the box.

◆ **Check box.** Click or tap the box to turn on or off the option. A checked box means the option is selected; a cleared box means it's not.

◆ **List box.** Click or tap the list arrow to display a list of options, and then click or tap the option you want.

◆ **Text box.** Click or tap in the box and type the requested information.

◆ **Command buttons.** Click or tap a button to perform a specific action or command. A button name followed by an ellipsis (...) opens another dialog box. OK executes the options and closes the dialog box. Cancel ignores the options and closes the dialog box. Apply executes the options and leaves the dialog box open.

◆ **Preview box.** Many dialog boxes show an image that reflects the options you select.

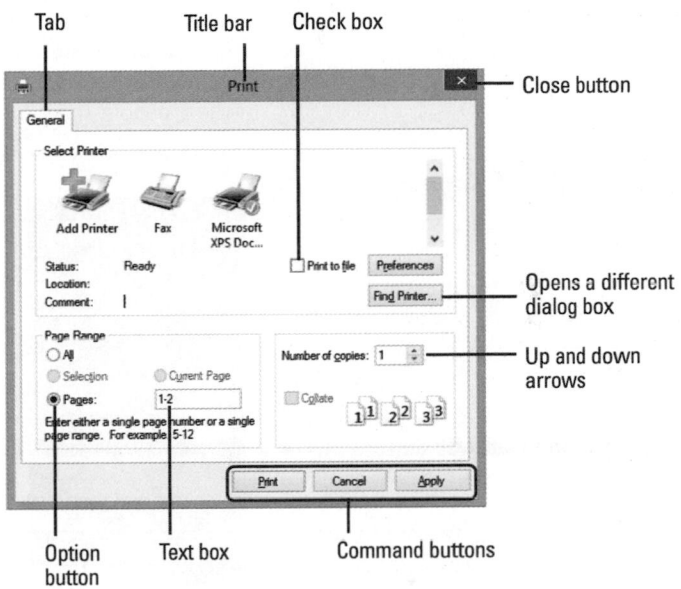

Tab    Title bar    Check box

Close button

Opens a different dialog box

Up and down arrows

Option button    Text box    Command buttons

## For Your Information

### Navigating a Dialog Box

Rather than clicking or tapping to move around a dialog box, you can press the Tab key to move from one box or button to the next. You can also use Shift+Tab to move backward, or Ctrl+Tab and Ctrl+Shift+Tab to move between dialog box tabs.

# Using Windows Help and Support

When you have a question about how to do something in Windows 8.1, you can usually find the answer with a few clicks of your mouse or taps of your finger. Microsoft Help and Support is a resource of information, training, and support to help you learn and use Windows 8.1. You can get online help from Microsoft web sites or local help from Windows Help and Support. You can access Help by using Settings on the Charms bar from the Start screen, desktop, or any app. Help and Support is local help like a book stored on your PC with additional links to the Internet, complete with a search feature, and a table of contents to make finding information easier. You can get online help from a support professional at Microsoft or from other users in Windows communities (a forum where people share information).

## Get Online Help and Support

1. Display the Start screen.

2. Point to the lower- or upper-right corner and move up or down (on a computer) or swipe left from the right edge of the screen (on a mobile device).

3. Click or tap the **Settings** button on the Charms bar.

4. Click or tap **Help** on the Settings panel.

   Your web browser opens, displaying a Microsoft site with specified help information.

5. Click or tap a topic of interest.

6. Read the help information, or click or tap any links to access other information.

7. To close your web browser, point to the top of the screen (cursor change to a hand), and then drag (on a computer) or swipe (on a mobile device) to the bottom of the screen.

## See Also

See "Getting Help+Tips for Windows 8.1" on page 522 for information to help you quickly get started, including what's new in Windows 8.1

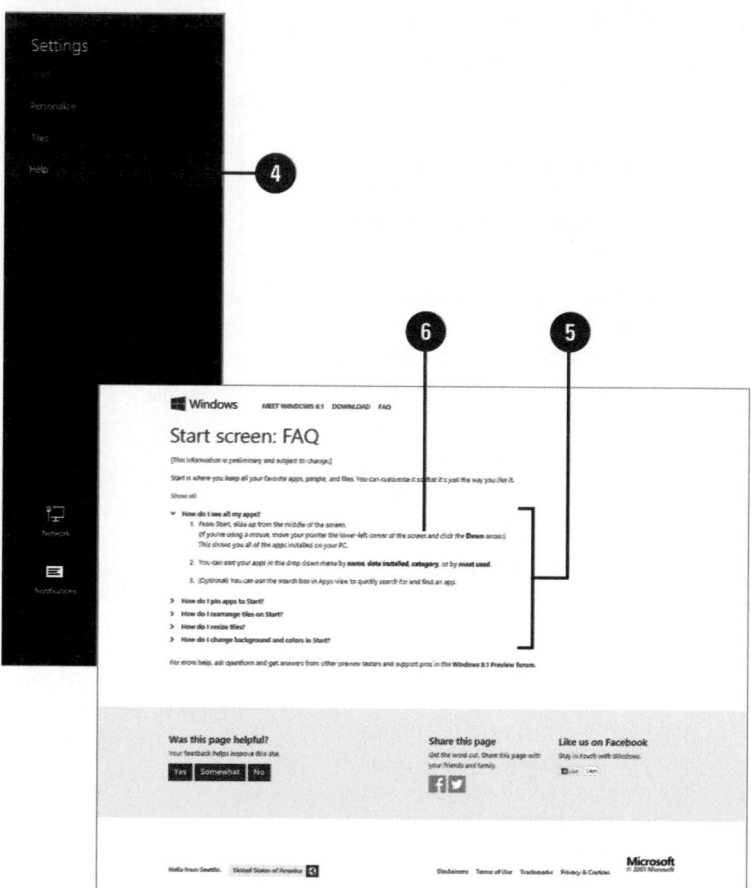

## Use Help and Support

**1** Open the Desktop screen.

**2** Point to the lower- or upper-right corner and move up or down (on a computer) or swipe left from the right edge of the screen (on a mobile device).

**3** Click or tap the **Settings** button on the Charms bar.

**4** Click or tap **Help** on the Settings panel.

**TIMESAVER** *Press Win+F1 (Start screen) or F1 (desktop) to open Windows Help and Support.*

**5** Click or tap a link with the type of help you want to use:

◆ **Help home.** Displays the main help page.

◆ **Browse help.** Displays a table of contents.

◆ **Contact support.** Displays information to help you find answers.

**6** Click or tap the item of interest.

**7** Read the information.

**8** If you can't find the information you need, click or tap the **Search Help** box, type a word or phrase, and then press Enter.

**9** If you need additional online help, click or tap an Internet resource link to access the web site.

**10** To go back to the previous page, click or tap the **Back** button.

◆ To go forward to a page you previously viewed, click or tap the **Forward** button.

**11** Click or tap the **Close** button.

Print button

Settings button

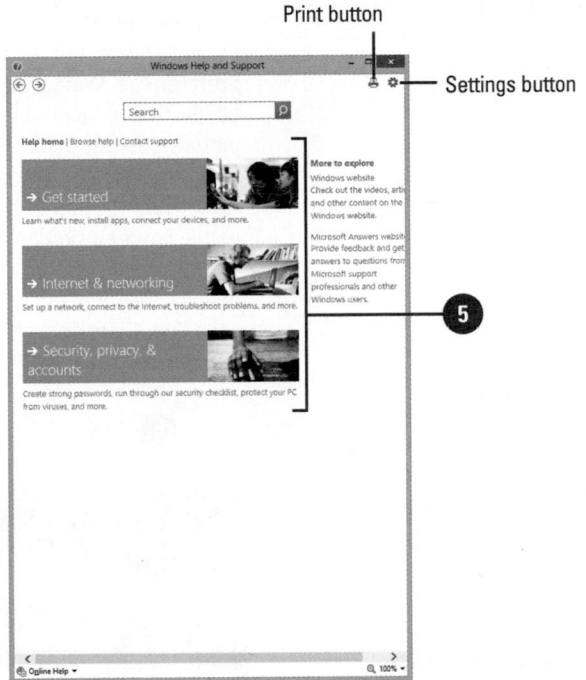

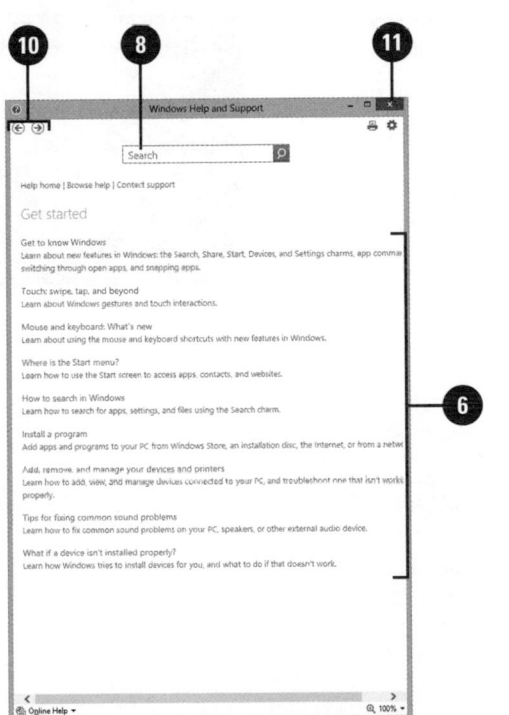

# Switching Users

Many users are able to share the same PC computer or mobile device. Their individual Windows identities allow them to keep their files completely private and to customize the operating system with their own preferences. Windows manages these separate identities, or accounts, by giving each user a unique username and password, either text or picture gesture. When a user selects an account and types a password or uses a gesture (if enabled), Windows starts with that user's configuration settings and network permissions. When you want to change users, you can sign out, (which closes all running programs, saves your settings, and signs you off the PC computer) or switch users, which quickly switches between users without having to close programs and saves your current settings.

## Switch Users Quickly

**1** Display the Start screen.

**2** Click or tap the **User Account** (username and picture).

**3** Click or tap the name of the user to which you want to switch.

**4** Type your password. Be sure to use the correct capitalization.

♦ **Sign-in options.** Click or tap **Sign-in options**, if available.

♦ **Picture password.** Click or tap icon; drag a sequence of gestures. Click or tap **Switch to password** to type a password.

**5** Click or tap the **Submit arrow**, or press Enter.

The Start screen appears for the user.

### Did You Know?

*You can change user account options in the Settings.* In the Start screen, click or tap the Settings button on the Charms bar, click or tap Change PC Settings, click or tap Accounts, click or tap a category, and then select the options you want.

## Sign Out and Sign In

**1** Display the Start screen.

**2** Click or tap the **User Account** (username and picture).

**3** Click or tap **Sign out** to close all your programs, save your settings, and sign off.

**4** If the Lock screen appears, drag your mouse anywhere on the screen, move your finger sideways from the edge, or press a key to dismiss it.

**5** Click or tap your username or picture, if necessary.

**6** Type your password. Be sure to use the correct capitalization.

◆ **Sign-in options.** Click or tap **Sign-in options**, if available.

◆ **Picture password.** Click or tap icon; drag a sequence of gestures. Click or tap **Switch to password** to type a password.

**7** Click or tap the **Submit arrow**, or press Enter.

The Start screen appears for the user.

## Did You Know?

*You can lock the screen and stay signed in.* In the Start screen, click or tap the User Account, and then click or tap Lock.

*You can use Ctrl+Alt+Del to lock, switch users, sign out, and power down.* When you press Ctrl+Alt+Del on a system, a screen appears with commands: Lock, Switch user, Sign out, Task Manager, Power button, and Ease of Access button.

## For Your Information

### Using the Lock Screen without Unlocking

When your screen locks, you can still access some apps without having to unlock your PC. When you display the Lock screen, you can answer Skype calls, take photos or see a slide show of your photos without having to unlock it first (**New!**). In the Start screen, click or tap the User Account, and then click or tap Lock to manually lock your PC.

### Using the Power User Menu

When you right-click the Start button, a power user menu appears with options to perform computer administration and open the Task Manager, Control Panel, File Explorer, Search, Run, and Desktop. You can also use it to shutdown or sign out of your device. Right-click the Start button (or lower-left corner), point to Shut down or sign out (**New!**), and then click an option: Sign out, Sleep, Shut down, or Restart.

# Powering Down

When you finish working on your device, you need to make sure to turn off, or shut down, it properly. This involves several steps: saving and closing all open files, exiting all running programs, shutting down Windows itself, and finally, turning off the device. However, if you shut down your device before or while installing Windows updates (download must be complete), Windows will automatically complete the install before shutting down, so you don't have to wait around. Shutting down your device makes sure Windows and all its related programs are properly closed and avoid potential problems in the future. In addition to the Shut down option, you can put your PC in sleep (useful for short periods) or hibernate (useful for longer periods) mode, or restart to reset your device if problems occur.

## Power Down Your Device

1. Point to the lower- or upper-right corner and move up or down (on a computer) or swipe left from the right edge of the screen (on a mobile device).

2. Click or tap the **Settings** button on the Charms bar.

3. Click or tap the **Power** button on the Settings panel.

4. Click or tap the option on the menu you want (confirm as prompted):

   ◆ **Sleep.** Saves your session to memory and switches to low-power mode; you can press the hardware power button to wake.

   ◆ **Hibernate.** Saves your session to memory and hard disk, and then exits Windows. Press the hardware power button to restore your session.

   ◆ **Shut down.** Exits Windows 8.1 and prepares the PC to be turned off.

   ◆ **Restart.** Exits Windows 8.1 and restarts the PC.

   **IMPORTANT** *Options vary depending on Windows settings.*

## For Your Information

### Setting Power and Sleep Options

You can specify how long your screen waits before it turns off or goes to sleep to save power. To set these options, click or tap the Settings button on the Charms bar, click or tap Change PC settings, click or tap PC and devices, click or tap Power and sleep (**New!**), and then specify the timing you want.

# Working with Windows Metro Apps

## Introduction

Now that you know how to work with the graphical elements that make Windows 8.1 work, you're ready to work with apps. An **app** (short for application), also known as a program, is software you use to accomplish specific tasks, such as browsing the web using the Internet Explorer app or communicating with others using the Skype app. When you display the Start screen on Windows 8.1, you will notice live tiles, which you can use to get quick status information for apps or open them in full screen view. The apps on the Start screen are a new generation of full screen apps, known as **metro apps**, that are primarily designed for use on Windows 8.1.

The apps available on the Start screen are not all the apps installed on your PC computer or mobile device. Windows 8.1 comes with additional built-in Windows Accessories and System tools that, although not as feature-rich as many apps sold separately, are extremely useful for completing basic tasks. For those who are familiar with Windows 7, you'll recognize them. They include Paint, WordPad, Windows Media Player, Windows Media Center, Calculator, Character Map, and Command Prompt to name a few.

This chapter shows you how to locate and access your Windows apps (and to customize this access). It also shows you how to work with multiple apps at the same time, share information between apps, and install or update apps from the Windows Store.

## What You'll Do

**Display All Your Apps**

**Search for Apps**

**Use Different Apps**

**Start and Close Apps**

**Use the App Bar**

**Change App Settings**

**Work with Multiple Apps**

**Work with Apps Side by Side**

**Share Between Apps**

**Install Apps from the Store**

**Update Apps**

**Uninstall Apps**

**Customize Apps on the Start Screen**

**Group Apps on the Start Screen**

**Set Notification Options for Apps**

**Set Search Options for Apps**

**Set Privacy Options for Apps**

# Displaying All Your Apps

When you display the Start screen on Windows 8.1, you will notice live tiles, which you can use to get quick status information for apps or open them in full screen view. The apps available on the Start screen are not all the apps installed on your PC computer or mobile device. Windows 8.1 comes with additional built-in Windows Accessories and System tools that, although not as feature-rich as many apps sold separately, are extremely useful for completing basic tasks. For those who are familiar with Windows 7, you'll recognize them. They include Paint, WordPad, Windows Media Player, Windows Media Center, Calculator, Alarms, Character Map, and Command Prompt to name a few. When you install an app, it appears in Apps view (**New!**), not the Start screen unless you choose to pin it to the Start screen. You can display all the available apps on your device by accessing the Apps screen (**New!**) from the Start screen.

## Display All Your Apps

1. Display the Start screen, and then move the pointer or tap the screen as needed to show the button.

   The Apps view button appears (**New!**) at the bottom of the Start screen.

2. Click or tap the **Apps view** button down arrow (**New!**) (on a computer) or swipe up from the bottom of the Start screen (on a mobile device).

   The Apps screen appears.

3. To sort your apps in Apps view, click or tap the **Sort by** list arrow (next to Apps title) (**New!**), and then click or tap an option: **by name**, **by date installed**, **by most used**, or **by category**.

4. To exit Apps screen, move your mouse or tap the screen to display the button, as needed, click or tap the **Apps view** button up arrow.

## Display All Your Apps by Categories

1. Display the Start screen, and then move the pointer or tap the screen as needed to show the button.

   The Apps view button appears (**New!**) at the bottom of the Start screen.

2. Click or tap the **Apps view** button (**New!**) (on a computer) or swipe up from the bottom of the Start screen (on a mobile device).

   The Apps screen appears.

3. Point to the lower-right corner, and then click or tap the **Zoom** button (on a computer) or pinch in (on a mobile device).

   The Apps screen zooms out to display categories with alphabetical and Windows labels.

4. Click or tap a category.

   The Apps screen zooms in to display the apps organized by the category.

   **TIMESAVER** *In Apps view, click the Sort by list arrow, and then click by Category (**New!**) to view all categories.*

Apps screen                     Search box

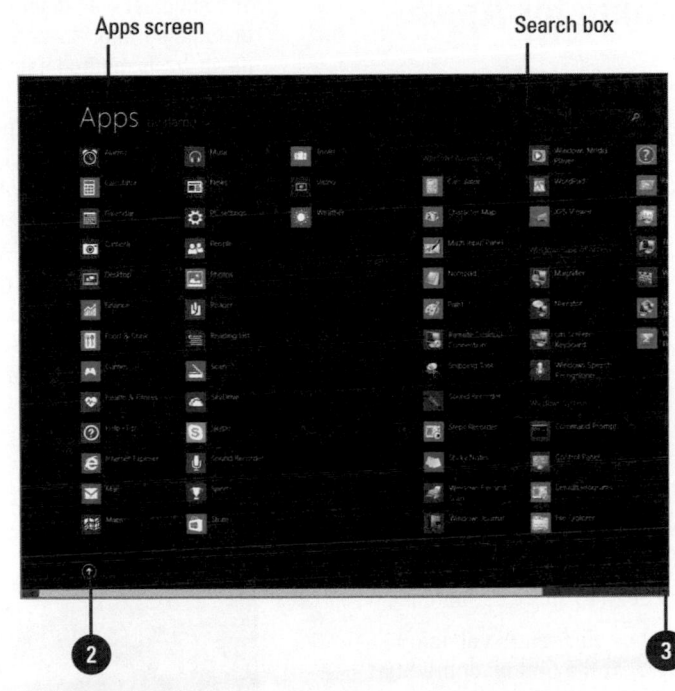

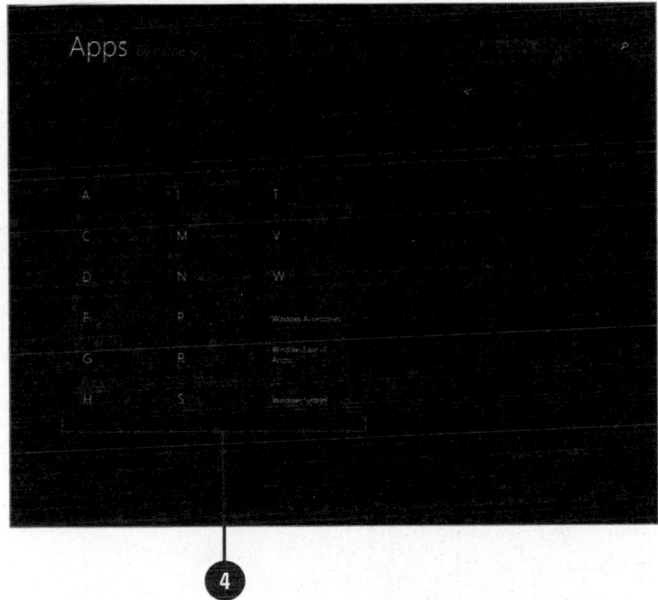

# Searching for Apps

The simplest way to look for a specific app is to scroll through the Start or Apps screen. However, when you have a lot of apps installed on your device, this method can be too time consuming. A more direct way is through the Search box in Apps screen (**New!**), or simply typing text from the Start screen. The Search panel is a centralized place to search for apps, settings, and files in Windows 8.1. The Search panel includes a Search box where you can enter the name of item you want to find, search categories (**New!**)—either Everywhere, Settings, Files, Web images or videos—where you can narrow down a search, and a list of apps where you can specify a specific place to perform a search. As you type the search criteria in the Search box, Windows narrows down and displays the search results for the specified category. The Search panel also displays the number of matches found for each category if you want to look in other places.

## Search for Apps

1. Display the Start screen, and then move the pointer or tap the screen as needed to show the button.

   The Apps view button appears (**New!**) at the bottom of the Start screen.

2. Click or tap the **Apps view** button down arrow (**New!**) (on a computer) or swipe up from the bottom of the Start screen (on a mobile device).

   The Apps screen appears.

3. Click or tap in the Search box (**New!**).

4. Type the first few characters for the app you want to find. You can continue typing or edit the text to narrow down your search.

   The Search screen displays a list of results.

5. To open an app, click or tap the app's tile.

6. To cancel the search, delete the search text in the Search box.

## Search Using an App

**1** Start the app that you want to use for your search or use the Start screen.

**2** Point to the lower- or upper-right corner and move up or down (on a computer) or swipe left from the right edge of the screen (on a mobile device).

**3** Click or tap the **Search** button on the Charms bar.

**TIMESAVER** *Press Win+Q to display the Search panel.*

The Search pane appears, displaying a Search box.

**4** To select a search type, click or tap the **Search** list arrow (**New!**), and then click or tap an option: **Everywhere**, **Setting**, **Files**, **Web images** or **Web videos**, or a specific app to use for the search.

**5** Type the first few characters for the information or item you want to find.

The Search panel displays a list of suggestions.

**6** Click or tap a suggestion, or continue typing, and then click or tap the **Search** button.

**7** To cancel the search, delete the search text in the Search box.

### See Also

*See "Setting Search Options for Apps" on page 45 for more information on customizing the use of the Search panel.*

Search using an app

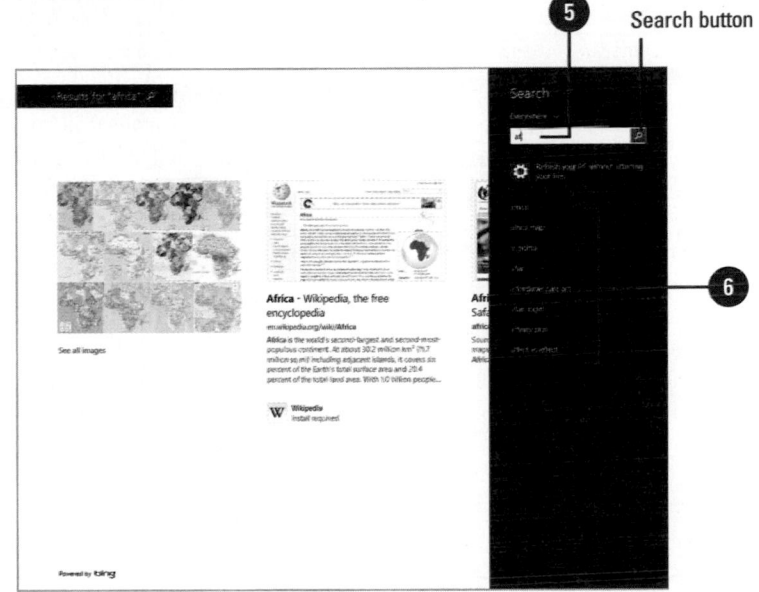

Search button

# Using Different Apps

Windows 8.1 comes with several built-in metro apps (**New!**) that are extremely useful for completing everyday tasks. You can access the metro apps from the Start screen. The live tiles on the Start screen provide quick status information that relates to the app. For example, the tile for the Finance app displays current stock information from the different exchanges. The information on the live tiles continually changes. However, you can clear the tile information by using the Tiles command on the Settings panel; click or tap the Settings button on the Charms bar. You can start an app on the Start or Apps screen by simply clicking or tapping the app's tile.

## Start Screen Default Metro Apps

| Program | Description |
| --- | --- |
| Alarms (**New!**) | Sets alarms and uses a timer or stopwatch |
| Calculator (**New!**) | Calculates numbers using a standard, scientific, or converter calculator |
| Calendar | Creates and manages events and appointments in a calendar |
| Camera | Takes and manages photos using a camera |
| Desktop | Provides access to the Windows desktop |
| Finance | Provides financial information from popular services |
| Food & Drink (**New!**) | Provides food and drink information from popular services |
| Games | Provides access to games and online services |
| Health & Fitness (**New!**) | Provides health and fitness information from popular services |
| Help+Tips (**New!**) | Provides quick help, tips, and what's new for Windows 8.1 |
| Internet Explorer | Browses the web |
| Mail | Sends and receives electronic messages to contacts |
| Maps | Provides maps and directions |
| Music | Provides access to music and online services |
| News | Provides news information from popular services |
| People | Creates and manages contact information |
| Photos | Works with pictures and photos |
| Reader | Displays PDF and XPS documents |
| Reading List (**New!**) | Keeps track of articles you want to read on the web or in apps |
| Scan (**New!**) | Scans pages and information from a connected scanner |
| Skype (**New!**) | Sends and receives online calls and messages to contacts |
| Sports | Provides sports information from popular services |
| SkyDrive | Stores and manages files on a Microsoft cloud service |
| Store | Purchases, installs, and updates apps |
| Travel | Provides travel information from popular services |
| Video | Provides access to videos and online services |
| Weather | Provides weather information |

# Starting and Closing Apps

Starting an app is pretty straight forward in Windows 8.1. You can start an app from the Start screen, Apps view screen, or Apps search results with a simple click of a mouse or tap of your finger. When you click or tap an app tile, the app opens in full screen view, where you can start using it. Some apps even allow you to start multiple instances (**New!**). As you work with an app in full screen view, you'll notice it doesn't display a visual way to close it. You can close an app with a drag from the top edge of the screen to the bottom edge of the screen. When you close an app, it's no longer active, however it's put to sleep —or tombstoned—(**New!**) to run in the background. This is helpful when you want to stream music or video, or receive notifications. When you reopen a tombstoned app, you can start where you left off. You can still close an app for good. Windows 8.1 is designed to work with multiple apps at the same time, so closing an app is not as necessary unless your device is low on memory. Each time you start an app, it uses device memory, known as RAM (Random Access Memory). When you reach the memory limit for your device, you can't open anymore apps unless you close one or more to free up memory space.

## Start and Close an App

1. Display the Start or Apps view screen.

2. Scroll as needed to display the tile for the app you want to start.

   ◆ **Scrolling.** Move the pointer to show the scroll bars, click or tap the scroll arrows or swipe right or left from the middle of the screen (on a mobile device).

3. To open an app in full screen view, click or tap the app's tile.

4. To close the app, use the following:

   ◆ **Close and sleep.** Point to the top edge of the screen (cursor changes to a hand), and then drag down to the bottom edge of the screen.

   ◆ **Close for good.** Point to the top edge of the screen (cursor changes to a hand), and then drag down to the bottom of the screen and hold until the tile flips around.

# Using the App Bar

When you're working on the Start screen or other metro apps in Windows 8.1, you can access commands and other options from the App bar. You can display the App bar within a metro app by right-clicking the screen on a PC computer or clicking or tapping a minimized App bar (if available for an app, such as Calendar) (**New!**), or swiping up from the bottom or down from the top of the screen on a mobile device. The App bar appears at the bottom of the screen, however, some apps, such as the Weather app, also display a bar at the top of the screen with additional options.

## Use the App Bar

1. Open an app or display the Start screen.

2. Right-click a blank area of the screen (on a computer) or swipe up from the bottom edge or down from the top edge of the screen (on a mobile device).

   Some apps display a minimized App bar with three dots (**New!**) on the right side. You can click or tap any where on the the minimized App bar to expand it.

   **TIMESAVER** *Press Win+Z to display the App bar.*

3. Click or tap a button on the App bar.

4. If a menu appears, click or tap a command.

5. To dismiss the panel, click or tap a blank area off the bar, or press Esc.

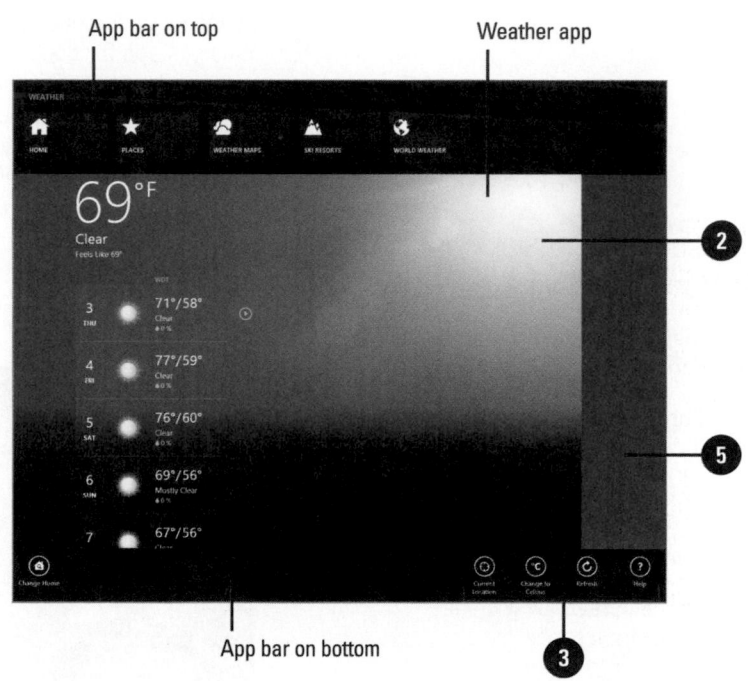

App bar on top — Weather app — App bar on bottom

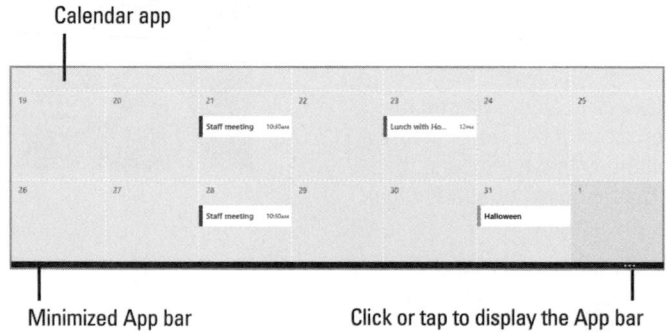

Calendar app — Minimized App bar — Click or tap to display the App bar

# Changing App Settings

In addition to the App bar, you can also change app settings by using the Settings button on the Charms bar. With the app open, the Settings button opens the Settings panel with options specific to the app. For example, Internet Explorer displays four options: Options, Privacy, About, Help, Accounts, and Permissions. When you select an option, the panel displays app specific settings. You can use the Back button in the upper-left corner of the panel to go back to the previous panel.

## Change App Settings

1. Open an app or display the Start screen.

2. Point to the lower- or upper-right corner and move up or down (on a computer) or swipe left from the right edge of the screen (on a mobile device).

3. Click or tap the **Settings** button on the Charms bar.

   **TIMESAVER** *Press Win+I to display the Settings panel.*

4. Click or tap an option on the Settings panel for the open app.

5. Change the options you want for the app. To display more options, if available, move the pointer to display a scroll bar in the panel.

6. To go back to the previous panel, click or tap the **Back** button.

7. To dismiss the panel, click or tap a blank area off the panel, or press Esc.

Internet Explorer app settings

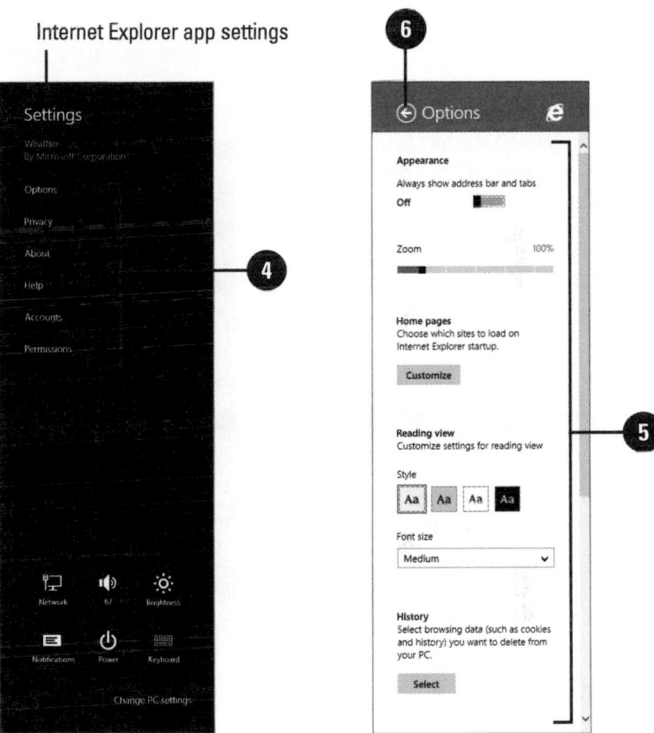

# Working with Multiple Apps

Windows 8.1 is designed to work with multiple apps at the same time, so closing an app is not as typical as with previous versions of Windows. After you open an app, you can switch to Start screen, and then open another one. After you open multiple apps, you can quickly switch between open apps with a click or swipe. You can click the lower- or upper-left corner on a PC computer or swipe right from the left edge on a mobile device to switch between open apps and the Start screen, unless you turn off the options under PC settings.

## Switch Between Apps

◆ **Switch between the Start screen and the most recently used apps.** Click the lower-left corner (on a computer) or swipe right from the left edge (on a mobile device).

◆ **Switch between all open apps.** Click the upper-left corner (on a computer) or swipe right from the left edge (on a mobile device).

**TIMESAVER** *Press Alt+Tab to cycle through open apps or press Alt+Shift+Tab to reverse the order.*

◆ **Use the Start bar to switch between apps.** Point to the upper- or lower-left corner (on a computer) or swipe in slightly from the left edge and then back quickly (on a mobile device).

If you have more than two apps open, move down from the top or up from the bottom to display thumbnails.

You can click or tap a thumbnail to display the app.

Open apps on the Start bar

Start button on the Start bar

### Did You Know?

*You can modify app switching options.* In the Start screen, click or tap the Settings button on the Charms bar, click or tap Change PC Settings, click or tap Corners and edges, and then drag the slider options under App switching to turn them on or off.

# Working with Apps Side by Side

Windows 8.1 was designed to work with multiple full screen apps at the same time. You can quickly switch between open apps with a click or swipe. However, sometimes you want to display more than one full screen app on the screen at the same time. For example, you might want to view your SkyDrive on one part of the screen while you work with files in File Explorer on the desktop on another part of the screen. The snap feature enables you to display up to four apps (**New!**) side by side by splitting the screen with dividers, known as Separation bars, as you drag one app next to another. The number of apps you can use, depends on your display resolution (**New!**); four apps need a large screen resolution of 2,560 x 1,600. You can adjust the position of the Separation bar (**New!**) to show more or less of an app as you need it. The screen with multiple apps acts like a single app, not separate ones. For example, when you switch apps, only the single screen appears.

## Display Apps Side by Side

1. Open one of the apps that you want to use from the Start screen.

2. Point to the top of the screen (cursor changes to a hand) and drag down (on a computer) or swipe in slowly from the left edge (on a mobile device), and then drag to the right or left edge.

   A Separation bar appears to indicate a split screen. The app displays on one side while the Start screen displays on the other.

3. Open another app from the Start screen to fill in the split screen; you can repeat for up to four apps (**New!**), and drag app to place.

   ◆ You can also right-click a thumbnail on the Start bar, and then click or tap **Insert Left**, **Insert Right**, or **Replace**.

4. To adjust the size of a side, point to the Separation bar, and then drag left or right (**New!**) to adjust it.

5. To remove an app from the split screen, point to the Separation bar, and then drag left or right to the edge towards the app you want to remove.

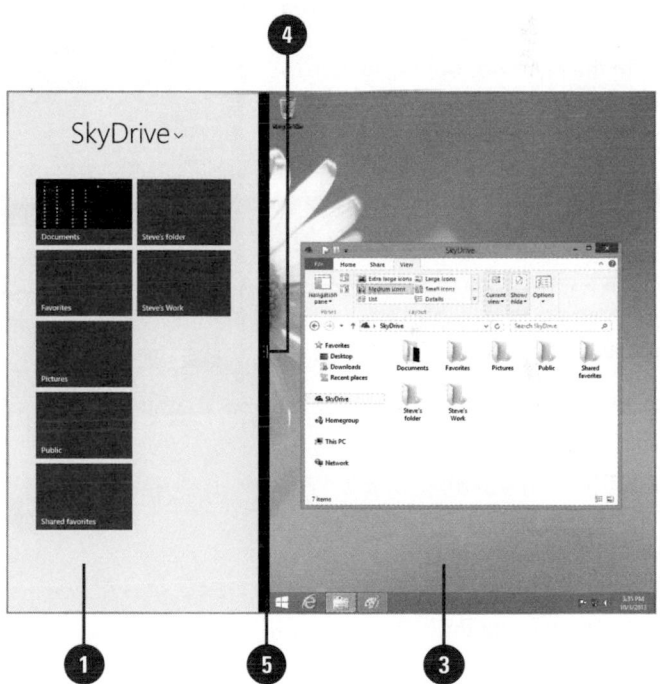

## Sharing Between Apps

Windows 8.1 makes it easy to share information, either text or pictures, using other apps. For example, you can select text or pictures on a web page in Internet Explorer, and then share it with others in an email using Mail. The default sharing app is Mail, however, you can also install and use other online services, such as Twitter and Facebook. The process is pretty simple. Open an app with the content you want to share, display or select the information or item, click or tap the Share button on the Charms bar, and then select the sharing app you want to use.

### Share Between Apps

1 Open the app with the content you want to share.

2 Display or select the information or item you want to share.

3 Point to the lower- or upper-right corner and move up or down (on a computer) or swipe left from the right edge of the screen (on a mobile device).

4 Click or tap the **Share** button on the Charms bar.

   **TIMESAVER** *Press Win+H to display the Share panel.*

5 Click or tap the app that you want to use.

   **TROUBLE?** *If a sharing app is not available, make sure it is installed using the Windows Store.*

6 Use the app to send the information to another person.

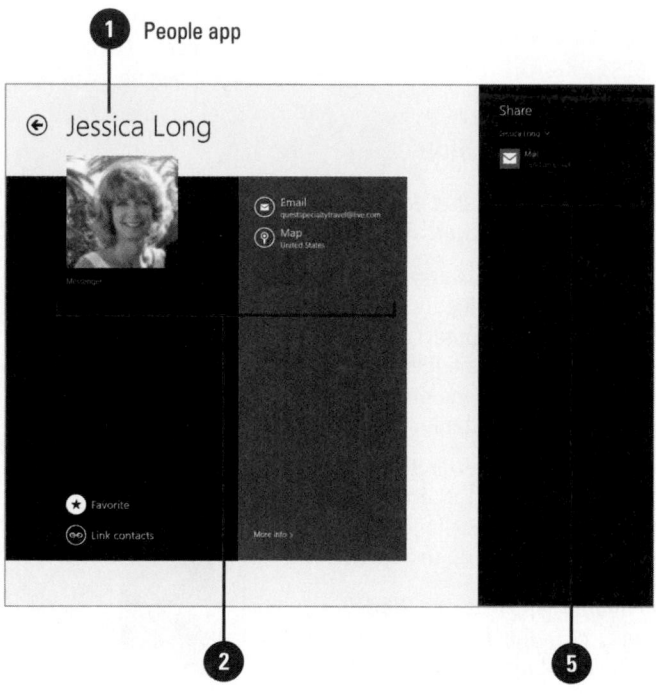

1 People app

2

5

### Did You Know?

*You can use a keyboard shortcut to take a screenshot.* In any app, press Win+PrtScn (Print Screen) to take a screenshot and automatically save it in the Pictures folder in the Screenshots folder as a PNG file.

## Change Share Settings

① Display the Start screen.

② Point to the lower- or upper-right corner and move up or down (on a computer) or swipe left from the right edge of the screen (on a mobile device).

③ Click or tap the **Settings** button on the Charms bar.

④ Click or tap **Change PC settings** on the Settings panel.

⑤ Click or tap **Search and apps** under PC settings (**New!**), and then click or tap **Share** on the panel.

⑥ Specify from the following options:

◆ **Show apps I use most often at the top of the app list.** Drag the slider to turn on or off.

◆ **Show a list of how I share most often.** Drag the slider to turn on or off.

◆ **Items in list.** Specify the number of items you want or click or tap Clear list.

◆ **Use these apps to share.** Drag the slider to turn the app on or off for sharing.

⑦ To close the app, point to the top edge of the screen (cursor changes to a hand), and then drag down to the bottom edge of the screen.

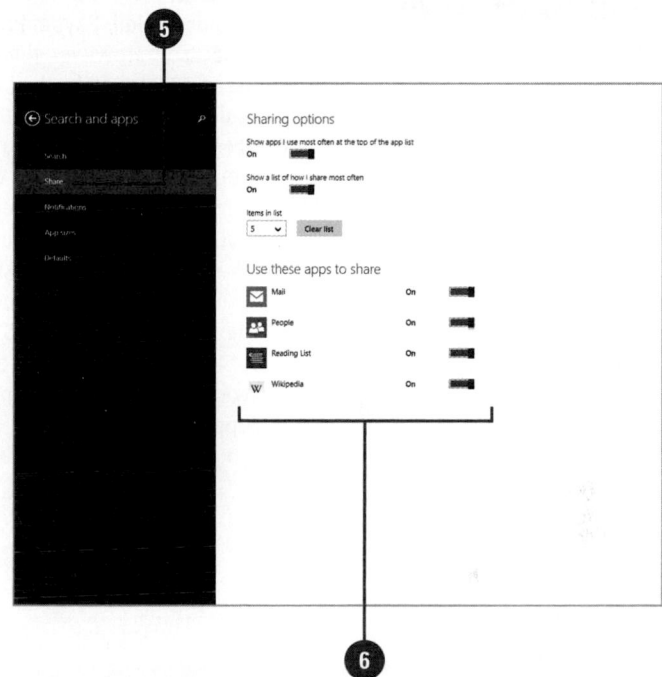

# Installing Apps from the Store

Windows 8.1 comes with a default set of apps, such as Internet Explorer, Mail, Skype, Photos, Video, and Music, developed by Microsoft. However, there are a lot more apps available for almost any need developed by third parties. You can purchase and install apps quickly and easily from the Windows Store. The Windows Store organizes apps by the main categories (**New!**), such as Featured, Picks for you, Trending, and New & Rising, and then further breaks them down into Top paid and Top free, to make apps easy to find and discover. If you're looking for a specific app, you can use Search box (**New!**). The Windows Store uses your Microsoft email (the one used to Sign-in to Windows 8.1) as the account to purchase apps. If you have multiple devices with Windows 8.1, you can install a purchased app on up to five of them using your Microsoft account. You can display a list of the apps you own on the Your apps screen. This doesn't include any Windows 8.1 apps installed along with operating system. From the Your apps screen, you can install or reinstall an app or an app update.

## Use the Windows Store

1 Click or tap the **Store** tile on the Start or Apps screen.

2 Scroll through the app categories to find the one you want.

3 To search for an app, click or tap in the Search box (**New!**), and then type an app name to find it.

4 Click or tap a category, such as **Featured**, **Picks for you**, **Trending**, **New & Rising**, **Top paid**, or **Top free**, as desired.

◆ **Options and All Categories.** Right-click (on a computer) or swipe down from the top of the Store (on a mobile device) to display options and categories (**New!**).

5 Click or tap a specific app tile.

6 Click or tap the **Install** button, and then follow any on-screen instructions as needed.

Windows starts installing the selected apps.

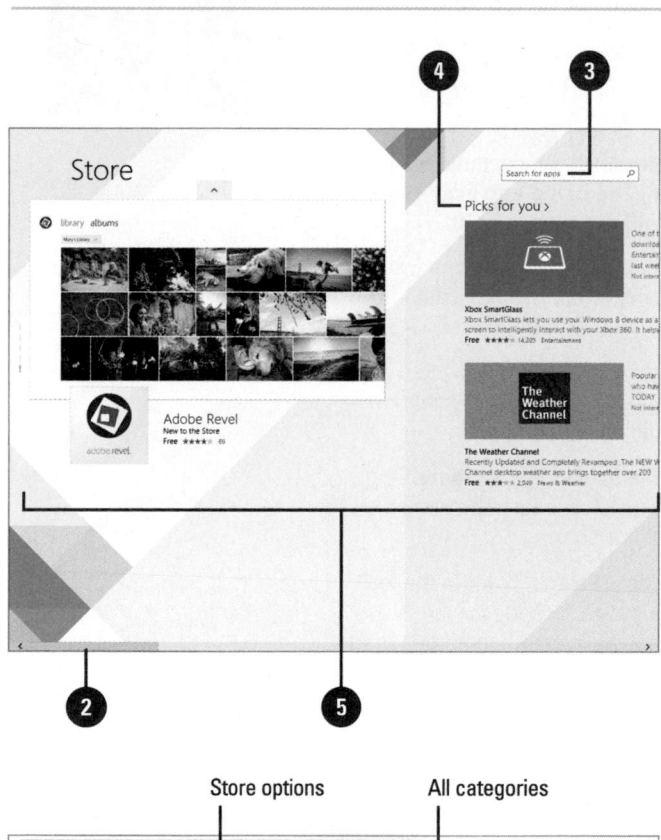

## View or Reinstall Your Apps from the Store

1. Click or tap the **Store** tile on the Start or Apps screen.

2. Right-click a blank area of the screen (on a computer) or swipe up from the bottom edge or down from the top edge of the screen (on a mobile device).

3. Click or tap **Your apps** on the App bar.

4. Click or tap the list arrow, and then select an option to filter the list.

   ◆ **All apps.**

   ◆ **Apps no installed on this PC.**

   ◆ **Apps installed on *device*.**

5. To install an app, click or tap an individual tile to select the app, click or tap the **Install** button, and then follow any on-screen instructions as needed.

   Windows starts installing the selected apps.

6. Click or tap the **Back** button to return to the previous screen.

7. To go back to the main Store screen, right-click a blank area of the screen (on a computer) or swipe up from the bottom edge or down from the top edge of the screen (on a mobile device), and then click or tap **Home** on the App bar.

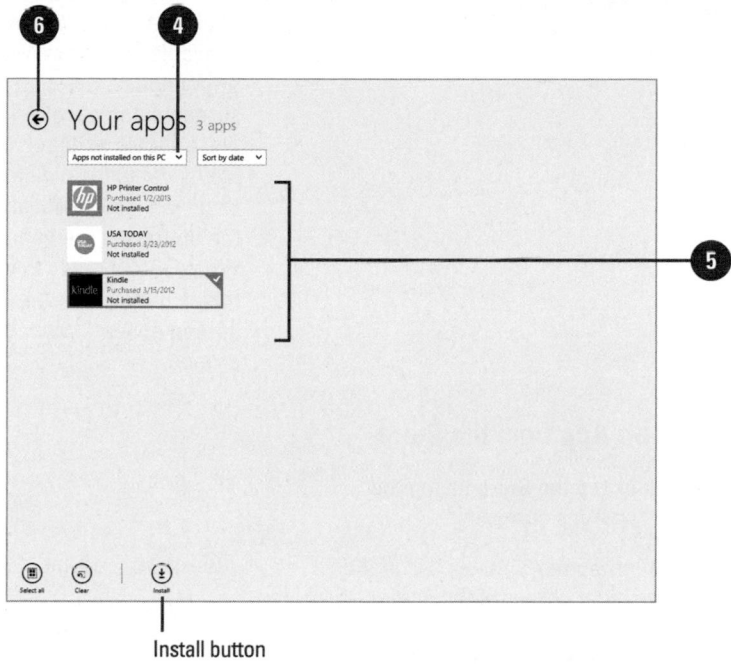

Install button

### Did You Know?

*You can view app disk space usage.* Click or tap the Settings button on the Charms bar, click or tap Change PC settings, click or tap Search and apps, and then click or tap App Sizes.

## For Your Information

### Viewing Your Account Information

Before you can purchase an app, you need to add a payment method to your Microsoft account. You can do this from your account in the Windows Store. Click or tap the Store tile on the Start or Apps screen, click or tap the Settings button on the Charms bar, click or tap Your account on the panel, click or tap Add payment method, and then follow the on-screen instructions. If you have a gift card or promotional code you can redeem it (**New!**). From your account, you can also change your user account and remove your user account from your device.

### Changing Store Preferences

You can change Store preferences to make it easier to find certain types of apps when you browse categories or view list of apps in the Store. You can set options to make it easier to find apps in my preferred languages or that include accessibility features. You can also set an option to have the Store recommend apps for you.

# Updating Apps

Developers, including Microsoft, continually update apps to provide additional features. If a new version of an app you have installed is available, Windows automatically generates an update link for you in the Windows Store on the App updates screen. The App updates screen automatically displays a list of apps with an available update. The updates appear with a check mark in the upper-right corner of the tile by default to indicate you want to install the update. You can click or tap an individual tile to deselect or select the app. You can also use the buttons at the bottom screen to clear, select, or view the updates. When you're ready to install the selected updates, click or tap the Install button. The App updates screen closes and Windows Store screen appears. Windows starts installing the app updates in the background.

## Update an App from the Store

1. Click or tap the **Store** tile on the Start or Apps screen.

2. Click or tap the **Updates** link in the upper-right corner of the screen.

   If the Updates link is not available, it means that all the apps you have installed on your device are up-to-date with the latest version.

   ◆ You can also click or tap the **Settings** button on the Charms bar, and then click or tap **App updates**.

3. Click or tap individual app tiles to deselect or select the app for updating.

4. Click or tap the **Install** button, and then follow any on-screen instructions as needed.

   Windows starts updating the selected apps.

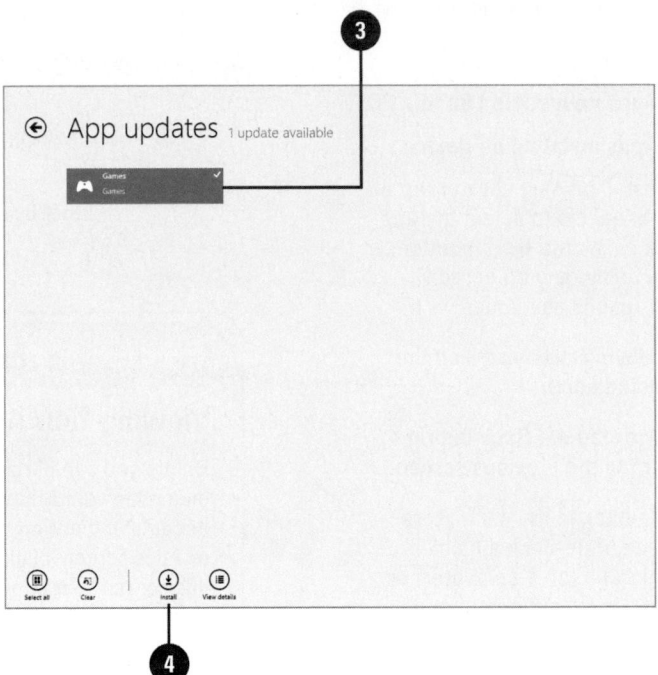

# Uninstalling Apps

When you install an app, including the ones that come by default with Windows 8.1, it takes up storage space on your PC computer or mobile device. If space becomes limited or you just don't use an app anymore, you can uninstall it to free up storage space. You can uninstall one or more apps at the same time from the Start or Apps screen. Simply select the one or more apps you want to uninstall, then use the Uninstall button on the App bar. After an alert message to confirm the uninstall, Windows 8.1 uninstalls the app. If you want to uninstall Windows accessories and system tools, you need to turn the Windows features off under Programs within the Control Panel from the desktop, which you'll learn about in a later unit.

## Uninstall an App from the Store

1. Display the Start or Apps screen.

   ◆ To display the Apps screen, click or tap the **Search** button on the Charms bar.

2. Right-click (on a computer) or tap-drag down slightly (on a mobile device) to select or deselect an app tile.

3. Click or tap the **Uninstall** button on the App bar.

4. Click or tap **Uninstall** to confirm the uninstall.

   The app tile is removed from the Start screen and Windows uninstalls the app from your device. However, as a purchased app, you can install it again in this or any other Windows 8.1 device.

# Customizing Apps on the Start Screen

The Start screen is the beginning point for accessing apps and features in Windows 8.1. Customizing the Start screen can save you time and effort by making it easier to find the apps or Windows accessories you use most often. You can add apps or accessories to the Start screen or customize the way the Start screen looks and functions. The Start screen contains pinned items from the Apps screen, which is the default location for installed apps (**New!**). Pinned items are shortcuts to make it easier to open an app or accessory.The Start screen comes with a default set of pinned items when you install Windows 8.1, however you can add your own. The pinned items remain on the Start screen, like a push pin holds paper on a bulletin board, until you unpin them. When you unpin an item, Windows removes the shortcut from the Start screen, however, it doesn't remove the app or accessory from your device. You can also change a few display options using the Start settings panel, such as personalizing the Start background (**New!**), showing accessories on the Start screen and clearing live tile information to maintain privacy.

## Customize Apps on the Start Screen

1. Display the Start screen, and then move the pointer or tap the screen as needed to show the button.

2. Click or tap the **Apps view** button (**New!**) (on a computer) or swipe up from the bottom of the Start screen (on a mobile device).

3. Right-click (on a computer) or tap-drag down slightly (on a mobile device) to select an app tile.

4. Click the **Pin to Start button** or **Unpin from Start button** button on the App bar.

### Did You Know?

*You can pin to or unpin from taskbar.* Display the Apps screen, right-click (on a computer) or tap-drag down slightly (on a mobile device) to select an app tile, and then click or tap the Pin to taskbar button or Unpin from taskbar button button on the App bar.

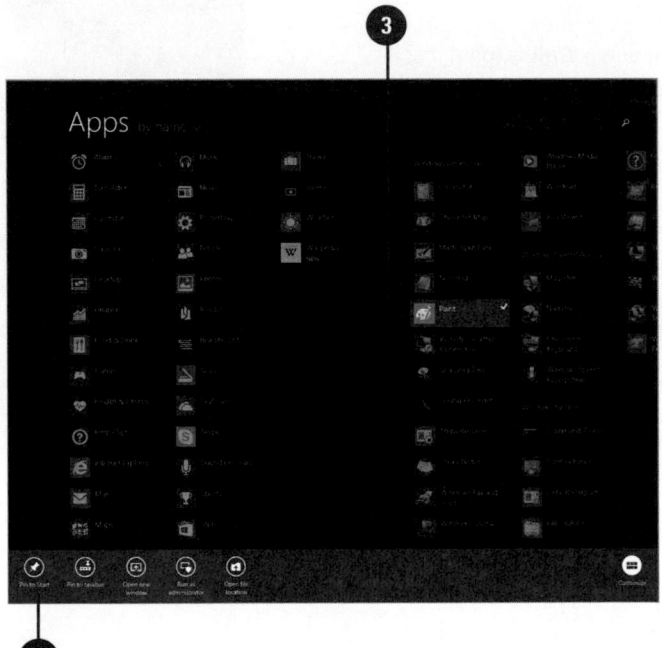

## Change Start Screen Settings

1. Display the Start screen.

2. Point to the lower- or upper-right corner and move up or down (on a computer) or swipe left from the right edge of the screen (on a mobile device).

3. Click or tap **Settings** button on the Charms bar.

4. Click or tap **Personalize (New!)** on the Settings panel.

5. Click or tap a background (**New!**), and then click or tap a background and accent color.

6. Click or tap the **Back** button on the Settings panel.

7. Click or tap **Tiles** on the Settings panel.

8. To show or hide Windows accessories and system tools on the Start screen, drag the **Show administrative tools** slider to turn it on or off.

9. To maintain privacy and clear information on tiles, click or tap the **Clear** button on the Tiles panel.

### Did You Know?

*You can turn live tile off.* On the Start screen, right-click (on a computer) or tap-drag down slightly (on a mobile device) to select an app tile, and then click or tap the Turn live tile off button on the App bar. Not all tiles can display live information

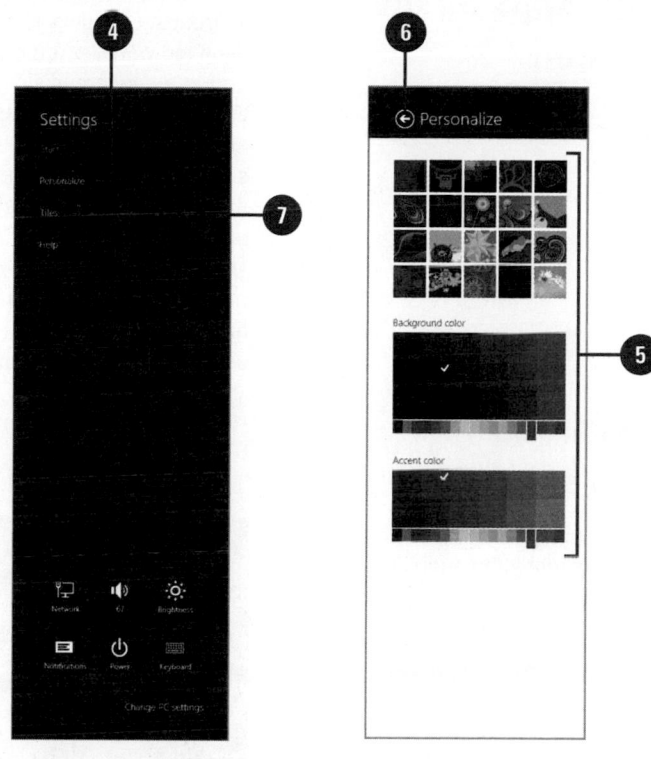

# Grouping Apps on the Start Screen

When you view the Start screen, you notice the app tiles are arranged in groups. Grouping apps together makes it easier to locate and use them individually. You can arrange app items within an existing group or create a new group simply by repositioning them on the Start screen. When you move app tiles into groups on the Start screen, Windows automatically arranges them in the group to fit in place. Because tile sizes vary, some are smaller squares while others are larger rectangles, they don't always fit seamlessly into place. If you want all the tiles to fit nicely in place, you can resize (**New!**) them to large, wide, medium, or small at any time. After you organize your apps into a group, you can name each group for easy identification (**New!**). If the name you originally chose for a group no longer fits, or you want to delete it, you can edit or remove the group name using the same method.

## Change App Tile Size

1. Display the Start screen.

2. Right-click (on a computer) or tap-drag down slightly (on a mobile device) to select one or more app tiles (**New!**).

3. Click or tap the **Resize** button (**New!**) on the App bar, and then click or tap an option (**New!**): **Large**, **Wide**, **Medium**, or **Small**.

### Did You Know?

*You can turn live tile off or on.* On the Start screen, right-click (on a computer) or tap-drag down slightly (on a mobile device) to select an app tile, and then click or tap the Turn live tile off or Turn live tile on button on the App bar. Not all tiles can display live information.

### See Also

*See "Customizing Apps on the Start Screen" on page 40 for more information on setting options to customize the Start screen.*

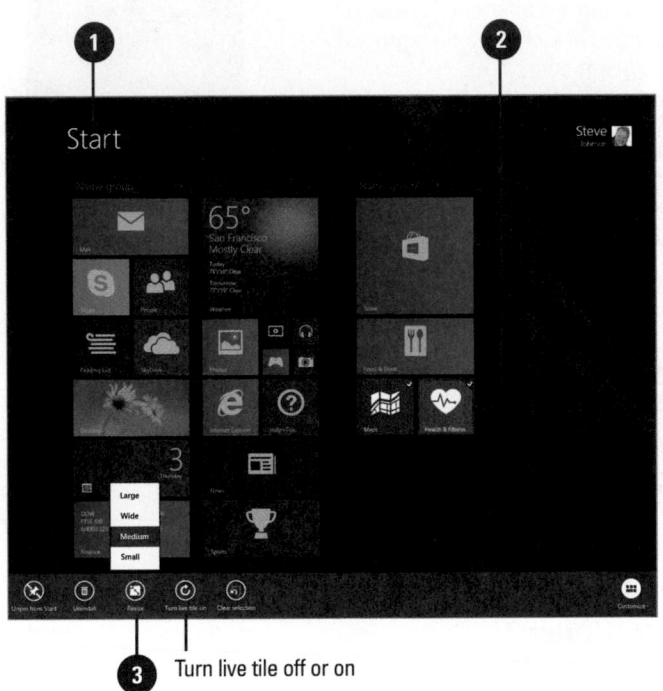

Turn live tile off or on

## Group Apps on the Start Screen

1. Display the Start screen.

2. Drag a tile to another existing group of tiles, or drag a tile to the blank area on the right side of the screen to create a new group.

3. Right-click a blank area of the screen (on a computer) or swipe up from the bottom edge or down from the top edge of the screen (on a mobile device).

4. Click or tap the **Customize** button on the App bar.

   **TIMESAVER** *When you select an app tile, you can also change any group names (**New!**).*

5. Click or tap in the Group Name box (**New!**), enter a name for the group, and then click or tap outside the box.

   ◆ **Remove group name.** Point to a group name, and then click the **Delete** button (x) (**New!**).

6. Click or tap in a blank area to exit Customize.

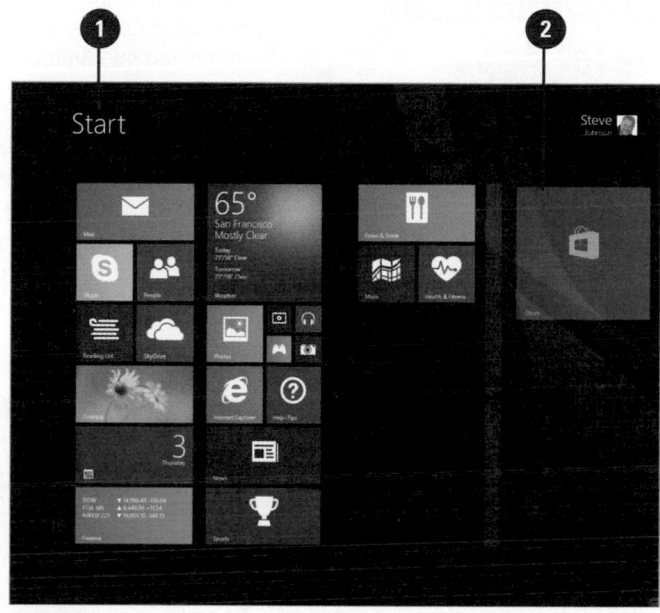

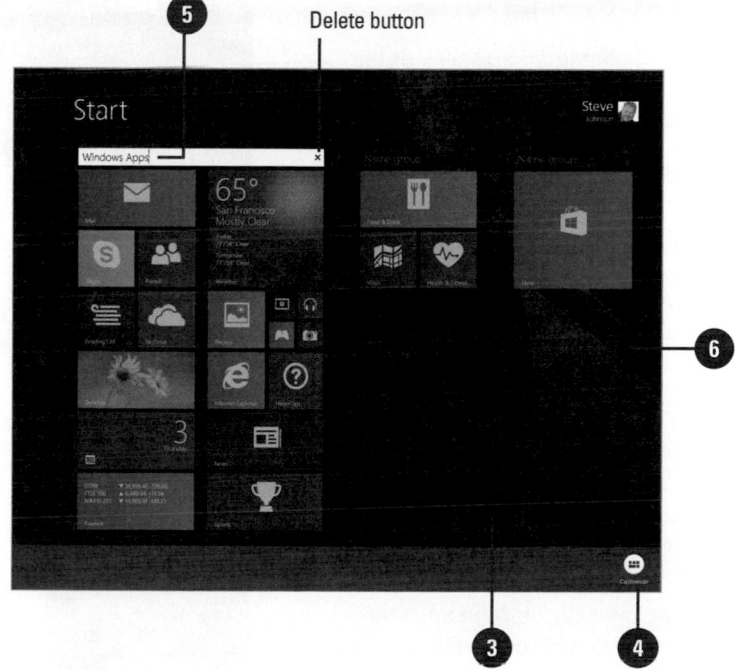

Delete button

# Setting Notification Options for Apps

Notifications are a way for Windows 8.1 and apps to communicate with you. When new information is available within an app or an action is requested by Windows, a notification appears. There are several types of notifications: a pop-up (also known as toast), start screen tile or badge, and lock screen icon. You can change notifications settings under Notifications or Lock screen to customize the way it works. You can enable or disable app notifications for all apps or just specific ones and play sounds. You can also specify a quiet time (**New!**) to stop notifications and calls when you're away. For the Lock screen, you can specify up to seven apps to show notifications and status. If you're getting to many notifications, you can temporarily hide them for 1, 3, or 8 hours.

## Set Notification Options for Apps

1. Display the Start screen.

2. Point to the lower- or upper-right corner and move up or down (on a computer) or swipe left from the right edge of the screen (on a mobile device).

3. Click or tap the **Settings** button on the Charms bar.

4. To hide notifications, click or tap the **Notifications** button, and click or tap **Hide for 1 hour, Hide for 3 hours**, or **Hide for 8 hours**. Click or tap again to show them.

5. Click or tap **Change PC settings** on the Settings panel.

6. Click or tap **Search and apps** under PC settings (**New!**), and then click or tap **Notifications** on the panel.

7. Drag the slider to turn notification options (**New!**) on or off.

8. Set options to stop notifications and receive calls during quiet times (**New!**).

9. Drag the slider for the app you want to enable or disable.

10. To close the app, point to the top edge of the screen (cursor changes to a hand), and then drag down to the bottom edge of the screen.

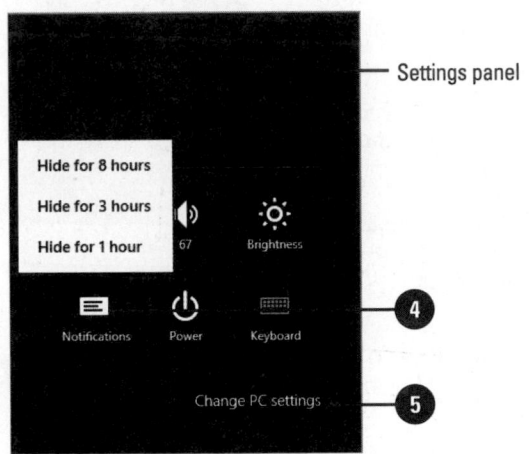

Settings panel

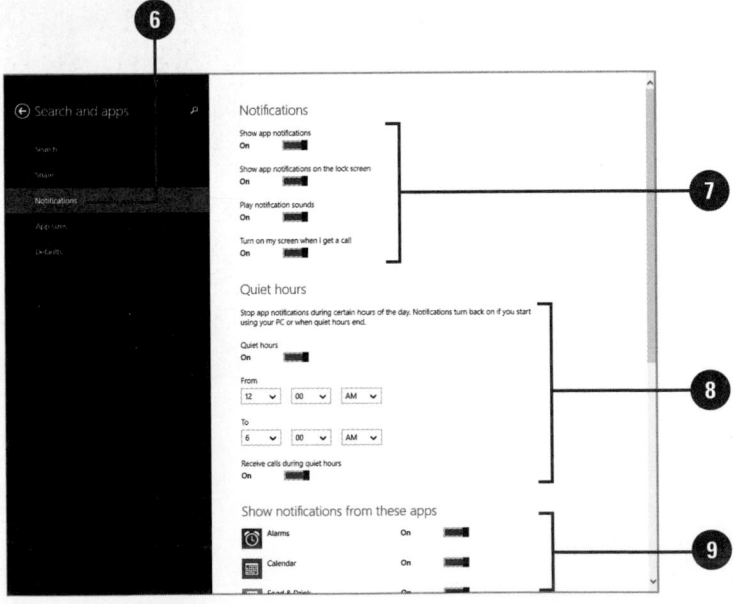

# Setting Search Options for Apps

When you use the Search button on the Charms bar to location information on the web or within an app, you can set options under PC settings to customize the way it works. You can set options to use Bing to search online, get personalized results from Bing (**New!**), filter search results (**New!**), get search suggestions for metered connections (**New!**), or clear the search history in Windows.

## Set Search Options for Apps

**1** Display the Start screen.

**2** Point to the lower- or upper-right corner and move up or down (on a computer) or swipe left from the right edge of the screen (on a mobile device).

**3** Click or tap the **Settings** button on the Charms bar.

**4** Click or tap **Change PC settings** on the Settings panel.

**5** Click or tap **Search and apps** under PC settings (**New!**), and then click or tap **Search** on the panel.

**6** To clear the search history in Windows, click or tap **Clear**.

**7** Drag the slider on or off to use Bing to search online.

**8** Click or tap a Search Experience option to get personalized results from Bing or not.

**9** Click or tag a SafeSearch option to filter the search: **Strict**, **Moderate**, or **Off**.

**10** Drag the slider on or off for search option for Metered Connections.

**11** To close the app, point to the top edge of the screen (cursor changes to a hand), and then drag down to the bottom edge of the screen.

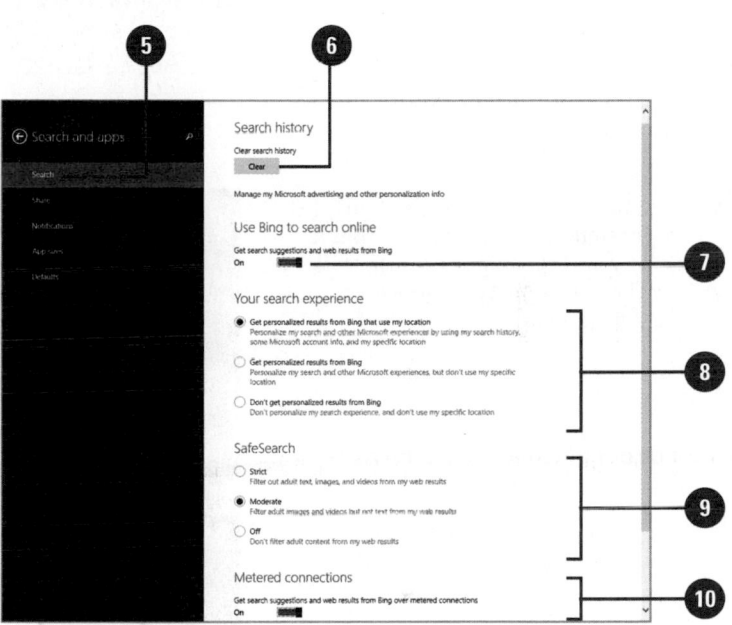

# Setting Privacy Options for Apps

When you use apps (which you can specify), such as Maps or Skype, the app includes functionality that uses information from Windows, such as my name and account picture, my location, my webcam (**New!**), my microphone (**New!**), and other devices (**New!**). For example, the Maps app uses your current location (my location) to pin point it on a map, and the Skype app displays your name (my name) and account picture and uses a webcam and microphone during calls and conversations. You can set privacy settings to enable or disable these and other options to specify the level of protection you want and the apps you want to use.

## Set Privacy Options for Apps

1. Display the Start screen.

2. Point to the lower- or upper-right corner and move up or down (on a computer) or swipe left from the right edge of the screen (on a mobile device).

3. Click or tap the **Settings** button on the Charms bar.

4. Click or tap **Change PC settings** on the Settings panel.

5. Click or tap **Privacy** under PC settings (**New!**), and then click or tap **General** on the panel.

6. Drag the slider to turn general privacy options (**New!**) on or off.

7. Click or tap **Location**, **Webcam** (**New!**), **Microphone** (**New!**), or **Other Device** (**New!**).

8. Drag the slider on or off to let windows and app use my location, webcam, microphone, or device.

9. When turned on, drag the slider for the app (**New!**) you want to enable or disable the use.

10. To close the app, point to the top edge of the screen (cursor changes to a hand), and then drag down to the bottom edge of the screen.

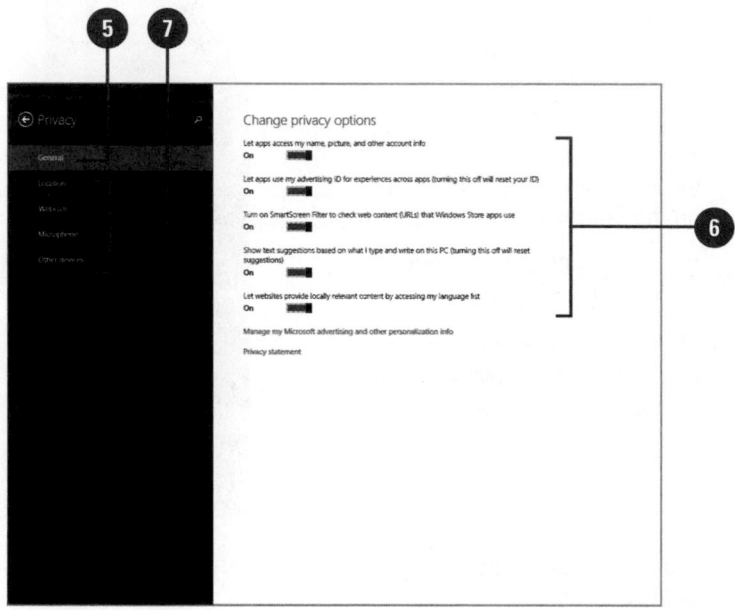

## For Your Information

### Changing Location Settings in the Control Panel

In the Control Panel, you can use the Location Settings icon to set options to let users control how apps use their location. In the Start screen, click or tap the Apps view button, click or tap Control Panel, and then click or tap the Location settings icon in Small icons or Large icons view. Select or clear the Turn on the Windows Location platform check box, where you can let users choose their own location settings for apps. If you want to help Microsoft with location services, you can select the Help Improve Microsoft Location Services check box. When you're done, click or tap Apply.

# Managing Files and Folders

## Introduction

File management is organizing and keeping track of files and folders, helping you stay organized, so information is easily located. A **folder** is a container for storing programs and files, similar to a folder in a file cabinet. As with a file cabinet, working with poorly managed files is like looking for a needle in a haystack—it is frustrating and time-consuming to search through irrelevant, misnamed, and out-of-date files to find the one you want. Windows allows you to organize folders and files in a file hierarchy, imitating the way you store paper documents in real folders. Just as a file cabinet contains several folders, each containing related documents with dividers grouping related folders together, so the Windows file hierarchy allows you to organize your files in folders, and then place folders in other folders. File Explorer comes with four libraries: Documents, Music, Pictures, and Videos. Libraries are special folders that catalog folders and files in a central location. A library includes and displays folders that are stored in different locations on your PC computer, Homegroup, or network.

Using the file management tools, you can save files in folders with appropriate names for easy identification, quickly and easily create new folders so you can reorganize information and delete files and folders that you no longer need. You can also search for a file when you cannot remember where you stored it, create shortcuts to files and folders for quick and easy access, and even compress files and folders to save space.

A folder can hold different types of files, such as text, spreadsheets, and presentations. The Documents folder is the main location in File Explorer where you store your files. However, there are some special folders, such as Pictures and Music, designed with specialized features to store specific types of files.

## What You'll Do

**Use the Explorer Window**

**Change the Explorer Window View**

**Use the Ribbon and Choose Commands**

**Open and View This PC**

**Work with Libraries**

**Navigate Between Folders**

**View the Folders List**

**Customize the Navigation Pane**

**Organize, Sort, and Group Files**

**Search for Files and Folders**

**Add Properties and Tags to Files**

**Create and Rename Files and Folders**

**Copy and Move Files and Folders**

**Delete and Restore Files and Folders**

**Create a Shortcut to a File or Folder**

**Change Folder Options**

**Change File and Folder List Views**

**Customize Personal Folders**

**Share Folders or Files with Others**

**Compress Files and Folders**

**Manage Files Using a CD or DVD**

# Using the Explorer Window

Explorer windows, such as File Explorer, are powerful easy-to-use tools for working with files in the desktop in Windows 8. Explorers give you more information and control while simplifying how you work with your files. The experience is easy and consistent, whether you're browsing documents or photos or even using the Control Panel. Key elements of the Explorer windows in the desktop are designed to help you get to the information you need, when you need it. Each Explorer window includes the following elements:

◆ **Toolbar.** Use to access frequently used commands, known as the Quick Access Toolbar.

◆ **Ribbon.** Use to access buttons or options organized in groups on tabs.

◆ **Back, Forward, and Up buttons.** Use to navigate between previously viewed folders.

◆ **Address bar.** Use to navigate directly to a different location, including local and network disks, folders, and web locations.

◆ **Search box.** Use to perform instant searches, which show only those files that match what you typed in the Search box for the current folder and any of its subfolders.

◆ **Navigation pane.** Use to display common folders, such as Favorites, SkyDrive (**New!**), Homegroup (a shared network), This PC (**New!**), and Network, using a Folder list tree structure.

◆ **SkyDrive, This PC, or Libraries.** Use to access common folders, such as Documents, Music, Pictures, and Videos located on your SkyDrive (**New!**) on the Microsoft cloud, or local PC (**New!**). A library is a collection of files and folders linked from different locations—such as a SkyDrive or This PC by default—into a central place. A file or folder can be stored in one location, yet linked to a library for easy access in one place.

◆ **Status bar.** Displays number of items and selected items in a folder, and Details and Icons view buttons.

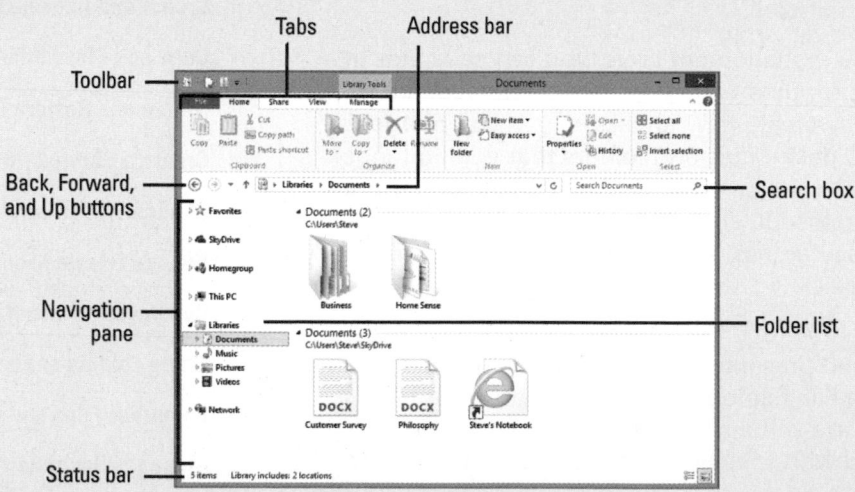

# Changing the Explorer Window View

The Explorer window displays the contents of a drive or folder in different ways to help you find the information you are looking for about a file or folder. The available views on the View tab of an Explorer window include Extra Large, Large, Medium and Small Icons, List, Details, Tiles, and Content.

**Icons** view displays icons in different sizes (Extra Large, Large, Medium, and Small), sorted alphabetically in horizontal rows with the name of the file or folder below each icon. When you view files using one of the Icon views, Live icons—thumbnails—display the first page of documents, the image of a photo, or the album art for individual songs, making it easier to find exactly what you are looking for.

**List** view displays small icons, sorted alphabetically into vertical columns with the name of the file or folder next to each icon.

**Details** view displays small icons, sorted alphabetically in a vertical column with the name of the file or folder and additional infor-

mation, such as file size, type, and date, in columns to the right.

**Tiles** view displays icons, sorted alphabetically into vertical columns, with information about the file next to each icon.

**Content** view displays medium icons in a vertical column with date modified information.

## Switching Between Views

You use the Layout options on the View tab in an Explorer window to quickly switch between window views. When you point to a Layout option—such as Extra large icon, Large icon, Medium icons, Small icons, List, Details, Tiles or Content—on the View tab, File Explorer displays a live preview of the option change so that you can see exactly what your change will look like before committing to it. You can also quickly change between Details and the current icons view by using the Details View and Icons View buttons on the Status bar.

Views button

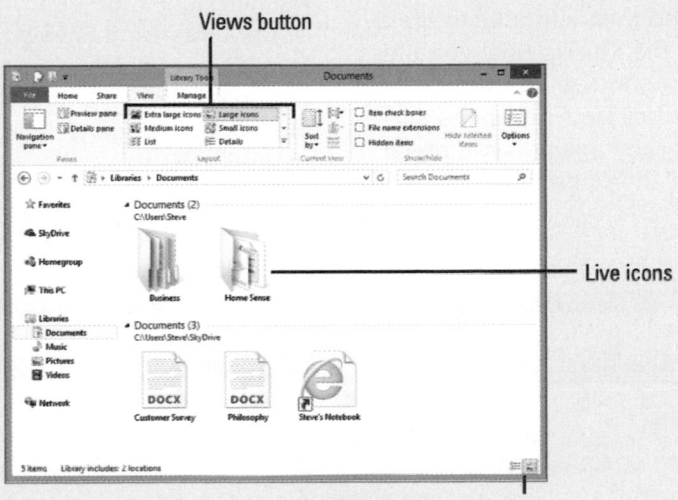

Live icons

View buttons on Status bar

# Using the Ribbon

The **Ribbon** is a results oriented way of working in File Explorer. The Ribbon is located at the top of the window and is comprised of **tabs** that are organized by task or objects. The controls on each tab are organized into **groups**, or subtasks. The controls, or **command buttons**, in each group execute a command, or display a menu of commands or a drop-down gallery. Controls in each group provide a visual way to quickly make document changes. The File tab on the left side of the Ribbon displays a menu of files related commands.

> **TIMESAVER** *To minimize the Ribbon, click or tap the Minimize the Ribbon button (Ctrl+F1) or double-click or double-tap the current tab. Click or tap a tab to auto display it (Ribbon remains minimized). Click or tap the Expand the Ribbon button (Ctrl+F1) or double-click or double-tap a tab to maximize it.*

If you prefer using the keyboard instead of the mouse to access commands on the Ribbon, File Explorer provides easy to use shortcuts. Simply press and release the ⟨Alt⟩ or ⟨F10⟩ key to display **KeyTips** over each feature in the current view, and then continue to press the letter shown in the KeyTip until you press the one that you want to use. To cancel an action and hide the KeyTips, press and release the ⟨Alt⟩ or ⟨F10⟩ key again. If you prefer using the keyboard shortcuts found in previous versions of Windows, such as Ctrl+C (for Copy) and Ctrl+V (for Paste), all the keyboard shortcuts and keyboard accelerators work exactly the same in File Explorer.

## Tabs

File Explorer provides three types of tabs on the Ribbon. The first type is called a **standard** tab—such as File, Home, Share, and View—that you see whenever you use File Explorer. The second type is called a **contextual** tab—such as Library Tools, Picture Tools, or Video Tools—that appears only when they are needed based on the type of task you are doing. File Explorer recognizes what you're doing and provides the right set of tabs and tools to use when you need them. The third type is called a **program** tab that replaces the standard set of tabs when you switch to certain views or modes, such as Homegroup, This PC, or Network.

## Live Preview

When you point to some options, such as a Layout option—Extra large icon, Large icon, Medium icons, Small icons, List, Details, Tiles or Content—on the View tab on the Ribbon, File Explorer displays a live preview of the option change so that you can see exactly what your change will look like before committing to it.

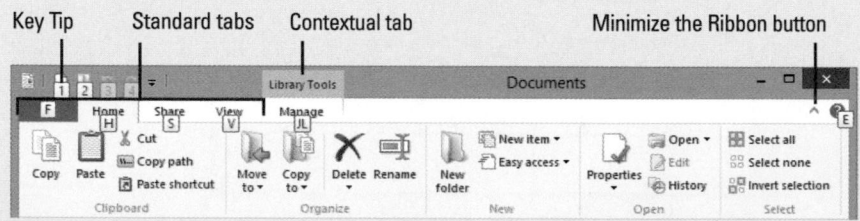

Key Tip     Standard tabs     Contextual tab          Minimize the Ribbon button

# Choosing Commands

File Explorer commands are organized in groups on the Ribbon and Quick Access Toolbar. Commands are available as buttons or options on the Ribbon, or as menus on button or option arrows or the File tab. The Quick Access Toolbar displays frequently used buttons that you may be already familiar with from other Microsoft programs, while the File tab on the Ribbon displays file related menu commands. In addition to the File tab, you can also open a shortcut menu with a group of related commands by right-clicking or tap holding an element.

## Choose a Menu Command Using the File Tab

1. In File Explorer, click or tap the **File** tab on the Ribbon.

2. If the command is followed by an arrow, point to the command to see a list of related options.

3. Click or tap a command.

   **TIMESAVER** *You can use a shortcut key to choose a command. Press and hold down the first key and then press the second key. For example, press and hold the Ctrl key and then press W (or Ctrl+W) to select the Close command.*

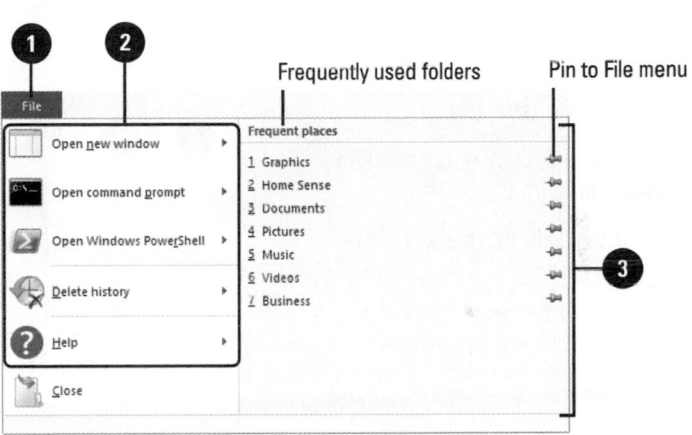

Frequently used folders    Pin to File menu

## Choose a Menu Command from a Shortcut Menu

1. In the desktop or File Explorer, right-click or tap-hold an icon.

   **TIMESAVER** *Press Shift+F10 to display the shortcut menu for a selected command.*

2. Click or tap a command on the shortcut menu. If the command is followed by an arrow, point to the command to see a list of related options, and then click or tap the option you want.

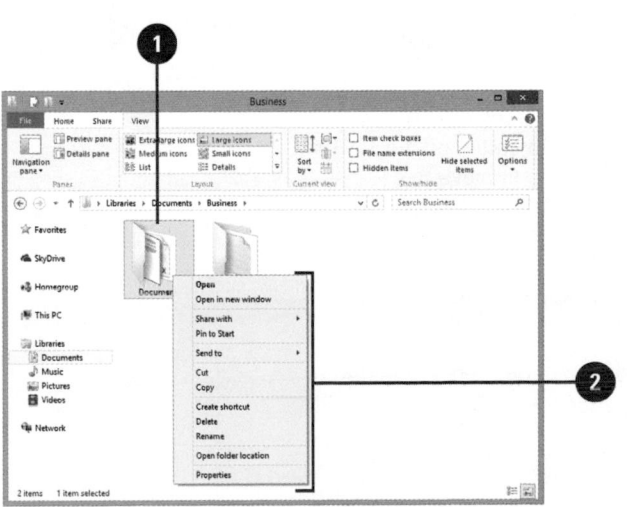

# Opening and Viewing This PC

The This PC window is the starting point to access every disk, folder, and file on your PC computer. You can access the This PC window from File Explorer. The This PC window displays local folders (**New!**) and several types of local, removable, and network drives. Drives and folders are represented by icons. Each drive is assigned a drive letter, denoted with parentheses and a colon, such as Local Disk (C:), to make it easier to identify. Typically, the floppy is drive A, the hard (also known as local) disk is drive C, and the CD or DVD is drive D. If your PC computer includes additional drives, your PC computer assigns them letters in alphabetical order. Once you open more than one drive or folder, you can use buttons on the Ribbon to help you move between folders.

## Open and View This PC

1. In the desktop, click or tap the **File Explorer** icon on the taskbar.

2. Click or tap **This PC** (**New!**) in the Navigation pane.

   ◆ In the Start screen, you can also click or tap **Apps view** button, and then click or tap **This PC**.

   TIMESAVER *Press Win+E to display the This PC window.*

3. Click or tap a drive to select it.

4. To review the drive details, click or tap the **Details pane** button on the View tab.

5. Double-click or double-tap the drive to open it.

6. Click or tap the **Back** or **Forward** button or the **Up** button on the toolbar to return or move to a previously visited window.

   TIMESAVER *You can press the Backspace key to go back to a previous folder you visited.*

7. When you're done, click or tap the **Close** button.

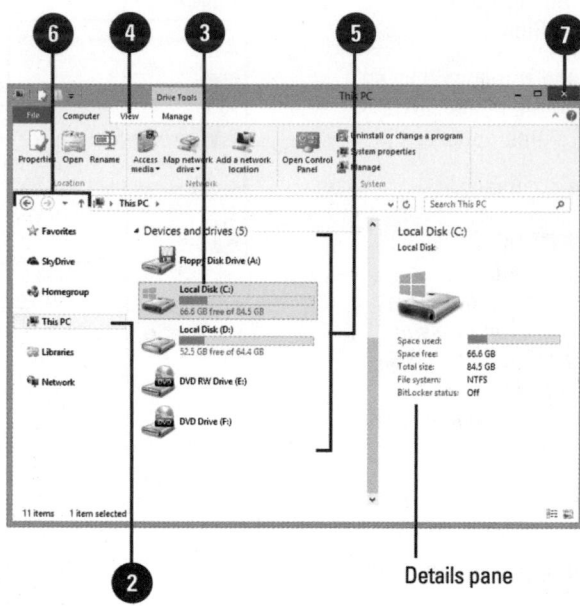

Details pane

## Did You Know?

*You can add the Computer icon to the desktop.* In the desktop, right-click or tap-hold the desktop in a blank area, click or tap Personalize, click or tap Change Desktop Icons in the left pane, select the Computer check box, and then click or tap OK.

*You can find Windows system information in This PC.* In File Explorer, click or tap This PC in the Navigation pane, click or tap System Properties on the Computer tab. You can also right-click or tap-hold the lower-left corner, and then click or tap System, or press Win+Pause/Break.

*You can find drive or device properties in This PC.* In File Explorer, click or tap This PC, click or tap the drive or device, click or tap Properties on the Computer tab.

## See Also

*See "Changing the Explorer Window View" on page 49 for information on changing the display of a folder's contents.*

## Typical Disk Drives on a Computer

| Icon | Type Description |
| --- | --- |
| Local | A hard magnetic disk (or hard disk) on which you can store large amounts of data. The Local Disk (C:) stores all the files on your PC computer. |
| Floppy | A soft removable magnetic disk that comes in a 3½-inch size, which stores up to 1.44 MB of data. Floppy disks are slower to access than a hard disk, but are portable and much less expensive. |
| Removable | A removable magnetic disk on which you can store PC computer data, such as a Zip disk (requires software). Another is a Flash memory card the size of a large stamp that holds128, 256, 512 MB or greater. Flash drives connect directly into a USB plug without software. |
| CD-ROM | **Compact Disc-Read-Only Memory**   An optical disk on which you can stamp, or burn, up to 1 GB (typical size is 650 MB) of data in only one session. The disc cannot be erased or burned again with additional new data. |
| CD-R | **Compact Disc-Recordable**   A type of CD-ROM on which you can burn up to 1 GB of data in multiple sessions. The disc can be burned again with new data, but cannot be erased. |
| CD-RW | **Compact Disc-Rewriteable**   A type of CD-ROM on which you can read, write, and erase data, just like a hard disk. |
| DVD | **Digital Video Disc**   A type of DVD-ROM that holds a minimum of 4.7 GB, enough for a full-length movie. |
| DVD-R | **Digital Video Disc-Recordable**   A type of DVD-ROM on which you can burn up to 4.7 GB of data in multiple sessions. The disc can be burned again with new data, but cannot be erased. |
| DVD-RW | **Digital Video Disc-Rewriteable**   A type of DVD-ROM on which you can read, write, and erase data, just like a hard disk. |
| HD-DVD DVD-ROM | **High Density Digital Video Disc**   A type of high density on which you can read data; the disc appears as a high density drive. |
| Blu-ray | **High Density Blu-ray Disc**   A type of high density DVD-ROM on which you can read data; the disc appears as a high density drive. |

# Viewing and Opening Documents

Windows makes it easy to manage the personal and business files and folders you work with every day. You can access your Documents folder from File Explorer, which displays the Documents library folder. The Documents library folder links and displays files and folders from different locations on your PC computer and SkyDrive in a central place, which includes your Documents folder located in your personal folder. In the folder, you can view file information, organize files and folders, and open files and folders. Once you open more than one folder, you can use buttons to help you move quickly between folders. Depending on previous installation, devices installed, or other users, your personal folders might differ.

## View and Open Documents

1. In the desktop, click or tap the **File Explorer** icon on the taskbar.

2. Click or tap **Document** in the Navigation pane.

3. Double-click or double-tap a folder to navigate to the document location.

4. Click or tap the document file to select it.

5. To review document details, click or tap the **Details pane** button on the View tab.

6. To open the document file, double-click or double-tap the file icon.

7. When you're done, click or tap the **Close** button.

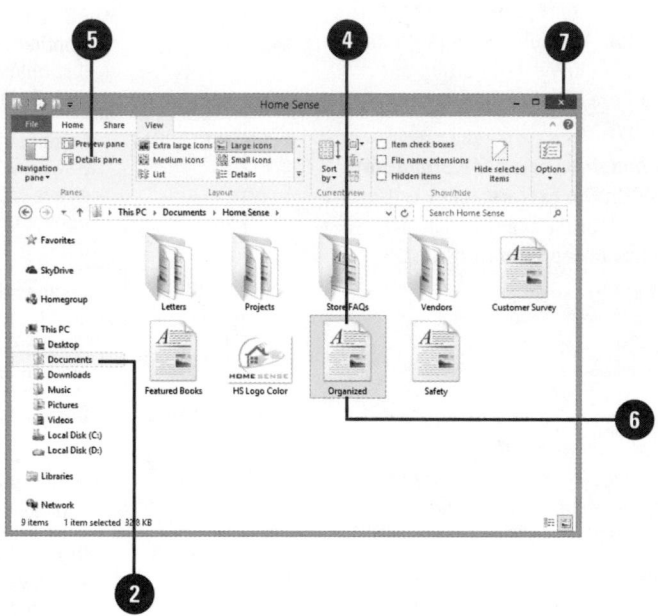

### Did You Know?

*Windows creates a separate Documents folder for each user.* When you share a PC, Windows creates a separate Documents folder and stores personalized settings for each user. Each user's Documents folder is located in the Documents And Settings folder under the user's name on the local hard disk.

## Open Any Folder and Switch Between Folders

**1** In the desktop, click or tap the **File Explorer** icon on the taskbar.

**2** Click or tap any other Explorer window, such as **Documents**, **Videos**, **Pictures**, or **Music**, in the Navigation pane.

**3** Double-click or double-tap the folder to open it.

**4** Click or tap the **Back** or **Forward** button or the **Up** button on the toolbar to return or move to a previously visited window.

**5** When you're done, click or tap the **Close** button.

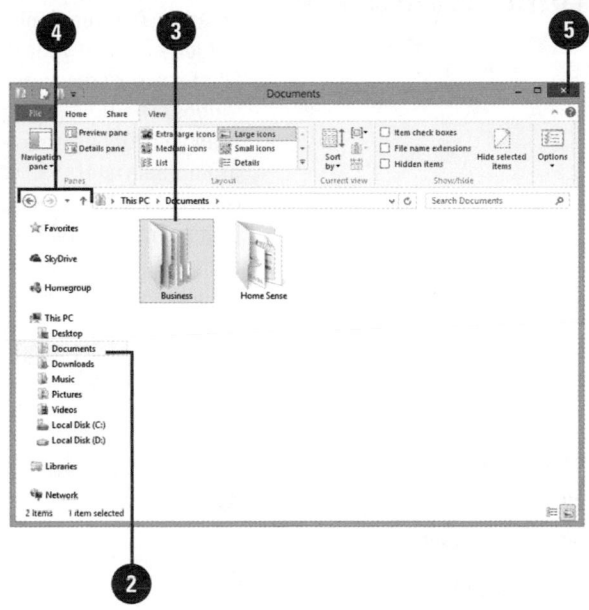

## Did You Know?

***Windows stores music and picture files in separate folders in your personal folder.*** Windows stores music files in the Music folder and pictures in the Pictures folder in your personal folder, which you can access from the Music and Pictures libraries.

## See Also

*See "Changing the Explorer Window View" on page 49 for information on changing the display of a folder's contents.*

*See "Working with Libraries" on page 56 for information on using and creating libraries.*

## For Your Information

### Opening a Document with a Different Program

Most documents on your desktop are associated with a specific program. For example, if you double-click or double-tap a document whose file name ends with the three-letter extension ".txt," Windows automatically opens the document with Notepad, a text-only editor. There are situations, though, when you need to open a document with a program other than the one Windows chooses, or when you want to choose a different default program. For example, you might want to open a text document in WordPad rather than Notepad so that you can add formatting and graphics. To do this, right-click or tap-hold the document icon you want to open, point to Open With, and then click or tap the application you want to use to open the document, or click or tap Choose Program to access more program options. Once you open a text file using WordPad, this option is automatically added to the Open With menu.

# Working with Libraries

Libraries are special folders that catalog folders and files in a central location. A library includes and displays folders that are stored in different locations on your PC computer, SkyDrive, Homegroup, or network. File Explorer comes with four libraries: Documents, Music, Pictures, and Videos. The Documents library, for example, includes files and folders from your Documents—This PC and SkyDrive (**New!**)—folders, which are actually stored in your Users folder. Instead of navigating to separate folders, you can quickly navigate to one central place, the Documents library. You can create additional libraries at any time and include folders from different locations or remove them. After you open a library, you can arrange all files and folders included in a library by folder (the default) or other properties based on the library type (General Items, Documents, Music, Pictures, or Videos). When you save a file to a library, you can specify which folder it actually gets stored in.

## Open and View a Library

1. In the desktop, click or tap the **File Explorer** button on the taskbar.

2. To show libraries, click or tap the **Navigation pane** button on the View tab, and then click or tap **Show libraries (New!)**.

3. Click or tap a library folder in the Navigation pane or double-click or double-tap a library folder.

4. To change the library display, right-click or tap-hold a blank area, point to **Arrange by**, and then click or tap an option.

   - ◆ **Folder.** File and folders.
   - ◆ **General Items.** Date modified, Tag, Type, or Name.
   - ◆ **Documents.** Author, Date modified, Tag, Type, or Name.
   - ◆ **Pictures.** Month, Day, Rating, or Tag.
   - ◆ **Music.** Album, Artist, Song, Genre, or Rating.
   - ◆ **Video.** Year, Type, Length, or Name.
   - ◆ **Clear changes.** Clears any arrange by modifications.

5. To sort or group items, click or tap the **Sort by** or **Group by** button on the View tab, and then click or tap an option.

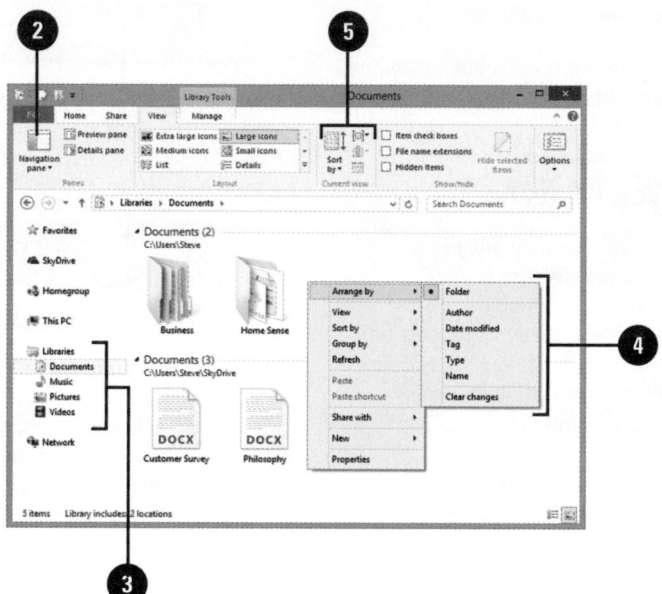

## Create a New Library and Include or Remove Folders

1. In the desktop, click or tap the **File Explorer** button on the taskbar.

2. Click or tap the **Libraries** in the Navigation pane.

3. Click or tap the **New item** button on the Home tab, click or tap **Library**, type a library name, and then press Enter.

   ◆ To delete a library, select it, click or tap the **Delete** button on the Home tab, click or tap **Permanently delete**, and then click or tap **Yes**.

4. To include a folder in a library, navigate to the folder location, click or tap the **Easy access** button on the Home tab, point to **Include in library**, and then select the library you want.

5. To remove a folder from a library, open the library, click or tap the **Manage library** button on the Manage tab, select the folder you want to remove, click or tap **Remove**, and then click or tap **OK**.

### Did You Know?

*You can change the save location.* Open the folder you want to change the save location, click or tap the Manage tab, click or tap the Set save location button, and then select a folder location. A check mark appears to the left of the selected folder location.

New library

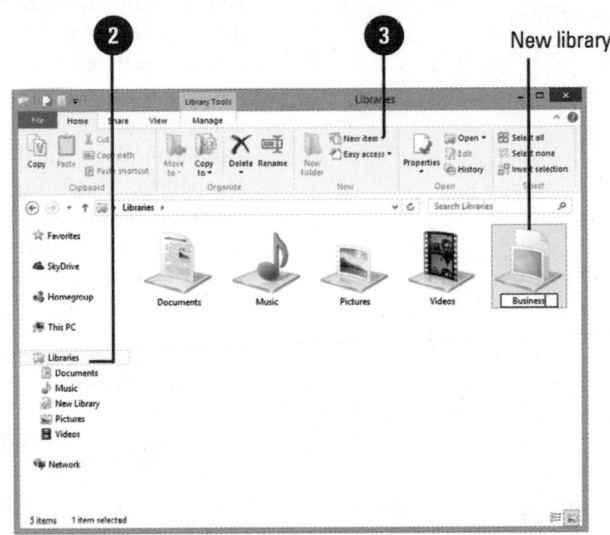

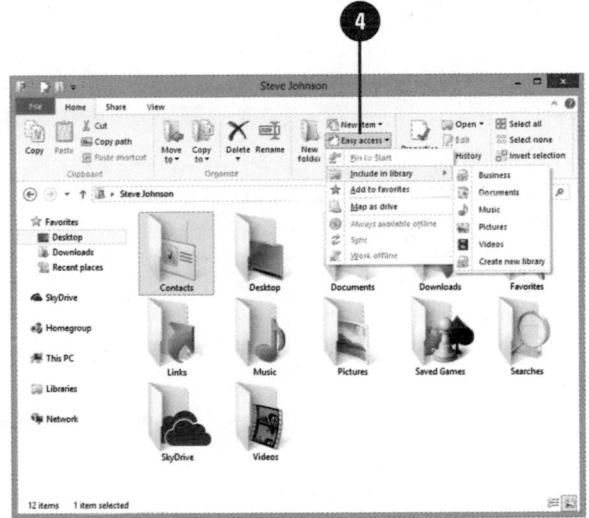

# Working with Personal Folders

File Explorer comes with a personal folder that stores your most frequently used folders in one location. The personal folder appears in File Explorer with the name of the person logged on to the PC computer. The personal folder only contains files and folders associated with a user account and are unique for each user. The personal folder includes a variety of folders: Contacts, Desktop, Downloads, Favorites, Links, Documents, Music, Pictures, Videos, Saved Games, Searches, and SkyDrive (**New!**). You can access these folders using the personal folder from File Explorer under Desktop. The Documents, Pictures, Music, and Videos folders are included in the Documents, Pictures, Music, and Videos libraries respectively, so you can also access them by name in File Explorer.

## View and Open a Personal Folder

1. In the desktop, click or tap the **File Explorer** button on the taskbar.

2. Click or tap the **Desktop** in the Navigation pane.

3. Double-click or double-tap the folder with the user account's name to open it.

4. Double-click or double-tap a folder to open it.

5. When you're done, click or tap the **Close** button.

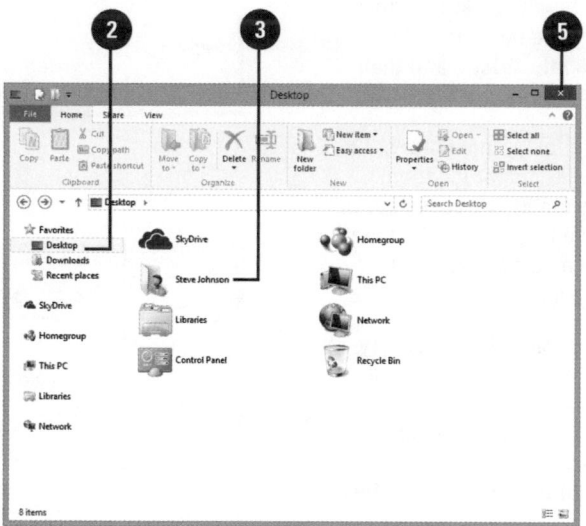

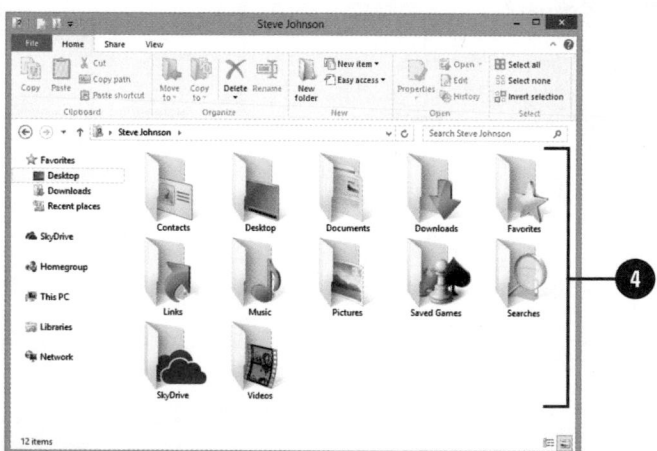

# Navigating Between Folders

The Address bar appears at the top of every Explorer window and displays the current location on your PC computer, skyDrive, or network. The location appears as a series of links separated by arrows. You can change your current location by either typing a new location—even a web address on the Internet—or selecting one using the Address bar. You can also use the Back and Forward buttons to the left of the Address bar to switch between locations you have previously visited.

## Navigate to a Location

- **Click or tap a location**. Use either of the following methods:
  - **Visible folder location**. To go directly to a location visible in the Address bar, click or tap the location name.
  - **Visible subfolder location**. To go to a subfolder of a location visible in the Address bar, click or tap the arrow to the right, and then click or tap the location name.

- **Type a location**. Click or tap a blank space (to the right of text) in the Address bar, and then type the complete folder name or path to the location, and then press Enter.

  You can type common locations and then press Enter. The common locations include: This PC, Contacts, Control Panel, Documents, Favorites, Games, Music, Pictures, Recycle Bin, and Videos.

  If you type a web address (URL) in the Address bar, the Explorer window switches to Internet Explorer.

Click a location        Address bar

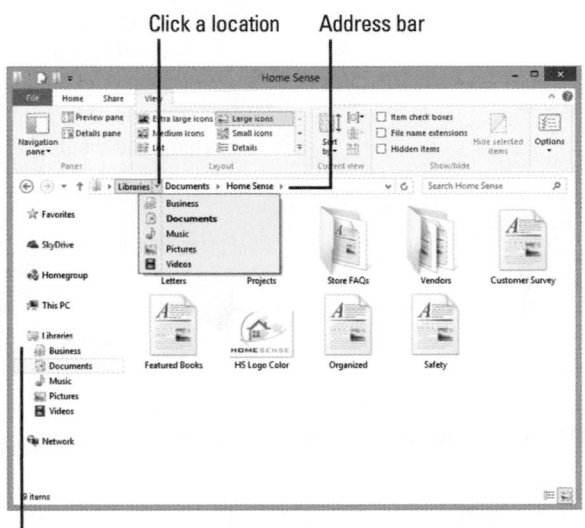

Navigation pane

# Viewing the Folders List

Windows offers a useful feature for managing files and folders, called the **Folders list**, which is integrated under categories—Favorites, SkyDrive (**New!**), Homegroup, This PC (**New!**), Libraries, and Network—into the Navigation pane. The Folders list displays the window in two panes, or frames, which allows you to view information from two different locations. The Navigation pane displays the file hierarchy of all the drives and folders on the PC computer, and the right pane displays the contents of the selected drive or folder. This arrangement enables you to view the file hierarchy of your PC computer and the contents of a folder simultaneously making it easy to copy, move, delete, and rename files and folders. Using the non filled arrow and the filled arrow to the left of an icon in the Folders list allows you to display different levels of the drives and folders on your PC computer without opening and displaying the contents of each folder.

## View the Folders List

1. In the desktop, click or tap the **File Explorer** button on the taskbar.

2. Open any folder window.

3. In the Navigation pane, point to an item to display the navigation arrows.

4. Perform the commands you want to display folder structure and contents:

   ◆ To show the file and folder structure, click or tap the non filled arrow.

   ◆ To hide the file and folder structure, click or tap the filled arrow.

   ◆ To display the contents of a folder, click or tap the folder icon.

Folder list tree structure

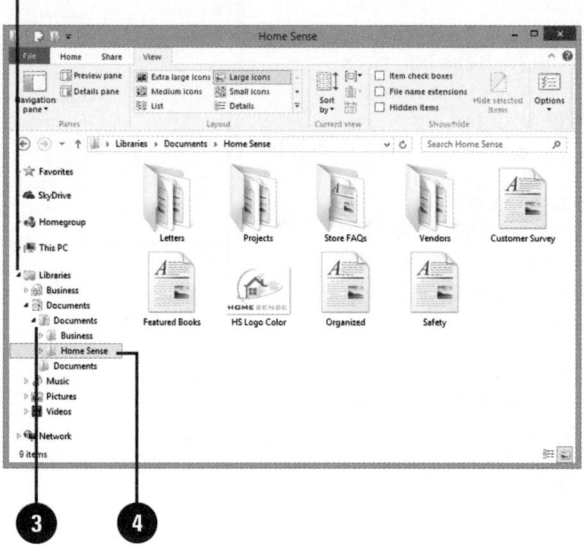

### Did You Know?

*You can quickly determine if a folder contains folders.* When an arrow doesn't appear next to an icon in the Folders list, the item has no folders in it.

# Changing the Explorer Layout

File Explorer gives you the option to customize the layout for each Explorer window depending on the information the window contains. The layout for each Explorer window includes a Preview pane, Details pane, and Navigation pane. The Preview pane provides a preview of the selected item, such as a picture. The Details pane a thumbnail preview and information about the selected item, such as the file name, type, date modified, dimensions, size, and date created. The Navigation pane provides a tree structure to navigate folders and drives on your SkyDrive, This PC, or libraries. The Details and Navigation panes appear by default. The Panes group on the View tab provides options to show or hide the Explorer layout elements (**New!**).

## Change the Explorer Layout

1. In the desktop, click or tap the **File Explorer** button on the taskbar.

2. Open the folder window you want to change.

3. Click or tap the **View** tab.

4. Select the layout pane button you want to show or hide: **Preview Pane**, **Details Pane**, or **Navigation Pane** (and then click or tap **Navigation pane**).

5. Click or tap the **Navigation Pane** button, and then click or tap an option to show or hide items in the Navigation pane: **Show all folders**, **Show libraries (New!)**, or **Show favorites**.

Layout options vary depending on the type of Explorer window.

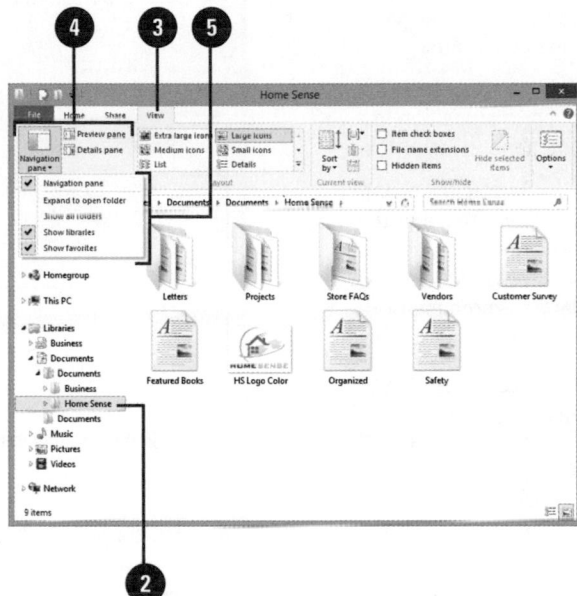

# Customizing the Navigation Pane

The Navigation pane provides links to commonly used drives and folders to reduce the number of clicks or taps it takes to locate a file or folder. File Explorer provides a default list of favorites, libraries, homegroups, and networks in the Navigation pane. You can customize the list of favorites for your own purposes. You can move current links, add or rename folders, or remove an item. If the Navigation pane gets cluttered, you can restore it back to the original default items. You can also set Navigation pane options to show all folders like the Folder list and automatically expand the folder list to the current folder.

## Customize the Navigation Pane

◆ **Move a link.** Drag an item in the Navigation pane to a higher or lower position in Favorites.

◆ **Add a link.** Drag an item from its original location to a position in the Navigation pane in Favorites.

◆ **Rename a link.** Right-click or tap-hold the link in Favorites, and then click or tap **Rename**. Type a new name, and then press Enter. The original folder or search is not renamed, only the Navigation link.

◆ **Remove a link.** Right-click or tap-hold the link in Favorites, and then click or tap **Remove**. The original folder or search is not removed, only the Navigation link.

◆ **Restore default links.** Right-click or tap-hold the Favorites link in the Navigation pane, and then click or tap **Restore favorite links**.

◆ **Show all folders like the folders list.** Click or tap the **Options** button on the **View** tab, click or tap **Change folder and search options**, select the **Show all folders** check box on the General tab, and then click or tap **OK**.

◆ **Automatically expand the folder list to the current folder.** Click or tap the **Options** button on the **View** tab, click or tap **Change folder and search options**, select the **Automatically expand to current folder** check box on the General tab, and then click or tap **OK**.

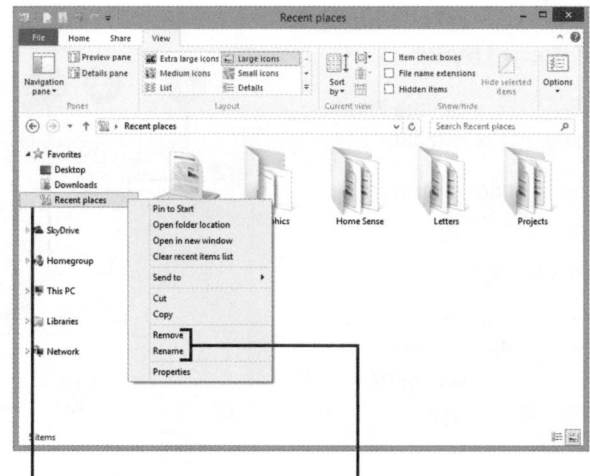

Favorites in the Navigation pane          Remove and Rename a link

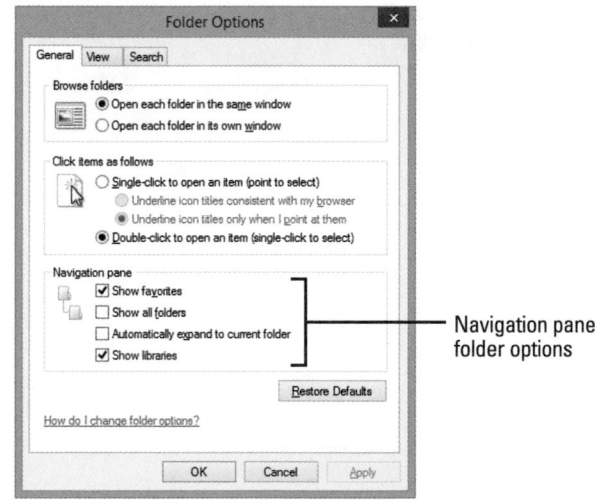

Navigation pane folder options

# Organizing Files by Headings

In Explorer windows, files and folders appear in lists with headings at the top in Details view. You can use the headings to change how files are displayed in the window. You can use filtering and sorting to display the files and folders you want. Filtering displays only files and folders with the properties you select by heading type. For example, the A - H filter for file and folder names displays only files and folder that start with A - H. Sorting displays the files and folders in ascending or descending order by heading type. For example, the sort by name displays files and folders from A to Z or Z to A. You can apply a filter and sort a column to achieve the results you want.

## Organize Files Using Filtering or Sorting

1. In the desktop, click or tap the **File Explorer** button on the taskbar.

2. Open the folder that contains the files you want to sort or filter.

3. Click or tap **Details** on the View tab, or click or tap the **Details** button.

4. To sort files by headings, click or tap the heading title you want to sort by. An arrow in the middle of the heading indicates the sort direction, ascending and descending.

5. Point to the heading you want to filter by.

6. Click or tap the arrow to the right of the heading you want to filter by.

7. Select the property check boxes you want to filter by.

8. Click or tap in a blank area to close the search menu.

   A check mark replaces the arrow to indicates a filter is in place.

   ◆ To cancel the search, you can also press Esc.

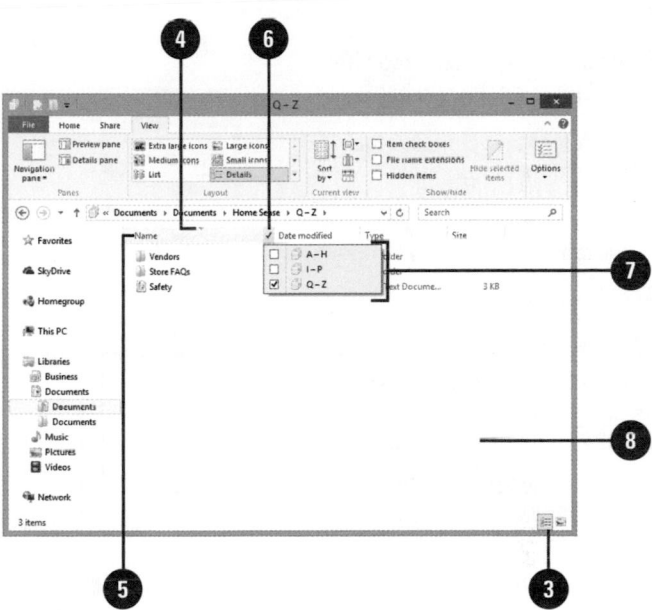

# Sorting and Grouping Files

In Explorer windows, files and folders appear sorted or grouped by different attributes, such as name or type, in the different views, such as Icons (Extra large, Large, Medium, or Small), List, Details, Tiles, and Content. You can select the attributes you want to use and then select whether to display the files and folders in ascending (A-Z) or descending (Z-A) order. You can use the Sort by or Group by buttons on the View tab to specify the options you want to apply to the current folder. The Sort by and Group by options are the same. However, the available options vary depending on the selected folder type, such as a Documents or Pictures folder.

## Sort Files and Folders

1. In the desktop, click or tap the **File Explorer** button on the taskbar.

2. Open the folder that contains the files you want to group.

3. Click or tap the **Sort by** button on the View tab.

4. Select a sort by option on the menu.

   ◆ **Options.** Select an option, such as name, Date, Size, Type, Date modified, and Dimensions.

   The available options vary depending on the selected folder type.

   ◆ **Ascending.** Select to sort items in ascending order A-Z.

   ◆ **Descending.** Select to sort items in descending order Z-A.

   ◆ **Choose columns.** Select to customize the columns shown in Details view.

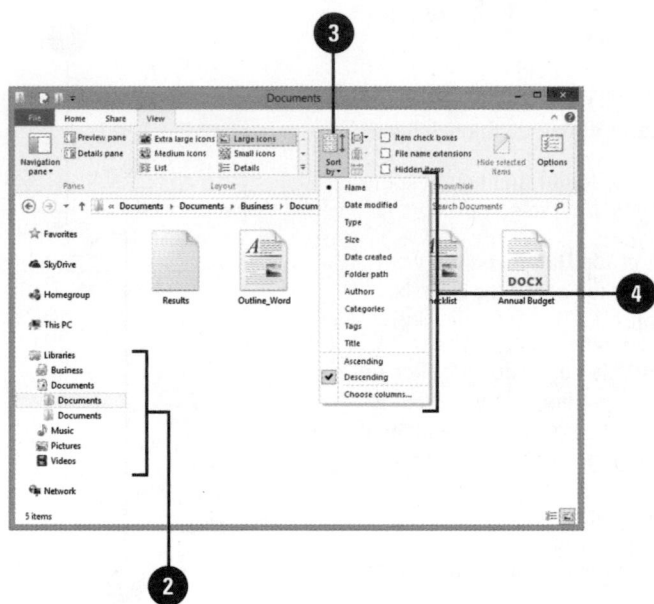

## See Also

*See "Changing File and Folder List Views" on page 80 for more information on setting options for customizing the columns shown in Details view.*

## Group Files and Folders

**1** In the desktop, click or tap the **File Explorer** button on the taskbar.

**2** Open the folder that contains the files you want to group.

**3** Click or tap the **Group by** button on the View tab.

**4** Select a group by option on the menu.

◆ **Options.** Select an option, such as name, Date, Size, Type, Date modified, and Dimensions.

The available options vary depending on the selected folder type.

◆ **(None).** Select to remove the group by option.

◆ **Ascending.** Select to group items in ascending order A-Z.

◆ **Descending.** Select to group items in descending order Z-A.

◆ **Choose columns.** Select to customize the columns shown in Details view.

**5** Click the **Collapse** or **Expand** arrow next to the heading to collapse or expand the grouping.

### Did You Know?

*You can size all columns to fit their contents in Details view.* In File Explorer, open the folder you want to size columns, click or tap Details on the View tab, and then click or tap the Size All Columns To Fit button on the View tab.

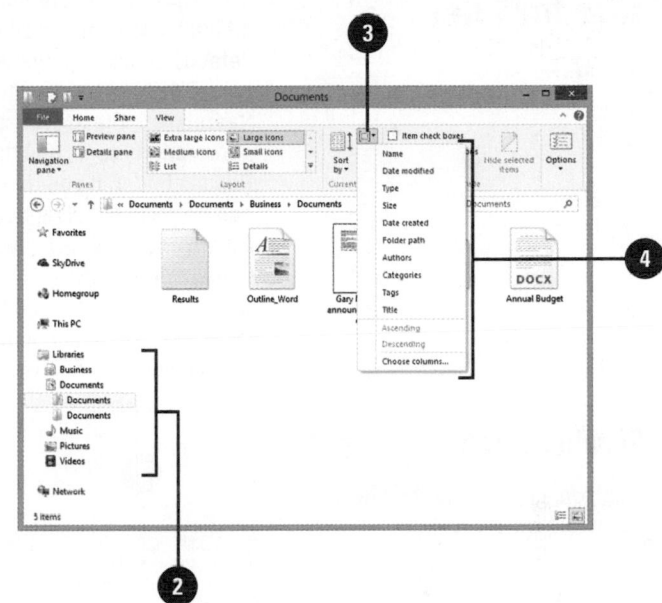

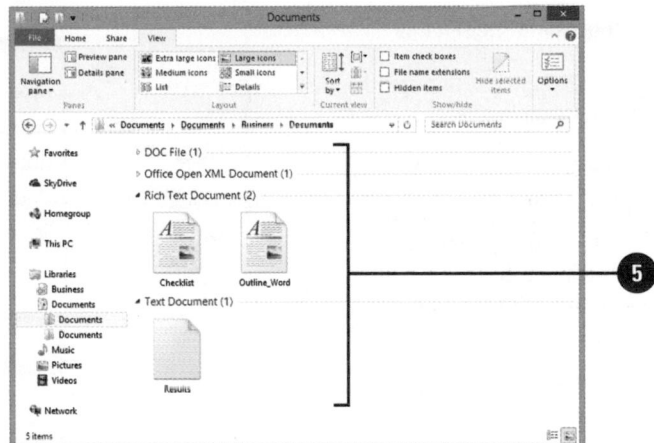

## Searching for Files and Folders

Sometimes remembering precisely where you stored a file can be difficult. File Explorer allows you to use Windows Search Explorer (by default) to help you find and view all of your files or folders in one place. You start a search by using the Search box. As you type in a Search box, the search looks for matches in the file name, contents, and property tags, and displays the highlighted results in a Search Results folder. If you don't find the file or folders you're looking for, you can perform an advanced search using a menu from the Search box. An advanced search gives you the option to find files or folders by type, name, title, location, date (taken, modified, or created), size, or property tag. The search locates files and programs stored anywhere in indexed locations, which includes personal folders, e-mail, offline files, and web sites in your History list.

### Create a Simple Search

① In the desktop, click or tap the **File Explorer** button on the taskbar.

② Open an Explorer window in the location where you want to search.

③ Click or tap in the Search box.

A search tab appears. Disregard the tab for a simple search.

④ Type a word or part of a word.

As you type, programs and files that match your text appear highlighted in the Search Results window. You don't have to press Enter.

**TROUBLE?** *In the Search box, you must press Enter to start a search for non-indexed files.*

⑤ To clear and close the search, click or tap the **Close** button (x) on the Search tab or in the Search box.

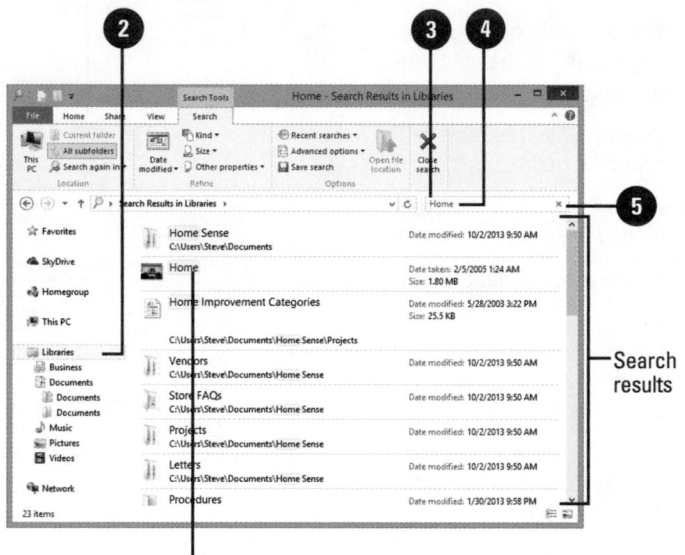

Highlighted search results

Search results

## Create an Advanced Search

1. In the desktop, click or tap the **File Explorer** button on the taskbar.

2. Open an Explorer window in the location where you want to search.

3. Click or tap in the Search box.

   A Search tab appears with advanced options.

4. Click or tap the **This PC**, **Current folder**, or **All subfolders** to specify a search location.

5. Click or tap the Refine buttons you want on the Search tab, and then select an option.

   ◆ **Date modified.** Searches by date modified.

   ◆ **Kind.** Searches by kind of file, such as Document, E-mail, Video, or Instant Message.

   ◆ **Size.** Searches by file size.

   ◆ **Other properties.** Searches by file type, name, folder path, or property tag.

6. To set additional options, click or tap the **Advanced options** button, and then click or tap **Partial matches**, **File contents**, **System files**, or **Zipped (compressed folders)** to enable or disable.

7. Type in search criteria in the Search box or select from the available criteria.

8. To search again in other locations, click or tap the **Search again in** button, and then click or tap **Homegroup**, **Libraries**, or **Internet**.

9. To clear and close the search, click or tap the **Close** button (x) on the Search tab or in the Search box.

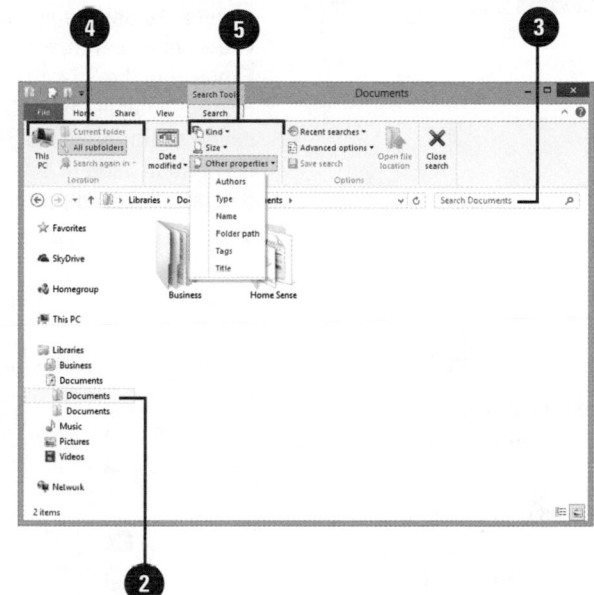

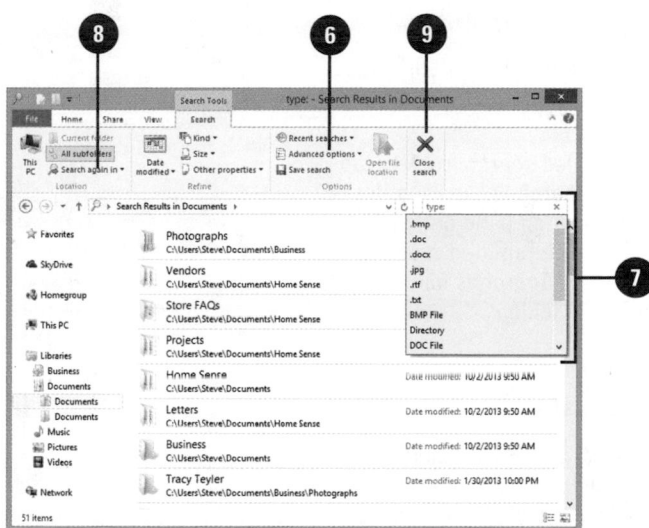

# Saving a Search

If you frequently perform the same search, you can save your search results like any file and perform or modify the search again later. When you save a search, the search is saved by default with Window Search Explorer in the Searches folder in your personal folder and added to the Favorites folder in the Navigation pane. Like any link, you can move a saved search from the Searches folder to the Favorites category in the Navigation pane to make it more accessible. To run a saved search, display the saved search link, and then click or tap it.

## Save a Search

1. In the desktop, click or tap the **File Explorer** button on the taskbar.

2. Open an Explorer window in the location where you want to search.

3. Click or tap in the Search box, specify the criteria you want, and then perform the search.

4. Click or tap the **Save search** button on the Search tab.

5. Type a name for the search.

6. Click or tap **Save**.

7. To use a saved search, click or tap the saved search link in Favorites in the Navigation pane or double-click or double-tap the saved search in the Searches folder in the personal folder.

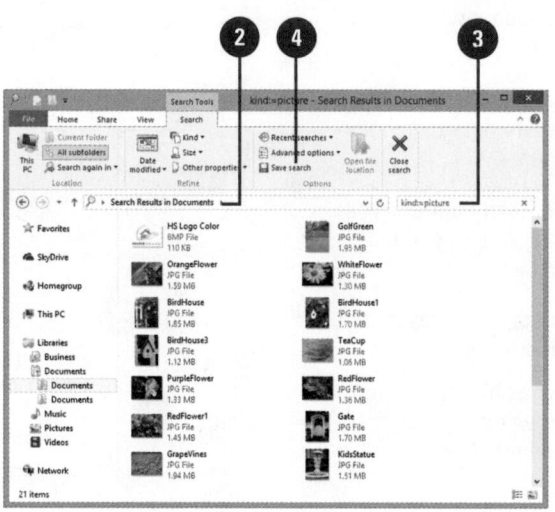

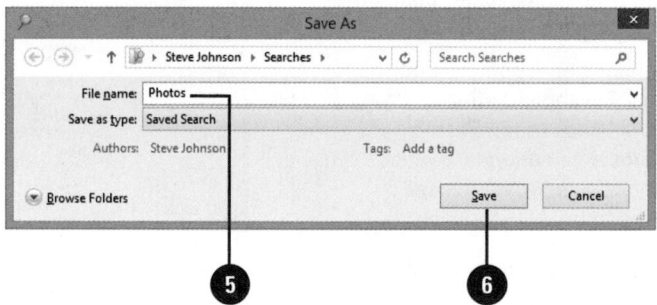

## Did You Know?

*You can quickly perform a recent search.* Click in the Search box to the display the Search tab. Click or tap the Recent Searches button, and then select a recent search. If the list gets cluttered, you can clear items. Click or tap the Recent Searches button, and then click or tap Clear Search History.

# Changing Search Options

When you perform a search for files or folders, File Explorer uses the search options to help customize the search results. You can specify whether you want to search for file names and content or just for file names and whether to include subfolders. For non-indexed searches, you can set options to include system directories or compressed files (ZIP, CAB...), or always search file names and contents. The search options are available in the Folder Options dialog box under the Search tab.

## Change Search Options

1. In the desktop, click or tap the **File Explorer** button on the taskbar.

2. Click or tap the **Options** button on the View tab, and then click or tap **Folder and search options**.

3. Click or tap the **Search** tab.

4. Select or clear the check boxes under How to search:

   ◆ **Don't use the index when searching in file folders for system files (searches might take longer).**

5. Select or clear the check boxes under When searching non-indexed locations:

   ◆ **Include system directories.**

   ◆ **Include compressed files (ZIP, CAB, ...)**

   ◆ **Always search file names and contents (this might take several minutes)**

6. Click or tap **OK**.

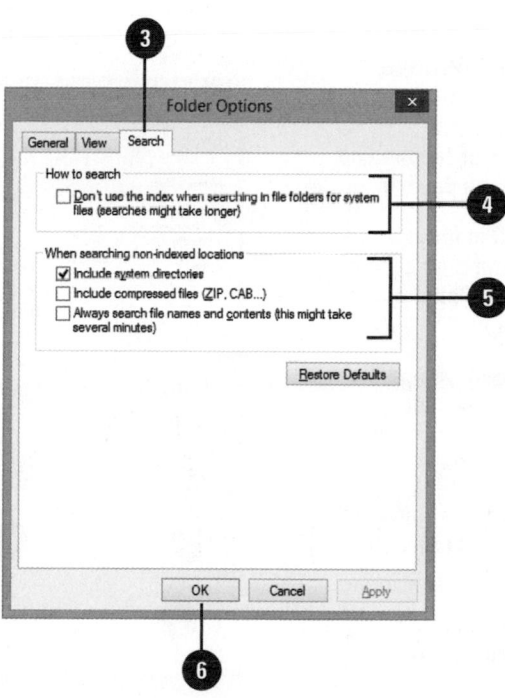

# Modifying the Index to Improve Searches

Windows keeps track of files in indexed locations and stores information about them in the background using an index, like the one found in the back of this book, to make locating files faster and easier. You can use Indexing Options in the Control Panel to view, pause, add, remove, and modify indexed locations, indexed file types, and other advanced index settings. For example, if a file type is not recognized by the index, you can add it; if you want to stop indexing new content for 15 minutes to specify options, you can pause it; or if you're having problems with the search index, you can rebuild or restore it.

## View, Pause, Add, or Remove Indexed Locations

1. In the desktop, click or tap the **File Explorer** button on the taskbar.

2. Click or tap **This PC** in the Navigation pane, and then click or tap the **Open Control Panel** button on the Computer tab.

   ◆ In the Start screen, you can also click or tap **Apps view** button, and then click or tap **Control Panel**.

3. Click or tap the **Indexing Options** icon in Small icons or Large icons view.

4. To pause new indexing for 15 minutes, click or tap **Pause**.

5. Click or tap **Modify**.

6. If you don't see all the locations, click or tap **Show all locations**.

7. If a folder location contains subfolders, click or tap the Expand arrow to expand it.

8. Select or clear the check box next to the folder locations you want to add or remove from the index.

9. Click or tap **OK**.

10. Click or tap **Close**.

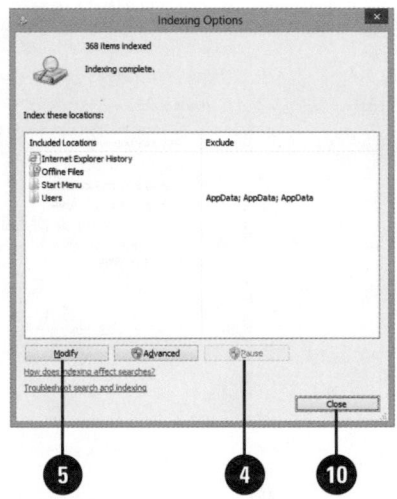

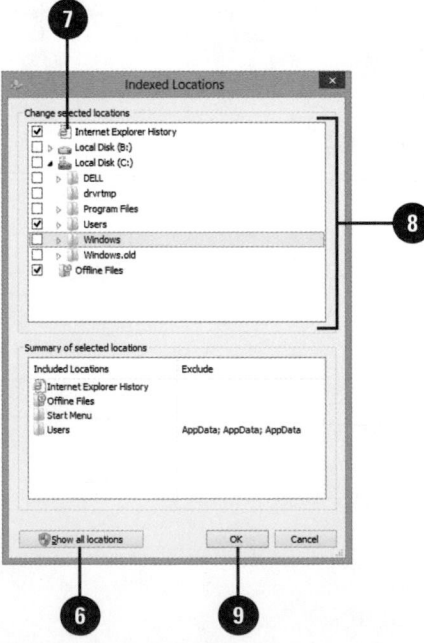

## Set Advanced Indexing Options

1. In the desktop, click or tap the **File Explorer** button on the taskbar.

2. Click or tap **This PC** in the Navigation pane, and then click or tap the **Open Control Panel** button on the Computer tab.

3. Click or tap the **Indexing Options** icon in Small icons or Large icons view.

4. Click or tap **Advanced**.

5. Click or tap the **Index Settings** tab.

6. Select or clear the following check boxes:

    ◆ **Index encrypted files.**

    ◆ **Treat similar words with diacritics as different words.**

7. For index troubleshooting, use either of these buttons:

    ◆ To re-index selected locations, click or tap **Rebuild**.

    ◆ To restore your index to its original settings, click or tap **Restore Defaults**.

8. If you need to change the Index Location, specify a new location or click or tap **Select new**.

9. Click or tap the **File Types** tab.

10. Select or clear the check boxes with the file types you want to include or exclude in the index.

11. For each selected file type, click or tap the option to specify how the file should be indexed.

12. Click or tap **OK**.

13. Click or tap **Close**.

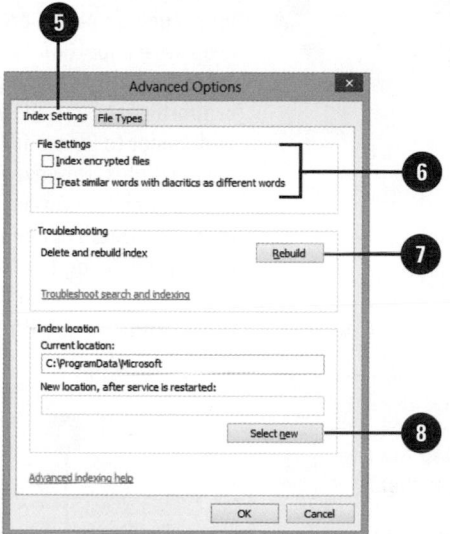

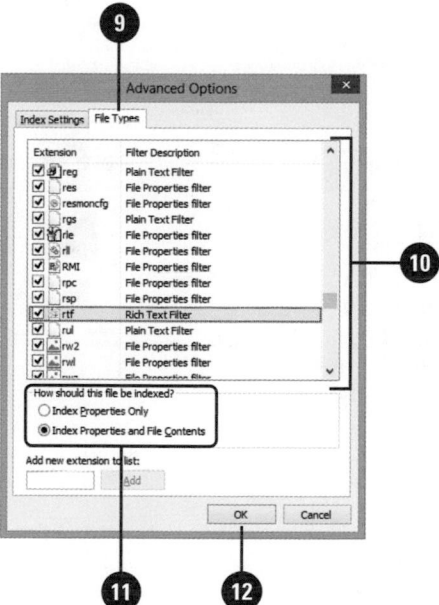

# Adding Properties and Tags to Files

When you create a file, Windows automatically adds properties to the files, such as name, creation date, modified date, and size. These properties are important to Windows, however, they may not be useful when you are searching for a file. You can add or modify common file properties and create or modify custom tag properties to make it faster and easier to locate files in the future. You can add or modify properties for most files. However, there are some exceptions, such as plain text (.txt) or rich text format (.rtf) files. You can add or modify properties using the Details pane in an Explorer window, the Details tab in the Properties dialog box, or in some Save As dialog boxes. If you want to remove some or all of the property information in a file, you can quickly remove it using the Properties dialog box.

## Add or Modify Properties

1. In the desktop, click or tap the **File Explorer** button on the taskbar.

2. Click or tap the file you want to add or modify properties.

3. In the Details pane, click or tap the tag you want to change, and then type the new tag.

   ◆ To display the Details pane, click or tap the **Details pane** on the View tab.

   ◆ If you want to work with more properties and tags, right-click or tap-hold the file, click or tap **Properties**, and then click or tap the **Details** tab. When you're done, click or tap **Apply**.

4. To add more than one tag, separate each entry with a semicolon.

5. To rate a file using the rating property, click or tap the star that represents the rating you want to give the file.

6. Click or tap **Save**.

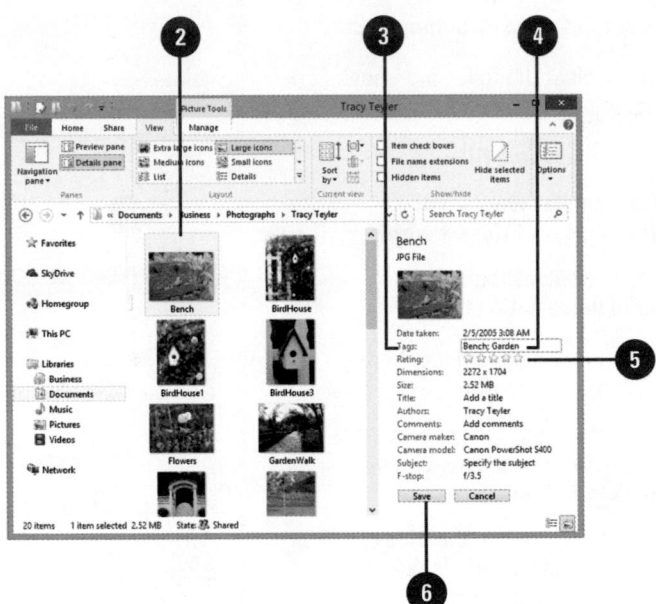

## Remove Properties

1. In the desktop, click or tap the **File Explorer** button on the taskbar, and then locate the file in which you want to change.

2. Select the file you want to remove properties.

3. Click or tap the **Properties** button on the Home tab, and then click or tap **Remove properties**.

4. Click or tap the **Create a copy with all possible properties removed** option or click or tap the **Remove the following properties from this file:** option.

5. Select or clear the check boxes for each property.

6. Click or tap **OK**.

### Did You Know?

*You can add properties while you save a file.* In some Save As dialog boxes, such as Microsoft Word, you can specify properties, such as Author and Tags.

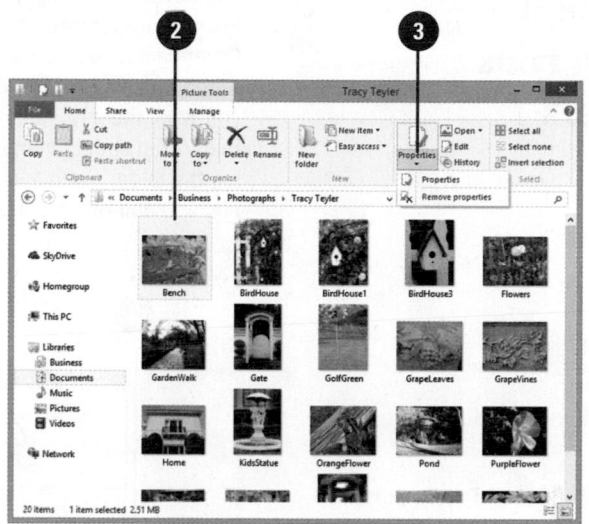

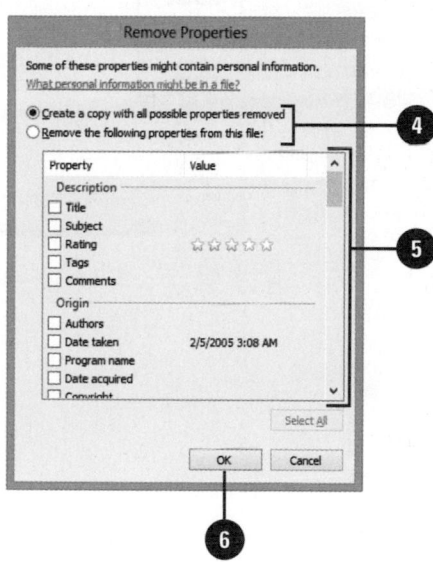

# Creating and Renaming Files and Folders

The keys to organizing files and folders effectively within a hierarchy are to store related items together and to name folders informatively. Creating a new folder can help you organize and keep track of files and other folders. In order to create a folder, you select the location where you want the new folder, create the folder, and then lastly, name the folder. You should name each folder meaningfully so that just by reading the folder's name you know its contents. After you name a folder or file, you can rename it at any time.

## Create a Folder

1. In the desktop, click or tap the **File Explorer** button on the taskbar.

2. Open the drive or folder where you want to create a folder.

3. Click or tap the **New Folder** button on the Home tab.

   **TIMESAVER** *Right-click or tap-hold a blank area of the window, point to New, and then click or tap New folder.*

4. With the New Folder name selected, type a new name.

5. Press Enter or tap in a blank area.

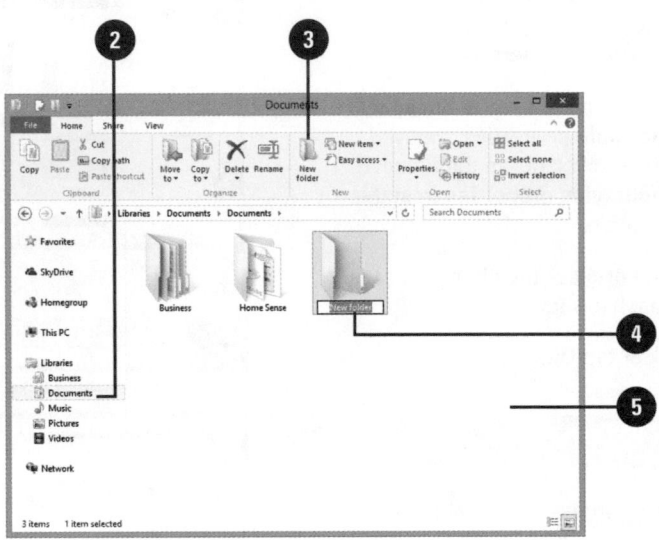

### Did You Know?

*File names can be up to 255 characters.* You can use spaces and underscores in names, but you can't use the following characters: @ * : < > | ? " \ or /. Remember the best way to keep your files organized is with a consistent naming convention.

## Rename a File or Folder

1. In the desktop, click or tap the **File Explorer** button on the taskbar.

2. Select the file or folder you want to rename.

3. Click or tap the **Rename** button on the Home tab.

4. With the name selected, type a new name, or click or tap to position the insertion point, and then edit the name.

5. Press Enter or tap in a blank area.

**TIMESAVER** *Right-click or tap-hold the file or folder you want to rename, click or tap Rename, type a name, and then press Enter or tap in a bland area. You can also select the file, click or tap the file name, type a name, and then press Enter or tap in a blank area.*

### Did You Know?

***You can rename a group of files.*** In File Explorer, select all the files you want to rename, right-click or tap-hold one of the selected files, click or tap Rename from the shortcut menu, type a name, and then press Enter or tap in a blank area. The group name appears with numbers in consecutive order.

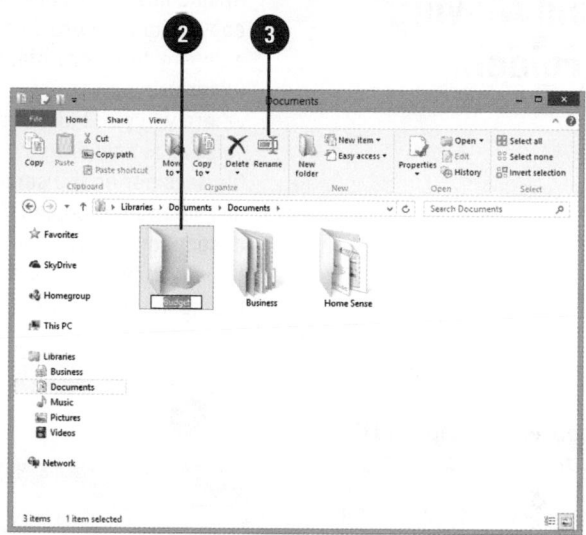

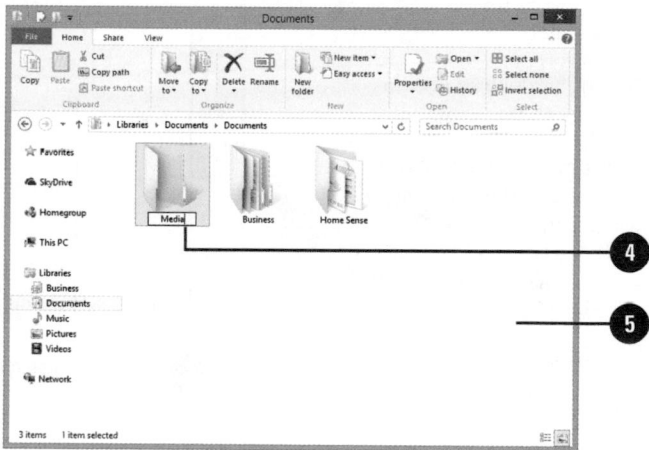

# Copying and Moving Files and Folders

Sometimes you will need to move a file from one folder to another, or copy a file from one folder to another, leaving the file in the first location and placing a copy of it in the second. You can move or copy a file or folder using a variety of methods. If the file or folder and the location where you want to move it are visible in a window or on the desktop, you can simply drag the item from one location to the other. Moving a file or folder on the same disk relocates it whereas dragging it from one disk to another copies it so that it appears in both locations. When the destination folder or drive is not visible, you can use the Move to or Copy to commands or the Cut (to move), Copy, and Paste commands on the Home tab to move or copy the items.

## Copy or Move a File or Folder

1. In the desktop, click or tap the **File Explorer** button on the taskbar.

2. Open the drive or folder containing the file or folder you want to copy.

3. Select the files or folders you want to copy or move.

4. Click or tap the **Copy** or **Cut** (to move) button on the Home tab.

5. Display the destination folder where you want to copy or move the files or folder.

6. Click or tap the **Paste** button on the Home tab.

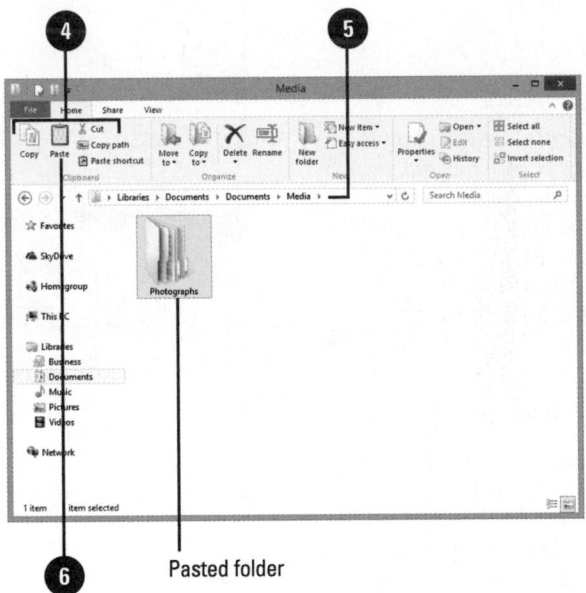

Pasted folder

## Did You Know?

*You can copy or move directly to a folder or drive.* In File Explorer, select the files or folder you want to copy or move, click or tap the Copy to or Move to button on the Home tab, and then select a destination or click or tap Choose location to select the one you want.

## Copy or Move a File or Folder Using Drag and Drop

1. In the desktop, click or tap the **File Explorer** button on the taskbar.

2. Open the drive or folder containing the file or folder you want to copy or move.

3. Select the files or folders you want to copy or move.

4. In the Navigation pane, point to a folder list to display the expand and collapse arrows.

5. Click or tap the arrows to display the destination folder.

6. Right-click or tap-hold the selected files or folders, drag to the destination folder, and then click or tap **Copy Here** or **Move Here**.

   **TIMESAVER** *To move the selected items, drag them to the destination folder. To copy the items, hold down the Ctrl key while you drag.*

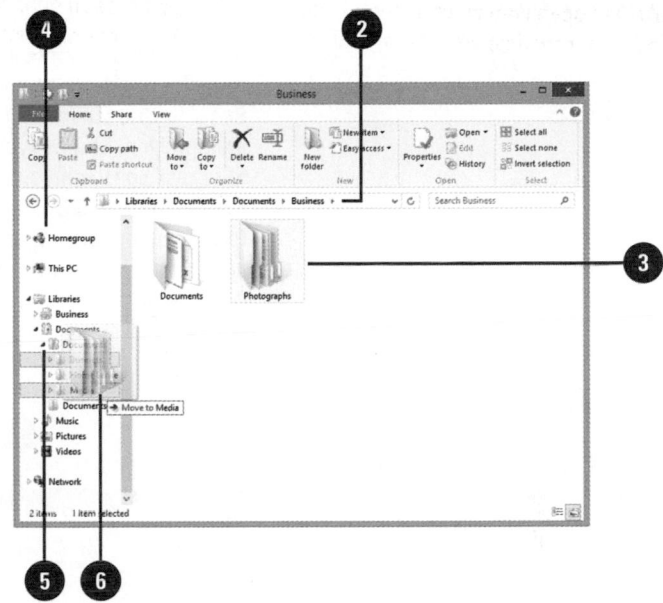

### Did You Know?

***You can transfer files using a disk.*** You can copy files from your PC computer to a disk if you need to either transfer files from one stand-alone PC computer to another. You can also save a copy of important files to prevent losing them in the event of a power failure or a problem. You can use several methods: copy and paste, drag and drop, and the Send To command.

### For Your Information

#### Sending Files and Folders

When you right-click or tap-hold most objects on the desktop or in This PC or File Explorer, the Send To command, located on the short-cut menu, lets you send, or move, a file or folder to a new location on your PC computer. For example, you can send a file or folder to a removable disk to make a quick backup copy of the file or folder, to a mail recipient as an electronic message, or to the desktop to create a shortcut. You can also use the Send To command to move a file or folder from one folder to another. To send a file or folder, right-click or tap-hold the file or folder you want to send, point to Send To on the shortcut menu, and then click or tap the destination you want.

# Deleting and Restoring Files and Folders

When you organize the contents of a folder, disk, or the desktop, you might find files and folders that you no longer need. You can delete these items or remove them permanently. If you delete a file or folder from the desktop or from the hard disk, it goes into the Recycle Bin. The **Recycle Bin**, located on your desktop, is a temporary storage area for deleted files. The Recycle Bin stores all the items you delete from your hard disk so that if you accidentally delete an item, you can remove it from the Recycle Bin to restore it. Be aware that if you delete a file from a removable disk or use the Permanently delete command, it is permanently deleted, not stored in the Recycle Bin. The files in the Recycle Bin do occupy room on your PC computer, so you need to empty it to free up space.

## Delete Files and Folders

1. In the desktop, click or tap the **File Explorer** button on the taskbar.

2. Select the files and folders you want to delete.

3. Click or tap the **Delete** button arrow on the Home tab, and then click **Recycle** or **Permanently delete**.

   **TIMESAVER** *Press the Delete key to recycle the items or press Shift+Delete to permanently delete the items.*

4. If prompted, click or tap **Yes** to confirm the deletion and place the items in the Recycle Bin.

   ◆ **Enable delete confirmation.** Click or tap the **Delete** button arrow on the Home tab, and then click or tap **Show recycle confirmation**.

5. In the desktop, right-click or tap-hold the **Recycle Bin** icon, and then click or tap **Empty Recycle Bin**.

   Your device permanently removes the items.

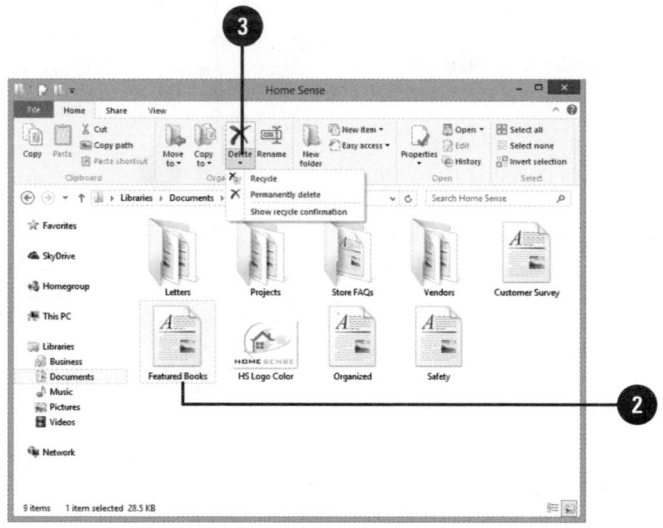

Recycle Bin icon

## Restore Files and Folders

**1** In the desktop, double-click or double-tap the **Recycle Bin** icon on the desktop.

**2** Select the item or items you want to restore.

**3** Click or tap the **Restore this item** or **Restore all items** button on the Manage tab.

◆ Empty Recycle Bin. Click or tap the **Empty Recycle Bin** button on the Manage tab, and then click or tap **Yes** to confirm.

**4** If prompted, click or tap **Yes** to confirm the restore or click or tap **No** to cancel it.

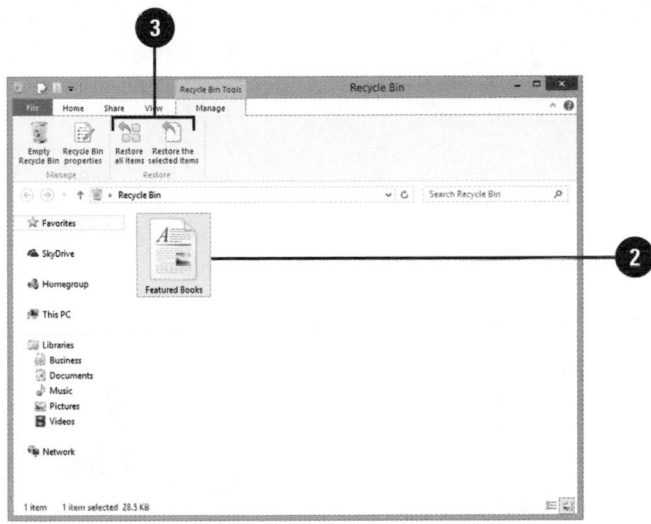

### Did You Know?

**You can undo a deletion.** If you accidentally delete a file, click or tap the Undo button on the Quick Access toolbar. Windows remembers your last three actions.

**You can't open a deleted folder and restore selected items.** When you've deleted a folder, you have to restore the entire folder.

---

### For Your Information

#### Changing Recycle Bin Properties

You can adjust several Recycle Bin settings by using the Properties option on the Recycle Bin shortcut menu or the Recycle Bin properties button on the Manage tab in the Recycle Bin window. For example, if you want to delete files immediately rather than place them in the Recycle Bin, right-click or tap-hold the Recycle Bin, click or tap Properties, and then select the Don't Move Files To The Recycle Bin check box. Also, if you find that the Recycle Bin is full and cannot accept any more files, you can increase the amount of disk space allotted to the Recycle Bin by increasing the Maximum size (MB) amount.

# Changing File and Folder List Views

You can display files and folders in a variety of different ways, depending on what you want to see and do. When you view files and folders in Details view, a default list of file and folder information appears, which consists of Name, Size, Type, and Date Modified. If the default list of file and folder details doesn't provide you with the information you need, you can add and remove any file and folder information from the Details view. If you need to change the way Windows sorts your files and folders, you can use the column indicator buttons in the right pane of Details view. Clicking or tapping one of the column indicator buttons, such as Name, Size, Type, or Date Modified, in Details view sorts the files and folders by the type of information listed in the column.

## Change File Details to List

1. In the desktop, click or tap the **File Explorer** button on the taskbar.

2. Open the folder you want to change in Details view.

3. Click or tap the **Add column** button on the View tab, and then click or tap a column (select or clear check mark) or click or tap **Choose columns**.

4. Select the check boxes with the details you want to include and clear the ones you don't.

5. Click or tap the **Move Up** or **Move Down** buttons to change the order of the selected items.

6. Click or tap the **Show** or **Hide** buttons to show or hide the selected items.

7. Specify the width in pixels of the column for the selected items.

8. Click or tap **OK**.

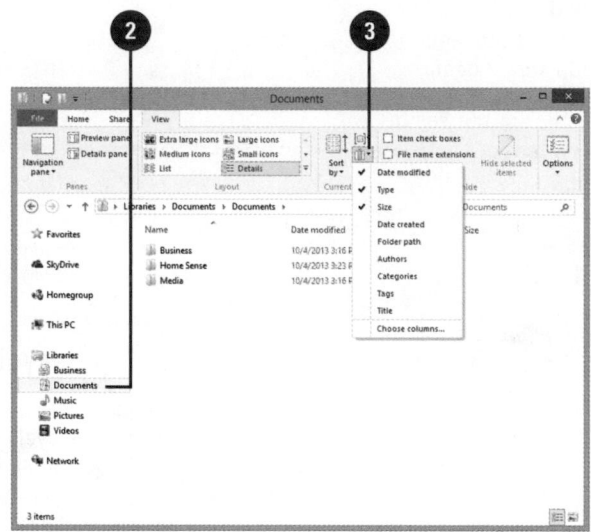

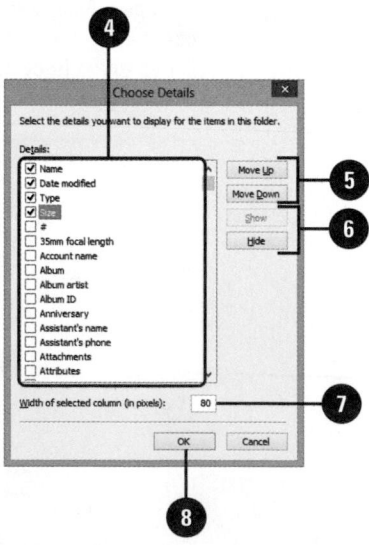

### Did You Know?

***An ellipsis indicates information is hidden.*** To show the information, drag the edge of the column indicator button to resize the column.

# Hiding Files and Folders

If you want to hide files and folders for added privacy purposes, you can do it by setting two separate options: one to set the option to hide specific files and folders, and the other to set a general folder option to show or hide files and folders. If you set the option to hide specific files and folders and the Show hidden files and folders option is set, the hidden files and folders appear transparent. If the general option is set to Do not show hidden files and folders, the hidden files and folders are actually hidden. The only way to view them again is to set the general option to Show hidden files and folders again. Anyone can show hidden files and folders, so it shouldn't be used for security purposes.

## Show or Hide Hidden Files and Folders

1. In the desktop, click or tap the **File Explorer** button on the taskbar.

2. Select the files or folders you want to hide or unhide.

3. Click or tap the **Hide selected items** button on the View tab.

4. Select the **Hidden items** check box on the View tab to show hidden files or folders. To hide hidden items, clear the check box.

   The hidden files or folders appear transparent.

5. To unhide hidden files or folders, select them, and then click or tap the **Hide selected items** button on the View tab.

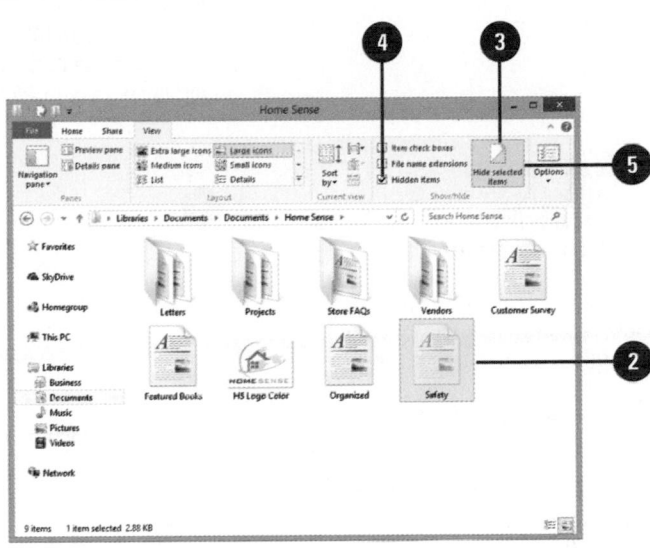

### Did You Know?

*You can set options to show or hide files and folders.* In File Explorer, click or tap the Options button on the View tab, click or tap Change folder and search options, click or tap the Do Not Show Hidden Files And Folders or Show Hidden Files And Folders option, click or tap Apply to Folders, and then click or tap OK.

# Changing Folder Options

When you work with files and folders, Windows displays folder contents in a standard way, known as the **default**. The default folder view settings are as follows: Tiles view displays files and folders as icons; common task links appear in the left pane; folders open in the same window; and items open when you double-click or double-tap them. Depending on previous installation or users, your folder view settings might differ. Instead of changing the folder view to your preferred view—Icons, List, or Details—each time you open a folder, you can change the view permanently to the one you prefer. In addition to the defaults, you can change options such as folder settings to show or hide file extensions for known file types, show or hide hidden files and folders, show or hide protected operating system files, and show pop-up descriptions of folders and desktop items. You can also set Navigation pane options to show all folders like the Folder list and automatically expand the folder list to the current folder.

## Change Folder Options

1. In the desktop, click or tap the **File Explorer** button on the taskbar.

2. Click or tap the **Options** button on the View tab, and then click or tap **Change folder and search options**.

3. Click or tap the **General** tab.

4. Select a Browse folders option to display each folder in the same window or its own window.

5. Select a Click items as follows option to single-click or double-click items.

6. Select the Navigation pane check boxes option to **Show all folders** or **Automatically expand to current folder**.

7. Click or tap **OK**.

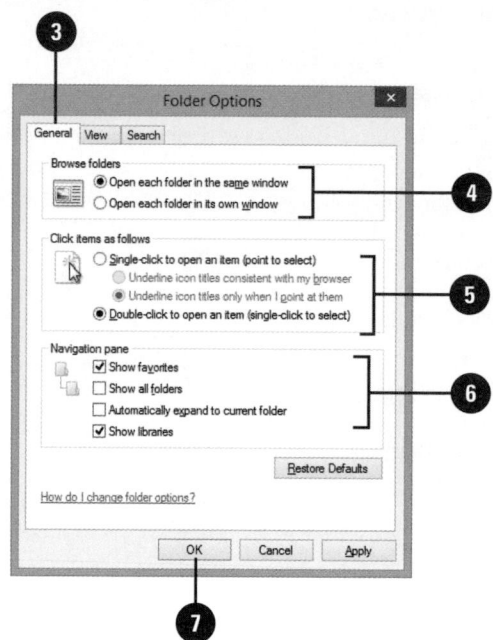

### Did You Know?

*You can restore all folder options to default Windows settings.* On the General tab in the Folder Options dialog box, click or tap Restore Defaults.

## Change the Folder View

**1** In the desktop, click or tap the **File Explorer** button on the taskbar.

**2** Click or tap the **Options** button on the View, and then click **Change folder and search options**.

**3** Click or tap the **View** tab.

**4** To set the current view to all folders, click or tap **Apply to Folders**.

**5** Select the check boxes for the options you want, and clear the check boxes for the ones you don't. Some common options include:

- ◆ **Always show menus**.
- ◆ **Hidden files and folders**.
- ◆ **Hide extensions for known file types**.
- ◆ **Hide protected operating system files (Recommended)**.
- ◆ **Show encrypted or compressed NTFS files in color**.
- ◆ **Show pop-up description for folder and desktop items**.

**6** Click or tap **OK**.

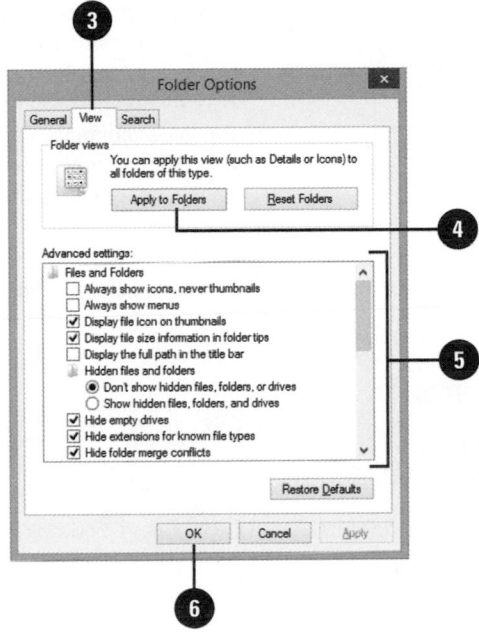

### Did You Know?

*You can reset folder views to original Windows settings.* On the View tab in the Folder Options dialog box, click or tap Reset Folders.

---

### For Your Information

#### Understanding File Extensions

The program Windows uses to open a document depends on a three-letter extension to the document's file name, called a **file extension**. You might have never seen a document's file extension because your system might be set up to hide it. The file extension for simple text files is ".txt" (pronounced "dot t-x-t"), and many graphic files have the extension ".bmp". This means that the full name for a text file named Memo is Memo.txt. If you double-click or double-tap a document whose file name ends with the three-letter extension ".txt," Windows automatically opens the document with Notepad, a text-only editor. If you want to display file extensions in dialog boxes and windows, select or clear the File Name Extensions check box on the View tab in File Explorer. If you want to change the program Windows automatically starts with a given file extension, open the Control Panel (click or tap This PC in File Explorer, and then click or tap the Open Control Panel button on the Computer tab), click or tap Default Programs in Small or Large icons view, click or tap Default Programs, click or tap Associate A File Type Or Protocol With A Program, select the file type, and then click or tap Change Program to see the list of the file extensions Windows recognizes and the programs associated with each of them, and then make changes as appropriate.

# Customizing Library Folders

In your library folders, you can customize view options based on the contents. In the tab of the Pictures and Music library folders, Windows provides buttons with file management activities specifically related to the contents of the folder, such as Slide Show in the Pictures library, or Play All in the Music library. The Arrange by options are also related to the folder contents, such as Rating in the Pictures library, or Artist in the Music library. When you create a new library folder, you can customize it for documents, pictures, music, and videos by applying a folder template, which is a collection of folder tasks and viewing options. When you apply a template to a folder, you apply specific features to the folder, such as specialized tasks and viewing options for working with documents, pictures, music, and videos.

## Customize a Library Folder

1 In the desktop, click or tap the **File Explorer** button on the taskbar.

2 Open the library folder you want to change.

3 Click or tap the **Properties** button on the Home tab.

4 Click or tap the **Optimize this library for** list arrow, and then select the type of folder you want: **General Items, Documents, Music Pictures**, or **Videos**.

   **TIMESAVER** *Click or tap the Optimize library for button on the Manage tab, and then select an option.*

5 To show or hide the library in the Navigation pane, select or clear the **Shown in navigation pane** check box.

6 To restore library default settings for this folder, click or tap **Restore Defaults**.

7 Click or tap **OK**.

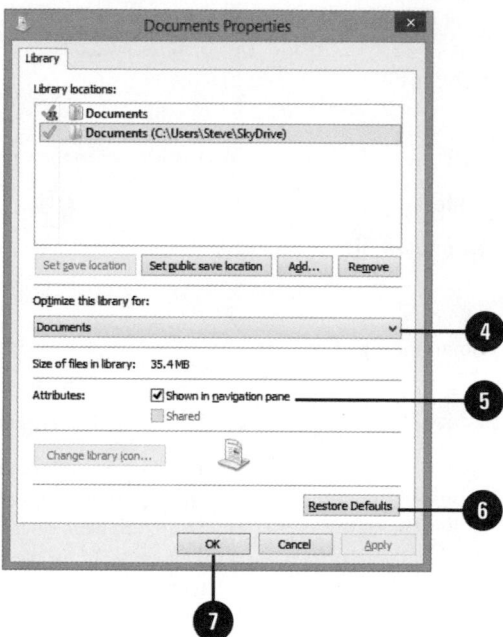

# Customizing Personal Folders

In your personal folders, you can create your own folders and customize view options based on the contents. In the toolbar of the Pictures and Music folders, Windows provides buttons with file management activities specifically related to the contents of the folder, such as Slide Show in the Pictures folder, or Play All in the Music folders. When you create a new folder, you can customize it for documents, pictures, music, and videos by applying a folder template, which is a collection of folder tasks and viewing options. When you apply a template to a folder, you apply specific features to the folder, such as specialized tasks and viewing options for working with documents, pictures, music, and videos.

## Customize a Folder

1. In the desktop, click or tap the **File Explorer** button on the taskbar.

2. Open the folder you want to change.

3. Click or tap the **Properties** button on the Home tab.

4. Click or tap the **Customize** tab for a folder.

5. Click or tap the **Optimize this folder for** list arrow, and then select the type of folder you want: **General Items**, **Documents**, **Pictures**, **Videos**, or **Music**.

6. Select the **Also apply this template to all subfolders** check box to apply the option.

7. To select a picture for display on the folder icon, click or tap **Choose File.**

8. To restore the default picture for the folder, click or tap **Restore Default**.

9. Click or tap **OK**.

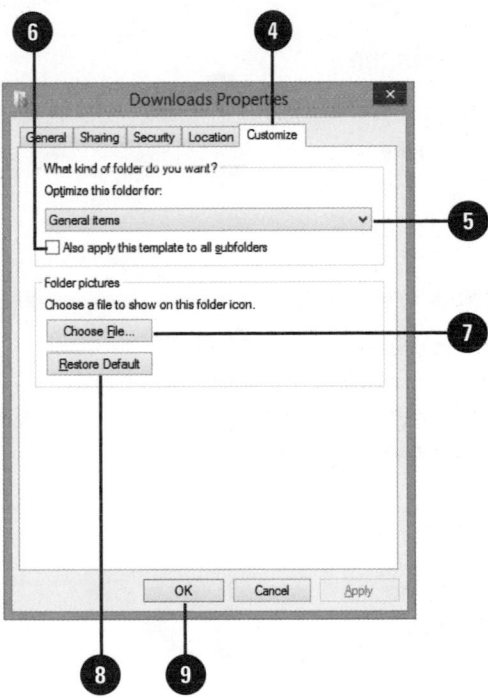

# Sharing Folders or Files with Others

File Explorer maintains a set of personal folders and options for everyone on your PC computer to make sure the contents of each user's personal folders remain private. The contents of your personal folders are private, unless you decide to share the contents with others who use your PC computer or SkyDrive. If you want the other users to have access to shared files, you can place those files in a shared folder on your SkyDrive (**New!**) called the Public folder that users can access online. If you're connected online, the files in the public folder are available to users. You can also share files from any folder on your PC computer that you want to designate as a shared folder to those connected to your network or Homegroup, a shared network. When you specify a shared folder, you can also set access permission levels for a person or group. If you no longer want to share a folder, you can stop sharing.

## Share a File or Folders from the Public Folder on SkyDrive

1. In the desktop, click or tap the **File Explorer** button on the taskbar.

2. Open the drive or folder containing the files or folders you want to share.

3. Select the files or folders you want to share.

4. In the Navigation pane, point to a folder list to display the expand and collapse arrows.

5. Click or tap the arrow next to the **SkyDrive (New!)** to display the Public folder, and then click or tap the arrow next to the **Public** folder (if available) to display the Public subfolders.

6. Drag the selected items onto the Public folder or subfolder where you want to share files.

### See Also

*See "Setting Network Sharing Options" on page 403 for information on controlling access to a public folder over a network*

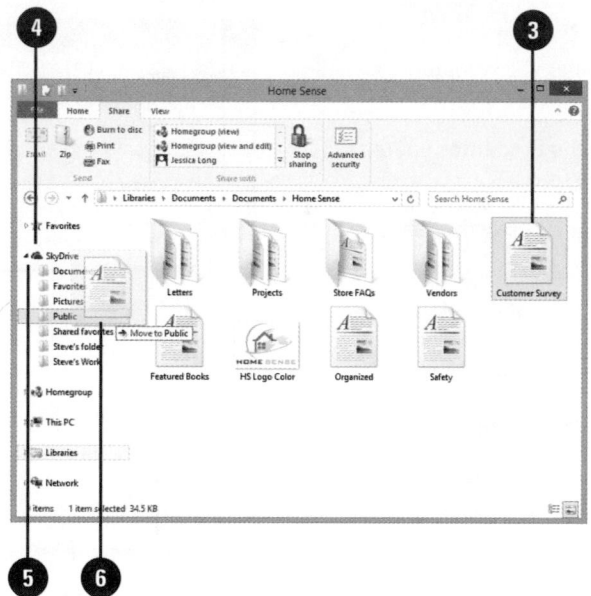

## Share or Unshare a Folder

**1** In the desktop, click or tap the **File Explorer** button on the taskbar.

**2** Select the folders you want to share or unshare.

**3** Click or tap **Specific people** on the Share tab to set multiple options.

- ◆ **Share with options.** Click or tap Homegroup (view) or Homegroup (view and edit) or a contact.

- ◆ **Unshare a folder.** Click or tap the **Stop sharing** button.

**4** Do any of the following:

- ◆ Type the name of the person with whom you want to share files, and then click or tap **Add**.

- ◆ Click or tap the arrow to the right of the text box, click or tap the person's name, and then click or tap **Add**.

**5** Click or tap the arrow next to the permission level for the person or group, and then select a sharing permission:

- ◆ **Read.** Allows viewing only.

- ◆ **Read/Write.** Allows viewing, adding, changing, and deleting all files.

- ◆ **Remove.** Deletes the current permission setting.

**6** Click or tap **Share**, and then wait while Windows sets up sharing.

**7** If you want, click or tap the e-mail or copy link to notify people you have shared this folder and files.

**8** Otherwise, click or tap **Done**.

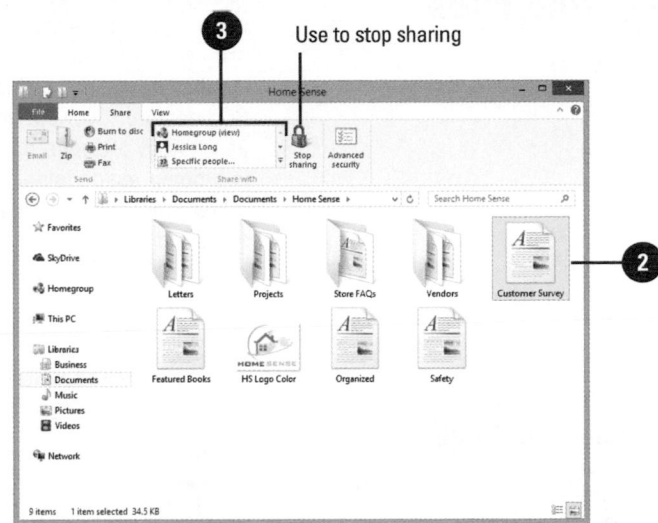

Use to stop sharing

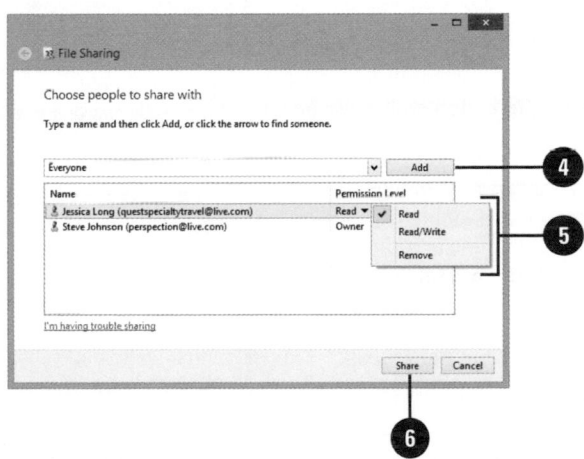

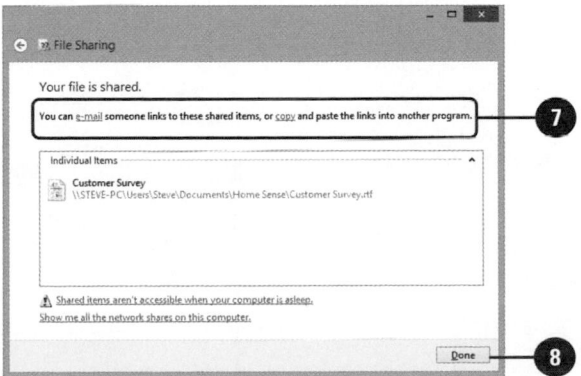

# Compressing Files and Folders

You can compress files in special folders that use compressing software to decrease the size of the files they contain. Compressed folders are useful for reducing the file size of one or more large files, thus freeing disk space and reducing the time it takes to transfer files to another PC computer over the Internet or network. A compressed folder is denoted by a zippered folder icon. You can compress one or more files in a compressed folder by simply dragging them onto the compressed folder icon. When a file is compressed, a copy is used in the compression, and the original remains intact. You can uncompress, or extract, a file from the compressed folder and open it as you normally would, or you can open a file directly from the compressed folder by double-clicking or double-tapping it. When you open a file directly, Windows extracts the file when it opens and compresses it again when it closes.

## Compress Files and Folders

1. In the desktop, click or tap the **File Explorer** button on the taskbar.

2. Select the files and folders you want to copy to a compressed folder.

3. Click or tap the **Zip** button on the Share tab.

   ◆ Right-click or tap-hold one of the selected items, point to **Send to**, and then click or tap **Compressed (zipped) folder**.

4. If you want, rename the compressed folder, and then press Enter or tap a blank area.

5. To copy additional files or folders to the compressed folder, drag the files onto the compressed folder.

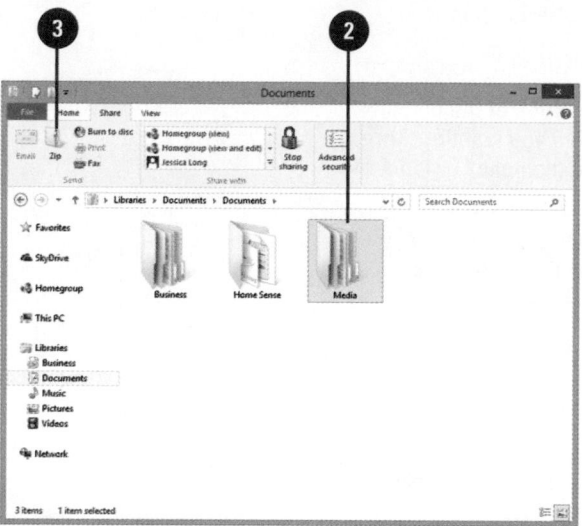

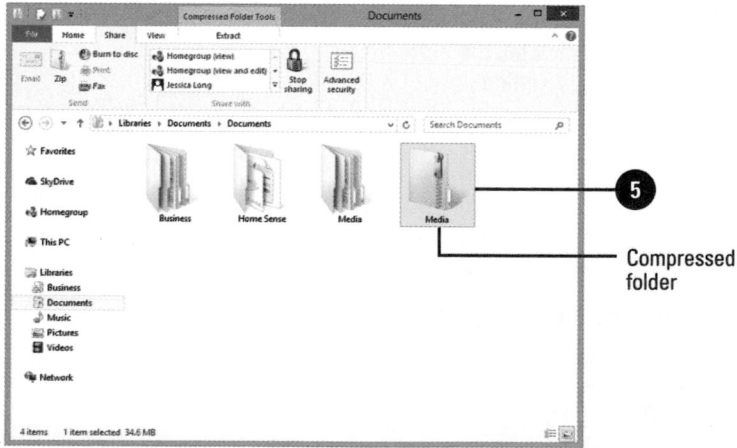

Compressed folder

## View Compressed Files

1. In the desktop, click or tap the **File Explorer** button on the taskbar.

2. Double-click or double-tap the compressed folder to open it.

3. Double-click or double-tap an item in the folder to open it using its associated program.

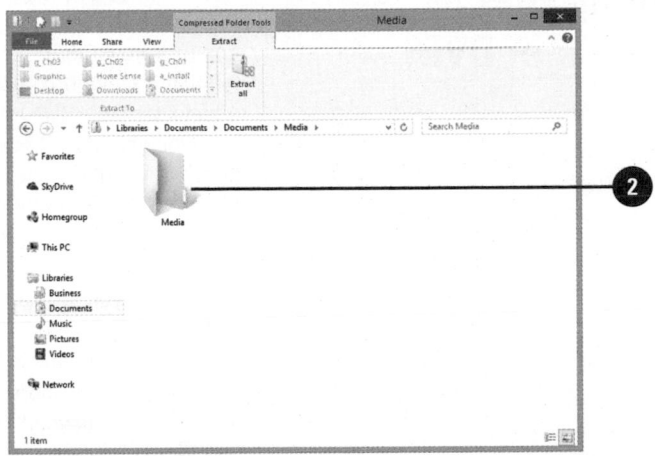

## Uncompress Files and Folders

◆ **Individual files or folders.** In File Explorer, double-click or double-tap the compressed folder to open it, select the files and folders you want to uncompress, and then drag the selection from the compressed folder to a new location in an uncompressed folder.

◆ **All files.** In File Explorer, double-click or double-tap the compressed folder, and then click or tap the **Extract all** button on the Extract tab, and then step through the Extraction Wizard.

Extract all button

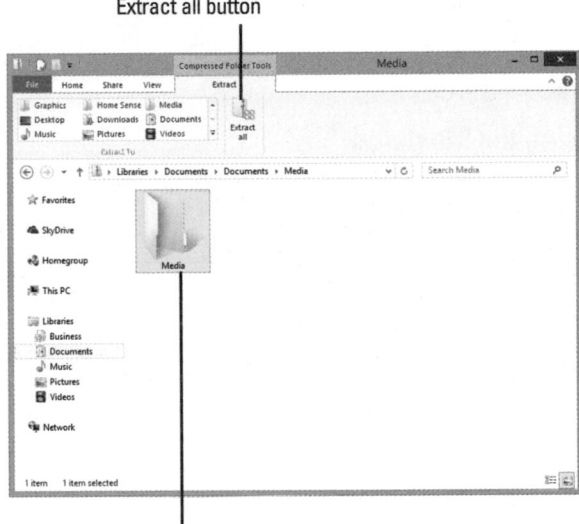

Opened compressed folder

### Did You Know?

*You can also compress file attributes in a folder.* Select the folder, click or tap the Properties button on the Home tab, click or tap Properties, click or tap the General tab, click or tap Advanced, select the Compress Contents To Save Disk Space check box, and then click or tap OK twice.

# Managing Files Using a CD or DVD

The low cost and large storage size of discs, either CD or DVD, makes creating and using CDs or DVDs an effective way to back up information or transfer large amounts of information to another PC computer without a network. Before you can create a CD or DVD, you must have a blank writable disc and a recorder (also known as a writer or burner) installed on your PC computer. You can copy, or write, files and folders to either a writable disc (CD-R or DVD-R) or a rewriteable disc (CD-RW or DVD-RW). With writable discs, you can read and write files and folders many times, but you can't erase them. With rewriteable discs, you can read, write, and erase files and folders many times, just like a hard disk. When you burn a disc, Windows needs disk space on your hard disk equal to the capacity of the disc. For a typical CD, this is between 650 and 740 megabytes (MB) and for a DVD, this is about 4.7 gigabytes (GB). Do not copy more files and folders to the CD or DVD than it will hold; anything beyond the limit will not copy. You can burn a disc using one of two formats: Live File System or Mastered. The **Live File System** format (*Like a USB flash drive* option) allows you to copy files to a disc at any time, while the **Mastered** format (*With a CD/DVD player* option) needs to copy them all at once. If you need a disc and want the convenience of copying files at any time, the Live File System is the best choice. When you need a compatible disc for older PC computers, the Mastered format is the better choice.

## Burn a Disc Using the Mastered Format

1. Insert a writable CD or DVD into your CD or DVD recorder.

2. Click or tap **Burn files to disc** in the notification or click or tap the **Burn to disc** button on the Share tab in File Explorer.

3. Type a name for the disc.

4. Click or tap the **With a CD/DVD player** option.

5. Click or tap **Next** to continue.

6. Open the folder that contains the files you want to burn, and then drag the files onto the empty disc folder.

7. Click or tap **Finish burning** button on the Manage tab, and then follow the wizard steps.

   The disc recorder tray opens when the disc is complete.

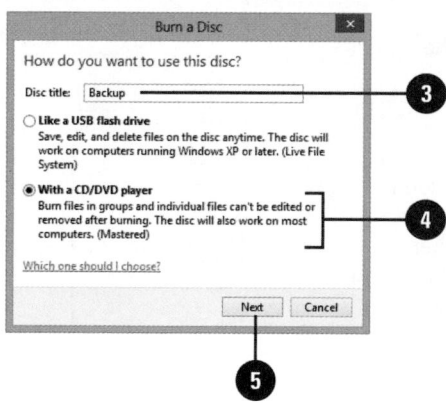

## Burn a Disc Using the Live System Format

1. Insert a writable CD or DVD into your CD or DVD recorder.

2. Click or tap **Burn files to disc** or click or tap the **Burn to disc** button on the Share tab in File Explorer.

3. Type a name for the disc.

4. Click or tap the **Like a USB flash drive** option.

5. Click or tap **Next** to continue.

    Windows names, formats, and prepares the disc for use.

6. Upon completion, open the folder with the files you want to burn.

7. Drag the files into the disc folder.

    As you drag files, they are copied automatically to the disc.

8. To close the session and prepare the disc for use, display the disc folder, click or tap the **Eject** button on the Manage tab.

    After you close a session, you can still add files to the disc. However, you need to close the session.

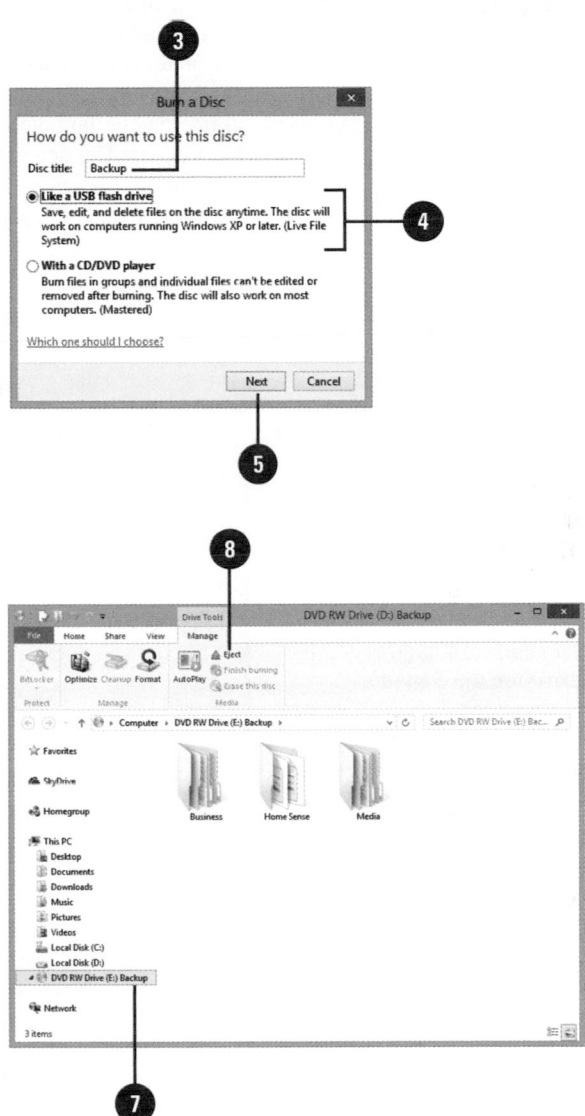

### Did You Know?

*You can erase some or all of the files on a disc.* Insert the writable disc with the Live File System format, click or tap This PC in File Explorer, click or tap the writable drive, and then click or tap Erase This Disc on the Manage tab to erase all the files. Double-click or double-tap the writable drive, select the files you want to delete, and then click or tap the Delete button on the Home tab.

# Creating a Shortcut to a File or Folder

It could take you a while to access a file or folder buried several levels down in a file hierarchy. To save some time, you can create shortcuts to the items you use frequently. A **shortcut** is a link that you can place in any location to gain instant access to a particular file, folder, or program on your hard disk or on a network just by double-clicking or double-tapping. The actual file, folder, or program remains stored in its original location, and you place an icon representing the shortcut in a convenient location, such as in a folder or on the desktop.

## Create a Shortcut to a File or Folder

1. In the desktop, click or tap the **File Explorer** button on the taskbar.

2. Select the file or folder in which you want to create a shortcut.

3. Click or tap the **New item** button on the Home tab, and then click or tap **Shortcut**.

4. To change the shortcut's name, select it, click or tap the **Rename** button on the Home tab, type a new name, and then press Enter or tap in a blank area.

5. Drag the shortcut to the desired location.

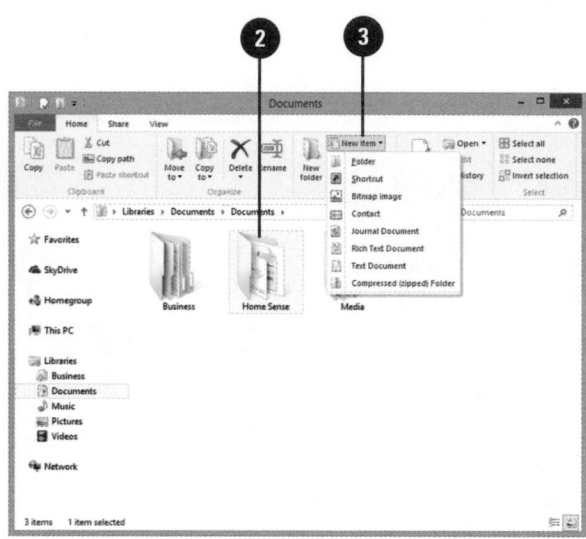

### Did You Know?

*You can pin a folder or file to the Start screen.* In File Explorer, select the folder or file you want to pin, click or tap the Easy access button on the Home tab, and then click or tap Pin to Start.

---

## For Your Information

### Placing Shortcuts on the Desktop or Taskbar

You can place shortcuts to frequently used files, folders, and programs on the desktop or toolbar on the taskbar. To do this, simply drag the shortcut file, folder, or program to the desktop. You can also drag a shortcut to a toolbar on the taskbar using the same method. When you release the mouse or finger, the item appears on the desktop or toolbar.

# Exploring the Internet

**4**

## Introduction

The **Internet** is a global collection of more than a billion computers (and growing) linked together to share information. The Internet's physical structure includes telephone lines, cables, satellites, and other telecommunications media. Using the Internet, users can share many types of information, including text, graphics, sounds, videos, and programs. The **World Wide Web** (also known as the web) is a part of the Internet that consists of web sites located on different computers around the world.

A **web site** contains web pages linked together to make searching for information on the Internet easier. **Web pages** are documents that contain highlighted words, phrases, and graphics, called **hyperlinks** (or simply **links**) that open other web pages when you click or tap them. Some web pages contain frames. A frame is a separate window within a web page that lets you see more than one web page at a time. **Web browsers** are software programs that you use to "browse the web," or access and display web pages. Browsers make the web easy to navigate by providing a graphical, point-and-click or tap environment.

Microsoft Internet Explorer (IE) is a popular browser from Microsoft that is built-in to Windows 8.1. Windows 8.1 comes with two versions of Internet Explorer: a metro app and a traditional desktop program. With a web browser, you can display web pages from all over the world, display web content on the desktop, view web feeds, use links to move from one web page to another, play audio and video clips, search the web for information, make favorite web pages available offline (when you're not connected to the Internet), and print text and graphics on web pages.

## What You'll Do

**Start the Internet Explorer App**

**View the Internet Explorer App Window**

**Navigate the Web with the IE App**

**Search the Web with the IE App & Bing**

**Change IE App Settings**

**Start Internet Explorer from the Desktop**

**View the Internet Explorer Window**

**Change Your Home Page**

**Browse the Web**

**Use Compatibility View**

**Use and Manage Accelerators**

**Get Suggestions for Web Sites**

**Add a Web Page to the Favorites List**

**View and Maintain a History List**

**Read and Subscribe to Feeds**

**Search the Web**

**Preview and Print a Web Page**

**Save Pictures or Text from a Web Page**

**Save a Web Page**

**Download Files from the Web**

**Connect to the Internet**

**Create an Internet Connection**

**Set Up Windows Firewall**

# Starting the Internet Explorer App

Windows 8.1 comes with two versions of Internet Explorer (version 11): a metro app and a traditional desktop program. You can start the Internet Explorer metro app from the Start screen, like any other metro app. After you start the Internet Explorer app, you might need to establish a connection to the Internet by selecting a dial-up service and entering a username and password. Internet Explorer starts in full screen view and loads your home page, which is a page that you set to display when you start the app. The elements of the Internet Explorer app window allow you to view and search for information on the Internet.

## Start the Internet Explorer App from the Start Screen

① Click or tap the **Internet Explorer** tile on the Start or Apps screen.

② If necessary, click or tap **Connect** to dial your ISP. You might need to type your username and password before Internet Explorer will connect to the Internet.

The Internet Explorer app window opens in full screen view with the Address bar at the bottom.

### Did You Know?

*You can switch to Internet Explorer on the desktop.* In the Internet Explorer app, click or tap the Page Tools button on the Address bar, and then click or tap View On The Desktop.

*You can pin a web page to the Start screen.* In the Internet Explorer app, display the web page you want to pin, click or tap the Favorites button on the Address bar, and then click or tap Pin Site button on the Favorites bar.

*You can view downloads from the web in Internet Explorer.* In the Internet Explorer app, click or tap the Page Tools button on the Address bar, and then click or tap View Downloads (**New!**).

# Viewing the Internet Explorer App Window

**Navigation arrow**
Displays an arrow to navigate back and forward between web pages.

**Browser pane**
Displays the current web page, document, or folder contents.

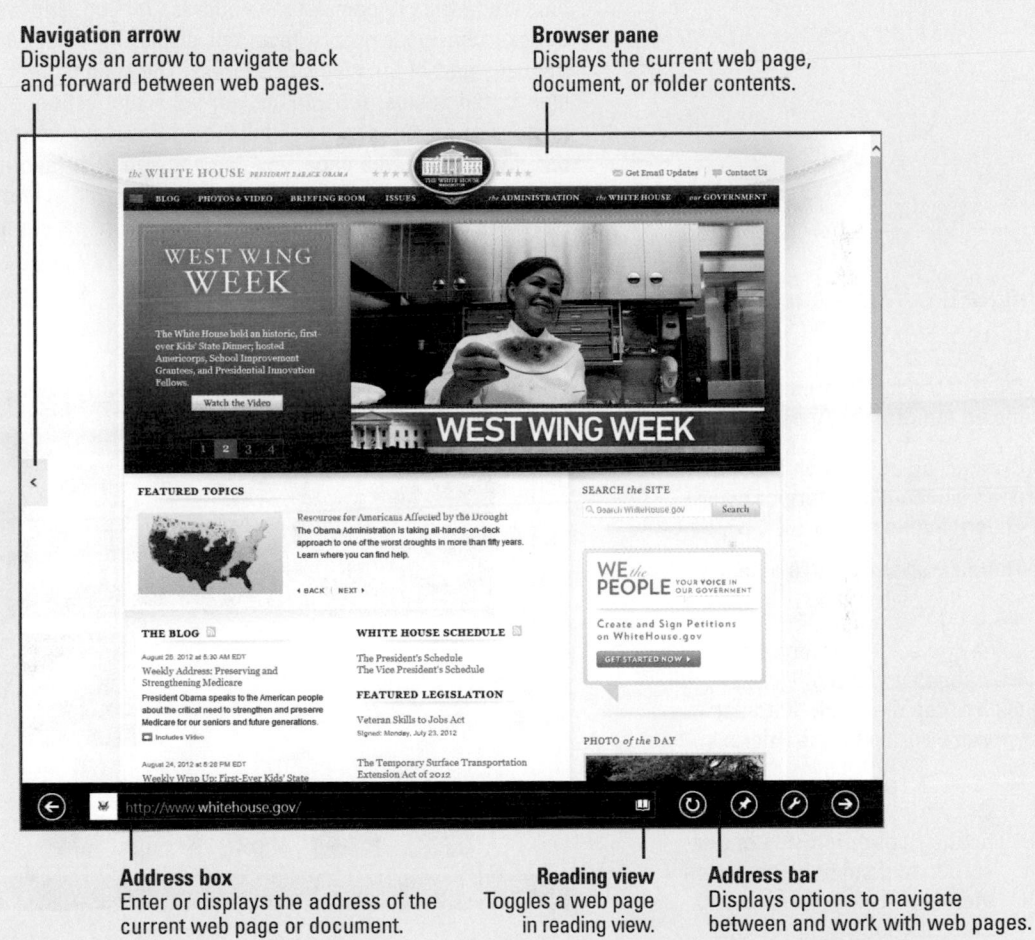

**Address box**
Enter or displays the address of the current web page or document.

**Reading view**
Toggles a web page in reading view.

**Address bar**
Displays options to navigate between and work with web pages.

# Navigating the Web with the IE App

With the Internet Explorer app, you can navigate the web by clicking or tapping a web page link, such as a picture or colored, underlined text, or use the Address bar to enter a web address. If the Address bar is minimized (at the bottom of the screen with three dots on the right), click or tap it to expand it (**New!**). When you use the Address bar, the Internet Explorer app displays frequently-used web sites. When you enter a web address, the Internet Explorer app provides suggestions and tries to complete the address for you using AutoComplete. If you have recently entered the web page address, AutoComplete remembers it and tries to complete the address for you. The smart Address bar searches your history, favorites, displaying a bar with matches from any part of the web site address. The suggested matches are highlighted in blue. You can click or tap a suggestion, the correct address or continue to type until the address you want appears in the bar. If you like a web page, you can add it to your favorites for easy access in the future. If a web page contains article, you can switch to Reading view (**New!**), which displays the page article for easy reading.

## Navigate the Web Pages with the IE App

1. Click or tap the **Internet Explorer** tile on the Start or Apps screen.

2. Click or tap any link on the web page, such as a picture or colored, underlined text.

   The pointer changes to a hand when it is over a link.

3. To navigate back or forward to web pages you already visited, click or tap the **Back** button or **Forward** button on the Address bar.

   ◆ **Use arrows.** Move your pointer on the right or left side of the screen to display an arrow, and then click or tap the arrow to navigate back or forward.

   ◆ **Use gestures.** Swipe left or right to navigate back or forward.

4. To view pages in Reading view, click or tap the **Reading view** button (**New!**). click or tap the button again to exit.

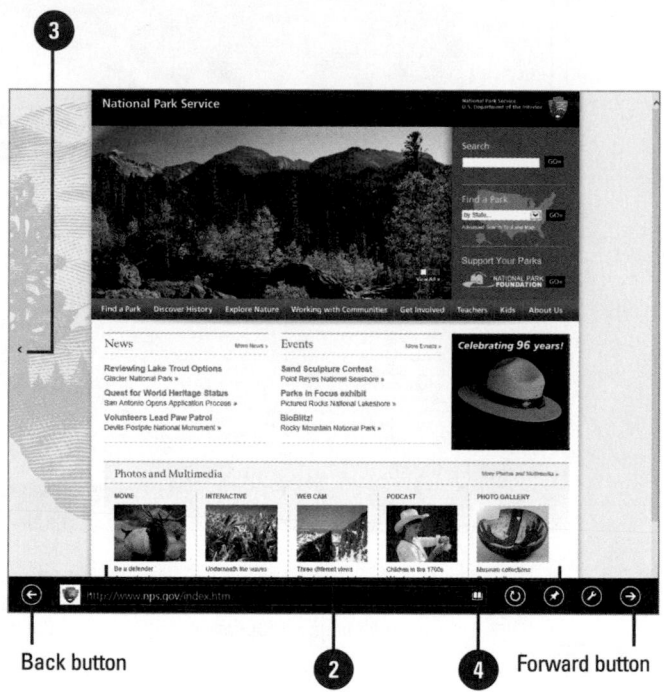

Back button

2

4

Forward button

## Navigate the Web Addresses with the IE App

1. Click or tap the **Internet Explorer** tile on the Start or Apps screen.

   The Address bar appears at the bottom of the screen. If the Address bar is minimized, click or tap it to expand it (**New!**).

2. Click or tap in the Address bar.

3. To use a Frequent web address, click or tap the tile.

4. In the Address bar, type the web address.

   As you type, the app displays suggestions and tries to complete the address using AutoComplete.

5. Click or tap a suggestion, the correct address or continue to type until the address you want appears in the bar.

6. Click or tap the **Go** button or press Enter.

   ◆ To cancel the address, click or tap the **Close** button (x) in the Address bar.

7. To use a Favorites web address, click or tap the **Favorites** button, on the Address bar, and then click or tap the tile.

   ◆ **Add to Favorites.** Display the web page, click the **Add to Favorites** button on the Favorites bar, specify options, and then click or tap **Add**.

### Did You Know?

***You can remove a frequent or favorite web page.*** In the Internet Explorer app, click or tap in the Address bar, right-click or tap-hold a frequent or favorite tile, and then click or tap Remove.

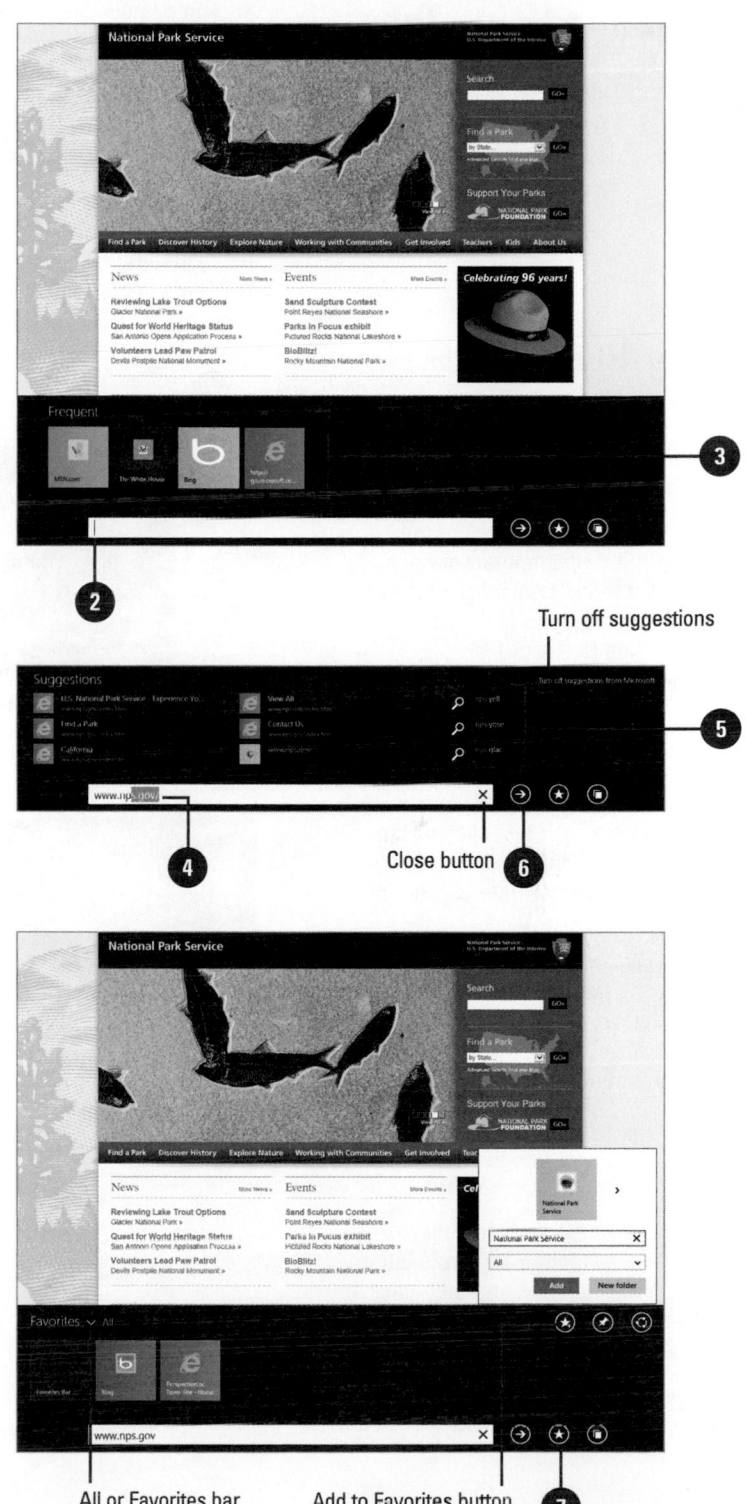

Turn off suggestions

Close button

All or Favorites bar    Add to Favorites button

# Navigating Using Tabs with the IE App

As you open web sites with the Internet Explorer app, you can use separate tabs for each one, so you can view multiple web sites in a single window. With the App bar, you can open web pages on new tabs, use InPrivate browsing on a new tab, and close tabs. After you open a tab, you can click or tap a tab to quickly switch between them or click or tap the Close button on the tab to remove it. InPrivate browsing doesn't retain or keep track of browsing history, searches, temporary Internet files, form data, cookies, and usernames and passwords. You can start InPrivate browsing by creating a new InPrivate tab. When you're done InPrivate browsing, close the InPrivate tab to exit it.

## Navigate Using Tabs with the IE App

1. Click or tap the **Internet Explorer** tile on the Start or Apps screen.

2. Right-click a blank area of the screen (on a computer) or swipe up from the bottom edge or down from the top edge of the screen (on a mobile device).

   ◆ **Display tabs**. From the Favorites bar, you can click the **Tabs** button (**New!**) to display tabs.

3. To create a new tab, click or tap the **New Tab** button on the App bar, and then navigate to the web page you want.

   **TIMESAVER** *Press Ctrl+T to create a new tab.*

4. To open to a tab, click or tap the tab thumbnail on the App bar.

5. To close a tab, click or tap the **Close** button (x) on the tab on the App bar.

   ◆ **Reopen the last closed tab**. Click or tap the **Tab tools** button on the App bar, and then click or tap **Reopen closed tab** (**New!**).

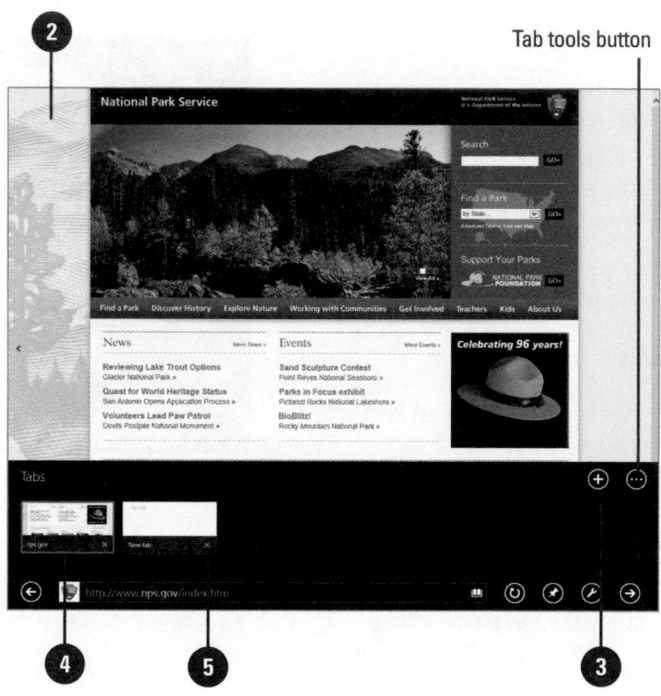

Tab tools button

## Navigate Privately with the IE App

1. Click or tap the **Internet Explorer** tile on the Start or Apps screen.

2. Right-click a blank area of the screen (on a computer) or swipe up from the bottom edge or down from the top edge of the screen (on a mobile device).

3. Click or tap the **Tab tools** button on the App bar, and then click or tap **New InPrivate tab.**

   The InPrivate tab opens, displaying information about the tab. An InPrivate icon appears in the Address bar to indicate InPrivate browsing is active.

4. Click or tap in the Address bar, type the web address, and then Click or tap the **Go** button or press Enter.

   ◆ You can also select a suggestion, or a Frequent web site tile.

5. To close a tab, click or tap the **Close** button (x) on the tab on the App bar.

### Did You Know?

*You can open a frequent or favorite web page. in a new tab.* In the Internet Explorer app, click or tap in the Address bar, right-click or tap-hold a frequent or favorite tile, and then click or tap Open In New Tab.

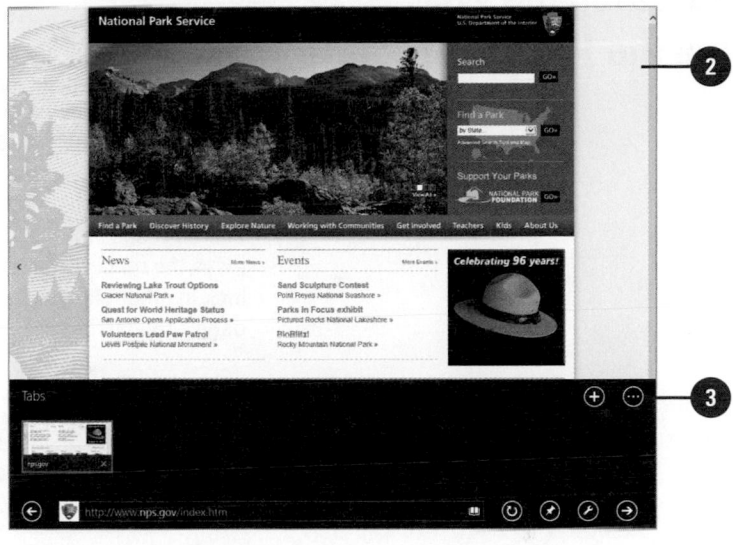

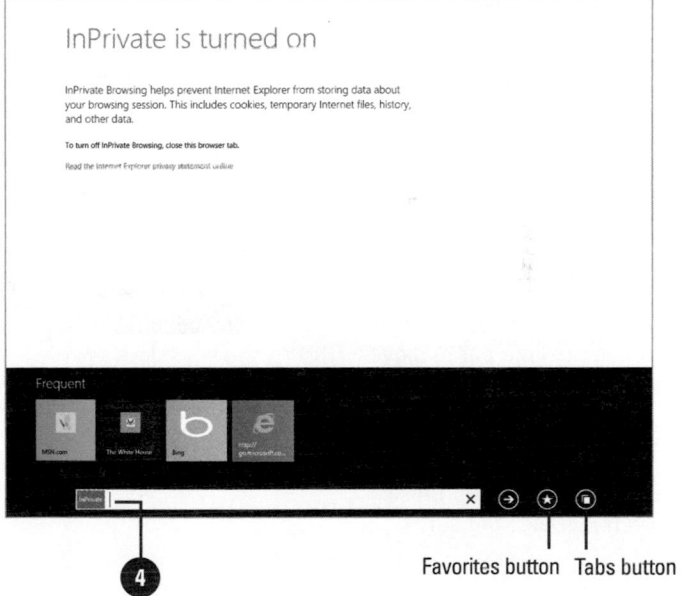

Favorites button   Tabs button

## Searching the Web with the IE App & Bing

With the Internet Explorer app, you can find text on the current web page or search the web with the Microsoft Bing search engine using the bing.com web site or the Search panel in Windows. With the Search panel, which you can access from the Charms bar, you can enter the name of item you want to find in the Search box, search categories, where you can narrow down a search, and a list of apps where you can specify a specific place to perform a search. As you type the search criteria in the Search box, Windows narrows down and displays the search results for the specified category. The Search panel also displays the number of matches found for each category if you want to look in other places. If you need to find information on the current web page, you can use the Find on page command to highlight it.

### Find Information on a Web Page with the IE App

1 Click or tap the **Internet Explorer** tile on the Start or Apps screen.

2 Click or tap the **Page tools** button on the Address bar, and then click or tap **Find on page**.

3 In the Find box, type the text or phrase you want to find.

As you type, the information is highlighted on the page.

◆ To clear the Find box, click or tap **Close** button (x).

4 Click or tap the **Previous** or **Next** button on the Find bar to move back and forward to the occurrences of the text or phrase.

5 To exit, click or tap the **Close** button (x) on the Find bar.

### Did You Know?

*You can share web sites.* In Internet Explorer, click or tap the Share button (**New!**) on the Favorites bar, and then click or tap the app to share from the Share panel from Windows.

## Search the Web with the IE App and Bing

1. Click or tap the **Internet Explorer** tile on the Start or Apps screen.

2. To use Bing.com, enter *www.bing.com* in the Address bar, and then go to Step 6.

3. To use the Search panel, point to the lower- or upper-right corner and move up or down (on a computer) or swipe left from the right edge of the screen (on a mobile device).

4. Click or tap the **Search** button on the Charms bar.

   The Search panel appears, displaying a Search box and a list of areas to search. The Internet Explorer app is selected as the search app.

5. Click or tap the **Search** list arrow (**New!**), and then click or tap **Internet Explorer**.

6. Type the first few characters for the information or item you want to find.

7. Click or tap a suggestion, or continue typing, and then click or tap the **Search** button.

8. To cancel the search, delete the search text in the Search box.

### See Also

*See "Setting Search Options for Apps" on page 45 for information on setting Bing and safe search options.*

*See "Protecting Privacy with IE App" on page 374 for information on setting privacy and web services options.*

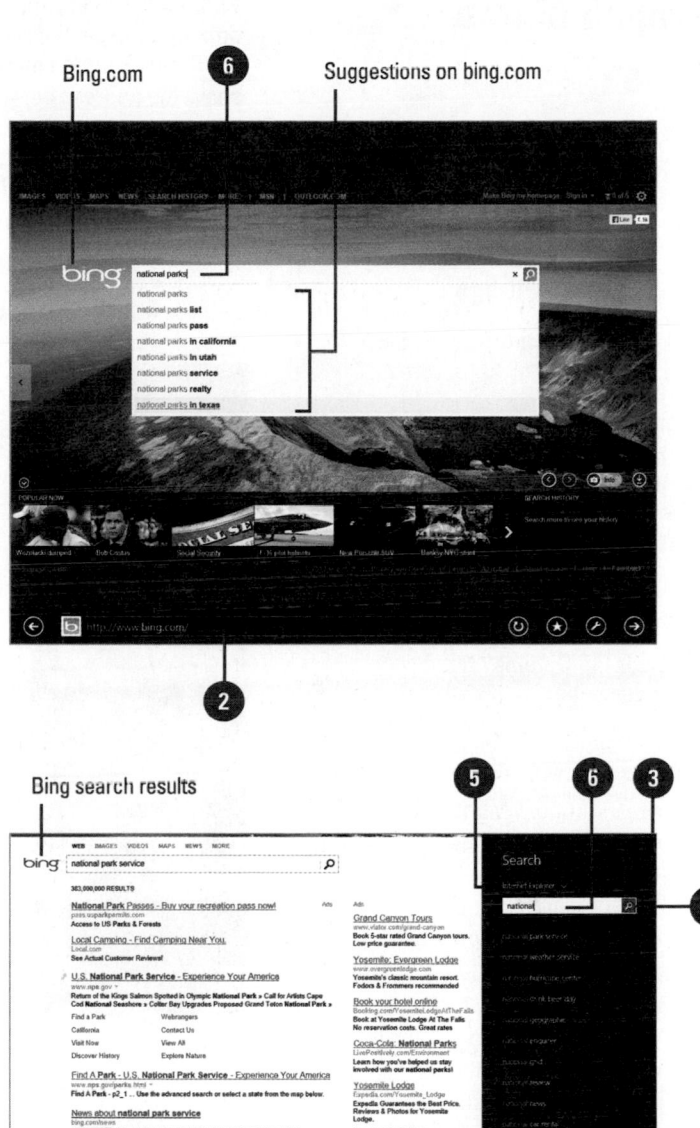

Bing.com    ⑥    Suggestions on bing.com

② 

Bing search results    ⑤    ⑥    ③

⑦

Suggestions on Search panel

# Changing IE App Settings

With the Internet Explorer app, you can set some basic level Internet options by using the Internet Options panel, which you can access from the Settings button on the Charms bar. You can set options to always show the address bar and tabs (**New!**), specify a default zoom, set home pages (**New!**), customize reading view (**New!**), delete browsing data types (**New!**), save and manage passwords (**New!**), detect phone numbers to make calls (**New!**), and select language script, web or fixed width fonts) and language encoding, and reading direction (**New!**).

## Change IE App Settings

**1** Click or tap the **Internet Explorer** tile on the Start or Apps screen.

**2** Point to the lower- or upper-right corner and up or move down (on a computer) or swipe left from the right edge of the screen (on a mobile device).

**3** Click or tap the **Settings** button on the Charms bar.

**4** Click or tap **Options** on the Settings panel.

**5** Specify any of the following options (**New!**):

   ◆ **Appearance.** Drag the slider on or off to always show the address bar and tabs.

   ◆ **Home pages.** Click or tap **Customize** to add pages.

   ◆ **Reading view.** Select a style and font size.

   ◆ **Delete Browsing Data.** Click or tap **Select** to delete data, such as cookies and history.

   ◆ **Passwords.** Drag the slider on or off to save passwords, and click or tap **Manage** to view or remove passwords.

   ◆ **Phone numbers.** Drag the slider on or off to detect phone numbers to make calls.

   ◆ **Fonts and Encoding.** Click or tap **Select** to set fonts and encoding language formats.

**6** Click or tap a blank area of the screen to exit the panel.

Internet Explorer app settings

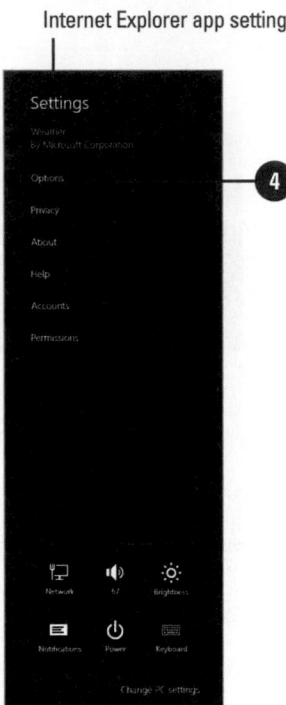

Back button to Settings panel

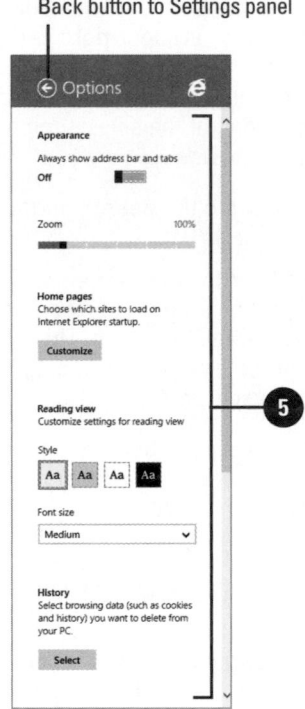

# Starting Internet Explorer from the Desktop

Windows 8.1 comes with two versions of Internet Explorer (version 10): a metro app and a traditional desktop program. You can start Internet Explorer from the desktop by using the Internet Explorer button on the taskbar. Internet Explorer starts and loads your home page, which is a page that you set to display when you start the program. After you start Internet Explorer, you might need to establish a connection to the Internet by selecting a dial-up service and entering a username and password. If you have problems running Internet Explorer—sudden crash—due to add-on programs, only that tab is affected while the other tabs remain stable. The affected tab is automatically reloaded.

## Start Internet Explorer from the Desktop

1. Click or tap the **Desktop** tile on the Start or Apps screen.

2. Click or tap the **Internet Explorer** button on the taskbar.

3. If necessary, click or tap **Connect** to dial your ISP. You might need to type your username and password before Internet Explorer will connect to the Internet.

   The Internet Explorer window opens.

### Did You Know?

***You can turn off the alert asking to make Internet Explorer the default.*** Click or tap the Tools button, and then click or tap Internet Options. Click or tap the Advanced tab, clear the Tell Me If Internet Explorer Is Not The Default Web Browser check box, and then click or tap OK.

***You can start Internet Explorer with tabs from the last session.*** Click or tap the Tools button, and then click or tap Internet Options. Click or tap the General tab, click or tap the Start With Tabs From The Last Session option, and then click or tap OK.

## For Your Information

### Browsing with Protected Mode

Internet Explorer includes protected mode, which makes it difficult for hackers using a web site to install malicious software, yet makes it easy for you to install wanted software using the Standard user account (with security enabled) instead of the Administrator user account (with security disabled). When a web page tries to install unwanted software, a warning message appears on the Status bar. If you need to disable or enable it (on by default), click or tap the Tools button, click or tap Internet Options, click or tap the Security tab, clear or select the Enable Protected Mode (requires restarting Internet Explorer) check box, and then click or tap OK.

# Viewing the Internet Explorer Window

The Internet Explorer window for the desktop provides a streamline interface with an Address bar, tabs, and toolbar buttons (Home, Favorites, and Tools). You can access frequently used menu commands using the toolbar buttons. However, you can access these and additional commands by using the Menu bar, Favorites bar, Command bar, or Status bar. You can show or hide these bars by right-clicking or tap-holding the title bar, and then choosing the command from the context menu. A check mark appears on the menu when the element is shown. The elements of the Internet Explorer window allow you to view, print, and search for information on the web.

**Address bar**
Displays the address of the current web page or document you are viewing or trying to access.

**Tabs**
Displays multiple web sites in a single browser window.

**Favorites bar**
Displays favorite sites, RSS feeds, and web slices.

**Browser pane**
Displays the current web page, document, or folder contents.

**Status bar**
Indicates the progress of loading a web page, as well as other messages about selected actions.

# Changing Your Home Page

Your **home page** in Internet Explorer is the page that opens when you start the program. When you first install Internet Explorer, the default home page is the Microsoft Network (MSN) web site. If you want a different page to appear when you start Internet Explorer and whenever you click or tap the Home button, you can change your home page. With the introduction of tabbed browsing, you can display multiple home pages in tab sets. You can choose one of the millions of web pages available through the Internet, or you can select a particular file on your hard drive.

## Change the Home Page

1. In Internet Explorer (desktop), open the web page or multiple web pages you want to be the new home page.

2. Click or tap the **Tools** button, and then click or tap **Internet options**.

3. Click or tap the **General** tab.

4. Use any of the following options:

   ◆ **Enter or edit addresses.** Type or edit each address on its own line to create home page tabs.

   ◆ **Use current.** Sets the current web page as the home page.

   ◆ **Use default.** Sets the default MSN web page as the home page.

   ◆ **Use new tab.** Sets a new tab as the home page. Select the default tab, and then enter an address.

5. Click or tap the **Start with home page** option.

6. To remove a web page as one of your home pages, select it, and then press Delete or clear it.

7. Click or tap **OK**.

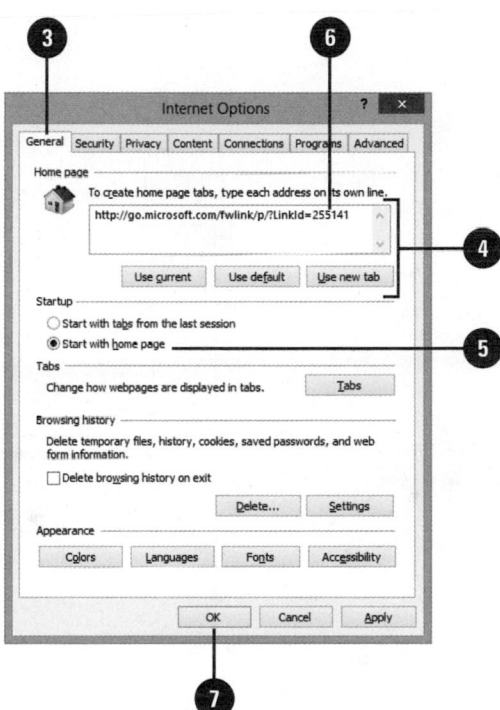

# Browsing the Web

A **web address** (also known as a URL, which stands for Uniform Resource Locator) is a unique place on the Internet where you can locate a web page. With Internet Explorer, you can browse sites on the web with ease by entering a web address or by clicking or tapping a link. Each method is better at different times. For example, you might type an address in the Address bar to start your session. Then you might click or tap a link on that web page to access a new site. When you type an Internet address in the Address bar, Internet Explorer uses **AutoComplete** to search for a recently visited page, favorite, and RSS feed that matches  what you've typed so far. If Internet Explorer finds one or more matches, it displays a drop-down menu and highlights them in blue. You can also use AutoComplete to fill out forms on the web, including single-line edits, and usernames and passwords.

## View a Web Page

In Internet Explorer (desktop), use any of the following methods to display a web page:

◆ In the Address bar, type the web address, and then click or tap the **Go** button or press Enter.

If you have recently entered the web page address, AutoComplete remembers it and tries to complete the address for you. The smart Address bar searches your history, favorites, displaying a drop-down menu with matches from any part of the web site address. The suggested matches are highlighted in blue. Click or tap the correct address or continue to type until the address you want appears in the Address list.

If you want to get rid of suggestions in the drop-down menu, you can delete them. Point to a menu item, and then click or tap the **Delete** button (red X).

◆ Click or tap any link on the web page, such as a picture or colored, underlined text. The pointer changes to a hand when it is over a link.

Type a web address          Address bar arrow

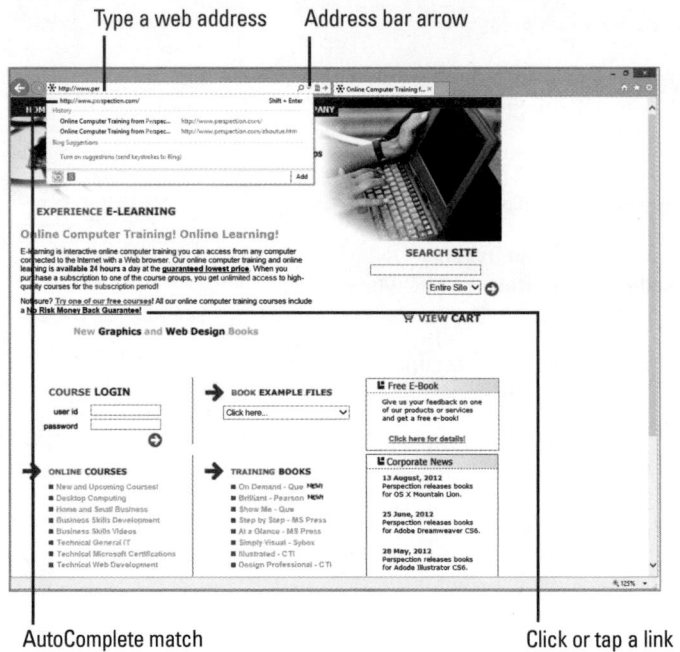

AutoComplete match          Click or tap a link

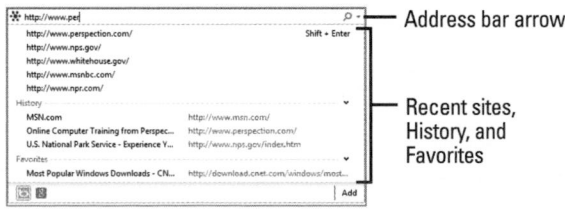

Address bar arrow

Recent sites, History, and Favorites

## Change AutoComplete Options

1. In Internet Explorer (desktop), click or tap the **Tools** button, and then click or tap **Internet options**.

2. Click or tap the **Content** tab.

3. Click or tap **Settings**.

4. Select or clear the AutoComplete options you want to turn on or off.

5. To delete AutoComplete history, click or tap **Delete AutoComplete history**, select the check boxes with the options you want, and then click or tap **Delete**.

6. Click or tap **OK**.

7. Click or tap **OK**.

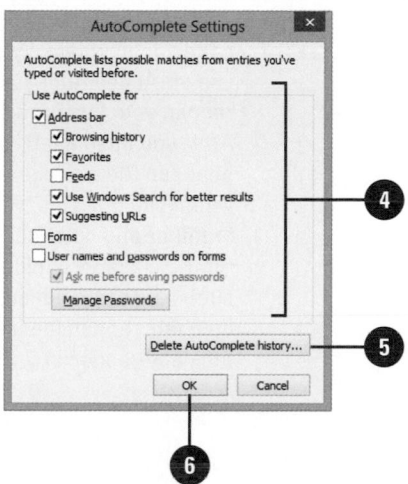

### Did You Know?

*You can have AutoComplete quickly complete a web address.* In the Address bar, type the name of the web site, such as *perspection*, and then press Ctrl+Enter. AutoComplete adds the "www." and ".com".

*You can use the Address bar to search for information.* In the Address bar, type a word or phrase, and then click or tap the Go button or press Enter.

*You can browse using your keyboard.* With caret browsing, you can use the navigation keys—Home, End, Page Up, Page Down, and the arrow keys. Press F7 or click or tap the Tools button, point to File, click or tap Caret Browsing, and then click or tap Yes.

## For Your Information

### Understanding a Web Address

The address for a web page is called a URL. Each web page has a unique URL that is typically composed of four parts: the protocol (a set of rules that allow systems to exchange information), the location of the web site, the name that maintains the web site, and a suffix that identifies the type of site. A URL begins with a protocol, followed by a colon, two slashes, the location of the web site, a dot, the name of the web site, a dot, and a suffix. The web site is the system where the web pages are located. At the end of the web site name, another slash may appear, followed by one or more folder names and a file name. For example, in the web site address, http://*www*.perspection.com/ downloads/main.htm, the protocol is *http* (HyperText Transfer Protocol), the location of the web site is *www* (World Wide Web), the name of the web site is *perspection*, and the suffix is *com* (a commercial organization); a folder at that site is called */downloads*; and within the folder is a file called *main.htm*.

# Browsing with Tabs

As you open web sites, you can use separate tabs for each one, so you can view multiple web sites in a single window. You can open web pages on new tabs by using the redesigned New Tab page with links—use an Accelerator, use InPrivate browsing, reopen closed tabs, and reopen your last browsing session—to help you get started quickly. After you open a tab, you can click or tap a tab to quickly switch between them or click or tap the Close button on the tab to exit it. When you open a new tab from another tab, the new tab is grouped together and color coded, which you can always ungroup later. You can right-click or tap-hold a tab to quickly perform a variety of operations, such as close a tab or tab group, ungroup a tab, refresh tabs, open a new tab, reopen the last tab closed, or see a list of all recently closed tabs and reopen any or all of them.

## Use Tabbed Browsing

In Internet Explorer (desktop), use any of the following methods to use tabbed browsing:

- **Open a blank tab.** Click or tap the **New Tab** button, or press Ctrl+T.

  On the new tab, click or tap a Frequent tile to open the page.

  **TIMESAVER** *In the Address bar, type a URL and then press Alt+Enter to open it in a new tab.*

- **Switch between tabs.** Click or tap a tab, or press Ctrl+Tab.

- **Close a tab.** Click or tap the **Close** button on the tab, or press Ctrl+W.

- **Close other tabs.** Right-click or tap-hold the tab you want open, and then click or tap **Close other tabs**.

- **Reopen closes tabs.** Click or tap the **New Tab** button, click or tap the **Reopen Closed tabs** arrow, and then click or tap a site or **Open all closed tabs**.

- **Reopen last session.** Click or tap the **New Tab** button, and then click or tap the **Reopen last session** link to reopen all tabs when Internet Explorer was last closed.

Open tabs      New Tab button

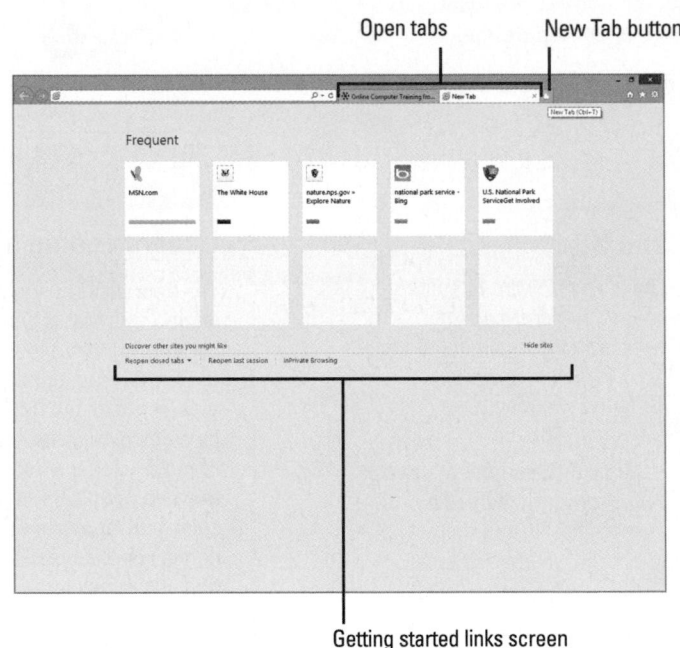

Getting started links screen

## Group or Ungroup Tabs

◆ **Open a new tab in a group (in background).** Press Ctrl+click a link or right-click or tap-hold a link, and then click or tap **Open in new tab**.

◆ **Open a new tab in a group (in foreground).** Press Ctrl+Shift+click a link.

◆ **Ungroup a tab.** Right-click or tap-hold a tab in a group, and then click or tap **Ungroup this tab**.

Click or tap to close this tab group     Tabbed group in color

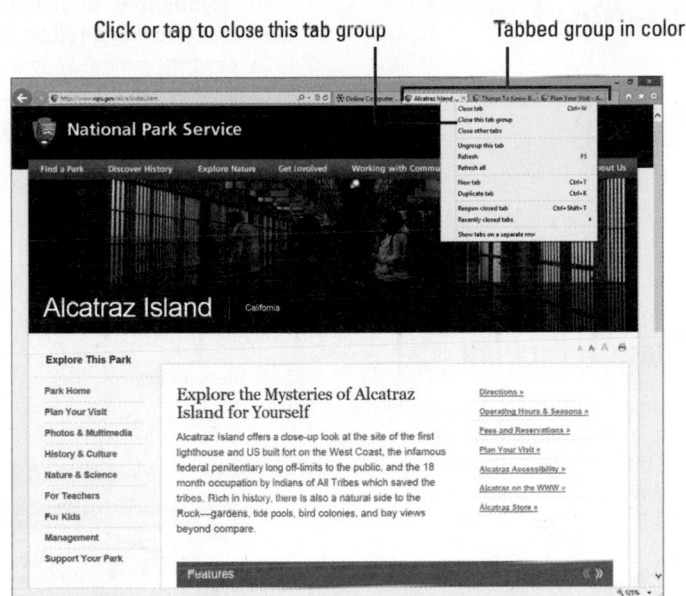

## Set Tabbing Options

1 In Internet Explorer (desktop), click or tap the **Tools** button, and then click or tap **Internet options**.

2 Click or tap **Tabs** on the General tab.

3 To enable or disable tabs, select or clear the **Enable Tabbed Browsing** check box.

4 If enabled, select the options that you want. Some options require you to restart Internet Explorer. Some common ones include:

◆ **Warn me when closing multiple tabs.**

◆ **When a pop-up is encountered.**

◆ **Open links from other programs in.**

5 To restore default settings, click or tap **Restore defaults**.

6 Click or tap **OK**.

7 Click or tap **OK**.

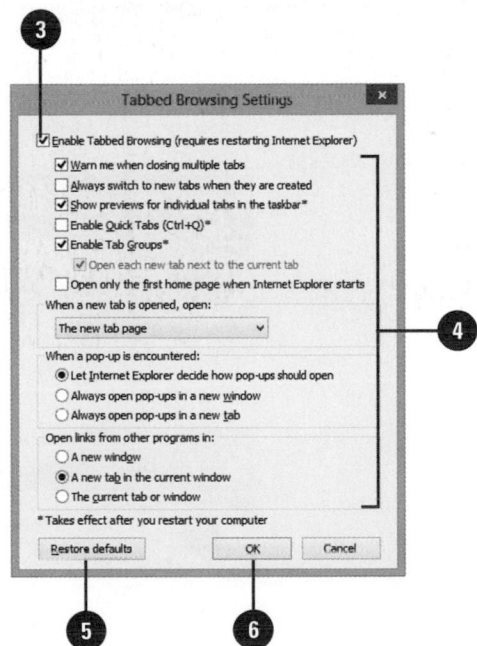

# Navigating Basics

As you browse the web or your local hard disk, you may want to retrace your steps and return to a web page, document, or hard disk you've recently visited. You can move backward or forward one location at a time. When you go back, sometimes it takes you to the start of an application, such as a map. Now Internet Explorer takes you back to the right page. After you start to load a web page, you can stop if the page opens too slowly or if you decide not to access it. If a web page loads incorrectly or you want to update the information it contains, you can reload, or **refresh**, the page. If you get lost on the web, you can start over with a single click or tap of the Home button.

## Move Back or Forward

◆ To move back or forward one web page or document at a time, click or tap the **Back** button or the **Forward** button on the Address bar.

   TIMESAVER  *To move back, press Alt+left arrow. To move forward, press Alt+right arrow.*

Back button

Forward button

## Stop, Refresh, or Go Home

◆ Click or tap the **Stop** button on the Address bar.

   TIMESAVER  *Press Esc.*

◆ Click or tap the **Refresh** button on the Address bar.

   TIMESAVER  *Press F5.*

◆ Click or tap the **Home** button on the toolbar.

   TIMESAVER  *Press Alt+Home.*

Refresh button

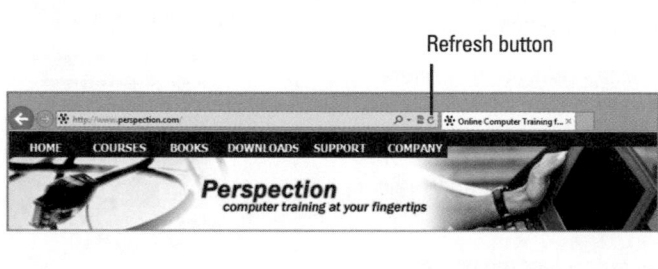

Stop button

# Browsing Privately

If you're using a system at a friend's house, another office, hotel, or an Internet cafe and you don't want to leave any trace or evidence of your web activity, you can use InPrivate browsing. InPrivate browsing doesn't retain or keep track of browsing history, searches, temporary Internet files, form data, cookies, and usernames and passwords. You can start InPrivate browsing from a new tab or use the Tools button on the toolbar. When you start InPrivate browsing, Internet Explorer opens a new browser window. An InPrivate indicator icon appears in the Address bar when the feature is turned on. When you're done, simply close the browser window to end the InPrivate browsing session.

## Browse the Web Privately

1. In Internet Explorer (desktop), start an InPrivate browsing session using any of the following:

   ◆ **Tools button.** Click or tap the **Tools** button, point to **Safety**, and then click or tap **InPrivate Browsing**.

   ◆ **New tab.** Click or tap the **New Tab** button to open a new tab, and then click or tap **InPrivate Browsing**.

   ◆ **Shortcut.** Press Ctrl+Shift+P.

   A new window opens, where you can browse the web.

2. Browse the web.

   The InPrivate indicator appears in the Address bar.

3. To end InPrivate browsing, click or tap the **Close** button to close the browser window.

New tab or inPrivate browsing    **1** New tab

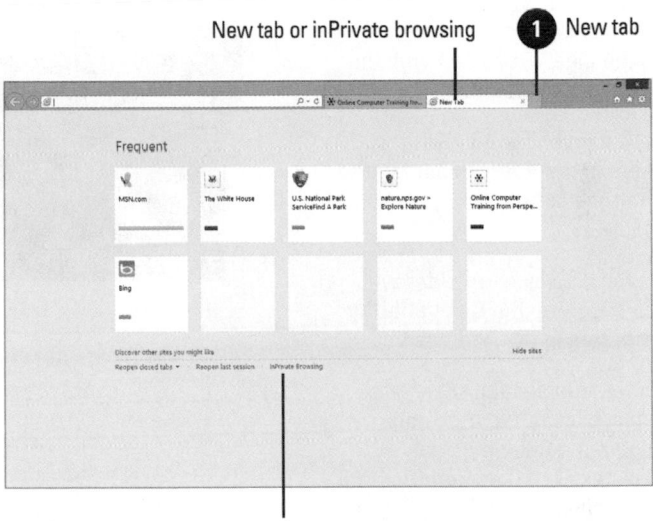

Click or tap to start InPrivate browsing

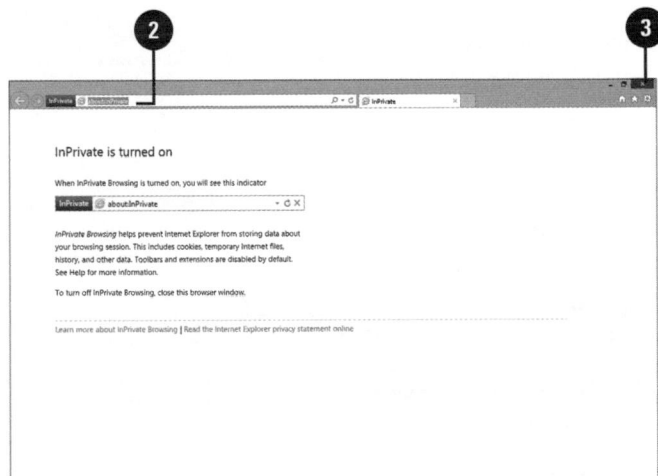

# Using Compatibility View

If you visit an older web site that doesn't display correctly—misaligned text, images, and text boxes—in Internet Explorer, you can quickly fix it, in most cases, with Compatibility view. When you open an older site that Internet Explorer recognizes, the Compatibility View button appears in the Address bar, near the Refresh button. The button appears on a per site basis. However, once you click or tap the button for a site, you don't have to do it again. Internet Explorer maintains a list of sites with Compatibility view, which you can customize.

## Fix the Display of Older Web Sites

**1** In Internet Explorer (desktop), open the older web page with the display you want to fix.

If the Compatibility View button appears in the Address bar next to the Refresh button, the option is available.

**2** To fix the display of an older web site, click or tap the **Compatibility View** button in the Address bar.

**3** To change Compatibility view settings, click or tap the **Tools** button on the Command bar, and then click or tap **Compatibility View Settings**.

**4** To remove a site, select the site, and then click or tap **Remove**.

**5** To enable other options, select the check boxes you want.

**6** Click or tap **Close**.

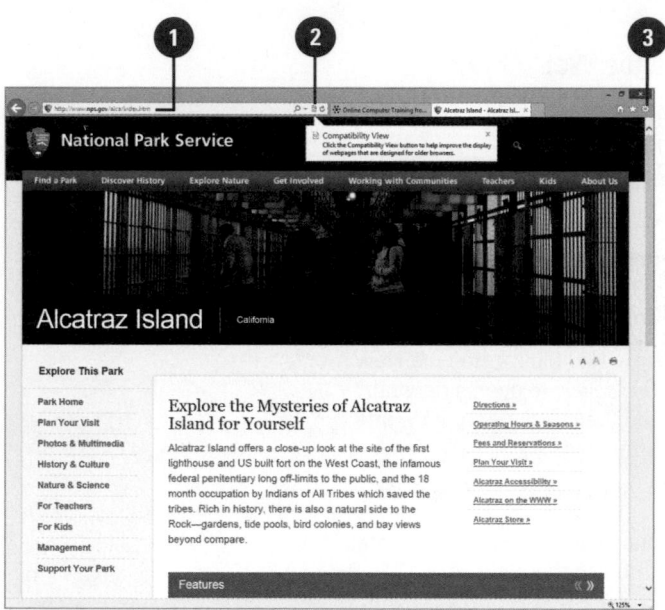

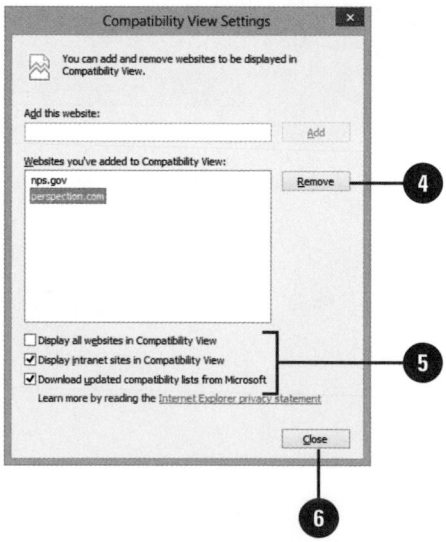

> ## Did You Know?
>
> ***You can show or hide toolbars the Internet Explorer (desktop) window.*** Right-click or tap-hold a blank area on the title bar, and then select Menu bar, Favorites bar, Command bar, or Status bar to show or hide it.

# Zooming the View In and Out

Working with the Zoom tools gives you one more way to control exactly what you see in a web page. Internet Explorer uses Adaptive Page Zoom tools that allow you to enlarge or reduce everything on the page, including text and images, by relaying out the page. You can adjust the zoom from 10% to 1000%. The Zoom tools are located in the bottom-right corner of the window on the Status bar or available on the Zoom submenu on the Tools button. If you have a mouse with a wheel, hold down the Ctrl key, and then scroll the wheel to zoom in or out.

## Change the View

1. In Internet Explorer (desktop), use any of the following zoom options:

   ◆ **Zoom In or Out.** Click or tap the **Change Zoom Level** button arrow on the Status bar, and then click or tap a percentage.

   **TIMESAVER** *Press Ctrl+(+) to zoom in by increments of 10%, or press Ctrl+(-) to zoom out by increments of 10%. Press Ctrl+0 to restore the zoom to 100%.*

   ◆ **Zoom Level.** Click or tap the **Change Zoom Level** button on the Status bar to cycle through 100%, 125%, and 150%.

   ◆ **Zoom Custom.** Click or tap the **Change Zoom Level** button arrow on the Status bar, click or tap **Custom**, type a zoom value, and then click or tap **OK**.

2. To toggle the view to full screen, click or tap the **Tools** button, point to **File**, and then click or tap **Full Screen**. You can also press F11.

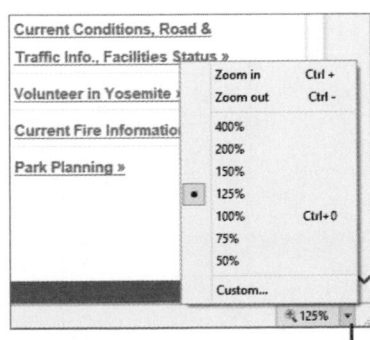

Change Zoom Level button arrow on the Status bar

### Did You Know?

*You can change web page text size to make it easier to read.* Click or tap the Page button on the Command bar, point to Text Size, and then click or tap the size you want. When you change the text size, graphics and controls remain unchanged, so you can focus on text.

# Using and Managing Accelerators

An **Accelerator** allows you to perform everyday tasks without having to navigate to other web sites. Internet Explorer comes with default Accelerators that make it easy to get driving directions on a map, translate and define words, e-mail information to others, and search for content. However, you can add more Accelerators, such as Bing, eBay, Yahoo!, Wikipedia, Amazon and Facebook, by adding them from the Internet Explorer Gallery. All you need to do is highlight text from any web page and then click or tap the blue Accelerator icon that appears near your selection to obtain a window with the information you need. If you no longer want to use an Accelerator, you can use the Manage Add-ons dialog box to delete or disable it, or change defaults.

## Use and Manage Accelerators

1. In Internet Explorer (desktop), select the text you want to use with an Accelerator, such as a phrase, address, or email address.

2. Click or tap the blue **Accelerator** button, and then point an accelerator from the default menu or point to **All Accelerators**, and then point to an accelerator.

   The Accelerator displays a window with the results, such as a definition, translation, or map.

3. Click or tap in the Accelerator window, if available, to open it.

4. To add an Accelerator, click or tap the blue **Accelerator** or **Page** button on the Command bar, point to **All Accelerators**, and then click or tap **Find More Accelerators**; click or tap **Add to Internet Explorer** for the Accelerator you want.

5. To manage Accelerators, click or tap the blue **Accelerator** or **Page** button on the Command bar, point to **All Accelerators**, and then click or tap **Manage Accelerators**, click or tap Accelerators in the left pane, select an Accelerator, and then click or tap **Set as default** or **Remove as default**, **Disable**, or **Remove**.

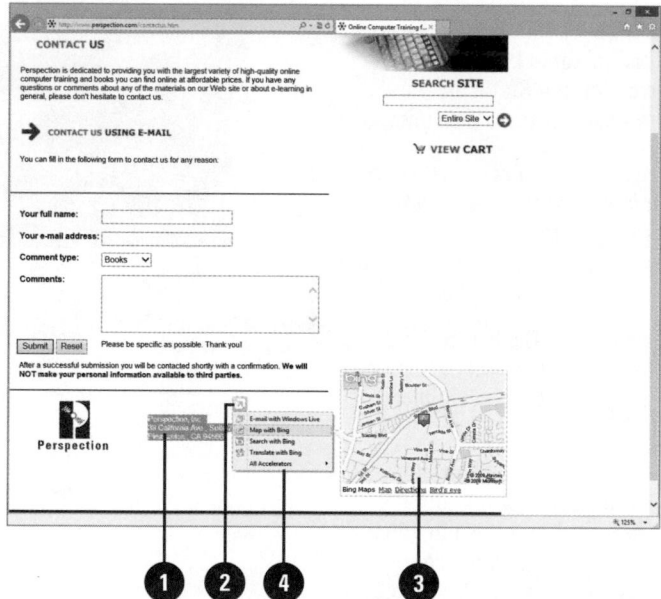

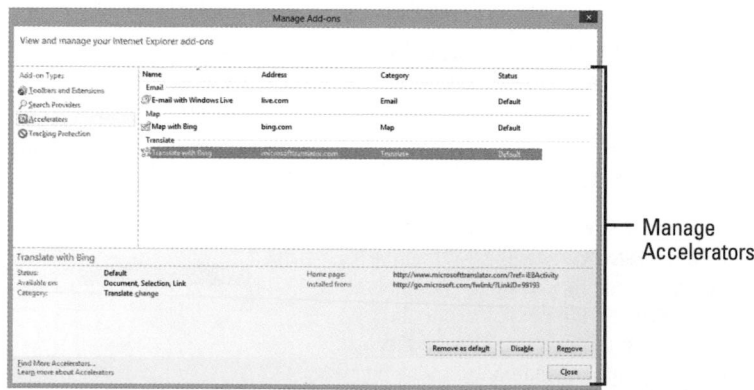

Manage Accelerators

# Getting Suggestions for Web Sites

If you're not sure what good sites are out there based on your own browsing history, then you might want to try Suggested Sites, a free online service from Microsoft. When enabled, Microsoft uses your browsing history to give you suggestions. Simply, click or tap the See Suggested Sites the Favorites Center to see a list of suggestions. The more places you visit, the better the suggested sites. You can also delete sites from your history. If you no longer want the service, you can choose to turn it off at any time.

## Use Suggested Sites

1. In Internet Explorer (desktop), click or tap the **Tools** button, point to **File**, click or tap **Suggested Sites,** and then click or tap **Yes**.

   ◆ You can also click or tap **Turn on Suggested Sites** in the Favorites Center.

   Suggested Sites is enabled.

2. Click or tap the **Favorites Center** button.

3. Click or tap the **See Suggested Sites**.

   A web site opens, displaying suggested sites based on your browsing history.

4. View the suggested sites that you want.

5. To turn off Suggested Sites, click or tap the **Tools** button, point to **File**, click or tap **Suggested Sites**.

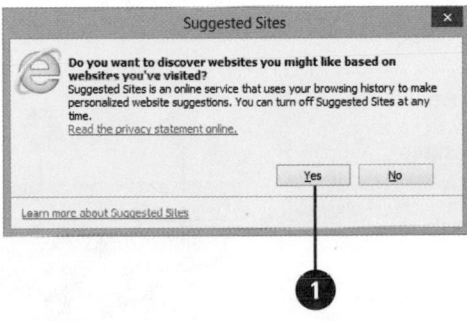

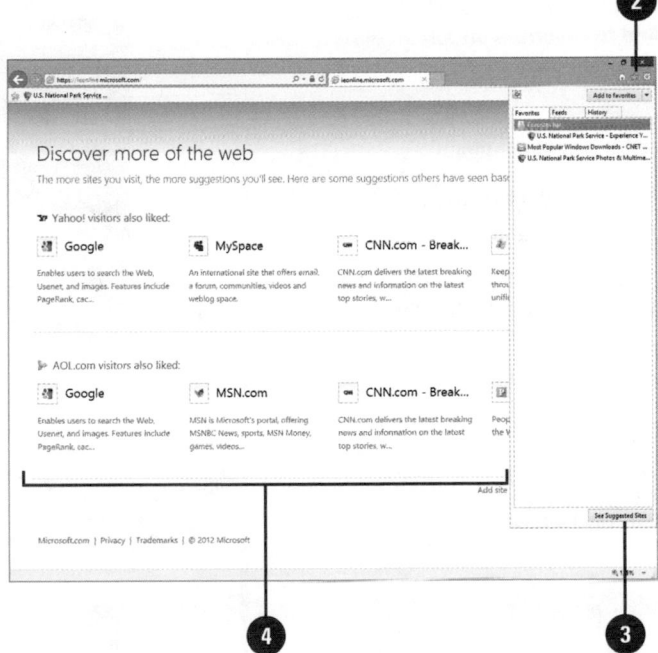

# Adding a Web Page to the Favorites List

Rather than memorizing URLs or keeping a handwritten list of web pages you want to visit, you can use the Favorites Center or Favorites bar to store and organize the addresses. The Favorites Center provides easy access to favorites, RSS feeds, and browsing history. When you display a web page that you want to display again at a later time, you can add the web page to the Favorites bar with one click or tap or to the Favorites Center. Once you add the web page to the Favorites bar or Center, you can quickly return to the page. To open all the favorites in a folder at the same time, click or tap the blue arrow to the right of the folder. If your list of favorites grows long, you can delete favorites you don't visit anymore or move favorites into folders.

## Add and Delete Favorites

1. In Internet Explorer (desktop), open the web site you want to add to your Favorites list.

2. Click or tap the **Favorites Center** button, and then click or tap **Add to Favorites**.

   ◆ You can also click or tap the **Add to Favorites** button on the Favorites bar.

3. Type the name for the site, or use the default name supplied.

4. Click or tap **Create In** arrow, and then select a location.

5. To create a new folder, click or tap **New Folder**, type a folder name, and then click or tap **OK**.

6. Click or tap **Add**.

7. To remove an item from the Favorites bar or Favorites Center, right-click or tap-hold it, and then click or tap **Delete**.

## Did You Know?

*You can import favorites.* Click or tap the Favorites Center button, click or tap the Add to Favorites button arrow, click or tap Import and Export, and then follow the wizard steps.

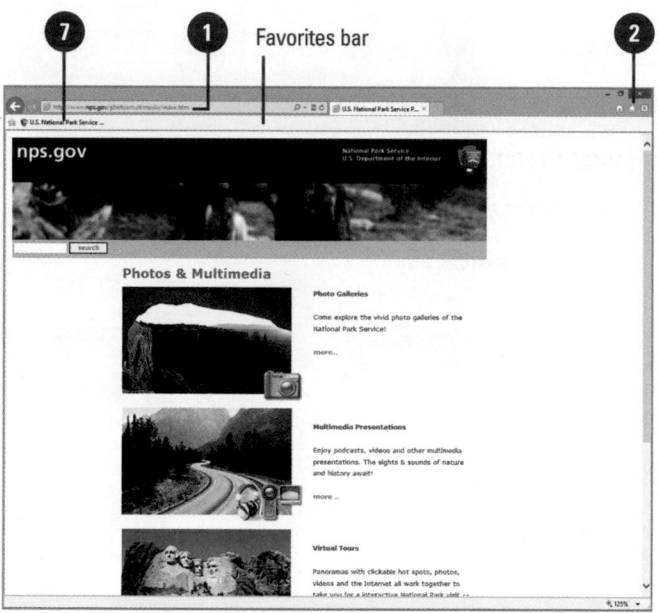

Favorites bar

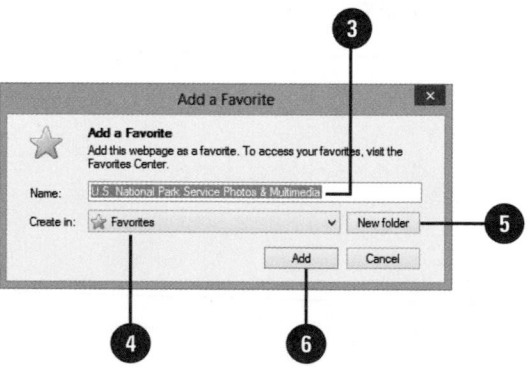

## Access Favorites

① In Internet Explorer (desktop), click or tap the **Favorites Center** button.

The Favorites Center pane appears with the Favorites tab. The pane is not pinned (locked) to the window.

② To pin the pane to the window, click or tap the **Pin the Favorites Center** button (green arrow).

When the pane is pinned, the Close button appears on the pane.

③ Click or tap a folder, if necessary.

④ To open all the favorites in a folder at the same time, click or tap the blue arrow next to the folder.

⑤ Click or tap the page you want.

⑥ Click or tap off the pane or click or tap the **Close** button.

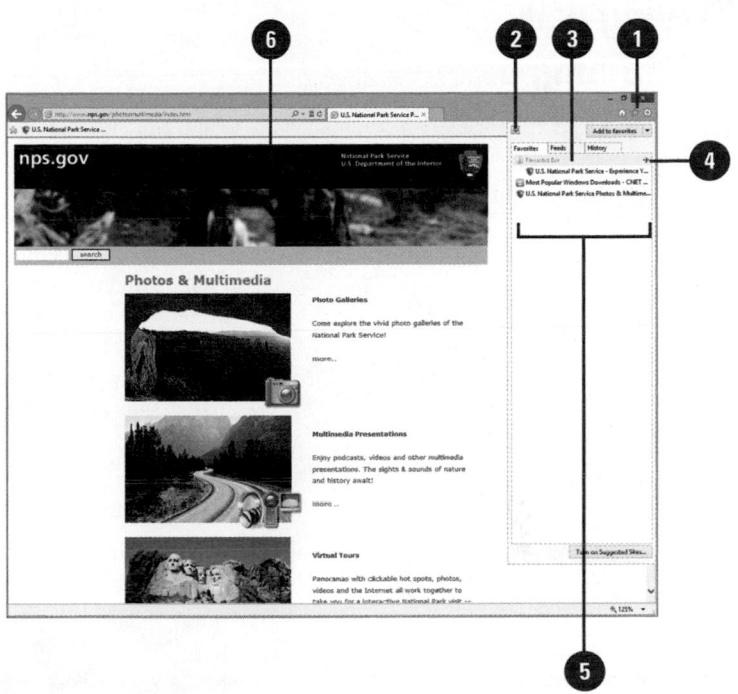

## Organize Favorites

① In Internet Explorer (desktop), click or tap the **Favorites Center** button, click or tap the **Add to Favorites** button arrow, and then click or tap **Organize Favorites**.

② Select one or more favorites.

③ Do any of the following:

◆ **New Folder**. Click or tap **New Folder**, type the new folder name, and then press Enter.

◆ **Move**. Click or tap **Move**, select a folder, and then click or tap **OK**.

◆ **Rename**. Click or tap **Rename**, type a new name, and then press Enter.

◆ **Delete**. Click or tap **Delete**.

④ When you're done, click or tap the **Close** button.

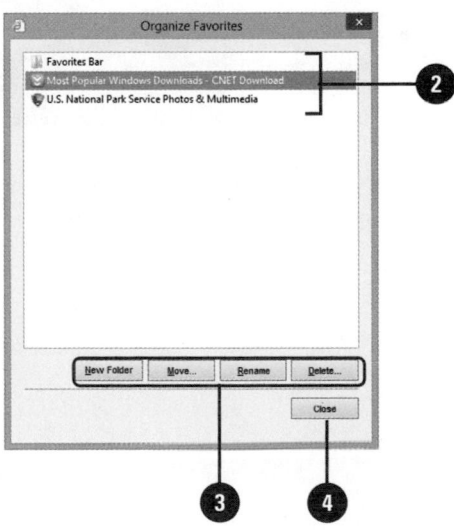

# Viewing and Maintaining a History List

Sometimes you run across a great web site and simply forget to add it to your Favorites list. With Internet Explorer there's no need to try to remember all the sites you visit. The History feature keeps track of where you've been by date, site, most visited, or order visited today, which you can now sort by. To view the History list, click or tap the History button in the Favorites Center, select a sort option, and then click or tap a link (if necessary) in the pane to expand the list of web sites visited. You can also search for pages in the History list by typing keywords. Because the History list can grow to occupy a large amount of space on your hard drive, it's important to control the length of time you retain web sites in the list. Internet Explorer deletes the History list periodically, based on the settings you specify. When you delete your History list, you can now protect and preserve your related data for trusted sites in your favorites list.

## View and Change the History List

1. In Internet Explorer (desktop), click or tap the **Favorites Center** button.

2. Click or tap the **History** tab.

3. To change the history view, click or tap the **Sort** button, and then select the view option you want.

   - **View By Date.**
   - **View By Site.**
   - **View By Most Visited.**
   - **View By Order Visited Today.**
   - **Search History.** Type a keyword to search for a page, and then click or tap **Search Now**. Click or tap **Stop** to end the search.

4. If view By Date, click or tap a week or day to expand or compress the list of web sites visited.

5. If necessary, click or tap the folder for the web site you want to view, and then click or tap a page within the web site.

6. Click or tap off the pane or click or tap the **Close** button.

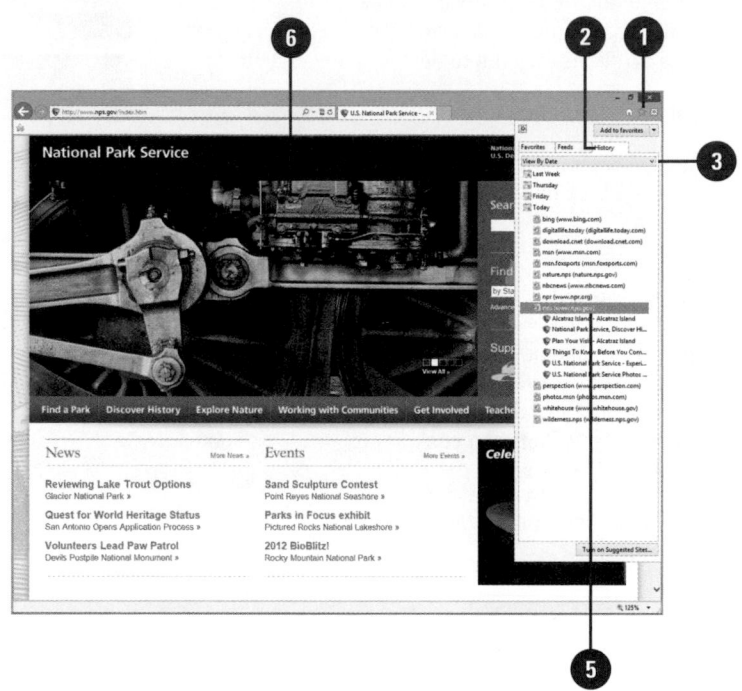

## Change the Number of Days Pages Are Saved

1. In Internet Explorer (desktop), click or tap the **Tools** button, and then click or tap **Internet options**.

2. Click or tap the **General** tab.

3. In the Browsing history section, click or tap **Settings**.

4. Click or tap the **History** tab.

5. Specify the total number of days you want to keep links listed in history.

6. Click or tap **OK**.

7. Click or tap **OK**.

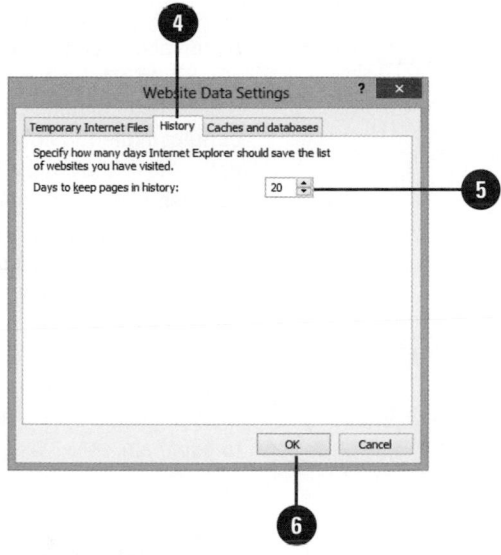

## Clear the History List

1. In Internet Explorer (desktop), click or tap the **Tools** button, point to **Safety**, and then click or tap **Delete Browsing History**.

   ◆ You can also open this dialog by clicking or tapping **Delete** on the **General** tab in the Internet Options dialog box.

   ◆ To delete browsing history on exit, click or tap the **Tools** button, click or tap **Internet options**, select the **Delete browsing history on exit** check box, and then click or tap **OK**.

2. To preserve cookies and temporary Internet files for sites in your Favorites folder, which are trusted sites, select the **Preserve Favorites website data** check box.

3. Select the **History** check box to clear the history list.

4. Click or tap **Delete**.

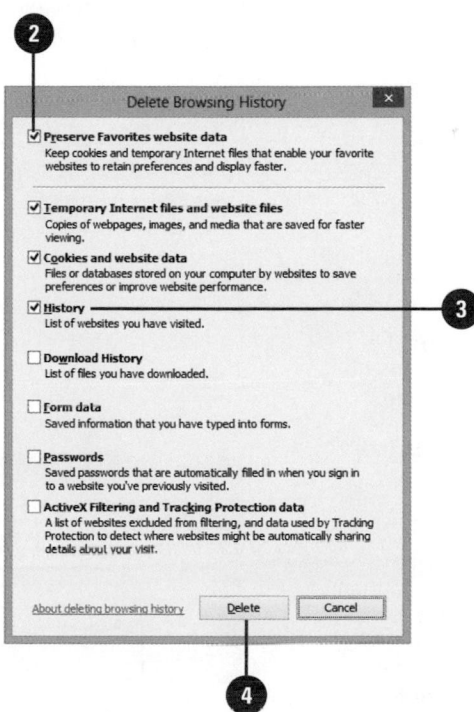

# Reading and Subscribing to Feeds

A **feed** delivers frequently updated web content to your browser on a continuous basis. A feed, also known as RSS (Really Simple Syndication) feed, XML feed, syndicated content, or web feed, is usually offered on a subscription basis and typically free of charge. A feed can deliver text content in the form of news headlines or blogs, or digital content in the form of pictures, audio, and video. When audio content is delivered usually in the MP3 format, it's referred to as a podcast. When you visit a web site, Internet Explorer checks for available feeds. If it discovers a feed, the orange Feeds button appears on the Command bar. You can view an individual feed or subscribe to one to get content automatically. When you subscribe to a feed, Internet Explorer checks the web site and downloads new content so you always stay updated with the latest site content. You can also add an RSS feed to your Favorites Center, making it easy to view updates. Internet Explorer manages a common feeds list, which allows other programs, such as e-mail, to use them.

## View and Subscribe to a Feed

1. In Internet Explorer (desktop), visit a web site with a feed.

   The Feeds button changes color and plays a sound.

   **TIMESAVER** *You can also press Alt+J to check for feeds.*

2. Click or tap the **Feeds** button arrow on the Command bar, and then select an available feed.

3. If available, click or tap the feed you want to see.

   A web page opens, displaying a lists of articles and other elements you can read and subscribe to.

4. Click or tap the **Subscribe to this Feed** button, and then click or tap **Subscribe to this Feed**, if necessary.

5. Type a name for the feed, and then select a location for the feed.

6. To add the feed to the Favorites bar, select the **Add to Favorites Bar** check box.

7. Click or tap **Subscribe**.

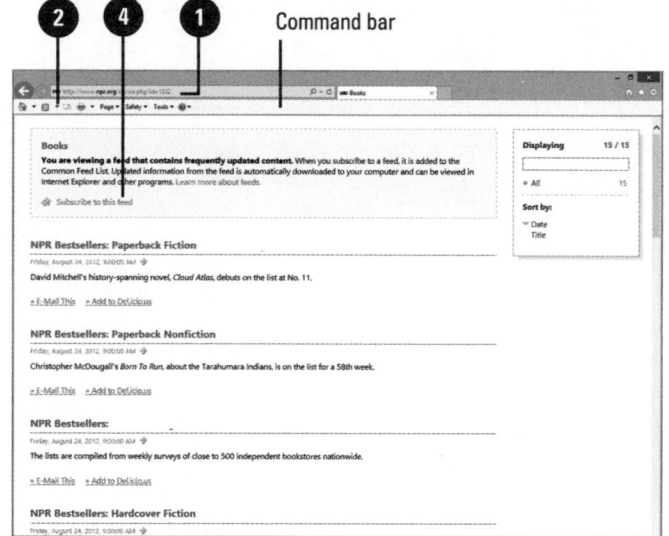

Command bar

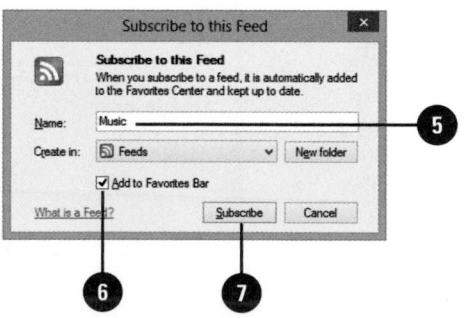

## View Subscribed Feeds

**1** In Internet Explorer (desktop), if available, click or tap the **Feed** button on the Favorites bar, and then click or tap a specific feed.

◆ If the feed button on the Favorites button is bold, the feed has been updated.

**2** Click or tap the **Favorites Center** button.

**3** Click or tap the **Feeds** tab.

**4** If needed, click or tap a folder to display related feeds.

**5** Click or tap the feed to visit the web site for the feed.

**6** Click or tap off the pane or click or tap the **Close** button.

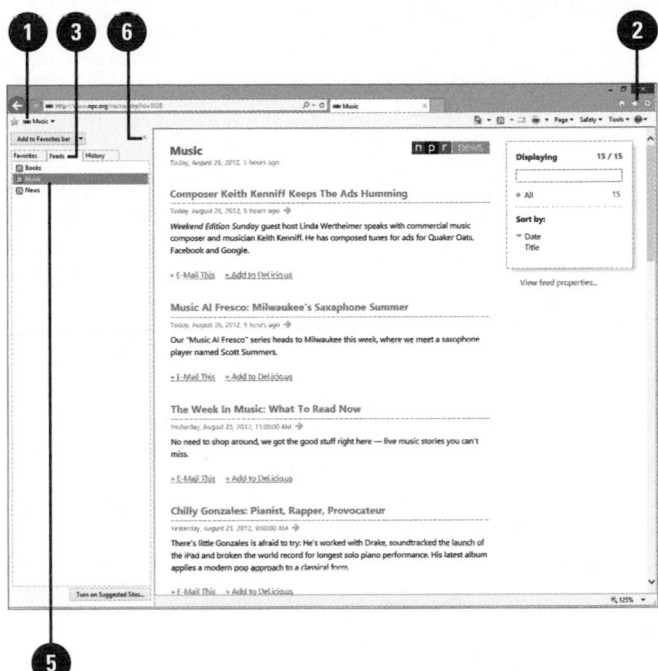

## Did You Know?

***What formats are feeds available in?*** The most common formats are RSS and Atom. All web feed formats are based on XML. XML (Extensible Markup Language) is a platform-independent language that enables you to create documents in which data is stored independently of the format. XML is a markup language just like HTML. You mark up a document to define the structure, meaning, and visual appearance of the information.

***You can change feed settings.*** Click or tap the Tools button, click or tap Internet Options, click or tap the Content tab, click or tap Settings in the Feeds and Web Slices section, specify the options you want, and then click or tap OK twice.

## For Your Information

### Resetting Internet Explorer Settings

If you installed another web browser after installing Internet Explorer, some of your Internet Explorer settings may have changed. You can reset your Internet Explorer settings to their original defaults, including your home page and search pages, and choice of default browser, without changing your other browser's settings. To reset Internet Explorer settings, click or tap the Tools button, click or tap Internet Options, click or tap the Advanced tab, click or tap Reset, read the dialog box carefully, and then click or tap Reset again.

# Searching the Web

You can find all kinds of information on the web using the Address box on the Address bar. The best way to find information is to use a search engine. A **search engine** is a program you access through a web site and use to search through a collection of Internet information to find what you want. Many search engines are available on the web, such as Bing, Wikipedia, Google, and Yahoo, which you can add-on to Internet Explorer. When performing a search, the search engine compares keywords with words that if finds on various Internet web sites. **Keywords** are words or phrases that best describe the information you want to retrieve. As you type in the Address box, the search engine displays a menu list of text and visual suggestions for the matched sites. These matched sites are sometimes called **hits**. The search results of different search engines vary. If you're looking for information on a page, you can use the Find toolbar to help highlight the text you want to find.

## Search the Web

1. In Internet Explorer (desktop), click or tap in the Address box.

   **TIMESAVER** *Press Ctrl+E to go to the address box.*

2. To use a specific search provider for this session only, click or tap the **Address** box arrow, and then click or tap the provider you want.

3. Type the information you want to find. Use specific words, eliminate common words, such as "a" or "the", and use quotation marks for specific phrases.

   As you type, a drop-down menu appears with text and visual suggestions.

4. Click or tap a suggestion or continue to type. Click or tap the **Go** button. You can also press Enter or press Alt+Enter to display the search results in a new tab.

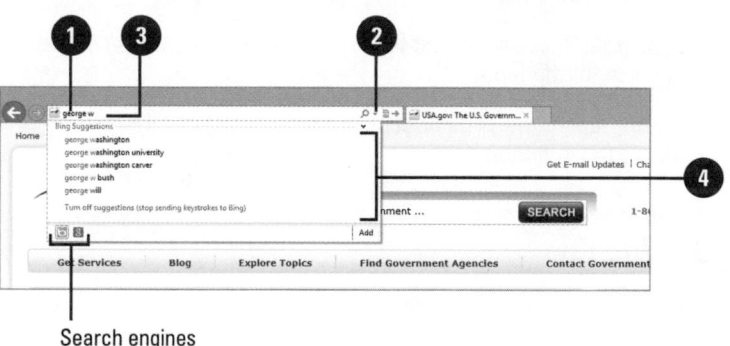

Search engines

Results

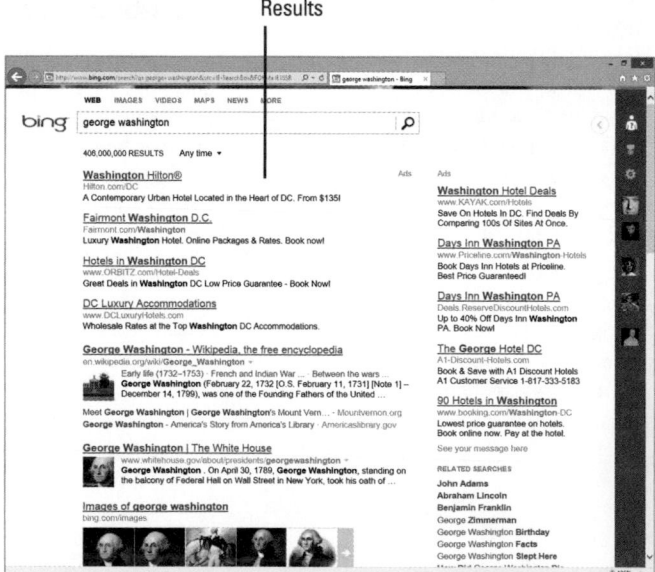

## Add or Change Search Providers

1. In Internet Explorer (desktop), click or tap the **Address** box arrow, and then click or tap the Search Provider's icon.

   ◆ To add search providers, click or tap the Address box arrow, click or tap **Add**, and then follow the web site instructions.

2. To set search provider options, click or tap the **Tools** button, click or tap **Manage add-ons**, click or tap **Search Providers**, select a search provider, click or tap **Set as default** or **Remove**, and then click or tap **Close**.

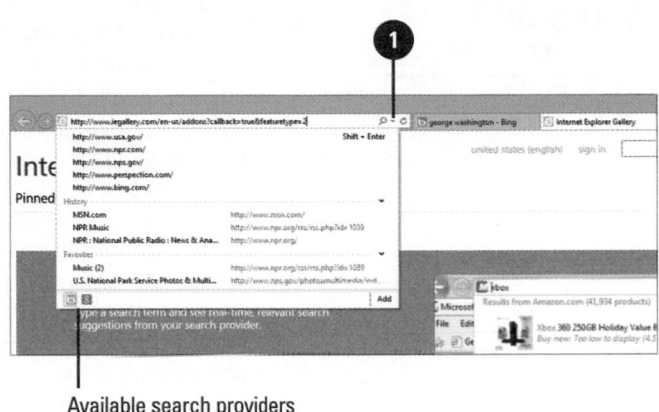

Available search providers

## Find Text on a Page

1. In Internet Explorer (desktop), click or tap the **Tools** button, point to **File**, and then click or tap **Find on this page** to display the toolbar.

   **TIMESAVER** *Press Ctrl+F to find text on this page.*

2. Click or tap the **Highlight all matches** button to turn highlighting in yellow on or off.

3. Click or tap the **Options** button, and then click or tap **Match whole word only** or **Match case** to turn them on or off.

4. Type text in the Find box. As you type, the search displays the results on the page.

5. Click or tap the **Previous** or **Next** button to go to the results.

6. Click or tap the **Close** button on the toolbar.

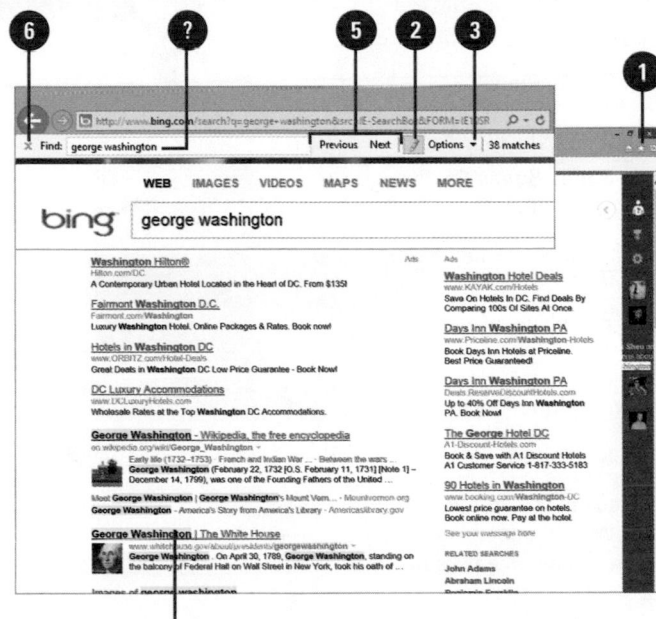

Highlighted results

# Previewing and Printing a Web Page

Web pages are designed for viewing on a screen, but you can also print all or part of one. Before you print, you should verify that the page looks the way you want. You save time, money, and paper by avoiding duplicate or wasteful printing. Printing now scales web pages to fit the paper you're using. Print Preview shows you exactly how the web page will look on the printed page, and gives you more control over margins and scaling. This is especially helpful when you have multiple pages to print. When you are ready to print, Internet Explorer provides many options for printing web pages. For web pages with frames, you can print the page just as you see it, or you can elect to print a particular frame or all frames. You can even use special Page Setup options to include the date, time, or window title on the printed page. You can also choose to print the web addresses from the links contained on a web page.

## Preview a Web Page

1. In Internet Explorer (desktop), click or tap the **Tools** button, point to **Print**, and then click or tap **Print Preview**.

2. Use the Print Preview toolbar buttons to preview or print the web page:

   ◆ **Print the document.**

   ◆ **Portrait** or **Landscape.**

   ◆ **Page Setup.** Opens the Page Setup dialog box.

   ◆ **Turn headers and footers on and off.**

   ◆ **View Full Width** or **View Full Page.**

   ◆ **Show Multiple Pages.**

   ◆ **Change the Print Size.**

3. Use options at the bottom of the Print Preview to specify the page to display or switch between pages.

4. Drag a margin adjust handle to fine tune the page margins.

5. When you're done, click or tap the **Close** button.

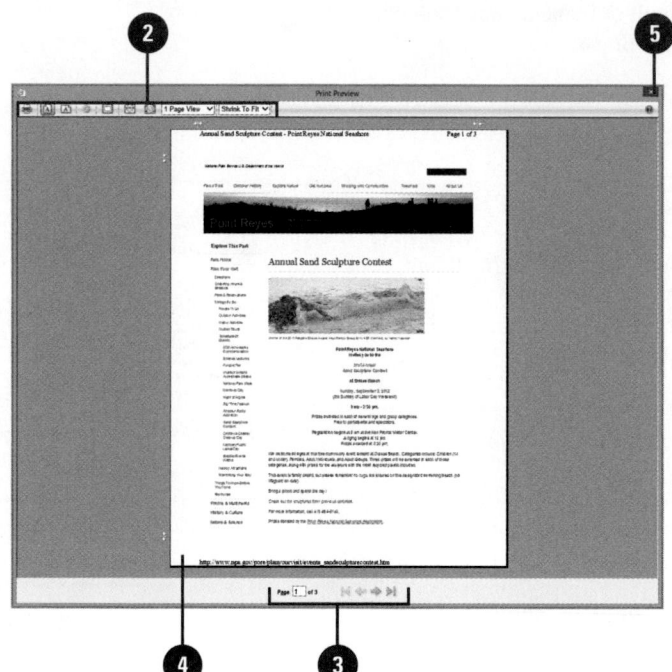

## Print a Web Page

1. In Internet Explorer (desktop), click or tap the **Tools** button, point to **Print**, and then click or tap **Print**.

    **TIMESAVER** *To print the current page with the current print settings, click or tap the Print button on the Command bar.*

2. Click or tap a printer to select it for use.

3. Specify the range of pages you want to print.

4. Specify the number of copies you want to print.

5. Click or tap the **Options** tab.

6. If the page contains frames, select the print frames option you want.

7. Select or clear the **Print all linked documents** and **Print table of links** check boxes.

8. Click or tap **Print**.

### See Also

*See Chapter 15, "Printing, Faxing, and Scanning" on page 417 for information on installing and using a printer.*

*See "Previewing and Printing a Document" on page 279 for more information on using the Preview window and the Print dialog box.*

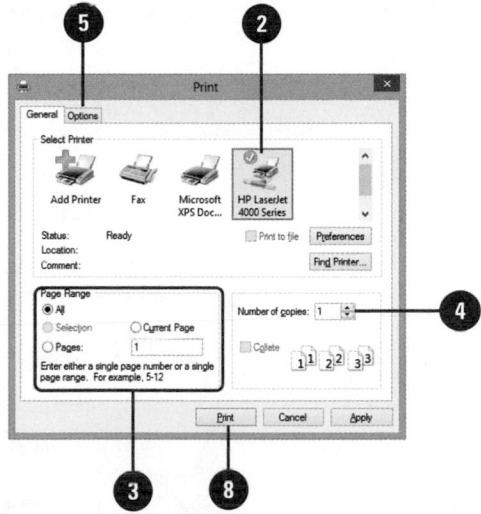

## For Your Information

### Setting Up the Page Format

When you print a web page, you can use the Page Setup dialog box to control the printing of text and graphics on a page. To open the Page Setup dialog box, click or tap the Tools button, point to Print, and then click or tap Page Setup. The Page Setup dialog box specifies the printer properties for page size, orientation, and paper source; in most cases, you won't want to change them. From the Page Setup dialog box, you can also change header and footer information. In the Headers and Footers text boxes, you can type text to appear as a header and footer of a web page you print. In these text boxes, you can also use variables to substitute information about the current page, and you can combine text and codes. For example, if you type **Page &p of &P** in the Header text box, the current page number and the total number of pages print at the top of each printed page. Check Internet Explorer Help for a complete list of header and footer codes.

# Saving Pictures or Text from a Web Page

If you find information on a web page that you want to save for future reference or share with others, you can copy and paste it to another document or save it on your system. When you copy information from a web page, make sure you're not violating any copyright laws.

## Save a Picture from a Web Page

1. In Internet Explorer (desktop), open the web page with the picture you want to save.

2. Right-click or tap-hold the picture, and then click or tap **Save picture as**.

3. Select the drive and folder in which you want to save the file.

4. Type a name for the file, or use the suggested name.

5. To change the format of a file, click or tap the **Save as type** arrow, and then click or tap a file format.

6. Click or tap **Save**.

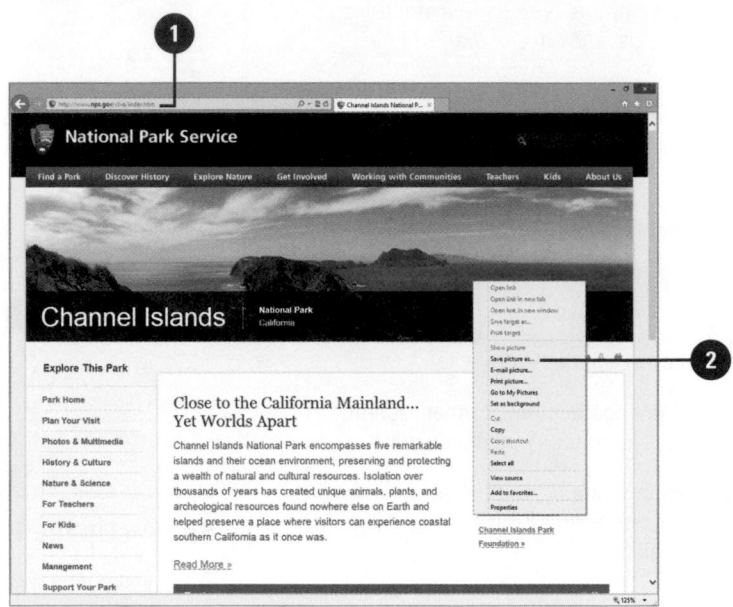

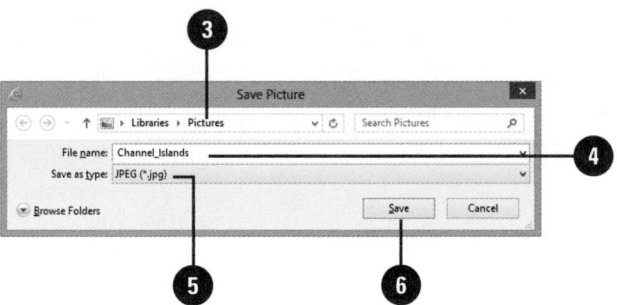

### Did You Know?

*You can save a page or picture without opening it.* Right-click or tap-hold the link for the item you want to save, and then click or tap Save Target As.

*You can create a desktop shortcut to the current web page.* Right-click or tap-hold in the web page, click or tap Create Shortcut, and then click or tap Yes.

## Set a Picture from a Web Page as the Background Picture

1. In Internet Explorer (desktop), open the web page with the picture you want to use.

2. Right-click or tap-hold the picture, and then click or tap **Set As Background**.

## Copy Text from a Web Page

1. In Internet Explorer (desktop), open the web page with the text you want to copy.

2. Select the text you want to copy.

    **TROUBLE?** *The I-beam cursor may or may not appear. You can still select the text.*

3. Right-click or tap the selected text, and then click or tap **Copy**, or press Ctrl+C.

    ◆ You can also access an Accelerator from the shortcut menu where you can use the selected text in an e-mail, blog, search, or translate.

4. Switch to where you want to paste the text.

5. Click or tap the **Edit** menu, and then click or tap **Paste**, or press Ctrl+V.

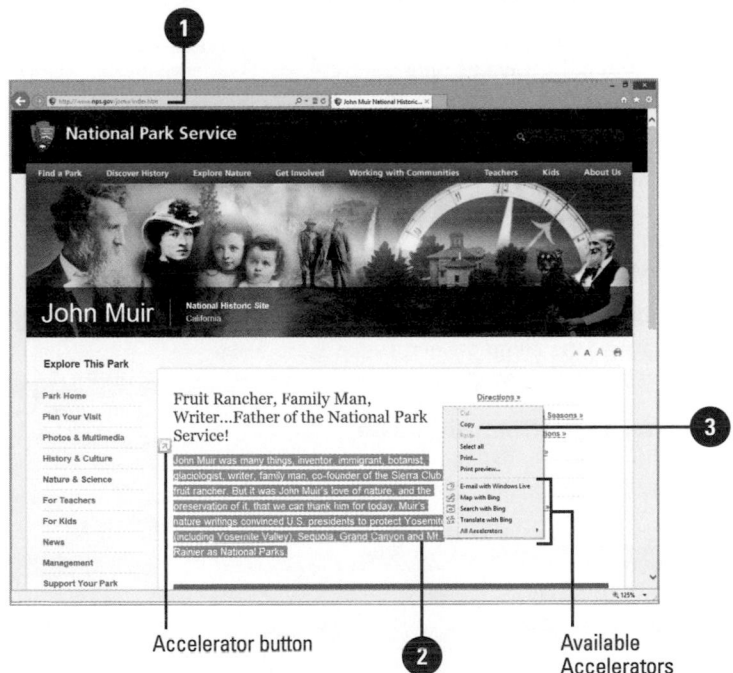

Accelerator button

Available Accelerators

# Saving a Web Page

You can save a web page you want to view offline even if you don't need to share it with others or update its content, such as a published article whose content will not change. There are several ways you can save the web page, from saving just the text to saving all of the graphics and text needed to display that page as it appears on the web. When you save a complete web page, Internet Explorer saves all the graphic and text elements in a folder. If you need to send a web page to a friend or co-worker, you can save all the elements of the web page in a single file to make the process easier.

## Save a Web Page

1. In Internet Explorer (desktop), open the web page you want to save.

2. Click or tap the **Tools** button, point to **File**, and then click or tap **Save as**.

3. Select the drive and folder in which you want to save the file.

4. Type a name for the file, or use the suggested name.

5. Click or tap the **Save as type** arrow, and then click or tap one of the following:

   ◆ **Web Page, complete** to save the formatted text and layout with all the linked information, such as pictures, in a folder.

   ◆ **Web Archive, single file** to save all the elements of the web page in a single file.

   ◆ **Web Page, HTML only** to save the formatted text and layout without the linked information.

   ◆ **Text File** to save only the text.

6. Click or tap **Save**.

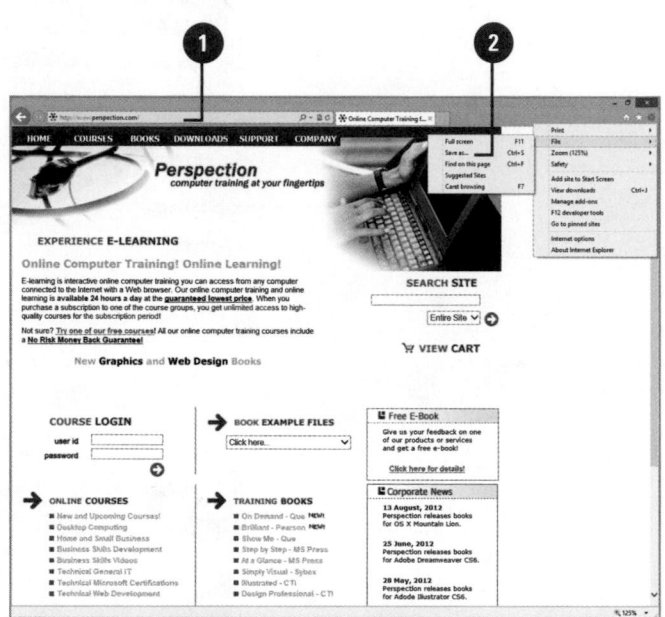

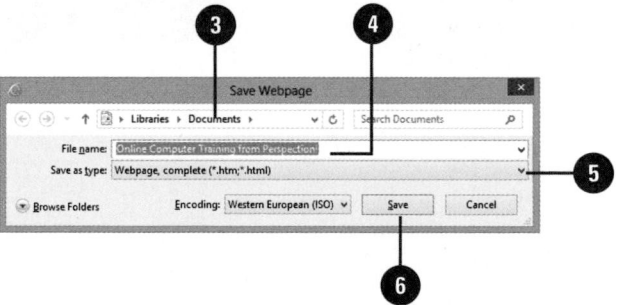

# Sending a Page or Link by E-mail

If you come across a web page that you want to share with a friend or co-worker, you can send the page or a link to the page directly from Internet Explorer using your default e-mail program. When you use the Send page by e-mail and Send link by e-mail commands on the Page button on the Command bar, Internet Explorer automatically opens your default desktop e-mail program, such as Outlook or Windows Live Mail, and creates a new message with the web page or link.

## Send a Page or Link by E-mail

1. In Internet Explorer (desktop), open the web page with the picture you want to send.

2. Click or tap the **Page** button arrow on the Command bar, and then click or tap **Send page by e-mail** or **Send link by e-mail**.

    Internet Explorer opens your default desktop e-mail program, such as Outlook or Windows Live Mail, and creates a new message.

3. Address and send the message.

### See Also

*See "Sharing Between Apps" on page 34 for information on sending information to others using apps, such as Mail.*

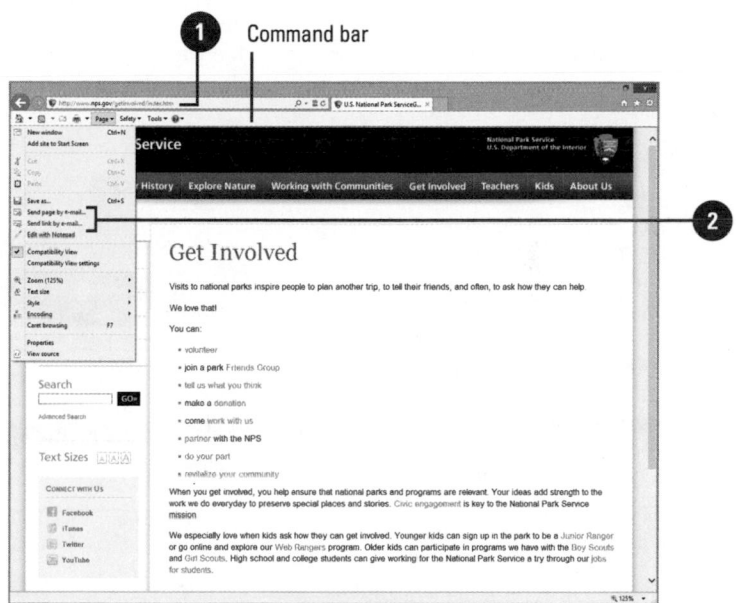

Command bar

## For Your Information

### Accessing E-mail from Internet Explorer

If you installed an e-mail program, such as Microsoft Outlook or Windows Live Mail program (*http://download.live.com*), you can access it directly from Internet Explorer. All you need to do is click or tap the Read Mail button on the Command bar to access and open the mail program on your system. If you want access e-mail with Outlook or Windows Live through Internet Explorer, you can access it online. Click or tap the Page button on the Command bar, and then click or tap E-mail with *program name* to access the web site, log in, and work with your mail.

# Downloading Files from the Web

There are tons of sites on the web offering all sorts of files you can download to your system. You can download files from any web site by finding the file you want, right-clicking or tap-holding the link, and telling Internet Explorer where you want to save the file. Some web sites are designed with specific links to make it easier to download files. When you click or tap a download link, a Message bar appears, asking you to run or don't run the file from the Internet or save the file. Internet Explorer checks to see whether there are any irregularities with the file or a potential for harm based on the file type, and provides strong warning and guidance to help you understand more about the file you are downloading. Just beware of viruses which can come from downloaded files off the Internet.

## Download a File from a Web Page

1. In Internet Explorer (desktop), open the web page from which you want to download a file.

   **IMPORTANT** *Before you download files, make sure your antivirus software is up-to-date.*

2. Click or tap the download link.

   A Message bar appears at the bottom of the screen.

   ◆ You can also right-click or tap-hold the link pointing to the actual file, and then click or tap **Save target as**.

3. Click or tap **Save**.

   ◆ To specify a download location, click or tap **Save** arrow, click or tap **Save as**, specify a location, and then click or tap **Save**.

   ◆ To execute the file after the download, click or tap **Run**, and then follow the on-screen instructions.

   The Message bar displays the estimated time to download the file, along with the estimated transfer time.

4. To view the downloaded item, click or tap **View download**.

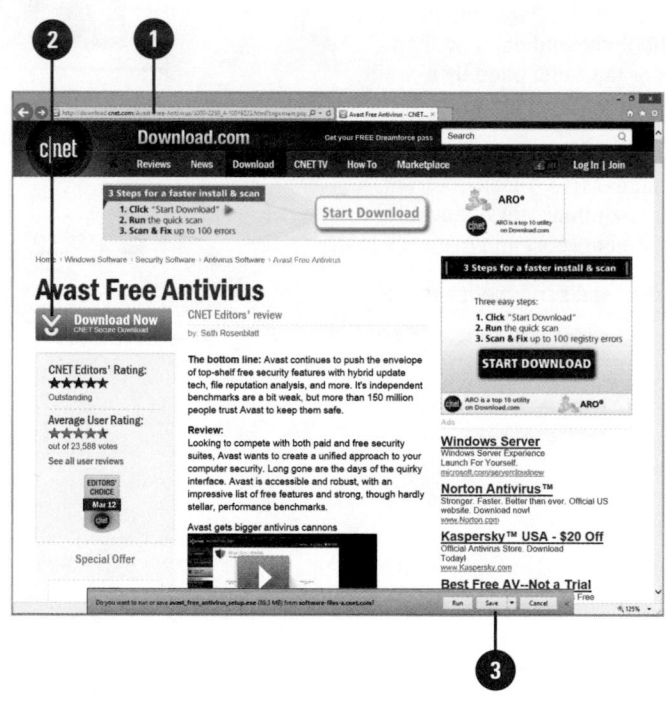

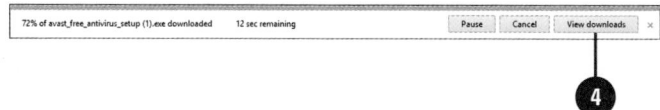

## View Downloads

1. In Internet Explorer (desktop), click or tap the **Tools** button, and then click or tap **View Downloads**.

   **TIMESAVER** *Press Ctrl+J to view downloads.*

2. To execute a downloaded file, click or tap **Run**, and then follow the on-screen instructions.

   **IMPORTANT** *Before you download files, make sure your antivirus software is up-to-date.*

3. To open the folder where the downloaded file is stored, click or tap the **Downloads** link.

4. To change the default download location, click or tap the **Options** link, specify a location, and then click or tap **OK**.

5. To clear the downloads list, click or tap **Clear list**.

6. Click or tap **Close**.

### Did You Know?

*You can access a site with lots of files to download.* Try these sites to find plenty of files to download: *http://www.download.com* and *http://www.shareware.com*.

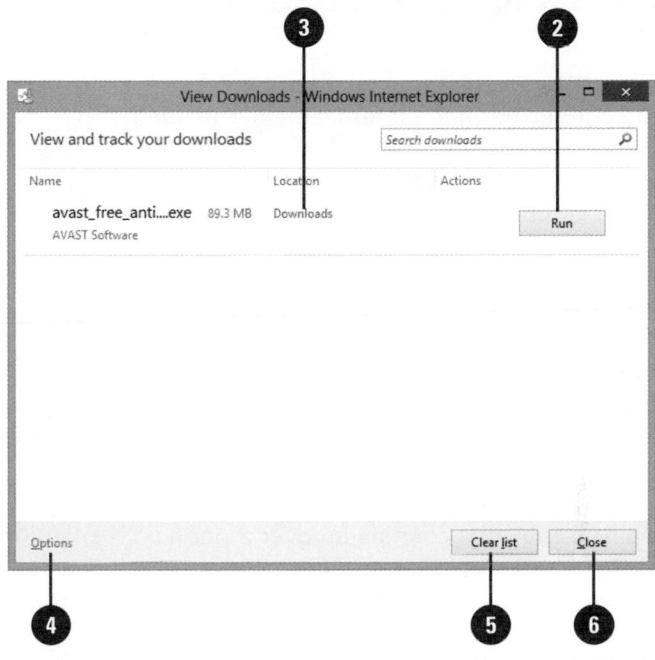

Download options

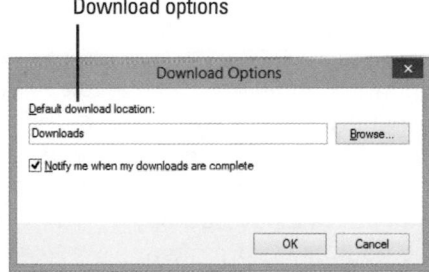

# Connecting to the Internet

Universities and large companies are most likely connected to the Internet via high-speed wiring that transmits data very quickly. As the Internet continues to explode around the world, several high-speed connection options are becoming more available and affordable for business and home use: DSL (Digital Subscriber Lines), wires that provide a completely digital connection; and cable modems, which use cable television lines. DSL and cable modems, also known as broadband connections, are continually turned on and connected and use a network setup. If a broadband connection is not available, you need to establish a connection over a phone line using a dial-up modem. Data travels more slowly over phone lines than over digital lines and cable modems. Whether you use a phone line, a DSL line, or a cable modem, Windows can help you establish a connection between your system and the Internet using the Connect to the Internet wizard. First, you need to select an ISP (Internet Service Provider), which is a company that sets up an Internet account for you and provides Internet access. ISPs maintain servers connected directly to the Internet 24 hours a day. You pay a fee, sometimes by the hour, but more often a flat monthly rate. To connect to the Internet, you need to obtain an Internet account and connection information from your ISP or your system administrator. For details, see "Creating an Internet Connection" on page 133. If you are working on a network, you can also share one Internet connection with everyone. For information on creating an Internet Connection Sharing (ICS), see "Sharing an Internet Connection" on page 402.

## Protecting your System with a Firewall

When you connect to the Internet, you can access web sites on the Internet, but other users on the Internet can also access information on your system and potentially infect it with harmful viruses and worms. For more information, see "Avoiding Viruses and Other Harmful Attacks" on page 360.

You can prevent this by activating Windows Firewall, another security layer of protection. A **firewall** is a security system that creates a protective barrier between your system or network and others on the Internet. Windows Firewall monitors all communication between your system and the Internet and prevents unsolicited inbound traffic from the Internet from entering your system. Windows Firewall blocks all unsolicited communication from reaching your system unless you specifically allow it (unblock) to come through, known as an exception. For example, if you run a program that needs to receive information from the Internet or a network, Windows Firewall asks if you want to block or unblock the connection. If you choose to unblock it, Windows Firewall creates an exception so the program can receive information. For details, see "Setting Up Windows Firewall" on page 134.

If you send and receive e-mail, Windows Firewall doesn't block spam or unsolicited e-mail or stop you from opening e-mail with harmful attachments. Windows Firewall helps block viruses and worms from reaching your system, but it doesn't detect or disable them if they are already on your system or come through e-mail. To protect your system, you need to install antivirus software.

# Creating an Internet Connection

Sometimes connecting your system to the Internet can be the most difficult part of getting started. The Connect to the Internet wizard simplifies the process, whether you want to set up a new connection using an existing account or select an Internet service provider (ISP) to set up a new account. In either case, you will need to obtain connection information from your ISP or your system administrator.

## Create an Internet Connection

1. In the File Explorer (desktop), click or tap **This PC**, and then click or tap the **Open Control Panel** button.

2. Click or tap the **Network and Sharing Center** icon in Small icons or Large icons view.

3. Click or tap **Set up a connection or network**, click or tap **Connect to the Internet**, and then click or tap **Next**.

4. Click or tap **Set up a new a connection**, or **Set up a new connection anyway** to set up a second connection.

5. Click or tap the option with the way you want to connect: **Wireless**, **Broadband (PPPoE)**, or **Dial-up**.

   ◆ For the wireless option, select a network, and then go to Step 10.

6. Type the name and password from your ISP. For a dial-up connection, type a dial-up phone number.

7. For the password, select or clear the **Show characters** or **Remember this password** check boxes.

8. Type a connection name.

9. Select or clear the **Allow other people to use this connection** check box.

10. Click or tap **Connect**.

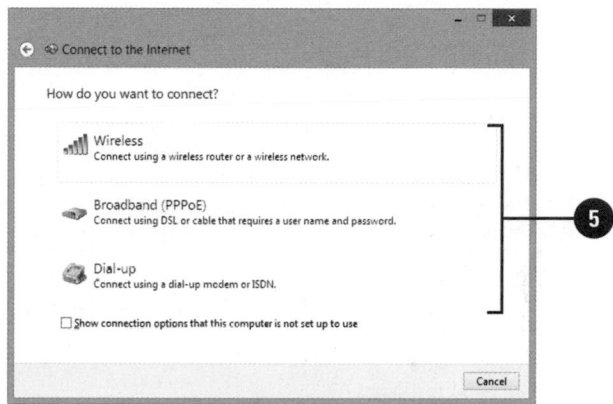

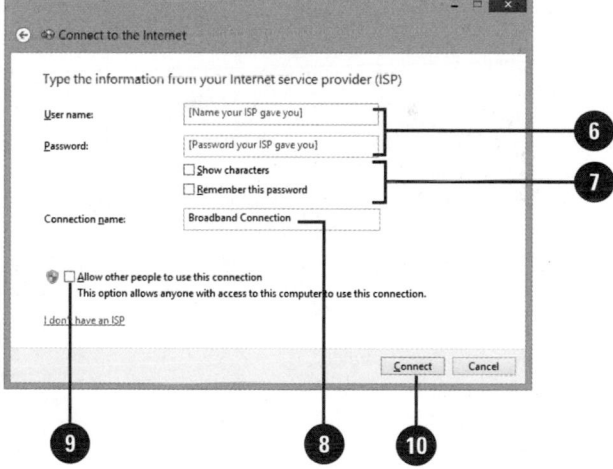

# Setting Up Windows Firewall

If your system is directly connected to the Internet, you need Windows Firewall to protect it from unauthorized access from others on the Internet for each network location you use. Windows Firewall is enabled by default for all Internet and network connections. However, some manufacturers and administrators might turn it off, so you need to check it. When Windows Firewall is enabled, you might not be able to use some communication features, such as sending files with a messaging program or playing an Internet game, unless the program is listed on the Exceptions list in Windows Firewall. If you use multiple Internet and networking connections, you can enable or disable individual connections.

## Set Up Windows Firewall

1. In the File Explorer (desktop), click or tap **This PC**, and then click or tap the **Open Control Panel** button.

2. Click or tap the **Windows Firewall** icon in Small icons or Large icons view.

3. In the left pane, click or tap **Turn Windows Firewall on or off**.

4. Select the **Turn on Windows Firewall** check box for each networks.

5. To set maximum protection, select the **Block all incoming connections, including those in the list of allowed programs** check box or clear it to make exceptions for each network.

6. Click or tap **OK**.

7. To make program exceptions, click or tap the **Allow a program or feature through Windows Firewall** in the left pane, select the check boxes with the exceptions you want; if necessary, click or tap **Allow another app** to add it, and then click or tap **OK**.

8. To restore default settings, click **Restore defaults** in the left pane, click or tap **Restore defaults**, and then click or tap **Yes**.

9. Click or tap the **Close** button.

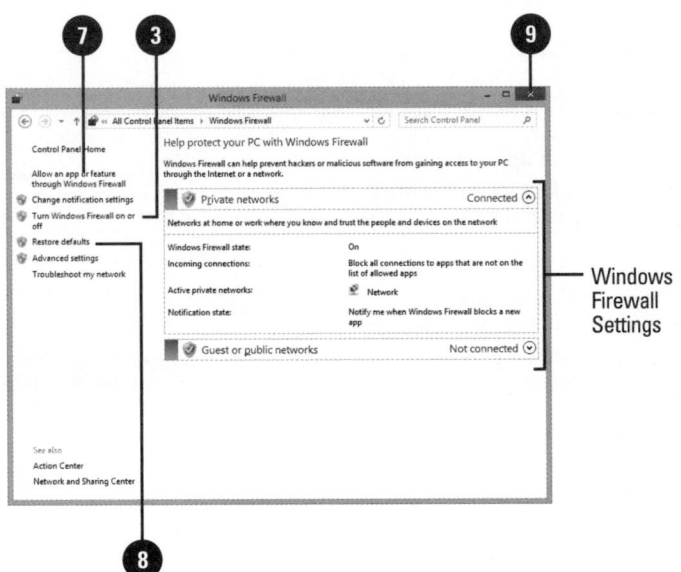

Windows Firewall Settings

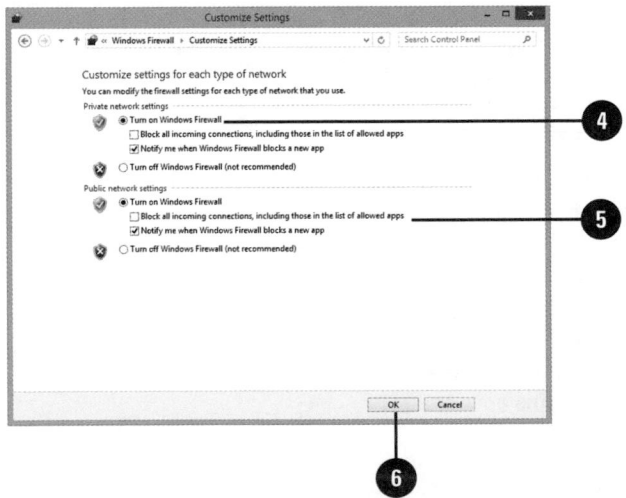

# Working with Contacts and Calendars

**5**

## Introduction

A contact is a person or company with whom you communicate. Windows 8.1 uses the People app as a centralized place to add and manage contact information, including a person's name, address, phone, and email, which you can use in other apps, including Mail and Skype, to communicate with others. You can create and manage contacts in the People app and add contacts from other online service accounts, such as Facebook, Outlook.com (Hotmail, Live or MSN), Twitter, Microsoft Exchange, LinkedIn, and Google. When you setup Windows 8.1, you also setup or specify a Microsoft account, which becomes your default account and profile in the People app.

In addition to the People app, Windows 8.1 includes a Calendar app, an electronic version of the familiar paper daily planner. The Calendar app allows you to update the appearance and organization of events on your calendar in order to make things less cluttered and easier to read. You can use the Calendar app to schedule time for completing specific tasks, appointments, meetings, vacations, holidays, or for any other activity. You can adjust the Calendar Home screen to show events using the What's Next, Day, Work Week, Week, or Month view. The Calendar app comes with multiple calendars for different purposes, which include Main (with the username), Birthday, Personal, Holidays, and Work. When you create a calendar event, you can specify a specific calendar, where and when the event takes place, how long the event will last, how often the event occurs, whether you want to a reminder notice, your status, and whether to make the event private.

## What You'll Do

**Start the People App**

**View the People App Window**

**Add Contacts from Online Accounts**

**View Contacts**

**Sort or Filter Contacts**

**Create Favorite Contacts**

**Add or Edit Contacts**

**Delete Contacts**

**Link Contacts**

**Start the Calendar App**

**Change Calendar Views**

**Schedule Events**

**Schedule Recurring Events**

**Schedule Events with Reminders**

**Edit or Delete Events**

**Set Calendar Options**

# Starting the People App

Windows 8.1 comes with a built-in app that allows you to work with contacts. The People app is a centralized place to add and manage contact information, including a person's name, address, phone, and email, which you can use in other apps, including Mail and Skype, to communicate with others. You can create and manage contacts in the People app and add contacts from other online social media accounts, such as Outlook.com (including Hotmail.com, Live.com, or MSN), Facebook, Twitter, Exchange (including Microsoft Exchange, Office 365, or Outlook.com), Google, LinkedIn, and Sina Weibo (**New!**). When you setup Windows 8.1, you also setup or specified a Microsoft account, which becomes your default account and profile in People. Like other metro apps, you can start it from the Start screen.

## Start the People App

① Click or tap the **People** tile on the Start or Apps screen.

The People app window opens in full screen view.

On first use, a list of social media accounts appear on the left side of the Home screen.

② If you want to add contacts from an online social media account, click or tap the account you want, or click or tap **View all in Settings** to display a complete list of accounts.

③ To dismiss the list of accounts on the Home screen, click or tap the **No thanks** link.

### See Also

*See "Adding Contacts from Online Accounts" on page 138 for information on adding contacts to the People app from social media accounts.*

# Viewing the People App Window

**Accounts**
Displays a list of online accounts to get info and updates from you contacts.

**Favorites & Contacts**
Displays a list of favorites and buttons to access all your contacts.

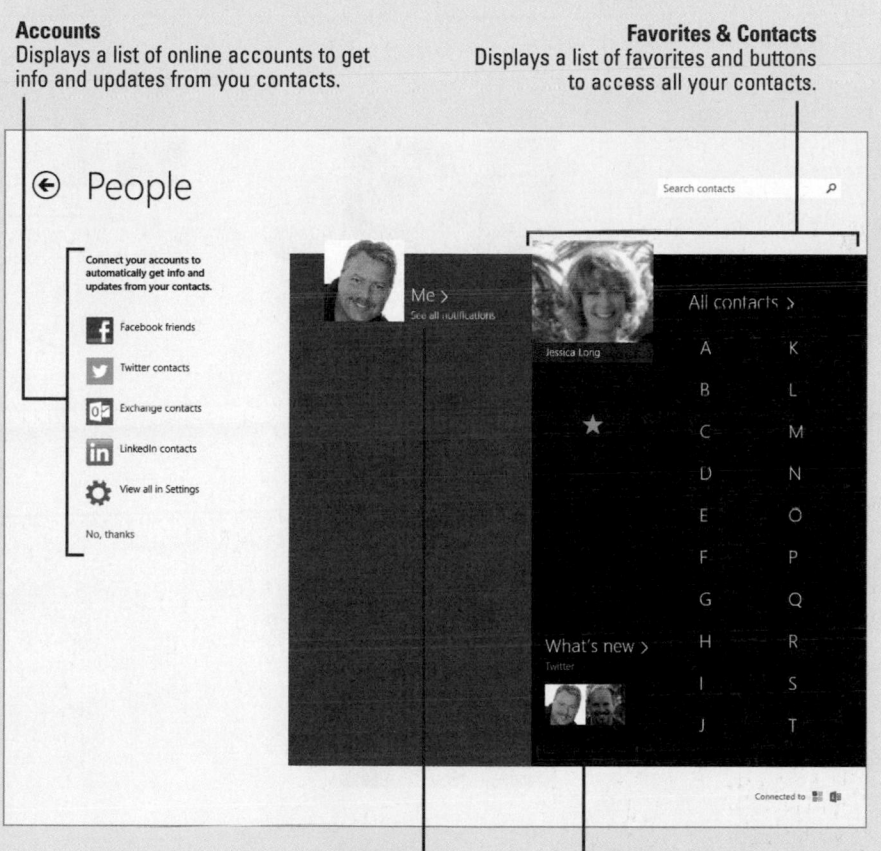

**Me Contact**
Displays a profile image and provides access to your contact information.

**What's new & View Notifications**
Provides access to view your friends on social networks and notifications.

# Adding Contacts from Online Accounts

With the People app, you can add contacts from other online media accounts, such as Outlook.com (including Hotmail.com, Live.com, or MSN), Facebook, Twitter, Exchange (including Microsoft Exchange, Office 365, or Outlook.com), Google, LinkedIn, and Sina Weibo (**New!**). When you setup Windows 8.1, you also setup or specified a Microsoft account, which becomes your default account and profile in People. When you start the People app for the first time, a list of accounts appears on the Home screen for easy access. If it's not there, you can access accounts from Settings on the Charms bar.

## View and Manage Online Accounts

**1** Click or tap the **People** tile on the Start or Apps screen.

> **TIMESAVER** *Icons appear in the upper-right corner with the connected online accounts.*

**2** If available on the People Home screen, click or tap **View all in Settings** to display a complete list of accounts. If not available, continue with Steps 3-5.

**3** Point to the lower- or upper-right corner and move up or down (on a computer) or swipe left from the right edge of the screen (on a mobile device).

**4** Click or tap the **Settings** button on the Charms bar.

**5** Click or tap **Accounts** on the Settings panel.

> The accounts connected to the People app appear on the Accounts panel.

**6** To edit account information, click or tap the account name on the Accounts panel, and then make the changes you want.

**7** To go back to the previous panel, click or tap the **Back** button.

> To exit the panel, click or tap off the panel, or press Esc.

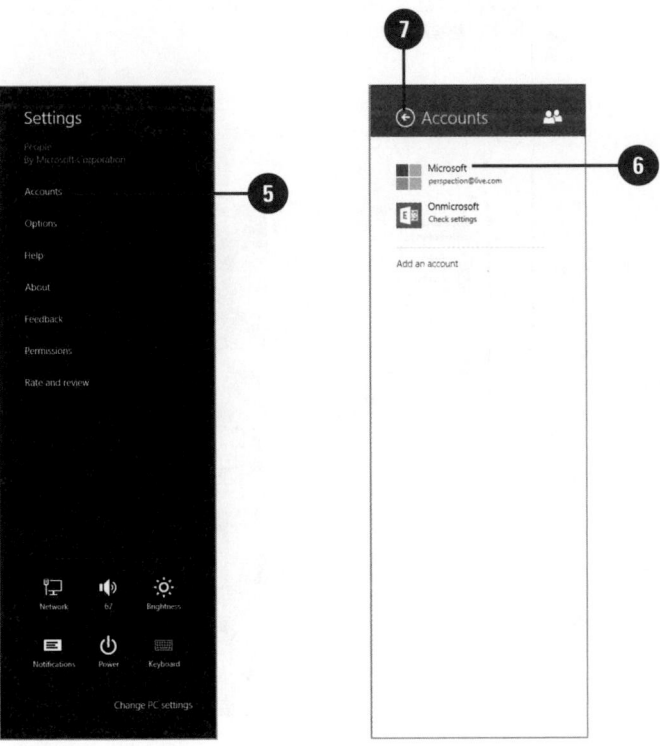

## Add Contacts from Online Accounts

**1** Click or tap the **People** tile on the Start or Apps screen.

**2** If an accounts list appears on the People Home screen, click or tap the account you want to add, and then skip to Step 8.

◆ To dismiss the accounts list on the People Home screen, click or tap the **No thanks** link.

**3** Point to the lower- or upper-right corner and move up or down (on a computer) or swipe left from the right edge of the screen (on a mobile device).

**4** Click or tap the **Settings** button on the Charms bar.

**5** Click or tap **Accounts** on the Settings panel.

The accounts connected to the People app appear on the Accounts panel.

**6** Click or tap the **Add an account** link on the Accounts panel.

**7** Click or tap the account from which you want to add contacts on the Add an account panel.

Your web browser opens, displaying instructions to connect to the online account.

**8** Follow the on-screen instructions to connect to the online account; steps vary depending on the account you select.

If necessary, use the Mail app to confirm the use of your online account.

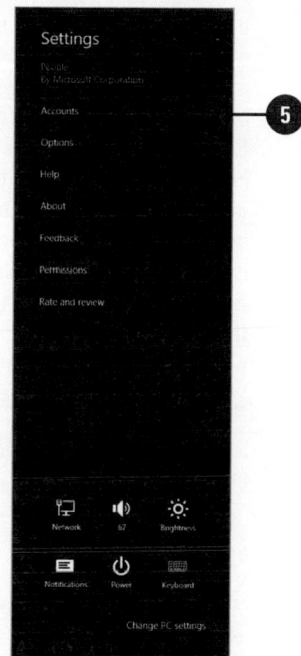

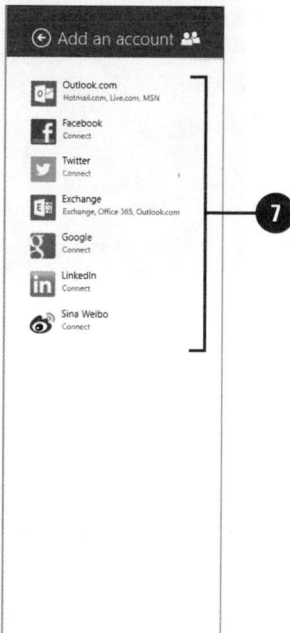

# Viewing Contacts

A **contact** is a person or company that you communicate with. One contact can often have several mailing addresses, phone numbers, or e-mail addresses. You can store this information in the People app along with other detailed information, such as job title, cell phone number, and web page addresses. You can add contacts directly within the People app for local use or from online media accounts, such as Facebook, Hotmail, Twitter, Outlook, LinkedIn, and Google. You can view all contacts or only the ones organized by A to Z (**New!**). If you don't see the contact you want, you can use the Search box (**New!**) to find it. The list of contacts also includes your Me contact, which displays contact information for the current user account for Windows 8.1. With the Me contact, you can view profile information as well as updates and notifications from a centralized place.

## View Contacts

1. Click or tap the **People** tile on the Start or Apps screen.

2. To search for a contact, click in the Search box (**New!**), enter a search contact name, and then click or tap a contact from the list.

3. Click or tap **All Contacts** or click or tap **A to Z** (**New!**) on the People Home screen.

   ◆ **View a favorite.** Click or tap a favorite tile (**New!**) on the People Home screen.

4. Click or tap the contact icon or name you want to view.

5. To go back to the previous screen, click or tap the **Back** button.

Favorite contact    Add a Favorite button

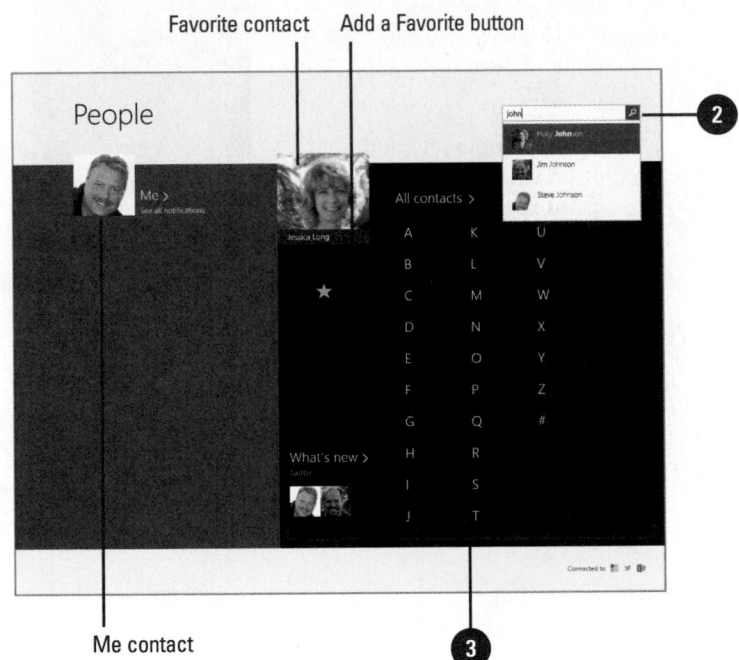

Me contact

### Did You Know?

***You can remove a favorite.*** In the People app, click the favorite contact tile, and then click the Favorites button to toggle it off.

## View a Contact and Profile

1. Click or tap the **People** tile on the Start or Apps screen.

2. Click or tap **All Contacts** or click or tap **A to Z (New!)** on the People Home screen.

3. Click or tap a contact icon or name you want to view.

   The contact appears with additional options to send an email or instant message, or view the contact's profile.

4. Click or tap **More info** or **View profile**, if available, for an account.

5. To go back to the previous screen, click or tap the **Back** button.

6. To respond to available posts from social networks, click or tap the appropriate button, and then respond to the post.

7. To go back to the Home screen, right-click a blank area of the screen (on a computer) or swipe up from the bottom edge or down from the top edge of the screen (on a mobile device), and then click or tap the **Home** button on the App bar.

### Did You Know?

*You can view your Me contact.* The Me contact is the contact for the current user account on your system. To view your Me contact, click or tap the Me contact on the People Home app. You can view What's new and Notifications. For more information, click or tap More info or View profile (if available).

All contacts shown

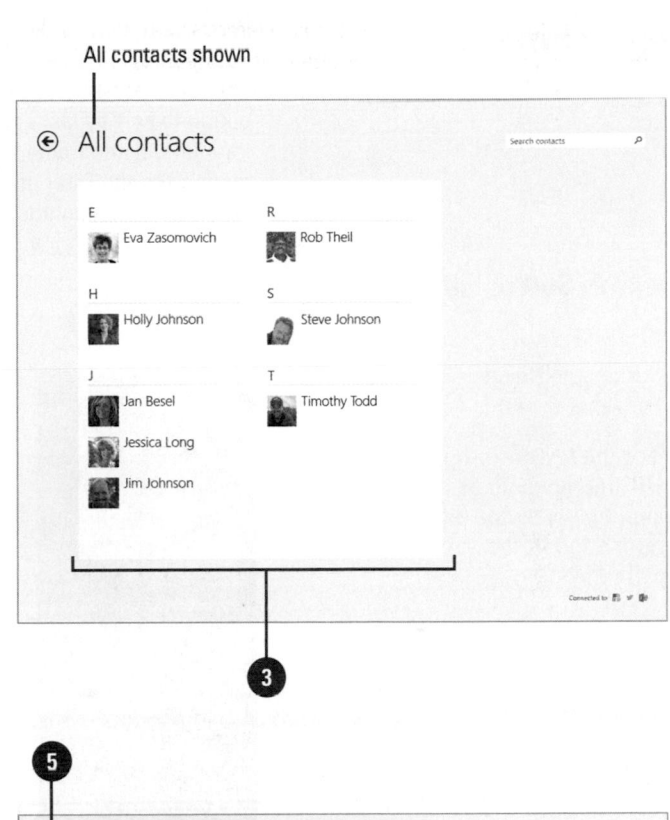

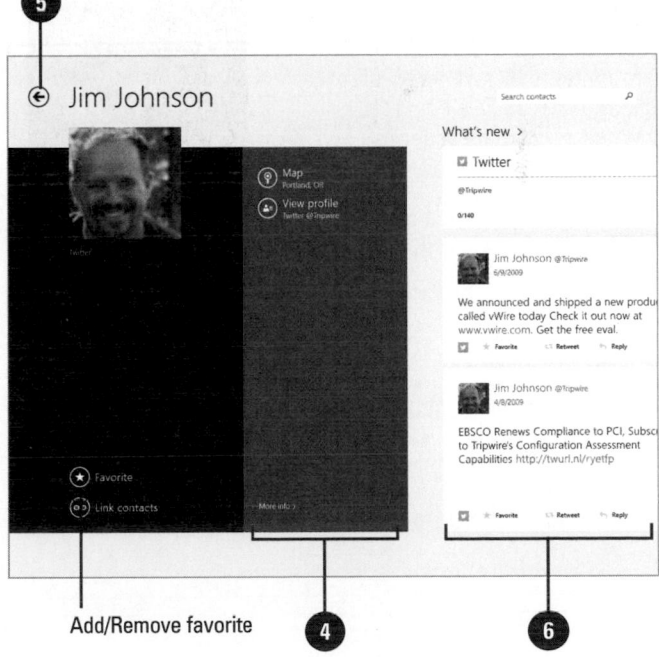

Add/Remove favorite

# Sorting or Filtering Contacts

With the Options panel in the People app, you can sort or filter contacts on the People Home screen. When you open the People app, contacts are sort by first name by default. However, you can change the Sort option to sort by last name. When you add online media accounts to the People app, the Home screen can become cluttered with a lot of contacts. With the Filter option, you can show or hide contacts for a specific type of account to work with the ones you want.

## Set Options to Sort or Filter Contacts

1. Click or tap the **People** tile on the Start or Apps screen.

2. Point to the lower- or upper-right corner and move up or down (on a computer) or swipe left from the right edge of the screen (on a mobile device).

3. Click or tap the **Settings** button on the Charms bar.

4. Click or tap **Options** on the Settings panel.

   The Options panel appears.

5. To sort contacts by last name, drag the slider to **On**. To sort contacts by first name, drag the slider to **Off**, the default.

6. To filter contacts by specific accounts, select or clear the account check boxes.

7. To go back to the previous panel, click or tap the **Back** button.

   To exit the panel, click or tap off the panel, or press Esc.

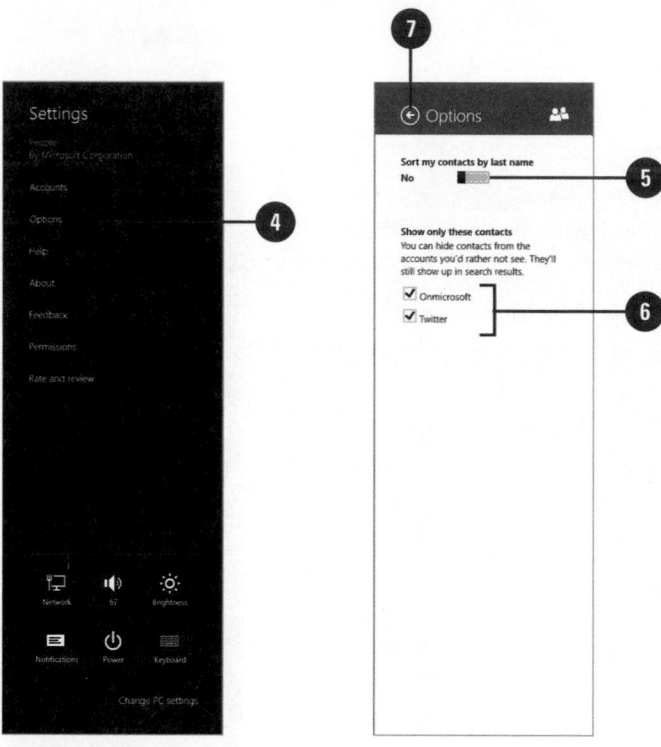

# Creating Favorite Contacts

Like Internet Explorer, you can create favorites in the People app. With a simple click or tap, you can create a favorite with any of your contacts. Favorites appear on the People Home screen for easy access along with the Add a Favorites (with Star icon) button (**New!**) to quickly add one or more favorites. When you use the People app from other apps, such as Mail and Skype, favorite contacts appear at the top of the list with a star for easy access. If you want easy access to a specific contact, you can pin it to the Start screen.

## Create a Favorite Contact

1. Click or tap the **People** tile on the Start or Apps screen.

2. Click or tap the Favorite tile (with the Star icon) (**New!**) on the People Home screen.

3. Click or tap one or more contacts to select them.

4. Click or tap the **Add** button.

   ◆ **Add or remove a favorite.** You can also open a contact, and then click the **Favorite** button (**New!**) to toggle a favorite on and off.

5. Click or tap the **Back** button to go back to the People Home screen.

   Your favorite contacts appear on the People Home screen.

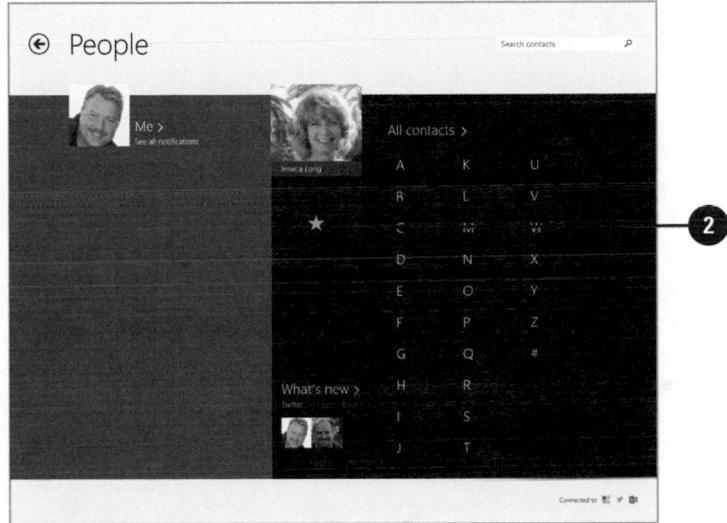

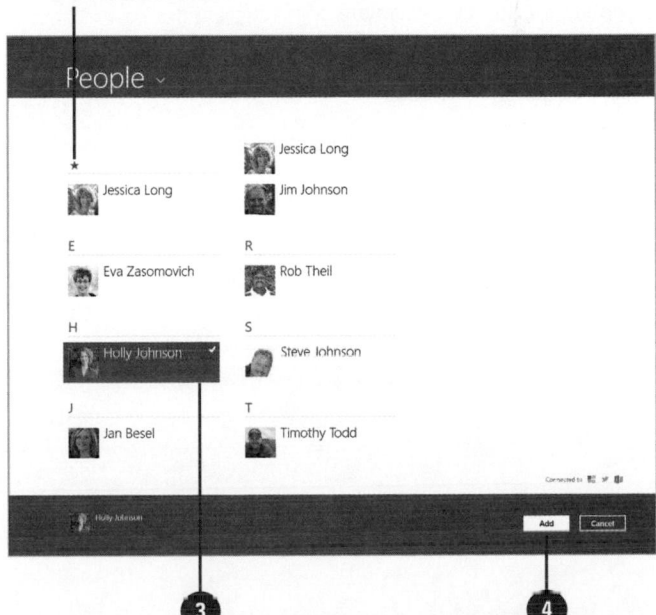

Favorite contacts

# Adding or Editing Contacts

A **contact** is a person or company that you communicate with. One contact can often have several mailing addresses, phone numbers, or e-mail addresses. You can store this information in the People app along with other detailed information, such as job title, mobile phone number, web page addresses, and other notes. This information can be used to send emails and instant messages. You can use the App bar to quickly add a new contact or edit an existing one.

## Add a New Contact

1. Click or tap the **People** tile on the Start or Apps screen.

2. Right-click a blank area of the screen (on a computer) or swipe up from the bottom edge or down from the top edge of the screen (on a mobile device).

3. Click or tap the **New** button on the App bar.

4. Click or tap **Account** list arrow, and then click or tap an account.

5. Enter the contact's information, including name, company, e-mail, and phone.

6. To add information for a category, click or tap the **Add** button, click or tap an option for the specified type of information.

7. Enter any additional information for a new category.

8. Click or tap the **Save** button.

   ◆ To cancel the new contact, click or tap the **Cancel** button.

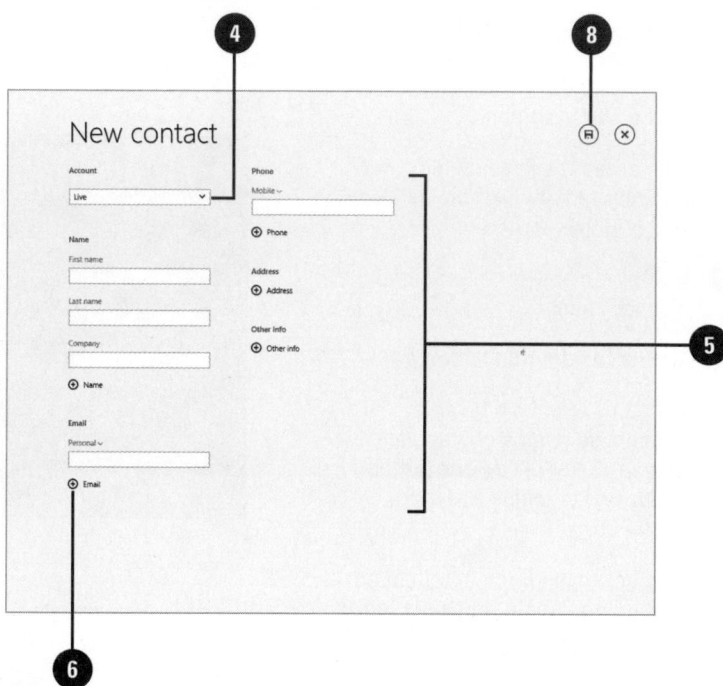

## Edit a Contact

1. Click or tap the **People** tile on the Start or Apps screen.

2. Click or tap the contact that you want to edit.

3. Right-click a blank area of the screen (on a computer) or swipe up from the bottom edge or down from the top edge of the screen (on a mobile device).

4. Click or tap the **Edit** button on the App bar. If multiple contacts are available, click or tap the contact you want to edit.

   ◆ If your contact originates online, your web browser opens, where you can edit the contact information. When you're done, close your web browser.

5. Edit the contact's information as desired.

6. Click or tap the **Save** button.

   ◆ To cancel the operation, click or tap the **Cancel** button.

### Did You Know?

*You can pin a contact to the Start screen.* In the People app, click or tap the contact you want to pin, right-click a blank area of the screen (on a computer) or swipe up from the bottom edge or down from the top edge of the screen (on a mobile device), click or tap the Pin to Start button on the App bar, enter a tile name, and then click or tap Pin to Start.

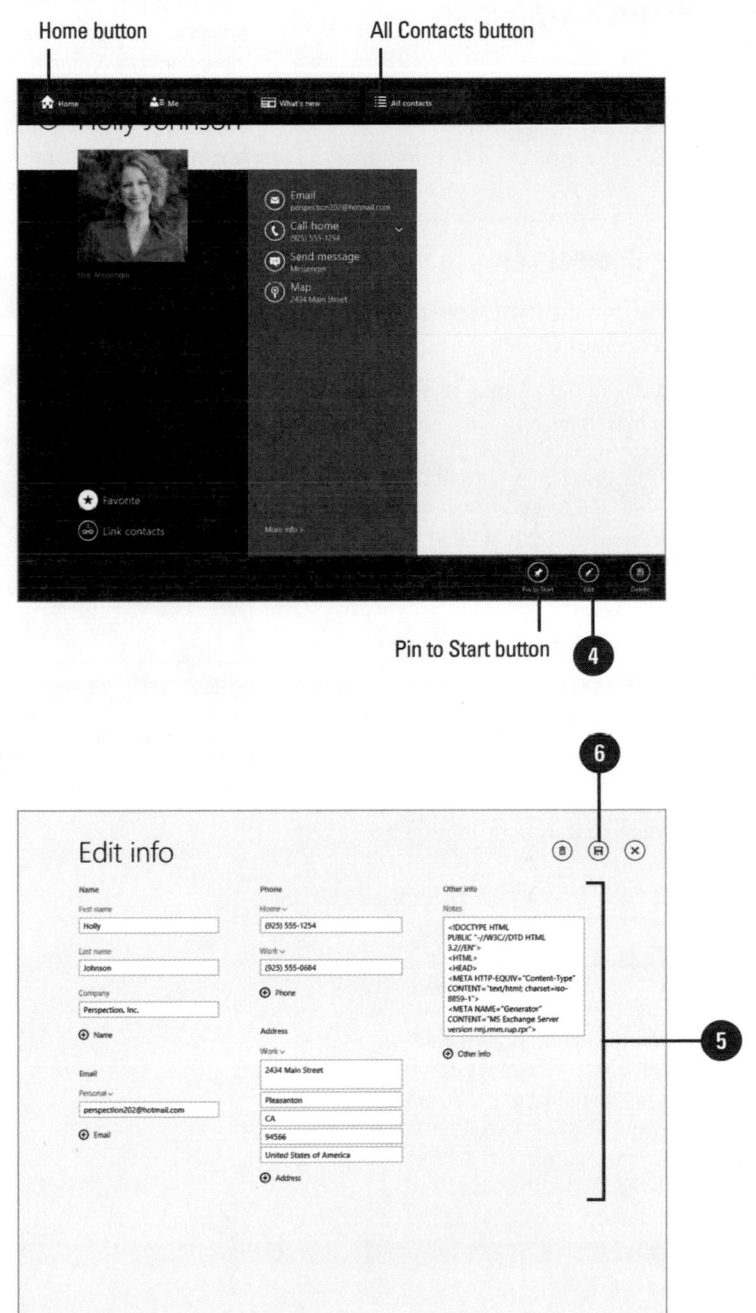

Home button    All Contacts button

Pin to Start button    4

6

Edit info

# Deleting Contacts

If you contacts list is getting to large or you no longer need a contact anymore, you can delete it from the People app. With a few simple clicks or taps, you can delete a contact using the App bar. When you delete a contact, the People app asks for a confirmation, so you don't delete a contact by mistake. Since, your user account is linked to your Me contact, you cannot delete it in the People app. You would need to remove the user account in Settings for Windows 8.1.

## Delete a Contact

1. Click or tap the **People** tile on the Start or Apps screen.

2. Click or tap the contact that you want to delete.

3. Right-click a blank area of the screen (on a computer) or swipe up from the bottom edge or down from the top edge of the screen (on a mobile device).

4. Click or tap the **Delete** button on the App bar.

5. Click or tap the check boxes (**New!**) to deselect the addresses you don't want to delete.

6. Click or tap **Delete** to confirm the deletion.

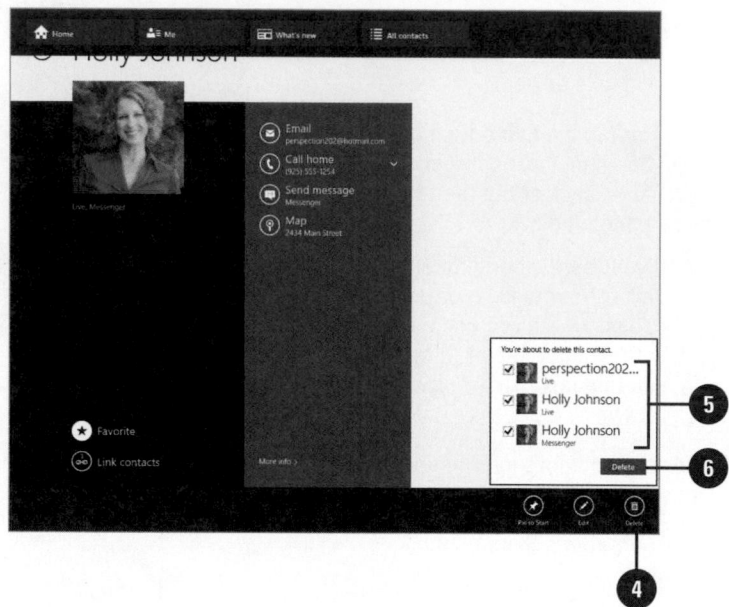

### Did You Know?

*You can get Help in the People app.* In the People app, point to the lower- or upper-right corner and move up or down (on a computer) or swipe left from the right edge of the screen (on a mobile device), click or tap the Settings button on the Charms bar, click or tap Help, and then click or tap a link.

# Linking Contacts

A contact can be linked with other profiles and contacts in the People app. With a few simple clicks or taps, you can link a contact with other information. You can view your current links as well as add new ones by using the Link button on the App bar for a specific contact. For those of you using Messenger, friends can't be linked to each other.

## Link a Contact

**1** Click or tap the **People** tile on the Start or Apps screen.

**2** Click or tap the contact that you want to link.

**3** Click or tap the **Link contacts** button.

**4** Click or tap the **Add** button for Choose a contact.

The People app display contacts to which you want to link.

**5** Select the contacts you want, and then click or tap **Add**.

**6** Click or tap the **Save** button.

◆ To cancel the operation, click or tap the **Cancel** button.

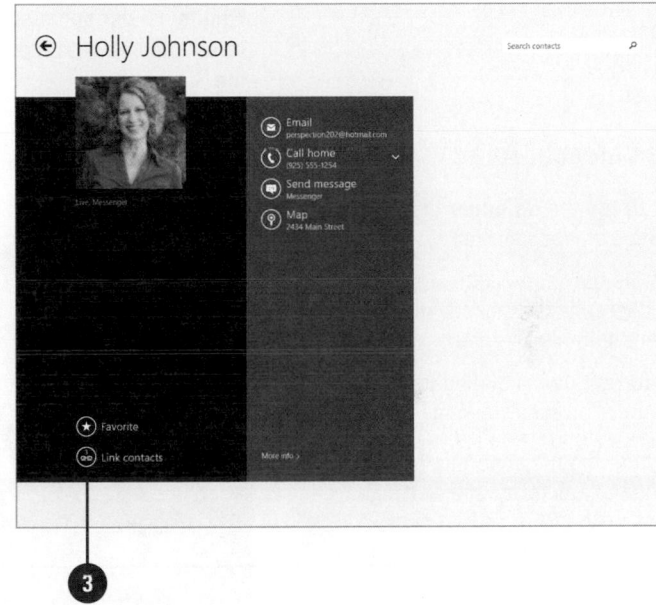

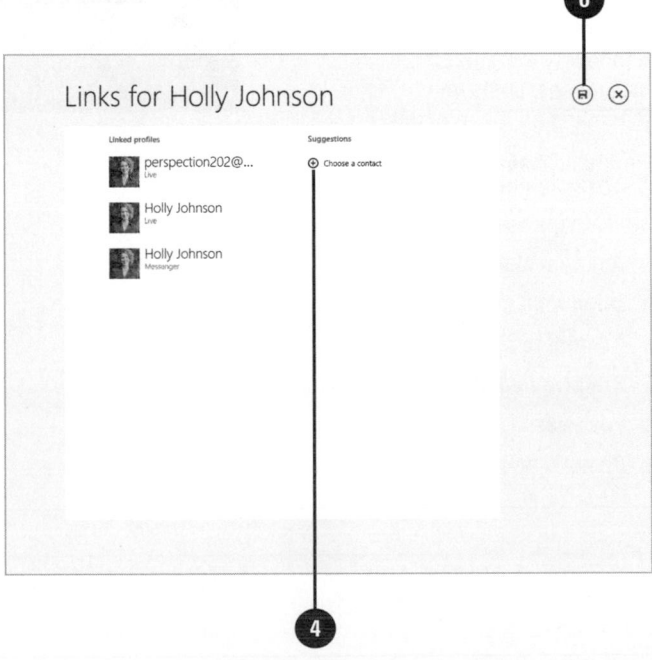

# Starting the Calendar App

Windows 8.1 comes with a built-in calendar app that allows you to manage your schedule. The Calendar app is an electronic version of the familiar paper daily planner that allows you to schedule time for completing specific tasks, appointments, meetings, vacations, holidays, or for any other activity. You can add or modify calendars from other online accounts, such as Hotmail (Hotmail.com, Live.com, or MSN), Outlook (Microsoft Exchange, Office 365, or Outlook.com), and Google. Each calendar appears in a different color to make things less cluttered and easier to read. Like other metro apps, you can start it from the Start screen.

## Start the Calendar App

**1** Click or tap the **Calendar** tile on the Start or Apps screen.

The Calendar app window opens in full screen view, displaying the current month's calendar.

The current day is highlighted in dark grey for easy viewing.

**2** To add or modify accounts for calendar, click or tap the **Settings** button on the Charms bar, click **Accounts**, and then do any of the following:

◆ **Add an Account.** Click the **Add an account** link, click or tap the account you want to add, and then follow the on-screen instructions; steps vary depending on the account.

◆ **Modify an Account.** Click an account, and then specify the options you want:

- ◆ **Account Name.**
- ◆ **Download new email.**
- ◆ **Content to sync.**
- ◆ **Preferred email address.**
- ◆ **Password.**
- ◆ **Remove account.**

# Changing the Calendar View

With the Calendar app, you can adjust the Calendar app Home screen to show events using the What's next (**New!**), Day, Work Week (**New!**), Week, or Month view. When you display the Calendar Home screen using the Day view, you can view events for the current day, as well as what is going on tomorrow. After viewing other dates in the calendar, you can use the Today button to quickly display today's date in the current view. The current day is highlighted in dark grey for easy viewing. You can switch between the different views by using buttons on the App bar or keyboard shortcuts. You can also use the View list arrow (**New!**), Back or Forward arrow or swipe left or right to navigate the calendar.

## Change the Calendar View

1. Click or tap the **Calendar** tile on the Start or Apps screen.

2. Right-click a blank area of the screen (on a computer) or swipe up from the bottom edge or down from the top edge of the screen (on a mobile device).

3. Click or tap one of the View buttons on the App bar.

   ◆ **What's next.** Displays a list of the next events (**New!**) from the current day.

   ◆ **Day.** Displays an hourly schedule for the selected day and day after.

   ◆ **Work Week.** Displays an hourly schedule for the 5-day work week (**New!**).

   ◆ **Week.** Displays an hourly schedule for the 7-day week.

   ◆ **Month.** Displays a monthly schedule.

   **TIMESAVER** *Press Ctrl+1 (What's next), Ctrl+2 (Day), Ctrl+3 (Work Week), Ctrl+4 (Week), and Ctrl+5 (Month) to display views.*

4. To navigate backward and forward in the calendar, move the pointer, and then click or tap the **Back** or **Forward** arrow, or swipe left or right. Click the **View** list arrow (**New!**) to navigate calendars and select a day or today.

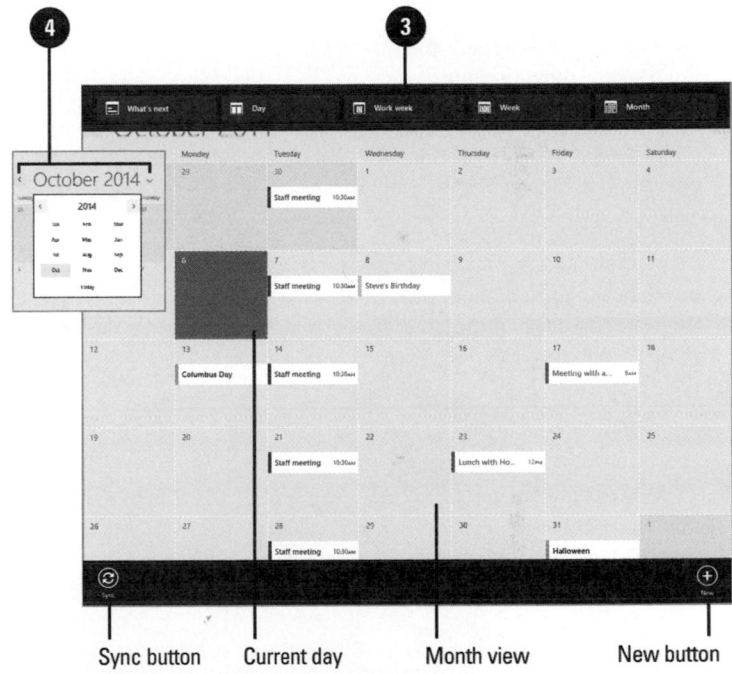

Sync button    Current day    Month view    New button

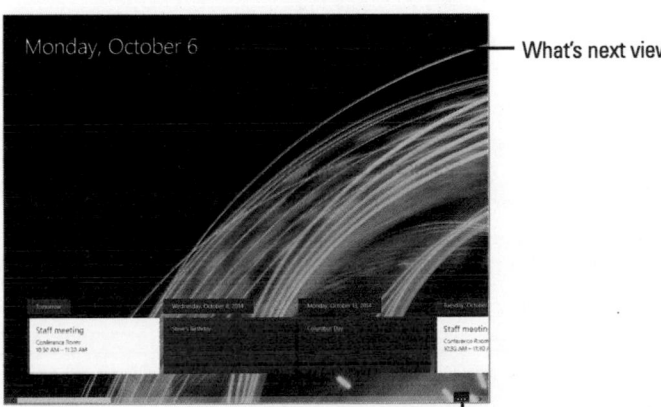

What's next view

Click or tap to display App bar

# Scheduling Events

The Calendar app comes with multiple calendars for different purposes, which include Main (with the username), Birthday, Personal, Holidays, and Work. When you create a calendar event, you can specify a specific calendar, where and when the event takes place, how long the event will last, how often the event occurs, whether you want to a reminder notice, your status (Free, Busy, tentative, Out of office, or Working elsewhere), and whether to make the event private. If an event recurs on a regular basis, such as a meeting, you can set the How Often option. If you need a reminder, you can also set the amount of time you need. If you don't want others to see an event, you can make it private.

## Schedule a New Event

**1** Click or tap the **Calendar** tile on the Start or Apps screen.

**2** To quickly add an event or appointment, click or tap the day you want, and then skip to Step 5.

**3** Right-click a blank area of the screen (on a computer) or swipe up from the bottom edge or down from the top edge of the screen (on a mobile device).

**4** Click or tap the **New** button on the App bar.

**5** Type a subject and a message, as desired.

**6** Specify any of the following:

◆ **Calendar.** Select the calendar for the event.

◆ **When.** Specify when you want the event.

◆ **Start.** Specify the start time for the event.

◆ **How Long.** Specify the length for the event.

◆ **Where.** Specify where you want to hold the event.

◆ **Who.** Enter email addresses (separated by a semi-colon).

**7** Click or tap the **Save this event** button.

◆ To cancel, click the **Back** button.

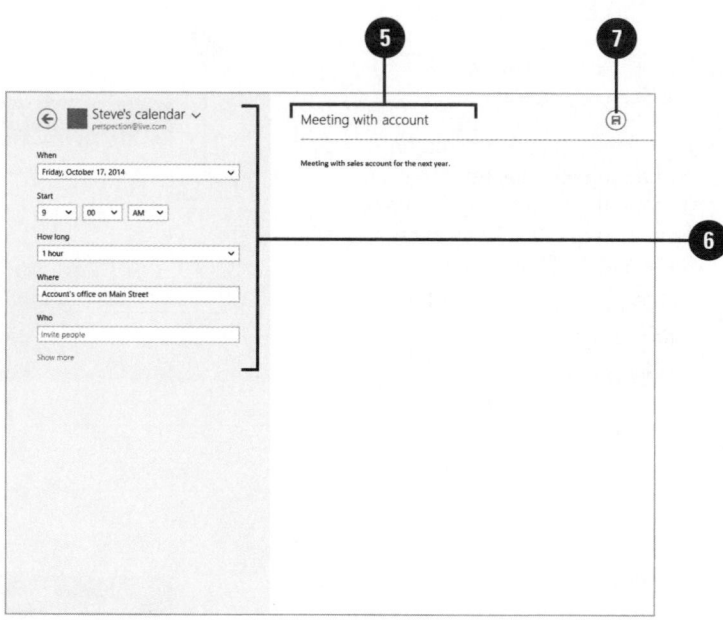

## Schedule a New Detailed Event

1. Click or tap the **Calendar** tile on the Start or Apps screen.

2. Right-click a blank area of the screen (on a computer) or swipe up from the bottom edge or down from the top edge of the screen (on a mobile device).

3. Click or tap the **New** button on the App bar.

4. Type a subject and a message, as desired.

5. Specify any of the following:

   ◆ **Calendar.** Select the calendar for the event.

   ◆ **When.** Specify when you want the event.

   ◆ **Start.** Specify the start time for the event.

   ◆ **How Long.** Specify the length for the event.

   ◆ **Where.** Specify where you want to hold the event.

   ◆ **Who.** Enter email addresses (separated by a semi-colon).

6. Click or tap the **Show more** link.

7. Specify any of the following:

   ◆ **How often.** Select Once for a one time event or an option for a recurring event.

   ◆ **Reminder.** Select None for no reminder, or an option for when you want a reminder.

   ◆ **Status.** Specify your status (Free, Busy, tentative, Out of office, or Working elsewhere).

   ◆ **Private.** Select to create a private event.

8. Click or tap the **Save this event** button.

   ◆ To cancel, click the **Back** button.

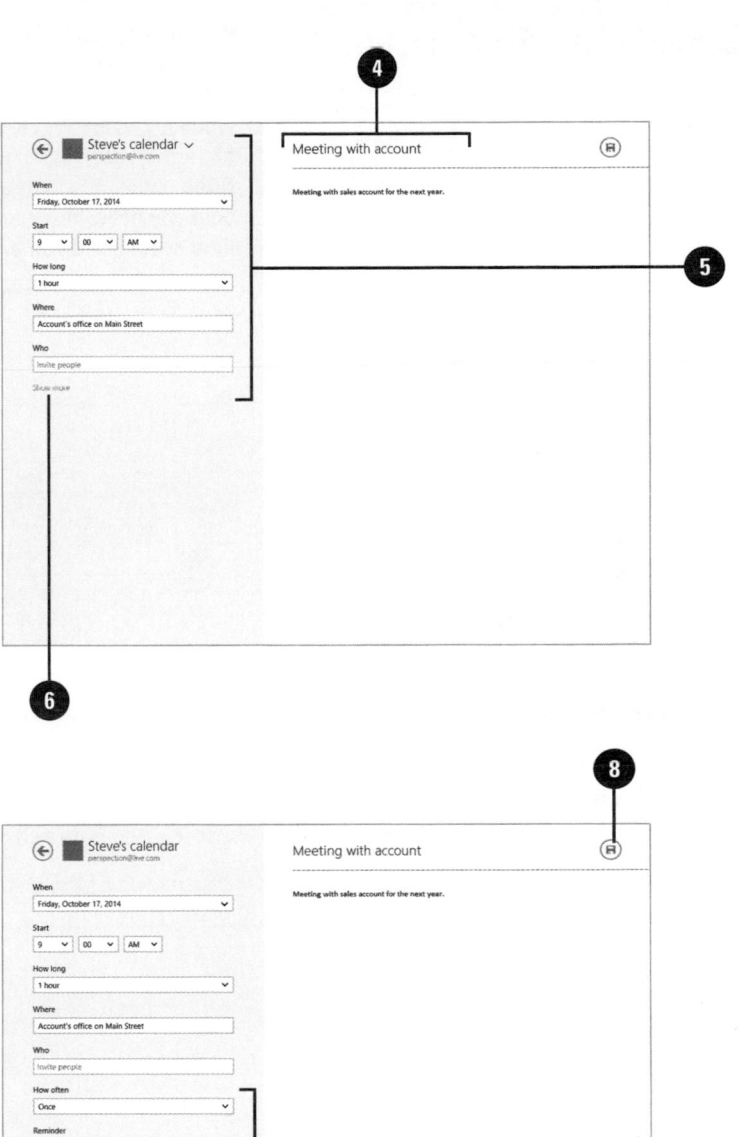

# Scheduling Recurring Events

If an event recurs on a regular basis, such as a meeting, you can set the How Often option to specify the interval in which you want to schedule it. You can specify the following intervals: Every day, Every weekday, Every week, Every month, or Every year. If you want to change a recurring event to an individual event, you can select the Once option. If you need a reminder, you can also set the amount of time you need. You can set the How Often option when you create a new event or edit an existing one.

## Schedule a Recurring Event

1. Click or tap the **Calendar** tile on the Start or Apps screen.

2. Click or tap the day you want to create a new event or an existing one.

3. Type a subject and a message, as desired.

4. Specify any of the following information: **Calendar**, **When**, **Start**, **How Long**, **Where**, and **Who**.

5. Click or tap the **Show more** link.

6. Click or tap the **How often** list arrow, and then select a recurring option for the event: **Every day**, **Every weekday**, **Every week**, **Every month**, or **Every year**.

   ◆ To change a recurring event to an individual event, select the **Once** option.

7. Specify any of the following information: **Reminder**, **Status**, or **Private**.

8. Click or tap the **Save this event** button.

   ◆ To cancel, click the **Back** button.

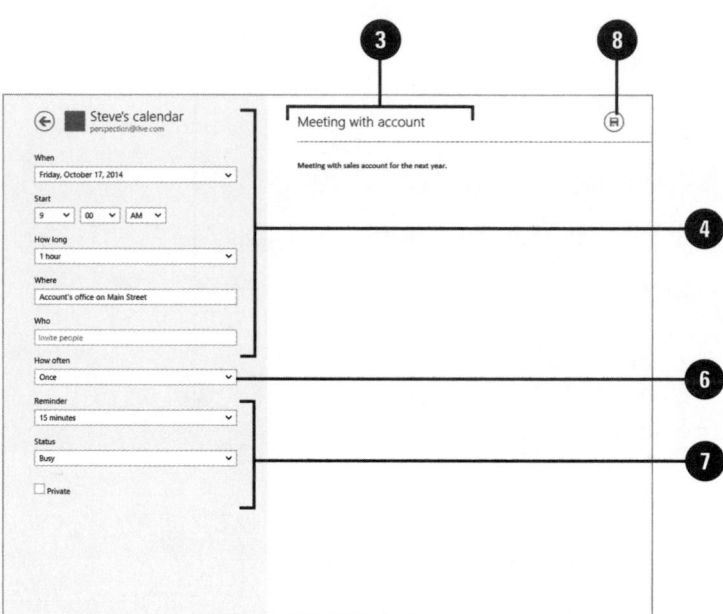

# Scheduling Events with a Reminder

If you have an event, such as a meeting, in the Calendar app, you can invite others to attend and provide a reminder. When you create a new event or edit an existing one, you can set the amount of time you need for a reminder and enter email addresses or select contacts from the People app in order to send email invitations. When the timing for the reminder takes place, a notification appears in the upper-right corner of the screen, where you can click or tap the notification to view the event.

## Schedule an Event with a Reminder

1. Click or tap the **Calendar** tile on the Start or Apps screen.

2. Click or tap the day you want to create a new event or an existing one.

3. Type a subject and a message, as desired.

4. Specify any of the following information: **Calendar**, **When**, **Start**, **How Long**, **Where**, and **Who**.

   ◆ To send email invites, enter the email addresses you want (separated by a semi-colon).

5. Click or tap the **Show more** link.

6. Click or tap the **How often** list arrow, and then select a recurring option.

7. Click or tap the **Reminder** list arrow, and then select the amount of time you want.

   ◆ To turn off the reminder, select the **None** option.

8. Specify any of the following information: **Status** or **Private**.

9. Click or tap the **Save this event** button or click or tap the **Send invite** button (if you added email addresses or contacts in Step 7).

   ◆ To cancel, click the **Back** button

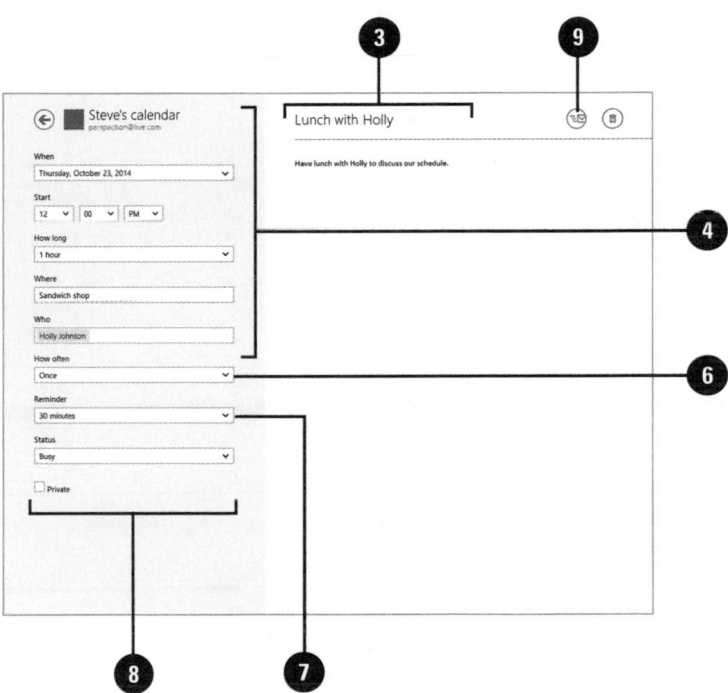

# Editing or Deleting Events

After you create an event, you edit it at any time. With a simple click or tap, you can open an event and make any changes that you want or delete it from the calendar. When you open an recurring event, the Calendar app asks you whether you want to open the individual event or the entire series. After you make changes to an individual or recurring event, you simply save it. If you no longer need an individual or recurring event, you can delete it from the calendar.

## Edit an Event

1. Click or tap the **Calendar** tile on the Start or Apps screen.

2. Navigate to the event you want to edit.

   ◆ To navigate backward and forward in the calendar, move the pointer, and then click or tap the **Back** or **Forward** arrow, or swipe left or right.

3. Click or tap the event to open it, and then click or tap **Open one** or **Open series**.

4. Make the changes you want for the event.

5. Click or tap the **Save this event** button.

   ◆ To cancel, click the **Back** button.

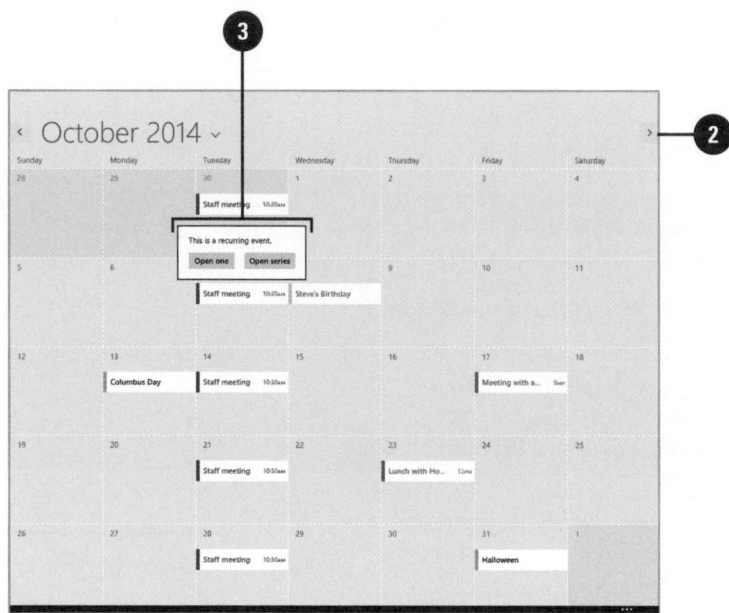

## Did You Know?

*You can sync calendar events to update them on all devices.* In the Calendar app, press F5 or click the Sync button on the App bar.

## Delete an Event

① Click or tap the **Calendar** tile on the Start or Apps screen.

② Navigate to the event you want to delete.

◆ To navigate backward and forward in the calendar, move the pointer, and then click or tap the **Back** or **Forward** arrow, or swipe left or right.

③ Click or tap the event to open it, and then click or tap **Open one** or **Open series**.

④ Click or tap the **Delete** button.

⑤ Click or tap the **Delete** to confirm the deletion.

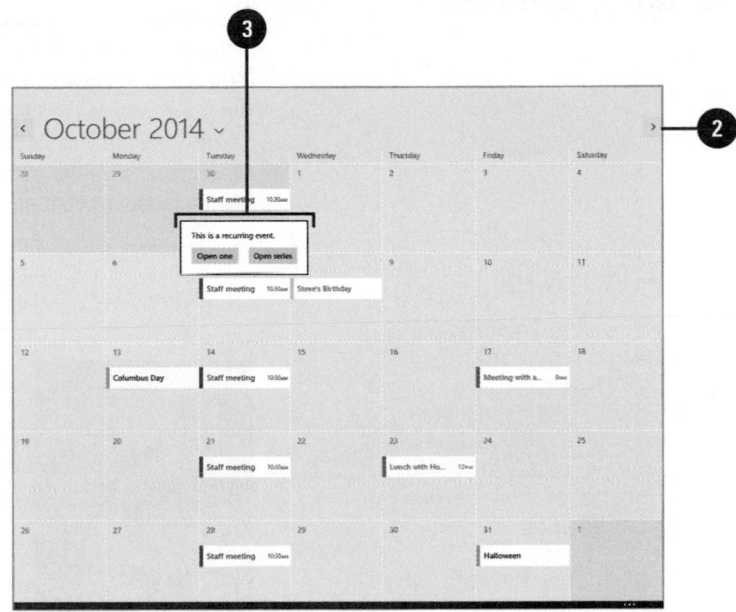

### Did You Know?

*You can get Help in the Calendar app.* In the Calendar app, point to the lower- or upper-right corner and move up or down (on a computer) or swipe left from the right edge of the screen (on a mobile device), click or tap the Settings button on the Charms bar, click or tap Help, and then click or tap a link.

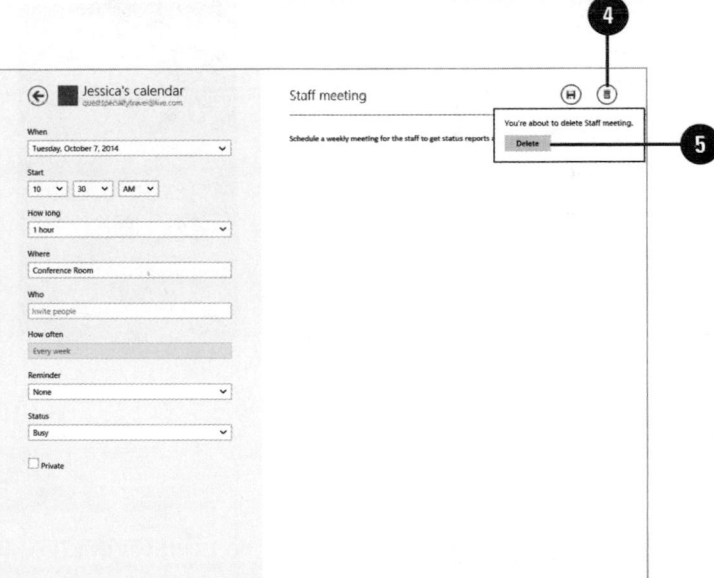

# Changing Calendar Options

With the Options panel in the Calendar app , you can show or hide the main calendar (indicated by the user account name) as well as other calendars from online accounts that are linked to the Calendar app. When you show a calendar, you can change the color of the scheduled events in any of the calendar views. When you hide a calendar, the color option is disabled. Forward and Back buttons (**New!**) appear when you move the pointer. If you want to always show the navigation buttons, you can set an option to do so.

## Change Calendar Options

**1** Click or tap the **Calendar** tile on the Start or Apps screen.

**2** Point to the lower- or upper-right corner and move up or down (on a computer) or swipe left from the right edge of the screen (on a mobile device).

**3** Click or tap the **Settings** button on the Charms bar.

**4** Click or tap **Options** on the Settings panel.

**5** Specify the following calendar options for the available accounts:

◆ **Show or hide a calendar.** Drag the slider to **Show** or **Hide**.

◆ **Change a calendar's color.** Click or tap the calendar's list arrow, and then select a color.

**6** To show or hide Forward and Back buttons (**New!**), drag the slider to **Show** or **Hide**.

**7** To go back to the previous panel, drag the slider to click or tap the **Back** button.

To exit the panel, click or tap off the panel, or press Esc.

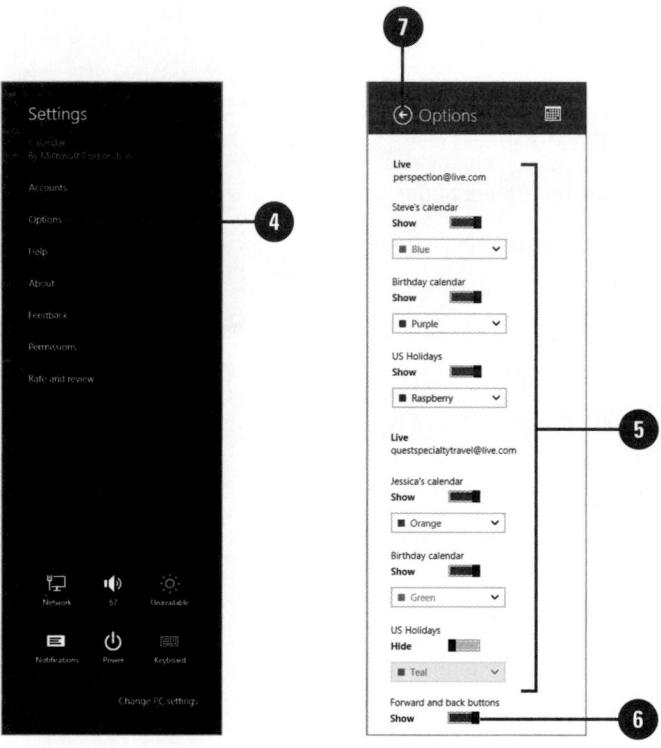

# Exchanging Mail

## Introduction

If you're like many people today who are using the Internet to communicate with friends and business associates, you probably have piles of information (names, email addresses, phone numbers, etc.) that you need often. Unless this information is in one convenient place, and can be accessed immediately, the information becomes ineffective and you become unproductive. The Mail app that comes with Windows 8.1 solves these problems by integrating management and organization tools into one simple system. The Mail app is a powerful program for managing **electronic mail** (known as email), and accessing contact information like names, and email addresses.

Using the Mail app with an Internet connection allows you to accomplish several tasks:

- Create and send email messages

- Manage multiple email accounts

- Use contacts from the People app to address emails messages

- Format email messages with emoticons

- Add signatures to email messages

- Attach a file to an email message

- Manage email messages with folders and favorites

- Remove unwanted email messages with delete, sweep, or junk

- Search for content within email messages

## What You'll Do

**Start the Mail App**

**Get Around the Mail Window**

**Add Mail Accounts**

**Modify Account Settings**

**Compose and Send Email**

**Format Email Messages**

**Create Email Signatures**

**Read and Reply to Email**

**Send and Retrieve a File**

**Manage Email**

**Remove Unwanted Email**

**Search for Email**

**Use Windows Live Essentials**

# Starting the Mail App

Whether you want to exchange email with colleagues or friends, the Mail app that comes with Windows 8.1 provides you with the tools you need. When you setup Windows 8.1, you also setup or specified a Microsoft account, which becomes your default email account in the Mail app. So, when you start the Mail app, you are ready to go. Like other metro apps, you can start the Mail app from the Start screen. You can also add more email accounts, such as Hotmail (Hotmail.com, Live.com, or MSN), Outlook (Microsoft Exchange, Office 365, or Outlook.com), and Google.

## Start the Mail App

1. Click or tap the **Mail** tile on the Start or Apps screen.

   The Mail app window opens in full screen view.

   When you setup Windows 8.1, you also setup or specified a Microsoft account, which becomes your default email account in the Mail app.

### Did You Know?

*You can pin a contact to the Start screen.* In the Mail app, click or tap the contact you want to pin, right-click a blank area of the screen (on a computer) or swipe up from the bottom edge or down from the top edge of the screen (on a mobile device), click or tap the Pin to Start button on the App bar, enter a tile name, and then click or tap Pin to Start

*You can get Help in the Mail app.* In the Mail app, click or tap the Settings button on the Charms bar, click or tap Help, and then click or tap a link.

# Getting Around the Mail Window

After you start the Mail app, you can use the full-screen window to work with email messages. Along the left side of the window is the **Folders pane**, which contains folders to store and manage messages. The Folders pane provides easy access to the Inbox with new messages, Favorites (**New!**) sent from a person, Flagged (**New!**) messages, Newsletters (**New!**) from messages (such as Xbox Live), Social Updates (**New!**) from messages (such as Facebook, Twitter, and Linkedin), and all Folders (Inbox, Drafts, Sent, Outbox, Junk, and Deleted). At the bottom of the Folders pane is a list of active email accounts you can use to switch between them. The **Messages pane** to the right of the Folders pane displays a list email messages. You can click or tap or use the check boxes (**New!**) to select and work with messages. The **Reading pane** displays the contents of the selected message in the Messages pane. At the bottom of the screen is a minimized App bar, which you can access with a click or tap (**New!**).

## Get Around the Map Window

1. Click or tap the **Mail** tile on the Start or Apps screen.

2. To switch email accounts, click or tap an account on the Folders pane.

3. Click or tap a folder in the Folders panel. Click or tap the **Expand/Collapse** arrow to show or hide options.

   ◆ The Folders icon displays a panel with all folders.

   ◆ On first use, the Favorites icon displays a panel, where you can add favorites.

4. Click or tap a message in the Messages pane.

   ◆ **Check Boxes.** Select the message check boxes to use options on the App bar.

   ◆ **Options.** When you point to a message, you can click or tap an icon to **Mark Read/Unread**, **Add/Remove Flag**, or **Delete**.

5. Read the selected message in the Reading panel.

6. To access more options, click or tap the minimized App bar.

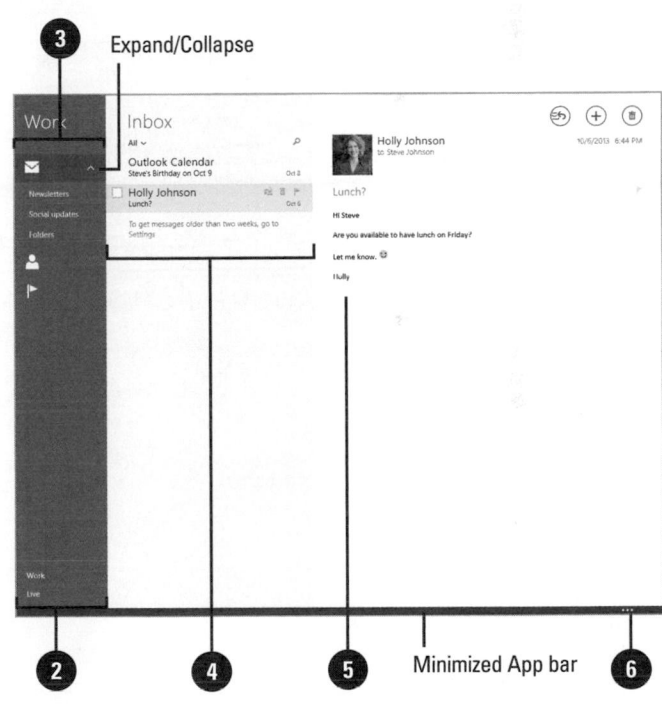

Expand/Collapse

Minimized App bar

# Adding Mail Accounts

When you setup Windows 8.1, you also setup or specified a Microsoft account, which becomes your default email account in the Mail app. So, when you start the Mail app, you are ready to go. However, if you have other email accounts, you can set up multiple accounts in the Mail app. You can add email accounts, such as Hotmail (Hotmail.com, Live.com, or MSN), Outlook (Microsoft Exchange, Office 365, or Outlook.com), and Google. When you add an email account, the Mail app does all the work for you, unless it needs your help with additional information. For some account types, such as Exchange, you need additional information, such as your account name, password, email server type, and the names of your incoming and outgoing email servers from your ISP or network administrator. The Mail app allows you to send and retrieve email messages from different types of email servers, which are the locations where your email is stored before you access it.

## Add a Mail Account

1. Click or tap the **Mail** tile on the Start or Apps screen.

2. Point to the lower- or upper-right corner and move up or down (on a computer) or swipe left from the right edge of the screen (on a mobile device).

3. Click or tap the **Settings** button on the Charms bar.

4. Click or tap **Accounts** on the Settings panel.

5. Click or tap **Add an account** on the Accounts panel.

6. Click or tap an account type.

   ◆ To go back to the previous panel, click or tap the **Back** button.

   ◆ To exit the panel, click or tap off the panel, or press Esc.

7. Enter the email address and password for the account.

8. Click or tap the **Show more details** link.

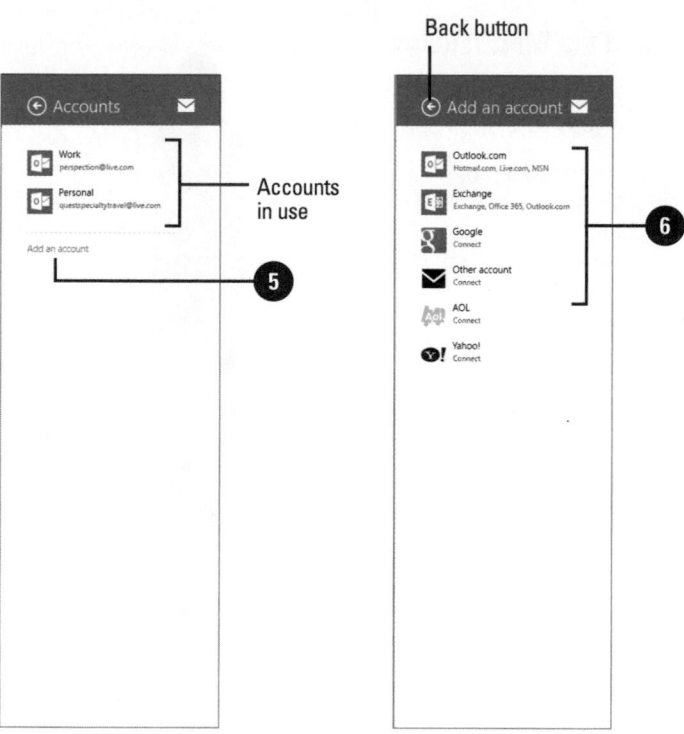

Back button

Accounts in use

**9** Enter the information requested for the account; the information varies depending on the account type.

- ◆ **Username.** Enter the username associated with the account.

- ◆ **Incoming (IMAP) email server.** Specify the incoming web address and port number; see host administrator.

- ◆ **Incoming server requires SSL.** Select if security is required by the host administrator.

- ◆ **Outgoing (SMTP) email server.** Specify the outcoming web address and port number; see host administrator.

- ◆ **Outgoing server requires SSL.** Select if security is required by the host administrator.

- ◆ **Outgoing server requires authentication.** Select if security authentication is required by the host administrator.

- ◆ **Use the same username and password to send and receive email.** Select to use the same user authentication for the incoming and outgoing server.

**10** Click or tap **Connect**.

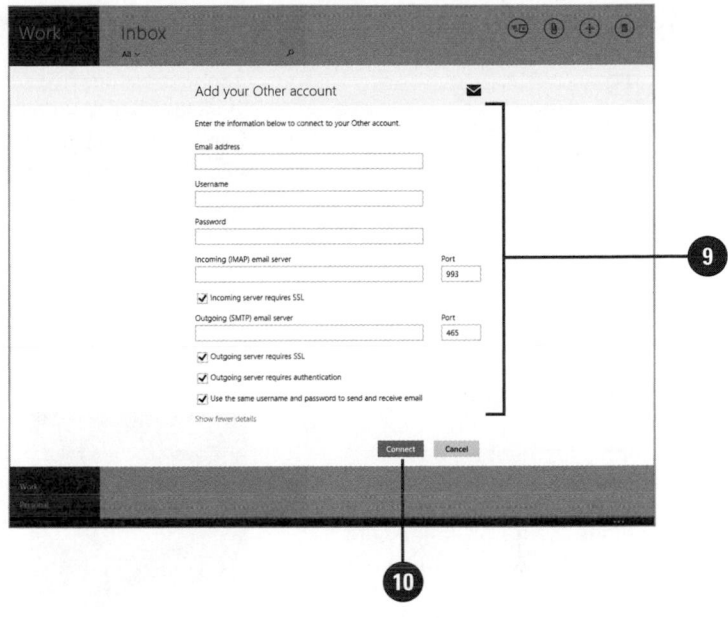

## For Your Information

### How Do I Choose an Email Server?

The Mail app supports three types of incoming email servers: **POP3** (Post Office Protocol), **IMAP** (Internet Message Access Protocol), and **HTTP** (Hypertext Transfer Protocol). A protocol is a set of rules and standards that control the transmission of content, format, sequencing, and error management for information over the Internet or network much like rules of the road govern the way you drive. POP3 servers allow you to access email messages from a single Inbox folder, while IMAP servers allow you to access multiple folders. HTTP servers are used on web sites, and allow you to send and receive email messages on a web site. When you use POP3 or IMAP email servers, you also need to provide an outgoing email server. **SMTP** (Simple Mail Transfer Protocol) is generally used to send messages between email servers.

# Modifying Account Settings

With the Mail app, you want to change options for the default Microsoft account or for any ones that you have added. You can change email account options by using an accounts panel, which you can access from the Settings panel on the Charms bar. In an accounts panel, you can change the account name, specify how and when to download email, specify whether to synchronize content—such as email, contacts, or calendar—with this account, whether to show newsletters (**New!**) or social updates (**New!**) in the folders pane, how to show email notifications (**New!**), specify whether to use an email signature at the end of a message, show or hide email notifications for this account, or remove this account.

## Modify Account Settings

1. Click or tap the **Mail** tile on the Start or Apps screen.

2. Point to the lower- or upper-right corner and move up or down (on a computer) or swipe left from the right edge of the screen (on a mobile device).

3. Click or tap the **Settings** button on the Charms bar.

4. Click or tap **Accounts** on the Settings panel.

5. Click or tap the account that you want to change.

6. Enter the information requested for the account; the information varies depending on the account type.

   - **Account name.** Specify a name for the account in the Mail app.

   - **Download new email.** Click or tap the list arrow, and then select an option to download new email.

   - **Download email from.** Click or tap the list arrow, and then select a download interval option.

   - **Content to sync.** Select or clear the check boxes to enable or disable synchronizing content type (such as Email, Contacts, or Calendar).

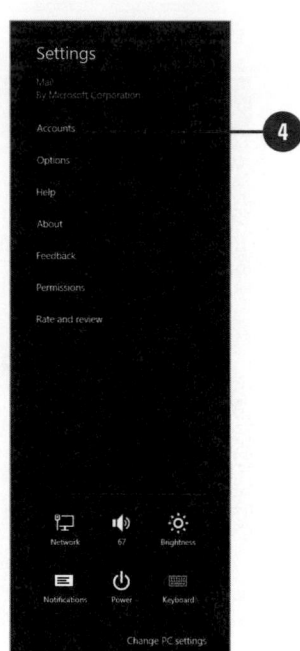

- **Organize your email.** Select or clear the check boxes (**New!**) to show or hide email newsletters or social updates separately.

- **Show email notification.** Select an option (**New!**) to show notifications: All email, Email from favorites, or Never.

- **Automatically download external images.** Drag the slider to On or Off.

- **Use an email signature.** Drag the slider to Yes or No. Enter the a signature.

- **Email address.** Identifies the email address for the account.

- **Password.** Enter the access password for the email address account.

- **Remove account.** Click or tap to remove the account.

    If you want to remove the default Microsoft account, you need to go Change PC Settings on the Settings panel.

7 To go back to the previous panel, click or tap the **Back** button.

To exit the panel, click or tap off the panel, or press Esc.

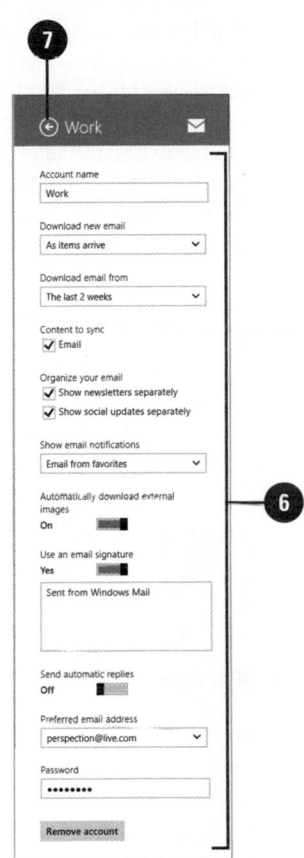

# Composing and Sending Email

Email is becoming the primary form of written communication for many people. Email messages in the Mail app follow a standard memo format, with fields for the sender, recipient, and subject of the message. To send an email, you need to enter the recipient's email address, type a subject, then type the message itself. The subject is the first information the recipient sees about the email, so it should provide a short, concise summary of the message content. For an added touch, you can add a signature at the end of a new email. You can send the same email to more than one individual. Before you send the email, you can set a priority level (high, normal, or low) to convey the message's importance. When you create a new message, Mail designates it as a draft (**New!**) (which you can save) until you send it.

## Compose and Send an Email

1 Click or tap the **Mail** tile on the Start or Apps screen.

2 Click or tap the **New** button.

> **TIMESAVER** *Press Ctrl+ N to create a new email message.*

3 If you have multiple accounts, click or tap the **Accounts** list arrow, and then select the From account.

- ◆ Click or tap the **More** link, if necessary, to show all the options.

4 Enter an email address (separate by a semi-colon) or name. As you type, any address or name matches appear in a drop-down menu.

Or click or tap the **Add** button for the To, Cc, or Bcc to select contacts from the People app, and then click or tap **Add**.

- ◆ **To.** Use if you want the recipient to receive the message.

- ◆ **Cc (Carbon Copy).** Use if you want the recipient to receive a copy of the message.

- ◆ **Bcc (Blind Carbon Copy).** Use if you want the recipient to receive a copy of the message but not be listed as a recipient on any copy of the message.

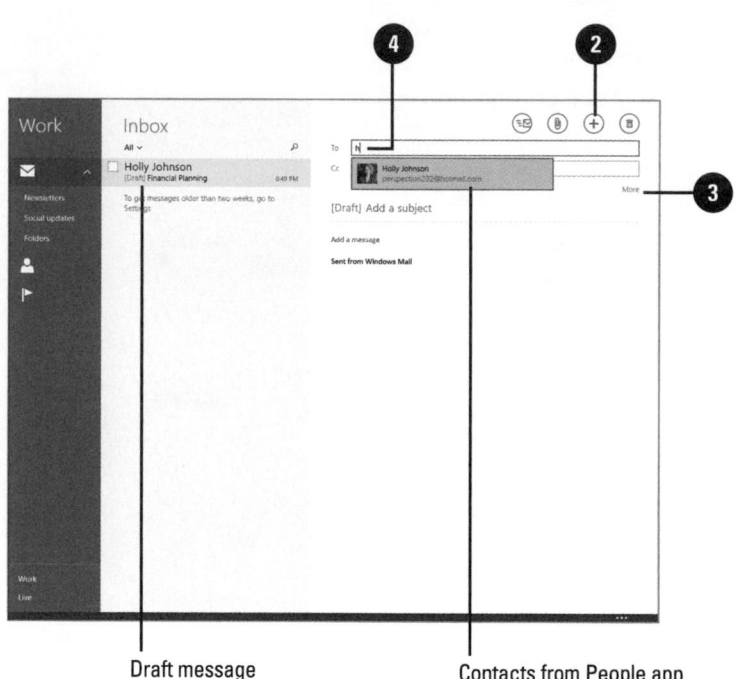

Draft message                    Contacts from People app

**5** If you want, click or tap the **Priority** list arrow, and then click or tap **High priority**, **Normal priority**, or **Low priority**.

**6** Click or tap in the **Add a subject** box, and then enter a brief description of your message.

**7** Click or tap in the **Add a message** box, and then type the text of your message.

◆ If a red line appears under a word, right-click or tap-hold the misspelled word, and then click or tap a suggested word, **Add to dictionary**, or **Ignore**.

**8** If you want, select the text you want to format and then use the commands on the App bar to customize your message.

**9** Click or tap the **Send** button.

The email message is sent, and then Home Mail screen appears.

◆ Save draft. or Delete draft. Click or tap the **Save draft** button on the App bar.

◆ Delete draft. Click or tap the **Delete** button.

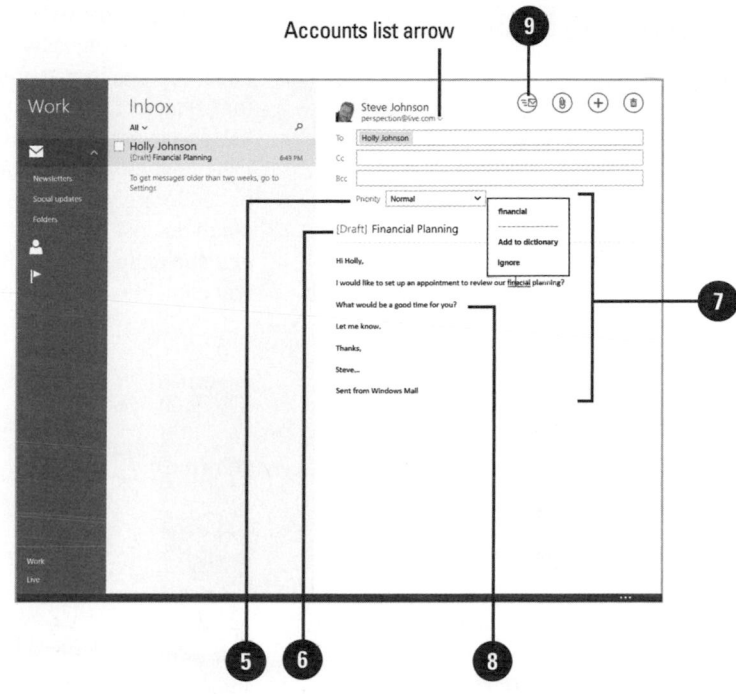

Accounts list arrow

### Did You Know?

*You can view a saved draft message to finish and send later.* In the Mail app, click or tap Folders in the Folders pane, and then click or tap the Drafts folder (**New!**). Select the email message to edit it, and then click or tap the Send button or Save draft button on the App bar.

## For Your Information

### Checking the Spelling in Email

Before you send an email message, you should spell check the text and read through the content to make sure your spelling is accurate and your content conveys the message you want to the recipient(s). The Mail app automatically checks your email message as you type it. When a red line appears under a word or phrase, the app dictionary doesn't recognize it. You can correct the word or phrase spelling, add the word or phrase to the dictionary, or ignore it.

# Formatting Email Messages

When you create an email message, you can quickly enter the text you want to send. However, if you want to add some emphasis to your message, you can format it with options on the App bar. The options include font, highlight (**New!**), bold, italic, underline, color, bulleted or numbered list, and hyperlink (**New!**). In addition, you can insert graphical symbols called **emoticons**, such as a happy face, which help convey your emotions. Before you can format text, you need to select it or click or tap to place the insertion point first. If you don't like the formatting changes, you can undo (reverse) it or clear formatting. If you want to multitask, you can open a message in a side by side window (**New!**).

## Format an Email Message

1. Click or tap the **Mail** tile on the Start or Apps screen.

2. Click or tap the **New** button.

3. Address the email message, and then enter a subject.

4. In the Message box, select the text you want to format or click or tap the place the insertion point.

5. Right-click a blank area of the screen (on a computer) or swipe up from the bottom edge or down from the top edge of the screen (on a mobile device).

6. Click or tap the formatting button you want on the App bar.

   ◆ **Font.** Select a font type and size.

   ◆ **Text color.** Formats text in the selected color.

   ◆ **Highlight**, **Bold**, **Italic**, or **Underline.** Formats text in highlight, bold, italic, or underline.

   ◆ **List.** Creates a bulleted or numbered list.

   ◆ **Emoticons.** Opens a panel where you select an icon.

   ◆ **Link.** Creates a hyperlink.

   ◆ **Open in a new window.** Opens message in side by side window.

   ◆ **More.** Access commands Undo, Redo, and Clear formatting.

7. Type any text, as desired.

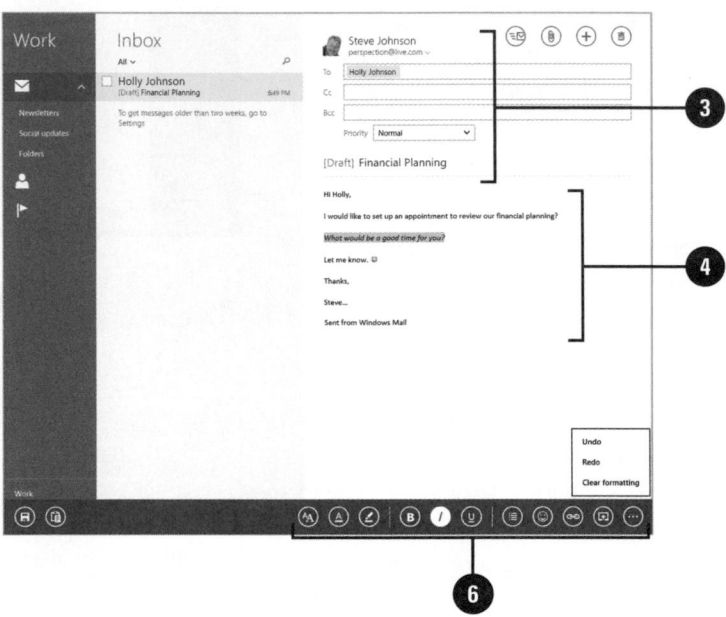

## For Your Information

### Setting the Default Message Font

You can set a default message font, size, and color for new email messages. Click or tap the Settings button on the Charms bar, click or tap Options (**New!**), and then select a font, font size, and font color. to exit the panel, click or tap off the panel or press Esc.

# Creating Email Signatures

Instead of typing the same ending signature and other personal or business card information, such as address, phone number, or web site, at the end of your email messages, you can have the Mail app automatically insert it for you. You can enable and create a signature for each email account used in the Mail app. You can enable and create a signature by using an accounts panel, which you can access from the Settings panel on the Charms bar.

## Use an Email Signature

1. Click or tap the **Mail** tile on the Start or Apps screen.

2. Point to the lower- or upper-right corner and move up or down (on a computer) or swipe left from the right edge of the screen (on a mobile device).

3. Click or tap the **Settings** button on the Charms bar.

4. Click or tap **Accounts** on the Settings panel.

5. Click or tap the account that you want to change.

6. Drag the Use an email signature slider to **Yes**.

7. Enter the signature you want to use for this account.

8. To go back to the previous panel, click or tap the **Back** button.

   To exit the panel, click or tap off the panel, or press Esc.

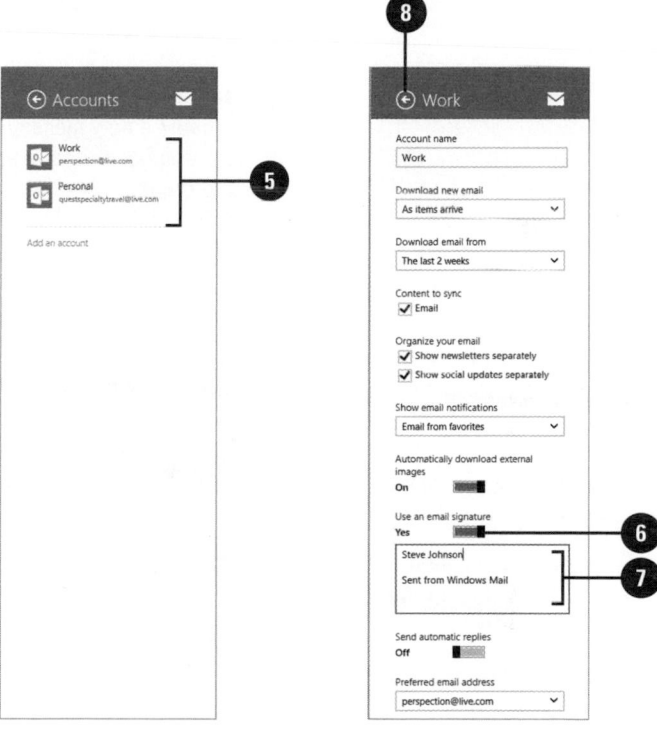

# Reading and Replying to Email

You can receive email anytime—even when your PC is turned off. You can retrieve your email manually or set the Mail app to do so automatically. When you start the Mail app, the program checks for new email. It continues to check periodically while the app is open. New messages appear in boldface in the Inbox along with any messages you haven't moved or deleted. Message flags may appear next to a message, which indicate a priority, the need for follow up, or an attachment. The Mail app blocks images and other potentially harmful content from automatically downloading in an email message from unknown people. Blocked items are replaced with a red "x". Any email messages identified as junk mail is automatically moved to the Junk folder. You can respond to a message in two ways: reply to it, which creates a new message addressed to the sender(s) and other recipients; or forward it, which creates a new message you can send to someone else. In either case, the original message appears in the response and all related messages are grouped together in a conversation (**New!**). When you reply to a message that had an attachment, the attachment isn't returned to the original sender. You can forward the message to the original sender if you need to send the attachment back.

## Open and Read an Email

1. Click or tap the **Mail** tile on the Start or Apps screen.

2. Click or tap the account you want to work to use.

3. To manually check for email messages, click or tap the **Sync** button on the App bar.

4. Click or tap the **Inbox** folder for the mail account you want.

5. Click or tap an email message to read it in the Reading pane. If you select a conversation, it expands or collapses to display or hide the conversation email messages.

   ◆ **Selection Mode.** Select the message check box (**New!**) to select it and display the App bar.

6. To mark an email message as unread, click or tap the **Mark unread** button on the App bar.

7. To flag a message for action, click the **Flag** button on the App bar.

Click or tap to expand/collapse conversation

Line indicates a conversation

Selection mode toggled on

## Reply to an Email

1. In the Mail app, click or tap the email message you want to reply to.

2. Click or tap the account you want to work to use.

3. Click or tap the **Respond** button, and then click or tap **Reply** to respond to the sender only, or click the **Reply all** to respond to the sender and to all recipients.

   **TIMESAVER** *Press Ctrl+R to reply to the message author.*

4. Click or tap the **Change** link, if needed, and then add or delete names from the To or the Cc box.

5. Type your message.

6. Click the **Send** button.

Reply email (RE:)

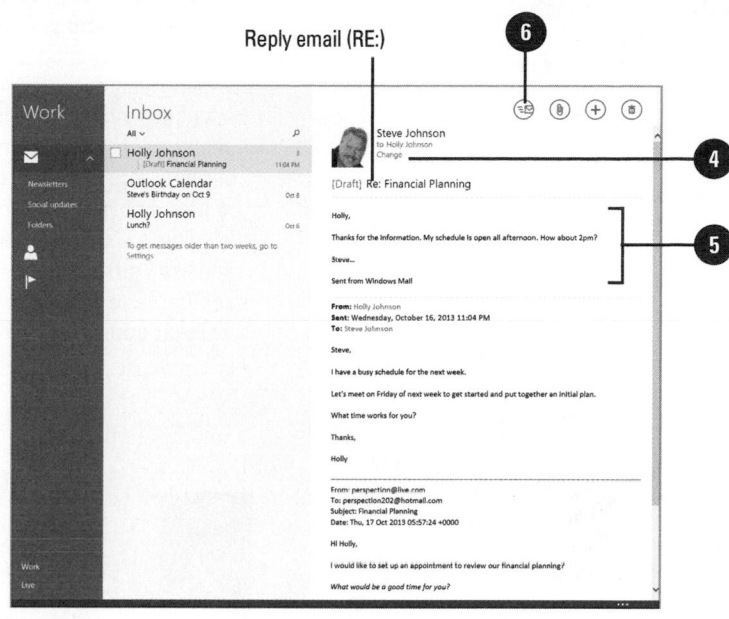

## Forward an Email

1. In the Mail app, click or tap the email message you want to forward.

2. Click or tap the account you want to work to use.

3. Click or tap the **Respond** button, and then click or tap the **Forward**.

4. Type the name(s) of the recipient(s), or click the **Add** button for To or Cc, and then select the recipient(s).

5. Type your message.

6. Click the **Send** button.

Forward email (FW:)

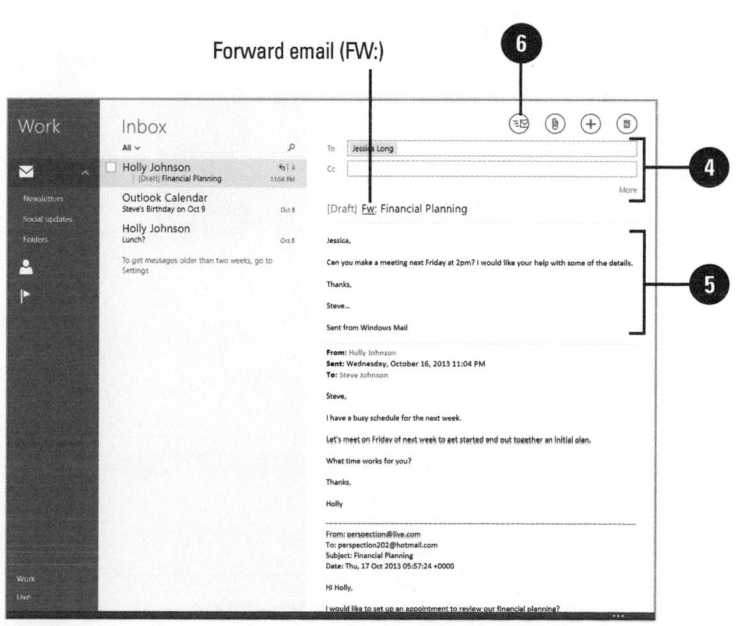

# Sending and Retrieving a File

With the Mail app, you can use email to easily share a file, such as a picture or a document by attaching it to an email from a folder, network, device (such as a camera), or SkyDrive. Upon receiving the email, the recipient can open the file in the program that created it or save it. Make sure you know and trust the sender before you open it, because it might contain a virus or other security threat. It's important to keep your antivirus software up-to-date. If an attachment is considered safe, the Mail app makes it completely available to you. Examples of safe attachments are text files (.txt) and graphic files, such as JPEGs (.jpg) and GIFs (.gif). Beware of potentially unsafe attachments, such as an executable program (.exe), screensavers (.scr) or script files (including .vbs) that could put your device at risk of problems.

## Send a File in an Email

1. In the Mail app, compose a new message or reply to an existing message.

   **IMPORTANT** *Some ISPs have trouble sending large attachments; check with your ISP.*

2. Click the **Attachments** button.

3. Click or tap the **Files** list arrow, and then select the drive and folder that contains the file you want to attach.

4. Click or tap to select the files you want to attach and send.

5. Click or tap **Attach**.

6. Click the **Send** button.

Attached file

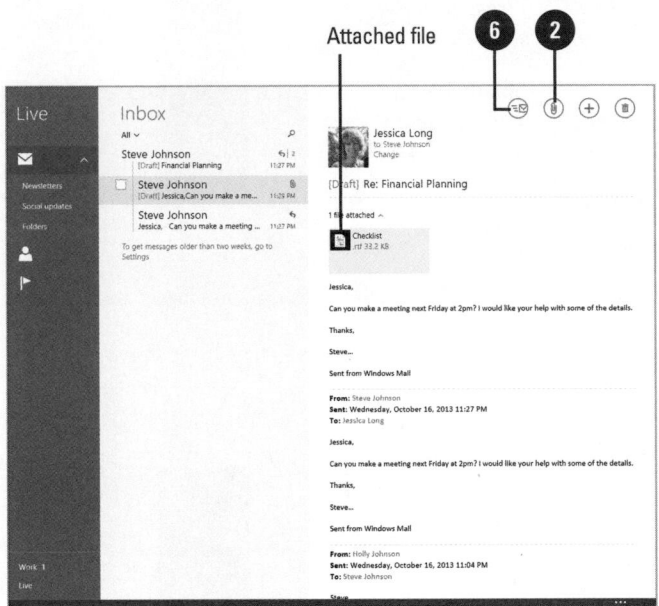

### Did You Know?

*You can set message conversation options.* In the Mail app, click or tap the Settings button on the Charms bar, click or tap Options, and then drag the slider on or off to group messages by conversation (**New!**) or show messages from sent items in conversations (**New!**).

## Download a File in an Email

① In the Mail app, select the message with the attached file.

**IMPORTANT** *If you're not sure of the source of an attachment, don't open it, because it might contain a virus or worm. Be sure to use anti-virus software.*

② Click or tap the **Download** link, if available.

The file is downloaded to your device.

### See Also

*See "Avoiding Viruses and Other Harmful Attacks" on page 360 for information on how to avoid getting a virus and other harmful threats.*

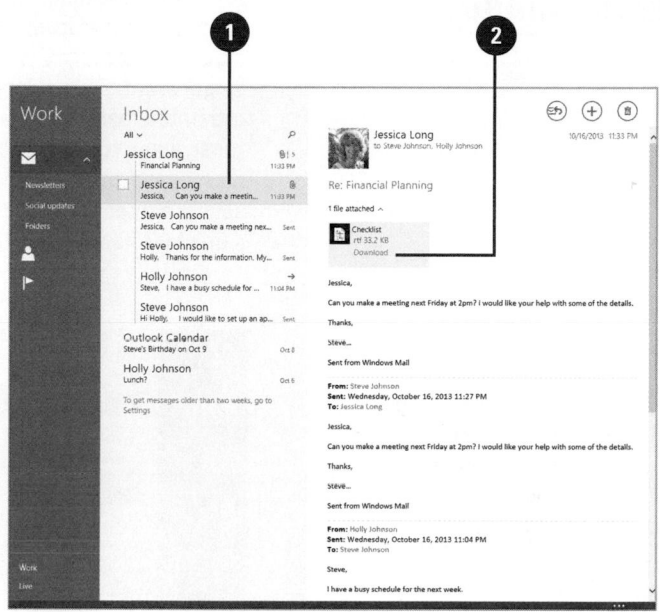

## Open or Save Files in an Email

① In the Mail app, select the message with the attached and downloaded file.

② To open the file with the default app, click or tap the attached file.

③ To open with or save, right-click or tap-hold the attached file, and then select any of the following:

◆ **Open with.** Select an option to specify how to open the attached file.

◆ **Save.** Enter a name for the file or use the existing one, use the Files list arrow to specify a location, and then click or tap Save.

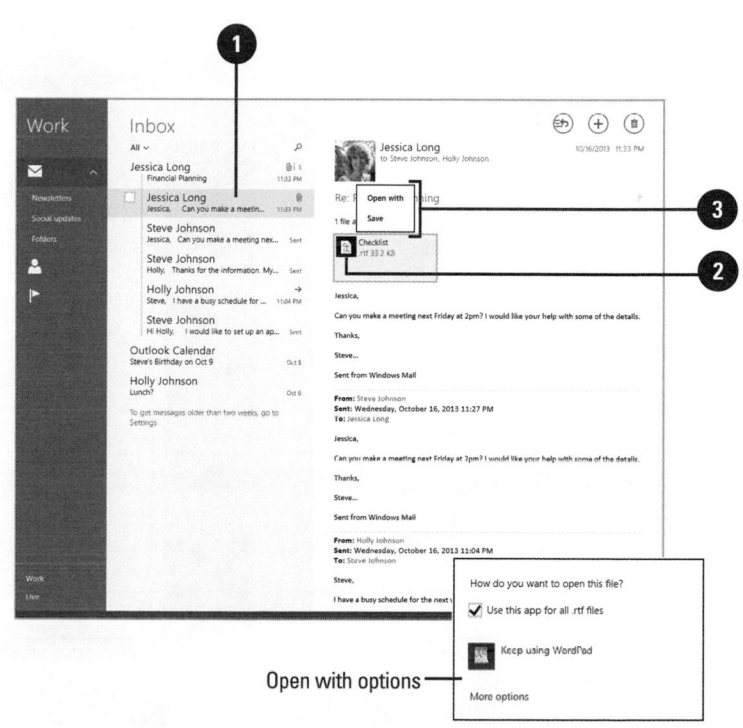

Open with options

# Managing Email

A common problem with using email is an overcrowded Inbox. To keep your Inbox organized, you should create folders or subfolders and then move the messages you want to the folders or delete messages you no longer want. Storing incoming messages in other folders and deleting unwanted messages make it easier to see the new messages you receive and to keep track of important messages. If you receive email messages from the same person, you can make them a favorite (**New!**) so you can easily view them from the Folders pane. You can also do the same for folders (**New!**), so you can access them more easily.

## Create a Folder and Move Emails to a Folder

1. In the Mail app, click or tap the **Folders** folder in the Folders pane, and then click or tap the folder where you want the new folder.

    ◆ Click or tap the **Expand/Collapse** arrow to show or hide options.

2. To create a folder, click the **Manage folders** button on the App bar, click or tap **Create folder** or **Create subfolder**, enter a folder name, and then click or tap **OK**.

3. Navigate to a folder, and then select the email messages that you want to move.

4. Click or tap the **Move** button on the App bar.

5. Click or tap the folder in the Folders pane where you want to move the email messages.

### See Also

See "Removing Unwanted Email" on page 174 for more information on deleting, sweeping, or junking email messages.

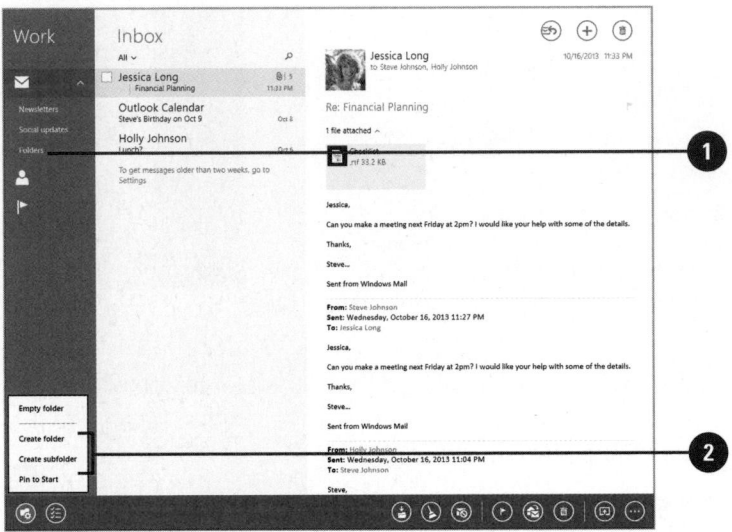

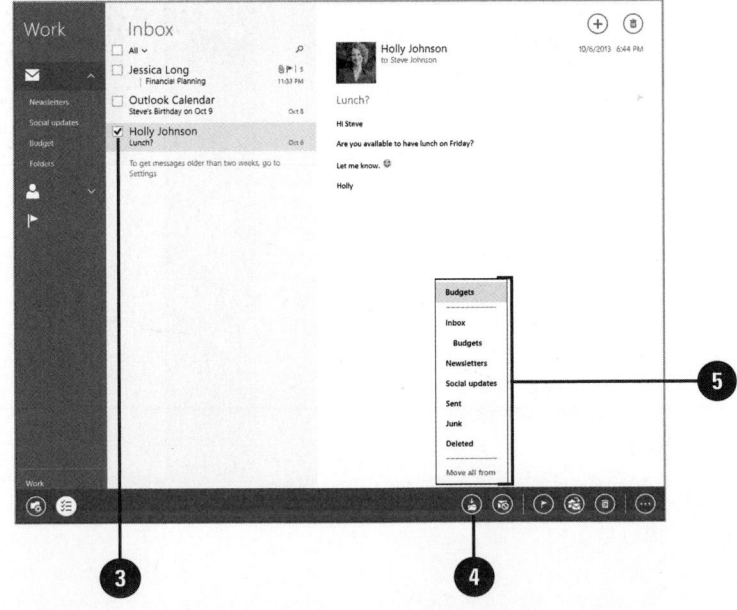

## Make a Folder a Favorite

1. In the Mail app, click or tap the **Folders** folder in the Folders pane.

2. Click or tap the **Star** icon (becomes filled) on the All Folders panel.

   The folder appears on the Folders pane under the Folders icon where you can quickly access it.

3. To remove a favorite, click or tap the **Star** icon (becomes unfilled) on the All Folders panel.

Favorite folder

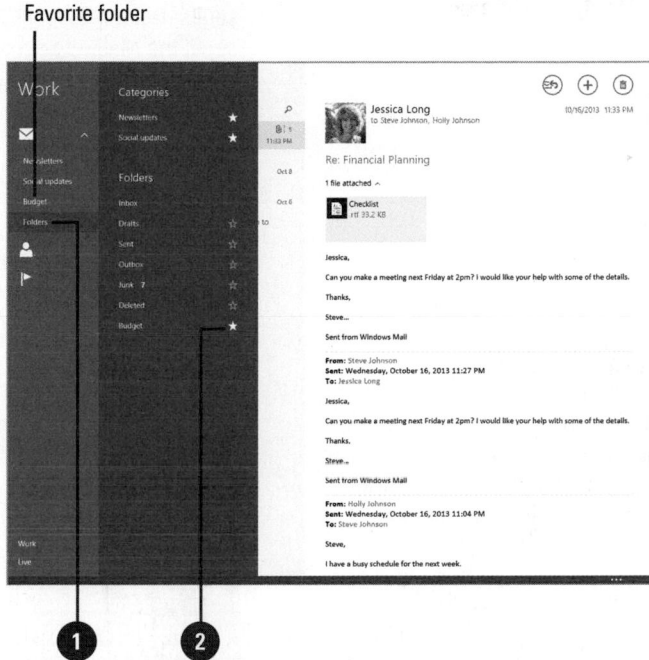

## Make a Contact a Favorite

1. In the Mail app, click or tap **Expand/Collapse** arrow for the **Favorites** folder in the Folders pane, and then click or tap **People**.

   ◆ **On First Use.** Click or tap the Favorites folder in the Folders pane.

2. To add a favorite contact, click or tap **Browse contacts**, select a contact, and then click or tap **Add**.

3. To show the favorite contact on the Folders pane, click or tap the **Star** icon (becomes filled) on the Favorites panel.

4. Click or tap the **Favorites** folder to show all email messages for all favorites or a contact name to show only its email messages.

# Removing Unwanted Email

The Mail app provides three ways to remove unwanted email messages: Delete, Sweep (**New!**), or Junk. When you delete an email message, the Mail app simply moves it into the Deleted items folder. If you want to recover a deleted message, you just have to retrieve it from the Deleted items folder. To get rid of a message permanently, you need to open the Deleted items folder, select the message, and then click Delete. If you want to delete messages from a specific person—past, present, or future—you can sweep (**New!**) them out (only available for Outlook.com). If you receive junk mail, you can mark it as junk, so it's automatically moved into the Junk folder, which you can unjunk with the Not Junk button on the App bar from the Junk folder if you wanted.

## Delete, Sweep, or Junk Unwanted Email

① In the Mail app, select one or more unwanted email messages; for a sweep, select from one person.

② Do any of the following:

   ◆ **Delete.** Click or tap the **Delete** button on the App bar or in the upper-right corner to move it to the Deleted folder.

   **TIMESAVER** *Press Delete or Ctrl+D to delete the message(s).*

   ◆ **Sweep.** Click or tap the **Sweep** button on the App bar, select the options you want, and then click or tap **Sweep**.

   ◆ **Junk.** Click or tap the **Junk** button on the App bar to move it to the Junk folder.

③ Click or tap the **Folders** folder in the Folders pane, and then click or tap **Deleted** or **Junk** folder on the All Folders pane.

④ Do any of the following to permanently delete messages:

   ◆ **Delete Selected.** Select the email messages, and then click or tap the **Delete** button.

   ◆ **Delete All.** Click the **Manage folders** button on the App bar, click or tap **Empty folder**, and then click or tap **Yes**.

Delete button

# Searching for Email

If you can't find a message, you can use the Search box in the Mail app to quickly find it. You can access the Search box by clicking or tapping the Search button at the top of the Messages pane. You can search a specific folder or all folders. When you perform an email search, the results appear in the Messages pane. If you searched a specific folder and want to search all the folders, you can easily use the Search in all folders link. When you're finished working with the search results, you can click or tap the Close button in the Messages pane to cancel the search.

## Search for Email

1. In the Mail app, navigate to the folder you want to search. If you want to search all folder, you can use the Inbox.

2. Click or tap the **Search** button in the Messages pane.

3. Click or tap the **Search** list arrow, and then click or tap the folder name or **All folders**.

4. Type the text you want to search for in the Search box.

5. Click or tap the **Search** button or press Enter.

   The results for the search appears in the Messages pane.

6. If you searched a folder and want to search all the folders, click or tap the **Search in all folders** link.

7. To cancel the search, click or tap the **Close** button (x) in the Messages pane.

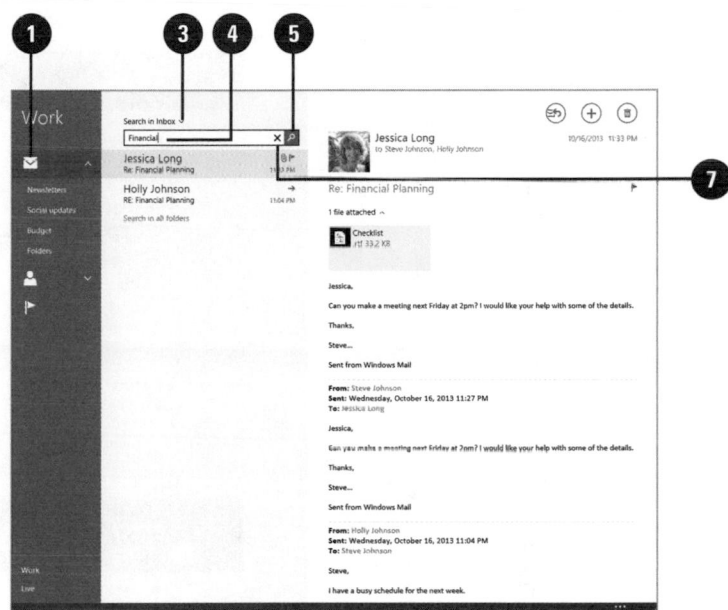

# Using Windows Live Essentials

If you want a more full featured Mail program, you can download and install Windows Live Essentials, which is a set of programs that allows you to communicate on the web and work with and share media. The Windows Live programs include Microsoft SkyDrive, Mail, Messenger, Photo Gallery, Movie Maker, and Writer. Many of these programs came installed along with Windows Vista, however in Windows 8.1, you need to download and install them. Installing the programs separately allows you to get and use the latest versions of the software. After you install Windows Live Essentials, you can access the Windows Live programs from the Start or Apps screen.

## Download and Install Windows Live Essentials

1. In Internet Explorer, visit the Windows Live Essentials web site at the following address:

   *http://download.live.com*

2. Click or tap **Download now**.

3. Click **Run** or **Save** to run the setup program or save it to your PC. If you click Save, select a location, click **Save**, and then click **Run**.

   The Windows Live setup program starts.

4. Click or tap **Choose the programs you want to install**, and then select the check boxes with the Windows Live programs you want to install.

5. Click or tap **Install**.

6. Follow the on-screen instructions to select additional tools and complete the installation.

7. When you're done, click or tap **Close**.

8. To access the Windows Live programs from the Start or Apps screen.

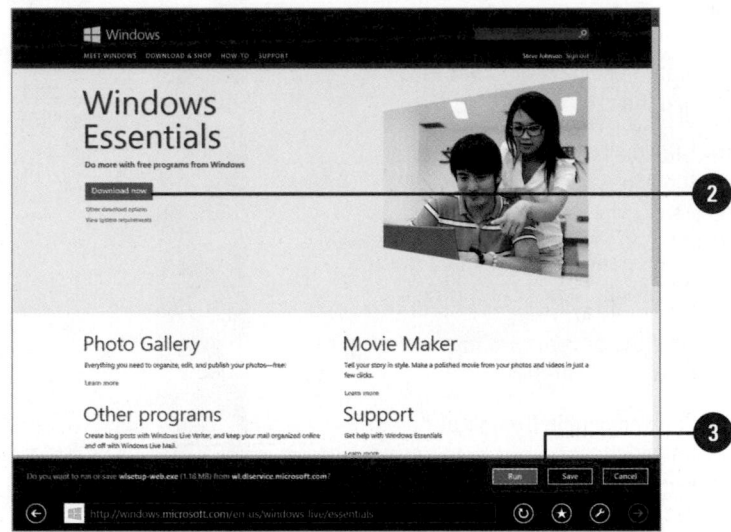

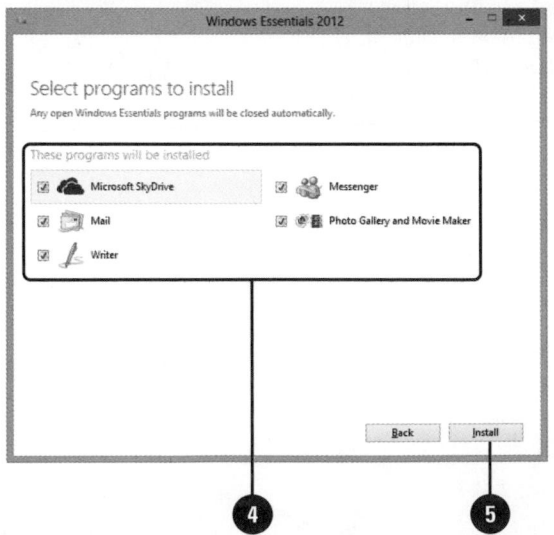

# Exchanging Calls and Instant Messages

## Introduction

Windows makes communicating with others over the Internet easier than ever with the Skype app. You can talk to others over the Internet (like you do on a telephone) and exchange instant messages. An **instant message** is an online typewritten conversation in real time between two or more contacts. Unlike an email message, instant messages require both parties to be online (like a phone call), and the communication is instantaneous. With the Skype app, you can send instant messages to any of your contacts from the People app or Skype who are online and have conversations with friends.

Using the Skype app with an Internet connection allows you to accomplish several tasks:

◆ Manage messaging accounts

◆ Make audio and video phone calls

◆ Use contacts to address instant messages

◆ Create and send instant messages

◆ Add emoticons to instant messages

◆ Invite others to instant messages

◆ Send files in instant messages

## What You'll Do

**Start the Skype App**

**View the Skype App Window**

**Modify Skype Profile Settings**

**Change Skype Options**

**Add Skype Contacts**

**Make Phone Calls**

**Send and Receive Instant Messages**

**Work with Contacts**

# Starting the Skype App

Whether you want to exchange calls (audio and video) or instant messages with colleagues and friends, the Skype app (**New!**) that comes with Windows 8.1 provides you with the tools you need. Like other metro apps, you can start the Skype app from the Start or Apps screen. If you have not signed in to Skype, you'll be prompted to enter an existing Skype account or specify your Microsoft account as a new user. During the process, an existing Skype account gets merged with your Microsoft account, which is what you'll use in the future to sign in.

## Start the Skype App and Sign In or Out

1. Click or tap the **Skype** tile (**New!**) on the Start or Apps screen.

   The Skype app window opens in full screen view.

2. If prompted, click or tap **Allow** or **Block** to use your webcam and microphone.

3. If you're not signed into Skype, click or tap **I have a Skype account** or **I'm new to skype**, and then follow the on-screen instructions to enter a username and password to complete the process.

   An existing Skype account is merged with your Microsoft account, which is what you'll use in the future to sign in.

4. To sign out and in with another account, click or tap **Settings** on the Charms bar, click or tap **Profile**, click or tap **Sign out**, and then click or tap another Microsoft account.

   **IMPORTANT** *In order to use another account, you must sign into Windows first.*

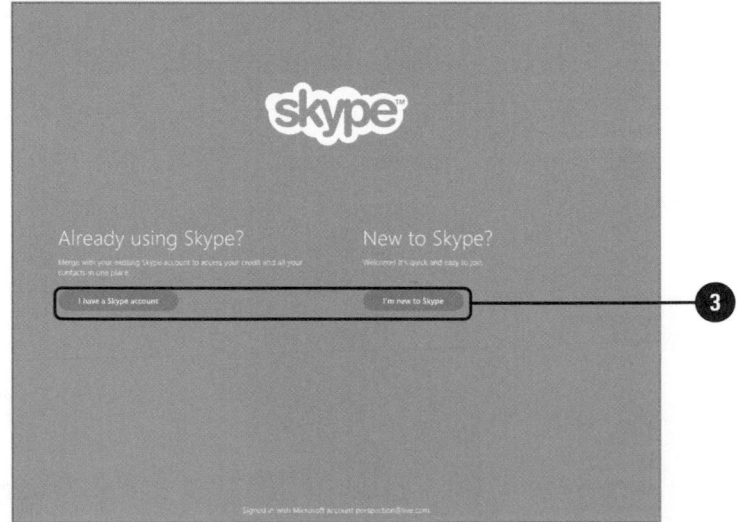

# Viewing the Skype App Window

**Options**
Buttons to make call or perform searches.

**Favorites**
Displays your favorites people for easy access.

**Status**
Displays your online status for other people.

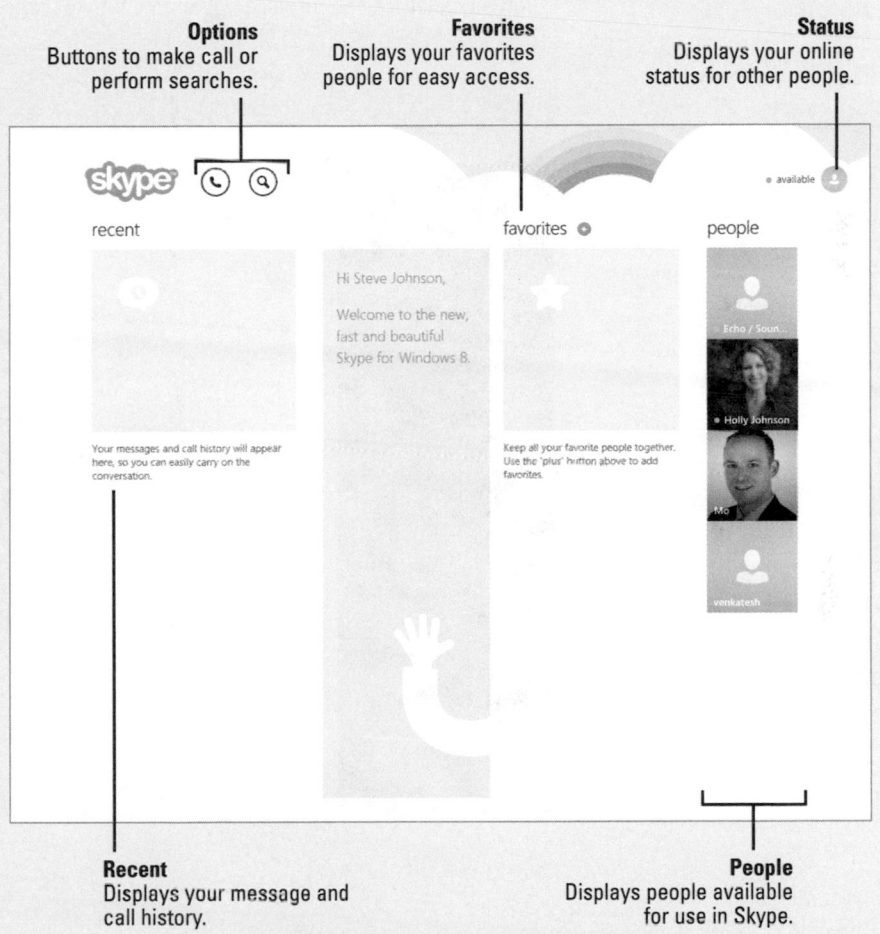

recent

Hi Steve Johnson,

Welcome to the new, fast and beautiful Skype for Windows 8.

Your messages and call history will appear here, so you can easily carry on the conversation.

favorites

Keep all your favorite people together. Use the 'plus' button above to add favorites.

people

Echo / Soun...

Holly Johnson

Mo

venkatesh

available

**Recent**
Displays your message and call history.

**People**
Displays people available for use in Skype.

# Modifying Skype Profile Settings

With the Skype app, you want to change Skype profile options (**New!**) and online account settings (**New!**). You can change profile options by using the Profile panel, which you can access from the Settings panel on the Charms bar. In a Profile panel, you can change your Skype picture, enter a mood message, change your online status, and access your account settings online with your web browser. With your online account, you can change personal and contact details, link and unlink accounts (such as Microsoft or Facebook), set notifications, change billing & payments, view usage history, and add more Skype features, such as caller ID, call forwarding, and voice messages.

## Modify Skype Profile Settings

1. Click or tap the **Skype** tile on the Start or Apps screen.

2. Point to the upper-right corner and move down (on a computer) or swipe left from the right edge of the screen (on a mobile device).

3. Click or tap the **Settings** button on the Charms bar.

4. Click or tap **Profile** on the Settings panel.

   **TIMESAVER** *Click the Status info on the Home screen to open the Profile panel.*

5. To change your picture, click or tap the placeholder or existing picture, navigate to and select a picture, and then click or tap **Open**.

6. To enter a mood message, enter the text in the box.

7. To change your status, click or tap **available** or **invisible**.

8. To go back to the previous panel, click or tap the **Back** button.

   To exit the panel, click or tap off the panel, or press Esc.

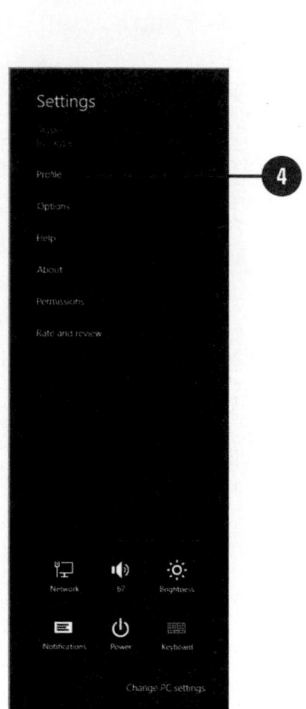

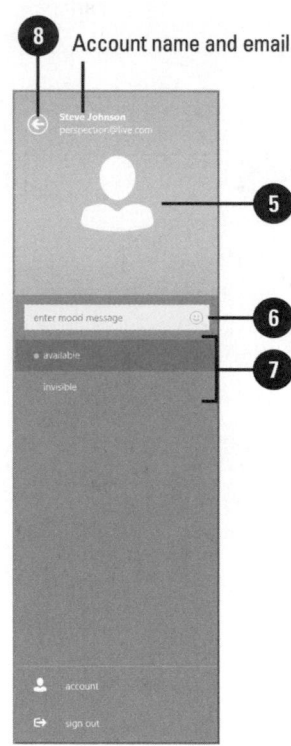

Account name and email

## Modify Skype Account Settings

**1** Click or tap the **Skype** tile on the Start or Apps screen.

**2** Point to the upper-right corner and move down (on a computer) or swipe left from the right edge of the screen (on a mobile device).

**3** Click or tap the **Settings** button on the Charms bar.

**4** Click or tap **Profile** on the Settings panel.

**5** Click or tap **Account** on the Profile panel.

Your default web browser opens, displaying your Skype account.

**6** Click or tap any of the following links or tiles:

◆ **Profile.** Enter personal information and contact details.

◆ **Account settings.** Change account information and notification settings.

◆ **Billing & payments.** View billing and payment data.

◆ **View usage history.** View usage minutes.

◆ **Caller ID.** Set up for caller ID.

◆ **Call forwarding.** Use call forwarding for a low fee.

◆ **Skype To Go.** Call from mobile or landline numbers.

◆ **Premium features.** Buy more features, like group video, for a monthly fee.

◆ **Skype Number.** Get a Skype number to use from mobile or landline phones.

◆ **Voice messages.** Activate voice messages.

Account name and email

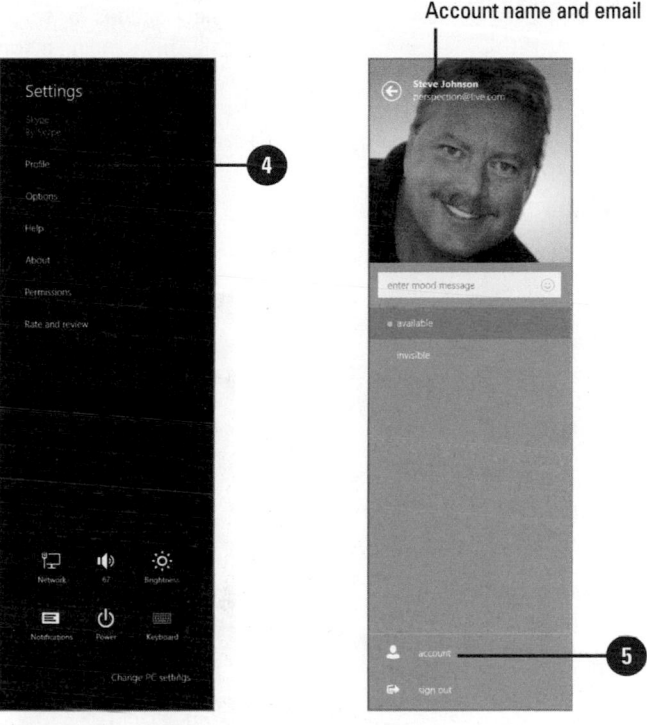

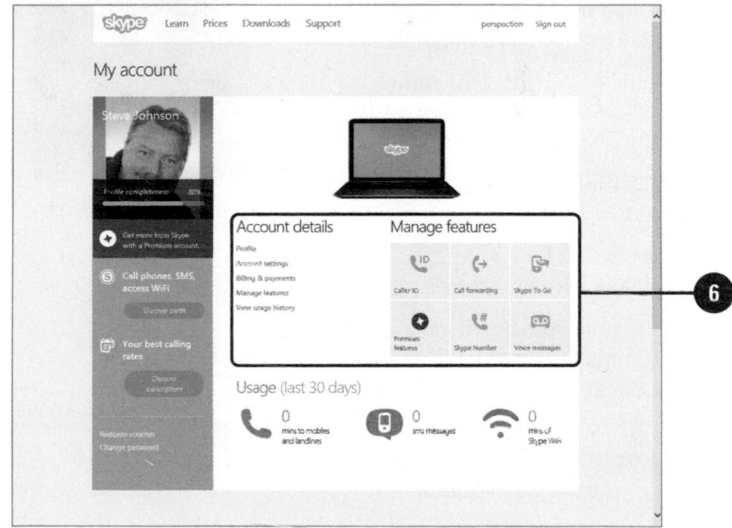

# Changing Skype Options

Before you get started with the Skype app (**New!**), it's a good idea to select options for settings audio and video hardware as well as making calls and sending instant messages while maintaining your privacy. You can use the Options panel (**New!**) in the Skype app to select the options you want. For audio, you can select an attached microphone and speakers and for video, you can select an attached camera.

## Change Audio and Video Options

1. Click or tap the **Skype** tile on the Start or Apps screen.

2. Point to the upper-right corner and move down (on a computer) or swipe left from the right edge of the screen (on a mobile device).

3. Click or tap the **Settings** button on the Charms bar.

4. Click or tap **Options** on the Settings panel.

5. Specify the following audio options:

    ◆ **Microphone.** Select **Use default device** or a specific one attached to your system.

    ◆ **Speakers.** Select **Use default device** or a specific one attached to your system.

6. Specify the following video options:

    ◆ **Camera.** Select a camera attached to your system.

    ◆ **Incoming video and screen sharing.** Select **Start automatically** or **Ask** to start sharing.

7. To go back to the previous panel, click or tap the **Back** button.

    To exit the panel, click or tap off the panel, or press Esc.

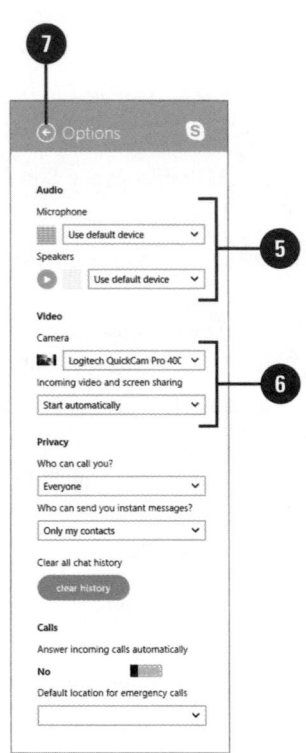

## Change Privacy and Call Options

**1** Click or tap the **Skype** tile on the Start or Apps screen.

**2** Point to the upper-right corner and move down (on a computer) or swipe left from the right edge of the screen (on a mobile device).

**3** Click or tap the **Settings** button on the Charms bar.

**4** Click or tap **Options** on the Settings panel.

**5** Specify the following privacy options:

◆ **Who can call you?** Select **Everyone** or **Only my contacts**.

◆ **Who can send you instant messages.** Select **Everyone** or **Only my contacts**.

◆ **Clear all chat history.** Click or tap **clear history** to erase it.

**6** Drag the slider **No** or **Yes** to answer incoming calls automatically.

**7** Select a default country location for emergency calls.

**8** To go back to the previous panel, click or tap the **Back** button.

To exit the panel, click or tap off the panel, or press Esc.

### Did You Know?

*You can get Help in the Skype app.* In the Skype app, click or tap the Settings button on the Charms bar, click or tap Help, and then click or tap a link to get help, support, or tips from the skype Community.

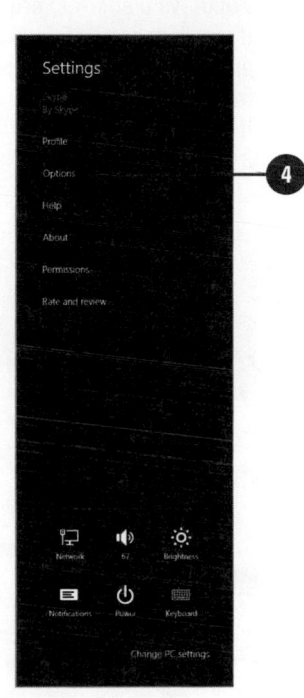

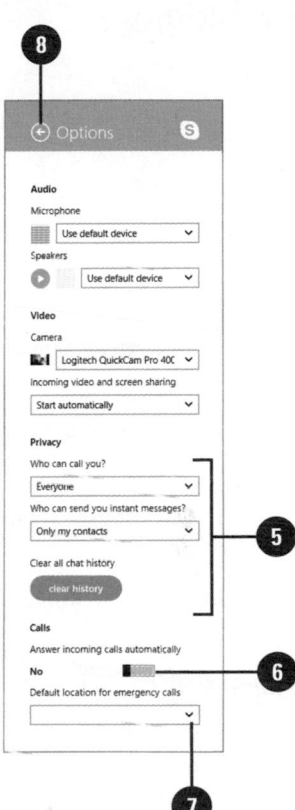

# Adding Skype Contacts

When you sign in to the Skype app (**New!**) with your Microsoft account, your Messenger buddies (the ones used with the Messaging app and Windows platforms) are added to your Skype contact list automatically. If you linked your Facebook account to Skype using the account option on the Profile panel, your contacts are added to your Skype contact list too. Your contacts show up in the People list on the Skype Home screen. If a contact is not available, you can search the Skype directory to find it. You can always enter a name and phone number to create a contact.

## Add Skype Contacts

**1** Click or tap the **Skype** tile on the Start or Apps screen.

**2** Right-click a blank area of the screen (on a computer) or swipe up from the bottom edge or down from the top edge of the screen (on a mobile device).

**3** Click or tap the **add contact** button on the App bar.

**4** Enter the name or email address you want in the Search box, and then click or tap the **Search** button or press Enter.

**5** Select the contact you want to add.

◆ If you don't see the contact you want, click or tap **search directory** to find it in the Skype directory.

**6** Click or tap **add to contacts**.

**7** Enter a send request message, and then click or tap **send** to send a request to the contact.

The contact is added to your contacts as offline until the person accepts your request.

**8** To accept a contact request, go to the Home screen, select the contact request under Recent on the Home screen, and then click or tap **accept**.

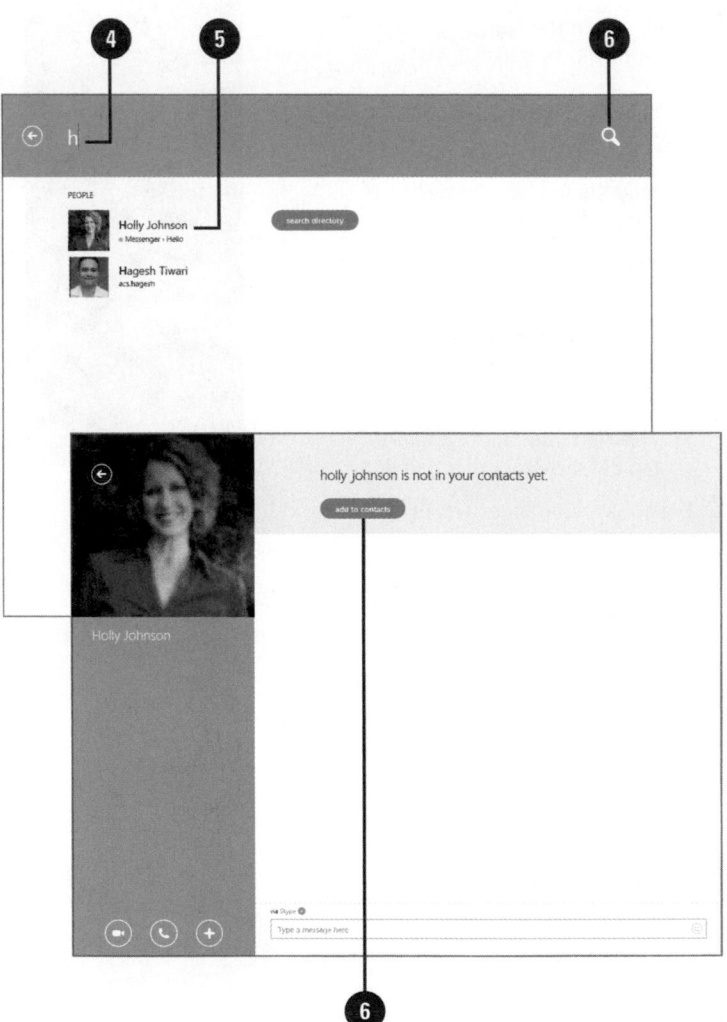

## Add a Mobile or Landline Contact

**1** Click or tap the **Skype** tile on the Start or Apps screen.

**2** Right-click a blank area of the screen (on a computer) or swipe up from the bottom edge or down from the top edge of the screen (on a mobile device).

**3** Click or tap the **save number** button on the App bar.

**4** Enter your contact's name.

**5** Click or tap the **Type** list arrow, and then select a type: **mobile**, **home**, **office**, or **other**.

**6** To change the country code, click or tap the **Code** icon, and then select a country code.

**7** Enter the number (without the country code).

**8** Click or tap **save**.

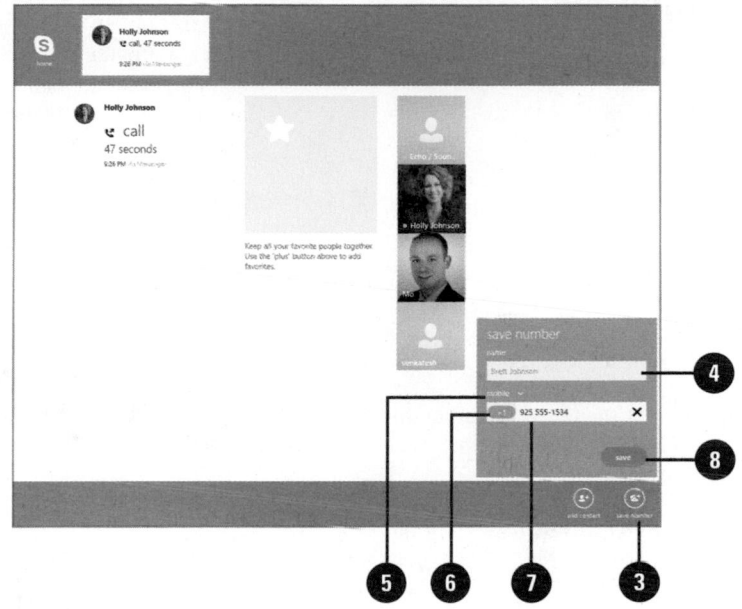

### Did You Know?

*You can search for contacts.* In the Skype app (Home screen), click or tap the Search button, type the contact name, and then click or tap the Search button or press Enter to display a list of matches. If you don't see the contact you want, click or tap search directory to find it.

*You can remove a contact.* In the Skype app (Home screen), select the contact under People, click or tap the Remove button on the App bar, and then click or tap Remove to confirm it.

*You can import contacts.* If you have the Skype for Windows (desktop) program, you can import contacts. You can't in the Skype app (metro).

# Making Phone Calls

In the Skype (**New!**) app, you can quickly make calls to available Skype contacts or use the dial pad to manually make them. A contact is available if a green circle icon status indicator appears next to their name. You can make an audio or video call to a Skype contact, mobile phone or landline phone. When you call a mobile or landline phone, there is a low rate fee, which you can pay for with Skype Credit or a subscription. As you make a call, you can also select options to start an instant message, open the dial pad, add participants, or send files.

## Make a Call with the Dial Pad

**1** Click or tap the **Skype** tile on the Start or Apps screen.

**2** Click or tap the **new call** button on the Skype Home screen.

> **TIMESAVER** To redial a recent call, click or tap the call button under recent calls on the Home or Dial Pad screen.

**3** To change the country code, click or tap the **Code** list arrow, and then select a country code.

**4** Click or tap the dial pad number to dial the phone number.

**5** Click or tap the **call** button in the window.

> Skype dials the call to the contact; wait for the receiver to accept or decline the call.

**6** Use any of the following options:

- ◆ **Webcam.** Turns it on and off.

- ◆ **Microphone.** Turns it on and off.

- ◆ **Options.** Show options to start an instant message, open the dial pad, add participants, or send files.

**7** To go back to the skype Home screen, click the **Back** button.

> To get back to the call screen, click or tap the small call window on the Home screen.

**8** To end the call, click the **end call** button.

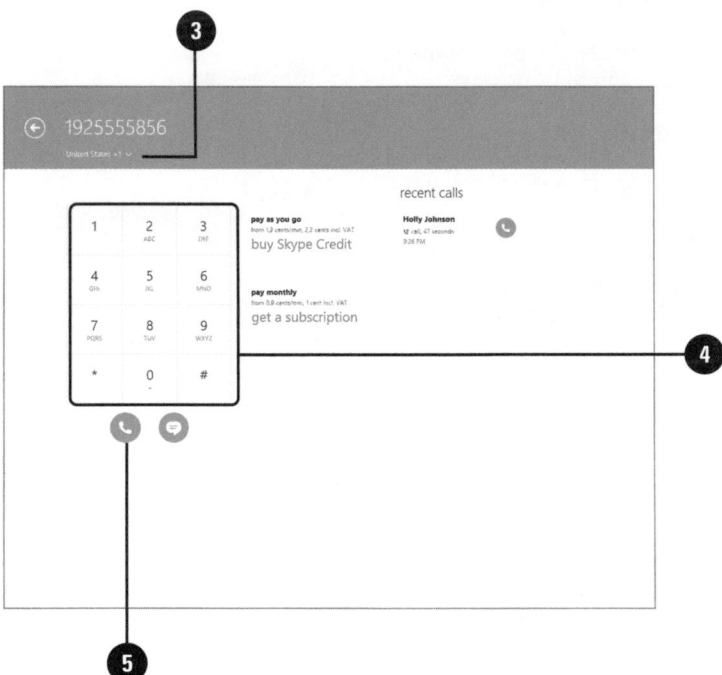

## For Your Information

### Changing My Status

When you sign in with the Skype app (**New!**), the program notifies your contacts that you are available to call or chat. In the Skype app window, your status appears in the upper-right corner along with your picture. A green circle icon also appears to the left of your status to indicate your available status. While you're signed in, you might need to leave for a meeting or lunch. Instead of closing the Skype app, you can change your online status to let your contacts know that you're not available at the moment. To change your status, click or tap your status or picture on the Skype Home screen to open the Profile panel, and then click or tap available or invisible.

## Make Audio or Video Calls to Contacts

**1** Click or tap the **Skype** tile on the Start or Apps screen.

**2** Click or tap an available contact (one with a green icon) under people or favorites.

**3** Click or tap the **call** (audio) or **video** button in the window, and then click or tap any of the following on the menu:

◆ **call Skype.** Use to call a contact with Skype.

◆ **Mobile.** Select the mobile number to call the phone (requires a fee).

◆ **Landline.** Select the landline number to call the phone (requires a fee).

Skype dials the call to the contact; wait for the receiver to accept or decline the call.

**4** Use any of the following options:

◆ **Webcam.** Turns it on and off.

◆ **Microphone.** Turns it on and off.

◆ **Options.** Show options to start an instant message, open the dial pad, add participants, or send files.

**5** To go back to the skype Home screen, click the **Back** button.

To get back to the call screen, click or tap the small call window on the Home screen.

**6** To end the call, click the **end call** button.

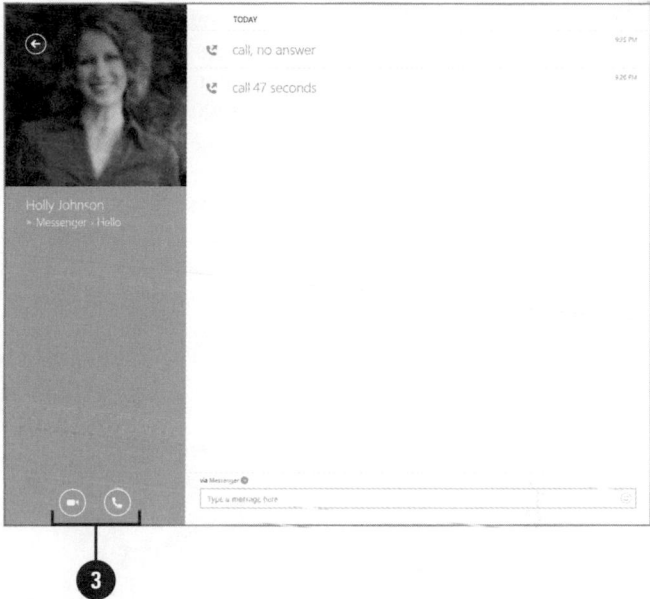

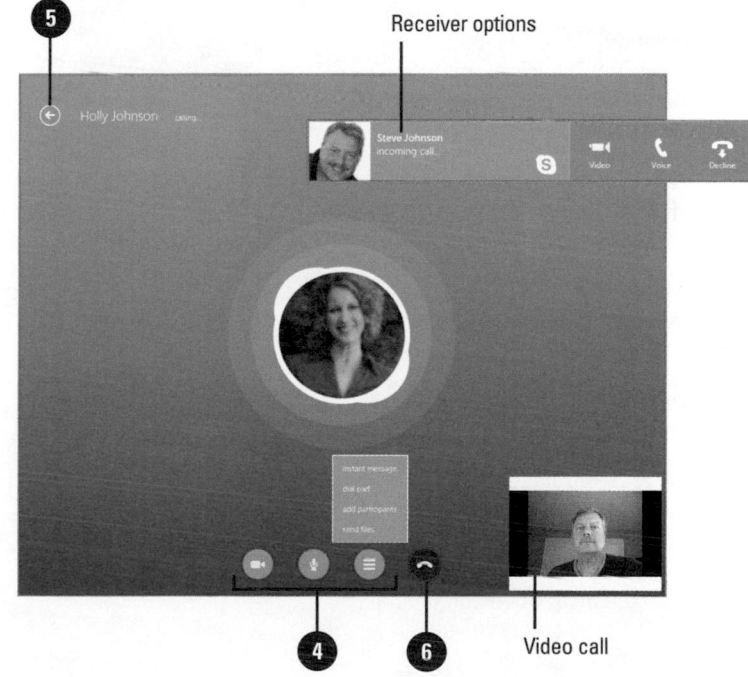

Receiver options

Video call

# Sending and Receiving Instant Messages

An instant message is an online typewritten conversation in real-time between contacts. You can select contacts directly from the Skype Home screen (**New!**). As you type an instant message, you can format your messages by adding graphical symbols called **emoticons**, such as a happy face, which help convey your emotions. In addition to text and symbols, you can also send one or more files in a message. When you send a message, Skype uses an instant messaging service, such as Messenger, Skype, or SMS (Short Message Service—a standard for mobile and landline phones, which requires a fee with Skype Credit or a subscription). You cannot send an instant message to more than one person with the Messenger service, however you can with the Skype service using the Add button (+) in the contact. This is also the case for sending files and video messages.

## Start a New Instant Message

1. Click or tap the **Skype** tile on the Start or Apps screen.

2. Click or tap an available contact (one with a green icon) under people or favorites.

3. To change the send method, click the **Method** list arrow, and then select **Messenger / Skype** (default) or **SMS**.

   ◆ **Default.** The default method (Messenger or Skype) changes based on the type of contact.

4. Click or tap in the Conversation box, type a message, and then press Enter.

5. If you want to add another person to the conversation (for Skype), click or tap the **Add** button (+), click or tap **add participants**, select the contacts, and then click or tap **add**.

6. Follow the instructions on the next page for send and receiving instant messages.

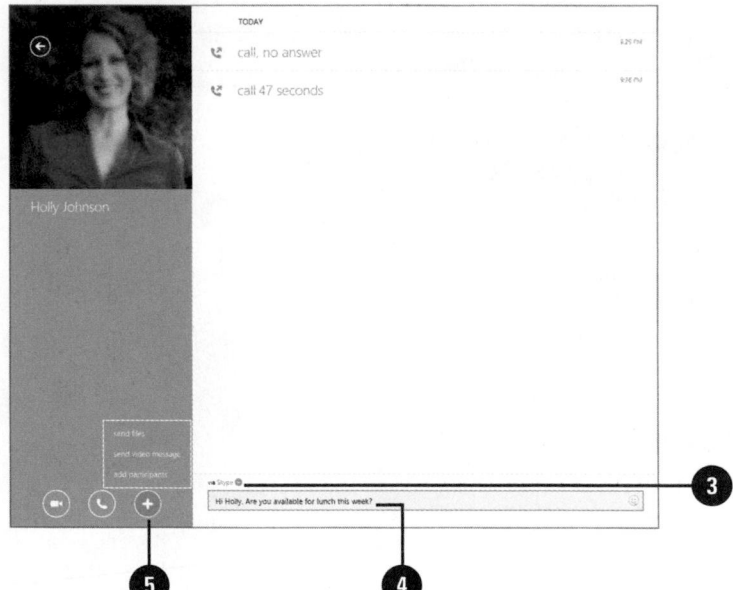

## Send and Receive Instant Messages

1. In a conversation for a contact in the Skype app, click or tap the conversation thread that you want to use.

   ◆ **Open existing conversation.** Click or tap the instant message tile on the App bar at the top.

   ◆ **Another conversation.** If you receive a message or call from someone else, an orange dot icon with the number of unread messages appears, which you can click or tap to view it.

2. Click or tap in the box at the bottom of the screen.

3. Type your message. When you get to the end of the first line, keep typing. The text will automatically wrap to the next line.

   To start a new line while typing, press Shift+Enter.

4. Press Enter, and then wait for a reply.

5. If you want to add an emoticon, click or tap the **Emoticon** button, and then click or tap an icon.

6. To send one or more files, click the **Add** button (+) click or tap **send files**, select the files you want, and then click or tap **Send**.

7. To exit a conversation, change your status to invisible on the Profile panel or close the Skype app.

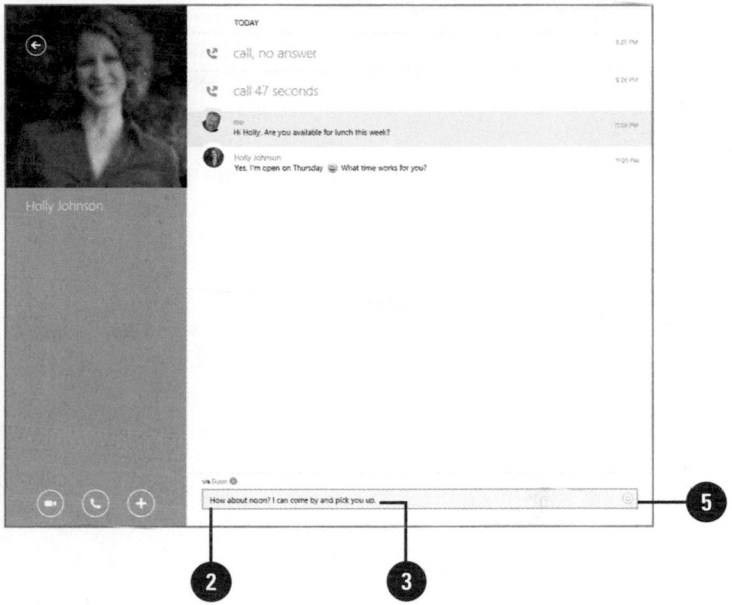

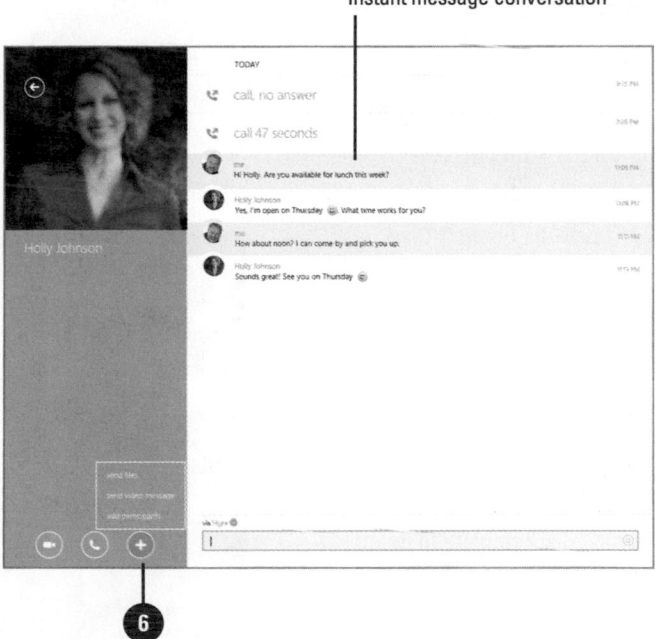

Instant message conversation

# Working with Contacts

As you make phone call or send and receive instant messages in the Skype app (**New!**) to more and more people, you many need to remove contacts you no longer use or block contacts you don't want. If you like a contact, you can make them a favorite for easy access on the Skype Home screen. If you need to change information for a contact, you can view and change the contact's profile in the People app. You can manage a contact by opening it and using options on the App bar.

## Work with Contacts

1. Click or tap the **Skype** tile on the Start or Apps screen.

2. To make a contact a favorite, click or tap the **add favorites** button (+) on the Skype Home screen, select a contact, and then click or tap **add**.

3. Click or tap the contact you want to change.

4. Right-click a blank area of the screen (on a computer) or swipe up from the bottom edge or down from the top edge of the screen (on a mobile device).

5. Click or tap any of the following button on the App bar:

   ◆ **favorite.** Adds the contact to your favorites on the Home screen.

   ◆ **view profile.** Opens the contacts in the People app in a side by side window.

   ◆ **block.** Select or clear options to remove from people (app) or report as spam, and then click or tap block.

   ◆ **remove.** Click remove to delete this person from contacts.

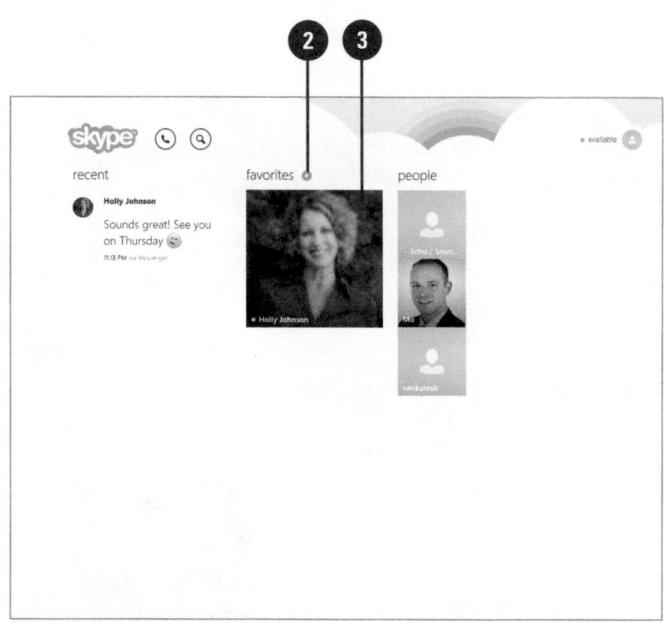

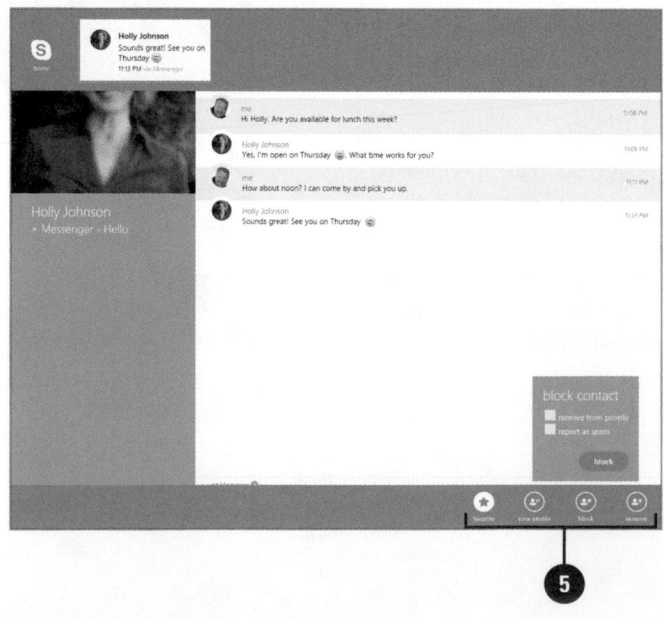

# Working with Photos and Pictures

8

## Introduction

Windows 8.1 comes with two main ways to work with photos and pictures. One is with the Photos app, available on the Start or Apps screen, and the other is with the Pictures folder in File Explorer, available on the desktop.

With the Photos app, you can display photos and pictures stored in the Pictures library, SkyDrive, and any attached devices, such as a camera. The Pictures library is stored locally on your device; you can manage photos and pictures in the Pictures library from File Explorer in the desktop. The SkyDrive is a cloud-based storage device where you can share photos and other documents; you can access and manage files on the SkyDrive from the SkyDrive app.

With the Pictures folder, you can view, organize, and share pictures with others. When you download and save pictures from your digital camera or scanner, Windows stores the digital images in the Pictures folder by default, however, you can specify an alternative location. You can view your picture files as a slide show or in the Extra-Large view, which displays a larger image above thumbnail images of the pictures. The Pictures folder also contains links to specialized picture tasks that help you share pictures with others, such as sending pictures in an email. You can also create your own pictures or edit existing ones in Paint, a Windows accessory program designed for drawing and painting. Paint is useful for making simple changes to a picture, adding a text caption, or saving a picture in another file format.

# Starting and Viewing the Photos App

The Photos app that comes with Windows 8.1 is a centralized place to view all your photos, pictures, and videos. You can display photos and pictures stored in the Pictures library, SkyDrive, and any attached devices, such as a camera. The Pictures library is stored locally on your device; you can manage photos and pictures in the Pictures library from File Explorer in the desktop. SkyDrive is a cloud-based storage device where you can share photos and other documents; you can access and manage files on the SkyDrive from the SkyDrive app. Like other metro apps, you can start the Photos app from the Start or Apps screen. After you start the app, you can change the view to display details (name, modify date, and size) or thumbnails with previews.

## Start the Photos App

1. Click or tap the **Photos** tile on the Start or Apps screen.

   The Photos app window opens in full screen view.

2. To change the view, click the **Details view** or **Thumbnails view** button; same button that toggles.

   **TIMESAVER** *Press Ctrl+Alt+1 to toggle between Details view and Thumbnails view.*

### Did You Know?

*You can set a shuffle option in the Photos app.* In the Photos app, click or tap the Settings button on the Charms bar, click or tap Options on the Settings panel, drag the slider On or Off for Shuffle photos on the app tile to enable or disable the option.

*You can no longer use Flickr or Facebook with the Photos app.* The integration of flickr and Facebook photos has been removed from the Photos app in Windows 8.1

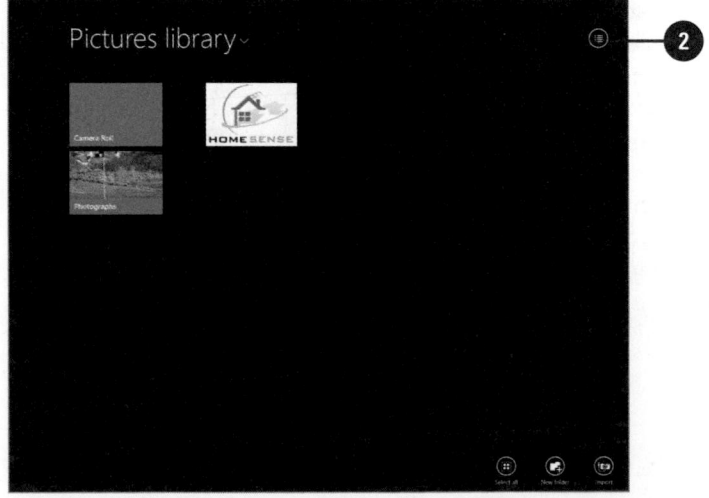

# Navigating in the Photos App

The Photos app allows you to view photos from your Pictures library, SkyDrive, or Devices in a central location in a full screen view. When you start the Photos app, you can select the stored location of the photos you want to view. You can navigate in the Photos app by simply clicking or tapping a folder or photo to open or display it. Within a folder, you can scroll left or right or zoom in or out. When you display a photo, you can use the Back or Forward arrow or a swipe left or right to quickly display each photo in the folder. To move back to the previous screen, you can use the Back button.

## Navigate in the Photos App

1. Click or tap the **Photos** tile on the Start or Apps screen.

2. Click or tap the **Location** list arrow, (**New!**) and then select a location, such as Pictures Library or SkyDrive.

   Folders or photos appear for display.

3. To open a folder, click or tap a folder to display its contents.

   ◆ **Scroll.** Move the pointer to display the scroll bar, and then click or tap the **Scroll** arrows or bar, or swipe left or right.

4. Click or tap a photo to display it in full screen.

5. To navigate through photos, move the pointer, and then click or tap the **Back** or **Forward** arrows, or swipe right or left.

6. To zoom, move the pointer to display the button, and then click or tap the **Zoom in** or **Zoom out** buttons or pinch in or out to gesture zoom..

7. To go back to previous screen, click or tap the screen, if needed to display the button, and then click or tap the **Back** button.

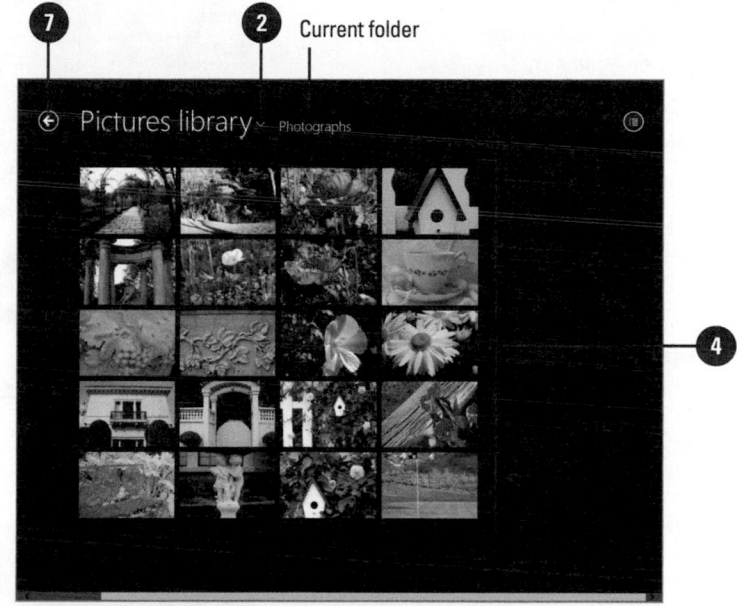

Current folder

# Importing Photos

When you connect a digital camera or other device with digital images, you can import them into a folder using the Photos app. After you connect the device and start the Photos app, you can use the Import button on the App bar to select the device and import the photos you want into a specified folder named with the current date.

## Import Photos

1. Connect your device with the photos to your PC computer or mobile device, and then turn it on.

2. Click or tap the **Photos** tile on the Start or Apps screen.

3. Click or tap to navigate to the location where you want to import the photos.

4. Right-click a blank area of the screen (on a computer) or swipe up from the bottom edge or down from the top edge of the screen (on a mobile device).

5. Click or tap the **Import** button on the App bar.

6. Click or tap the device on the menu.

7. Click or tap to select or deselect the photos you want to import.

   ◆ You can use the **Select all** and **Clear selection** buttons on the App bar to help with the selection.

8. Click or tap **Import**.

   The selected photos are imported into a folder with today's date.

### Did You Know?

*You can create a folder.* In the Photos app, click or tap the New folder button the App bar, enter a name, and then click or tap Create.

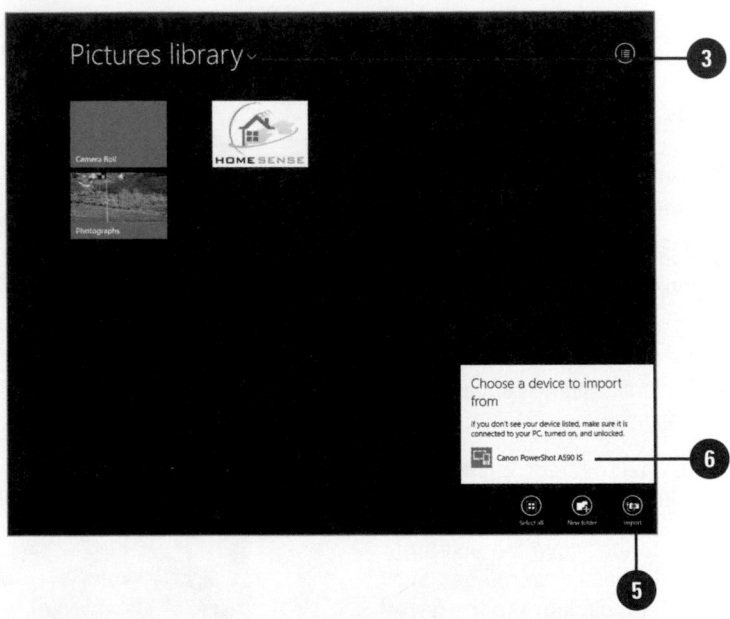

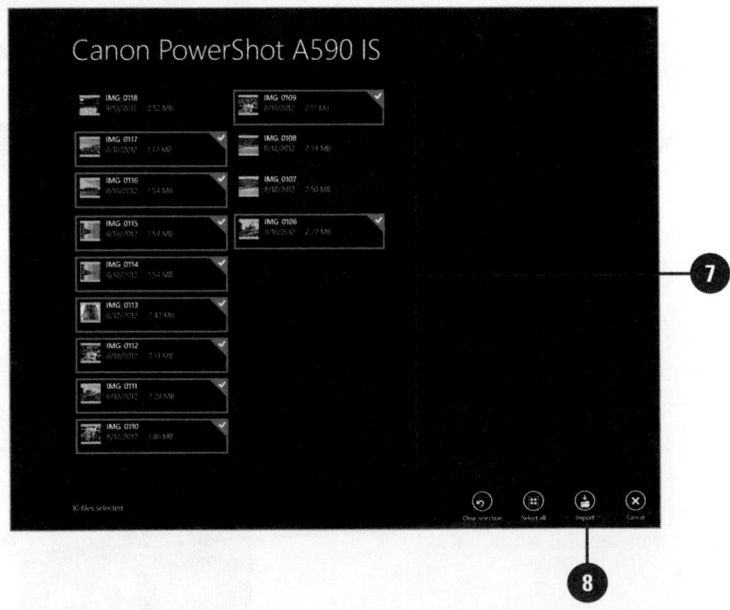

# Deleting Photos

If you no longer need some photos, you can use the Photos app to delete them. It's quick and easy to do. Simply, navigate to the folder location where the photos are stored, select the ones that you want to delete, and then click or tap the Delete button on the App bar. After a confirmation, the photo files are permanently removed from their location.

## Delete Photos

1 Click or tap the **Photos** tile on the Start or Apps screen.

2 Click or tap to navigate to the folder where you want to delete photos.

3 Right-click or tap-hold each photo you want to delete to select it.

◆ To select all photos in a folder, click or tap the **Select all** button on the App bar.

A check mark appears in the selected photo.

4 To clear an individual selection, right-click or tap hold the photo.

To clear the entire selection, click or tap the **Clear selection** button on the App bar.

5 Click or tap the **Delete** button on the App bar.

6 Click or tap **Delete** to confirm the deletion.

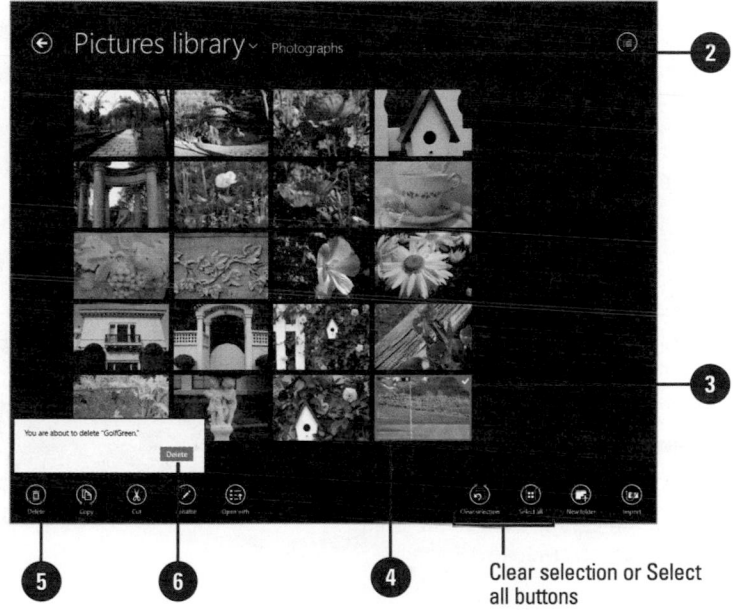

Clear selection or Select all buttons

## Did You Know?

***You can rename a photo.*** In the Photos app, select a photo, click or tap the Rename button on the App bar, enter a name, and then click or Rename.

***You can copy or move (cut) a photo.*** In the Photos app, select one or more photos, click or tap the Copy or Cut button on the App bar.

## For Your Information

### Using Windows Live Photo Gallery

Windows Live Photo Gallery allows you to view, locate, organize, open, and edit photos and pictures. Windows Live Photo Gallery shows all the pictures and videos located in the Pictures folder. In Windows Live Photo Gallery, you can also print photos, order photos through an online service, email photos and pictures using your email program, create CDs or DVDs, and make a movie using Windows Live Movie Maker. Windows Live Photo Gallery and Windows Live Movie Maker don't come installed with Windows 8.1; they are available for free online from Microsoft. You can download the programs from Windows Live at *http://download.live.com*.

# Editing Photos

In addition to viewing photos, you can also use the Photos app to edit and enhance (**New!**) a photo. You can use photo related options to automatically fix images (**New!**) or apply basic fixes (**New!**) like rotate, crop, remove red eye, or retouch. If you have an eye for editing photos, you can also apply brightness, contrast, highlights, shadows, temperature, tint, saturation, color enhance, vignette or selective focus.

## Crop and Rotate a Photo

**1** Click or tap the **Photos** tile on the Start or Apps screen.

**2** Click or tap to navigate to the folder with the photo you want to edit.

**3** Click the photo you want to edit.

**4** Right-click a blank area of the screen (on a computer) or swipe up from the bottom edge or down from the top edge of the screen (on a mobile device).

**5** Click or tap the **Crop** button (**New!**) on the App bar.

**6** Drag the corner point to the area you want to crop.

**7** Click or tap the **Apply** button on the App bar.

**8** Click or tap the **Save a copy** or **Update original** button on the App bar.

◆ You can also click or tap the **Undo** button, and then click or tap **Cancel anyway** to cancel it.

**9** To rotate the photo, click or tap the **Rotate** button (**New!**) on the App bar.

**10** To go back to previous screen, click or tap the screen, if needed to display the button, and then click or tap the **Back** button.

## Edit and Enhance a Photo

1. Click or tap the **Photos** tile on the Start or Apps screen.

2. Click or tap to navigate to the folder with the photo you want to edit.

3. Click the photo you want to edit.

4. Right-click a blank area of the screen (on a computer) or swipe up from the bottom edge or down from the top edge of the screen (on a mobile device).

5. Click or tap the **Edit** button on the App bar.

6. Click or tap the editing options (**New!**) on the left pane.

   ◆ **Auto fix.** Click a thumbnail to apply an auto fix.

   ◆ **Basic fixes.** Use buttons to rotate, crop, remove red eye, or retouch.

   ◆ **Light.** Use buttons to apply brightness, contrast, highlights, and shadows.

   ◆ **Color.** Use button to apply temperature, tint, saturation, or color enhance.

   ◆ **Effects.** Use buttons to apply a vignette or selective focus.

7. Click or tap the available editing options (**New!**) for the selected editing option.

8. Click or tap the **Save a copy** or **Update original** button on the App bar.

   ◆ You can also click or tap the **Undo** button, and then click or tap **Cancel anyway** to cancel it.

9. To go back to previous screen, click or tap the screen, if needed to display the button, and then click or tap the **Back** button.

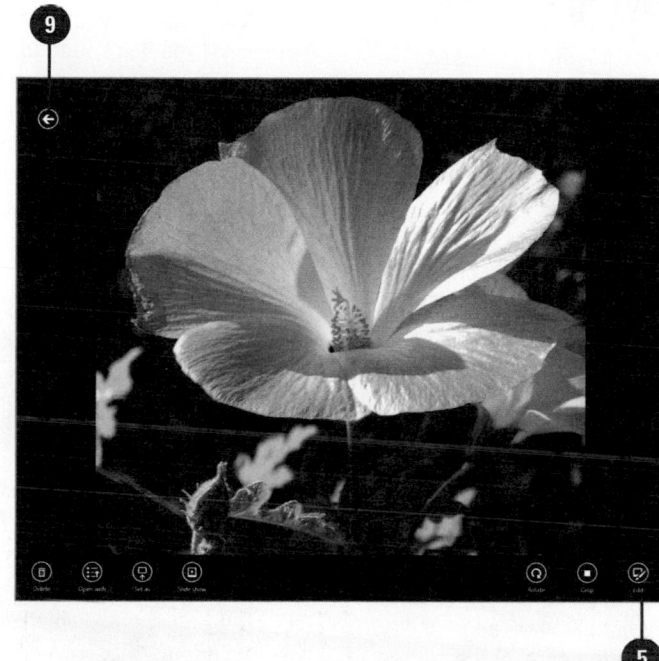

# Displaying a Slide Show

Instead of manually navigating through a set of photos in a folder, you can also display the photos as a slide show in the Photos app. That way, you don't need to manually scroll through each photo. The Photos app displays the photos for you every 3 to 4 seconds. The Photos apps uses the open folder for the contents of the slide show. However, you can start the slide show from any photo in the folder. The slide show continue to run until you stop it with a click or tap or press Esc.

## Display a Slide Show

1. Click or tap the **Photos** tile on the Start or Apps screen.

2. Click or tap to navigate to the folder you want to use for the slide show.

3. Click or tap the photo you want to use as the start image.

4. Right-click a blank area of the screen (on a computer) or swipe up from the bottom edge or down from the top edge of the screen (on a mobile device).

5. Click or tap the **Slide Show** button on the App bar.

6. To stop the slide show, click or tap the screen, or press Esc.

7. To go back to previous screen, click or tap the screen, if needed to display the button, and then click or tap the **Back** button.

# Setting a Photo as the Lock or Start Screen Tile

Instead of using one of the photos provided by Windows, you can select a photo in the Photos app as the lock screen or Photos app tile. The lock screen is the security screen that appears when you start Windows 8.1 or return to Windows 8.1 after signing out or going to sleep. So, the Lock screen option allows you to change the lock screen to a photo of your choice. The Photos tile option allows you to customized the Photos tile on the Start screen.

## Set a Photo as the Lock Screen or Photos App Tile

1. Click or tap the **Photos** tile on the Start or Apps screen.

2. Click or tap to navigate to the photo you want to use.

   The photo should fill most or the entire screen.

3. Right-click a blank area of the screen (on a computer) or swipe up from the bottom edge or down from the top edge of the screen (on a mobile device).

4. Click or tap the **Set as** button on the App bar.

5. Click or tap one of the following options on the menu:

   ◆ **Lock screen.** Changes the photo of the lock screen.

   ◆ **Photos tile.** Changes the photo of the Photos app tile on the Start screen.

6. To go back to previous screen, click or tap the screen, if needed to display the button, and then click or tap the **Back** button.

# Drawing a Picture

**Paint** is a Windows accessory you can use to create and work with graphics or pictures. Paint is designed to create and edit bitmap (.bmp or .dib) files, but you can also open and save pictures created in or for other graphics programs and the Internet using several common file formats, such as .jpeg, .gif, .tiff, or .png. A **bitmap** file is a map of a picture created from small black, white, or colored dots, or bits. When you start Paint, a blank canvas appears in the work area, along with a File menu and Ribbon at the top. The Ribbon with two tabs—Home and View—allows you to quickly select document related commands. Paint comes with a File menu with file related commands and a set of tools on the Ribbon that you can use for drawing and manipulating pictures. A tool remains turned on until you select another tool. In addition to the drawing tools, you can also add text to a picture. When you create a text box and type the text, you can edit and format it, but once you deselect the text box, the text becomes part of the picture, which you can't edit.

## Draw a Picture

1. In the Start screen, click or tap the **Apps view** button, and then click or tap **Paint**.

2. If you want, drag a resize handle on the canvas to resize it.

3. Click or tap a drawing tool.

    ◆ If available, use the **Outline**, **Fill**, and **Size** buttons for the selected tool.

4. Click or tap **Color 1** to select the foreground color or click or tap **Color 2** to select the background color.

5. Drag the shapes you want by holding down one of the following:

    ◆ The left mouse button to draw with the foreground color.

    ◆ The right mouse button to draw with the background color.

    ◆ The Shift key to constrain the drawing to a proportional size, such as a circle or square.

6. Click or tap the **File** menu, and then click or tap **Exit**.

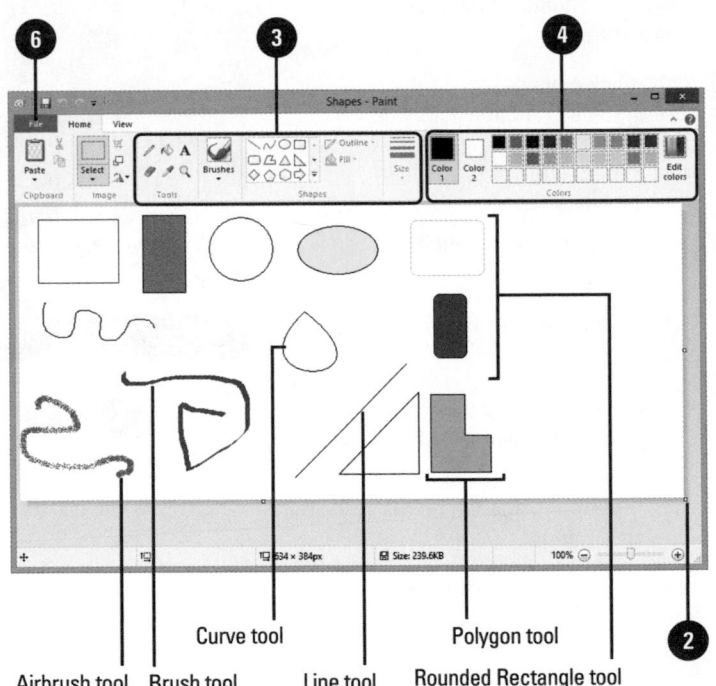

Airbrush tool  Brush tool  Curve tool  Line tool  Polygon tool  Rounded Rectangle tool

## Add Text to a Picture

1. In Paint, create or open the picture you want to modify.

2. Click or tap the **Text** tool on the Home tab.

3. Drag a text box.

4. Using the **Text** tab, select the font, font size, and any formatting you want to apply to the text.

5. Click or tap in the text box, if necessary, and then type the text.

6. Drag a text box resize handle to enlarge or reduce the text box.

7. Edit and format the text.

8. Click or tap outside the text box to deselect it and change the text to a bitmap.

> **IMPORTANT** *Once you click or tap outside the text box to place the text in the picture, the text becomes part of the picture.*

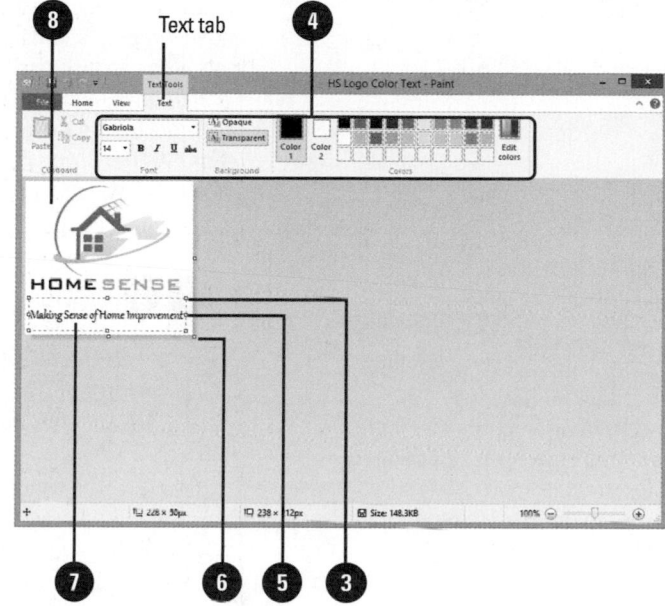

Text tab

## Save a Picture in Different Formats

1. In Paint, create or open the picture you want to save.

2. Click or tap the **File** tap, and then click or tap **Save as**. You can also point to Save as, and then select a format (PNG, JPEG, BMP, or GIF).

3. Select the drive and folder in which you want to save the file.

4. Type a name for the file, or use the suggested name.

5. Click or tap the **Save as type** list arrow, and then click or tap a file format.

6. Click or tap **Save**.

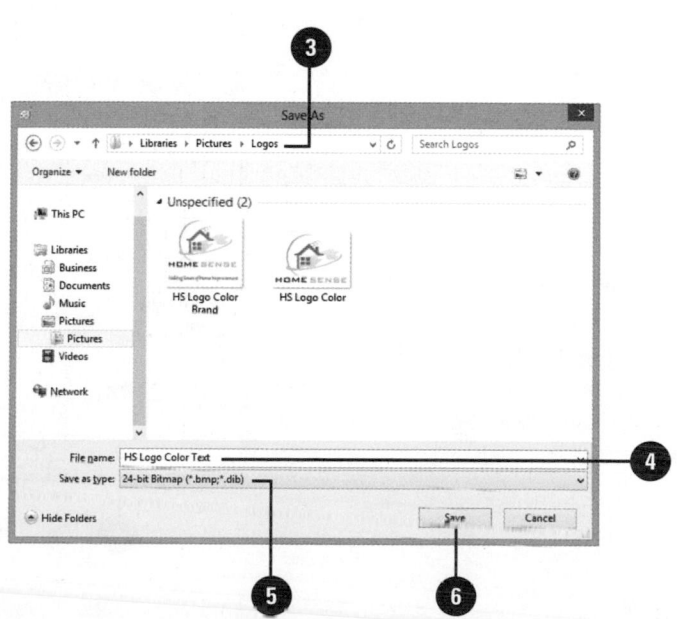

# Editing a Picture

After you create or open a picture, you can select all or part of the picture and use commands on the Image menu, such as rotate, stretch, and invert colors, to further modify it in Paint. In addition to the drawing tools, you can also use painting tools, such as Fill With Color, Airbrush, Brush, Pencil, and Pick Color, to transform the picture. The Fill With Color tool is useful if you want to color an entire item or recolor text letter by letter. If you need to remove part of a picture, you can use the Eraser tool, which comes in four different sizes.

## Modify a Picture

1. In Paint, create or open the picture you want to edit.

2. Click or tap the **Select** button arrow on the Home tab, and then click or tap **Free-form selection** tool to select irregular shapes, or click or tap the **Rectangular section** tool to select rectangle shapes.

3. Drag the selection area you want.

4. Click or tap the **Select** button arrow, and then click or tap **Transparent selection** to select it to use a transparent background or deselect it to use an opaque background.

   ◆ Copy selection. Hold down the Ctrl key, and then drag the selection.

5. In the Image area of the Home tab, click or tap any of the following buttons:

   ◆ **Rotate or flip.**

   ◆ **Resize and skew.**

   ◆ **Crop.**

   ◆ Invert colors. Right-click or tap-hold the selection, and then click or tap **Invert color**.

6. Click or tap **OK**, if necessary.

7. Save the picture and exit Paint.

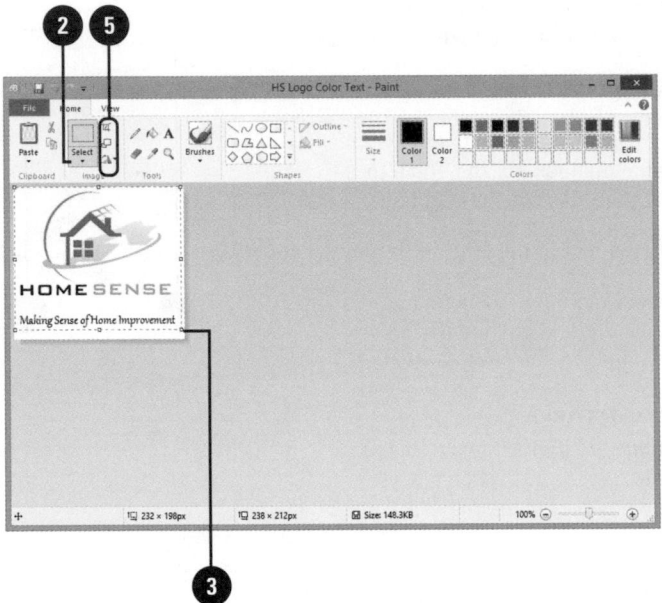

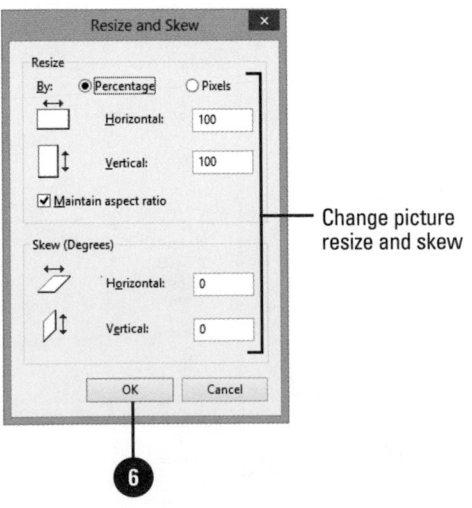

Change picture resize and skew

## Fill Part of a Picture

1. In Paint, create or open the picture you want to edit.

2. Click or tap the color you want to fill, or click or tap the **Color picker** tool and click or tap a color from the picture.

3. Click or tap the **Fill with color** tool.

4. Point the tip of the paint bucket to the area you want to fill, and then click or tap.

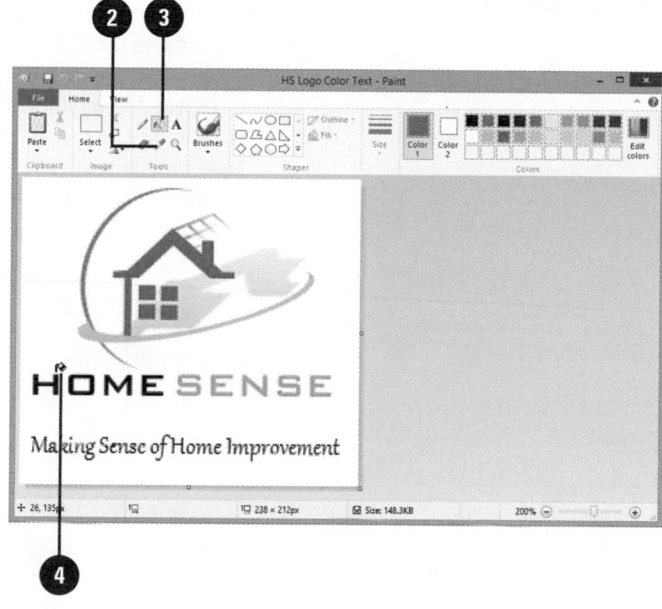

## Erase Part of a Picture

1. In Paint, create or open the picture you want to edit.

2. To magnify an area of the screen, click or tap the **Magnifier** tool, and then click or tap the area you want to magnify.

   ◆ You can also drag the **Zoom** slider to change the view size.

3. Click or tap the **Eraser** tool.

4. Drag the Eraser over the area you want to erase.

5. If you make a mistake, click or tap the **Undo** button on the Quick Access toolbar (on title bar) to restore your last action.

6. To restore the magnification, click or tap the **Zoom (-)** or **Zoom (+)** buttons.

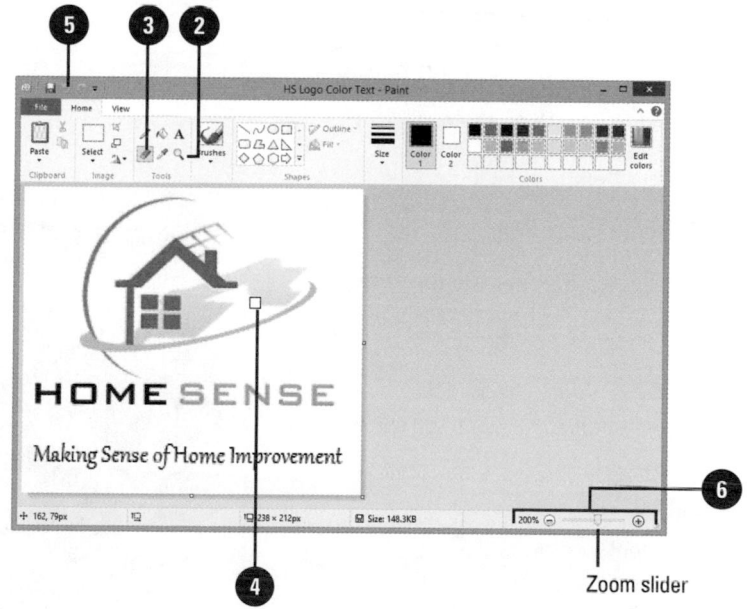

Zoom slider

# Viewing Pictures

Windows gives you several ways to view pictures. In a folder with pictures, you can use Extra Large Icons view to see a larger view of the pictures. In the Pictures folder, you can use the slide show feature to display pictures in a full screen slide show. If you want to preview pictures or open a picture to edit, you can double-click or double-tap the file icon to use the default program associated with the picture file type, or select the specific program—such as Paint, Photos app, or Windows Photo Viewer—you want to use to make changes.

## View a Picture

1. Click or tap the **Desktop** tile on the Start or Apps screen.

2. Click or tap the **File Explorer** icon on the taskbar.

3. Click or tap the **Pictures** folder in the Navigation pane in the Explorer window, and then navigate to the folder you want.

4. Click or tap the picture or photo you want to view.

   **TIMESAVER** *Press Win+ PrtScn to take a screenshot and save it in the Pictures folder.*

5. To display details about the selected picture or photo, click or tap the **View** tab, and then click or tap the **Details pane** button.

6. Click or tap the **Home** tab.

7. Click or tap the **Open** button arrow, and then click or tap the program you want to open the picture.

   ◆ **Paint.** Opens the selected picture in the Paint program.

   ◆ **Photos.** Opens the selected picture in the Photos app.

   ◆ **Windows Photo Viewer.** Opens the selected picture in the Windows Photo Viewer program.

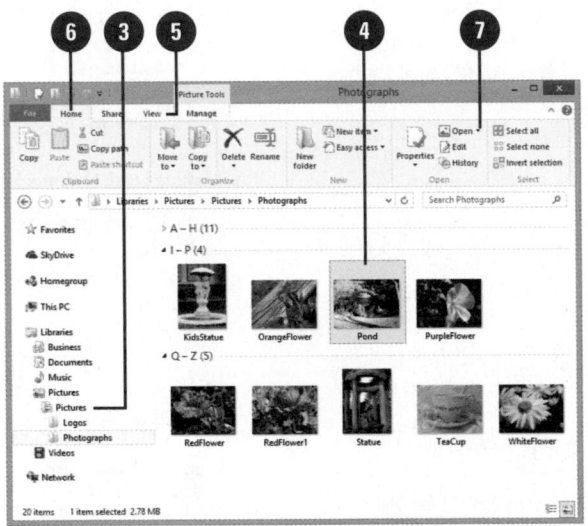

Preview in Windows Photo Viewer

## View Pictures as Extra Large Icons

1. In File Explorer (desktop), click or tap **Pictures** in the Navigation pane, or open any other folder with pictures you want to view.

2. Click or tap the **View** tab.

3. Click or tap **Extra large icons**.

   ◆ To preview a view change, point to the view.

   ◆ If the pictures are too large, you can also use **Large icons** and **Medium icons** to display pictures.

## View Pictures as a Slide Show

1. In File Explorer (desktop), click or tap **Pictures** in the Navigation pane, or open any other folder with pictures you want to view.

2. Select the pictures you want in the show, or click or tap one picture to see all the pictures.

3. Click or tap the **Manage** tab under Picture Tools.

4. Click or tap the **Slide show** button, and then watch the show.

5. To manually advance to the next slide, click or tap anywhere in the picture.

6. To control the slide show, right-click or tap the screen, and then click or tap the control you want, including **Shuffle**, **Loop**, or a **Slide Show Speed** (Slow, Medium, or Fast).

7. To exit the slide show, press Esc or right-click or tap-hold the screen, and then click or tap **Exit**.

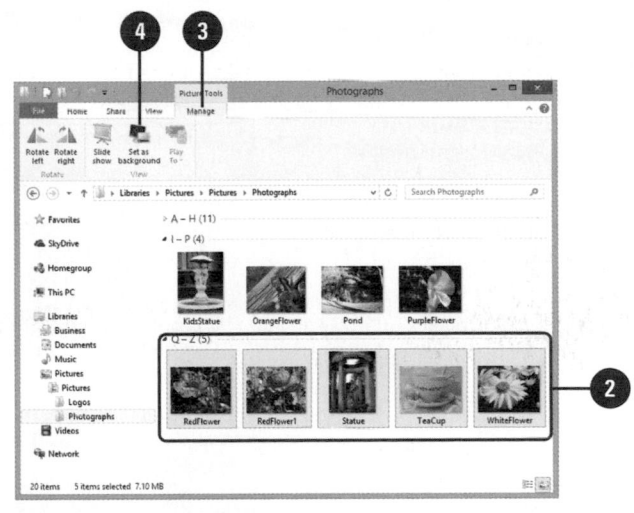

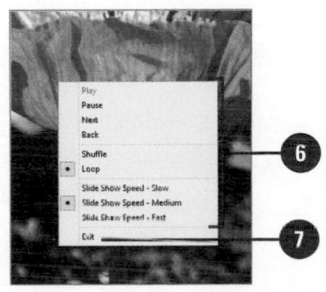

# Formatting and Printing Photos

Windows makes it easy to format and print photographs from Windows Photo Viewer, which allows you to print photographs. During the process, you can select the photo(s) to print, the paper type, and a page layout, such as full-page prints, contact-sheet prints, 4 x 6-inch prints, 5 x 7-inch prints, 8 x 10-inch prints, 3.5 x 5-inch prints, and wallet size prints. To print a photo, you need a color printer and special photo paper. In order to get the best results when you print photographs, set your printer resolution to the highest setting for the best quality output, and use high-quality glossy paper designed specifically for printing photographs. Check your printer documentation for the best resolution setting suited to print your photographs. When you print photographs with a high resolution setting, the printing process might take longer. Many printer manufacturers also make paper designed to work best with their printers; check your printer manufacturer's web site for more information.

## Format and Print a Photo

1. In File Explorer (desktop), click or tap **Pictures** in the Navigation pane, or open any other folder with pictures you want to use.

2. Select the photo you want to format and print.

3. Click or tap the **Print** button on the Share tab.

   ◆ You can also click or tap the **Open** button arrow on the Home tab, and then click or tap **Windows Photo Viewer**.

4. Click or tap the **Print** button on the toolbar, and then click or tap **Print**.

5. Specify the printer options (printer, paper size, quality resolution, or paper type) you want.

6. Specify a number of copies.

7. Select or clear the **Fit picture to frame** check box.

8. Click or tap **Print**, and then follow any printer specify instructions.

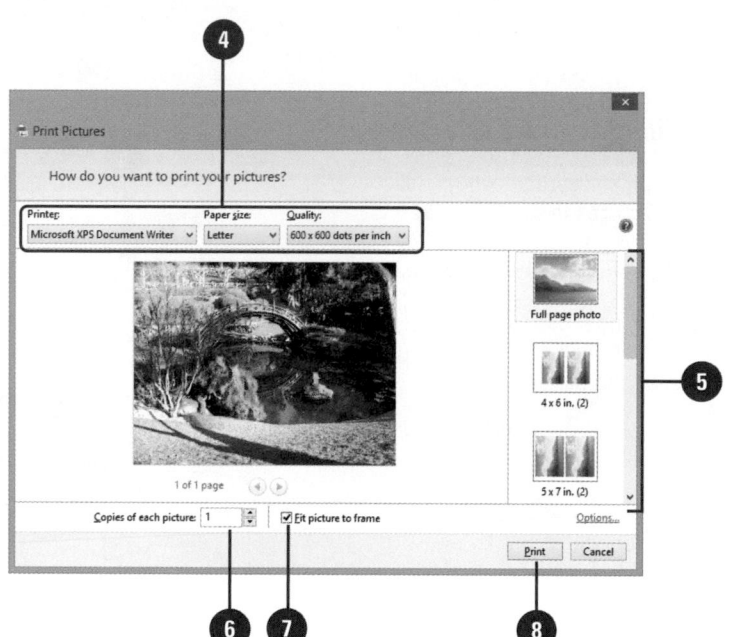

# Ordering Photo Prints from the Web

If you have digital photographs taken from a digital camera or scanned into your PC computer or mobile device, you can send your digital photographs to an online printing company, such as CVS/pharmacy, Fujifilm, HPs Snapfish, Kodak, or Shutterfly, where they create photo prints and send them to your mailing address. Windows makes the process easy from the Print Pictures wizard, which walks you through the ordering process. You'll need to provide print sizes, quantities, and billing and shipping information to complete the order.

## Order Photo Prints from the Web

1. In File Explorer (desktop), click or tap **Pictures** in the Navigation pane, or open any other folder with pictures you want to use.

2. Select the photo you want to send to an online printing company.

3. Click or tap the **Print** button on the Share tab.

   ◆ You can also click or tap the **Open** button arrow on the Home tab, and then click or tap **Windows Photo Viewer**.

4. Click or tap the **Print** button on the toolbar, and then click or tap **Order prints**.

5. Select the printing company you want to send your photos.

6. Click or tap **Send Pictures**.

7. If necessary, click or tap **Send**.

8. Follow the remaining steps to place an order with the specific printing company.

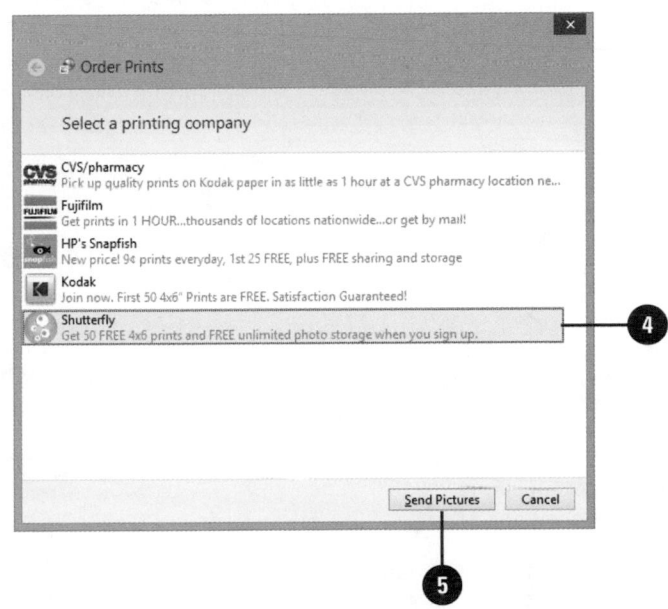

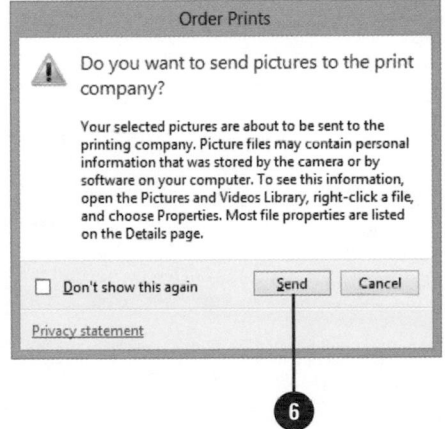

# Emailing a Picture

If you have one or more photos, pictures, or documents that you want to share with others, you can send them in an email as attachments. Before you send photos or pictures in an email as an attachment, you typically need to resize them in a separate graphics program so your recipient can view them with minimal scrolling, open your email program (non-metro app, such as Windows Live Mail), and then attach the files. You can send a photo or picture in an email message without having to resize it in a separate graphics program, or even open your email program. Using the Email button on the Share tab in any Explorer window or the E-mail button on the toolbar in Windows Photo Viewer, Windows opens an email message window with the attached files from your default email program. All you need to do is address the message, add any message text, and then send it.

## Email a Photo or Picture

1. In File Explorer (desktop), click or tap **Pictures** in the Navigation pane, or open any other folder with pictures you want to use.

2. Select the pictures or a folder with pictures you want to email.

3. Click or tap the **Email** button on the Share tab, or click or tap the **E-mail** button on the toolbar in Windows Photo Viewer.

   ◆ Click or tap the **Open** button arrow on the Home tab, and then click or tap **Windows Photo Viewer**.

4. Click or tap the **Picture size** list arrow, and then select a size.

5. Click or tap **Attach**.

   Your default email program (non metro app, such as Windows Live Mail) opens, displaying an email message with a file attachment.

6. Type an email address and a subject.

7. Click or tap **Send** on the toolbar.

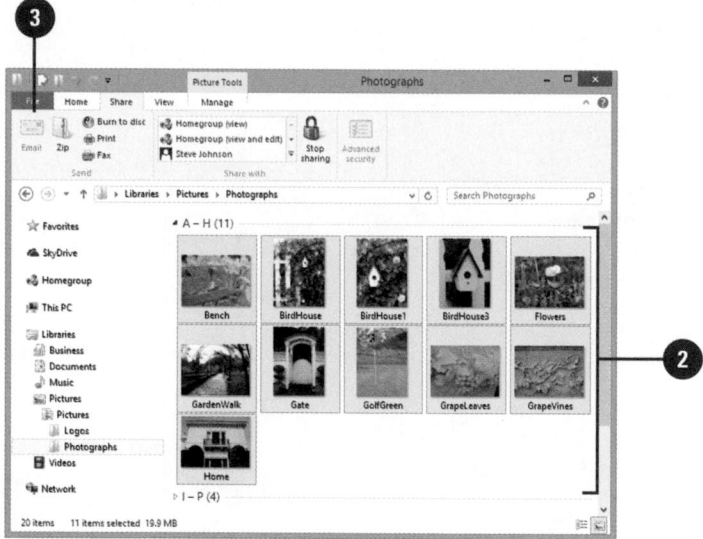

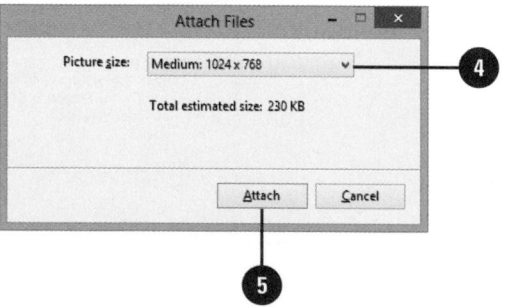

# Installing a Digital Camera or Scanner

Windows makes it easy to install a scanner or digital camera on your PC computer or mobile device using plug-and-play. In most cases, all you need to do is plug in the hardware device. Windows recognizes the new hardware and installs it. If the hardware provides it's own installation wizard, the program will automatically start. If for some reason Windows doesn't recognize the hardware, you can start a wizard, which walks you through the installation process.

## Install a Digital Camera or Scanner

1. Plug your camera or scanner into your PC to start the device installation wizard or the Scanner and Camera wizard.

   If the wizard doesn't open, open the Control Panel, click or tap the **Devices and Printers** icon in Small icons or Large icons view, and then click or tap the **Add a device** button on the toolbar.

2. Click or tap **Next** to continue.

3. Click or tap the device manufacturer you want to install, click or tap the device name, and then click or tap **Next** to continue.

4. Select a port and any device specific options, and then click or tap **Next** to continue.

5. Type a name for the device, or use the suggested one, and then click or tap **Next** to continue.

6. Click or tap **Finish**.

### Did You Know?

*You can remove a scanner or camera.* In the Control Panel, click or tap Devices And Printers in Small icons or Large icons view, select the device icon, and then click or tap the Remove Device button on the toolbar, and then or tap click or tap Yes.

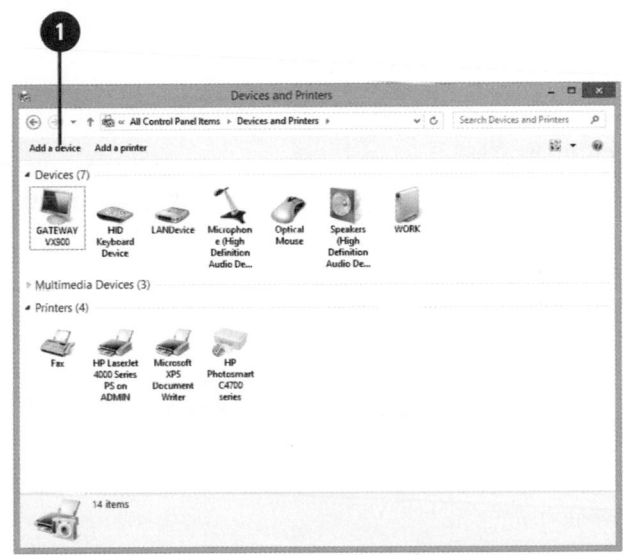

## For Your Information

### Scanning Pictures

After you connect and install a scanner, you can use the Scanner device in the Devices and Printer window in the Control Panel or start the Scan app (**New!**) in Apps view to scan pictures. In the Scan app, specify the scan settings (File Type, Color mode, Resolution (DPI), and Save folder), and then click or tap the Scan or Preview button. The Scan button scans and saves, while the Preview scans and previews. After the scan, you can click or tap View to see your scan. If you saved it as an image file, it automatically opens in the Photos app in a split window. If you want to edit the scan, use the Rotate, Crop, or Edit buttons on the App bar. See "Scanning a Document" on page 442 for more information on scanning document and pictures.

# Downloading Digital Camera Pictures

A **digital still camera** stores pictures digitally rather than on film. The major advantage of digital still cameras is that making photos is fast and inexpensive. In order to use the digital camera features of Windows, you need to have a digital still or video camera attached and installed on your PC computer or mobile device. When you connect a digital camera to your device, Windows 8.1 displays the AutoPlay pop-up notification, where you can choose to import files using the Photos app or view files from the device window using File Explorer. If you don't use AutoPlay, you can also use an Import pictures and videos command in the Computer window. You can use the device window to view pictures that you have already taken with the camera and copy them in a folder on your device, or delete pictures from your camera.

## Download Pictures from a Camera

① Connect the digital camera to your device, and follow instructions to install and recognize the camera.

② If the AutoPlay pop-up notification appears, click or tap the pop-up, click or tap **Open device to view files** (File Explorer) to import the pictures.

If the AutoPlay pop-up notification doesn't open, open File Explorer (desktop), and then click or tap **This PC** in the Navigation pane.

③ Right-click or tap-hold the digital camera icon, and then click or tap **Import pictures and videos**.

④ Click or tap the **Review, organize, and group items to import** or **Import all new items now** option.

⑤ To more import settings, click or tap the **More options** link, select the options you want, and then click or tap **OK**.

⑥ Click or tap **Import**.

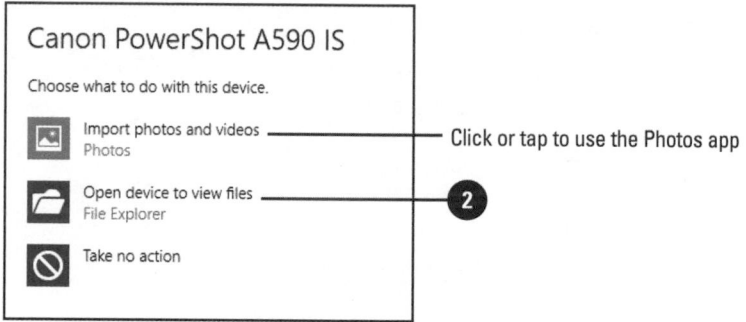

Click or tap to use the Photos app

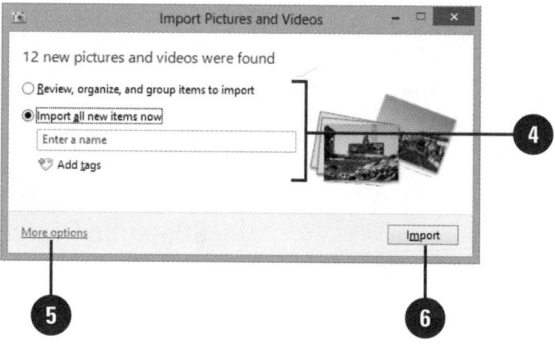

## Manage Pictures on the Camera

**1** Connect the digital camera to your PC computer or mobile device.

**2** If the AutoPlay pop-up notification appears, click or tap the pop-up, click or tap **Open device to view files** (File Explorer) to import the pictures, and then skip to Step 4.

If the AutoPlay dialog box doesn't open, continue.

**3** In File Explorer (desktop), click or tap **This PC** in the Navigation pane, and then double-click or double-tap the Camera icon associated with the digital camera.

**4** Double-click or double-tap the removable storage icon, and any folders to display the pictures stored on the digital camera.

**5** Click or tap a picture to select the one you want to work with.

**6** Perform any of the following commands:

◆ **Open.** Click or tap the **Open** button arrow on the Home tab, and then click or tap **Paint**, **Photos**, or **Windows Photo Viewer**.

◆ **Edit.** Click or tap the **Edit** button on the Home tab. Opens in the Paint where you can edit it.

◆ **Delete.** Click or tap the **Delete** button on the Home tab.

◆ **Move or Copy.** Click or tap the **Move to** or **Copy to** button on the Home tab, and then select a destination folder.

You can also right-click or tap-hold a picture, and then select an option.

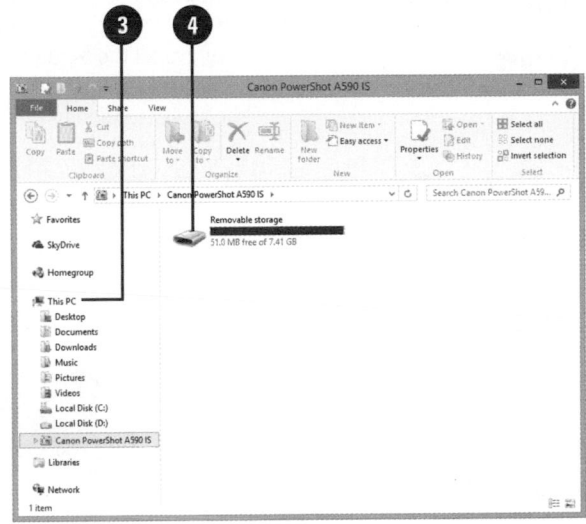

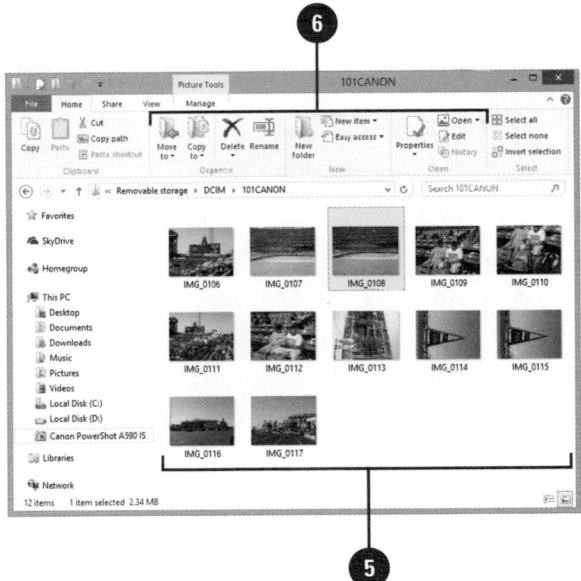

# Using Pictures as a Screen Saver

Instead of using standard screen savers provided by Windows, you can use your own pictures to create a slide show screen saver. Windows displays all the pictures, which you have designated in a folder, to create as a full screen slide show. You can add or remove pictures from the folder to modify the slide show.

## Use Pictures as a Screen Saver

1. In File Explorer (desktop), if you want to create a custom folder for pictures, create a folder, and then place the pictures you want to use in the slide show in the folder.

2. Right-click or tap-hold a blank area of the desktop, and then click or tap **Personalize**.

3. Click or tap **Screen Saver**.

4. Click or tap the **Screen Saver** list, and then click or tap **Photos**.

5. Click or tap **Settings**.

6. If necessary, click or tap **Browse**, select the folder with your pictures, and then click or tap **OK**.

7. Click or tap the **Slide show speed** list, select the speed you want, and then select or clear the **Shuffle pictures** check box.

8. Click or tap **Save**.

9. Click or tap **Preview**, and then click or tap the screen to stop it.

10. Click or tap **OK**.

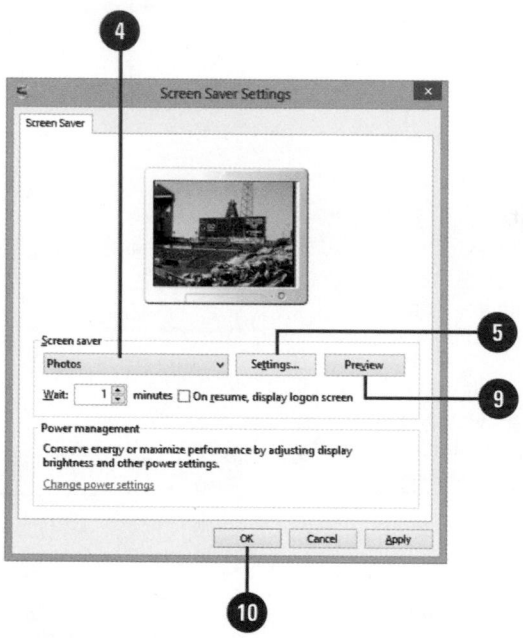

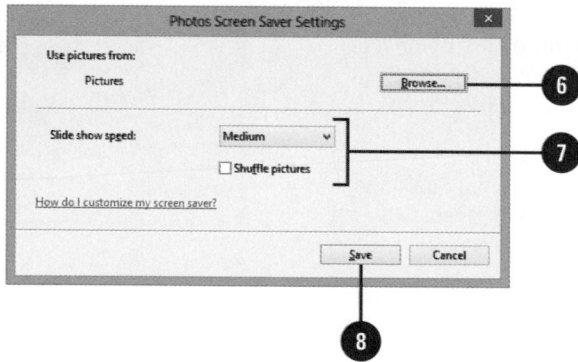

# Using a Picture as a Desktop Background

Instead of using one of the pictures provided by Windows, you can select a picture on your hard disk or from a web page as the desktop background. You can use Paint or any graphics program to create new background designs or change existing ones. Acceptable formats for background files are Bitmap (the format of a Paint file), JPEG (the format of an Internet graphic file), or HTM (the format of a web page). After you set a picture as the desktop background, Windows adds the picture to the Background list in the Desktop Background dialog box. When you use a picture from a web page, Windows saves it in the Background list as Internet Explorer Background. Each new picture from a web page you set as a background replaces the previous one.

## Set a Picture as the Desktop Background

1. In File Explorer (desktop), open the folder or the web page with the picture you want to set as the background.

2. Click or tap the picture you want to use.

3. Click or tap the **Set as background** button on the Manage tab under Picture Tools.

   If the picture doesn't appear on your desktop, continue.

4. Right-click or tap-hold a blank area of the desktop, and then click or tap **Personalize**.

5. Click or tap **Desktop Background**.

6. Click or tap the picture you set as the background.

7. Click or tap **Save changes**.

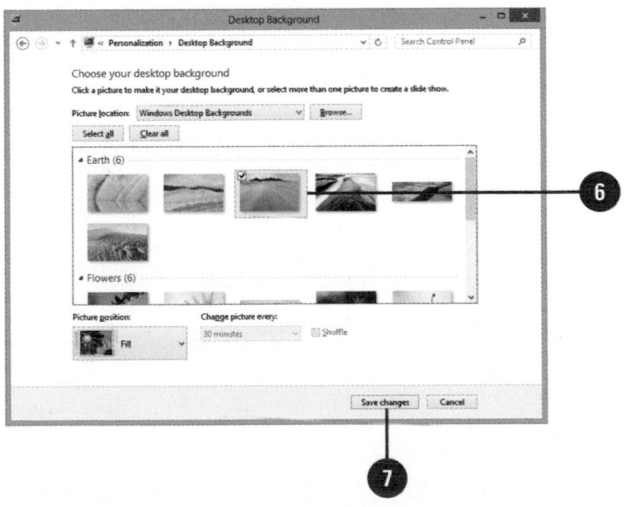

### Did You Know?

*You can save an web page picture as a background.* In your web browser, right-click or tap-hold the picture, click or tap Save as background, and then click or tap Yes.

# Understanding Picture File Formats

Each file type has a different format and rec-ommended use. JPG (Joint Photographic Experts Group; also known as JPEG) and PNG (Portable Network Graphics) are graphic file formats commonly used on web pages, while BMP (Bit-mapped) and TIF (Tagged Image File Format, also known as Tiff) are file formats used in documents. The format specifies how the information in the file is organized internally. JPG and PNG formats are com-pressible, which means that the file size is smaller and transfers over the Internet faster. Each file format uses a different compression method, which produces different results when you display the graphic files. JPG is designed for photographs and supports mil-lions of colors, but loses some image quality by discarding image data to reduce the file size. PNG is designed for web graphics and supports millions of color without losing image quality, but not all web browsers fully support its capabilities without using a plug-in, which is a software add-on installed on your PC computer or mobile device. TIF is designed for all graphics and colors and one of the most widely used graphic formats, but the file size is large. BMP is the standard Windows graphic format and is similar to TIF.

## Understanding 8-, 16-, and 32-Bit Images

Along with the file format is a number. Sometimes it's shown and sometimes it's not. The number indicates the colors available for displaying or printing each pixel in an image is called **bit depth**—also known as pixel depth or color depth. A higher bit depth means more available colors and more accurate color representation in an image. A bit depth setting of 2 bits displays 4 colors, 4 bits dis-plays 16 colors, 8 bits displays 256 colors, 16 bits displays 32,768 colors, and 24 bits and 32 bits both display 16.7 million colors. Most dig-ital images currently use 8 bits of data per channel. For example, an RGB image with 8 bits per channel is capable of producing 16.7 million (a 24-bit RGB image: 8 bits x 3 chan-nels) possible colors per pixel. While that may seem like a lot of color information, when it comes to color correction and adjustment, it isn't.

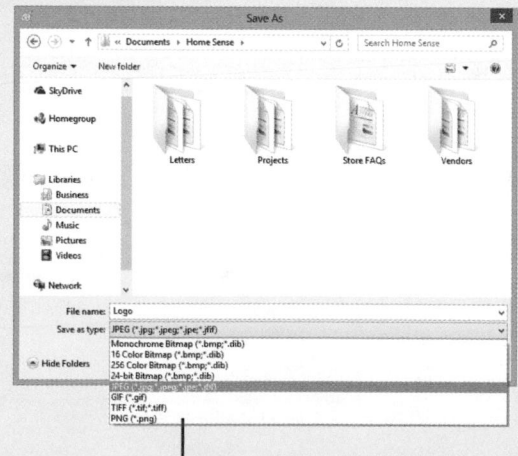

File formats with color depth in Paint

# Working with Windows Media

## Introduction

You can use Windows Media Player (WMP version 12) to play sounds, music, and digital movies. In addition, you can play and copy CDs, rip music from CDs, create your own CDs, play DVDs or VCDs, and copy music and videos to portable devices, such as portable digital audio players and portable PCs. If you have your media on another PC computer, you can use Remote Media Streaming to play it on your PC computer. Using Windows Media Player requires a sound card, speakers, and an Internet connection to view online content.

Windows also comes with Sound Recorder, a sound recording utility program you can use to create and modify a sound. You can use the sound to indicate a Windows event, such as starting Windows or if an error has occurred. Using Sound Recorder requires a sound card, speakers, and a microphone.

In addition to Windows Media Player, you can also use Windows Media Center to play media files on your PC computer or mobile device, or on the web. Windows Media Center is an entertainment system integrated into your PC computer that lets you watch live or recorded TV, play video and watch pictures, listen to music and radio using an FM tuner or the Internet, play and burn CDs or DVDs, browse online media, and play games. You can also use Windows Media Center Extenders to add entertainment devices—such as a TV, DVD player, digital camera, or Xbox 360—to your system and control each one from Windows Media Center within a networked environment.

If you have one of the Windows 8.1 N versions (**New!**), you need to download Windows Media Player and Windows Media Center from the Microsoft web site as a separate file.

## What You'll Do

**Start, Update, and View Windows Media Player**

**Play a Music CD, DVD, or VCD Movie**

**Control the Volume**

**Play Media Files and the Playlists**

**Rip CD Music**

**Copy Media Files to a CD or Portable Device**

**Stream Media**

**Enhance the Media Player Display**

**View and Play Music Files**

**Record a Sound File**

**Associate a Sound with an Event**

**Start and Navigate Windows Media Center**

**Change Windows Media Center Settings**

# Starting and Updating Windows Media Player

Before you can use Windows Media Player (WMP), you need to check to make sure you have the latest version (12 or later) installed on your PC computer using the About Windows Media Player command on the Help menu for the current player. If it's not, you can download and install it from the web at *www.microsoft.com/downloads*. You start Windows Media Player like any other Windows program from the Apps screen. After you start Windows Media Player, you should check for software updates on the Internet. Microsoft is continually adding features and fixing problems. You can use the Help menu in Windows Media Player to access the updates.

## Start and Update Windows Media Player

1. In the Start screen, click or tap the **Apps view** button, and then click or tap **Windows Media Player**.

2. If a setup dialog box appears, click or tap the **Recommended settings** option, and then click or tap **Finish**.

3. Click or tap the **Help** menu, click or tap **Check for updates**, and then follow the instructions to complete the upgrade. To show menus, see the DYK? below.

4. To use the player, click or tap the toolbar button or task tabs. You can use the **Back** and **Forward** button to retrace previous steps.

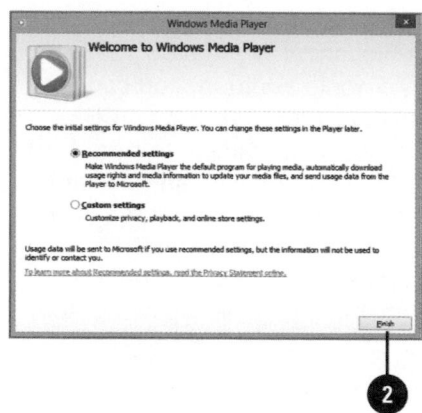

### Did You Know?

*You can show and hide the menu bar.* To show or hide the menu bar, click or tap the Organize button, point to Layout, and then click or tap Show Menu Bar.

*You can automatically check for software updates.* Click or tap the Organize button, click or tap Options, click or tap the Player tab, and then click or tap the Once A Day, Once A Week, or Once A Month option.

# Viewing the Media Player Window

## Now Playing View

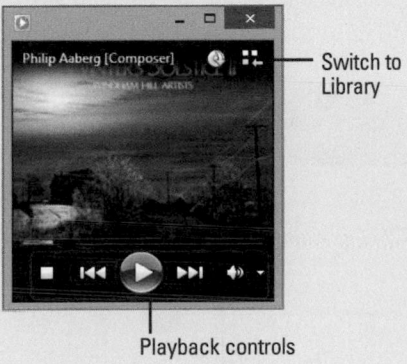

Switch to Library

Playback controls

## Library View

Search and layout options

Tabs

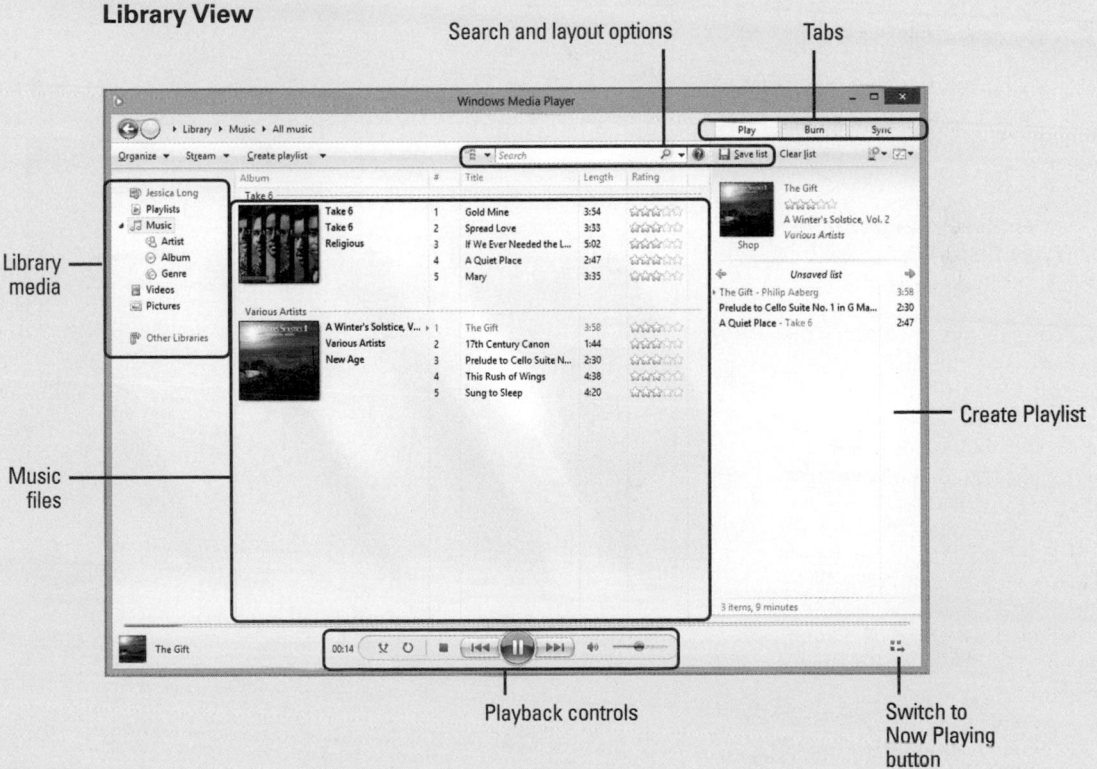

Library media

Music files

Create Playlist

Playback controls

Switch to Now Playing button

# Playing Music from CDs

Windows allows you to play music on your PC computer in the background while you work. After you insert a music CD into your CD-ROM drive and the music starts to play, you can minimize Windows Media Player and continue to work with other programs on your computer. If you are connected to the Internet when you play a music CD, Windows Media Player tries to locate information about the CD from the Internet, such as the name of the artist and the songs on the album. If the information is not available, the track number of each song displays instead.

## Play a Music CD

1. Insert a music CD into your CD-ROM drive.

2. If the Audio pop-up notification appears, click or tap the pop-up, and then click or tap **Play audio CD** (Windows Media Player).

   The Windows Media Player window appears, and the CD starts to play.

3. To play the music, click or tap the **Play** button.

   ◆ **Play in random order.** Click or tap the **Turn Shuffle On** button; click or tap again to turn off.

   ◆ **Play continuously.** Click or tap the **Turn Repeat On** button; click or tap again to turn off.

4. To stop the music, click or tap the **Stop** button.

   ◆ You can also right-click or tap-hold the song in the list, and then click or tap **Remove from list**.

5. To play a specific song, double-click or double-tap the song.

6. To play the previous or next song, click or tap the **Previous** or **Next** button.

7. Click or tap the **Minimize** button to continue to listen while you work, or click or tap the **Close** button to exit.

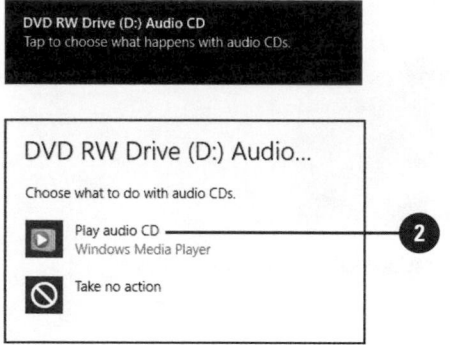

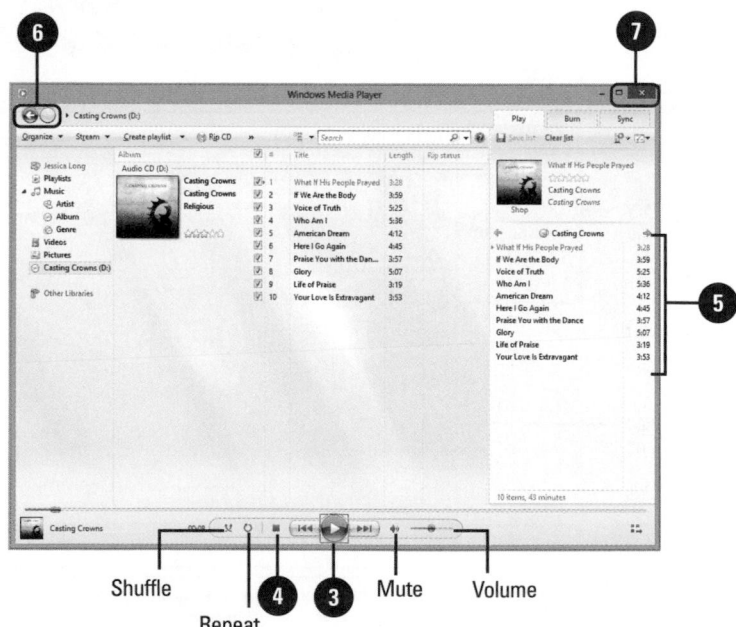

Shuffle

Repeat

Mute

Volume

# Playing a DVD or VCD Movie

If you have a DVD drive and decoder hardware or software on your PC computer, you can play DVD movies with Windows Media Player. If you don't have a decoder, you can purchase one from a third party manufacturer. If you only have a CD player, you can play VCD movies. A VCD is similar to a DVD, yet the video quality is not as high. When you play a DVD or VCD movie, a list of titles appear with a section of content from the movie. You can use the titles to browse through the contents of the DVD or VCD.

## Play a DVD or VCD Movie

1. Insert a DVD into your DVD drive or a VCD into your CD drive.

2. If the Audio pop-up notification appears, click or tap the pop-up, and then click or tap the option to play the DVD or VCD.

    The Windows Media Player window appears, and the DVD or VCD starts to play.

3. To expand the contents list of the DVD or VCD click or tap the plus sign (+).

4. To pause the movie, click or tap the **Pause** button.

5. To stop the movie, click or tap the **Stop** button.

6. To play a specific title, double-click or double-tap it in the list.

7. To play the previous or next section of the movie, click or tap the **Previous** or **Next** button.

8. Click or tap the **Close** button to exit.

### Did You Know?

*You can display captions and subtitles for a DVD.* Click or tap the Play menu, point to Lyrics, Captions, and Subtitles, and then click or tap Off (toggles on and off) or Defaults to select the language you want to use.

# Controlling the Volume

Windows comes with master volume controls that allow you to change the volume of all devices and applications on the PC at once. You can increase or decrease the volume, or you can mute (turn off) the sound. The volume control is available on the Settings panel from the Charms bar and in the notification area on the taskbar from the desktop. The Volume icon makes it easy to increase or decrease the volume or mute the sound. In addition to changing the master volume on your PC, you can also adjust the volume of specific devices, such as a CD or DVD player, without affecting the volume of other devices.

## Change the Volume from the Start Screen

1. In the Start screen, click or tap the **Settings** button on the Charms bar.

2. Click or tap the **Volume** button on the Settings panel.

3. Drag the slider to adjust the volume to the level you want.

4. To mute the sound, click or tap the **Mute** button.

5. Press Esc or click or tap off the menu to close the volume controls.

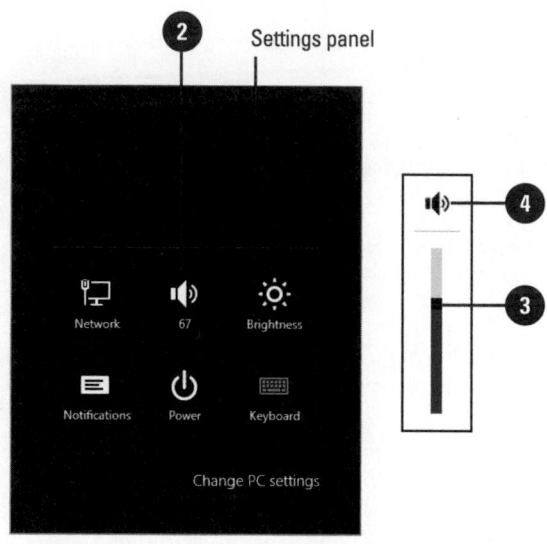

Settings panel

## Change the Volume from the Desktop

1. In the desktop, click or tap the **Volume** icon in the notification area on the taskbar.

   ◆ **Display volume.** Point to the Volume icon in the notification area.

2. Drag the slider to adjust the volume to the level you want.

3. To mute the sound, click or tap the **Mute** button.

4. Press Esc or click or tap off the menu to close the volume controls.

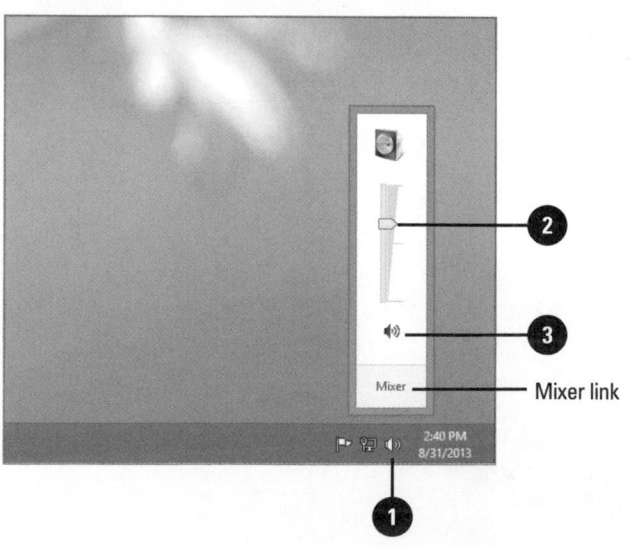

Mixer link

## Set Volume Levels
## for Specific Devices

**1** In the desktop, click or tap the **Volume** icon in the notification area on the taskbar.

**2** Click or tap the **Mixer** link.

**3** Drag the **Speakers** slider to adjust the settings for the sound level you want.

The volume for the speakers is the main volume control.

**4** Drag the other sliders to adjust the settings for the applications you want.

The volume for the speakers is the main volume control.

**5** When you're done, click or tap the **Close** button.

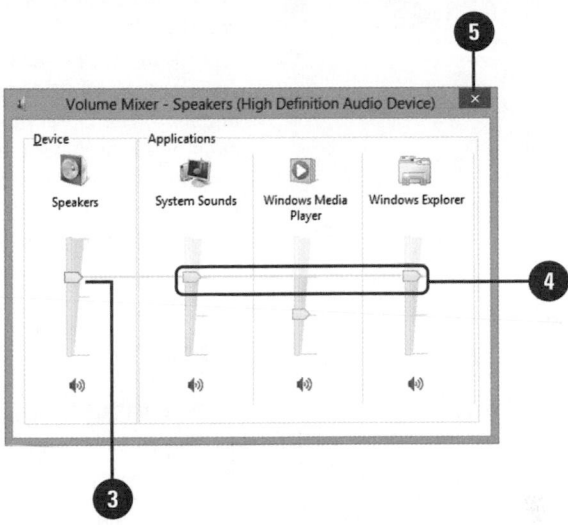

### Did You Know?

*You can display the Volume icon on the taskbar.* In the desktop, right-click or tap-hold the taskbar, click or tap Properties, click or tap Customize, click or tap the Turn System Icons On or Off link, set the Volume Behavior to On, and then click or tap OK.

*You can set the recording volume.* In the desktop, right-click or tap-hold the Volume icon, click or tap Recording Devices, click or tap a device, click or tap Properties, click or tap the Levels tab, adjust the volume level, and then click or tap OK twice.

### Troubleshooting

### Testing Your Sound Hardware

If your are having trouble hearing the sound from Windows Media Player, the best place to start is to test your sound hardware. In File Explorer (desktop), click or tap This PC in the Navigation pane, click or tap the Control Panel button on the Computer tab, and then click or tap the Sound icon in Small icons or Large icons view. Next, click or tap the Playback tab, select the hardware, click or tap Configure, click or tap Test, click or tap Next, and then follow the instructions to test the hardware. Once you have tested the hardware, click or tap Finish, and then click or tap OK.

# Playing Media Files

With Windows Media Player, you can play sound and video files on your PC. You can find and download sound and video files from the Internet or copy media files from a CD or DVD. WMP now supports more audio and video formats, including 3GP, AAC, AVCHD, DivX, MOV, and Xvid. The Library makes it easy to organize your media by category, such as Artist, Album, Genre, Rated Songs, or Year Released. You can quickly search for media by name or you can browse through the Library. If you want to do other things while you listen to media, you can switch to Now Playing view to use a smaller display.

## Perform a Quick Search

1 In Windows Media Player, click or tap a media library in the Navigation pane.

2 Click or tap in the **Search** box.

3 Type the text that you want to search by.

**TIMESAVER** *Click or tap Search Results in the Library list to display it at any time.*

4 To clear the search, click or tap the **Close** button in the Search box (x).

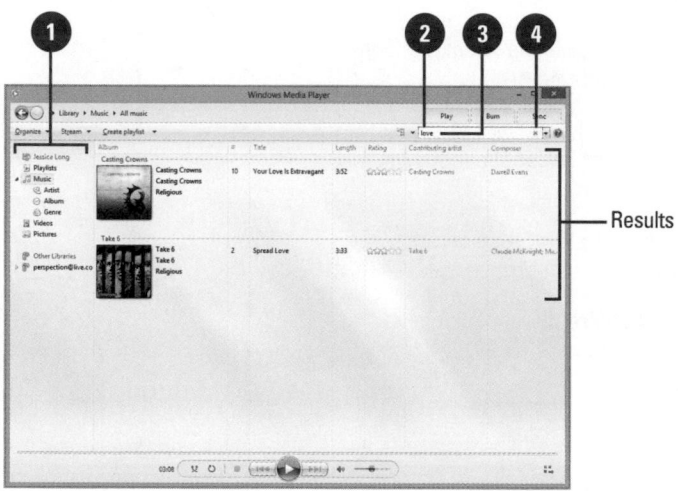

Results

## Browse Media Files

1 In Windows Media Player, click or tap a media library in the Navigation pane.

2 Click or tap the **Select a Category** button on the address bar, and then select a category.

3 Select a view of that category in the Navigation pane.

4 To change the view:

◆ **View More**. Click or tap the list arrow next to a button on the address bar, and then select a category.

◆ **View Less**. Click or tap a button on the address bar to the left.

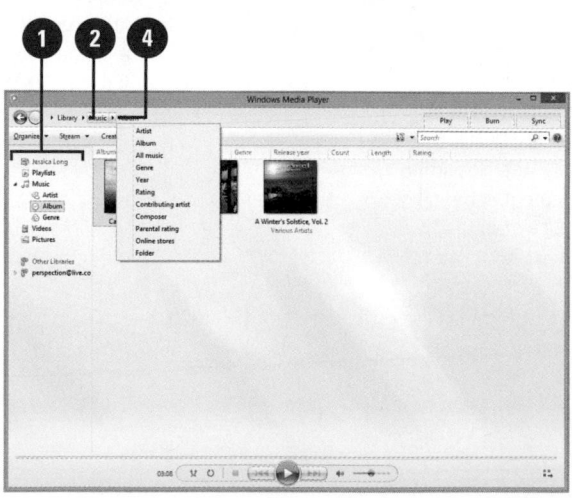

## Play Media Files from the Library

1. In Windows Media Player, click or tap a media library in the Navigation pane.

2. Click or tap an arrow next to the category you want to view.

3. Click or tap a category.

4. Double-click or double-tap the media file to play it.

### Did You Know?

*You can automatically add media files to the Library when played.* Click or tap the Organize button, click or tap Options, click or tap the Player tab, select the Add Local Media Files To Library When Played check box, and then click or tap OK.

## Play Media Files from a Playlist

1. In Windows Media Player, click or tap a media library in the Navigation pane.

2. Click or tap an arrow next to the **Playlists** category.

3. Double-click or double-tap a playlist to play it.

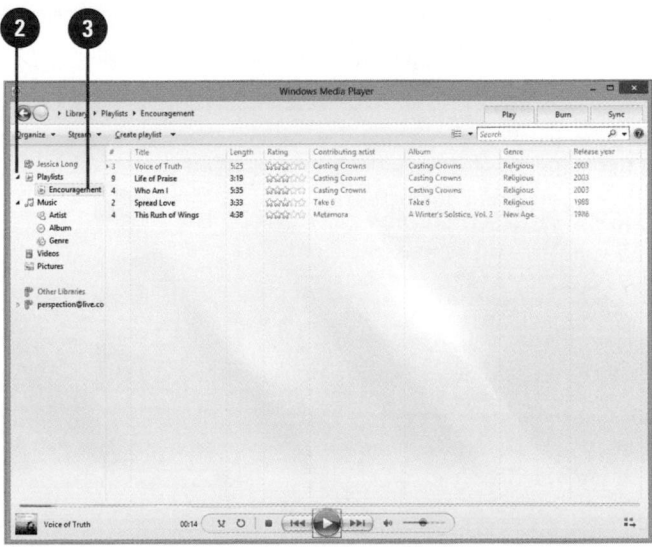

### Did You Know?

*You can delete a file from the library.* Click or tap a media library in the Navigation pane, right-click or tap-hold the file you want to remove, click or tap Delete, click or tap the Delete from Library Only or Delete From Library And My Computer option, and then click or tap OK.

# Playing Media Using a Playlist

Instead of playing digital media files, such as music tracks, video clips, or DVD segments, one at a time or in sequential order from a CD or DVD, you can use Windows Media Player to create a **playlist**. A playlist is a customized list or sequence of digital media that you want to listen to or watch. A playlist allows you to group together media files and specify the order in which you want to play back the media. You can mix and match the media files on your PC computer, a network, a CD, or the Internet, creating a personal juke box. You can create an easy access general playlist called Play list, create one with a specific name, or specify criteria to create an Auto Playlist.

## Create Playlist

1. Click or tap a media library in the Navigation pane.

2. Click or tap the **Play** tab.

3. To clear the Play list, click or tap the **Clear list** button.

   ◆ To create a blank new playlist, click or tap the **Create playlist** button, click or tap **Create playlist**, type a name, and then press Enter or tap away.

4. Drag items from the details pane to the Play tab. Use the Ctrl or Shift keys to select multiple items.

   ◆ To rearrange items, drag them up or down the list.

5. To save the list, click or tap the **Save list** button, type a name, specify a location, and then press Enter or tap away.

   ◆ To save a playlist in a another format, click or tap the **List options** button, and then click **Save list as**.

6. To hide the List pane, click or tap the **List options** button, and then click or tap **Hide list**.

7. To add more items to the playlist, drag them to the playlist, or right-click or tap-hold the the media files, point to **Add to**, and then select the playlist name.

Type playlist name

## Create an Auto Playlist

① Click or tap a media library in the Navigation pane.

② Click or tap the **Create playlist** button, and then click or tap **Create auto playlist**.

③ Type a name for the Auto Playlist.

④ Select the criteria options you want.

⑤ Click or tap **OK**.

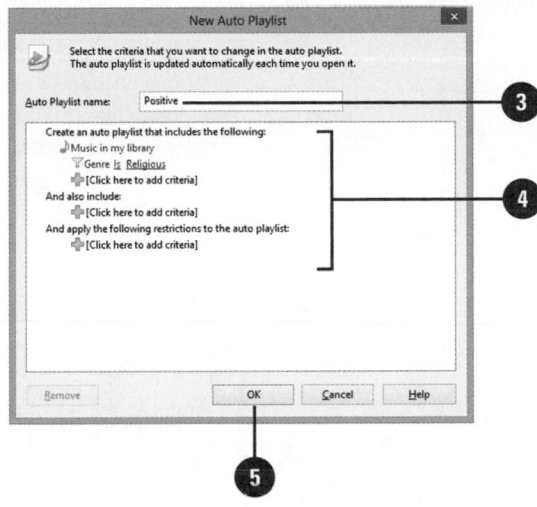

## Add Media Files from Your Hard Disk to a Playlist

① Open the folder window that contains the files or folders you want to add to a playlist.

② Select the file(s) or folder(s) you want to include in the playlist.

③ Right-click or tap-hold the selection, and then click or tap **Add to Windows Media Player list**.

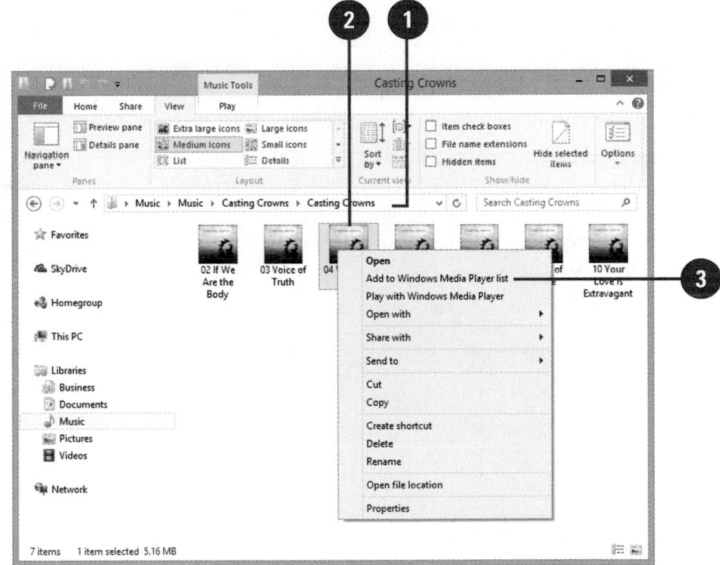

### Did You Know?

**You can delete a playlist.** Right-click or tap-hold the playlist in the Navigation pane, click or tap Delete, click or tap the Delete From Library Only or Delete From Library And My Computer option, and then click or tap OK.

**You can edit playlist.** Click or tap the playlist in the Navigation pane, drag new items to the list or right-click or tap-hold items in the list, and then click or tap Remove From List.

# Ripping CD Music

Windows Media Player (WPM) allows you to **rip**, or copy, one music track or an entire album from a music CD to your PC computer. When you rip music from a CD or download music from the web to your PC computer, Windows copies music by the same artist into one folder in the Music folder and creates subfolders for each album. Windows gives you several ways to play the music on your PC computer.

## Rip Tracks from a Music CD

1. Insert your music CD into the CD-ROM drive.

2. If the Autoplay pop-up notification appears, click or tap the pop-up, and then click or tap **Play audio CD** (Windows Media Player) to burn individual tracks, and then click or tap the **Stop** button.

   The WMP window opens, and starts to play the CD.

3. Use default options, or click or tap the **Rip settings** button, point to **Format** or **Audio Quality**, and then select the option you want.

4. Clear the check boxes next to the tracks you don't want to copy.

5. Click or tap **Rip CD** (toggles with Stop Rip).

   The music is copied to the Music folder unless you specify a different location.

6. To stop the copy at any time, click or tap **Stop Rip**.

Toggles to Start  6   3

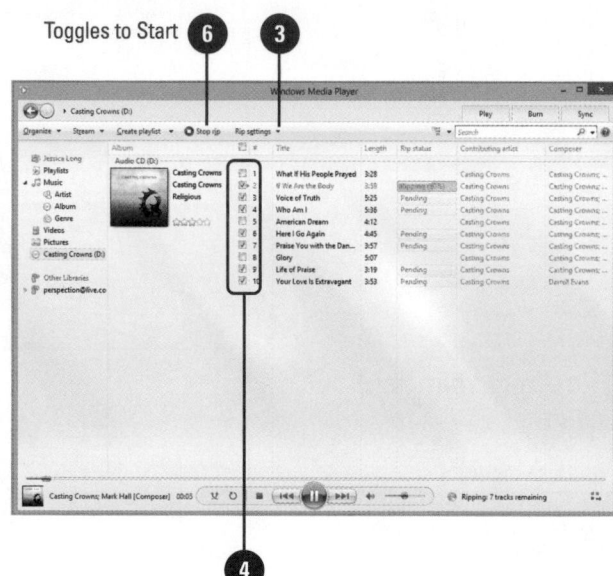

### Did You Know?

***You can use error correction during a copy.*** Click or tap the Tools menu, click or tap Options, click or tap the Devices tab, select the CD-ROM drive, click or tap Properties, click or tap Digital, select the Use Error Correction check box, and then click or tap OK.

## Select Rip Music Settings

1️⃣ Click or tap the **Rip settings** button on the toolbar, and then click or tap **More options**.

◆ You can also select Format and Audio Quality options directly from the Rip settings menu.

2️⃣ To change the location where Windows Media Player stores ripped music, click or tap **Change**, select a new folder location, and then click or tap **OK**.

3️⃣ Select the format and copy setting you want:

◆ **Windows Media Audio** or **Windows Media Audio Pro.** Most common WMA format with widest range of quality and file size.

◆ **Windows Media Audio (Variable Bit Rate).** High quality with variable file size.

◆ **Windows Media Audio Lossless.** Quality closest to the original with high file size.

◆ **MP3.** Common and flexible format.

◆ **WAV (Lossless).** Common alternate format.

4️⃣ Drag the slider to adjust audio quality.

5️⃣ Click or tap **OK**.

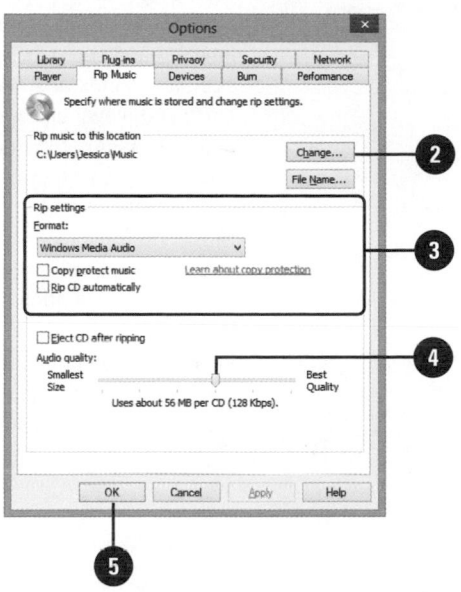

### Did You Know?

*You can turn off music copy protection.* Click or tap the Tools menu, click or tap Options, click or tap the Rip Music tab, clear the Copy Protect Music check box, and then click or tap OK.

### For Your Information

#### Getting a License to Copy Music

Most CD music is secured with a license to prevent illegal distribution. A license is a legal agreement that specifies whether the license expires or how you can use the file. The terms of the license are entirely dependent upon the person or company that provided the file. Windows Media Player cannot play licensed files without a license. When you copy music from a CD with the Acquire Licenses Automatically option selected, Windows Media Player searches the Internet for the license and copies it to your PC computer. If the license is not available, you can still acquire a license by copying the music and selecting the Copy Protect music check box on the Rip Music tab in the Options dialog box. As you copy the music, the licenses are issued. The license allows you to copy the music to your hard disk, a portable device, or a CD. If you want to view the license information for a file, right-click or tap-hold the file, click or tap Properties, and then click or tap the Media Usage Rights tab. If you copy music without a license, you could be violating the music's copyright. You can avoid license problems by backing them up.

# Copying Media Files to a CD or Portable Device

Windows Media Player makes it easy to burn (copy) music to a CD using a CD burner or copy the music and video you want to a portable device and keep it in sync. If you have a Portable Digital Media Player, such as an ipod or zune, you can download digital media from an online store and play it on the go. Windows Media Player verifies that there is enough space for the selected files on the portable device and then starts the copying process. As the music copies, the amount of used and free space on the portable device is displayed at the bottom of the Music On Device pane. You can synchronize music, video, and picture files to the device so you can bring your whole library with you. You can choose to automatically or manually sync your digital media between WMP and your device, known as a partnership. Set up sync once, and every time you connect your device to your PC computer, WMP updates the digital media between them, so devices that allow you to rate your music can automatically send them back to WMP.

## Copy Music to a CD

1. Insert a blank CD or DVD in your CD recorder.

   If the Autoplay pop-up notification appears, click or tap the pop-up, click or tap **Burn an audio CD**. If the Autoplay dialog box doesn't appear, click or tap the **Burn** tab.

   If you need to erase your disc, right-click or tap-hold the drive in the Navigation pane, and then click or tap **Erase disc**.

2. To select a disc type, click or tap the **Burn options** button, and then click or tap **Audio CD** or **Data CD or DVD**.

3. If you need to clear the List pane, click or tap the **Clear list** button.

4. Drag the files you want to burn from the Details pane to the List pane.

5. To remove a file from the list, right-click or tap-hold the file, and then click or tap **Remove from list**.

6. Drag the files in the list to arrange them in the order you want.

7. Click or tap the **Start burn** button.

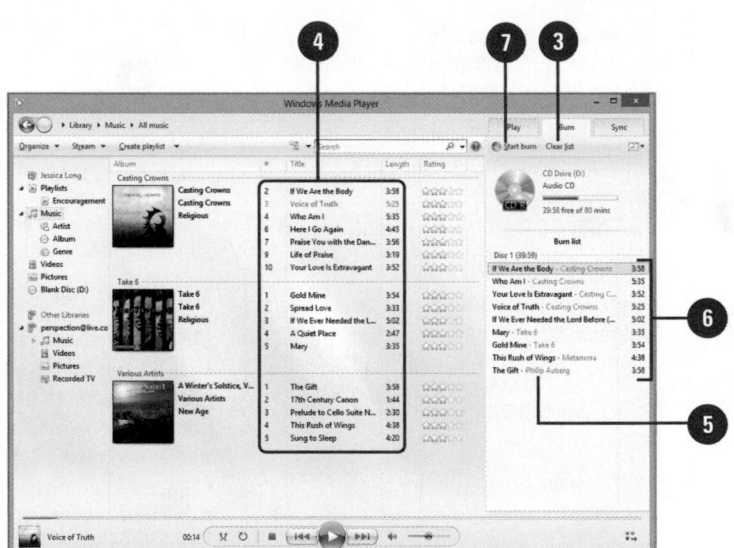

## Copy Music to a Portable Device

1. In Windows Media Player, and then connect the portable device to your PC computer.

2. If sync setup is needed for the device, follow the wizard instructions, and then click or tap **Finish**.

3. If you set up Auto Sync, synchronization begins, click or tap **Stop sync**.

4. Click or tap a media library in the Navigation pane.

5. Click or tap the **Sync** tab.

6. If you need to clear the List pane, click or tap the **Clear list** button.

7. Display and drag the media files you want to the sync list.

8. To remove a file from the list, right-click or tap-hold the file, and then click or tap **Remove from list**.

9. To change sync priority order, sync method, and other settings, click or tap the **Sync options** button, and then click or tap **Set up sync**, specify options, and then click or tap **OK**.

10. Click or tap the **Start sync** button.

11. If you want to stop the sync, click or tap **Stop sync**.

   Upon completion, status appears indicating success or failure.

### Did You Know?

*You can find a list of compatible portable devices.* Open your browser, go to *www.windowsmedia.com*, and then click or tap the Music Players link.

---

## For Your Information

### Changing the Media Player Look

Windows Media Player gives you the freedom of expression to change the look, known as the **skin**, of the Media Player. Windows Media Player includes several skins from which you can select the one you like the best. When you select a skin, Windows Media Player changes from full mode to skin mode. You can use skins only when Media Player is in skin mode. Skin mode displays a smaller player, which provides more room on the screen for other programs. To apply a skin, click or tap the View menu, click or tap Skin Chooser, click or tap a design, click or tap Apply Skin, and then use the controls to play a media file. To delete a skin, click or tap the Delete Selected Skin button, and then click or tap Yes. Press Shift+F10 to display a shortcut menu of convenient commands in skin mode. To return to the full window, click or tap the Return To Full Mode button. To switch back to skin mode, click or tap the View menu, and then click or tap Skin Mode.

# Streaming Media

## Prepare for Streaming Media

① To turn on basic streaming, click or tap the **Stream** button, and then click or tap **Turn on home media streaming**. (If the command is not available, it's turned on.) Click or tap **Turn on media streaming**, and then click or tap **OK**.

② Click or tap the **Stream** button, and then click or tap **More streaming options**.

③ Click or tap **Allow All** to allow all computers to stream, click or tap **Block All** to block all computers, or select **Allowed** or **Blocked** for each individual computer.

④ Click or tap **OK**.

⑤ Click or tap the **Stream** button, and then click or tap an option:

◆ **Allow Internet access to home media.** Click or tap to establish a link to an Online ID provider, such as Windows Live. Sign in and use your account to share files.

◆ **Allow remote control of my Player.** Click or tap to allow or not allow media streaming to another computer.

◆ **Automatically allow devices to play my media.** Click or tap to allow or not allow media streaming from another computer.

If you have a home network, you can use Windows Media Player to stream music and video to and from another PC computer and media devices—such as a networked digital stereo receiver, TV, or Xbox 360—in your home. You can also stream your music library from a home PC computer over the Internet to another PC computer. Before you can start, you need to turn on home media streaming and enable options to allow devices to access, play, or control your media. In Windows Media Player, you can use the Navigation pane to access and play streamed media from another PC computer or media device, or use the Play To button to push media to another PC computer or media device.

Select media types          Name of shared media

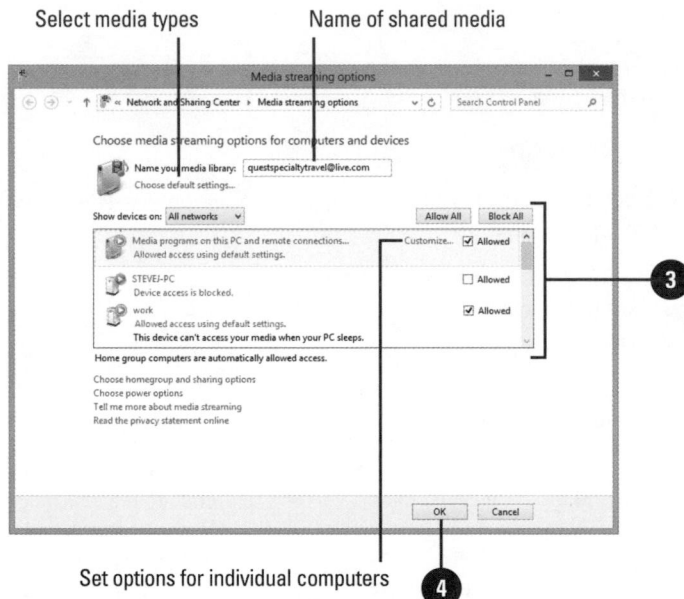

Set options for individual computers

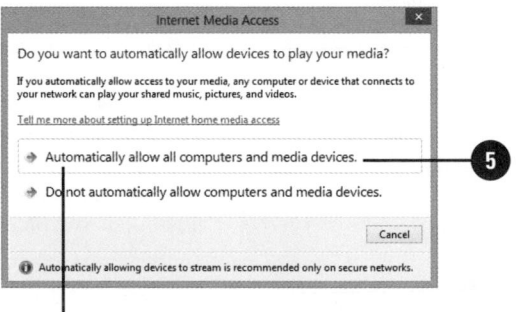

Automatically allow devices to play my media; click or tap on first use.

## Play Media Streamed to or from Another PC Computer

**1** In Windows Media Player, click or tap a media library in the Navigation pane.

◆ **Stream to.** Use your local PC computer under Library.

◆ **Stream from.** Use a networked computer under Other Libraries.

**2** Click or tap an arrow next to the PC computer you want to view, then click or tap a category.

**3** Use either of the following methods.

◆ **Stream to.** Click or tap the **Play To** button under the Play tab, then select a networked computer. This opens the Play To window to control the media.

◆ **Stream from.** Double-click or double tap the media file to play it.

### Did You Know?

*You cannot access or modify the content of a Player library.* The people accessing your media are only permitted to use your computer to play the items in your Player library and cannot add, remove, or modify any items.

*You may have problems on a public network.* If you're on a public network, such as a coffee shop, Windows Firewall might block the streaming process to your Player library. Check your Windows Firewall settings to make sure Windows Media Player is an allowed program. You can also check the Enabled Network Protocols on the Network tab in the Options dialog box. Click or tap the Organize button, and then click or tap Options to open it.

Local PC computer

Networked PC computer

Play To button

**2**

Music playing from networked computer

### For Your Information

#### Adding Functionality to Media Player

Windows Media Player allows you to add functionality to the player using plug-ins. Plug-ins add or enhance the media experience with audio and video effects, new rendering types, and visualizations. Before you can use a plug-in, you need to download it from the web and add it to the Media Player. You can find lots of Media Player plug-ins at *www.wmplugins.com*. Before you download a plug-in, read the online information about the plug-in for additional instructions. Click or tap the Organize button, click or tap Options, and then click or tap the Plug-ins tab. Select a plug-in category. Select a plug-in option, if available. To modify a plug-in, click or tap Properties. To remove a plug-in, click or tap Remove. Click or tap OK.

# Enhancing the Media Player Display

Visualizations are plug-ins that display geometric shapes and color on the Now Playing mode when you play music. Visualizations are grouped together into collections. You can add and remove visualizations or download additional collections from the web. You can also display special enhancement controls to change video settings, play speed, or audio levels with a graphics equalizer, choose color effects, and send a media link in an e-mail.

## Select Visualizations

1. In Windows Media Player, click or tap the **Switch to Now Playing** button.

2. Right-click or tap-hold the window, and then point to **Visualizations**.

3. Point to a category, and then click or tap the visualization you want to display.

4. To go back to the library, click or tap the **Switch to Library** button.

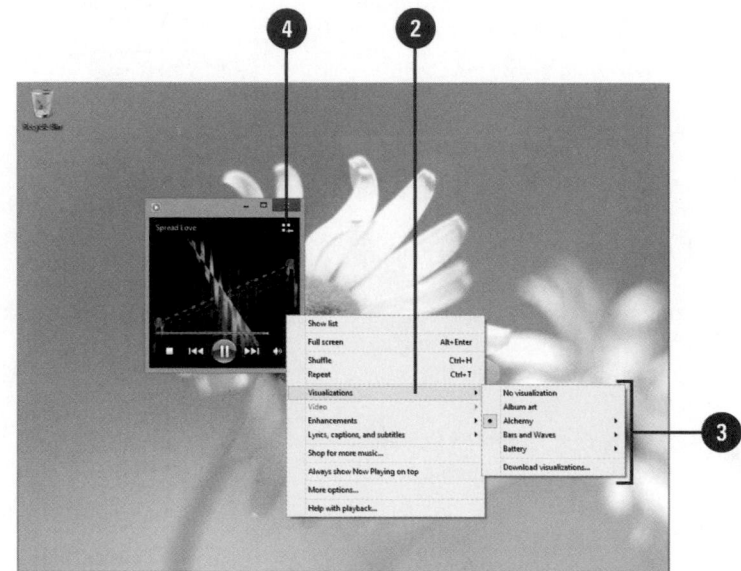

## Select Enhancements

1. In Windows Media player, click or tap the **Switch to Now Playing** button.

2. Right-click or tap-hold the window, and then point to **Enhancements**.

3. Click or tap the enhancement you want to display.

4. Adjust the enhancement controls.

5. When you're done, click or tap the **Close** button in the control.

6. To go back to the library, click or tap the **Switch to Library** button.

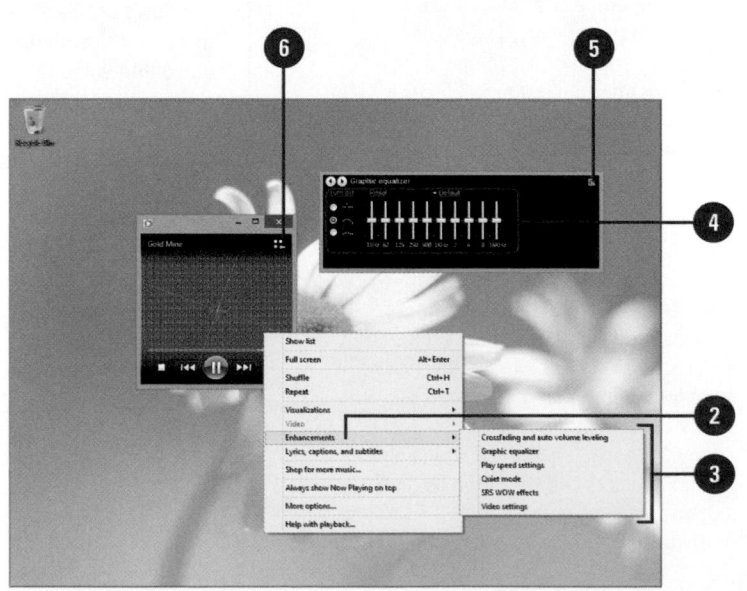

# Viewing and Playing Music Files

You can view and play music files with relative ease in the Music folder. The Music folder is a folder specifically designated to play and manage music files. When you copy music files from a CD or download them from the Internet, the files are copied to the Music folder by default unless you specify a different location. The Music folder contains links to specialized music tasks that can help you play the music you store on your PC computer. In the Music folder, you can click or tap Play All or Play on the Play tab or double-click or double-tap an individual music file to open and play the music in Windows Media Player. If you click or tap Play All in the Music folder, Windows Media Player opens and plays all the music in your Music folder and subfolder in random order. If you click or tap Play All in a subfolder within your Music folder, Windows Media Player opens and plays all the music in the folder in consecutive order. In addition to playing music, you can also add music files to a playlist in Windows Media Player.

## View and Play Music Files

1. In File Explorer (desktop), click or tap **Music** in the Navigation pane.

2. Select the music files or folder you want to play.

3. Click or tap the **Play** tab under Music Tools

4. To add the selected music files to a playlist, click the **Add to playlist** button.

   The files are added to a new playlist in Windows Media Player.

5. To play the selected music files or all the music files in the folder, click or tap the **Play** or **Play all** button.

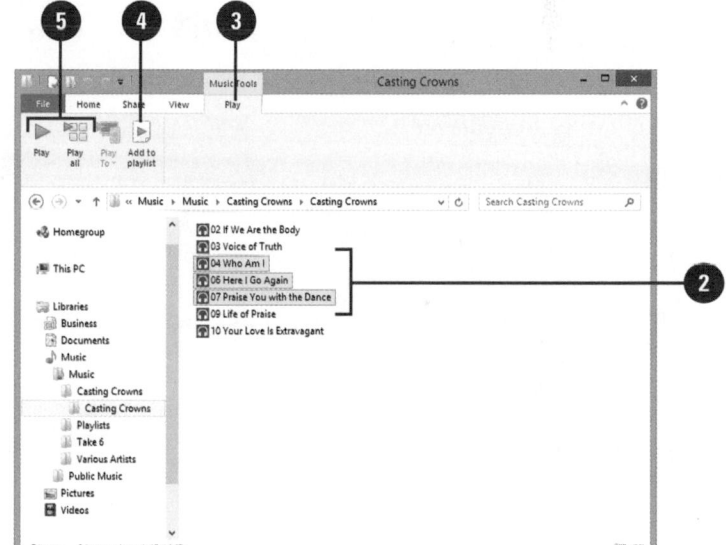

# Recording a Sound File

With the Sound Recorder app or Windows accessory and a microphone, you can record your own sound files. Sound Recorder creates Windows Media Audio files with the .wma file extension. Before you can use Sound Recorder, you need to have a sound card, speakers, and a microphone installed on your PC computer. When you open the Sound Recording app for the first time, you're asked to allow or block the use of your microphone. When you record a sound with the app, you can trim the start or end if you like, and play it back. If you don't like the way a sound came out or no longer want it, you can delete it at any time. Sound files are stored in an AppData folder; to locate it, perform a search in This PC in File Explorer (desktop). When you record a sound with the Windows accessory, you can save it where you want.

## Use the Sound Recorder Program

1. In the Start screen, click or tap the **Apps view** button, and then click or tap **Sound Recorder** (under Windows Accessories).

2. Click or tap the **Start Recording** button, and then record the sounds you want.

3. When you're done, click or tap the **Stop Recording** button.

4. Select a folder, type a name for the file, and then click or tap **Save**.

5. Click or tap the **Close** button.

Sound Recorder doesn't play sounds; you can play your recording in a digital media player, such as Windows Media Player.

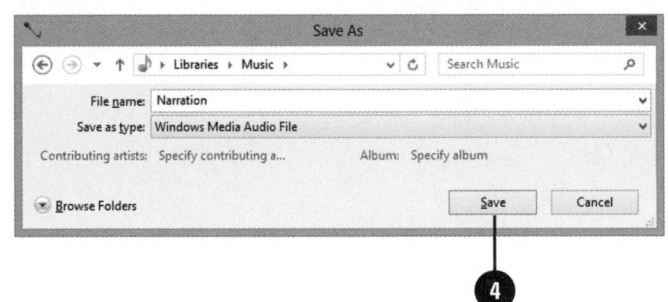

## Use the Sound Recorder App

1. In the Start screen, click or tap the **Apps view** button, and then click or tap **Sound Recorder** (app).

2. If prompted, click or tap **Allow** or **Block** to enable or disable the use of your webcam and microphone.

3. To record a sound, click or tap the **Microphone** button to start it, and then click or tap it again to stop it.

4. To rename the sound, click the **Rename** button on the App bar, enter a name, and then click or tap **Rename**.

5. To trim a sound, click or tap the **Trim** button on the App bar, drag the start or end handles, and then click or tap **OK**.

6. To play/pause a sound, select the sound, click or tap the **Play/Pause** button on the App bar.

   ◆ **Playhead.** You can drag the playhead to adjust the start position.

7. To delete a sound, select the sound, click or tap the **Delete** button on the App bar.

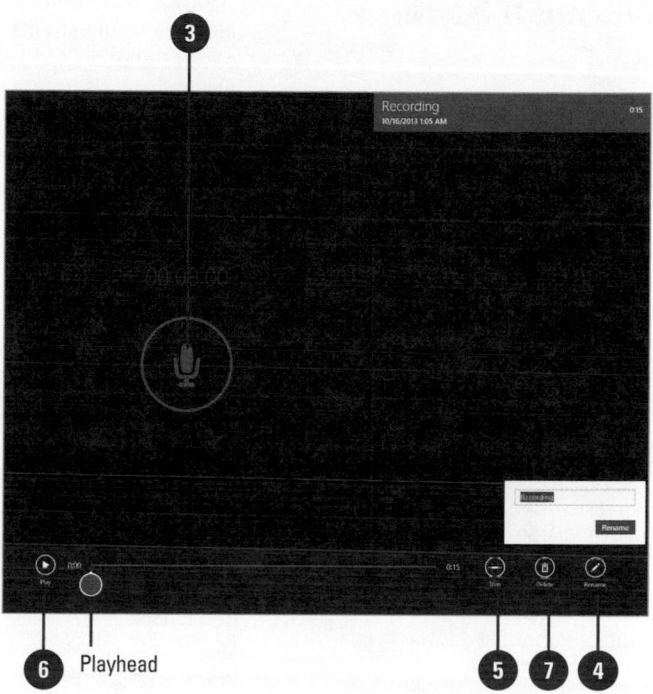

Playhead

# Associating a Sound with an Event

Besides customizing the desktop appearance of Windows, you can also add sound effects to common Windows commands and functions, such as starting and exiting Windows, printing complete, opening and closing folders, or emptying the Recycle Bin. You can select a sound scheme (a collection of sounds associated with events), or you can mix and match sound files to create your own sound scheme for your PC computer. You need to use Wave files with the .wav file extension. If you put WAV files in the Media folder, located in the Windows folder, the sound files appear in the Sounds list.

## Create and Select a Sound Scheme

1. In File Explorer (desktop), click **Computer** in the Navigation pane, click or tap the **Control Panel** button on the Computer tab, and then click or tap the **Sound** icon in Small icons or Large icons view.

   ◆ You can also click or tap the **Control Panel** tile on the Apps screen.

2. Click or tap the **Sounds** tab.

3. Click or tap an event to which you want to associate a sound.

4. Click or tap the **Sounds** list arrow, and then select a sound, or click or tap **Browse** and locate the sound file you want to use.

   ◆ Select **(None)** to remove a sound association.

5. Click or tap the **Test** button to preview the sound.

6. Click or tap **Save As**, type a name for the sound scheme, and then click or tap **OK**.

7. To select a sound scheme, click or tap the **Sound Scheme** list arrow, and then select a scheme.

8. Click or tap **OK**.

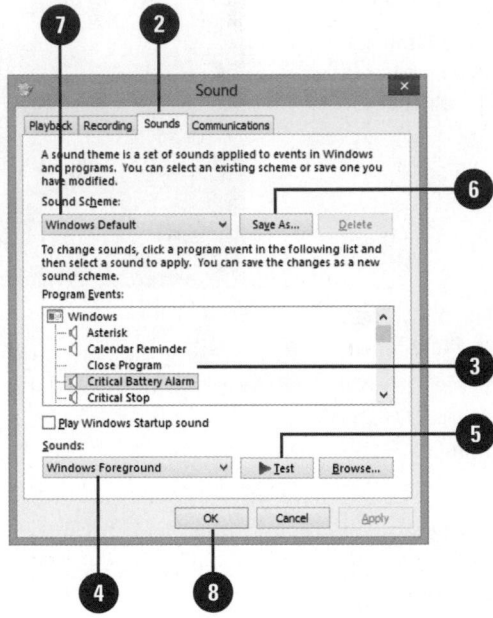

# Starting and Navigating Windows Media Center

Windows Media Center is an entertainment system integrated into your PC computer that lets you watch live or recorded TV, play video and watch pictures, create and play slide shows, listen to music and radio using an FM tuner or the Internet, play and burn CDs or DVDs, and play games. When you start Windows Media Center, the program uses the entire screen and doesn't use menus or toolbars. You navigate by using the up and down arrows to specify a main category, and then left and right arrows to specify a subcategory using Turbo Scroll. Play, Record, and other VCR/DVD type commands are available in the bottom right corner when you point to them. You can use your keyboard, mouse, a remote control, or touch screen to navigate the system. Before you can play FM radio or watch TV, you need additional hardware installed on your PC computer, an FM tuner and a TV tuner card along with a remote control. For some versions of Windows 8.1, you may need to download Windows Media Center from the Microsoft web site as a separate file or as part of Windows 8.1 Pro Pack.

## Start, Navigate, and Exit Windows Media Center

1. In the Start screen, click or tap the **Apps view** button, and then click or tap **Window Media Center**.

2. Press the Up or Down arrow keys or tap arrows to scroll the list of categories: **Extras**, **Pictures + Videos**, **Music**, **Movies**, and **TV**.

3. With the category you want, press the Left and Right arrow keys or tap arrows to display the subcategory you want, and then click or tap the option icon.

4. Click or tap the options you want to play music, movies, or videos, watch TV, display pictures, or create and display slide shows.

5. To get back to the main screen, point to the upper-left corner, and then click or tap the **Home** button. To go back to the previous screen, click or tap the **Back** button.

6. To exit, point to the upper-right corner, and then click or tap the **Close** button.

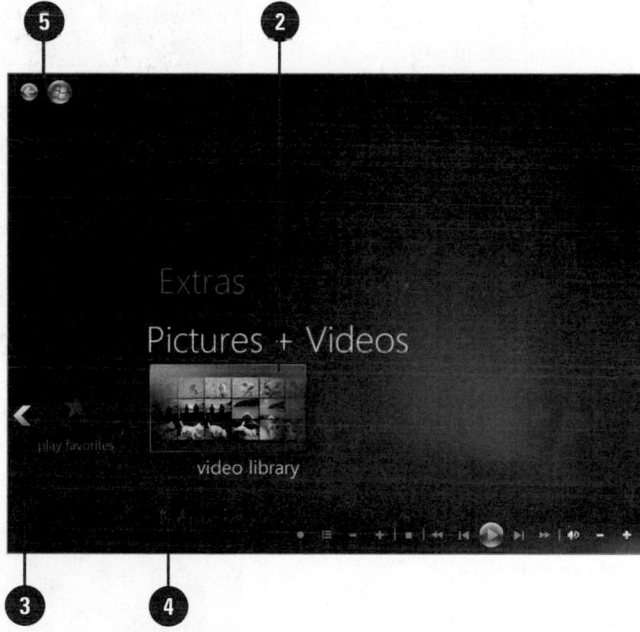

# Changing Windows Media Center Settings

You can set up and customize Windows Media Center by selecting Tasks on the start screen, and then selecting Settings. In the Settings area, you can set general options for Windows Media Center and specific options for each of the media types, including TV, Pictures, Music, and DVD. You can also set options for extenders and libraries. A Windows Media Center Extender is a device you connect to your PC computer, such as a TV, DVD player, digital camera, or Xbox 360, that you want to control from Windows Media Center within a networked environment. Before you get started with Windows Media Center, it's a good idea to set general options, which include startup and window behavior, visual and sound effects, program library options, Windows Media Center set up, automatic download options, optimization, and privacy. You can also block access to objectionable TV shows and movies with Family Safety controls in Windows Media Center.

## Change Windows Media Center Settings

1. In the Windows Media Center start screen, scroll to **Tasks**.

2. Display and click or tap **settings**.

3. Click or tap the type of settings you want to change: **General**, **TV**, **Pictures**, **Music**, **DVD**, **Start Menu and Extras**, **Extender**, or **Media Libraries**.

4. Click or tap the setting type you want to change.

5. Specify the options you want. Use the up and down arrow to display option screens.

   Depending on the option, follow the on-screen wizard to complete the setup or settings.

6. When you're done, click or tap **Save** or **Cancel**, if available.

7. Click or tap the **Back** button to navigate back to the previous screen, or click or tap the **Home** button to go back to the start screen.

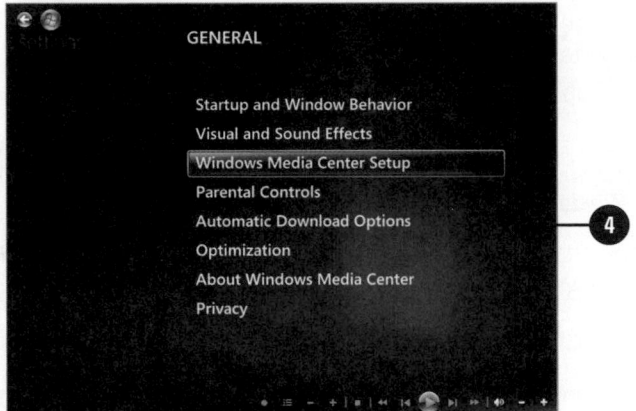

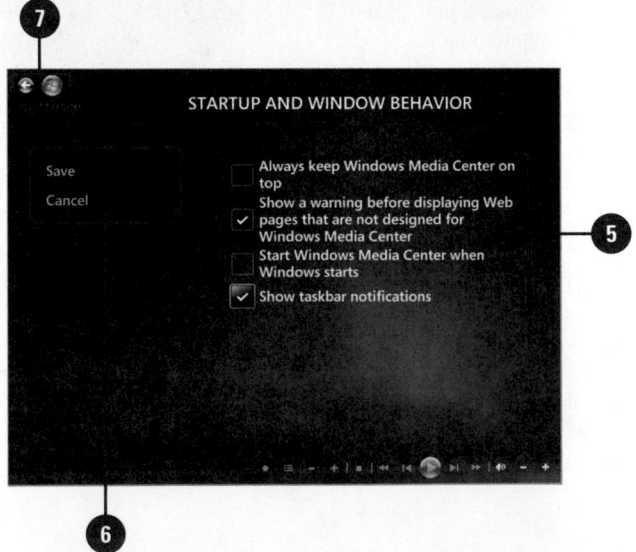

# Working with Online Media

## Introduction

Windows 8.1 comes with a host of media related apps that allow you to get specialized information, manage and share files online, capture photos and video, watch movies and tv shows, listen to music, and play games.

If you need information on a specific topic, Windows provides specialized apps, such as News, Finance, Travel, Sports, Weather, Food & Drink, Health & Fitness, and Maps, with the information you need. For example, if you want to find out the latest sports news, all you need to do is start the Sports app. This reduces the amount of searching you need to perform in order to find what you need. As you browse articles in apps and on the web, you can add them to the Reading List app in order to view later. If you have a PDF or XPS document, you can use the Reader app to view and read it.

In addition to the specialized information apps, you can use the SkyDrive app to work with files stored on a cloud-based file hosting service that you can sync with other devices, such as Windows Phone, iPhone, or Android. With the Alarms app, you can set alarms and use a timer or stopwatch. With the Camera app, you can use a digital camera, such as a webcam, to capture a still photo or video. After you capture a photo, you can crop it as desired; for a video, you can trim it.

Windows 8.1 integrates the use of Xbox Live in the Video, Music, and Games apps to let you watch movies and tv shows, listen to music, and play games (locally or on a connected Xbox 360 console). With an existing Xbox Live or Microsoft account, you can purchase online media content for use in any of these apps. You can also use the Devices button on the Charms bar within an app to work with devices, such as a printer or second screen, attached to your system.

## What You'll Do

**Get News Information**

**Get Financial Updates**

**Get Travel Information**

**Get the Latest Sports News**

**Get the Latest Weather**

**Get Food & Drink Information**

**Get Health & Fitness Information**

**Create Reading List**

**Read Documents**

**View Maps and Directions**

**Manage and Share Files with SkyDrive**

**Change SkyDrive Settings**

**Set Alarms**

**Capture a Photo or Video**

**Watch Videos**

**Play Games**

**Listen to Music**

**Use Devices with Apps**

# Getting News Information

The News app that comes with Windows 8.1 provides a centralized place to focus on news information from around the world. You can view top stories and the latest news in business, technology, entertainment, politics, and sports. If you you like to view your news from a specific source, you can select it from an organized list. If you're looking for a specific topic, you can search for it using the News app. The full screen app provides options—take a tour, customize, add a section—to help you get started as well as organizes information into easy to view and read categories (which you can customize) that you can view directly with the App bar or scroll through to find the information you want.

## Use the News App

1. Click or tap the **News** tile on the Start or Apps screen.

2. In the Get Started panel (**New!**), click or tap to take a tour, customize your news, add a section, or remove the panel.

3. To search for information, enter it in the Search box.

4. To navigate around, right-click the screen (on a computer) or swipe up from the bottom edge or down from the top edge of the screen (on a mobile device), and then click or tap a category or source.

5. To view sections, move the pointer to display the button, click or tap the **Zoom In** button, or pinch in, and then click or tap a section tile.

6. To scroll through sections, move the pointer to display the scroll bar and then drag the scroll bar or click or tap the arrows, or swipe left or right.

7. To go back to the previous screen, click or tap the **Back** button.

Quick access to news sources

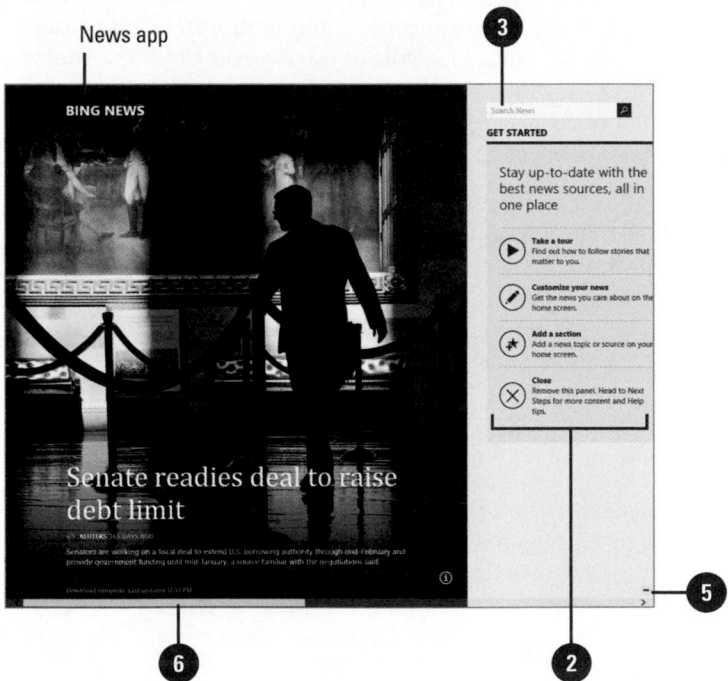

News app

## Customize the News App

① Click or tap the **News** tile on the Start or Apps screen.

② Click or tap **Customize your news** in the Get Started panel or click or tap the **Customize** button on the App bar.

③ To add content, click or tap any of the following **Add** buttons (+):

- ◆ **Topics.** Adds a topic.
- ◆ **Sources.** Adds a section from top news organizations.
- ◆ **Editors' Picks.** Adds a section from Editor's Picks.
- ◆ **International News.** Adds a section from International news sources.

④ To reorder or remove sections, do any of the following:

- ◆ **Reorder.** Drag a section to another position.
- ◆ **Delete.** Click or tap the Delete button (x) for the section.

⑤ To go back to the previous screen, click or tap the **Back** button.

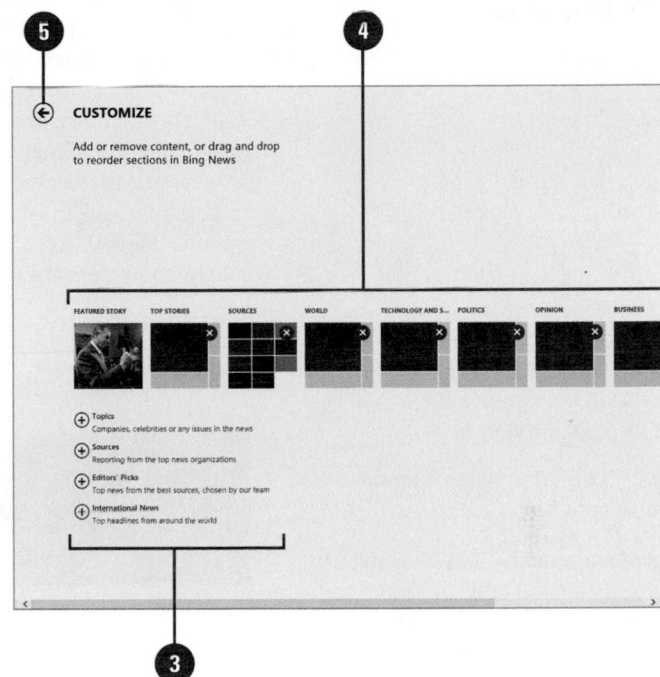

### Did You Know?

*You can change the language used for the News app and content.* In the News app, click or tap the Settings button on the Charms bar, click or tap Options, and then select a language for the app and content. To read articles online or offline, drag the slider on or off.

# Getting Financial Updates

The Finance app that comes with Windows 8.1 provides a centralized place to focus on financial information from around the world. You can view the latest financial news, industrial averages and indices, world markets, major currencies, stock watch lists and market movers, articles, current rates, and fund returns. The full screen app organizes information from Financial institutions, such as Morning star, into easy to view and read categories that you can view directly with the App bar or scroll through to find the information you want. In Personalization options (**New!**), you can set options to sync across devices, use information to personalize your experience, and control advertising settings.

## Use the Financial App

**1** Click or tap the **Finance** tile on the Start or Apps screen.

**2** To search for information, enter it in the Search box.

**3** To navigate around, right-click the screen (on a computer) or swipe up from the bottom edge or down from the top edge of the screen (on a mobile device), and then click or tap a category or source.

**4** To view sections, move the pointer to display the button, click or tap the **Zoom In** button, or pinch in, and then click or tap a section tile.

**5** To scroll through sections, move the pointer to display the scroll bar and then drag the scroll bar or click or tap the arrows, or swipe left or right.

**6** To go back to the previous screen, click or tap the **Back** button.

### Did You Know?

*You can change the language used for the Financial app and content.* In the Financial app, click or tap the Settings button on the Charms bar, click or tap Options, and then select a language for the app and content.

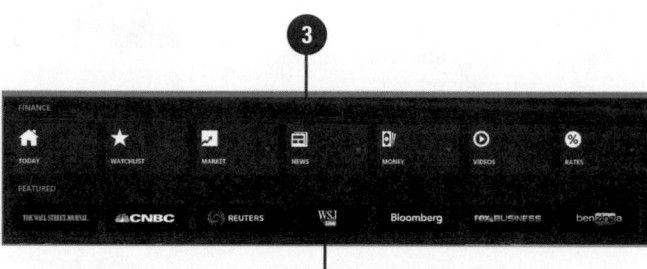

Quick access to financial sources

Financial market information

# Getting Travel Information

The Travel app that comes with Windows 8.1 provides a convenient place to focus on all things travel. You can discover the best of the web, view destinations, and book flights and hotels. You can find what's hot in travel today, look around at featured destinations, view panoramas, and and read magazine articles. The full screen app organizes information from Bing into easy to view and read categories that you can view directly with the App bar or scroll through to find the information you want.

## Use the Travel App

1 Click or tap the **Travel** tile on the Start or Apps screen.

2 To search for travel information, click or tap a tool or task, or enter a destination in the Search box.

3 To navigate around, right-click the screen (on a computer) or swipe up from the bottom edge or down from the top edge of the screen (on a mobile device), and then click or tap a category or source.

4 To view sections, move the pointer to display the button, click or tap the **Zoom In** button, or pinch in, and then click or tap a section tile.

5 To scroll through sections, move the pointer to display the scroll bar and then drag the scroll bar or click or tap the arrows, or swipe left or right.

6 To go back to the previous screen, click or tap the **Back** button.

Quick access to travel sources

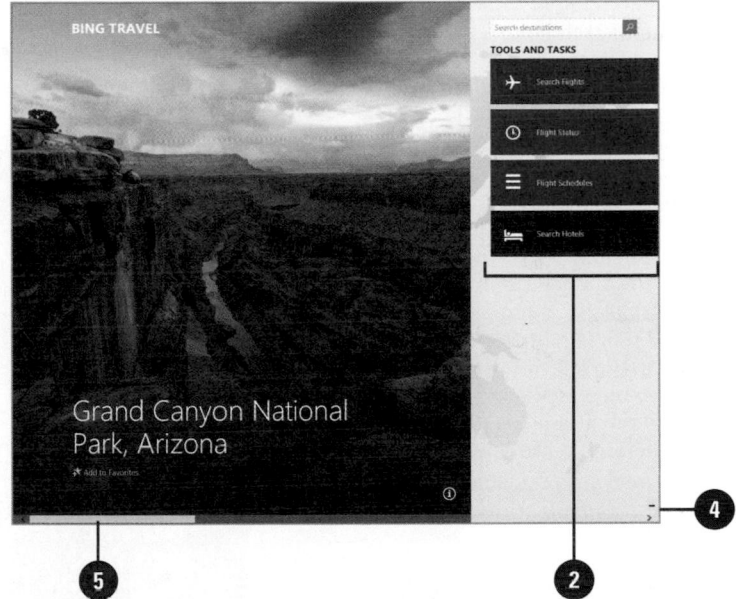

# Getting the Latest Sports News

If you're a sports nut, then you'll love the Sports app that comes with Windows 8.1. The Sports app allows you to view the latest news in the world of sports. You can read the top stories, get the latest news, look at schedules, and read magazine articles. You can also customize the Sports app to focus on your favorite teams. The full screen app provides options—take a tour and add your favorite sports—to help you get started as well as organizes information from Bing into easy to view and read categories that you can view directly with the App bar or scroll through to find the information you want. In Personalization options (**New!**), you can set options to sync across devices, use information to personalize your experience, and control advertising settings.

## Use the Sports App

1. Click or tap the **Sports** tile on the Start or Apps screen.

2. In the Get Started panel (**New!**), click or tap to take a tour, add your favorite sports, or remove the panel.

3. To search for information, enter it in the Search box.

4. To navigate around, right-click the screen (on a computer) or swipe up from the bottom edge or down from the top edge of the screen (on a mobile device), and then click or tap a category tile.

5. To view sections, move the pointer to display the button, click or tap the **Zoom In** button, or pinch in, and then click or tap a section tile.

6. To scroll through sections, move the pointer to display the scroll bar and then drag the scroll bar or click or tap the arrows, or swipe left or right.

7. To go back to the previous screen, click or tap the **Back** button.

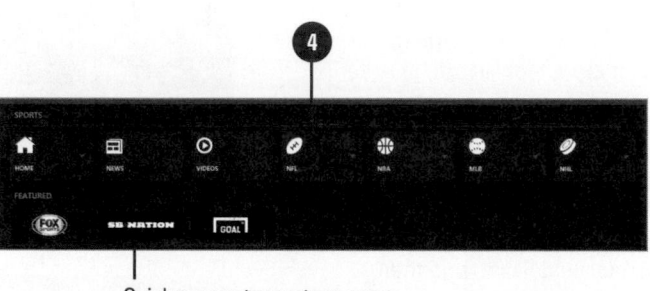

Quick access to sports sources

## Customize the Sports App for Your Favorite Teams

1. Click or tap the **Sports** tile on the Start or Apps screen.

2. Move the pointer to display the button, click or tap the **Zoom In** button, or pinch in, and then click or tap **Favorite Teams**.

3. Click or tap the **Add** button (+) under Favorite Teams.

4. Type the name of your favorite team.

   As you type a list of suggestions appears.

5. Click or tap **Add**.

6. When you're done adding teams, click or tap **Cancel**.

7. To go back to the previous screen, click or tap the **Back** button.

### Did You Know?

*You can change the language and auto refresh for the Sports app.* In the Sports app, click or tap the Settings button on the Charms bar, click or tap Options, and then select a language for the app and content.

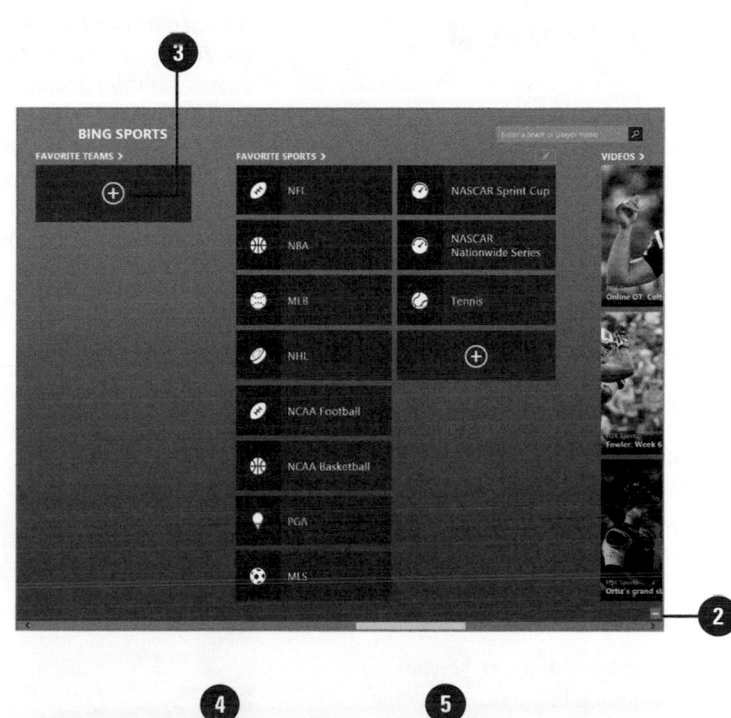

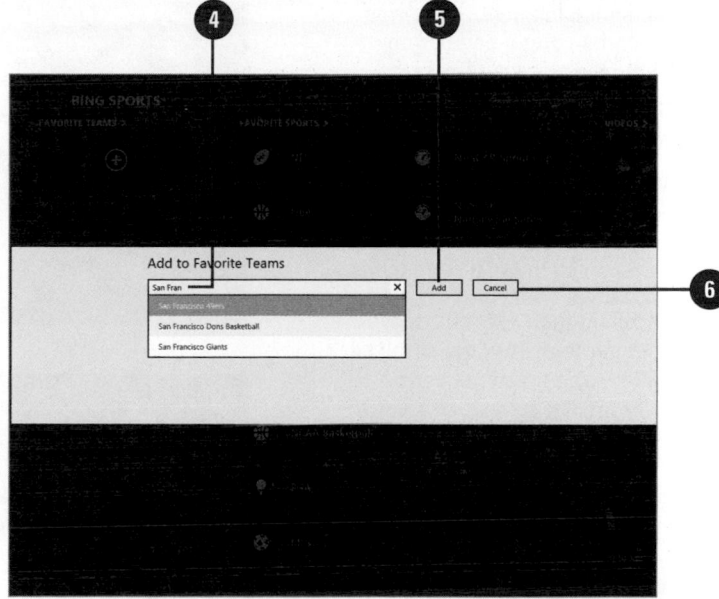

# Getting the Latest Weather

As you get ready to start the day or go on a trip, it's good to know what the weather is like, so you can prepare for it. With the Weather app that comes with Windows 8.1, you can get all the weather information you need from Bing for your local area or other areas that you might be going to visit. You can get hourly forecasts, maps, and historical weather. You can also customize the Weather app to display your local weather. The full screen app provides options—take a tour and add your favorite places—to help you get started as well as organizes information from Bing into easy to view and read categories that you can view directly with the App bar or scroll through to find the information you want.

## Use the Weather App

① Click or tap the **Weather** tile on the Start or Apps screen.

② In the Get Started panel (**New!**), click or tap to take a tour, add your favorite places, or remove the panel.

③ To navigate around, right-click the screen (on a computer) or swipe up from the bottom edge or down from the top edge of the screen (on a mobile device), and then click or tap a category tile.

④ To view sections, move the pointer to display the button, click or tap the **Zoom In** button, or pinch in, and then click or tap a section tile.

⑤ To scroll through sections, move the pointer to display the scroll bar and then drag the scroll bar or click or tap the arrows, or swipe left or right.

⑥ To go back to the previous screen, click or tap the **Back** button.

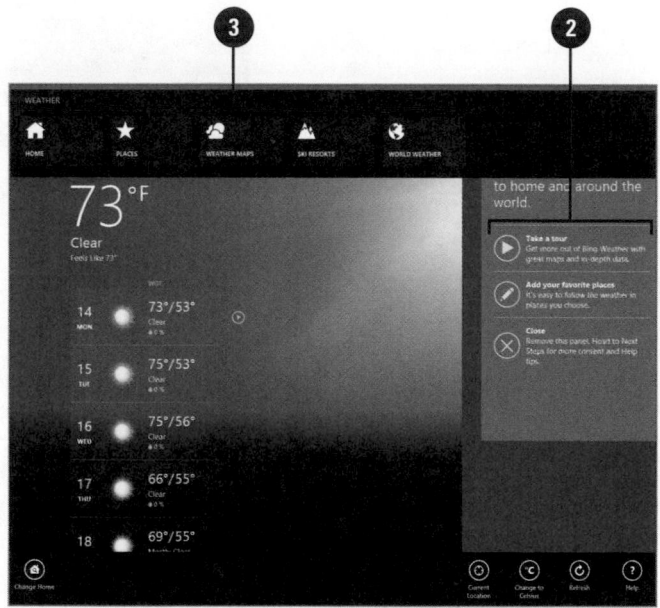

## Did You Know?

*You can view weather in celsius or fahrenheit.* In the Weather app, click or tap the Change To Celsius or Change To Fahrenheit button on the App bar; the button toggles back and forth.

## Customize the Weather App for Your Local Area

1. Click or tap the **Weather** tile on the Start or Apps screen.

2. Right-click the screen (on a computer) or swipe up from the bottom edge or down from the top edge of the screen (on a mobile device), and then click or tap **Places** on the App bar.

3. To add a favorite, click or tap the **Add** button (+).

4. Enter your location, and then select it from the list.

5. Click or tap **Add**.

6. To remove a favorite, click or tap the **Edit** button, and then click or tap the **Delete** button (x)..

7. To change the home default, click or tap the **Home** button, enter your location, select it from the list, and then click or tap **Confirm**.

8. To go back to the previous screen, click or tap the **Back** button.

### Did You Know?

*You can clear the search history for the Weather app.* In the Weather app, click or tap the Settings button on the Charms bar, click or tap Options, and then drag the slider to On or Off. To clear searches, click or tap Clear Weather Searches.

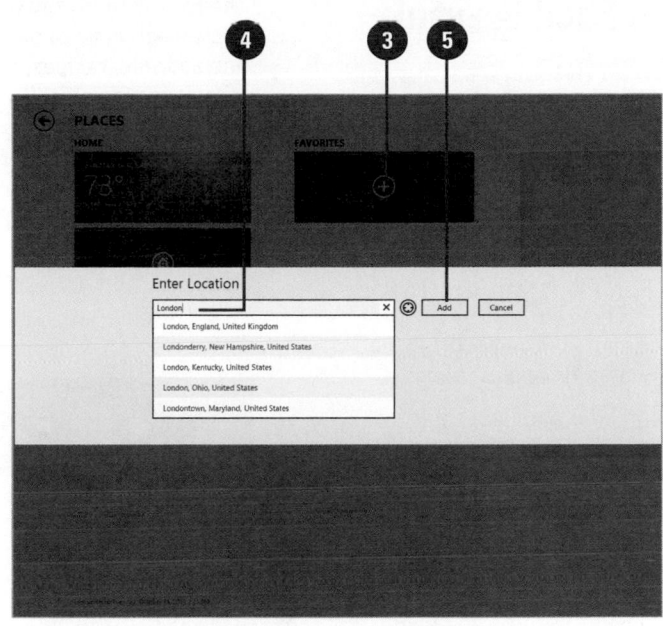

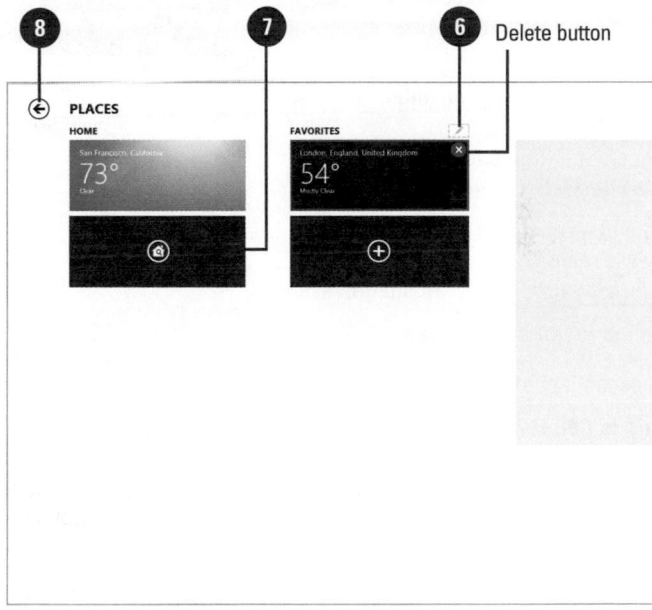

Delete button

# Getting Food & Drink Information

The Food & Drink app (**New!**) that comes with Windows 8.1 provides a convenient place to get information from Bing on food & drink. You can find and view recipes, even using hands-free mode by waving your hand in front of a camera. If you like a recipe, you can add it to a collection—like a bookmark—for easy reference in the future or add it to your meal planning for the week. If you have your own tried and true recipes, you can also add them to a collection. If you need ingredients for a recipe, you can add them to a shopping list that you can save or print out.

## Use the Food & Drink App

**1** Click or tap the **Food & Drink** tile on the Start or Apps screen.

**2** To search for a recipe, enter search text in the Search box.

**3** To navigate around, right-click the screen (on a computer) or swipe up from the bottom edge or down from the top edge of the screen (on a mobile device), and then click or tap a category tile.

♦ To edit or delete, use buttons on the App bar.

**4** To browse recipes, scroll, click or tap **Browse Recipes**, or a category, and then click or tap a filter as desired to narrow it down.

♦ To add a recipe, click or tap **Add a recipe**, enter a title, and take a picture or add an image.

**5** To view a recipe, click or tap it.

**6** Click or tap any of the following:

♦ **Add to Collections.** Add the recipe to a collection.

♦ **Add to Meal Planner.** Add the recipe a weekly meal planner.

♦ **Hands-Free Mode.** Wave your hand in front a camera to turn recipe pages.

♦ **Add to Shopping List.** Add ingredients to a shopping list.

**7** To go back to the previous screen, click or tap the **Back** button.

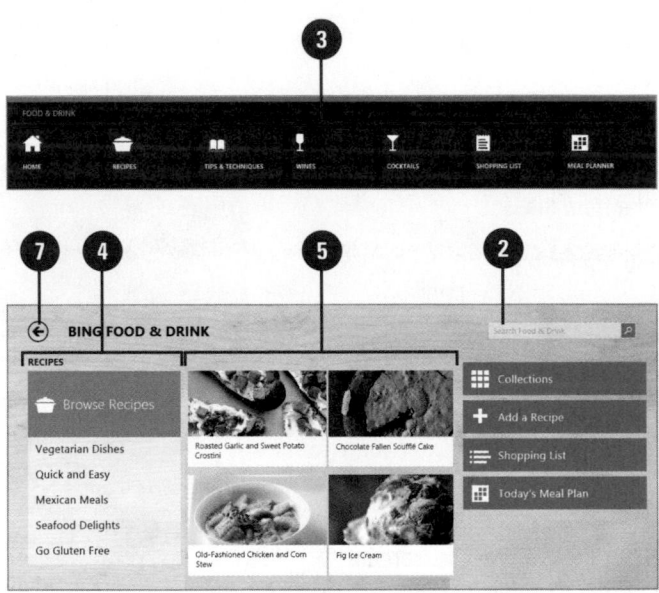

# Getting Health & Fitness Information

The Health & Fitness app (**New!**) that comes with Windows 8.1 provides a convenient place to to get information on health and fitness. You can find and track information on nutrition and calories, exercise, and health, including symptoms, drugs, and conditions. The full screen app organizes information from Bing into easy to view and read categories and videos that you can view directly with the App bar or scroll through to find the information you want. In My Profile options, you can specify your own information as a baseline for progress. In Personalization options, you can set options to sync across devices, use information to personalize your experience, and control advertising settings.

## Use the Health & Fitness App

1. Click or tap the **Health & Fitness** tile on the Start or Apps screen.

2. In the Get Started panel, click or tap to take a tour or remove the panel. In the Personalize panel, enter my profile information.

3. To search for information, enter search text in the Search box.

4. To navigate around, right-click the screen (on a computer) or swipe up from the bottom edge or down from the top edge of the screen (on a mobile device), and then click or tap a category tile.

5. To browse information, scroll, and then click or tap a category, topic, video, or article.

6. Click or tap any of the following:

   ◆ **Diet Tracker.** Track your calorie intake and dietary needs.

   ◆ **Nutrition and Calories.** Look up information.

   ◆ **Exercise Tracker.** Track your exercise program

   ◆ **Health Tracker.** Track your physical health.

   ◆ **Symptoms.** Check symptoms step by step using lists.

   ◆ **Drugs and Conditions.** Look up information.

7. To go back to the previous screen, click or tap the **Back** button.

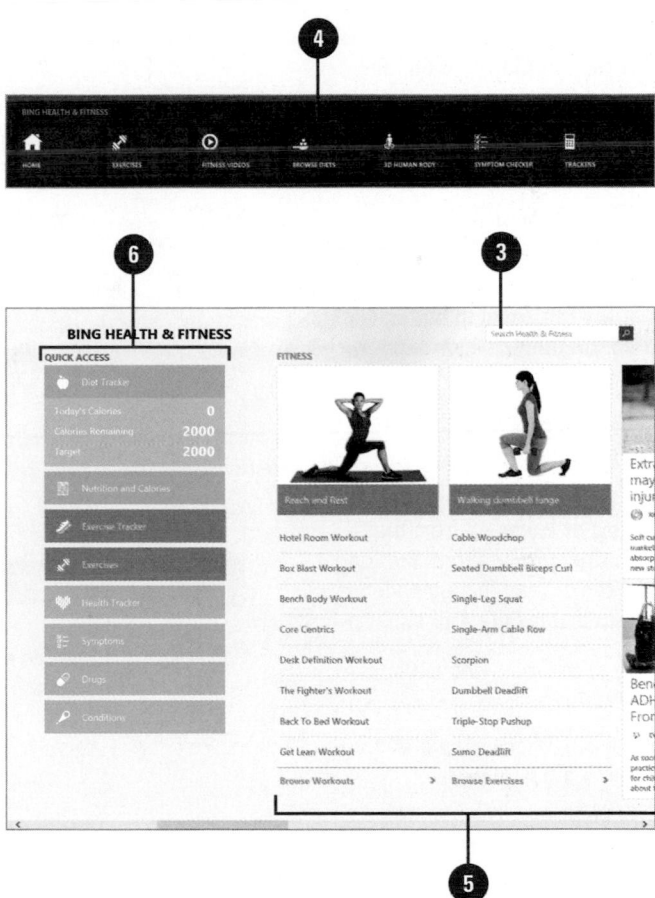

# Viewing Maps and Directions

With the Maps app that comes with Windows 8.1, you can view maps and get directions for any place in the world. The full screen app makes it easy to view maps, either at a high level with a big picture view or at a street level with a details view. When you open the Maps app for the first time, you're asked to allow or block the use of location services, which makes use of your location, a diamond on the map. The full screen app organizes information from Bing into easy to view and read categories that you can view directly with the App bar or scroll through to find the information you want. You can search for points of interest (**New!**), such as places to eat, see, shop, bank, or park.

## View Maps

1. Click or tap the **Maps** tile on the Start or Apps screen.

2. If prompted, click or tap **Allow** or **Block** to enable or disable location services.

3. To zoom in or out, move the pointer to display the buttons, and then click or tap the **Zoom In** button (+) or **Zoom Out** button (-), or pinch in or out.

    **TIMESAVER** *Press Ctrl+ + or Ctrl+ - to zoom in or out.*

4. Right-click the screen (on a computer) or swipe up from the bottom edge or down from the top edge of the screen (on a mobile device) to display the App bar.

5. Use any of the following options on the App bar.

    ◆ **Add a pin.** Click or tap and drag to place a pin (**New!**).

    ◆ **Map style.** Displays the map in Road view or Aerial view, or Show traffic.

    ◆ **My location.** Toggles my location (diamond) on (filled) or off (not filled).

    ◆ **Directions.** Provides directions from a start destination to an end destination.

    ◆ **Search.** Search for points of interest (**New!**).

Navigation tiles　　　My location

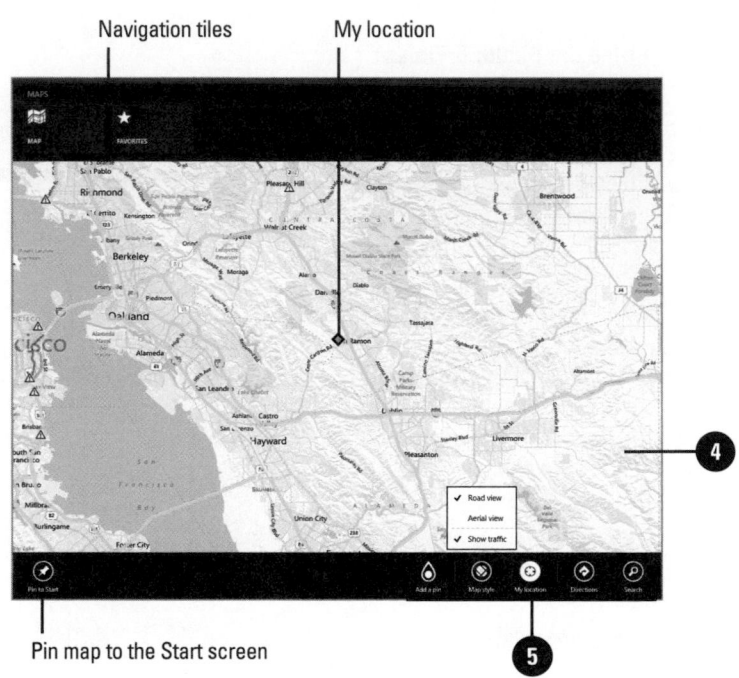

Pin map to the Start screen

## Get Directions with the Maps App

1. Click or tap the **Maps** tile on the Start or Apps screen.

2. Right-click the screen (on a computer) or swipe up from the bottom edge or down from the top edge of the screen (on a mobile device).

   The App bar appears.

3. Click or tap the **Directions** button on the App bar.

   **TIMESAVER** *Press Ctrl+D to get directions.*

4. Click or tap in the **Start** box (A), and then enter a start location.

   ◆ To cancel an entry, click the **Close** button (x) in the box.

5. Click or tap in the **End** box (B), and then enter a end location.

6. Click or tap the **Get directions** button.

   ◆ To switch the start and end destination, click or tap the **Get reverse directions** button.

7. Click or tap the travel method (Car, Bus, or Walk), and then drag the slider on or off for options to avoid highways or tolls.

8. Click or tap the directions on the map, or scroll the top banner.

9. To clear the map, click or tap the **Clear map** button on the App bar.

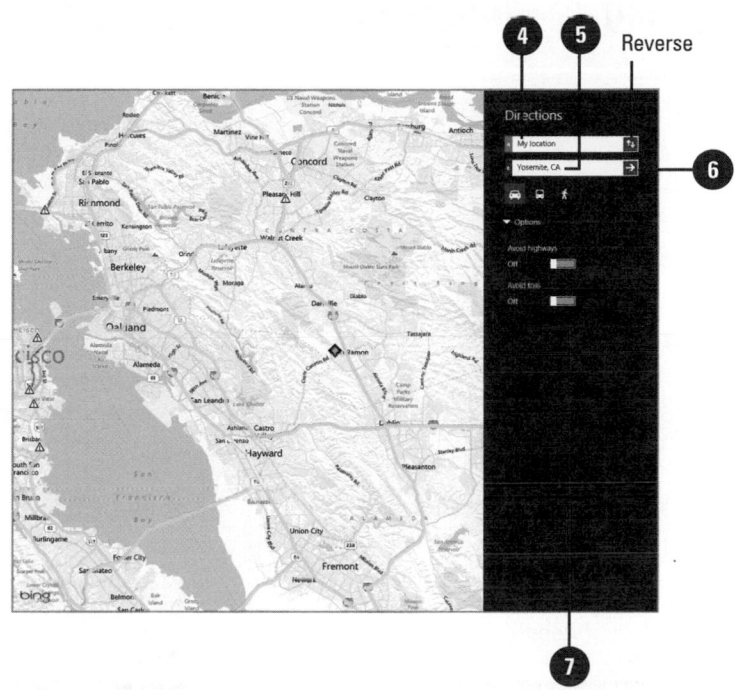

Reverse

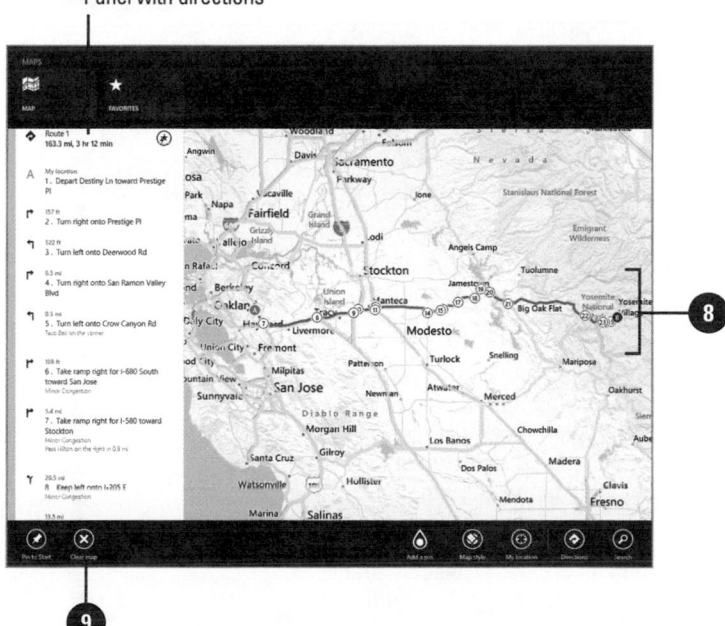

Panel with directions

# Creating Reading Lists

If you don't have time to read an article in an app or on the web, you can add it to your Reading List so you can come back to it later. The Reading List app (**New!**) helps you keep track of and share the articles you want to read. You can quickly add an article to your Reading List by using the Share button on the Charms bar. In the Reading List app, you can open and read new articles, or continue reading existing articles in a separate side by side window, or delete articles as you like.

## Use the Reading List App

1 To add an article to Reading List, open the app and display the article, click or tap the **Share** button on the Charms bar, click or tap **Reading List**, and then click or tap **Add**.

After you add articles, you can view and read them in the Reading List app.

2 Click or tap the **Reading List** tile on the Start or Apps screen.

3 To search for an article, click or tap the Search button, and then enter search text.

4 To view an article, click or tap the article or click or tap **Open** or **Continue viewing** for the Spotlight article.

Your web browser opens in a side by side screen, where you can read the article.

5 Move the point, and then click or tap the **Next** or **Previous** button, or swipe left or right.

6 To close the article in the side by side screen, point to the top edge of the screen (cursor changes to a hand), and then drag down to the bottom edge of the screen.

7 To delete an article, right-click or tap-hold an article to select it, and then click or tap the **Delete** button on the App bar.

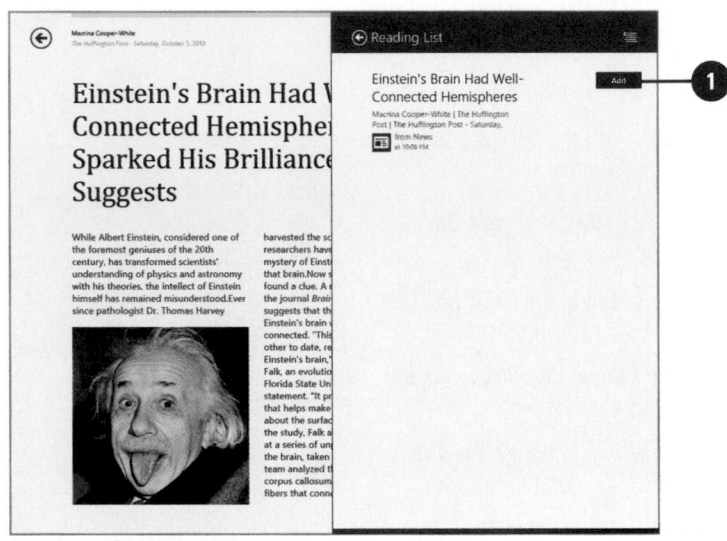

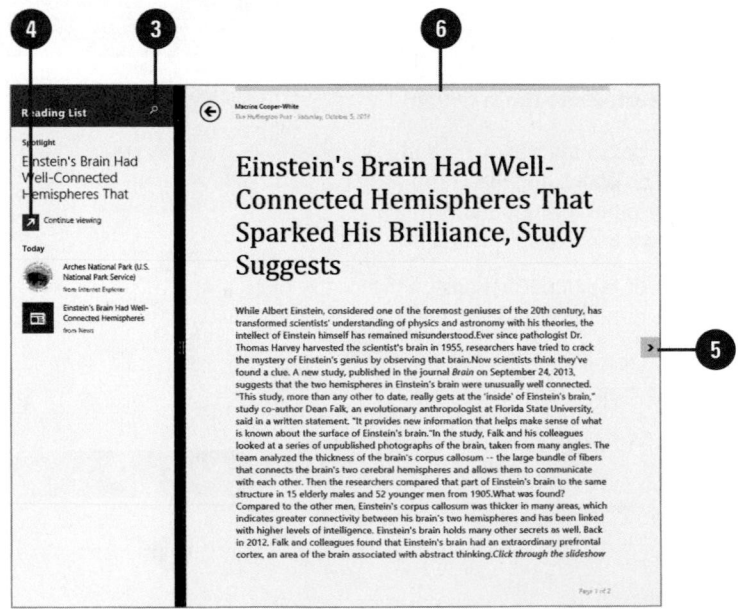

# Reading Documents

With the Reader app that comes with Windows 8.1, you can view PDF and XPS documents. The Reader app allows you to view PDF (Portable Document Format)—instead of using Adobe Reader—as well as view to view Microsoft's XPS (XML Paper Specification). In the Reader app, you can zoom in and out to view the document, search for words and phrases, take notes and fill in forms (with permission and rights), save your changes, and then print or share files with others.

## Use the Reader App

1. In the Start screen, click or tap the **Apps view** button, and then click or tap **Reader**.

2. Click or tap a recently opened document or click or tap the **Browse** button, select a file, and then click or tap **Open**.

3. Click or tap the **Zoom In** or **Zoom Out** button or pinch in or out.

4. Move the point, and then click or tap the **Next** or **Previous** button, swipe left or right, or use the page controls to navigate pages.

5. Right-click a blank area of the screen or swipe up from the bottom edge or down from the top edge, and then click or tap a button on the App bar.

   - ◆ **Find.** Search for text.

   - ◆ **One page or Two pages.** Display one or two pages. For two pages, click or tap Coverpage to display page one.

   - ◆ **Continuous.** Display one page and continuously scroll.

   - ◆ **Save or Print.** Save, Save as, or print the document.

   - ◆ **More.** Display a menu with Rotate and Info (document).

6. To highlight or add a note, select text, right-click the selection, and then click or tap **Highlight** or **Add a Note** and type. Click or tap it to remove/delete it.

7. To close a file, click the **Close** button (X) on the Tab bar.

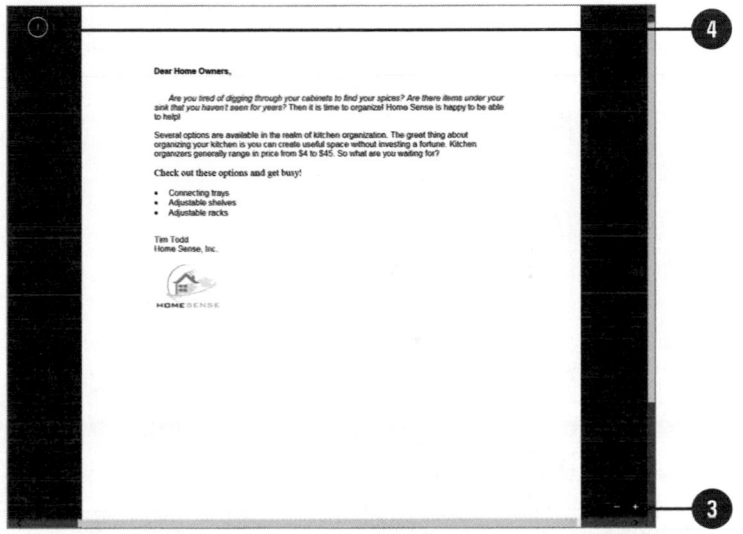

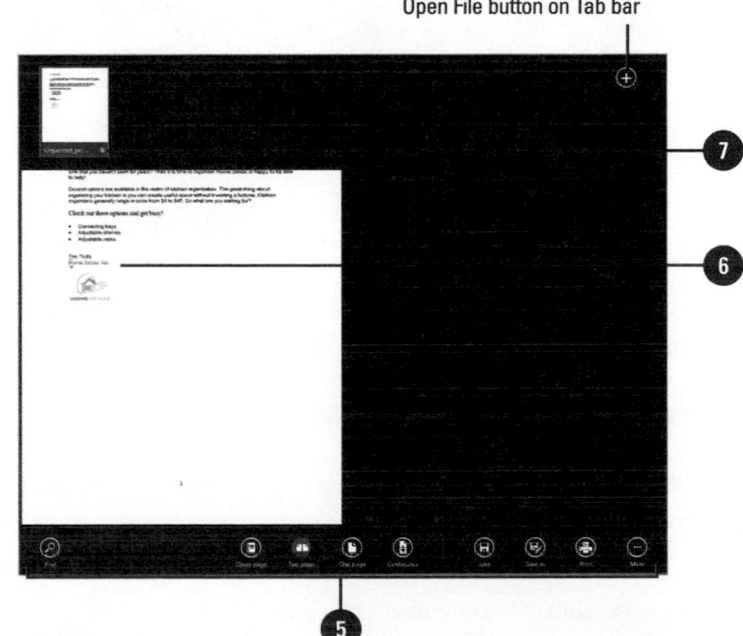

Open File button on Tab bar

# Managing Files with SkyDrive

SkyDrive is a cloud-based file hosting service that allows you to upload files to and download files from an online drive and sync files with other devices, such as Windows Phone, iPhone, or Android. You can use the SkyDrive app in Windows 8.1, a web browser at SkyDrive.com, or a mobile device using the SkyDrive app to access your online files using your Microsoft account. SkyDrive allows you to organize your files so that you can share them with contacts, or make them public, or keep them private. The cloud-based service offers 7 GB (gigabytes) of free storage for new users; however additional storage is available for purchase. SkyDrive comes with a default set of folders, Documents, Pictures, and Public (Shared), you can use to store your files. When you store files on SkyDrive, it automatically makes them available on other devices without having to sync them. The files you store in the Public (Shared) folder are available for anyone to view and edit.

## Use the SkyDrive App

1. Click or tap the **SkyDrive** tile on the Start or Apps screen.

2. To create a new folder, click or tap the **New folder** button on the App bar, enter a folder name, and then click or tap **Create folder**.

3. To display details in the folder tiles, click or tap the **Details** button on the App bar. You can click or tap the button again to toggle it off.

4. To find a folder or files, click or tap the **Search** button, and then enter a name search.

5. To open a folder, click or tap the folder tile.

6. To open a file, click or tap the file icon to view it.

   ◆ To open with a specific app, click or tap the **Open with** button on the App bar.

   If the document is from Microsoft Office, an Office WebApp opens in your web browser where you can view and edit the document.

7. To delete a file, right-click or tap-hold a file, click or tap the **Delete** button on the App bar, and then click or tap **Delete** to confirm.

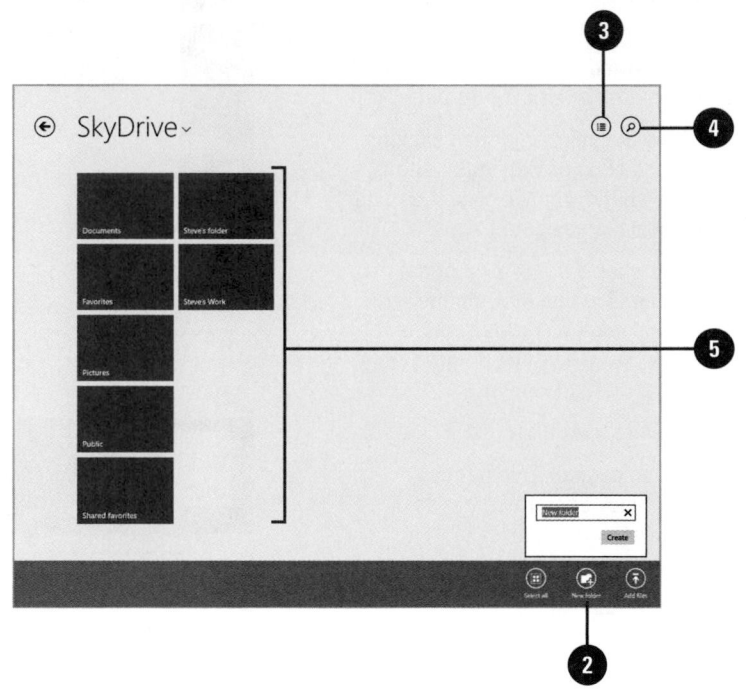

## Use SkyDrive.com

① Click or tap the **Internet Explorer** tile on the Start or Apps screen.

② Enter *www.skydrive.com* in the Address box, and the click or tap the **Go** button or press Enter.

③ Enter your username and password for your Microsoft account to access your SkyDrive, and then click or tap **Sign in**.

The SkyDrive web page opens, displaying your files.

④ To open a folder, click or tap **Files**, and then click or tap the folder tile.

⑤ To open a file, click or tap the file icon to view it.

⑥ Use any of the following options:

◆ **Create.** Use to create a new folder or Microsoft Office document.

◆ **Upload.** Use to upload file to the SkyDrive.

◆ **Search box.** Use to search for a files on the SkyDrive.

⑦ To manage storage or get SkyDrive apps (for Windows Phone, iPhone, or Android), click or tap the links.

⑧ To manage your account, profile, or sign out, click or tap the username (upper-right corner).

### Did You Know?

***You can manage SkyDrive storage online.*** In the SkyDrive app, click or tap the Settings button on the Charms bar, click or tap Options, and then click or tap Manage Storage. Your web browser opens, where you can manage your storage.

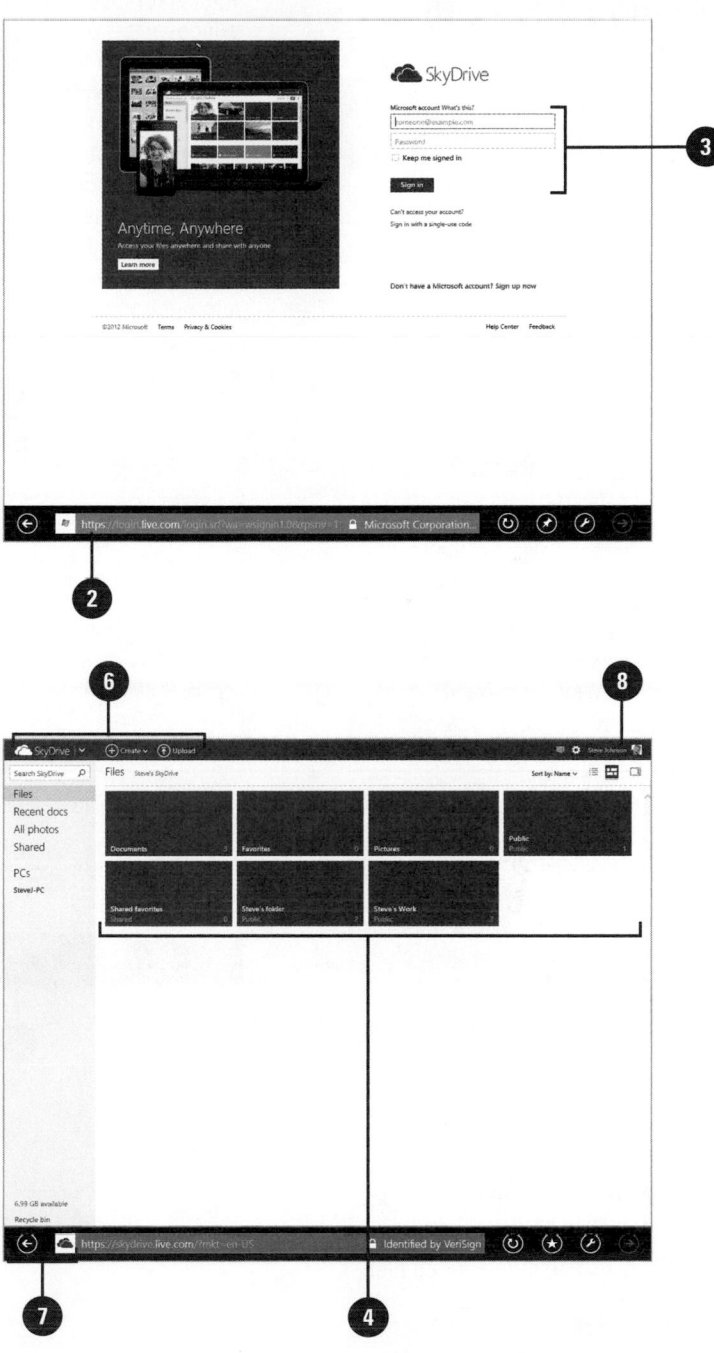

# Sharing Files with SkyDrive

You can upload (copy) files to your SkyDrive two different ways in Windows 8.1. One way is to select files within the SkyDrive app and then add them to a SkyDrive folder, or select the files in File Explorer (desktop) (**New!**), and then copy them to a SkyDrive folder in the Navigation pane. Either way, the files are available on the SkyDrive for use on other devices, such as Windows Phone, iPhone, or Android. If you have files on a SkyDrive and not on your PC, you can make them available offline (**New!**) so you can open and edit them even if your PC isn't connected to the Internet. If you don't want to have SkyDrive files on your PC, you can make them online-only (**New!**), which requires an Internet connection to access them.

## Make SkyDrive Files Online or Offline

1. Click or tap the **SkyDrive** tile on the Star or Apps screen.

2. Click or tap the folder tile where you want to change files.

3. Select the PC files you want o make online only or the SkyDrive files you want to make PC only.

   A check mark appears next to a selected file.

4. Click or tap the appropriate button (it changes based on the file selection):

   ◆ **PC Only.** Click or tap the **Make offline** button, and then click **Make offline**.

   This makes the selected files offline so you can open and edit them even if this PC isn't connected to the Internet.

   ◆ **SkyDrive Only.** Click or tap the **Make online-only** button, and then click **Make online-only**.

   This makes the selected files online-only; you need a connection to the Internet to access the online-only files.

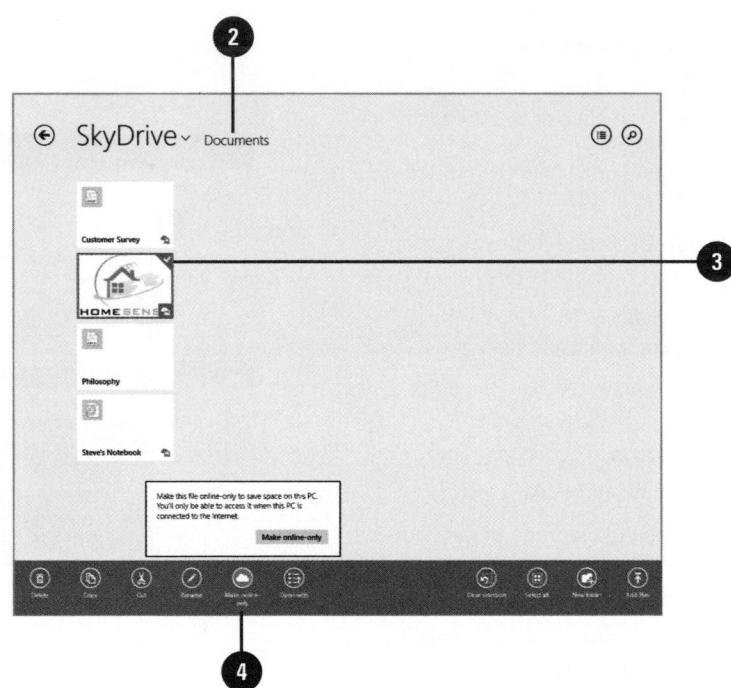

## Upload Files to the SkyDrive

① Click or tap the **SkyDrive** tile on the Star or Apps screen.

② Click or tap the folder tile where you want to upload files.

③ Right-click the screen (on a computer) or swipe up from the bottom edge or down from the top edge of the screen (on a mobile device) to display the App bar.

④ Click or tap the **Add files** button on the App bar.

The Files screen opens, where you can select one or more files.

⑤ Use any of the following options to navigate the Files screen:

- ◆ **Files down arrow.** Use to select a drive, folder, or device.

- ◆ **Go up.** Use to go up one level.

- ◆ **Sort by.** Use to sort by name or sort by date.

- ◆ **Select all.** Use to select all files in the current folder.

- ◆ **Clear selection.** Use to de-select the current selection.

⑥ Click or tap the files you want.

A check mark appears next to a selected file.

⑦ Click or tap **Copy to SkyDrive**.

The files get copied and uploaded to the SkyDrive.

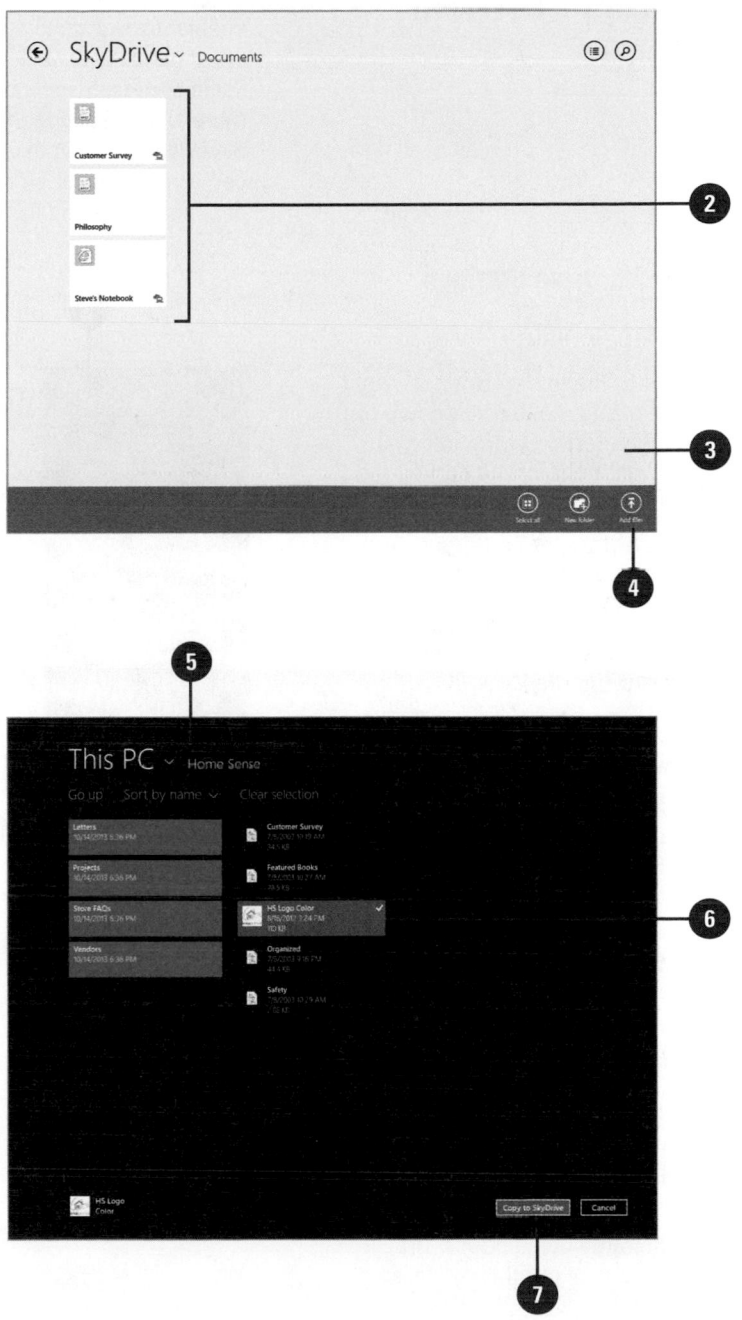

# Changing SkyDrive Settings

When you sign in to Windows 8.1 with a Microsoft account, you can enable the system to automatically synchronize your system and some app settings with other devices using SkyDrive that also sign in with the same Microsoft account. In PC settings, you can set SkyDrive options (**New!**) to customize the way files and settings are synced to your SkyDrive and other devices. In addition to these SkyDrive options, you can also turn on or off access to all files offline by opening the SkyDrive app, and displaying Options from the Settings panel.

## Change SkyDrive Settings

1. Display the Start screen.

2. Point to the lower- or upper-right corner and move up or down (on a computer) or swipe left from the right edge of the screen (on a mobile device).

3. Click or tap the **Settings** button on the Charms bar.

4. Click or tap **Change PC settings** on the Settings panel, and then click or tap **SkyDrive**.

5. Click or tap the following under SkyDrive (**New!**):

    ◆ **File storage**. Manage storage on SkyDrive.com, view SkyDrive files, and set an option to save documents to the SkyDrive by default.

    ◆ **Camera roll**. Set options to automatically upload photos and videos to the SkyDrive.

    ◆ **Sync settings**. Drag sliders on or off to enable or disable SkyDrive sync settings; see the topic on page 301 for more information on the sync settings.

    ◆ **Metered connections.** Drag sliders on or off for metered Internet connections.

6. To close the app, point to the top edge of the screen (cursor changes to a hand), and then drag down to the bottom edge of the screen.

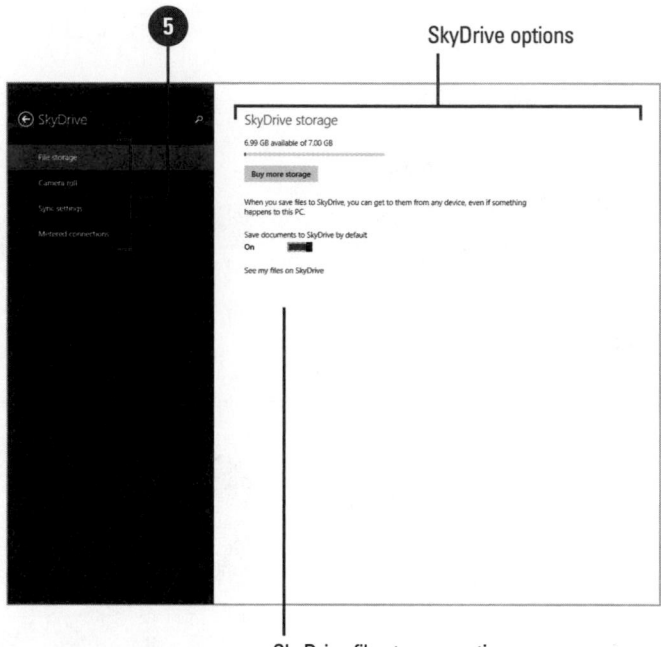

SkyDrive options

SkyDrive file storage options

# Setting Alarms

The Alarms app (**New!**) is useful for those who need to get up in the morning or need a reminder throughout the day. You can create alarms for different things and turn them on when you need them. You can create an alarm that happens only once or repeats on a consistent basis with the sound of your choice. In addition to alarms, the Alarms app also provides a timer to countdown and a stopwatch to keep track of time. It's important to note that notifications will only show if the PC is awake.

## Set Alarms and Use a Timer and Stopwatch

1. Click or tap the **Alarms** tile on the Apps screen.

2. Click or tap **Alarm**.

3. Use the following to open an alarm or create a new one:
   - ◆ **Open.** Click or tap an alarm.
   - ◆ **New.** Click or tap the **Add** button (+), and then change the name.

4. Drag the minutes and seconds playhead to the time you want, and then select **AM** or **PM**.

5. Specify the occurrence of the alarm (Once or Repeat with days),and a sound.

6. Click or tap the **Save** button.
   - ◆ You can use the **Delete** button to delete an alarm.

7. Click or tap the **On/Off** button for the alarm.

8. To use the timer, click or tap **Timer**, click or tap the **Add** button (+), if needed, drag the minutes and seconds playhead to the time you want, and then click or tap the **Play/Pause** button.

9. To use the stopwatch, click or tap **Stopwatch**, click or tap the **Reset** button (+), if needed, and then click or tap the **Play/Pause** button to start/resume the time. You can click or tap the **Laps/Splits** button to keep track of intervals.

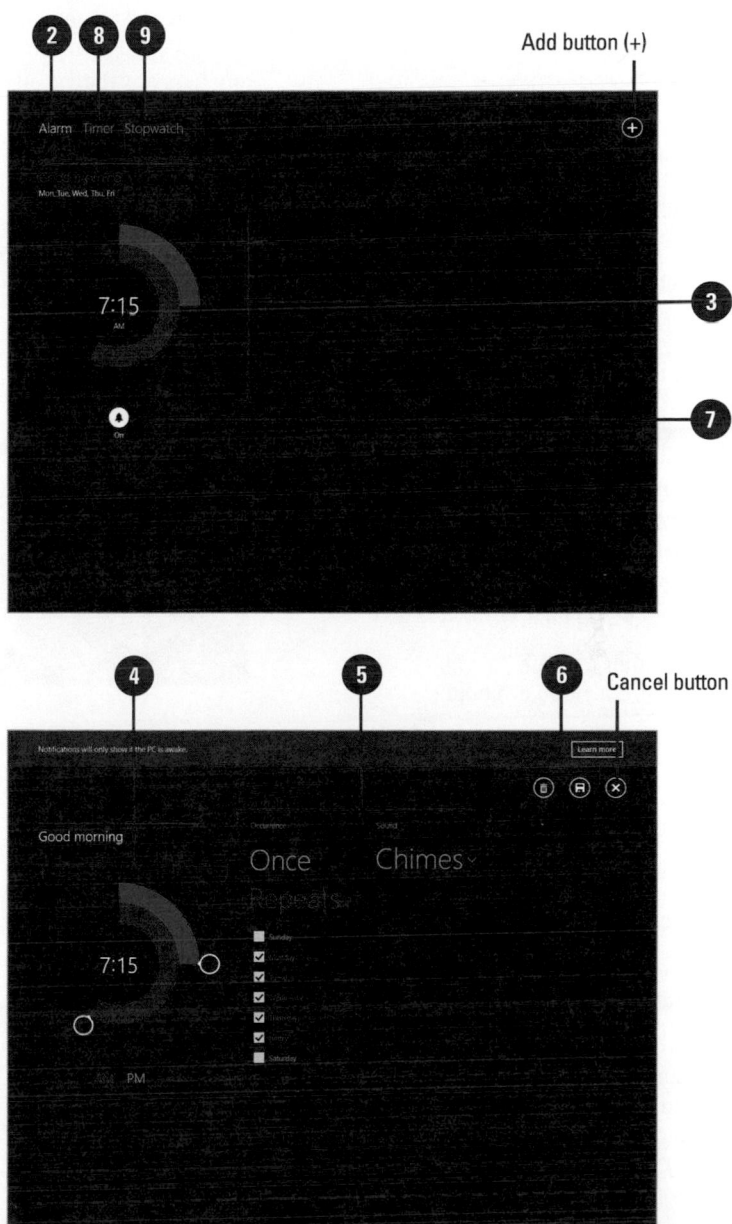

Add button (+)

Cancel button

# Capturing a Photo or Video

With the Camera app that comes with Windows 8.1, you can use a digital camera to capture a still photo or video. When you open the Camera app for the first time, you're asked to allow or block the use of your webcam and microphone. When you capture a photo, you can crop it as desired. When you capture a video, you can trim if you like, and play it back in the Camera app. After you capture a photo or video, it's automatically saved in the Camera Roll folder within the Pictures library folder. If you don't like the way a photo or video came out or no longer want it, you can delete it at any time. You can also view a photo or play a video and manage individual files in the Photos app or in File Explorer. Before you can use the Camera app, you need to have a digital camera such as a webcam, installed on your device.

## Use the Camera App

1. Click or tap the **Camera** tile on the Start or Apps screen.

2. If prompted, click or tap **Allow** or **Block** to enable or disable the use of your webcam and microphone.

3. To adjust the exposure, click the **Exposure** button on the App bar, and then adjust the level.

4. To display a 3-second timer count down before capturing a screen, click or tap the **Timer** button on the App bar; click or tap the button again to toggle it off.

5. Do either of the following to capture a video or photo:

   ◆ Video. Click or tap the **Video** button on the screen, click or tap the screen to start, and then click or tap again to end.

   ◆ Photo. Click or tap the **Photo** button on the screen, and then click or tap the screen.

6. To view photos/videos in Camera, click or tap the **Camera roll** button on the App bar.

7. To move between photos/videos, and the Home screen, move the pointer to display buttons, click or tap the **Back** or **Forward** button, or swipe left or right.

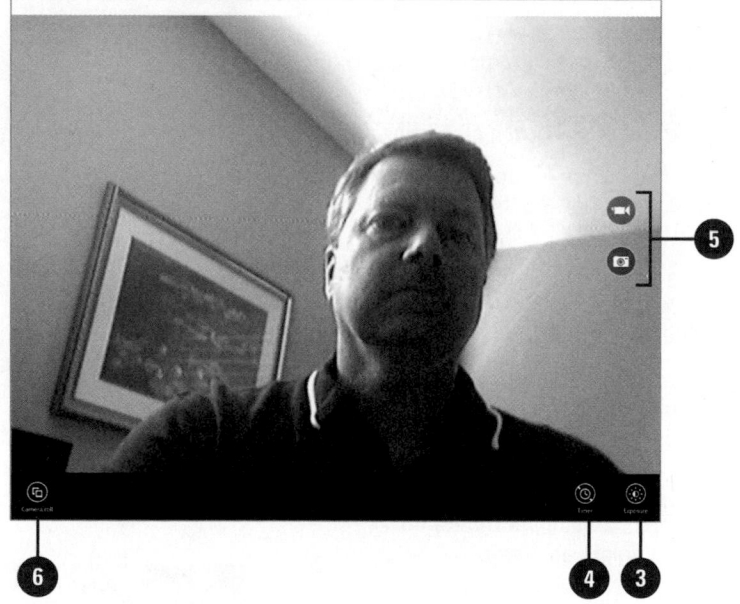

## Capture a Video

1. Click or tap the **Camera** tile on the Start or Apps screen.

2. Click or tap the **Video mode** button on the App bar to select it.

3. Click or tap the screen to start the video capture, and then click or tap the screen to end it.

4. Move the point and then click or tap the **Left** arrow or swipe right to display the video capture.

5. Click or tap the **Play/Pause** button or the screen.

6. Right-click or tap-hold the screen to display the App bar.

7. To trim the video, click or trap the **Trim** button on the App bar, drag the start or end points, and then click or tap the **Save as** button.

8. To delete the video, click or tap the **Delete** button on the App bar.

## Capture a Photo

1. Click or tap the **Camera** tile on the Start or Apps screen.

2. Click or tap the **Video mode** button on the App bar to deselect it,

3. Click or tap the screen to capture the still photo.

4. Move the point and then click or tap the **Left** arrow or swipe right to display the video capture.

5. Right-click or tap-hold the screen to display the App bar.

6. To crop the video, click or trap the **Crop** button on the App bar, drag the corner points, and then click or tap the **OK** button.

7. To delete the video, click or tap the **Delete** button on the App bar.

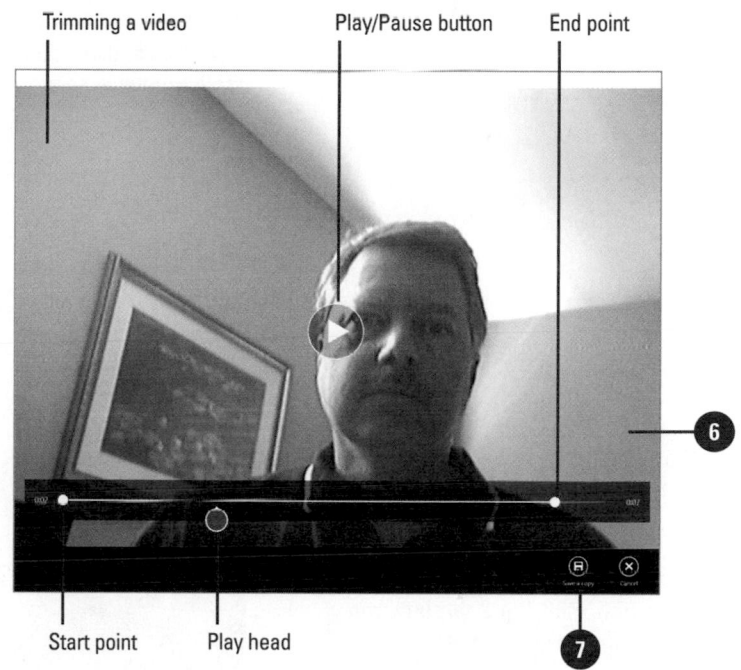

Trimming a video  Play/Pause button  End point

Start point  Play head

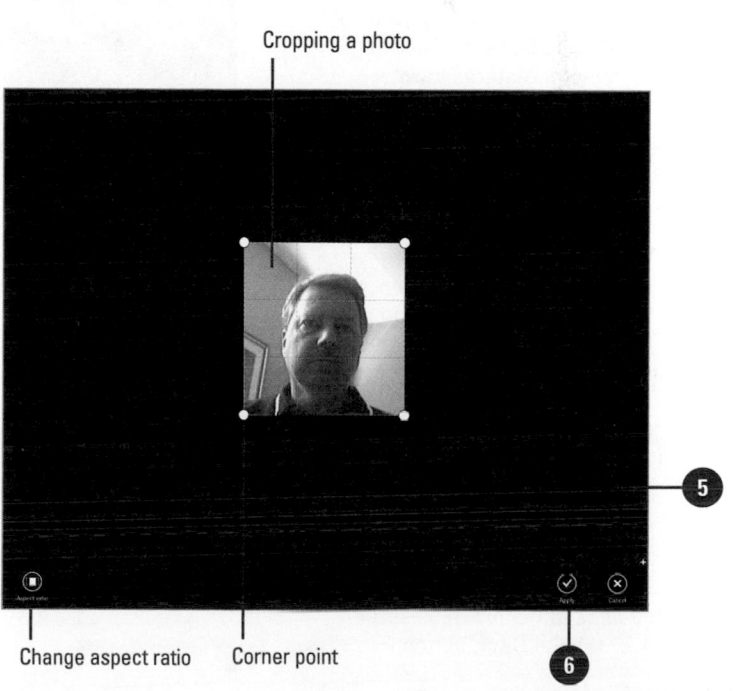

Cropping a photo

Change aspect ratio  Corner point

# Watching Videos

With the Video app that comes with Windows 8.1, you can watch videos located in the Videos library folder or on the Xbox Live online service. Xbox Live allows you to rent or buy and watch video from the movies store or television store, where videos are organized by featured, new releases, top selling, genres, free tv, and studios or networks. If you can't find a video, you can use the Search button on the Charms bar to locate it. In order to use Xbox Live and make purchases, you need to login with an existing Xbox account or your Microsoft account. If you have your Xbox 360 console connected to your device, you can get media for (requires the free Xbox SmartGlass app from the Windows Store) and play media on the console.

## Use the Video App

1 Click or tap the **Video** tile on the Start or Apps screen.

2 If needed, click or tap **Sign in**, and then enter your username and password.

3 To search, click the **Search** button, and then enter search text.

4 To scroll, move the pointer to display the scroll bar, and then drag the scroll bar or click or tap the arrows, or swipe left or right.

5 As desired, click or tap a category (personal videos, my movies, my tv, and new or features movies or tv).

6 Click or tap a media tile to view information, where you can click or tap Buy, Rent, or Play trailer.

◆ When prompted to make a purchase, sign in, and then follow the steps to buy and use Microsoft points.

7 To play videos, use button controls (**Repeat**, **Previous**, **Play/Pause**, **Next**, or **Play to**) on the App bar.

◆ If connected to Xbox 360 console, use the **Get for Xbox 360** or **Play on Xbox 360** buttons on the App bar.

8 To go back to the previous screen, click or tap the **Back** button.

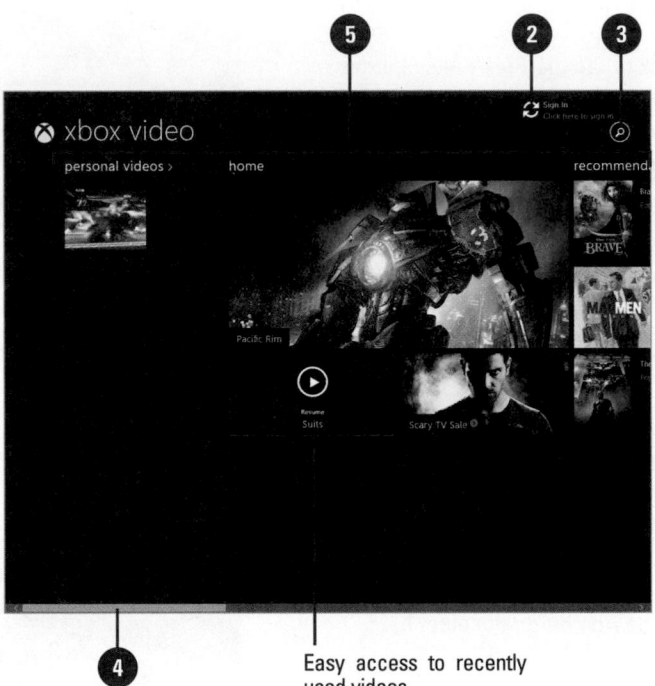

Easy access to recently used videos

# Playing Games

With the Games app that comes with Windows 8.1, you can play local or online games from the Windows games store or Xbox 360 games store. For Windows games, you can buy and install them using the Windows Store. For Xbox 360 games, you can buy a game for and play a game on Xbox 360. In order to use Xbox Live and make purchases, you need to login with an existing Xbox account or your Microsoft account. To play Xbox 360 games, you need to connect the console to your device and may need to install the free Xbox SmartGlass app from the Windows Store. If you can't find a game, you can use the Search button on the Charms bar to locate it. As a game player, you can create an avatar—a character that represents you—and profile for use during games, and view your gaming achievements.

## Use the Games App

1. Click or tap the **Games** tile on the Start or Apps screen.

2. To search, click the **Search** button, and then enter search text.

3. To scroll, move the pointer to display the scroll bar, and then drag the scroll bar or click or tap the arrows, or swipe left or right.

4. As desired, click or tap a category (game activity, windows games store, or xbox 360 games store).

5. Click or tap a game tile to view information, where you can click or tap Buy, Rent, Explore, or Play.

    ◆ When prompted to make a purchase, sign in, and then follow the steps to buy and use Microsoft points.

6. To play games, use button controls (**Repeat**, **Previous**, **Play/Pause**, **Next**) on the App bar.

7. To go back to the previous screen, click or tap the **Back** button.

8. To view game achievements, click or tap **Achievements**.

9. To communicate and play with friends, click or tap **Messages** or **Friends**.

## For Your Information

### Accessing Xbox Account Information

After you accept the terms of use for Xbox Live, you can use Account Preferences to view your Xbox account information. Click or tap the Settings button on the Charms bar, click or tap Account on the Settings panel, sign in if prompted, view account information, and then click or tap a link to an account area, such as Manage Payment Options, and Billing contact Information and History.

# Listening to Music

With the Music app (**New!**) that comes with Windows 8.1, you can listen to music located in the Music library folder or on the Xbox Music online service. Xbox Music allows you to explorer, buy, and play music from the Xbox Music store, create collections of music (**New!**) on your PC or in the cloud, and add and play Xbox Music radio stations (**New!**). You can also personalize your music by creating or importing playlists (**New!**). If you can't find an artist or song, you can use the Search button on the Xbox Music pane. In order to use Xbox Live and make purchases, you need to login with an existing Xbox account or your Microsoft account.

## Use the Music App

1. Click or tap the **Music** tile on the Start or Apps screen.

2. To search, click the **Search** button, and then enter search text.

3. As desired, click or tap a category on the Xbox Music pane:

    ◆ **Collection.** Create and view music collections based on albums, artists, and songs on this PC or in the cloud (**New!**).

    ◆ **Radio.** Add radio stations from Xbox Music and listen to them (**New!**).

    ◆ **Explore.** Browse new releases, and top albums.

4. Click or tap a media tile to view information, where you can click or tap Buy, Rent, or Play trailer.

    ◆ When prompted to make a purchase, follow the step-by-step instructions to buy and use Microsoft points.

5. To play music, use controls (**Playhead**, **Previous**, **Play/ Pause**, **Next**, **Volume**, **Shuffle**, or **Repeat**) on the App bar.

    The current song appears on the App bar for easy access.

6. To go back to the previous screen, click or tap the **Back** button.

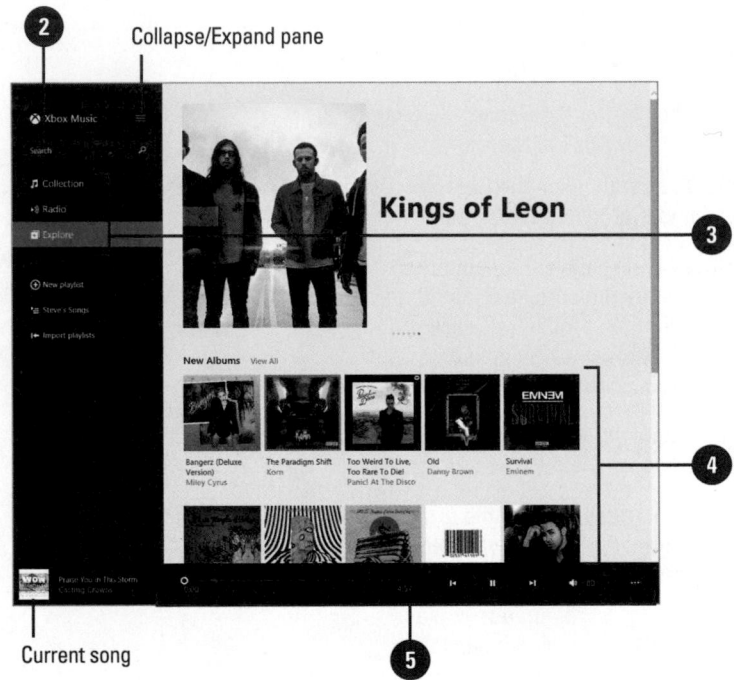

Collapse/Expand pane

Current song

## Create and Use a Playlist

1. Click or tap the **Music** tile on the Start or Apps screen.

2. to create a new playlist, click **New playlist** on the Xbox Music pane, enter a name, and then click or tap **Save** (**New!**).

   The new playlist appears on the Xbox Music pane.

3. To add songs to a playlist (**New!**), navigate to the album or song, click or tap the **Add** button (+), and then select a playlist on your PC or cloud.

4. Click or tap a playlist on the Xbox Music pane.

5. Click or tap the **Play** button to play the songs on the playlist.

   The current song appears on the App bar for easy access.

6. Use controls (**Playhead**, **Previous**, **Play/ Pause**, **Next**, **Volume**, **Shuffle**, or **Repeat**) on the App bar.

   The current song appears on the App bar for easy access.

7. To work with playlists, do any of the following:

   ◆ **Remove song**. Select the song, click or tap the **Remove** button (-) button.

   ◆ **Delete playlist**. Click or tap the **More** button, and then click or tap **Delete**.

8. To go back to the previous screen, click or tap the **Back** button.

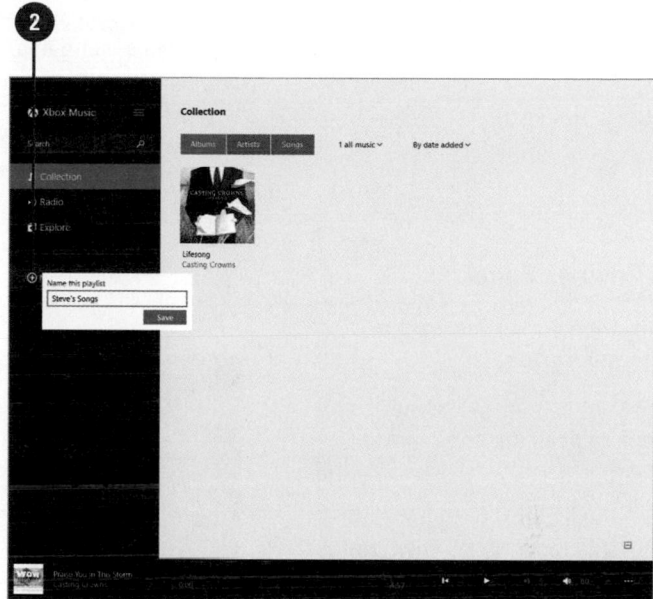

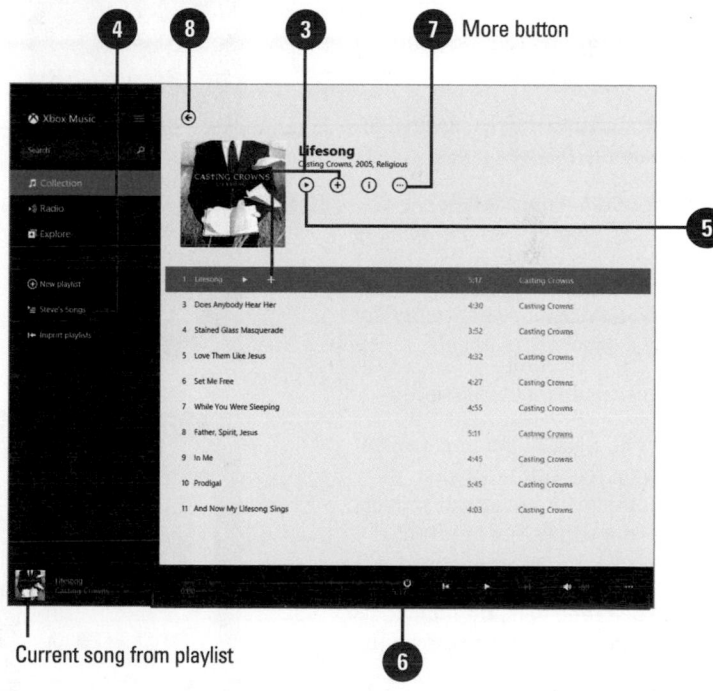

More button

Current song from playlist

# Using Devices with Apps

The Devices button on the Charms bar allows you to work with devices attached to your system when you work with metro apps. If you want to print from a metro app, configure a secondary display, use Play for displaying device-based media on a compatible television, or send files to portable devices using technologies, such as NFC, you can quickly do so with the Devices panel. For example, you can print directions in the Maps app or set options to use a second screen to display more information or have more screen space to play a game.

## Use the Devices Panel

1. Connect the device you want to use to your system.

2. In the Start screen, select the content or open the app you want to use.

3. Point to the lower- or upper-right corner and move up or down (on a computer) or swipe left from the right edge of the screen (on a mobile device).

4. Click or tap the **Devices** button on the Charms bar.

   **TIMESAVER** *Press Win+K to display the Devices panel.*

5. Click or tap a device type—**Play**, **Print**, or **Project**—on the Devices panel.

   **TIMESAVER** *Press Win+P to display the Project panel.*

6. Select the options you want.

   ◆ **Print.** Specify the options you want (click or tap **More settings** for additional settings), and then click or tap **Print**.

   ◆ **Project.** Click or tap an option: **PC screen only**, **Duplicate**, **Extend**, or **Second screen only**.

7. To go back to the previous panel, click or tap the **Back** button.

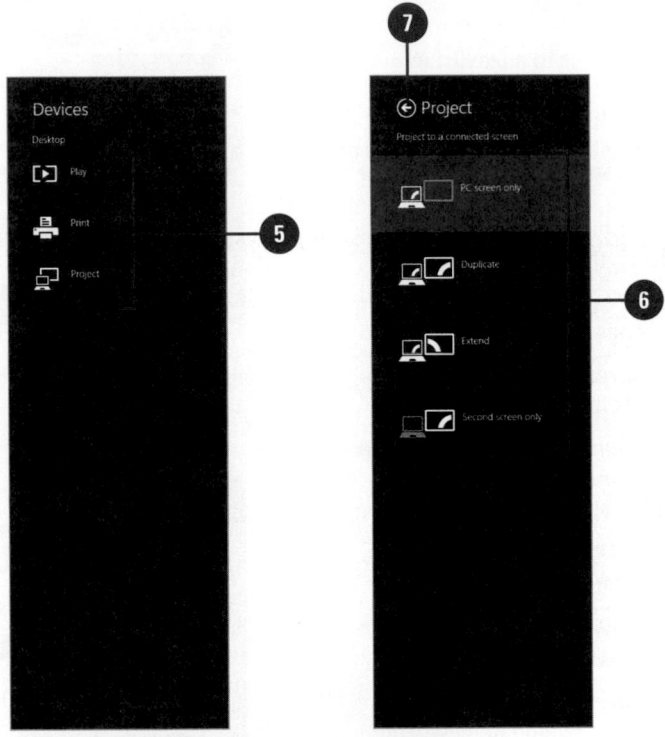

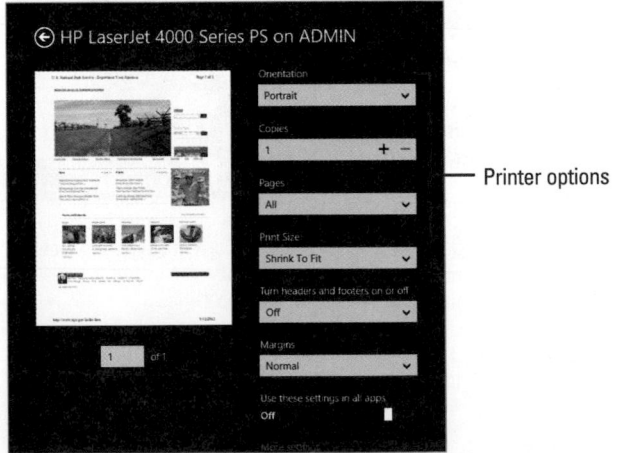

Printer options

# Working with Windows Accessories

## Introduction

Windows comes with several small programs, called **accessories**, that are extremely useful for completing basic tasks, such as creating a written document or performing basic calculations. In addition to the accessories, Windows 8.1 also includes system tools—such as Control Panel and Task Manager—to make it easier to work with Windows.

Windows 8.1 provides a number of ways for you to resolve some common problems. For example, you can use older programs (designed to run on previous versions of Windows) on your Windows device by changing specific settings. You can run commands from a text-based interface (called a command line), and Windows provides an interface for quitting a program that has stopped responding without turning off your PC computer or mobile device and losing information in other programs.

Using the Windows accessories and system tools allows you to accomplish several tasks:

- Create and edit documents with WordPad
- Insert symbols with Character Map
- Perform basic arithmetic, scientific, or statistical equations with Calculator
- Capture screen shots with Snipping Tool
- Capture a sequence of actions with Steps Recorder
- Create notes with Sticky Notes
- Take handwritten notes with Windows Journal
- Take math notes with Math Input Panel

## What You'll Do

Start and Exit Windows Accessories

Change the Way Programs Start

Use Windows Accessories

Create a Document

Edit and Format Text

Set Paragraph Tabs and Indents

Preview and Print a Document

Save and Close a Document

Insert Special Characters

Insert and Edit Information

Link and Update Information

Calculate Numbers

Run Commands

Snip the Screen

Record Steps

Create Sticky Notes

Handwrite Journal Entries

Use the Math Input Panel

Run Older Programs

Quit a Program Not Responding

## Starting and Exiting Windows Accessories

The most common way to start a Windows accessory or other system tool is to use the Apps screen (**New!**), which provides easy access to programs installed on your device. A Windows accessory or system tool is made for use on the desktop, so when you start a Windows accessory or system tool from the Apps screen, the desktop opens and then starts the program. When you're done working with a program, you should exit, or close it, to conserve your PC's resources.

### Start a Windows Accessory or System Tool

1. Display the Start screen.

2. Move the pointer or tap the screen as needed to show the button.

   The Apps view button appears (**New!**) at the bottom of the Start screen.

3. Click or tap the **Apps view** button down arrow (**New!**) (on a computer) or swipe up from the bottom of the Start screen (on a mobile device).

   The Apps screen appears.

4. Click or tap a tile for a Windows Accessories or Windows System tool.

   The desktop starts and the accessory or system tool opens. A taskbar button appears for the program, which you can pin to the taskbar for easy access later.

> ### Did You Know?
>
> **You can open a document and a program at the same time.** In File Explorer (desktop), double-click or double-tap the document icon. The document opens in the associated program.

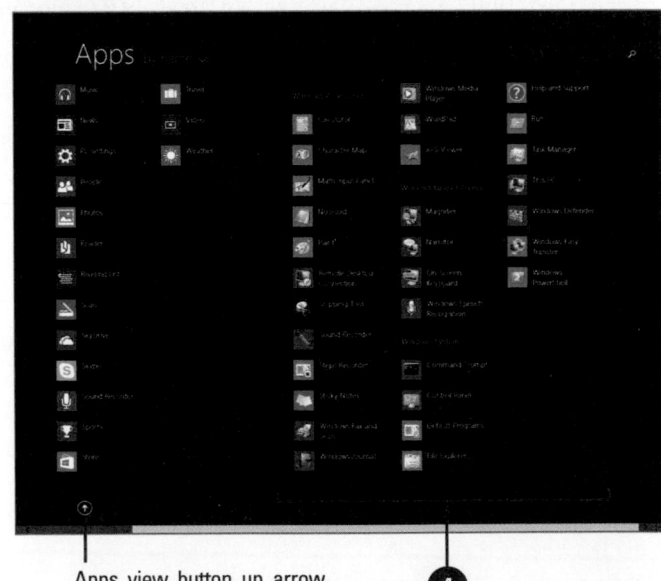

Apps view button up arrow returns you to Start screen

## Exit a Windows Accessory or System Tool

Windows provides several ways to exit a Windows accessory or system tool:

◆ Click or tap the **File** tab, and then click or tap **Exit**.

◆ Click or tap the **Close** button on the program's title bar.

◆ Double-click or double-tap the Control-menu on the program's title bar.

◆ Right-click or tap-hold the program's taskbar button, and then click or tap **Close window**.

### See Also

*See "Using Windows Accessories" on page 271 for information on using Windows built-in programs.*

Control menu                                              Close button

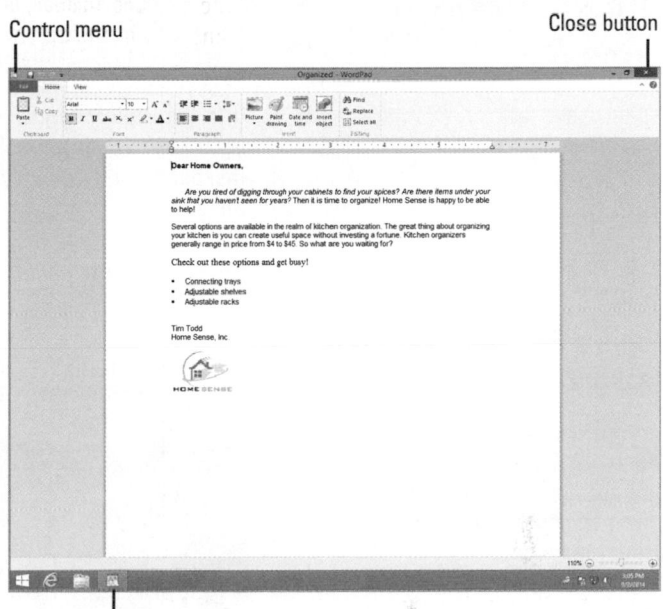

Taskbar button for WordPad

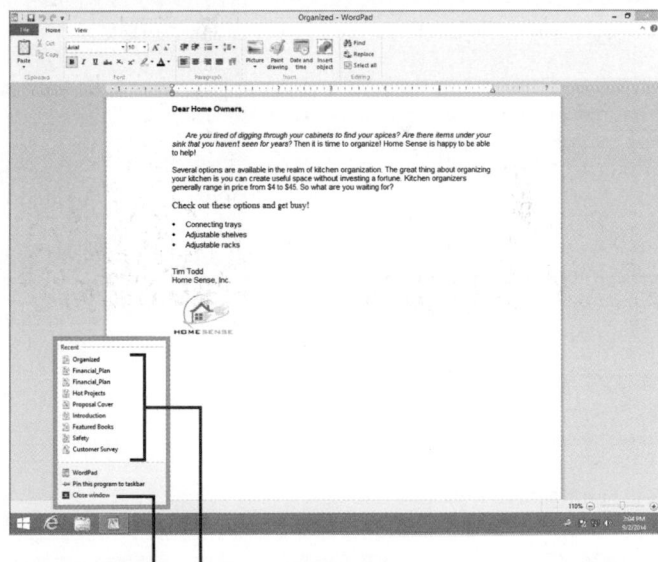

Close Wordpad    Jump list for WordPad

# Changing the Way Programs Start

In addition to pinning and unpinning programs to the Start screen, you can pin and unpin them to the taskbar. The pinned items remain on the Start screen or taskbar, like a push pin holds paper on a bulletin board, until you unpin them. The default programs pinned to the taskbar include Internet Explorer and File Explorer, however, you can customize it. When you right-click or tap-hold a taskbar button—such as WordPad—on the taskbar, a list of recently opened files or folders and related commands appear for easy access. Windows tracks recently opened files, known as jump lists, to programs on the taskbar, which you can pin or unpin to the list, or click or tap to open.

## Pin or Unpin a Program or Items on the Taskbar

◆ **Pin a program on the taskbar.** In the desktop, right-click or tap-hold an open program on the taskbar, and then click or tap **Pin this program to taskbar**.

You can also, right-click or tap-hold a program on the Start screen, and then click or tap the **Pin to taskbar** button on the App bar.

◆ **Unpin a program on the taskbar.** In the desktop, right-click or tap-hold a pinned program on the taskbar, and then click or tap **Unpin this program from taskbar**.

◆ **Pin or unpin an item on a jump list.** In the desktop, right-click or tap-hold a taskbar program, point to a jump list item, and then click or tap the **Pin** or **Unpin** icon.

◆ **Remove an item on a jump list.** In the desktop, right-click or tap-hold a taskbar program, right-click or tap-hold a jump list item, and then click or tap **Remove from this list**.

### See Also

*See "Customizing Apps on the Start Screen" on page 40 for more information on pinning or unpinning an app to the Start screen.*

Jump list for WordPad

Click or tap to pin to jump list

Pin WordPad to taskbar

# Using Windows Accessories

Windows comes with several accessories, built-in programs that are extremely useful for completing every day tasks.

One of the most useful features Windows offers is the ability to use data created in one file in another file, even if the two files were created in different Windows programs. To work with more than one program or file at a time, you simply need to open them on your desktop. A program button on the taskbar represents any window that is open on the desktop. When you want to switch from one open window to another, click or tap the program button on the taskbar. If you tile, or arrange open windows on the desktop so that they are visible, you can switch among them simply by click or taping or tapping in the window in which you want to work.

## Frequently Used Windows Accessories

| Program | Description |
|---|---|
| Calculator | Performs arithmetic calculations |
| Character Map | Identifies and inserts symbols and special characters into documents |
| Command Prompt | Executes MS-DOS commands |
| File (Windows) Explorer | Manages files and folders |
| Internet Explorer | Displays web (HTML) pages |
| Math Input Panel | Recognizes handwritten math expressions and inserts them into documents |
| Notepad | Creates, edits, and displays text only documents |
| Paint | Creates and edits bitmap pictures |
| Remote Desktop Connection | Connects to a remote desktop on your network or the Internet |
| Snipping Tool | Captures different parts of the screen |
| Sound Recorder | Creates and plays digital sound files |
| Sticky Notes | Creates color notes on the screen |
| Task Manager | Ends Windows tasks and displays Windows process, performance, app history, startup items, user information, services |
| Windows Fax and Scan | Sends and receives faxes or scanned pictures and documents |
| Windows Journal | Creates handwritten notes and drawn pictures to mimic a note pad |
| Windows Media Center | Provides entertainment options for digital and on-demand media |
| Windows Media Player | Plays sound, music, and video |
| WordPad | Creates, edits, and displays text, Rich Text Format, and Word documents |
| XPS Viewer | View an XPS document (XML Paper Specification); Microsoft's version of a PDF document |

# Creating a Document

A **document** is a file you create using a word processing program, such as a letter, memo, or resume. When you start WordPad, a blank document appears in the work area, known as the document window, along with a Ribbon, similar to Microsoft Office 2010, at the top. The Ribbon with two tabs—Home and View—allows you to quickly select document related commands. You can enter information to create a new document and save the result in a file, or you can open an existing file and save the document with changes. As you type, text moves, or **wraps**, to a new line when the previous one is full.

## Create a Document

1. In the Start screen, click or tap the **Apps view** button, and then click or tap **WordPad**.

   If WordPad is already open, click or tap the **File** tab, and then click or tap **New**.

2. Type your text.

3. Press Enter when you want to start a new paragraph.

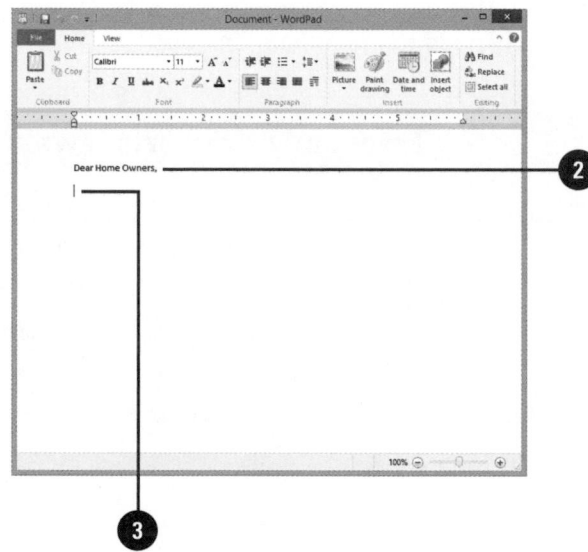

## Change the Page Setup

1. Click or tap the **File** tab, and then click or tap **Page setup**.

2. Specify the paper size and source.

3. Specify the page orientation, either portrait or landscape.

4. Specify the page margins.

5. Click or tap **OK**.

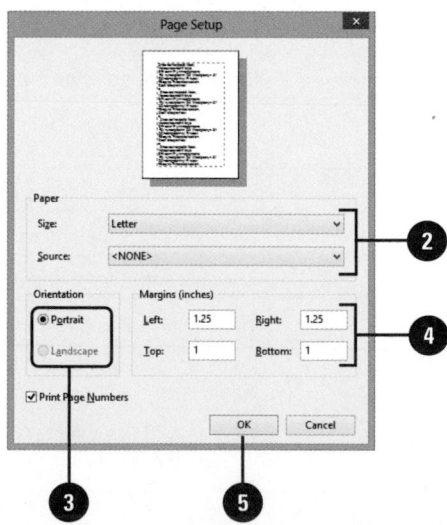

## Open an Existing Document from Within a Program

① Click or tap the **File** tab, and then click or tap **Open**.

② Click or tap the **Files name** list arrow, and then click or tap the file type you want to open.

③ Use the Navigation pane to navigate to the folder from which you want to open the file.

④ Click or tap the document you want to open.

⑤ Click or tap **Open**.

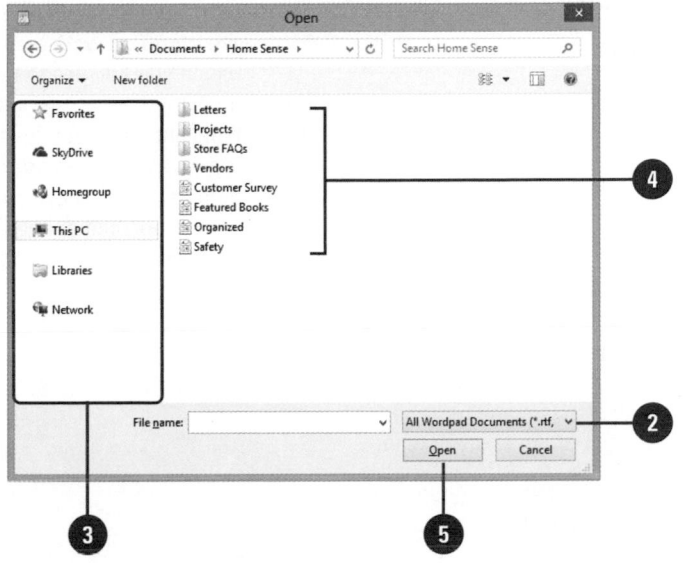

## Open a Recent Document from the File Tab or Taskbar

① Click or tap the **File** tab in the program or right-click or tap the program on the taskbar.

② Click or tap the recently opened document you want to re-open.

### Did You Know?

*You can remove recently used documents from a jump list..* Right-click or tap-hold a taskbar program, right-click or tap-hold a jump list item, and then click or tap Remove from this list.

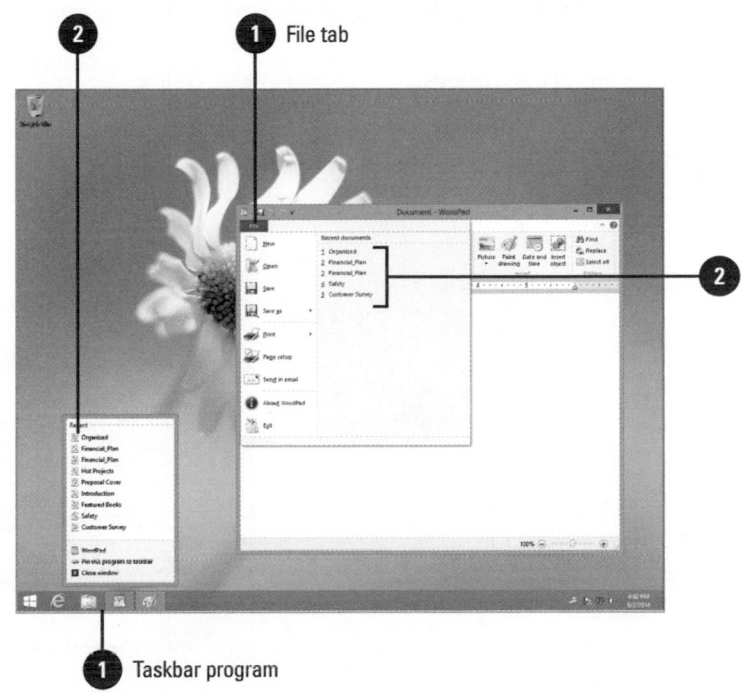

File tab

Taskbar program

# Editing Text

One of the advantages of using a word processing program is that you can edit a document or change the contents without re-creating it. In the WordPad work area, the pointer changes to the I-beam pointer, which you can use to reposition the insertion point (called navigating) and insert, delete, or select text. Before you can edit text, you need to highlight, or select, the text you want to modify. Then you can delete, replace, move (cut), or copy text within one document or between documents even if they're different programs. When you cut or copy an item, it's placed on the Clipboard, which stores only a single piece of information at a time. You can also move or copy selected text without storing it on the Clipboard by using drag-and-drop editing.

## Select and Edit Text

1. Move the I-beam pointer to the left or right of the text you want to select.

2. Drag the pointer to highlight the text.

   **TIMESAVER** *Double-click or tap or double-tap a word to select it; triple-click or tap or triple-tap a paragraph to select it.*

3. Perform any of the following:

   ◆ To replace text, type your text.

   ◆ To delete text, press the Backspace key or the Delete key.

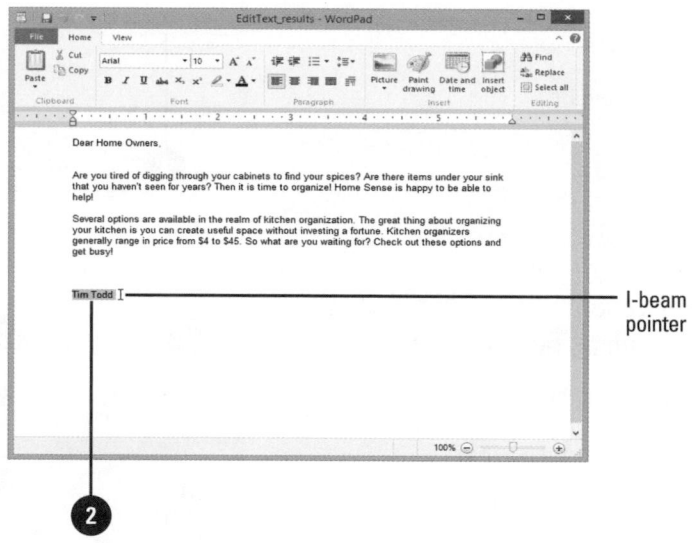

I-beam pointer

## Insert and Delete Text

1. Click or tap in the document to place the insertion point where you want to make the change.

   ◆ To insert text, type your text.

   ◆ To delete text, press the Backspace key or the Delete key.

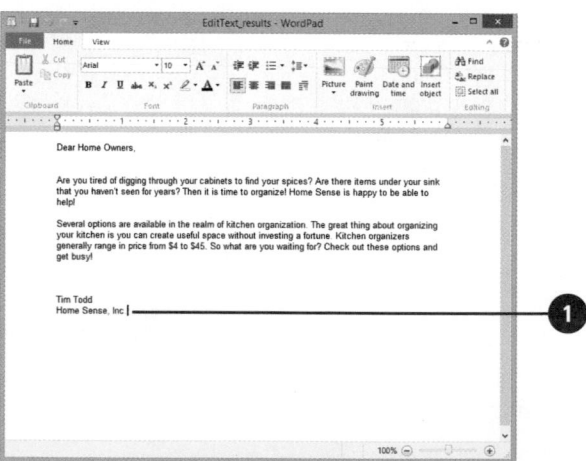

## Move or Copy Text

1. Select the text you want to move or copy.

2. Click or tap the **Cut** button or **Copy** button on the Home tab.

3. Click or tap where you want to insert the text.

4. Click or tap the **Paste** button on the Home tab.

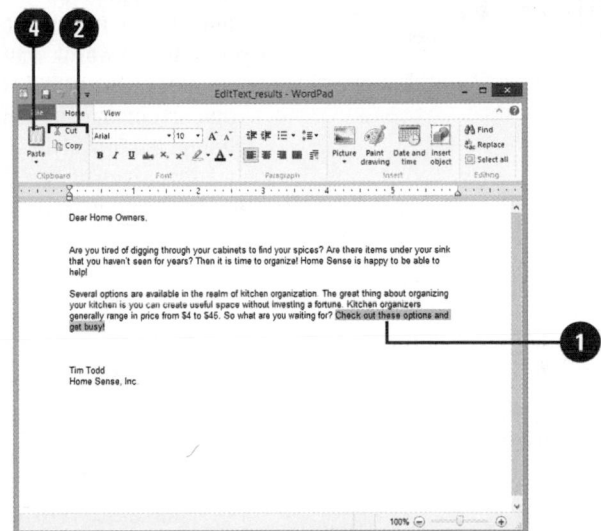

## Move or Copy Text Using Drag and Drop

1. Select the text you want to move or copy.

2. Point to the selected text, and then click or tap and hold the mouse button or finger.

   If you want to copy the text to a new location, also press and hold the Ctrl key. A plus sign (+) appears in the pointer box, indicating that you are dragging a copy of the selected text.

3. Drag the selected text to the new location, and then release the mouse button or finger (and the Ctrl key, if necessary).

4. Click or tap anywhere in the document to deselect the text.

Dear Home Owners,

Are you tired of digging through your cabinets to find your spices? Are there items under your sink that you haven't seen for years? Then it is time to organize! Home Sense is happy to be able to help!

Several options are available in the realm of kitchen organization. The great thing about organizing your kitchen is you can create useful space without investing a fortune. Kitchen organizers generally range in price from $4 to $45. So what are you waiting for? Check out these options and get busy!

Tim Todd
Home Sense, Inc.

Dear Home Owners,

Are you tired of digging through your cabinets to find your spices? Are there items under your sink that you haven't seen for years? Then it is time to organize! Home Sense is happy to be able to help!

Several options are available in the realm of kitchen organization. The great thing about organizing your kitchen is you can create useful space without investing a fortune. Kitchen organizers generally range in price from $4 to $45. So what are you waiting for?

Check out these options and get busy!

Tim Todd
Home Sense, Inc.

# Formatting Text

You can change the format or the appearance of text and graphics in a document so that the document is easier to read or more attractive. A quick and powerful way to add emphasis to parts of a document is to format text using bold, italics, underline, or color. For special emphasis, you can combine formats, such as bold and italics. In addition, you can change the font style and size. A **font** is a set of characters with the same typeface or design that you can increase or decrease in size. After formatting, you can create lists, and adjust text and line spacing.

## Format Text

1 Select the text or click or tap in the paragraph you want to format.

2 Use any of the formatting tools on the Home tab to style text:

- Font list arrow
- Font Size list arrow
- Grow Text
- Shrink Text
- Bold button
- Italic button
- Underline button
- Strikethrough button
- Subscript button
- Superscript button
- Text Highlight button
- Text Color button

3 Use any of the formatting tools on the Home tab to adjust text spacing:

- Indent buttons
- List button
- Line Spacing button
- Alignment buttons
- Paragraph button

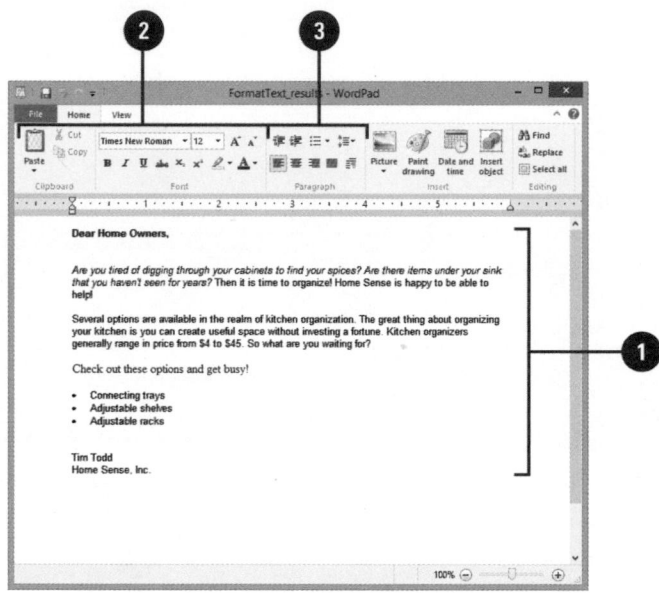

### Did You Know?

*Font size is measured in points.* One point is 1/72 of an inch high.

# Setting Paragraph Tabs

Tabs set text or numerical data alignment in relation to the edges of a document. A **tab stop** is a predefined stopping point along the document's typing line. Default tab stops are set every half-inch on the ruler, but you can set multiple tabs per paragraph at any location. Each paragraph in a document contains its own set of tab stops. The default tab stops do not appear on the ruler, but the manual tab stops you set do appear. Once you place a tab stop, you can drag the tab stop to position it where you want. If you want to add or adjust tab stops in multiple paragraphs, simply select the paragraphs first.

## Create and Clear a Tab Stop

1 Select the text or click or tap in the paragraph you want to format.

2 Click or tap the ruler where you want to set the tab stop.

◆ **View ruler.** Click or tap the **View** tab, and then select the **Ruler** check box.

3 To move a tab, drag the tab stop to position it where you want.

4 To clear a tab stop, drag it off the ruler.

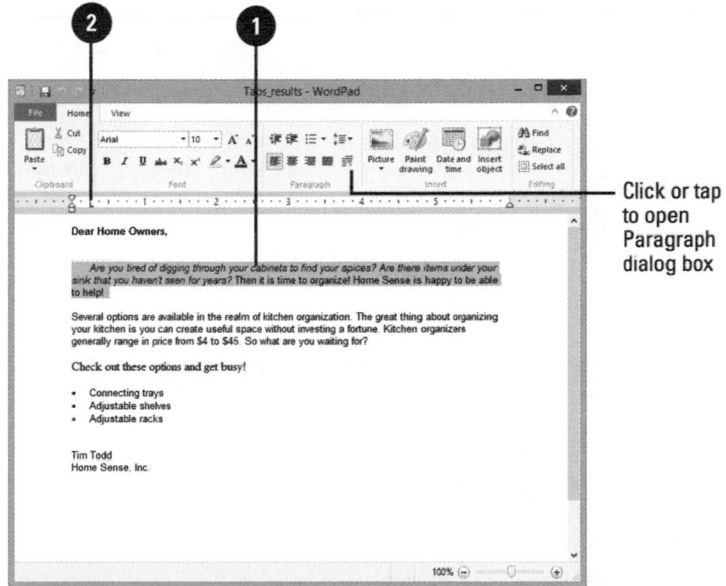

Click or tap to open Paragraph dialog box

## Did You Know?

*You can insert the date and time in WordPad.* Open a document in WordPad, click or tap to place the insertion point, click or tap the Date And Time button on the Home tab, select a format, and then click or tap OK.

## See Also

*See "Setting Paragraph Indents" on page 278 for information on changing the text alignment.*

---

## For Your Information

### Changing the Word Wrap Display

As you type a complete line of text, it wraps to the next line. Depending on your preference, you can change the Document window to display text wrapped to the window or ruler. To change word wrap options, click or tap the View tab, click or tap the Word Wrap button, and then click or tap the word wrap option you want. The wrapping options affect only how text appears on your screen. When printed, the document uses the margin settings specified in Page Setup.

# Setting Paragraph Indents

When you indent a paragraph, you move its edge in from the left or right margin. You can indent the entire left or right edge of a paragraph or just the first line. The markers on the ruler control the indentation of the current paragraph. The left side of the ruler has three markers. The top triangle, called the **first-line indent marker**, controls where the first line of the paragraph begins. The bottom triangle, called the **hanging indent marker**, controls where the remaining lines of the paragraph begin. The small square under the bottom triangle, called the **left indent marker**, allows you to move the first-line indent marker and the left indent marker simultaneously. When you move the left indent marker, the distance between the hanging indent and the first-line indent remains the same. The triangle on the right side of the ruler, called the **right indent marker**, controls where the right edge of the paragraph ends.

## Change Paragraph Indents

Select the text or click or tap in the paragraph you want to format.

- To view the ruler, click or tap the **View** tab, and then select the **Ruler** check box.

- To change the left indent of the first line, drag the First-Line Indent marker.

- To change the indent of the second and subsequent lines, drag the Hanging Indent marker.

- To change the left indent for all lines, drag the Left Indent marker.

- To change the right indent for all lines, drag the Right Indent marker.

As you drag a marker, the dotted guideline helps you position the indent accurately.

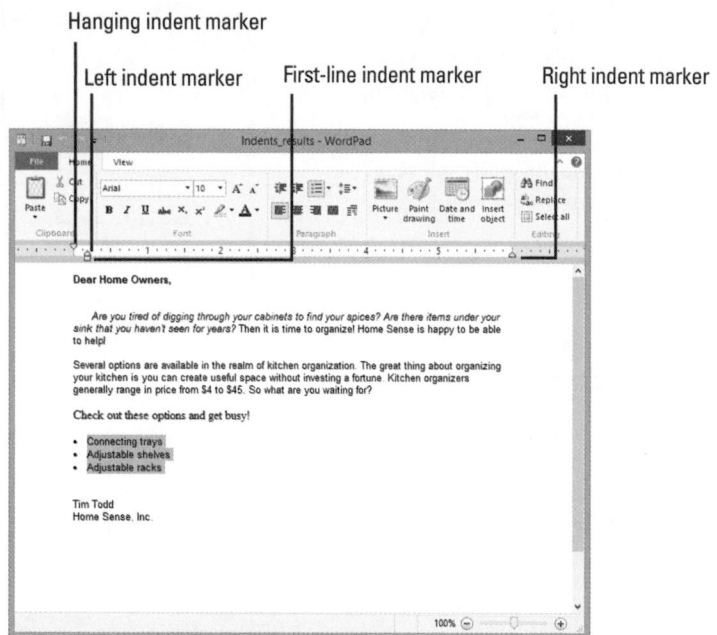

Hanging indent marker

Left indent marker    First-line indent marker    Right indent marker

### Did You Know?

*You can exact numbers for indents, line spacing, and tabs.* Click or tap the Paragraph button on the Home tab, specify the amounts you want, click or tap Tabs if desired, and then click or tap OK.

# Previewing and Printing a Document

Before printing, you should verify that the page looks the way you want. You save time, money, and paper by avoiding duplicate printing. Print Preview shows you the exact placement of your text on each printed page. Printing a paper copy is a common way to review and share a document. You can use the Print button on the toolbar to print a copy of your document using the current settings, or you can open the Print dialog box and specify the print options you want.

## Preview a Document

1. Click or tap the **File** tab, point to **Print**, and then click or tap **Print preview**.

2. Use the toolbar buttons to preview the document:

   ◆ To change the view size, click or tap the preview screen or **100%**.

   ◆ To view other pages, click or tap **Next Page** or **Prev Page**.

   ◆ To view two pages at a time, click or tap **Two Pages**.

   ◆ To print the document, click or tap **Print**.

3. When you're done, click or tap **Close print preview** button.

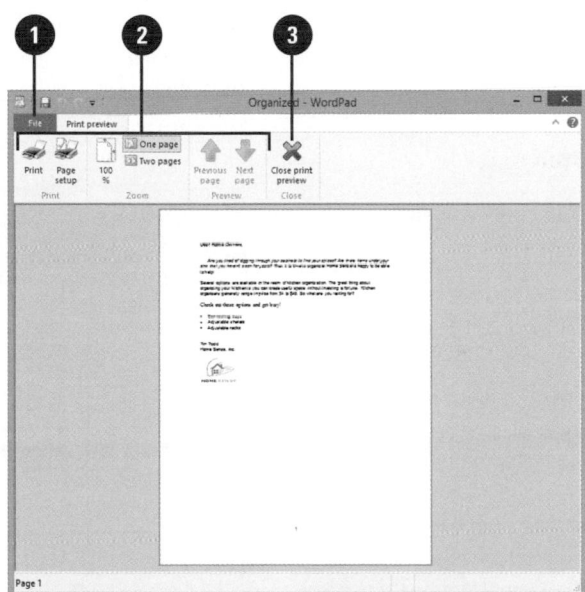

## Print All or Part of a Document

1. Click or tap the **File** tab, and then click or tap **Print**.

2. Click or tap a printer.

3. Specify the range of pages you want to print.

4. Specify the number of copies you want to print.

5. Click or tap **Print**.

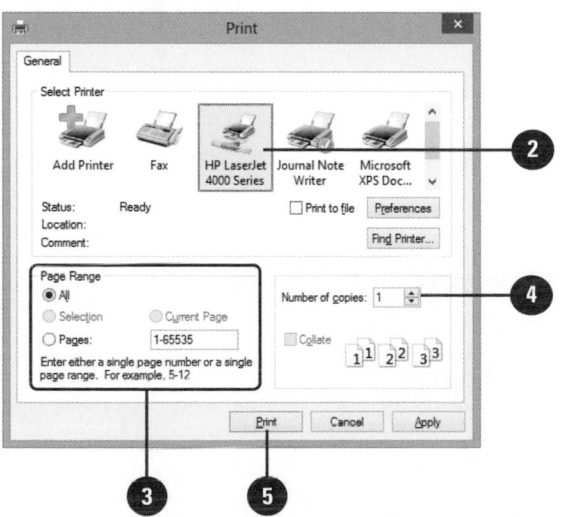

# Saving and Closing a Document

Saving your files frequently ensures that you don't lose work during an unexpected power loss. The first time you save, specify a file name and folder in the Save As dialog box. The next time you save, the program saves the file with the same name in the same folder. If you want to change a file's name or location, you can use the Save As dialog box again to create a copy of the original file. To conserve your PC's resources, close any file you are not working on. WordPad saves a document by default in the **Rich Text document (RTF)**. In addition to RTF, you can also save documents in **Office Open XML document (DOCX)**, which is for Microsoft Word 2010 or later, **OpenDocument text (ODT)**, which is for exchanging office documents, and **Plain Text Document (TXT)**, which is for plain text.

## Save a Document

1. Click or tap the **File** tab, and then click or tap **Save as**.

   ◆ You can also point to Save as, and then select a specific file format.

2. Use the Navigation pane to navigate to the drive or folder in which you want to save the file.

3. Type a name for the file, or use the suggested one.

4. To change the format of a file, click or tap the **Save as type** list arrow, and then click or tap a file format.

5. Click or tap **Save**.

New folder button

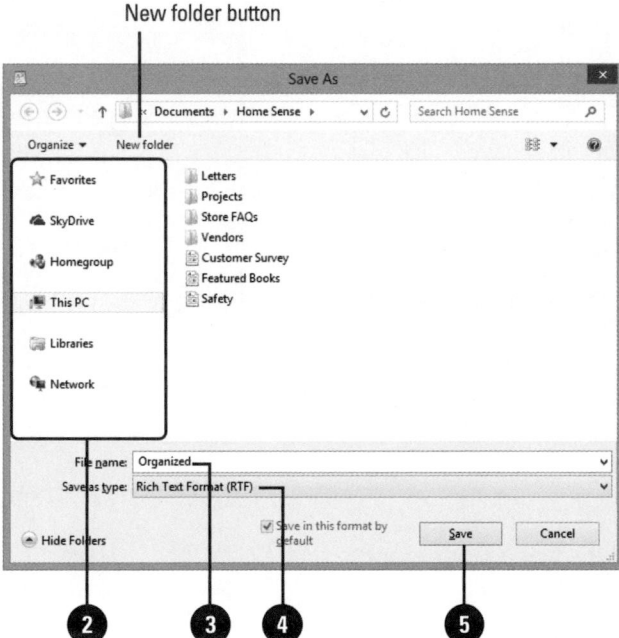

### Did You Know?

***You can save a file in a new folder.*** In the Save As dialog box, click or tap the New Folder button, type the new folder name, press Enter, click or tap Open, and then click or tap Save.

***You can close a document.*** Click or tap the Close button in the program window or click or tap the File tab, and then click or tap Close. If necessary, click or tap Yes to save your changes.

# Inserting Special Characters

When you need to insert special characters such as ©, ™, or ® that don't appear on your keyboard, you can use a special accessory program called Character Map to do the job. Character Map displays all the characters that are available for each of the fonts on your PC computer or mobile device.

## Insert a Special Character

1. In the Start screen, click or tap the **Apps view** button, and then click or tap **Character Map**.

2. Click or tap the **Font** list arrow, and then click or tap a font.

3. Double-click or double-tap the character you want to insert.

   **TIMESAVER** *Click or tap a character to see an enlarged view of it.*

4. Click or tap **Copy** to place the character on the Clipboard.

5. Click or tap the **Close** button.

6. Click or tap in the document to place the insertion point.

7. Click or tap the **Paste** button on the Home tab.

   **TIMESAVER** *Press Ctrl+V to quickly paste the contents from the Clipboard.*

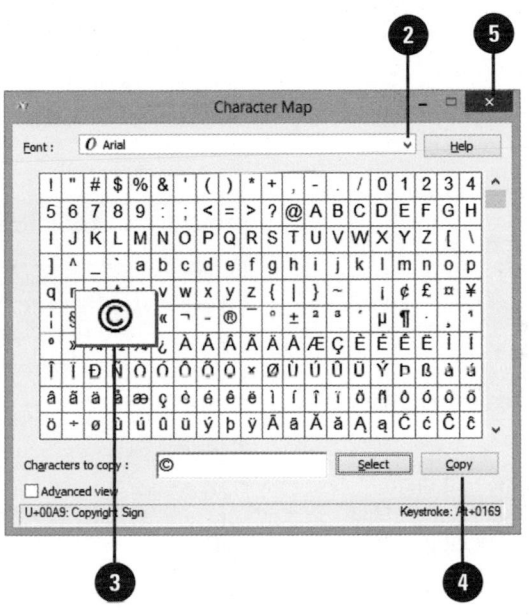

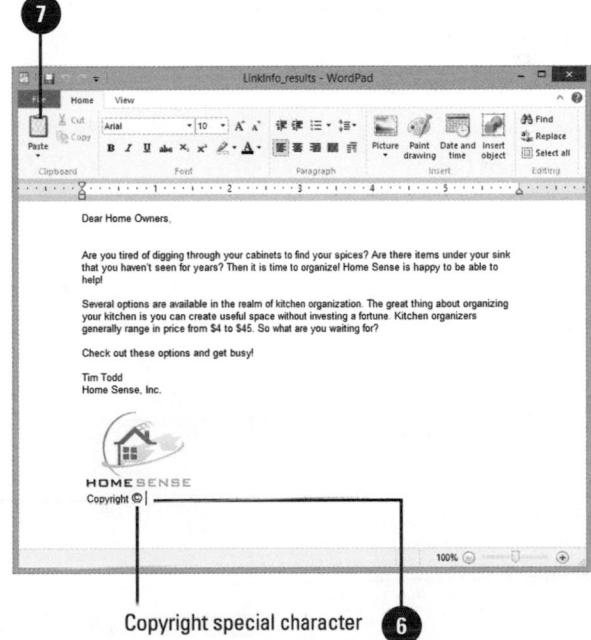

Copyright special character

# Inserting and Editing Information

Instead of switching back and forth between programs to copy and paste information, you can insert, or embed, the information. With **embedding**, a copy of the object becomes part of the destination file. If you want to edit the object, you make changes in the destination file, and the original file remains intact. Once you embed data, you can edit it using the menus and toolbars of the source program without leaving the program in which it's embedded (that is, the destination program). For example, you can create a picture in a program, such as Paint, or select an existing picture and insert it into a WordPad document. In WordPad, you can use the Paint drawing button on the Home tab to embed a new Paint object. The inserted picture is an object you can resize.

## Embed an Existing Object

1. Click or tap where you want to embed the object.

2. Click or tap the **Insert Object** button on the Home tab.

3. Click or tap the **Create from File** option.

4. Click or tap **Browse**, and then double-click or double-tap the file with the object you want to use.

5. Click or tap **OK**.

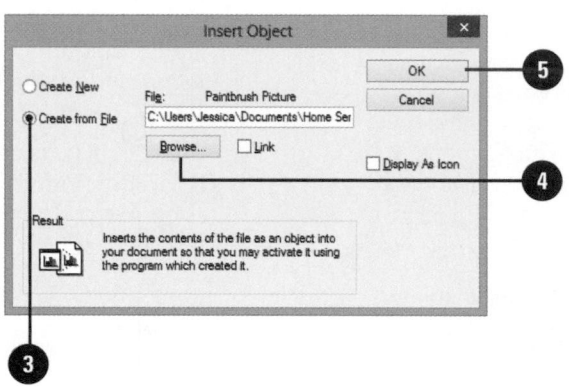

## Embed a New Object

1. Click or tap where you want to embed the object.

2. Click or tap the **Insert Object** button on the Home tab.

3. Click or tap the **Create New** option.

4. Double-click or double-tap the type of object you want to create.

5. Enter information in the new object using the menus and toolbars in the source program.

6. Click or tap the **Program** button, and then click or tap **Exit and return to document** to close the object.

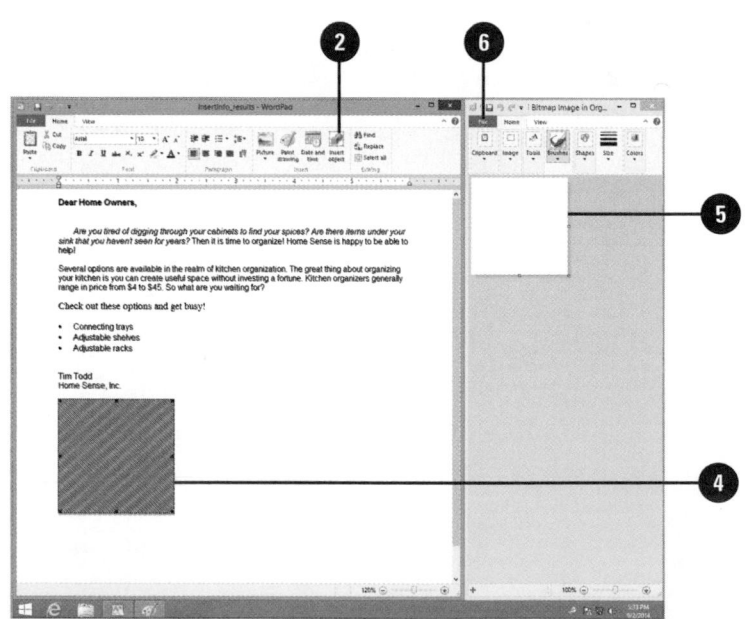

## Edit an Object

① Open the document with the object you want to edit.

② Double-click or double-tap the object.

③ Edit the object using the menus and toolbars in the source program.

④ Click or tap the **Program** button, and then click or tap **Exit and return to document** to close.

### Did You Know?

*You can use Paste Special to embed part of a file.* Select and copy the information, click or tap where you want to embed the copied information, click or tap the Paste button arrow on the Home tab, click or tap Paste Special, click or tap the Paste option, select a format, and then click or tap OK.

## Resize an Object

① Click or tap the object to select it.

② Drag a sizing handle to change the size of the object.

◆ Drag a corner sizing handle to change height and width simultaneously.

◆ Drag the top or bottom middle sizing handle to change height.

◆ Drag the left or right middle sizing handle to change width.

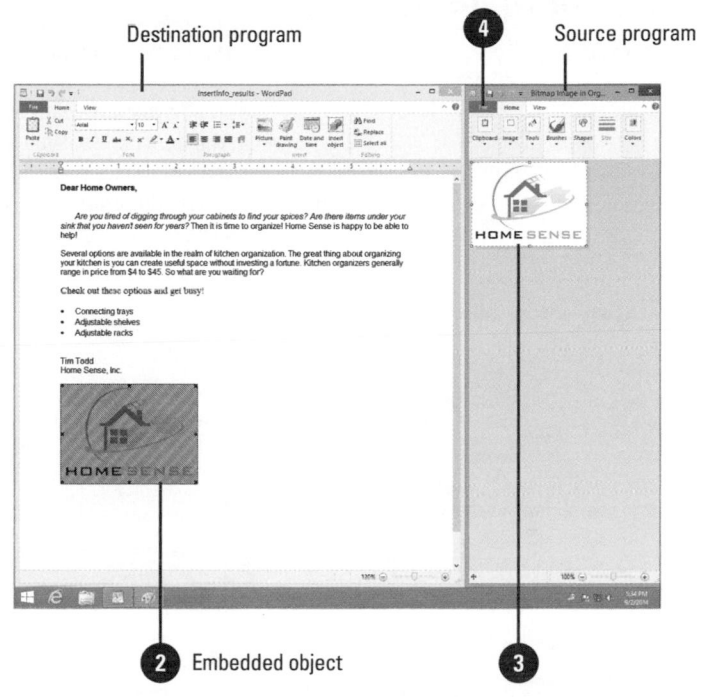

Destination program

Source program

Embedded object

Drag a sizing handle

# Linking and Updating Information

When you want to keep source and destination files in sync with each other, you can link the source file that created the object with the destination file that displays the object. **Linking** displays information stored in one document (the source file) into another (the destination file). You can edit the linked object from either file, although changes are stored in the source file. Only a representation of the object appears in the destination file; any changes made to the object are done in the source file, whether you access it by double-clicking or double-tapping the object in the destination file or by opening it in the source program.

## Link an Object Between Programs

1. Click or tap where you want to embed the object.

2. Click or tap the **Insert Object** button on the Home tab.

3. Click or tap the **Create from File** option.

4. Click or tap **Browse**, and then double-click or double-tap the file with the object you want to link.

5. Select the **Link** check box.

6. Click or tap **OK**.

### Did You Know?

*You can use Paste Special to link part of a file.* Select and copy the information, click or tap where you want to link the copied information, click or tap the Edit menu, click or tap Paste Special, click or tap the Paste Link option to link, select a format, and then click or tap OK.

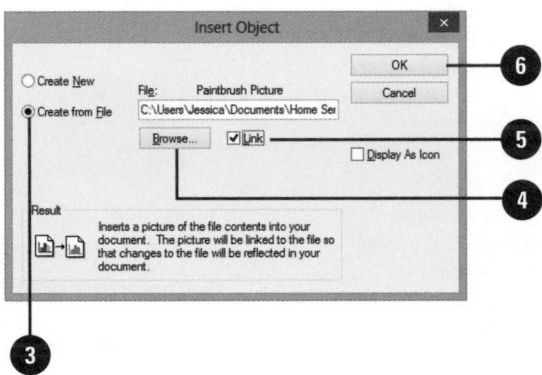

Linked object

## Update a Linked File

1. Open the file with the source program.

2. Edit the file using the source program's commands.

3. Click or tap the **Save** button on the toolbar.

4. Click or tap the **Close** button to exit the source program.

5. Open the linked file with the destination program.

   The object automatically updates.

6. Click or tap the **Save** button on the toolbar.

7. Click or tap the **Close** button to exit the destination program.

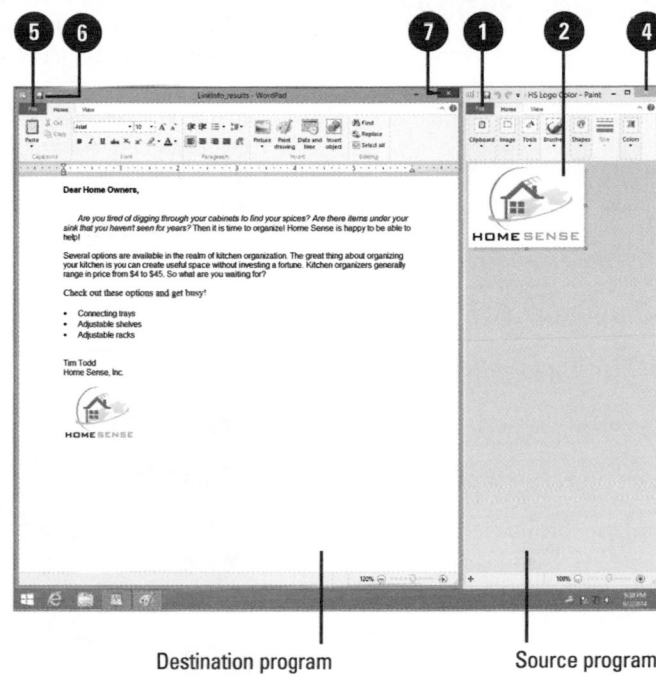

Destination program                    Source program

### For Your Information

## Finding, Changing, and Breaking a Linked Object

Instead of opening a linked object from the source file to make changes, you can open a linked object from the destination file using the Open Source button in the Links dialog box. The Open Source button finds the source file containing the linked object and opens that file. After making changes, you exit and return to the destination file. The Links dialog box keeps track of the source file location. You can change the linked source to a different file by using the Change Source button. If you want to disregard a link and change it to an embedded object, select the linked object in the destination file, right-click or tap-hold the object, click or tap Object Properties, click or tap the Link tab, click or tap Break Link, click or tap Yes in the message box, and then click or tap OK. On the Link tab in the Object Properties dialog box, you can also open or change the source file, change update options, and update the source for the selected object.

# Calculating Numbers

If you don't have a handheld calculator handy, you can use the Calculator app (**New!**) or desktop program provided by Windows to perform standard calculations or even more complex ones. Calculator performs basic arithmetic, such as addition and subtraction, functions found on a scientific calculator, such as logarithms and factorials, programmer conversions, such as Hex and Decimal, as well as functions for statistical analysis. You can also change the display to perform functions, including unit conversion, date calculation, and worksheets, such as mortgage, vehicle lease, or fuel economy (mpg or L/100 km).

## Use the Calculator App

**1** In the Start screen, click or tap the **Apps view** button, and then click or tap **Calculator** (metro app).

**2** Click or tap **Standard** or **Scientific**.

**3** Click or tap the number buttons.

**4** Click or tap a function button, and then enter another number.

**5** When you've entered all the numbers you want, click or tap the equals (=) button.

**6** To use the converter, select the conversion type, such as volume or weight, select the conversion units from and to, and then click or tap the number buttons.

**7** Click or tap the results, and then click or tap **Copy** to copy the result to the Clipboard to paste in a document.

**8** To close the app, point to the top edge of the screen (cursor changes to a hand), and then drag down to the bottom edge of the screen.

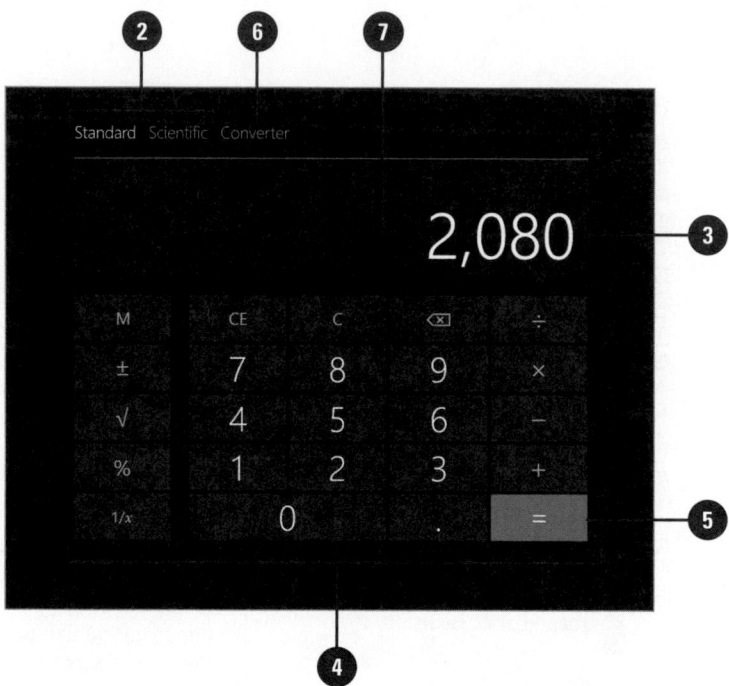

## Use the Calculator Program

**1** In the Start screen, click or tap the **Apps view** button, and then click or tap **Calculator** (under Windows Accessories)

**2** Click or tap the **View** menu, and then click or tap **Standard**, **Scientific**, **Programmer**, or **Statistics**.

**3** To change the view to display other functions, click or tap the **View** menu, and then click or tap **Basic**, **Unit conversion**, **Date calculation**, or point to **Worksheets**, and click or tap an option.

**4** Enter a number, or click or tap the number buttons.

◆ **Numeric keypad on keyboard.** Press the number, +, -, *, /, and Enter keys to quickly enter numbers and use the calculator.

**5** Click or tap a function button, and then enter another number.

**6** When you've entered all the numbers you want, click or tap the equals (=) button.

**7** Click or tap the **Edit** menu, and then click or tap **Copy** to copy the result to the Clipboard to paste in a document.

**8** When you're done, click or tap the **Close** button.

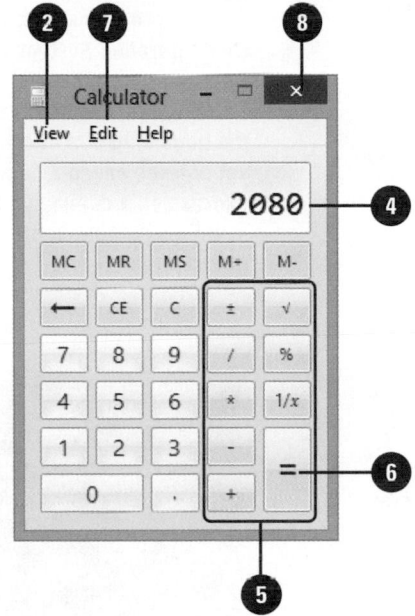

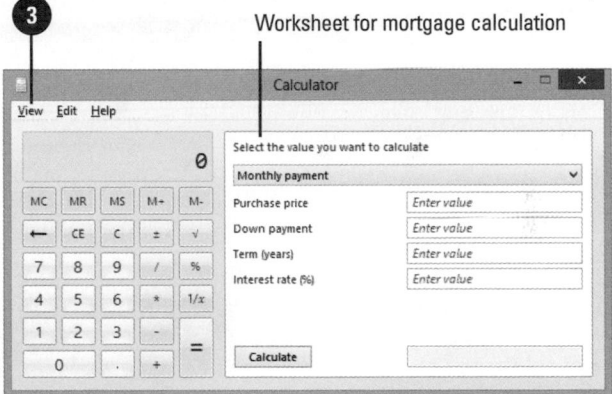

Worksheet for mortgage calculation

# Running Commands

Besides running Windows programs, you can also enter commands and run programs written in MS-DOS. **MS-DOS** stands for Microsoft Disk Operating System. MS-DOS, or DOS, employs a **command-line interface** through which you must type commands at a **command prompt** to run different tasks. A character such as a > or $ appears at the beginning of a command prompt. Each DOS command has a strict set of rules called a **command syntax** that you must follow when expressing a command. Many commands allow you to include switches and parameters that give you additional control of the command.

## Run a Command

1. In the Start screen, click or tap the **Apps view** button, and then click or tap **Command Prompt**.

   ◆ You can also right-click or tap-hold the lower-left corner, and then click or tap **Command Prompt**.

2. At the prompt, type a command including any parameters, and then press Enter.

3. When you're done, click or tap the **Close** button, or type **exit**, and then press Enter.

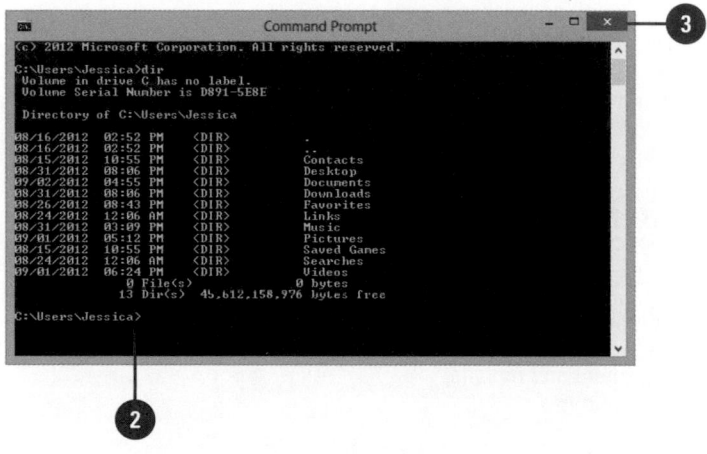

## Find a Command

1. In the Start screen, click or tap the **Apps view** button, and then click or tap **Command Prompt**.

2. At the prompt, type **help**, and then press Enter.

3. Read the list of commands. Use the scroll bar or scroll arrows to display additional information.

4. When you're done, click or tap the **Close** button, or type **exit**, and then press Enter.

Prompt

## Get Information About a Command

1. In the Start screen, click or tap the **Apps view** button, and then click or tap **Command Prompt**.

2. At the prompt, type a command followed by a space and **/?**, and then press Enter.

3. Read the information about the command. Use the scroll bar or scroll arrows to display additional information.

4. When you're done, click or tap the **Close** button, or type **exit**, and then press Enter.

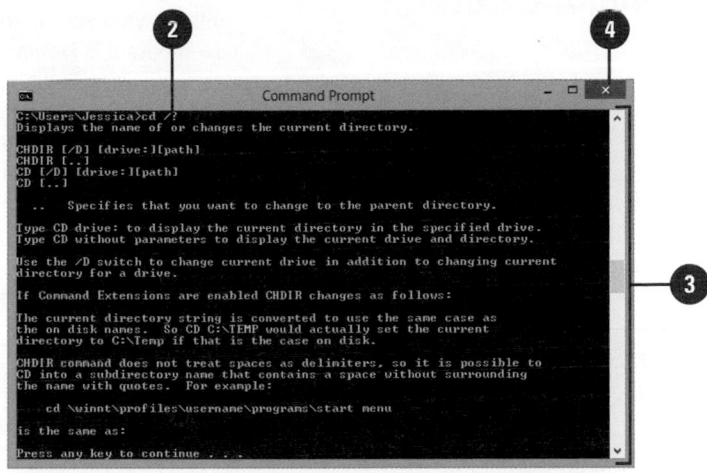

### Did You Know?

**You can use a wildcard character to change more than one file.** An asterisk is a wildcard and represents any number of characters. For example, the command *dir at\*.doc* matches atback.doc, ati.doc, and atlm.doc.

**You can change the appearance of the Command Prompt window.** Right-click or tap-hold the Command Prompt window title bar, and then click or tap Properties.

**You can ping a connection to make sure it works and find out an IP address.** Ping is a diagnostic network tool that verifies whether an IP address is accessible. To test a connection, type **ping *IP address*** at the command prompt, and then press Enter. To find an IP address, type **ipconfig /?** or type **ipconfig /all**, and then press Enter. To get a new IP address, type **ipconfig/release**, press Enter, type **ipconfig/renew**, and then press Enter.

### Common DOS Commands

| Command | Purpose |
|---------|---------|
| cd *foldername* | Changes to the specified folder |
| cls | Clears the screen |
| copy | Copies the specified files or folder |
| dir | Lists the contents of the current folder |
| *c*: (where c is a drive) | Switches to the specified drive |
| exit | Closes the Command Prompt window |
| rename | Renames the specified file or files |
| more *file name* | Displays the contents of a file, one screen of output at a time |
| type *file name.txt* | Displays the contents of the text file |

# Snipping the Screen

The Snipping Tool allows you to capture a screen shot of anything currently on your screen as an image file. After you capture the image, you can annotate, save and share it with others in an e-mail. You can capture the screen in different ways: draw a free-form shape around an object, draw a rectangle around an object, select a window, or take the entire screen. If you want to use a keyboard shortcut in any app, you can press Win+PrtScn (Print Screen) to take a screenshot and automatically save it in the Pictures folder as a PNG file.

## Use the Snipping Tool

1. In the Start screen, click or tap the **Apps view** button, and then click or tap **Snipping Tool**.

2. To change snipping options, click or tap the **Options** button, select the options you want, and then click or tap **OK**.

3. To capture a screen, click or tap the **New Snip** button arrow, and then select a capture option:

   ◆ **Free-form Snip.**

   ◆ **Rectangle Snip.**

   ◆ **Window Snip.**

   ◆ **Full-screen Snip.**

4. Drag a free-form or rectangle shape, or click or tap a window.

5. To annotate the image, use the **Pen**, **Highlighter**, and **Eraser** tools.

6. To share the image, use the **Send Snip** button.

7. Click or tap the **Save** button, select a save location, and then select a file format (PNG, GIF, JPEG, or MHT). MHT is for a single page web page.

8. To copy it to the Clipboard to paste in a document, click or tap the **Copy** button.

9. When you're done, click or tap the **Close** button.

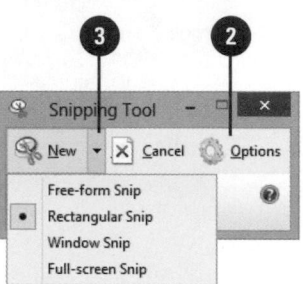

Annotation

# Recording Steps

Using Steps Recorder, you can record a series of actions you take on your system, including a text description of your steps and a picture of the screen during each step. After you capture the steps you want to take, you can save them in a ZIP file that you can use later or send to others in an email message. There are a few important notes to be aware of before you get started. You cannot record anything you enter and some full screen apps might not capture the entire screen. If you use two monitors, Steps Recorder will capture both screens, so you should adjustments as needed.

## Record a Series of Actions

1. In the Start screen, click or tap the **Apps view** button, and then click or tap **Steps Recorder**.

2. Click or tap the **Start Record** button, and then execute the steps you want.

3. When you're done, click or tap the **Stop Record** button.

   The Steps Recorder window opens, displaying a text description of your steps and a picture of the screen during each step,

4. Click or tap the **Save** button.

5. Select a folder, type a name for the file, and then click or tap **Save**.

   The recorded steps are saved in a ZIP file.

   ◆ **Email.** Click or tap to send the recorded steps as a file attachment in your default email program.

6. Click or tap the **Close** button.

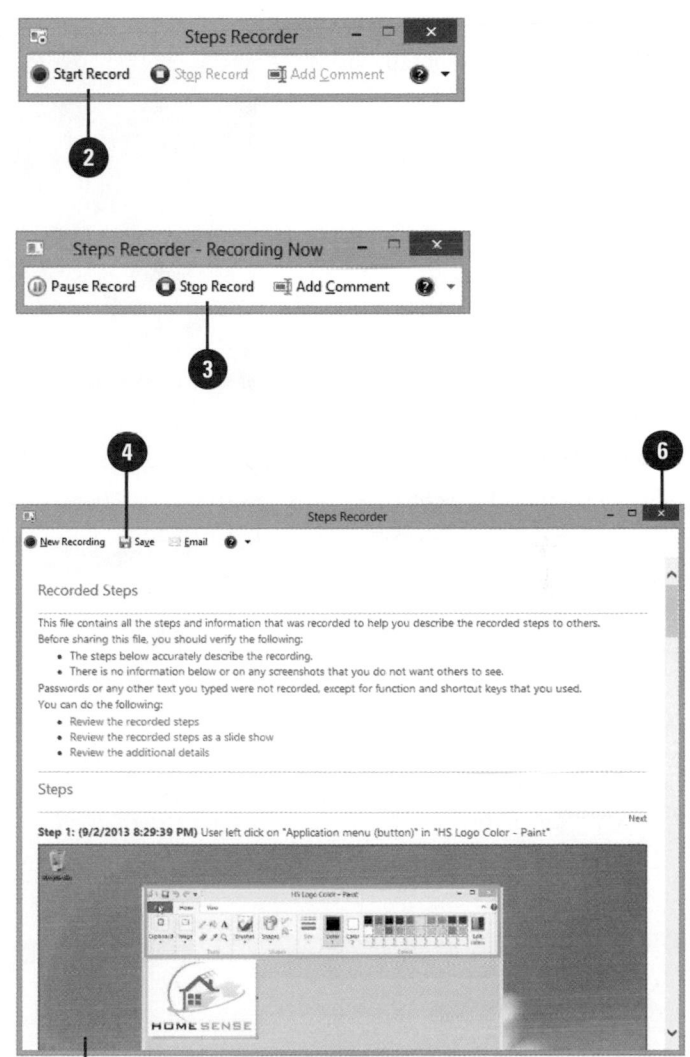

Text description and screen shots of the recorded steps

# Creating Sticky Notes

A sticky note is an electronic postem note. With Sticky Notes, you always have a not pad handy for jotting down things you want to remember or keep handy when you need them. When you start the Sticky Notes program, a new sticky note appears on the desktop along with the Sticky Notes button on the taskbar. You can add more notes or remove the ones you no longer need. The notes appear in yellow by default, however, you can change them to another color to make them easier to identify.

## Create and Manage Sticky Notes

1. In the Start screen, click or tap the **Apps view** button, and then click or tap **Sticky Notes**.

2. If a new sticky note appears, type the text you want in it.

3. To create a new sticky note in Sticky Notes, point to a notes, and then click or tap the **Add** button (+).

4. To delete a sticky notes, point to a notes, and then click or tap the **Delete** button (x).

5. To change a note color, right-click or tap-hold a note, and then select a color.

6. To move a note, drag the top of the note to another location on the desktop.

7. To exit, right-click or tap-hold the Sticky Notes program on the taskbar, and then click or tap **Close window**.

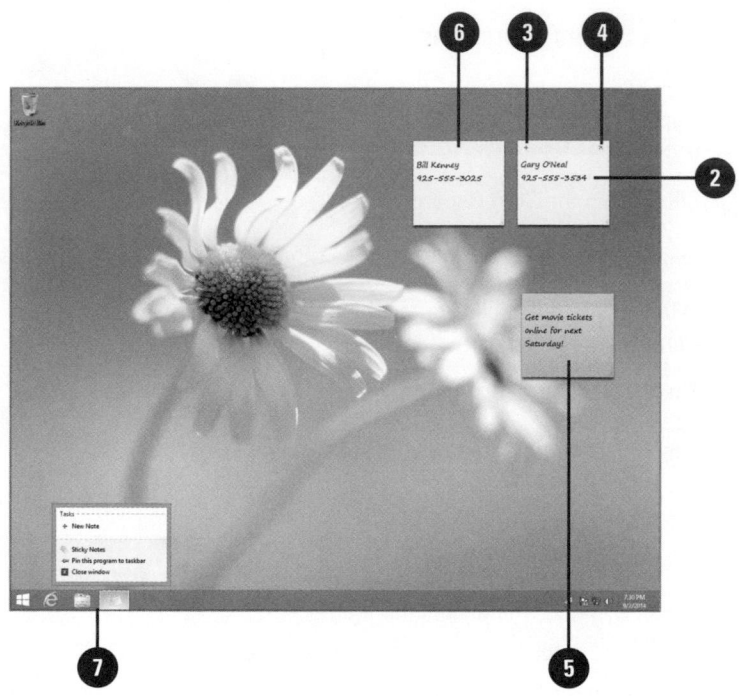

# Handwriting Journal Entries

With Windows Journal, you can handwrite notes and draw pictures to mimic a notebook pad. Since Windows 8.1 is designed for use with tablets and mobile devices, you can use a pen or finger to take handwritten notes. The program is available on a standard PC and you can use them with a mouse, but not as effectively. Windows Journal provides a toolbar with easy to use buttons that allow you to select a pen, highlighter, or eraser to create and save notes.

## Handwrite Journal Entries

1 In the Start screen, click or tap the **Apps view** button, and then click or tap **Windows Journal**.

◆ **Of first use.** Click or tap **Install** or **Cancel** to install the Journal Note Writer printer driver, which captures an image of the document.

2 Click or tap the **Pen** button arrow on the toolbar, and then select a pen style.

3 Handwrite notes or make a drawing.

4 To make corrections, click or tap the **Erase** button arrow, select an eraser size, and then drag to erase on the page.

5 Use many of the common tools on the toolbar and menus to create a handwritten document.

6 When you're done, click or tap the **Save** button on the toolbar, type a name, specify a location, and then click or tap **Save**.

7 Click or tap the **File** menu, and then click or tap **Exit**.

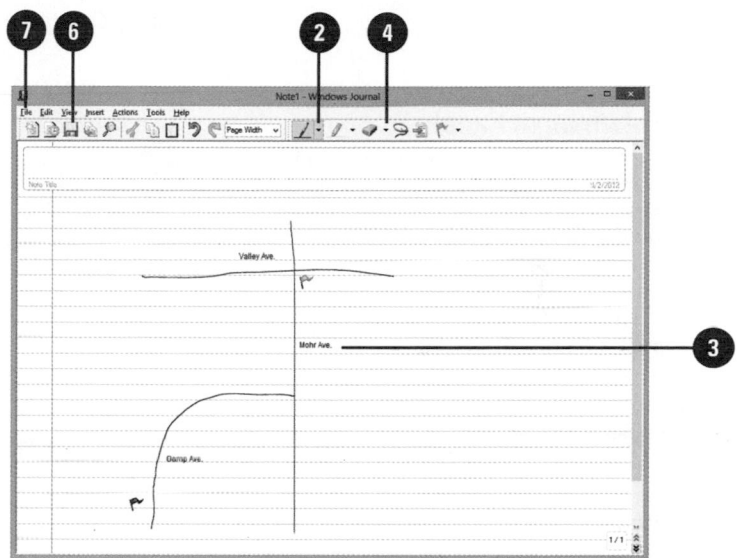

# Using the Math Input Panel

If you use Windows to take notes in math or you work in an engineering or scientific profession, then you need the Math Input Panel. The Math Input Panel recognizes handwritten math expressions and inserts them into other programs. The program needs to support Mathematical Markup Language (MathML). Just open the document in which you want to insert your math expressions, start Math Input Panel, handwrite your math expression, and then click or tap Insert. If you take notes in Windows Journal, you can convert your handwritten math expression to normal text that you can use in a word processing program. Simply drag the select expression directly into the Math Input Panel.

## Use the Math Input Panel

① Open the document in which you want to insert the math expression.

② In the Start screen, click or tap the **Apps view** button, and then click or tap **Math Input Panel**.

③ Handwrite the math expression you want.

As you write, the expression appears in the recognition box. The **Write** button is selected by default.

④ To correct a letter, click or tap the **Select and Correct** button, select a part of the expression, and then select a correction from the menu.

⑤ To erase the expression, click or tap the **Erase** button, and then drag to erase it.

⑥ To clear the expression and start over, click or tap the **Clear** button.

⑦ To undo or redo, click or tap the **Undo** or **Redo** button.

⑧ Click or tap **Insert** to place it in the open document.

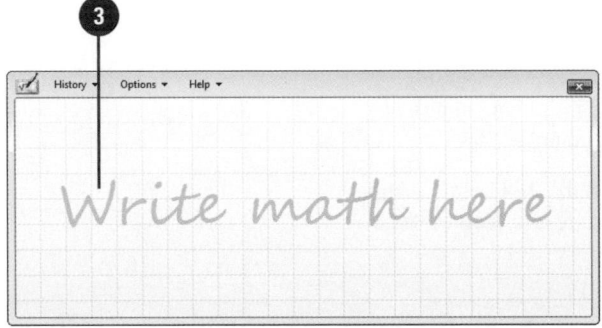

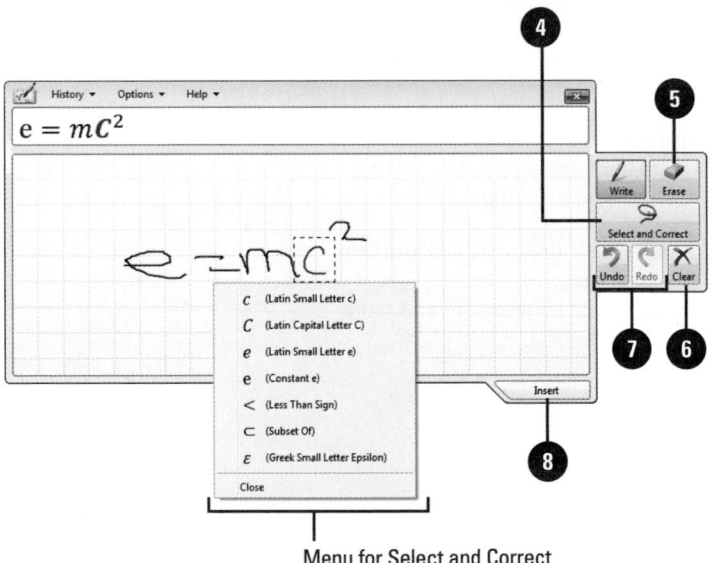

Menu for Select and Correct

# Running Older Programs

Some older programs are designed to run on earlier versions of Windows and don't work properly on Windows 8.1. You can set the compatibility of Windows 8.1 to act like an earlier version of Windows to run an older program. In addition, you can also set display resolution and color settings, and user privilege levels to provide the best level of compatibility for the program and the Windows 8.1 operating system. You set options in the Compatibility tab in the program's Properties dialog box.

## Set Compatibility for an Older Program

1. In the desktop, click or tap the **File Explorer** icon on the taskbar, and then locate the older program.

2. Right-click or tap-hold the program you want to run, and then click or tap **Properties**.

3. Click or tap the **Compatibility** tab.

4. Select the **Run this program in compatibility mode for** check box.

5. Click or tap the list arrow, and then click or tap the version of Windows in which the program was designed.

6. Select the check boxes for applying the appropriate settings to the display, based on the program's documentation.

7. Click or tap **OK**.

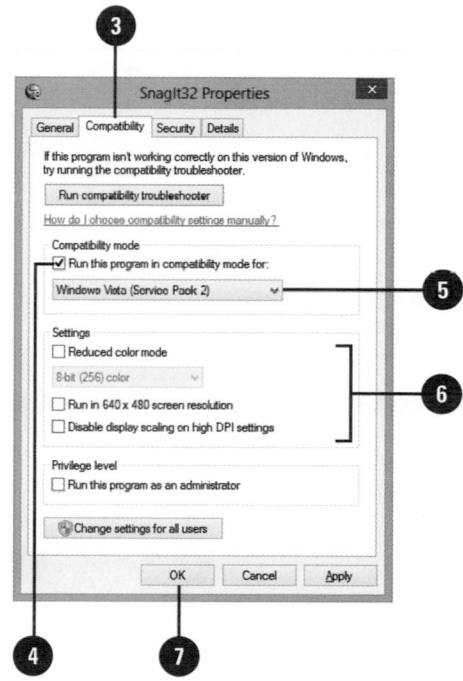

## Did You Know?

*You can test your program using the Program Compatibility troubleshooter.* In the Control Panel (desktop), click or tap the Troubleshooting icon in Small icons or Large icons view, and then click or tap the Run Programs Made For Previous Versions Of Windows link to start the Program Compatibility troubleshooter. Follow the on-screen instructions.

# Quitting a Program Not Responding

If a program stops responding while you work or freezes up, Windows provides you with the option to end the task. When you end a task, you'll probably lose any unsaved work in the problem program. If the problem persists, you might need to reinstall the program or contact product support to fix the problem. Pressing Ctrl+Alt+Delete or click or tapping the Close button closes the non responsive program and opens the Task Manager, where you can stop the program. You can also use the Task Manager to view system performance and log off users.

## End a Task Not Responding

① In the desktop, right-click or tap-hold the taskbar, and then click or tap **Task Manager**.

If Windows doesn't respond, press Ctrl+Shift+Esc or press Ctrl+Alt+Delete, and then click or tap **Task Manager**.

② Click or tap the **More details** or **Fewer details** to display more or less information.

③ Select the program not responding (on the Processor tab in More details view).

④ Click or tap **End task**. If you're asked to wait, click or tap **End now**.

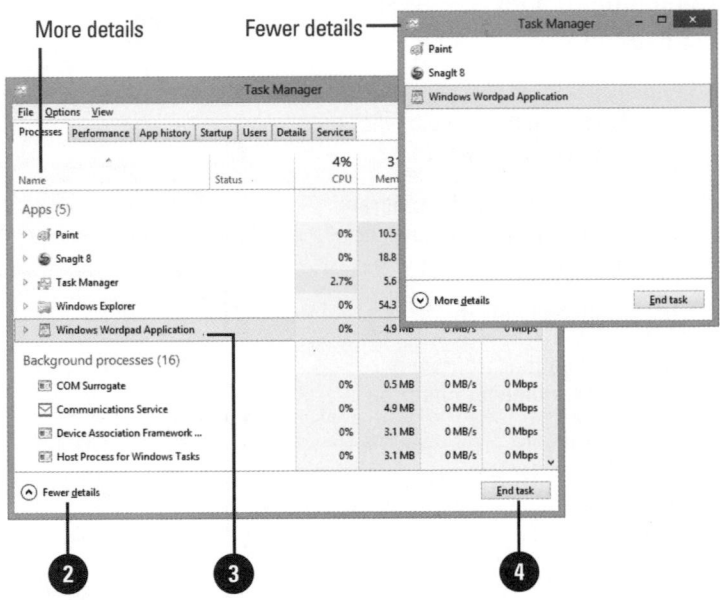

## End a Program Not Responding

① If a program is not responding, click or tap the **Close** button on the program's title bar. Click or tap several times, if necessary.

② If you see a dialog box telling you the program is not responding, click or tap **End Now**.

③ When a message appears, click or tap **Send Information** to send information about the error over the Internet to Microsoft, or click or tap **Cancel** to continue.

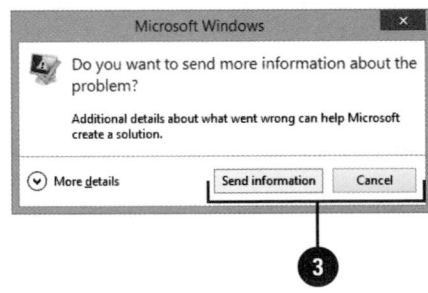

# Customizing Windows

## Introduction

Windows 8.1 gives you the ability to customize your work environment to suit your personal needs and preferences. You can customize Windows 8.1 by using PC settings or by using the Control Panel from the desktop. PC settings provide the options you need for using Windows in full-screen view with metro apps, while the Control Panel provides the options you need for customizing the desktop and other advanced Windows settings. Some options overlap between PC settings and Control Panel.

You can change the main Windows features through PC settings, which displays a list of categories, including Personalize, Users, Notifications, Search, Share, General, Privacy, Devices, Ease of Access, Sync your Settings, Homegroup, and Windows Update, where you can specify the options you want. For example, you can personalize the Lock screen, Start screen, and account picture, and specify general options to set the time, app switching, spelling, and language. You can also set options to refresh, remove, or reinstall Windows 8.1.

You can adjust most Windows features through the Control Panel, a central location for changing Windows settings. From the Control Panel you access the individual programs for changing the properties, or characteristics, of a specific element, such as the desktop or the taskbar. The Control Panel displays utilities in two different views: Category and Small or Large Icons. Control Panel Category view displays utilities in functional categories based on tasks with some direct links, while Small or Large Icons view displays an icon for each utility program. Each icon in the Control Panel represents an aspect of Windows that you can change to fit your own working habits and personal needs. Some Control Panel settings are vital to how you work (such as the Date and Time, or the Language settings) and others are purely aesthetic (such as the background picture).

## What You'll Do

**View Windows Settings**

**Personalize the Lock and Start Screen**

**Sync Options on Other Devices**

**Change General Options**

**View the Control Panel**

**Change the Desktop Background**

**Change the Desktop and Start Screen**

**Customize the Desktop**

**Use a Screen Saver**

**Change Text Size on the Screen**

**Change the Screen Display**

**Set the Date, and Time**

**Change Regional and Language Options**

**Work with Fonts**

**Display and Arrange Toolbars**

**Customize the Taskbar**

**Change the Way a Disc or Device Starts**

**Use the Ease of Access Tools**

**Use the Ease of Access Center**

**Listen to Your System**

**Recognize Your Speech**

**Set Ease of Access Options**

# Viewing Windows Settings

With PC settings, you can customize the use of Windows 8.1 in full screen view with metro apps. The PC settings screen displays a list of main categories (**New!**), including PC and devices, Accounts, SkyDrive, Search and apps, Privacy, Network, Time and language, Ease of Access, and Update and recovery, where you can specify the options you want. The main screen for PC settings displays links to the Lock screen, Account picture, Picture password, and other recently used settings for easy access. You can specify options to add devices and accounts, personalize corners and edges, check for Windows update, set spelling correction, time, and language. You can also set options to refresh, remove, or reinstall Windows 8.1.

## View and Change PC Settings

1. Display the Start screen.

2. Point to the lower- or upper-right corner and move up or down (on a computer) or swipe left from the right edge of the screen (on a mobile device).

3. Click or tap the **Settings** button on the Charms bar.

4. Click or tap **Change PC settings** on the Settings panel.

   The Personalize screen (**New!**) appears with easy access links.

5. To view recently used settings, click or tap the **View recently used settings** link (**New!**).

6. Click or tap a main category under PC settings.

7. Click or tap a subcategory under a category.

8. Specify the PC settings options you want.

9. Click or tap the **Back** button to back to the main categories.

10. To close the app, point to the top edge of the screen (cursor changes to a hand), and then drag down to the bottom edge of the screen.

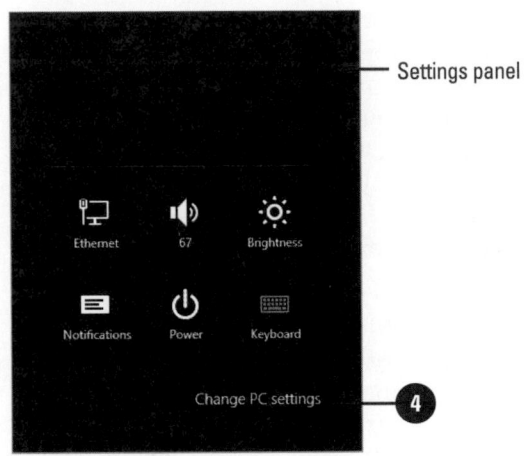

Settings panel

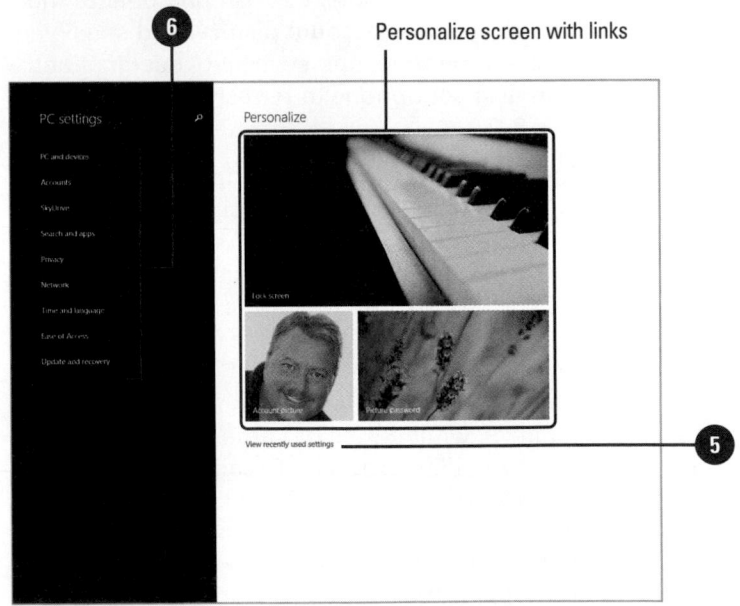

Personalize screen with links

# Personalizing the Lock Screen

The Lock screen appears when you start Windows 8.1, switch users, or put Windows to sleep. It's a security feature that helps prevent other from accessing your device. You can customize the Lock screen by changing it's picture, displaying status information, showing alarms (**New!**), playing a slide show (**New!**), or using a camera (**New!**). You can select up to seven apps to run in the background and show quick status and notification on the Lock screen, and select one app to display detailed status and one app to show alarms.

## Personalize the Lock Screen

1. Display the Start screen.

2. Point to the lower- or upper-right corner and move up or down (on a computer) or swipe left from the right edge of the screen (on a mobile device).

3. Click or tap the **Settings** button on the Charms bar.

4. Click or tap **Change PC settings** on the Settings panel, and then click or tap **PC and devices**.

5. Click or tap **Lock screen** under PC and devices.

6. Specify the options you want for use on the Lock screen.

   ◆ **Lock screen.** Click or tap an available screen or click or tap **Browse** to select one.

   ◆ **Slide Show.** Drag the slider On or Off to play a slide show (**New!**).

   ◆ **Lock screen apps.** Click or tap the **Add** icon (+) to add an app for status or show alarms (**New!**) or click or tap an icon to change or remove it.

   ◆ **Camera.** Drag the slider On or Off to use the camera with a swipe down (**New!**).

7. To close the app, point to the top edge of the screen (cursor changes to a hand), and then drag down to the bottom edge of the screen.

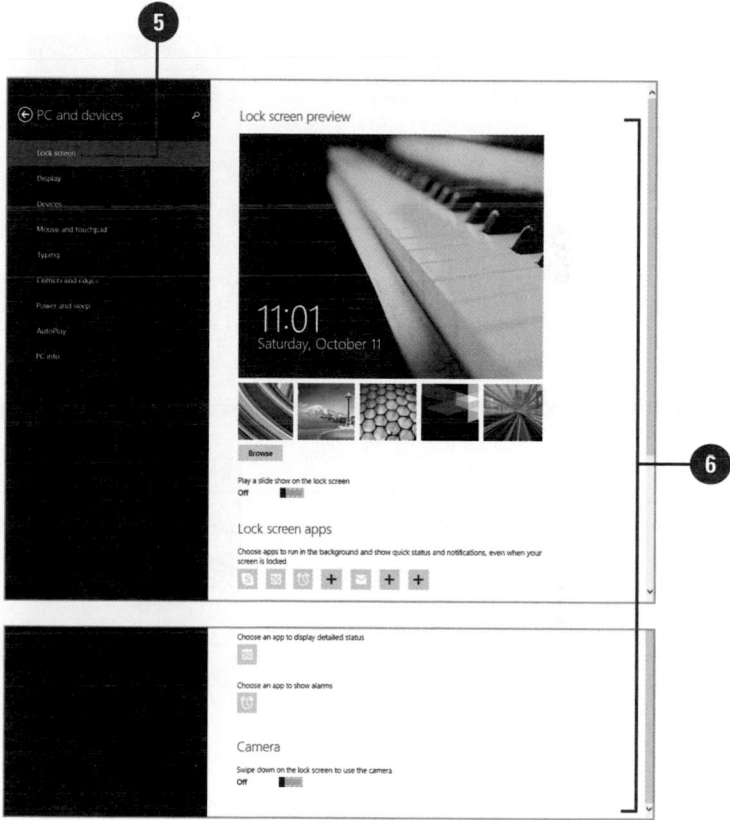

# Personalizing the Start Screen

The Start screen provides a central place to access apps, utilities, and device settings. When you start Windows 8.1 and sign-in, the Start screen appears, displaying app tiles in groups with information and notifications. You can customize the Start screen with a background design and color. You can even use the same background as your desktop screen (**New!**). The color changes the background design, colored text, and selection color in Windows 8.1.

## Personalize the Start Screen

1. Display the Start screen.

2. Point to the lower- or upper-right corner and move up or down (on a computer) or swipe left from the right edge of the screen (on a mobile device).

3. Click or tap the **Settings** button on the Charms bar.

4. Click or tap **Personalize** on the Settings panel.

    The Personalize panel appears, displaying background options (**New!**).

5. Click or tap the background design you want to use.

    ◆ **Desktop.** The list of background designs includes the current desktop background, which you can apply to the Start screen (**New!**).

6. Click or tap the background and access color (**New!**) you want to apply to the selected background.

7. Click or tap a blank area of the screen to exit the panel.

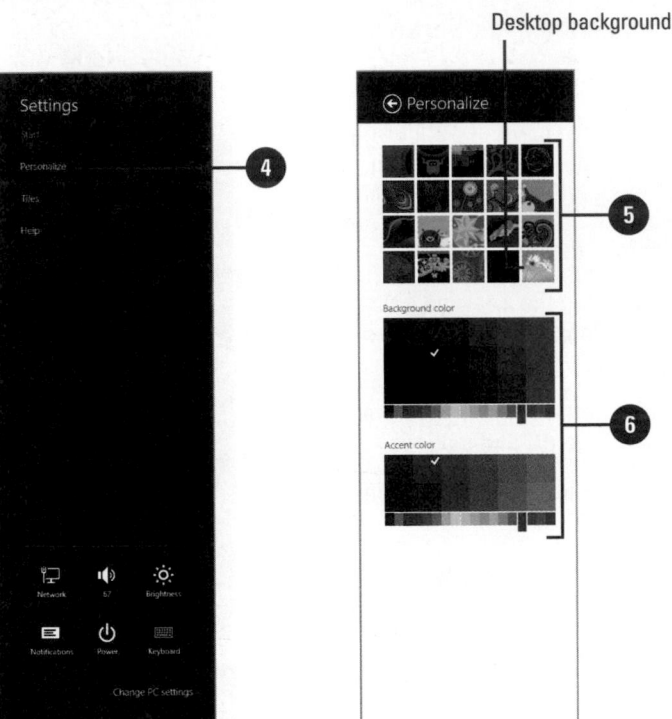

Desktop background

# Syncing Options on Other Devices

When you sign in to Windows 8.1 with a Microsoft account, you can enable the system to automatically synchronize your system and some app settings with other devices using SkyDrive (**New!**) that also sign in with the same Microsoft account. You can enable or disable sync settings for the entire device or enable or disable individual settings (**New!**). You can sync your settings on this device for personalize settings (Start screen, Appearance, and desktop personalization), app settings (Apps and App data), web browser, passwords, language preferences, Ease of Access, and other Windows settings (File Explorer, mouse, and more). You can also back up your settings (**New!**) to the SkyDrive for your PC, which you can restore at any time.

## Sync Options with Other Devices Using SkyDrive

1. Display the Start screen.

2. Point to the lower- or upper-right corner and move up or down (on a computer) or swipe left from the right edge of the screen (on a mobile device).

3. Click or tap the **Settings** button on the Charms bar.

4. Click or tap **Change PC settings** on the Settings panel, and then click or tap **SkyDrive**.

5. Click or tap **Sync settings** under SkyDrive.

6. Drag the slider On or Off for Sync settings on this PC.

7. Drag the sliders On or Off individual sync settings (when Step 6 is turned on):

   ◆ **Personalization.** Start screen, Appearance, and Desktop.

   ◆ **App.** Apps and App data.

   ◆ **Other.** Web browser, passwords, language, Ease of Access, and Windows settings.

   ◆ **Back up.** Back up settings.

8. To close the app, point to the top edge of the screen (cursor changes to a hand), and then drag down to the bottom edge of the screen.

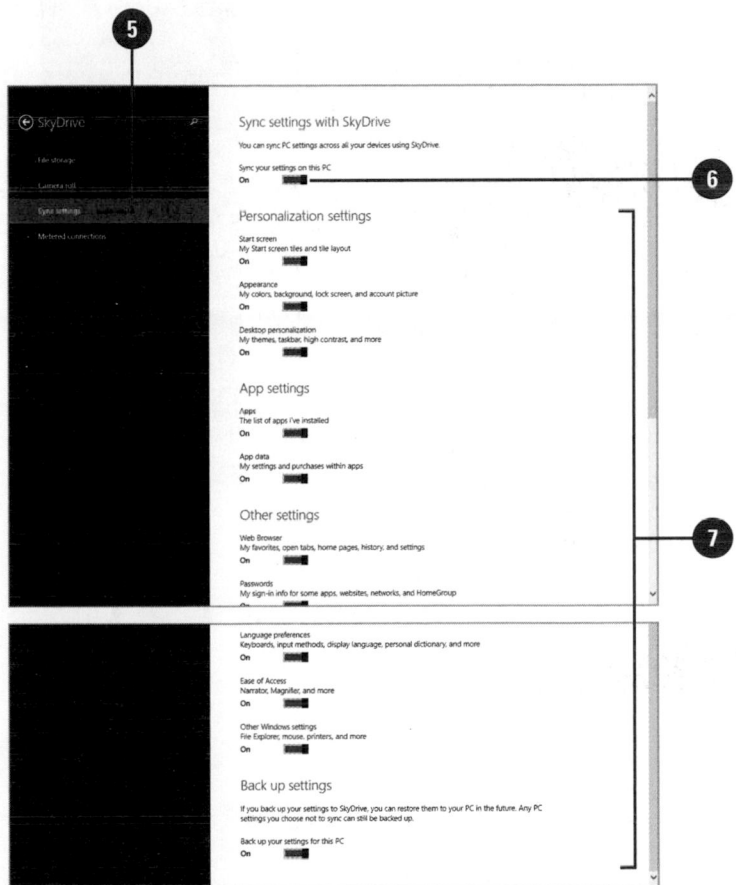

# Changing General Settings

In PC settings there are an array of options for general PC use, including app switching, corner navigation (**New!**), spelling, mouse and touchpad, time and date, and language. For example, you can specify how corner respond when you point or click (**New!**). For app switching, you can specify whether to allow switching between recent apps and how to do it. For date and time, you can specify the date and time in your area, formats, and whether to automatically adjust for daylight saving time.

## Change General Settings

1. Display the Start screen.

2. Point to the lower- or upper-right corner and move up or down (on a computer) or swipe left from the right edge of the screen (on a mobile device).

3. Click or tap the **Settings** button on the Charms bar.

4. Click or tap **Change PC settings** on the Settings panel, and then click or tap **PC and devices**.

5. Click or tap **Corners and edges** under PC and devices.

6. Specify the options you want:

   ◆ **App switching.** Drag the sliders On or Off app switching options. To clear app history, click or tap **Clear list**.

   ◆ **Corner navigation.** Drag the sliders On or Off corner navigation options (**New!**).

7. Click or tap the following under PC and devices.

   ◆ **Typing.** Drag the sliders On or Off to Autocorrect or highlight misspelled words.

   ◆ **Mouse and touchpad.** Select a primary button, mouse wheel to scroll option, and how many lines to scroll each time.

8. To close the app, point to the top edge of the screen (cursor changes to a hand), and then drag down to the bottom edge of the screen.

## Set Time and Language Options

1. Display the Start screen.

2. Point to the lower- or upper-right corner and move up or down (on a computer) or swipe left from the right edge of the screen (on a mobile device).

3. Click or tap the **Settings** button on the Charms bar.

4. Click or tap **Change PC settings** on the Settings panel, and then click or tap **Time and language**.

5. Click or tap **Date and time** under Time and language.

6. Specify the options you want:

   ◆ Date and time. Turn options On or Off or specify them.

      ◆ **Set time automatically.** Click or tap Change when off.

      ◆ **Time zone.**

      ◆ **Adjust for daylight saving time automatically.**

   ◆ Formats. Click or tap the **Change date and time formats** link to set format options (First day of week, short & long date, and short & long time).

7. Click or tap **Region and language** under Time and language.

8. Specify the options you want:

   ◆ Country or region. Select a country or region.

   ◆ Languages. Click or tap **Add a language** to select a language. Click or tap an existing icon to set as primary, change options, or remove it.

9. To close the app, point to the top edge of the screen (cursor changes to a hand), and then drag down to the bottom edge of the screen.

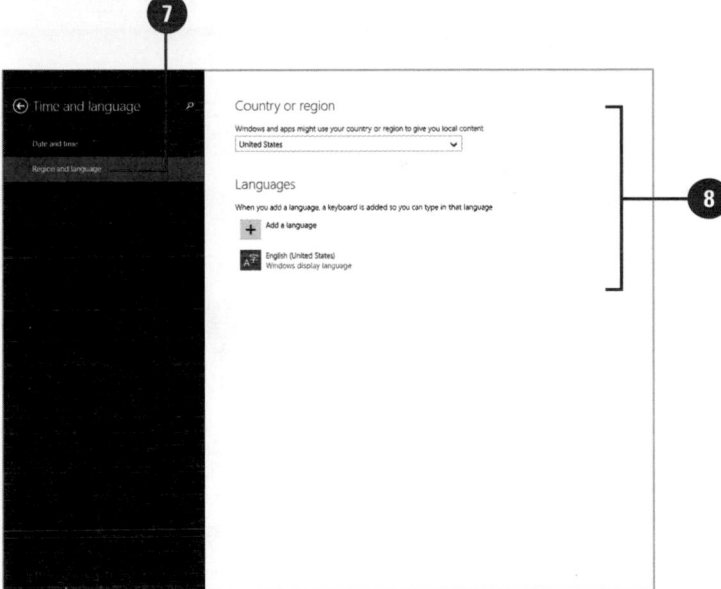

# Viewing the Control Panel

The Control Panel is a collection of utility programs that determine how Windows looks and works on your PC. The Control Panel displays utilities in two different views: Category and Small or Large Icons. Control Panel Category view displays utilities in functional categories based on tasks with some direct links, while Small or Large Icons view displays an icon for each utility program as in previous versions of Windows. You can change views by using the View by button in the Control Panel. If you're not sure where an option is located, you can search for it by using the Search box in the Control Panel.

## View the Control Panel

1. In the Start screen, click or tap the **Apps view** button, and then click or tap **Control Panel**.

   ◆ You can also right-click or tap-hold the lower-left corner, and then click or tap **Control Panel**.

2. Click or tap the **View by** button, and then click or tap a view: **Category**, **Small icons**, or **Large icons**.

3. Click or tap a Control Panel link or icon.

4. Click or tap the **Back** button on the toolbar to return to the previous Control Panel screen.

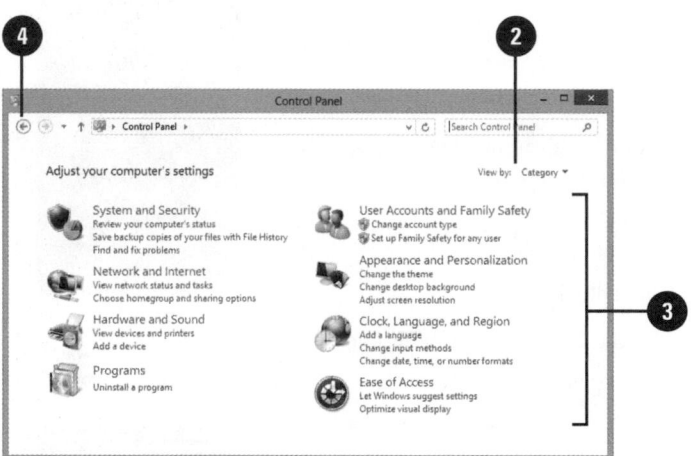

## Search for Options in the Control Panel

1. In the Start screen, click or tap the **Apps view** button, and then click or tap **Control Panel**.

2. Click or tap in the Search box.

3. Type a word or phrase related to the option you want.

4. Click or tap a Control Panel link or icon in the list of results.

5. Click or tap the **Back** button (when available) on the toolbar or click or tap the **Close** button (x) in the Search box.

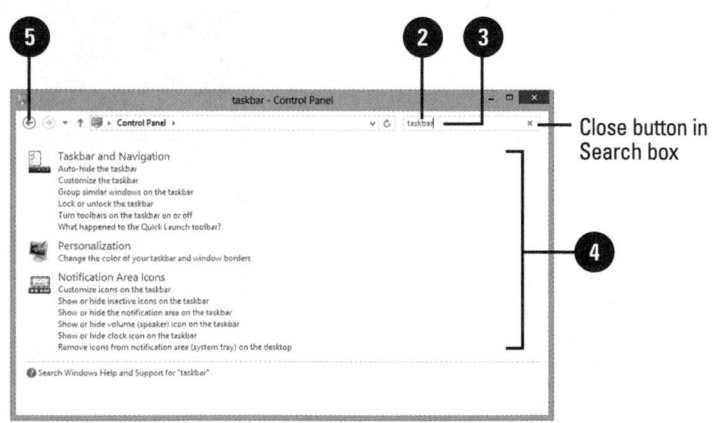

Close button in Search box

# Changing the Desktop Background

The desktop **background**, or wallpaper, is a picture that serves as your desktop's backdrop, the basic surface on which icons and windows appear. You can select one or more background pictures and change how it looks using the Desktop Background dialog box. If you select more than one picture, you can set a change picture interval in to display them in order or shuffle them. Once you select a background picture, you can display it on the screen five different ways: Fill, Fit, Stretch, Tile, or Center. Instead of selecting a background picture, which can sometimes make icons on the desktop difficult to see, you can also change the background to a color.

## Select a Desktop Background

1. In the desktop, right-click or tap-hold a blank area on the desktop, and then click or tap **Personalize**.

2. Click or tap **Desktop Background**.

3. Click or tap the **Picture location** list arrow and select a location, or click or tap **Browse**, select a picture in the location you want, and then click or tap **Open**. The default picture locations include:

   ◆ **Windows Desktop Backgrounds.**

   ◆ **Pictures Library.**

   ◆ **Top Rated Photos.**

   ◆ **Solid Colors.**

   ◆ **Computer.**

4. Point to a pictures, and then select the check box next next to it.

5. If you select more than one picture, select a **Change picture every** interval, the **Shuffle** check box.

6. Select the **Picture position** button, and then select the option you want: **Fill**, **Fit**, **Stretch**, **Tile**, or **Center**.

7. Click or tap **Save changes**.

8. Click or tap the **Close** button.

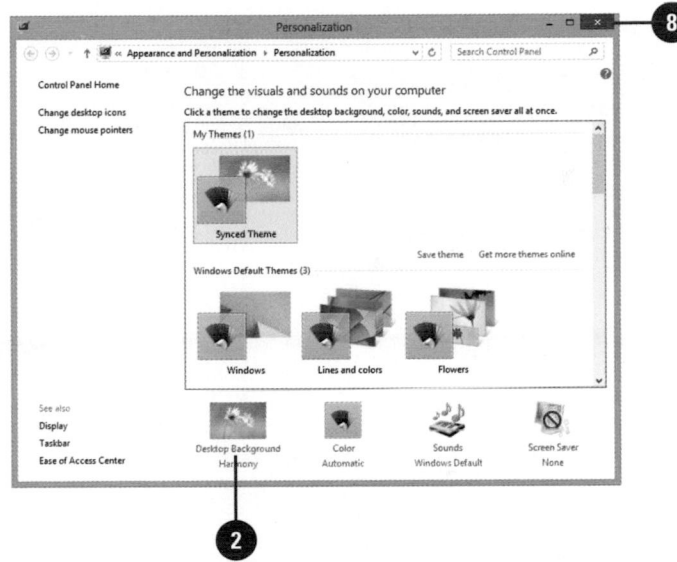

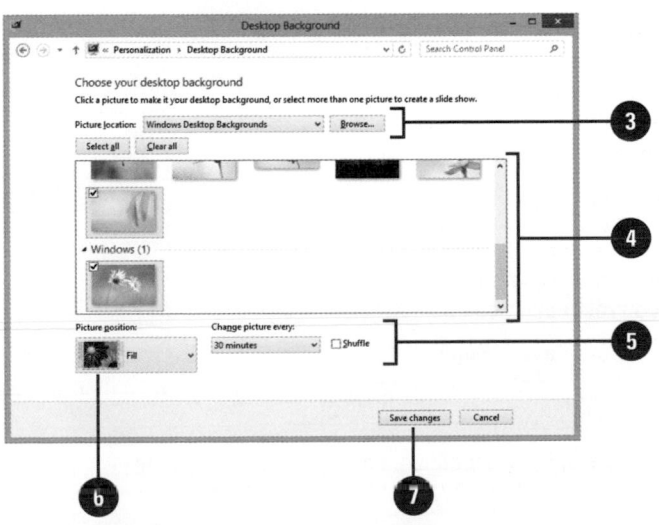

# Changing the Desktop Appearance

You can change the entire appearance of the desktop by using desktop themes. A desktop **theme** changes the desktop background, screen saver, pointers, sounds, icons, and fonts based on a set theme, such as Lines and color or Flowers. You can use one of the predefined desktop themes (Windows Default or High Contrast), a synced theme, or create and save your own. If a theme isn't exactly what you want, you can change the appearance of colors, fonts, and sizes used for major window elements such as title bars, icons, menus, borders, and the desktop itself. The theme options differ depending on the theme type, either Windows or high contrast. High contrast is helpful for those who need Ease of Access tools, which you can set in PC settings (**New!**).

## Select a Desktop Theme

1. In the desktop, right-click or tap-hold a blank area on the desktop, and then click or tap **Personalize**.

2. Click or tap a theme in the list.

   ◆ **Get more themes.** In the Theme list, click or tap the **Get more themes online** link, and then follow the on-screen instructions to download the themes.

3. Click or tap **Color**.

   You can also change the background, sound, and screen saver.

4. Make the changes you want based on the type of theme you selected:

   ◆ **Windows Theme.** Select a color, drag the **Color intensity** slider, and then use the color mixer to make any color adjustments.

   ◆ **High Contrast Theme.** Select an item in the display, and then change the color, size, or font for individual items for a high contrast color scheme.

5. Click or tap **Save changes**.

6. To save a theme, click or tap **Save theme** (under My Themes), name the theme, specify a location, and then click or tap **Save**.

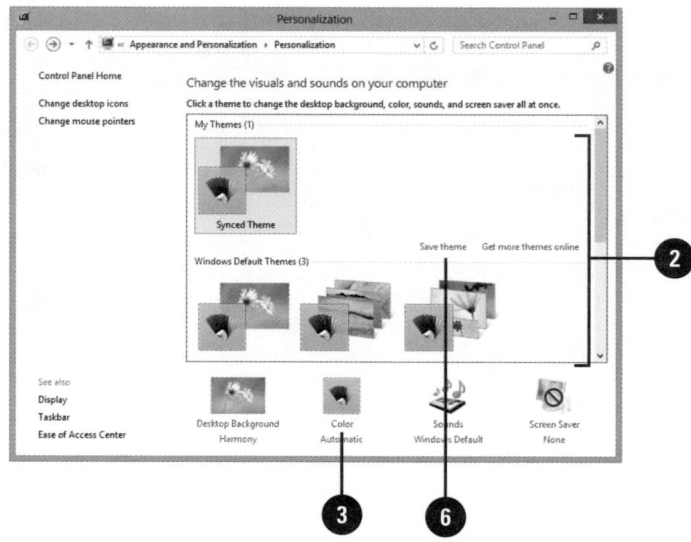

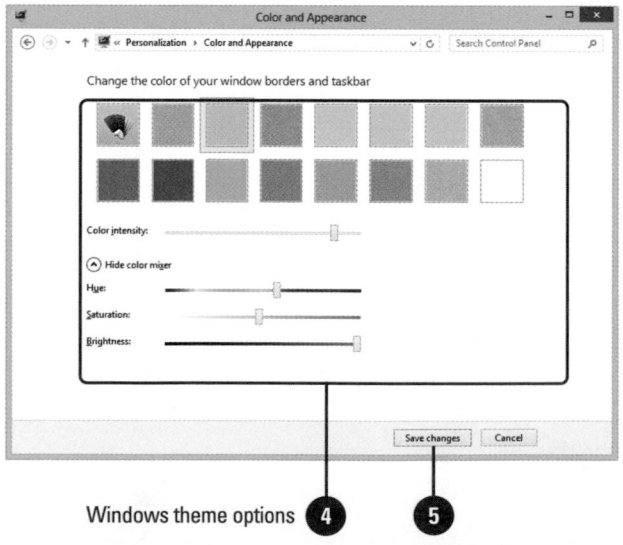

Windows theme options

# Starting with the Desktop

When you start windows 8.1, the default is set to display the Start screen; however, if you like using the desktop instead, you can by-pass the Start screen and go straight to the desktop. The Navigation tab (**New!**) in the Taskbar and Navigation Properties dialog box allows you to modify corner navigation (when you point or click in a corner) and Start screen options. For example, if you like a consisent look, you can set your desktop background as your Start screen.

## Set Navigation Options

1. In the desktop, right-click or tap-hold a blank area on the taskbar, and then click or tap **Properties**.

2. Click or tap the **Navigation** tab.

3. Select or clear the following check box options for the Start screen:

   ◆ **When I sign in or close all apps on a screen, go to the desktop instead of Start.**

   ◆ **Show my desktop background on Start.**

   ◆ **Show Start on the display I'm using when I press the Windows logo key.**

   ◆ **Show the Apps view automatically when I go to Start.**

   ◆ **When I sign in or close all apps on a screen, go to the desktop instead of Start.**

      ◆ **Search everywhere instead of just my apps when I search from the Apps view.**

   ◆ **List desktop apps first in the Apps view when it's sorted by category.**

4. Select or clear the check box options for Corner navigation.

5. Click or tap **OK**.

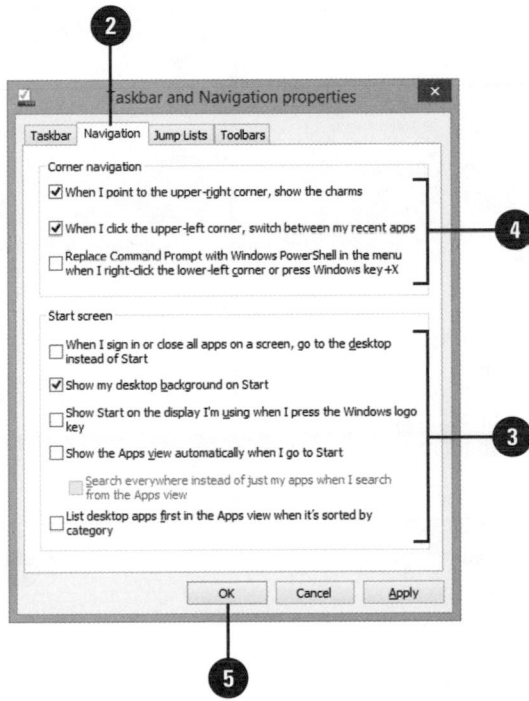

# Customizing the Desktop

The icons on the desktop provide easy access to programs, folders, and system related shortcuts. If your desktop is getting cluttered, you can quickly show or hide the desktop icons. In addition, you can customize the desktop to show or hide the familiar icons: Computer, User's Files, Network, Recycle Bin, or Control Panel. You can also quickly sort, resize, and rearrange desktop icons by right-clicking or tap-holding the desktop, and then using commands on the View and Sort By submenus.

## Display or Hide Desktop Icons

1. In the desktop, right-click or tap-hold a blank area on the desktop, and then click or tap **Personalize**.

   **TIMESAVER** *To show or hide all desktop icons, right-click or tap-hold the desktop, point to View, and then click or tap Show Desktop Icons.*

2. In the left pane, click or tap **Change desktop icons**.

3. Select or clear the check boxes to show or hide desktop icons.

4. To change the appearance of an icon, select the icon, click or tap **Change Icon**, select an icon, and then click or tap or tap **OK**.

5. Click or tap **OK**.

6. Click or tap the **Close** button.

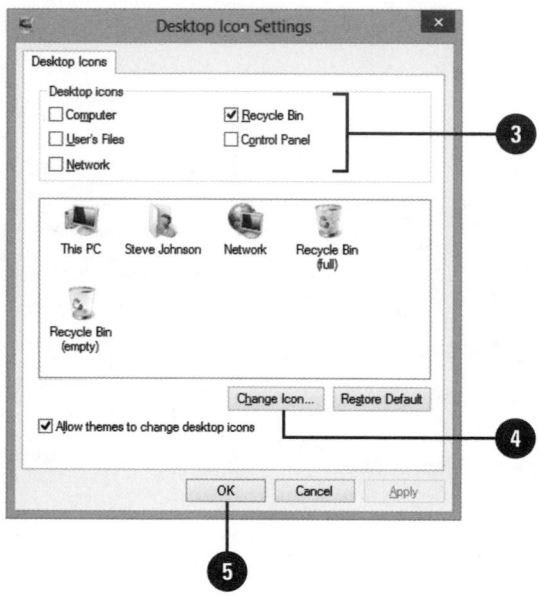

## Did You Know?

*You can use peek to preview the desktop.* In the desktop, right-click or tap-hold a blank area on the taskbar, and then click or tap Properties. On the Taskbar tab, select or clear the Use Peek To Preview The Desktop When You Move Your Mouse To Show Desktop Button At The End Of The Taskbar check box to enable or disable the option, and then click or tap OK.

## Customize the Desktop Appearance

◆ **Resize desktop icons.** Right-click or tap-hold a blank area on the desktop, point to **View**, and then click or tap **Large Icons**, **Medium Icons**, or **Small Icons**.

◆ **Auto arrange icons.** The Auto arrange icons option keeps icons organized so they don't overlap each other. Right-click or tap-hold a blank area on the desktop, point to **View**, and then click or tap **Auto arrange icons**. (the option toggles on and off)

◆ **Align icons to grid.** The Align icons to grid option aligns icons in a window according an invisible grid to keep them organized. Right-click or tap-hold a blank area on the desktop, point to **View**, and then click or tap **Auto arrange icons**. (the option toggles on and off)

◆ **Show or hide desktop icons.** Right-click or tap-hold a blank area on the desktop, point to **View**, and then click or tap **Show desktop icons**. (the option toggles on and off)

◆ **Sort desktop items.** Right-click or tap-hold a blank area on the desktop, point to **Sort by**, and then select an option.

◆ **Show the next desktop background.** With multiple backgrounds selected, right-click or tap-hold a blank area on the desktop, and then click or tap **Next desktop background**.

Desktop view options

Next desktop background     Sort by options

# Using a Screen Saver

In the past, you needed a screen saver, a continually moving display, to protect your monitor from burn in, which occurs when the same display remains on the screen for extended periods of time and becomes part of the screen. Those days are gone with the emergence of new display technology. Screen savers are more for entertainment than anything else. When you leave your system idle for a specified wait time, a screen saver displays a continuous scene, such as an aquarium, until you move your mouse or drag your finger to stop it.

## Select a Screen Saver

1 In the desktop, right-click or tap-hold a blank area on the desktop, and then click or tap **Personalize**.

2 Click or tap **Screen Saver**.

3 Click or tap the list arrow, and then click or tap a screen saver.

4 Click or tap **Settings**.

5 Select the options you want for the screen saver, and then click or tap **OK**.

6 Click or tap **Preview** to see the screen saver in full-screen view, and then move your mouse or drag your finger to end the preview.

7 Specify the time to wait until your system starts the screen saver.

8 Select or clear the **On resume, display logon screen** check box.

9 Click or tap **OK**.

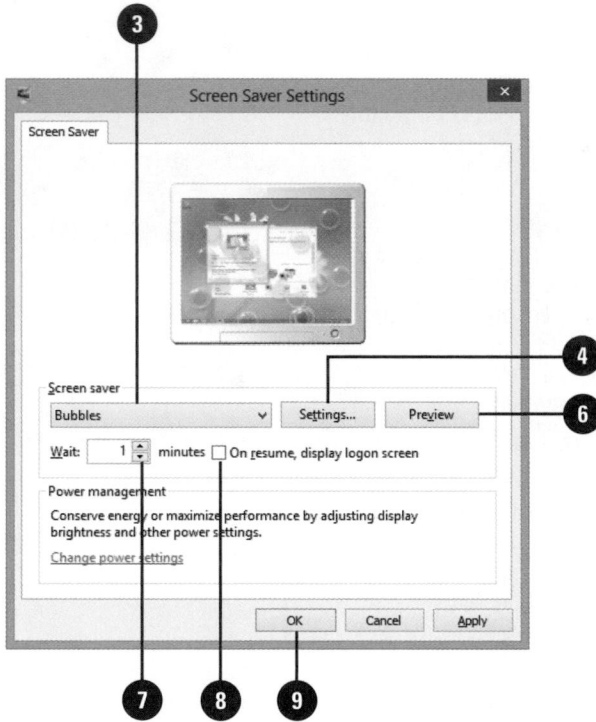

### Did You Know?

*You can turn off a screen saver.* On the Screen Saver tab, click or tap (None) from the Screen Saver list arrow.

# Changing Text Size on the Screen

If text and other items, such as icons, on the screen are not large enough for you to comfortably view, you can customize the screen to display items larger. Windows 8.1 allows you to increase the screen scaling option, known as the Dots Per Inch (DPI) scale, which is the number of dots that a device can display or print per linear inch. The greater the number, of dots per inch, the better the resolution. DPI is a standard measurement used to specify screen and printer resolution. The Smaller - 100% option is the default screen scale setting (96 DPI). If you want to make items on the screen larger, select the Medium - 125% or Larger - 150% option. After you change the screen scale option, you need to log off and restart Windows to see the change.

## Change the Screen Scaling Options

1. In the desktop, right-click or tap-hold a blank area on the desktop, and then click or tap **Screen resolution**.

2. Click or tap the **Make text and other items larger or smaller** link.

   ◆ You can also click or tap the **Display** icon in the Control Panel (desktop).

3. Drag the slider (between Smaller and Larger) or click or tap the **Let me choose one scaling level for all my displays** check box (**New!**).

4. Click or tap the **Smaller - 100% (default)**, or **Medium - 125%**, **Larger - 150%** or **Extra Large - 200% (New!)** option.

5. To adjust the DPI setting, if available for your display, click or tap **Set custom text size (DPI)** in the left pane, specify a scale percentage with a DPI, and then click or tap **OK**.

6. Click or tap **Apply**.

   To see the changes, close all your programs, and log off Windows.

7. If a message alert appears, click or tap **Log off now** or **Log off later** to log off now or later.

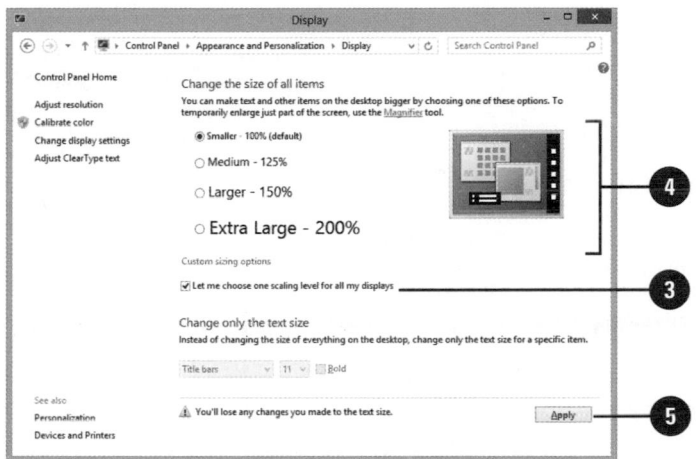

## For Your Information

### What's ClearType

ClearType is a font technology that improves the display on a monitor. ClearType makes on-screen text more clear, smooth, and detailed, which can reduce eye strain. ClearType is turned on by default in Windows. This is useful and most effective when you use LCD (Liquid Crystal Displays) devices, including flat-panel monitors, mobile PCs, and smaller hand-held devices. ClearType is optimized for use with some fonts, including Constantia, Cambria, Corbel, Candara, Calibri, and Consolas. To set the ClearType setting, open the Control Panel, click or tap Appearance and Personalization, click or tap Make text and other items larger or smaller link, click or tap Adjust ClearType text in the left pane, select the Turn On ClearType check box, click or tap Next, and then follow the on-screen instructions to complete it.

# Changing the Screen Display

If you find yourself frequently scrolling within windows as you work or squinting to read small text, you might want to change the size of the desktop on your monitor. A monitor displays pictures by dividing the display screen into thousands or millions of dots, or pixels, arranged in rows and columns. The pixels are so close together that they appear connected. The **screen resolution** refers to the number of pixels on the entire screen, which determines the amount of information your monitor displays. A low screen resolution setting, such as 640 by 480 pixels (width by height), displays less information on the screen, but the items on the screen appear relatively large, while a high setting, such as 1024 by 768 pixels, displays more information on the screen, but the items on the screen appear smaller. You can also change the screen orientation (Landscape, Portrait, or flipped) and color quality. The higher the color quality, the more colors the monitor displays, which requires greater system memory. The most common color quality settings are as follows: 16-bit, which displays 768 colors, and 24-bit and 32-bit, both of which display 16.7 million colors.

## Change the Display Size

1. In the desktop, right-click or tap-hold a blank area on the desktop, and then click or tap **Screen resolution**.

2. Click or tap the **Display** button, and then click or tap a display.

3. Click or tap the **Resolution** button, and then click or tap a screen size.

4. Click or tap the **Orientation** list arrow, and then click or tap an orientation option.

5. To change color quality, click or tap the **Advanced settings** link, click or tap the **Monitor** tab, select a color setting, and then click or tap **OK**.

   ◆ To eliminate flicker, click or tap the **Advanced settings** link, click or tap the **Monitor** tab, increase the screen refresh rate, and then click or tap **OK**.

6. Click or tap **OK**.

7. If a message alert appears, click or tap **Keep changes** or **Revert** to accept or decline the settings.

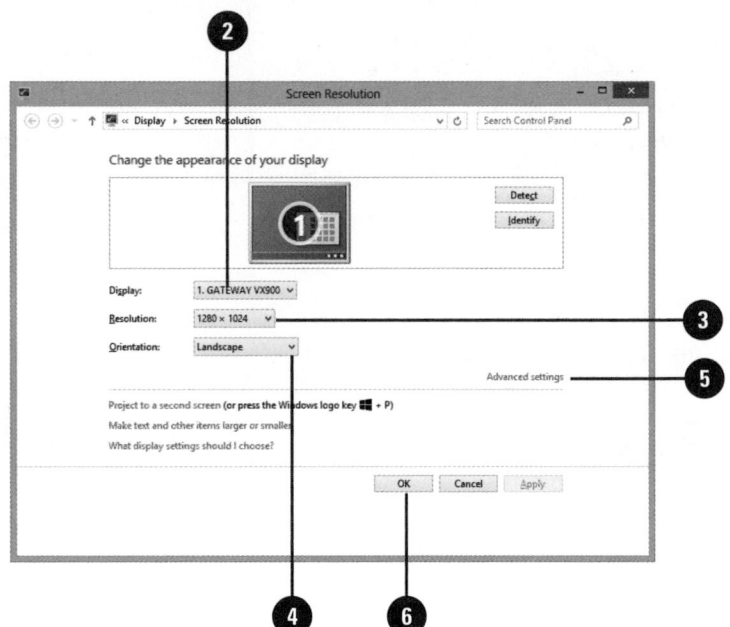

## Change Display Options in PC Settings

1. Display the Start screen.

2. Point to the lower- or upper-right corner and move up or down (on a computer) or swipe left from the right edge of the screen (on a mobile device).

3. Click or tap the **Settings** button on the Charms bar.

4. Click or tap **Change PC settings** on the Settings panel, and then click or tap **PC and devices**.

5. Click or tap **Display** under PC and devices

6. Drag, click or tap the **Resolution** bar to specify a screen size.

7. Click or tap the **Orientation** list arrow, and then click or tap an orientation option.

8. To change the size of apps, text, and other items on the screen, click or tap the list arrow, and then select an option.

   **NOTE** The option is only available for displays that support it.

9. Click or tap **Apply**.

10. To close the app, point to the top edge of the screen (cursor changes to a hand), and then drag down to the bottom edge of the screen.

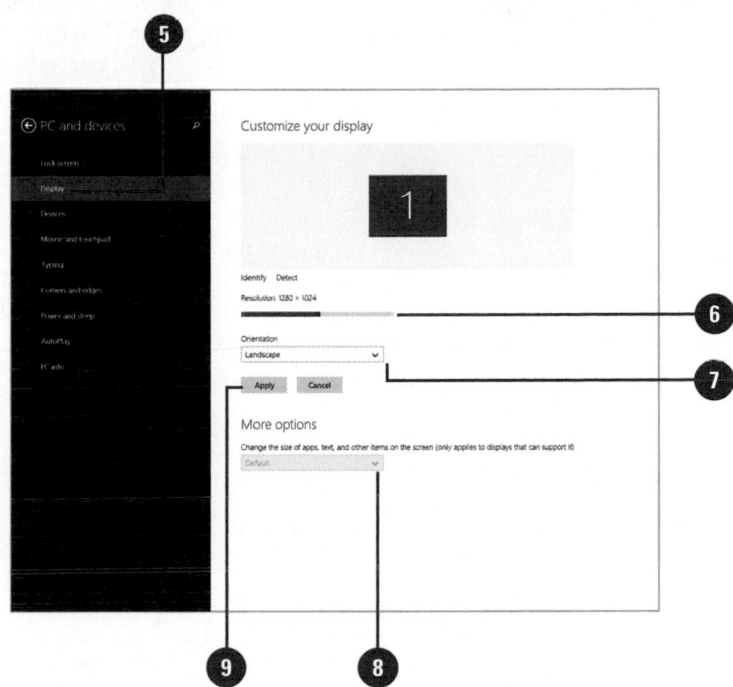

# Setting the Date and Time

The date and time you set in the Control Panel appear in the lower-right corner of the taskbar. When you click or tap or hover over the taskbar clock, the data appears. Programs use the date and time to establish when files and folders are created and modified. To change the date and time, you modify settings in the Date and Time dialog box. When you modify the time, it's important to also verify or update the time zone setting in the Time Zone Settings dialog box, which is used to accurately display creation and modification dates in a different time zone. With an Internet connection, you can set options on the Internet tab to make sure the time is accurate. If you need to know the time in other time zones, you can display additional clocks, which you can display by clicking, tapping, or hovering over the taskbar clock.

## Change the Date or Time

1 In the desktop, click or tap the time on the taskbar in the notification area, and then click or tap **Change date and time settings**.

2 Click or tap the **Date and Time** tab.

3 If needed, click or tap **Change time zone**, click or tap the list arrow, select a time zone, and then select or clear the **Automatically adjust clock for Daylight Saving Changes** check box, and then click or tap **OK**.

4 Click or tap **Change date and time**.

5 Click or tap the date arrows to select the month and year.

6 Click or tap a day, and then specify a time.

7 Click or tap **OK**.

8 Click or tap **OK**.

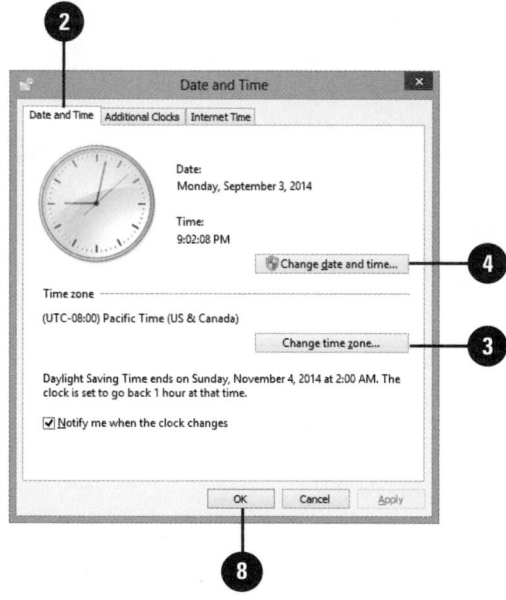

### See Also

*See "Changing General Settings" on page 302 for information on setting date and time options in PC settings.*

## Keep the Time Accurate

1. In the desktop, click or tap the time on the taskbar in the notification area, and then click or tap **Change date and time settings**.

2. Click or tap the **Internet Time** tab.

3. Click or tap **Change settings**.

4. Select the **Synchronize with an Internet time server** check box.

5. Click or tap the **Server** list arrow, and then click or tap a time server.

6. Click or tap **Update now**, and then wait for the time to update.

7. Click or tap **OK**.

8. Click or tap **OK**.

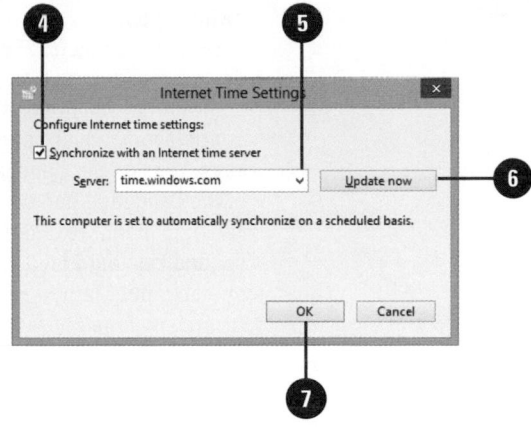

## Add Clocks

1. In the desktop, click or tap the time on the taskbar in the notification area, and then click or tap **Change date and time settings**.

2. Click or tap the **Additional Clocks** tab.

3. Select the **Show this clock** check box.

4. Click or tap the **Select time zone** list arrow, and then select a time zone.

5. Type a name.

6. If you want another clock, perform steps 3 through 5 for Clock 2.

7. Click or tap **OK**.

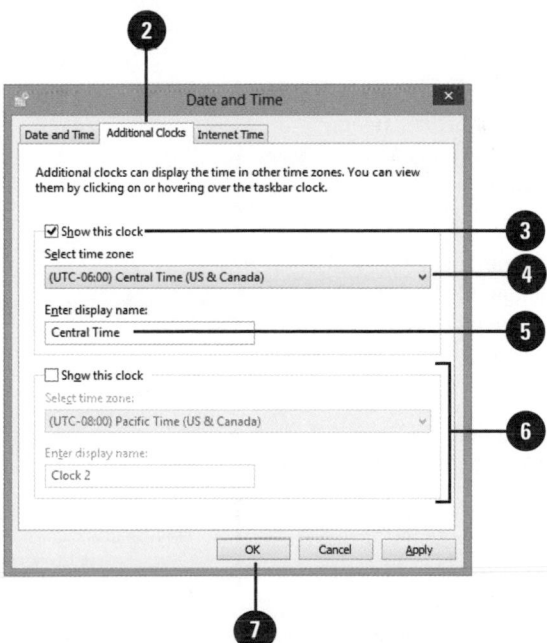

# Changing Language Options

You can also install multiple input languages on your system and easily switch between them. An **input language** is the language in which you enter and display text. When you install additional languages on your device, the language for the operating system doesn't change, only the characters you type on the screen. Each language uses its own keyboard layout, which rearranges the letters that appear when you press keys. You can set options to switch the input method, including the use of the Language bar, which appears on your desktop and in the Toolbars menu. Text services are text-related add-on programs for a second keyboard layout, handwriting recognition, speech recognition, and an Input Method Editor (IME), which is a system that lets you input Asian language characters with a standard 101-keyboard. You can switch between different language keyboard layouts using the Language bar or keyboard shortcuts.

## Add or Change Languages

1 In the Control Panel (desktop), click or tap the **Language** icon in Small icons or Large icons view.

2 To add a language, click or tap **Add a language**, select the language you want from the list, and then click or tap **Open**. If there are dialects, select one, and then click or tap **Add**.

3 To move language in the list, select a language, and click or tap **Move** up or **Move down**. The language at the top is the primary language.

4 To change language options, select the language, click or tap the **Options** link, specify the options you want, and then click or tap **Save**.

   ◆ **Add an input method.** Use to add a touch keyboard layout.

   ◆ **Personalize handwriting recognition.** Use to teach the recognizer your handwriting style.

5 To remove a language, select it, and then click or tap **Remove**.

6 Click or tap the **Close** button.

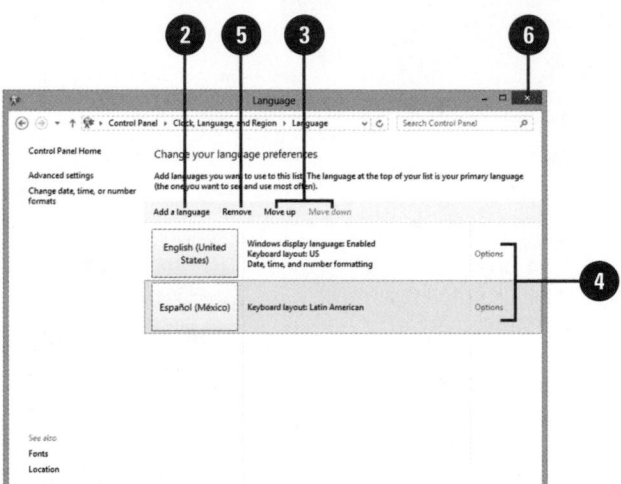

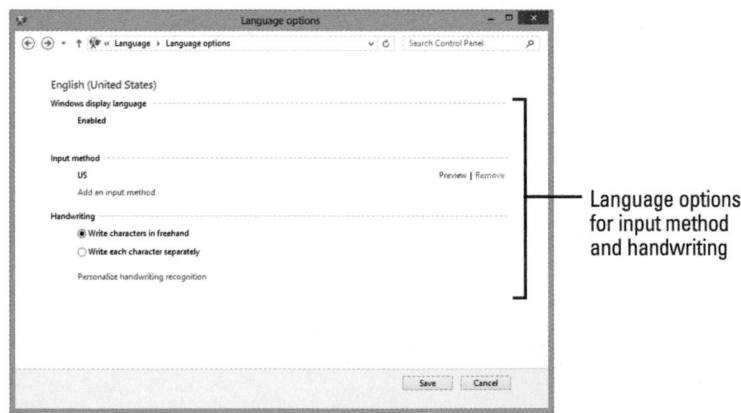

Language options for input method and handwriting

## Change the Advanced Options

1. In the Control Panel (desktop), click or tap the **Language** icon in Small icons or Large icons view.

2. Click or tap the **Advanced settings** link.

3. Select the options you want:

   ◆ **Override the display language or input method.** Select an override language.

   ◆ **Switch input methods.** Select options to set different options for different apps and use the Language bar.

   ◆ **Use personalization data.** Select to use or not automatic learning for improved handwriting recognition.

4. Click or tap **Save**.

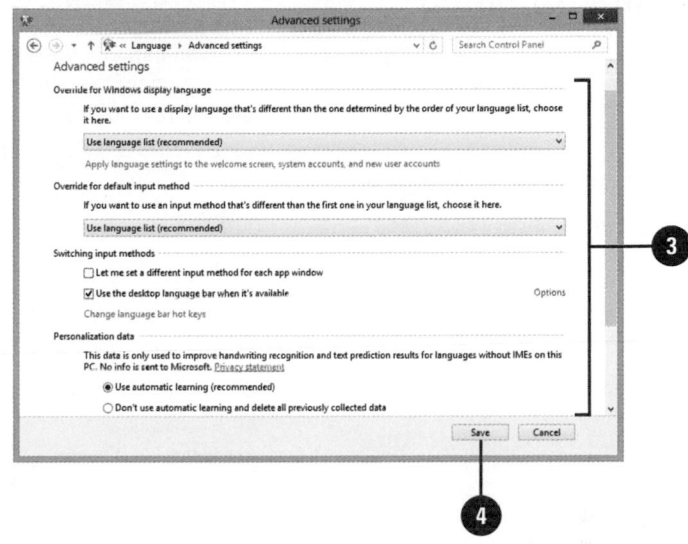

## Use the Language Bar

◆ To switch languages, click or tap the **Language bar**, and then click or tap a language.

◆ To change Language bar settings, click or tap the **Options** button (small white arrow) or right-click or tap-hold the **Language bar**, and then click or tap an option, such as transparency, vertical (orientation), and minimize.

◆ To change Text Services and Input Languages, right-click or tap-hold the **Language bar**, and then click or tap **Settings**.

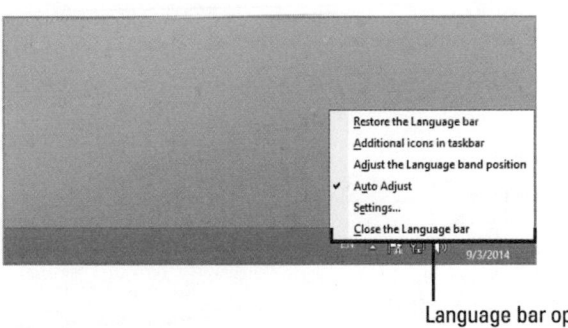

Language bar options

Languages

Language bar minimized

# Changing Regional Options

For those who work in international circles, you can change the format of the date, time, currency, and number into almost any form. For example, you can change the decimal symbol and list separator, the format used for negative numbers and leading zeros, and the measurement system (U.S. or metric).

## Change the Display for Dates, Times, Currency, and Numbers

1. In the Control Panel (desktop), click or tap the **Region** icon in Small icons or Large icons view.

2. Click or tap the **Formats** tab.

3. Click or tap the **Format** list arrow, and then click or tap a locale with the settings you want.

4. Click or tap the buttons to select the date and time formats you want.

5. Click or tap **Additional settings** to change individual settings.

6. Select the format options you want on the different tabs.

7. Click or tap **OK**.

8. Click or tap **OK**.

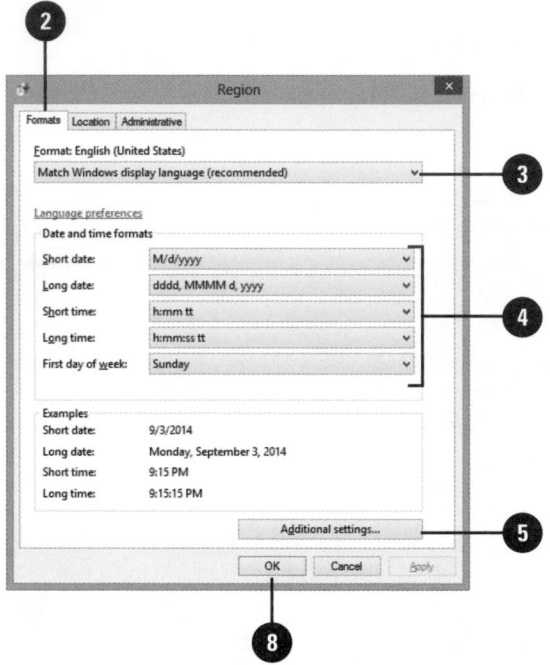

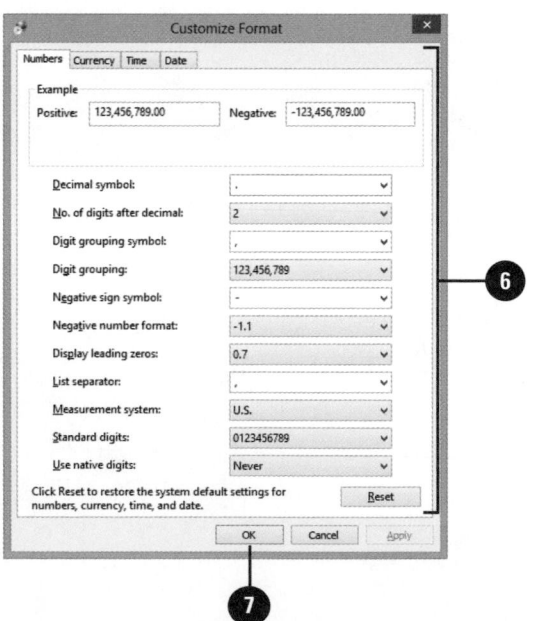

### Did You Know?

***You can change regional format by language and country.*** On the Location tab, click or tap the Current language list arrow, and then click or tap a language.

### See Also

*See "Changing Language Options" on page 316 for information on working with different languages.*

# Working with Fonts

Everything you type appears in a **font**, or typeface, a particular design set of letters, numbers, and other characters. The height of characters in a font is measured in points, each point being approximately 1/72 inch, while the width is measured by **pitch**, which refers to how many characters can fit in an inch. You might have heard common font names, such as Times New Roman, Arial, Courier, or Symbol. Windows comes with a variety of fonts for displaying text and printing documents. Using the Fonts window, you can view these fonts, see a sample of how a font appears when printed, and even install new fonts.

## View or Install Fonts

1. In the Control Panel (desktop), click or tap the **Fonts** icon in Small icons or Large icons view.

   The installed fonts appear in the Fonts window.

2. To install a font, drag the font into the Fonts window in the Control panel.

   - You can also right-click or tap-hold the font, and then click or tap **Install**.

3. To delete a font, select the font, and then click or tap the **Delete** button on the toolbar.

   - Use the Ctrl key to select more than one font.

4. To hide or show a font in your programs, select the font, and then click or tap the **Hide** or **Show** button on the toolbar.

5. To show and hide fonts based on language settings, install fonts using a shortcut, or restore default font settings, click or tap **Font settings** in the left pane.

6. To group fonts by font style, type, category, etc., right-click or tap-hold a blank area, point to **Group by**, and then select an option or click or tap **More**.

7. Click or tap the **Close** button.

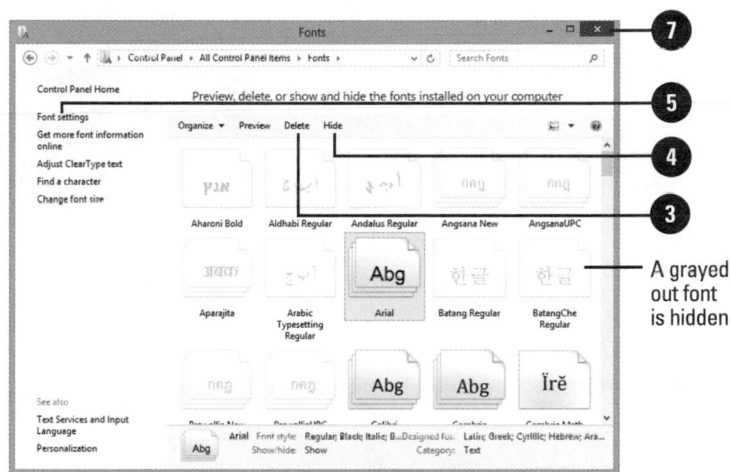

A grayed out font is hidden

---

## For Your Information

### What's the Difference Between the Fonts?

Everything you type appears in a font, a particular typeface design and size for letters, numbers, and other characters. Usually, each typeface, such as Times New Roman, is made available in four variations: normal, bold, italic, and bold italic. There are two basic types of fonts: scalable and bitmapped. A **scalable font** (also known as **outline font**) is based on a mathematical equation that creates character outlines to form letters and numbers of any size. The two major scalable fonts are Adobe's Type 1 PostScript and Apple/Microsoft's TrueType or OpenType. Scalable fonts are generated in any point size on the fly and require only four variations for each typeface. A **bitmapped font** consists of a set of dot patterns for each letter and number in a typeface for a specified type size. Bitmapped fonts are created or prepackaged ahead of time and require four variations for each point size used in each typeface. Although a bitmapped font designed for a particular font size will always look the best, scalable fonts eliminate storing hundreds of different sizes of fonts on a disk.

# Displaying and Arranging Toolbars

Toolbars provide easy access to commonly used tasks. Windows comes with a set of toolbars you can use to access programs, folders, documents, and web pages right from the taskbar. You can rearrange, resize, and move the toolbars to compliment your working style. When you move a toolbar, you can attach or dock it, to any of the sides on the desktop or you can float it in a window anywhere within the desktop.

## Show or Hide a Toolbar

①	In the desktop, right-click or tap-hold a blank area on the taskbar.

②	Point to **Toolbars**, and then click or tap a toolbar without a check mark.

	A toolbar with a check mark is already displayed.

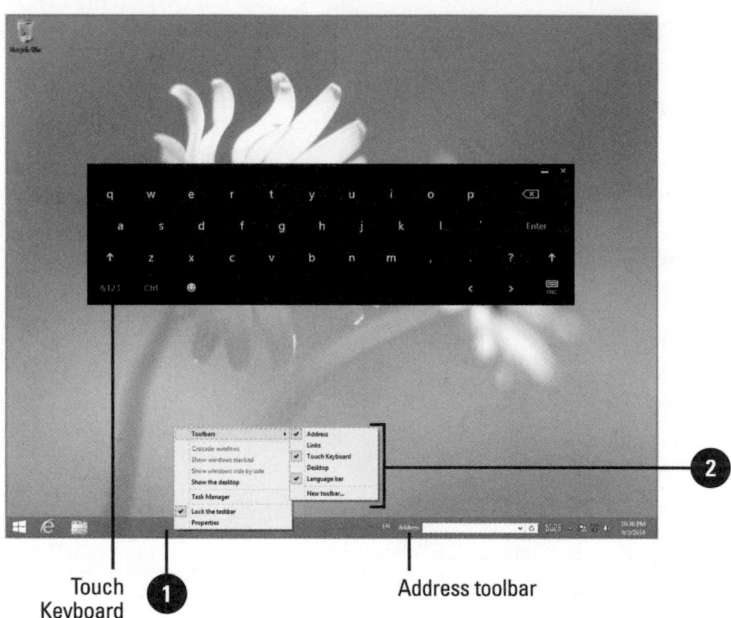

Touch Keyboard ①

Address toolbar ②

### Did You Know?

*You can display hidden buttons on a toolbar.* Click or tap the double-arrow at the end of the toolbar.

*You can display buttons on the taskbar.* Click or tap the up or down arrow on the taskbar to scroll through the taskbar buttons.

*You can also show or hide toolbars using the Taskbar Properties dialog box.* In the desktop, right-click or tap-hold the taskbar, click or tap Properties, click or tap the Toolbars tab, select or clear the toolbar check boxes, and then click or tap OK.

### See Also

*See "Customizing the Taskbar" on page 322 for information on modifying the taskbar.*

## Toolbars on the Taskbar

| Toolbar | Description |
|---|---|
| Address | Opens web pages, network locations, files, and folders using the Address bar from Internet Explorer |
| Links | Opens links using the Links toolbar from Internet Explorer |
| Touch Keyboard | Opens the Touch Keyboard to use as an input device |
| Desktop | Opens windows to files, folders, and shortcuts on the desktop |
| Language bar | Opens the Language bar toolbar to switch between languages (needs to be enabled in Advanced Language options in the Control Panel) |
| New Toolbar | Adds a new toolbar to Windows |

## Unlock or Lock the Taskbar

1. In the desktop, right-click or tap-hold a blank area on the taskbar.

2. Click or tap **Lock the taskbar**.

   ◆ Toolbars on the taskbar are locked when a check mark is displayed.

   ◆ Toolbars on the taskbar are unlocked when a check mark isn't displayed.

## Move a Toolbar

1. In the desktop, right-click or tap-hold a blank area on the taskbar, and then click or tap **Lock the taskbar** to remove the check mark, if necessary.

2. Point to the dotted bar or name of the toolbar, and then drag it to a new location on the desktop docked to the side or floating in the middle.

### Did You Know?

*You can resize a toolbar.* Unlock the taskbar, and then drag the small vertical bar at the beginning of the toolbar.

*You can expand or collapse a toolbar.* Unlock the taskbar, and then double-click or tap the small vertical bar at the beginning of the toolbar.

Dotted bar indicates taskbar is unlocked.

# Customizing the Taskbar

The taskbar is initially located at the bottom of the Windows desktop and is most often used to switch from one program to another. As with other Windows elements, you can customize the taskbar; for example, you can change its size and location, customize its display, or add or remove toolbars to help you perform the tasks you need to do. If you need more room on the screen to display a window, Auto-hide can be used to hide the taskbar when it's not in use. You can also combine similar windows—such as several WordPad documents—together on the taskbar to save space. If icons in the notification area are hidden when you want to see them, you can customize the notification area to always show the icons and notifications you want to use. In addition, you can also choose whether to show or hide common system icons, including Clock, Volume, Network, Power, and Action Center.

## Customize the Taskbar

1. In the desktop, right-click or tap-hold a blank area on the taskbar, and then click or tap **Properties**.

2. Click or tap the **Taskbar** tab.

3. Select the **Auto-hide the taskbar** check box to hide the taskbar when you're not using it.

   The taskbar appears when you move the pointer to where the taskbar would appear.

4. Select the **Use small taskbar button** check box to display small button icons on the taskbar.

5. Click or tap the **Taskbar location on screen** button, and then select a taskbar location: **Bottom**, **Left**, **Right**, or **Top**.

   ◆ You can also drag a taskbar. Unlock the taskbar, and then drag a blank area on the taskbar to a new location on any side of the desktop.

6. Click or tap the **Taskbar buttons** button, and then select a combine option: **Always combine, hide labels** (default), **Combine when taskbar is full**, or **Never combine**.

7. Click or tap **OK**.

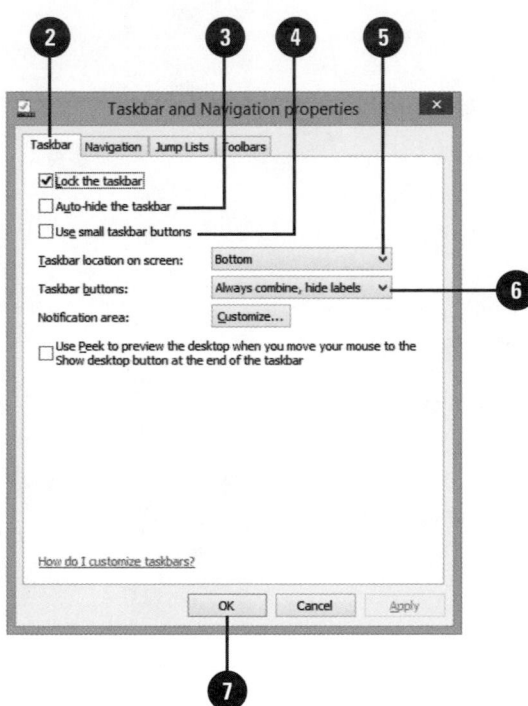

## Customize the Notification Area

**1** In the desktop, right-click or tap-hold a blank area on the taskbar, and then click or tap **Properties**.

**2** Click or tap the **Taskbar** tab.

**3** Click or tap **Customize**.

◆ You can also click or tap the **Show hidden icons** button in the notification area, and then click or tap **Customize**.

**4** To shows all icons and notifications in the notification area, select the **Always show all icons and notifications on the taskbar** check box.

**5** Specify the behaviors you want for the icons and notifications on the taskbar:

◆ **Show icon and notifications.**

◆ **Hide icon and notifications.**

◆ **Only show notifications.**

**6** To show or hide system icons on the notification area, click or tap the **Turn system icons on or off** link, select **On** or **Off** for the system icons, and then click or tap **OK**.

**7** Click or tap **OK**.

**8** Click or tap **OK**.

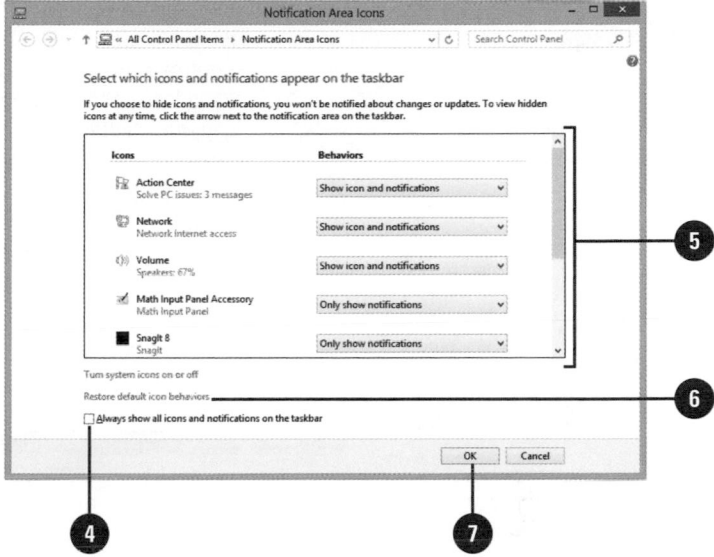

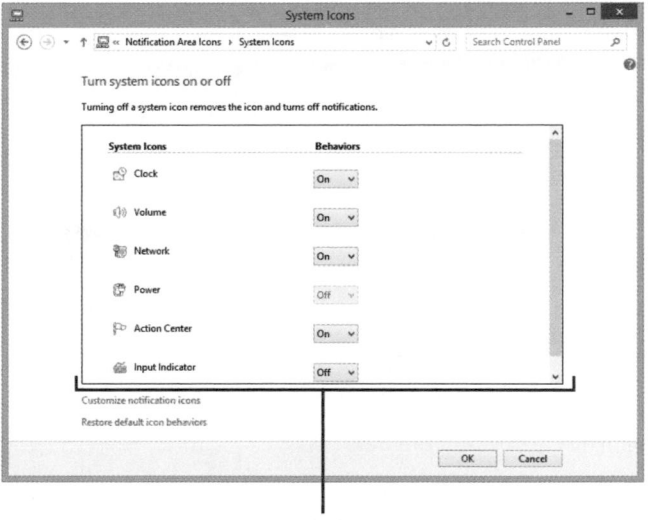

Default desktop icons

### Did You Know?

*You can show and hide icons by dragging them in the notification.* To show hidden icons, click or tap the Show Hidden Icons button in the notification area, drag a hidden icon to the notification area. To hide an icon, drag an icon to the Show Hidden Icons button, and then to the top of the menu.

# Setting Default Programs

When you double-click or double-tap an audio or video file, or click or tap a web link, a default program associated with that file type automatically starts and opens the file. The Default Programs icon in the Control Panel provides an easy way to change the default program used for specific file types. You can change file types, such as .bmp or .jpg, and set file associations for common activities, such as web browsing, sending e-mail, playing audio and video files, sending instant messaging, and using a search application, either Windows Search Explorer or a third-party one, such as Google Desktop Search. You can also specify which programs are available from the Start screen, the desktop, and other locations. To change default options, you need to have administrator privileges for your system. The options you set apply to all users on your PC computer or mobile device.

## Set Your Default Programs

1. In the Start screen, click or tap the **Apps view** button, and then click or tap **Default Programs**.

   ◆ In the Control Panel (desktop), you can also click or tap the **Default Programs** icon in Small icons or large icons view.

2. Click or tap **Set your default programs**.

3. Select a program.

4. Click or tap **Set this program as default**, or **Choose defaults for this program**.

5. If you select Choose defaults for this program, select the extension you want this program to open by default, and then click or tap **Save**.

6. When you're done, click or tap **Close**.

7. Click or tap **OK**.

8. Click or tap the **Close** button.

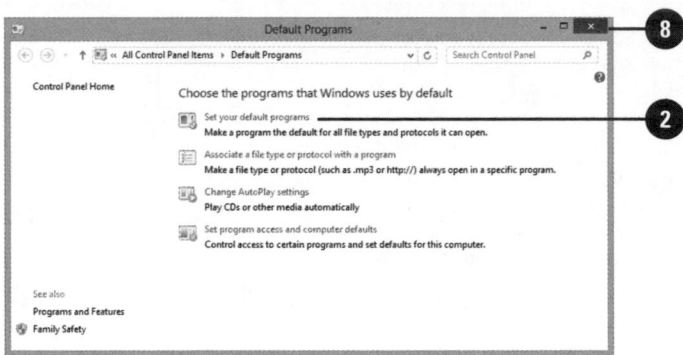

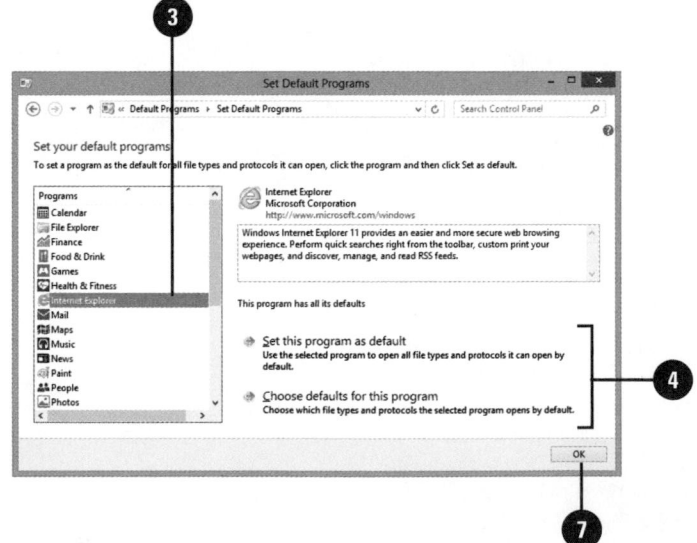

## Set Program Access and Computer Defaults

1. In the Start screen, click or tap the **Apps view** button, and then click or tap **Default Programs**.

2. Click or tap **Set program access and computer defaults**, and then enter administrator permissions, if requested.

3. Click or tap the option for the type of program you want to set: **Computer Manufacturer** (if available), **Microsoft Windows**, **Non-Microsoft**, or **Custom**.

4. Click or tap the option or select from a list the defaults you want to set.

5. Click or tap **OK**.

6. Click or tap the **Close** button.

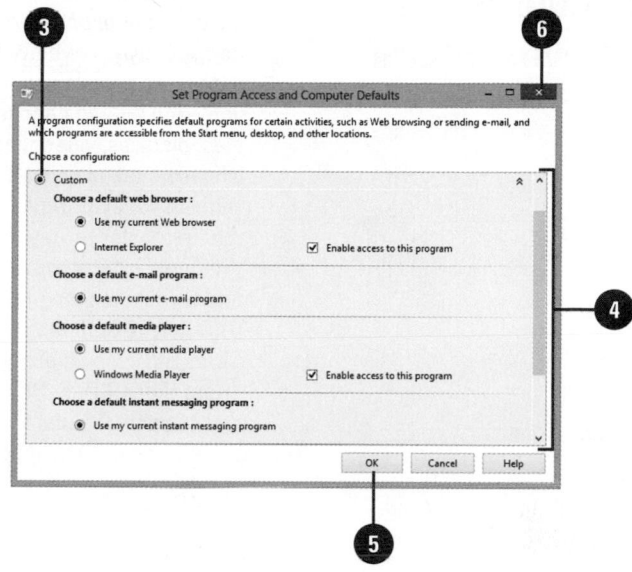

## Change File Type or Protocol Association with a Program

1. In the Start screen, click or tap the **Apps view** button, and then click or tap **Default Programs**.

2. Click or tap **Associate a file type or protocol with a program**.

3. Click or tap the extension.

4. Click or tap **Change program**.

5. Select the program you want to use; click or tap **Browse** if necessary to locate it.

6. Click or tap **OK**.

7. When you're done, click or tap **Close**.

8. Click or tap the **Close** button.

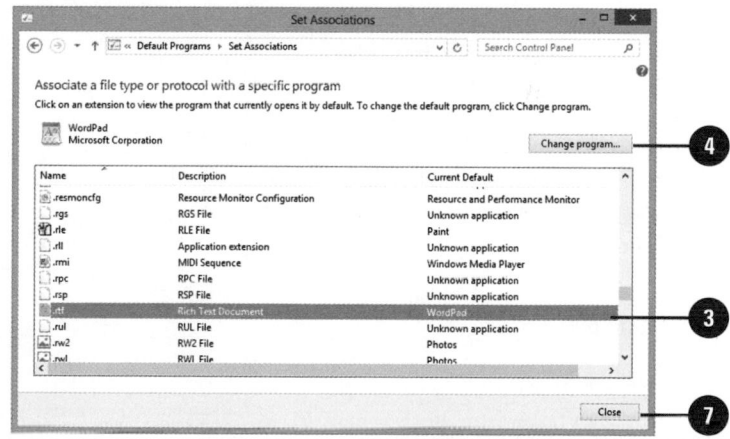

# Changing the Way a Disc or Device Starts

When you insert a CD or DVD disc into your drive or attach devices, such as digital cameras with a memory card or removable drives, you can specify how you want Windows to respond. You can have Windows detect the type of content on the disc and automatically start, or prompt you each time to choose an action. If you have CDs or DVDs with music files, pictures, video files, or mixed content, you can change the action Windows takes when it detects the content on the disc. You can have Windows play or rip a CD or DVD using Windows Media Player, open the first folder to view files using File Explorer, or take no action. Windows allows you to set AutoPlay options for a wide-variety of CDs and DVDs, including an audio or enhanced audio CD, DVD or enhanced DVD movie, Software and games, pictures, video and audio files, blank CD or DVD, mixed content, HD DVD or Blu-ray Disc movie, Video or Super Video CD. In PC settings (**New!**), you can turn on or off AutoPlay and choose defaults for removable drives and memory cards; click or tap PC and devices in PC settings, and then click or tap AutoPlay.

## Set AutoPlay Options

**1** In the Control Panel (desktop), click or tap the **Auto Play** icon in Small icons or Large icons view.

**2** To display the AutoPlay pop-up every time you insert a CD or DVD, select the **Use AutoPlay for all media and devices** check box.

**3** For each of the different media types, click or tap the list arrow, and then select the default action you want; options vary depending on the type of disc or device.

- ◆ To turn off AutoPlay for a specific media type, click or tap **Take no action**.

**4** To reset defaults, click or tap **Reset all defaults**.

**5** Click or tap **Save**.

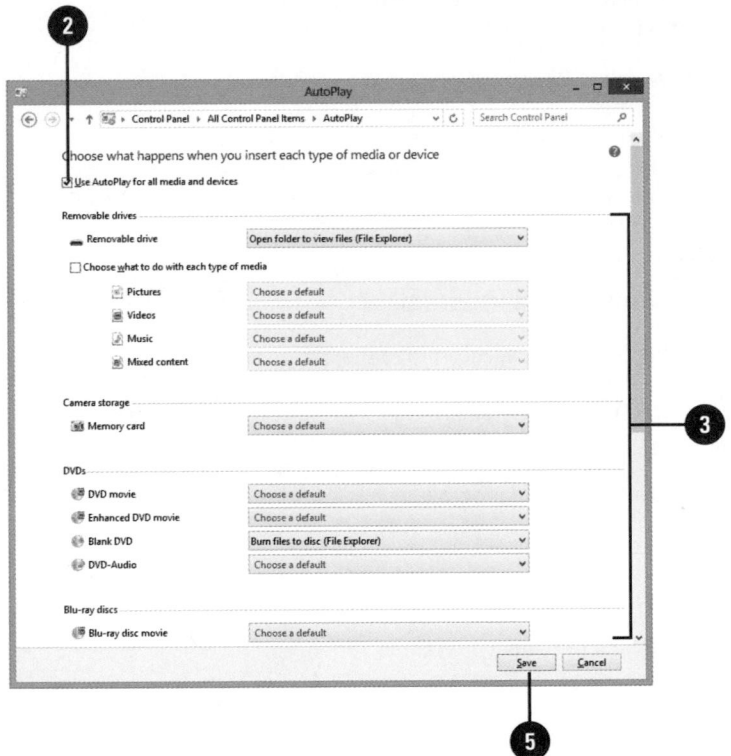

### Did You Know?

*You can stop Windows from performing an action on a CD or DVD.* Hold down the Shift key while you insert the CD or DVD.

# Using Ease of Access Tools

If you have difficulty using a mouse or typing, have slightly impaired vision, or are deaf or hard of hearing, you can adjust the appearance and behavior of Windows 8.1 to make your system easier for you to use. The Ease of Access Center helps you configure Windows for your vision, hearing, and mobility needs. You can also answer a few questions about your daily PC use that can help Windows recommend accessibility settings and programs for you. To open the Ease of Access Center, press Win+U, or click or tap the Apps view button on the Start screen, click or tap Control Panel, click or tap Ease of Access and then click Ease of Access Center. To use the Ease of Access questionnaire, click or tap Get recommendations to make your PC easier to use.

The Ease of Access Center provides utilities to adjust the way your keyboard, display, and mouse function to suit various vision and motor abilities. Some of the accessibility tools available include Magnifier, On-Screen Keyboard, Narrator, and High Contrast. You can also set accessibility options, such as StickyKeys, FilterKeys, ToggleKeys, Sound-Sentry, ShowSounds, and MouseKeys, that automatically turn off accessibility features, provide warning sounds, and determine when to apply the settings. The accessibility tools in Windows are intended to provide a low level of functionality for those with special needs. If these tools do not meet your daily needs, you might need to purchase a more advanced accessibility program.

## Ease of Access Center Tools

| Option | Description |
|---|---|
| Magnifier | Displays a separate window with a magnified portion of the screen; this is designed to make the screen easier to read for users who have impaired vision. In Windows, you can use full-screen and lens modes for added functionality. |
| On-Screen Keyboard | Displays an on-screen keyboard; this is designed to use the PC computer without the mouse or keyboard. |
| Narrator | Use the PC without a display; this is a text-to-speech utility program designed for users who are blind or have impaired vision. |
| High Contrast | Sets the desktop appearance to high contrast to make the monitor easier to see; this is designed to make the screen easier to read for users who have impaired vision. |
| StickyKeys | Enables simultaneous keystrokes while pressing one key at a time, such as Ctrl+Alt+Del. |
| FilterKeys | Adjusts the response of your keyboard; ignores repeated characters or fast key presses. |
| ToggleKeys | Emits sounds when you press certain locking keys, such as Caps Lock, Num Lock, or Scroll Lock. |
| SoundSentry | Provides visual warnings for system sounds. |
| ShowSounds | Instructs programs to provide captions. |
| MouseKeys | Enables the numeric keypad to perform mouse functions. |

# Using the Ease of Access Center

The Ease of Access Center allows you to check the status of and start or stop the Magnifier, Narrator, and On-Screen Keyboard accessibility programs. Magnifier is a utility that enlarges the full screen, the mouse area, or an area of the screen. Narrator is a text-to-speech utility that gives users who are blind or have impaired vision access to the PC. On-Screen Keyboard is a utility that displays a keyboard on the screen where users with mobility impairments can type using a mouse, joystick, or other pointing device. If you have administrator access, you can specify how the accessibility programs start when you log on, lock the desktop, or start the Ease of Access Center.

## Use the Ease of Access Center

1. Press Win+U to start the Ease of Access Center.

   ◆ In the Control Panel (desktop), you can also click or tap the **Ease of Access** icon in Small icons or Large icons view.

2. To get recommendations on what to use, click or tap **Get recommendations to make your computer easier to use**, and then follow the instructions.

3. To provide quick access to common tools, select the **Always read this section aloud** and **Always scan this section** check boxes.

4. Click or tap the utility program or the settings you want to manage.

5. Select or clear the check boxes you want to specify how you want the selected program to start or a setting to be applied.

6. Click or tap **Save** or exit the window.

7. When you're done, click or tap the **Close** button.

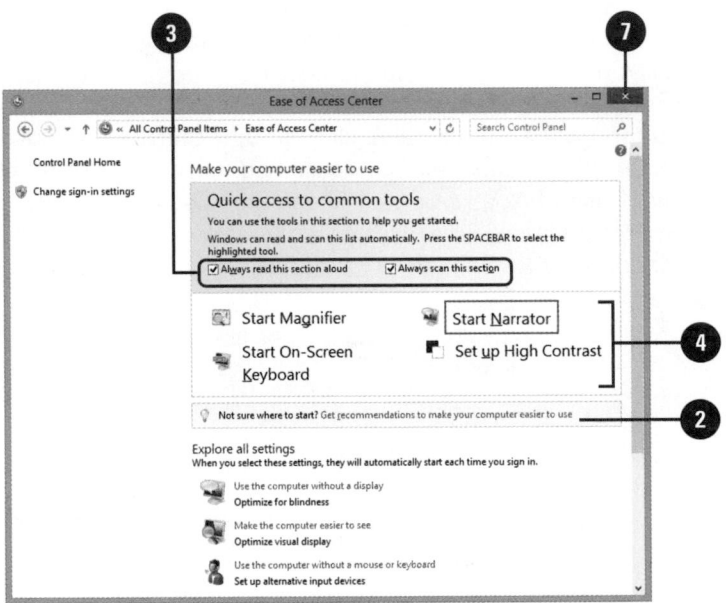

### Using Ease of Access from the Sign in Screen

When you start your system, the Sign in screen appears, where you can log into Windows 8.1. If you want to use Ease of Access features, you can quickly start or enable them with the Ease of Access button. When you click or tap the Ease of Access button, a menu appears where you can start Narrator, Magnifier, or On-Screen Keyboard, and turn on or off High Contrast, Sticky Keys, and Filter Keys.

## Use the Magnifier

1. In the Start screen, click or tap the **Apps view** button, and then click or tap **Magnifier**.

2. Click or tap the **Views** button, and then select a view: **Full screen**, **Lens**, or **Docked**.

3. Click or tap the **Options** button.

4. Drag the **Zooming** slider to adjust the view level.

5. Select or clear the **Turn on color inversion** check box.

6. Select or clear the check boxes with the tracking options to follow the mouse pointer or keyboard focus, or have Magnifier follow the text insertion point.

7. Click or tap **OK** to use the Magnifier program. When you're done, click or tap the **Close** button to close the program.

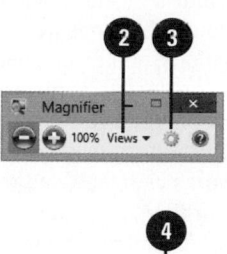

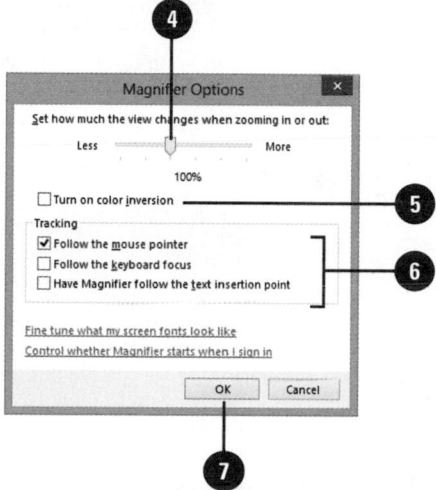

## Use the On-Screen Keyboard

1. Open the program in which you want to type.

2. In the Start screen, click or tap the **Apps view** button, and then click or tap **On-Screen Keyboard**.

3. Position the cursor, if necessary.

4. Type the text you want, or type keyboard commands.

5. When you're done, click or tap the **Close** button.

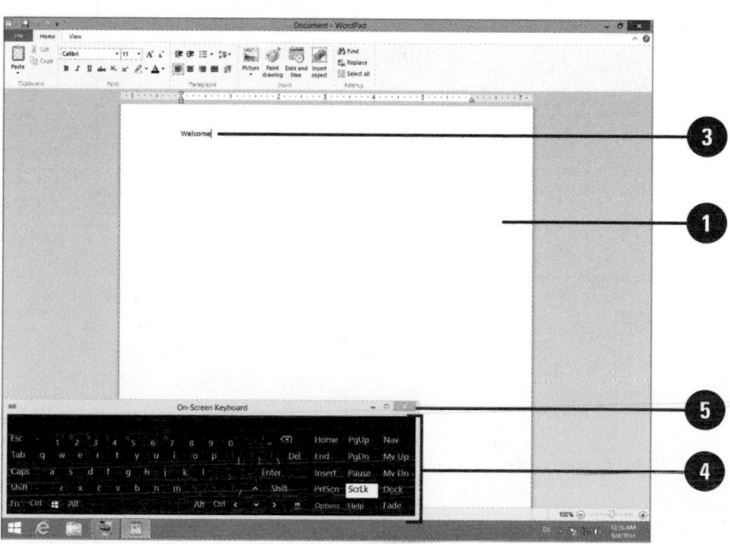

# Listening to Your System

Windows 8 comes with an accessibility tool called Narrator that reads aloud what appears on your screen, such as window items, menu options, and typed characters. Windows uses Text-to-Speech (TTS) technology to recognize text and play it back as spoken words using a synthesized voice, which is chosen from several pre-generated voices. Narrator is designed for those who are blind or have impaired vision and works with the Windows desktop and setup, Control Panel, Notepad, WordPad, and Internet Explorer. Narrator supports only the English language and might not read words aloud correctly in other programs. You can adjust the speed, volume, or pitch of the voice in Narrator and change other Text-to-Speech options using Speech properties in the Control Panel.

## Change Text-To-Speech Options

1. In the Control Panel (desktop), click or tap the **Speech Recognition** icon in Small icons or Large icons view.

2. In the left pane, click or tap **Text to Speech**.

3. Click or tap the **Voice selection** list arrow, and then select a voice.

4. Drag the **Voice speed** slider to adjust the speed of the voice.

5. Click or tap **Preview Voice**.

6. To set a preferred audio device as output for TTS playback, click or tap **Advanced**, make a selection, and then click or tap **OK**.

7. To adjust settings for your audio output devices, click or tap **Audio Output**, specify the options you want on the Playback, Recording, or Sounds tabs, and then click or tap **OK**.

8. Click or tap **OK**.

> ### See Also
>
> *See "Recognizing Your Speech" on page 332 for information on speech capabilities.*

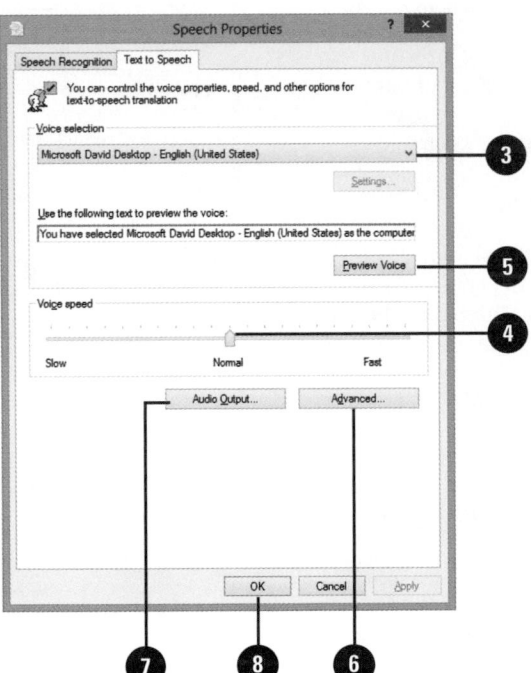

## Use the Narrator

1. In the Start screen, click or tap the **Apps view** button, and then click or tap **Narrator**.

   **TIMESAVER** *Press Win+Enter to start Narrator.*

2. Select the Narrator options you want:

   ◆ **General.** Select options to change how Narrator stars and other standard settings.

   ◆ **Navigation.** Select options to change how you interact with your PC using Narrator.

   ◆ **Voice.** Select options to change the speed, pitch, or volume of the current voice or choose a new voice.

   ◆ **Commands.** Select options to create your own keyboard shortcuts.

3. Click or tap **Save changes** or **Discard changes**.

4. Click or tap **Minimize** to use the Narrator program or click or tap **Exit** to close the program; restore the Narrator window, if necessary; and then click or tap **Yes**, if necessary.

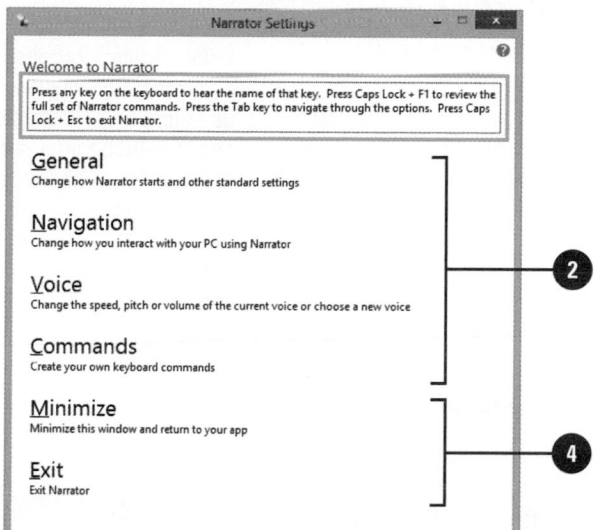

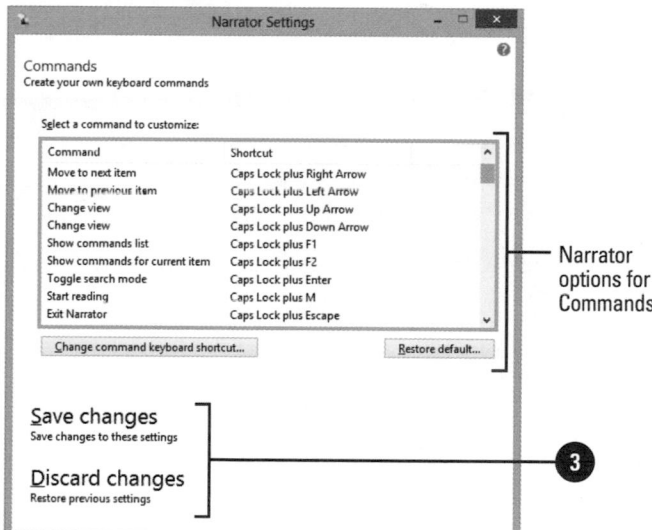

Narrator options for Commands

# Recognizing Your Speech

If you have a speech-enabled program, you can initialize and customize speech recognition options using Speech properties in the Control Panel. **Speech recognition** is the ability to convert a spoken voice into electronic text. Windows adapts to your speech, and speech recognition increases over time. You can use the speech recognition properties to select a language, create a profile to accommodate your speaking style and environment, and train your PC computer in as little as ten minutes to recognize and adapt to the sound of your voice, word pronunciation, accent, speaking manner, and new or distinctive words. Some programs use speech differently, so you need to check the speech-enabled program for details. Speech Recognition is not available in all languages.

## Set Up Speech Recognition

1. In the Control Panel (desktop), click or tap the **Speech Recognition** icon in Small icons or Large icons view.

2. Click or tap **Set up microphone**, and then follow the wizard instructions to adjust the microphone.

3. Click or tap **Take Speech Tutorial**, and then follow the instructions to take the 30 minute training tutorial to teach you the commands used with speech recognition.

4. Click or tap **Train your computer to better understand you**, and then follow the wizard instructions to train your voice.

5. When you're done, click or tap the **Close** button.

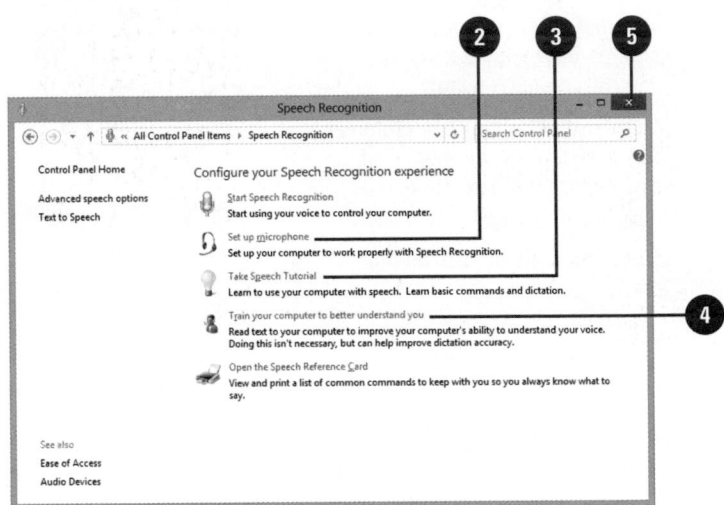

## Did You Know?

*You can view and print a Speech Recognition reference card.* In the Control Panel (desktop), click or tap the Speech Recognition icon in Small icons or Large icons view, and then click or tap Open and Speech Reference Card.

## Set Speech Recognition Options

① In the Control Panel (desktop), click or tap the **Speech Recognition** icon in Small icons or Large icons view.

② In the left pane, click or tap **Advanced speech options**.

③ Click or tap the **Speech Recognition** tab.

④ Click or tap the list arrow, and then select a language.

⑤ To start the Profile Wizard, click or tap **New**, type your name, click or tap **OK**, follow the wizard instructions to create a profile, adjust the microphone, and train your voice, and then click or tap **Finish**.

⑥ Select or clear the User Settings check boxes you do or don't want.

⑦ Click or tap **OK**.

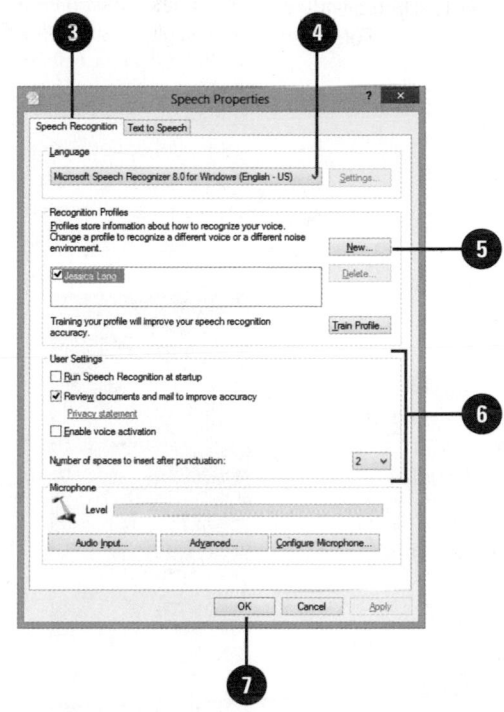

## Start Speech Recognition

① In the Start screen, click or tap the **Apps view** button, and then click or tap **Windows Speech Recognition**.

② If requested, follow the wizard instructions to create a profile, adjust the microphone, and train your voice, and then click or tap **Finish**.

③ Click or tap the **Speech Recognition** button to toggle between Sleeping/Listening mode.

> **TIMESAVER** *Right-click or tap-hold the Speech Recognition button to select command options.*

④ When you're done, click or tap the **Close** button.

Speech Recognition options

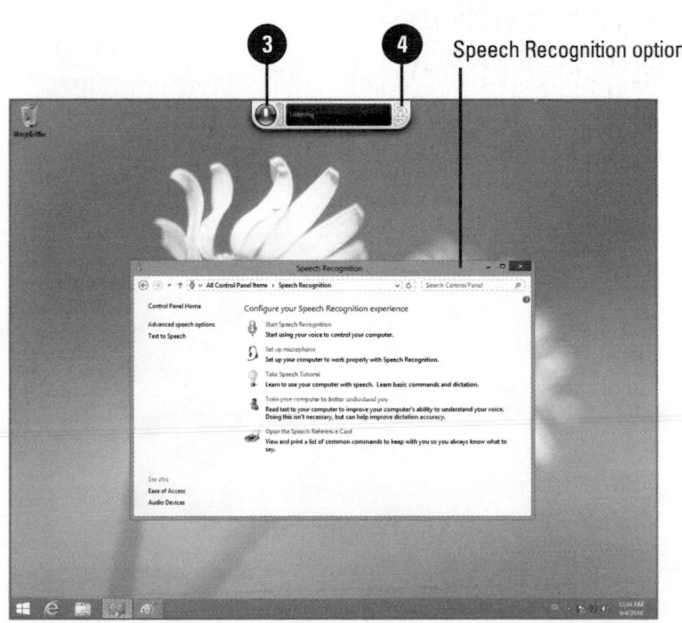

# Setting Ease of Access Options

With PC settings, you can set options to use Ease of Access. You can set options in the following areas (**New!**): Narrator, Magnifier, High contrast, Keyboard, Mouse, and Other, which includes settings to play animations, show background, show notifications, or for cursor thickness. You can turn features (Narrator, Magnifier, or On-Screen Keyboard) and individual options on or off or customize them to fit your needs. For example, you can use the High contrast color scheme and make everything on the screen bigger and easier to see.

## Set Ease of Access Options

1. Display the Start screen.

2. Point to the lower- or upper-right corner and move up or down (on a computer) or swipe left from the right edge of the screen (on a mobile device).

3. Click or tap the **Settings** button on the Charms bar.

4. Click or tap **Change PC settings** on the Settings panel, and then click or tap **Ease of Access**.

5. Click or tap the following under Ease of Access (**New!**):

   ◆ **Narrator**. Set options for Hear text and controls, Voice, Sounds you hear, or Cursor and keys.

   ◆ **Magnifier**. Set options for Magnify things on the screen or Tracking.

   ◆ **High contrast**. Choose a theme, customize, and apply.

   ◆ **Keyboard**. Set options for On-Screen Keyboard and Useful keys.

   ◆ **Mouse**. Set options for Pointer size & color and Mouse keys.

   ◆ **Other options**. Set options to play animations, show background, show notifications, or for cursor thickness.

6. To close the app, point to the top edge of the screen (cursor changes to a hand), and then drag down to the bottom edge of the screen.

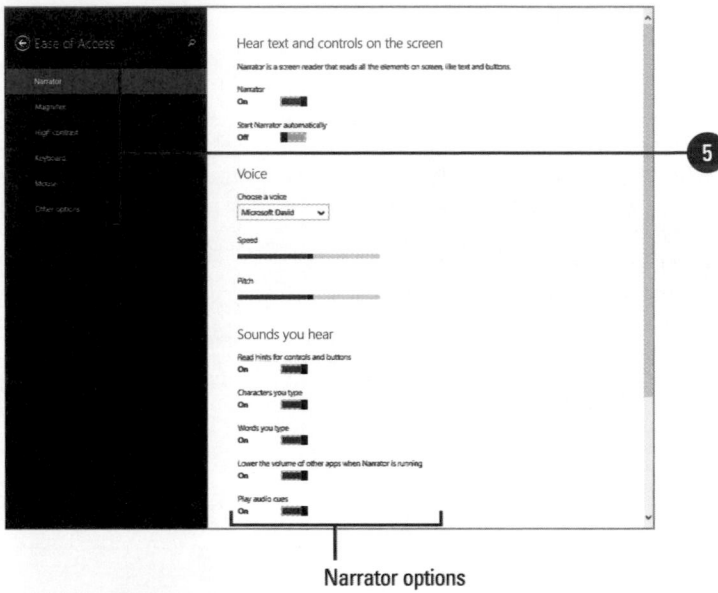

Narrator options

High contrast options

# Setting Up Accounts and Maintaining Security

**13**

## Introduction

With user accounts, you can customize and personalize Windows for each user on your system. Each user can have their own Documents folder and list of web favorites, customize system preferences, and protect private files. When you set up a new user account, the account appears on the Sign-in screen, where the new user can log on. You can use Accounts in PC settings or User Accounts in the Control Panel to add or delete user accounts, create a guest account, change a user's group or account type, change the way Windows starts, change the account picture, and set, change, and reset an account password.

Keeping your system safe and secure is a continuing battle. With the Windows Action Center, you can manage system security from one place. The Action Center makes it easy to find information about the latest virus or security threat, check the status of essential security settings, and quickly get support from Microsoft for a security-related issue.

While you're browsing the Internet or working in your email program, you need to be aware of viruses and other harmful attacks so you can protect your system from being infected by one. Internet Explorer include security enhancements to help you make your system more secure. In Internet Explorer, you can create security zones to designate trusted web sites, set web site ratings to restrict user access, clean up Internet files and information, and manage cookies to protect your personal identity from unauthorized access. If you're tired of closing unwanted pop-up ads, you can use Pop-up Blocker in Internet Explorer to prevent most pop-up windows from appearing.

## What You'll Do

**Explore Windows Security**

**Change User Account Settings**

**Add and Delete User Accounts**

**Change a User Account Type**

**Change the Start Up Screen**

**Set, Change, and Reset a Password**

**Lock the Screen**

**Manage Security in One Place**

**Defending Against Malicious Software**

**Set Family Safety Controls**

**Encrypt Files for Safety**

**Avoid Viruses and Other Harmful Attacks**

**Understand Security on the Internet**

**Create Security Zones and Set Ratings**

**Protect Internet Privacy and Identity**

**Block Content with Tracking Protection**

**Manage Add-Ons**

**Protect Privacy with IE App**

# Exploring Windows Security

Windows 8.1 provides several ways to secure your PC computer or mobile device.

## Create User Accounts

For a shared or workgroup system, there are four main types of user accounts: administrator, standard, child, and guest. For a domain network system, different account types (administrator, standard user, and restricted user) provide similar permissions as the ones on a shared or workgroup system.

The **administrator** account is for the person who needs to make changes to anything on the system as well as manage user accounts. An administrator account can install programs and hardware, make system-wide changes, access and read all non private files, create and delete user accounts, change other people's accounts, change your own account name, type and picture, and create, change, or remove your own password.

The **standard** account is for the person who needs to manage personal files and run programs. This account cannot install software or hardware, or change most system settings.

The **child** account (**New!**) is for a person that you want to manage and limit PC use with Family Safety. When you add a child account, it turns on Family Safety, which you can manage in the Control Panel.

The **guest** account doesn't have a password for easy access and contains more restrictions than the standard account. The guest account is disabled by default and needs to be turned on.

## Use Action Center

Use the Action Center to check your security settings, view security alerts, take actions about security and maintenance issues with and learn how to improve the security of your system.

If an option displays the Security icon next to it, you need to enter the administrator password or provide confirmation when prompted by the **User Account Control (UAC)**.

Icon indicates administrator privileges needed to access

Administrator account

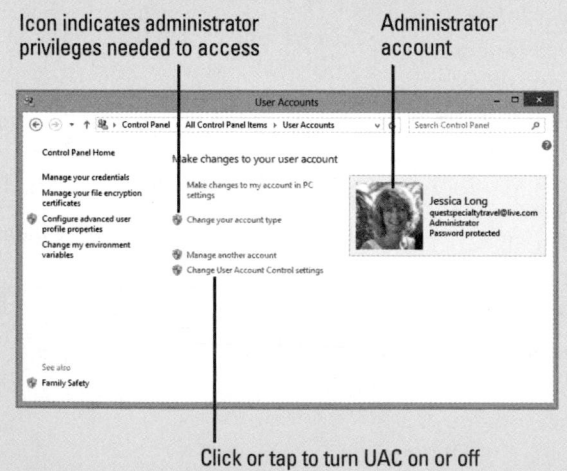

Click or tap to turn UAC on or off

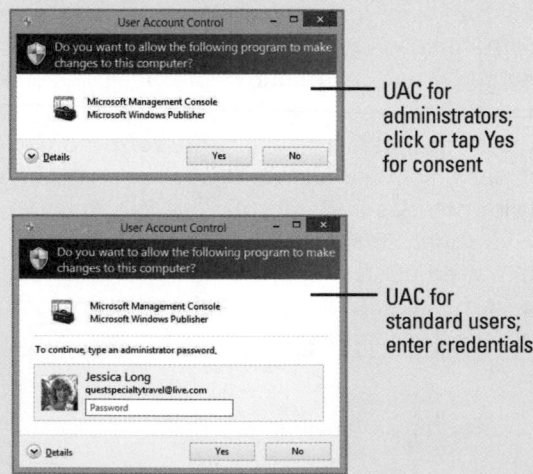

UAC for administrators; click or tap Yes for consent

UAC for standard users; enter credentials

This adds an additional level of security to keep your system secure. If you don't need the security (not recommended), you can turn it off in User Accounts.

## Enable Windows Firewall

Windows Firewall is a security system that creates a protective barrier between your PC or network and others on the Internet. Windows Firewall monitors all communication between your system and the Internet and prevents unsolicited inbound traffic from the Internet from entering your system. For more information on Windows Firewall, see "Connecting to the Internet" on page 133 and "Setting Up Windows Firewall" on page 134.

## Enable Automatic Updates

Windows Automatic Updates allows you to keep your system up-to-date with the latest system software and security updates over the Internet. For more information, see "Updating Windows" on page 458.

## Enable Internet Security Options

Internet Explorer provides security zones to browse secure web sites and a rating system to screen content, protects personal information and your privacy on the Internet, blocks pop-up ads, and displays information to help you make security decisions. For more information, see "Understanding Security on the Internet" on page 362.

## Enable Email Security Options

Email programs, such as Windows Live Mail, provide security zones to help you determine whether or not to run potentially harmful content from inside an email, prevents your email program from sending mail with your email address to your contacts (which is a common way to propagate a virus), and stops pictures and other content from automatically downloading inside and email to your system (which is a common way spammers confirm your email address to send more spam). For more information, see "Sending and Retrieving a File" on page 170, "Reading and Replying to Email" on page 168, or "Using Windows Live Essentials" on page 176.

## Protect Files and Folders

Another way to protect the files on your system is to use the built-in security provided by the NTFS file system. The NTFS file system is available for Windows NT-based systems, which doesn't include pre-Windows XP. You can select your hard disk in the Computer window and display Details view to determine whether your PC uses the NTFS file system.

The NTFS file system provides additional security for your files and folders. You can make a folder private, use the advanced Encrypting File System (EFS) to protect sensitive data files on your system. If someone tries to gain access to encrypted files or a folder on your system, a unique file encryption key prevents that person from viewing it. While these security options are more advanced, they could be helpful for securing very sensitive information. For more information, see "Encrypting Files for Safety" on page 358.

## Understand the Enemy

Knowing your enemy (harmful intruders) can help you make safe computing decisions that lead to a secure system rather than unsafe ones that lead to potential disaster. For information, see "Avoiding Viruses and Other Harmful Attacks" on page 360.

# Changing User Account Settings

With PC settings, you can change your account, sign in, and other user account settings. An account can be local using a username and password (no email) or online using your Microsoft email account. When you sign in with a Microsoft account, your account settings are maintained online. You can access and manage your Microsoft account online from PC settings. You can change online account options, including personal info, password and security info, aliases (other connected email addresses), notifications, permissions, billing, and even close the account. You can switch (disconnect and connect) between local and online accounts (**New!**) by using links in Your account under Accounts in PC settings.

## View User Account Settings

1. Display the Start screen.

2. Point to the lower- or upper-right corner and up or move down (on a computer) or swipe left from the right edge of the screen (on a mobile device).

3. Click or tap the **Settings** button on the Charms bar.

4. Click or tap **Change PC settings** on the Settings panel, and then click or tap **Accounts**.

5. Click or tap **Your account** under Accounts.

   The active user account appears.

6. To disconnect or connect to a Microsoft account, use the following:

   ◆ Disconnect. Click or tap the **Disconnect** link (**New!**) to create a local account.

   ◆ Connect. Click or tap the **Connect to a Microsoft account** link (**New!**), and then enter user name and password as prompted.

7. To close the app, point to the top edge of the screen (cursor changes to a hand), and then drag down to the bottom edge of the screen.

Uses an online Microsoft account

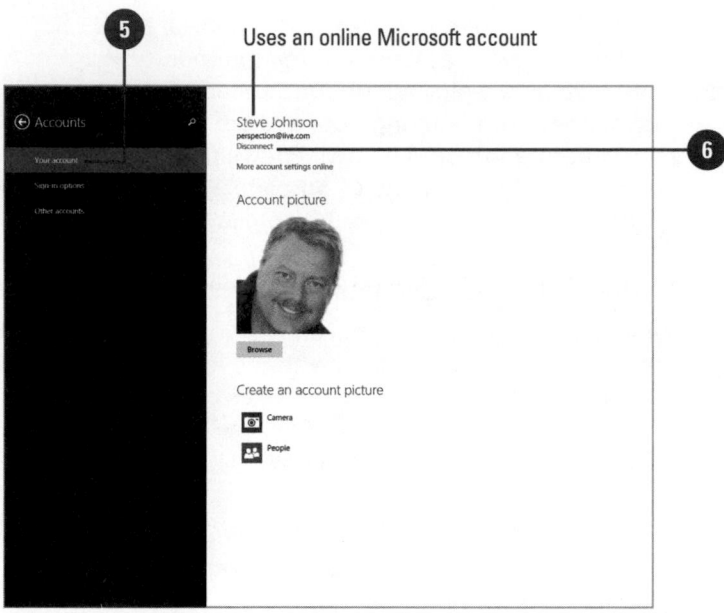

## Change User Account Online Settings

**1** Display the Start screen.

**2** Point to the lower- or upper-right corner and up or move down (on a computer) or swipe left from the right edge of the screen (on a mobile device).

**3** Click or tap the **Settings** button on the Charms bar.

**4** Click or tap **Change PC settings** on the Settings panel, and then click or tap **Accounts**.

**5** Click or tap **Your account** under Accounts.

**6** Click or tap the **More account settings online** link.

Your default web browser opens in a side by side window (**New!**), displaying your Microsoft account

**7** Specify the options you want.

◆ **Edit name.** Edit your first and last name.

◆ **Update email address.** Update your email address.

◆ **Edit personal info.** Change or add info, such as date of birth, profession, and addresses.

◆ **Change password.** Change your password.

◆ **Edit security info.** Change or add info, such as a phone number, alternate email, and security question.

◆ **Close account.** Deletes the online account.

**8** To close your web browser app, point to the top edge of the screen (cursor changes to a hand), and then drag down to the bottom edge of the screen.

Microsoft account settings online

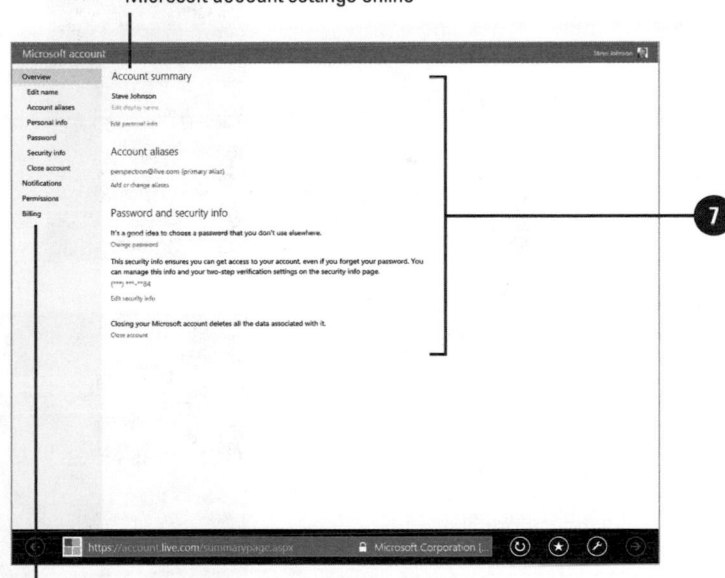

Additional options: Notifications, Permissions, and Billing

# Adding User Accounts

If you have an administrator account, you can create a new user account, either standard or child (**New!**)—needed to turn on Family Safety. An account can be local using a username and password (no email) or online using your Microsoft email account. When you add a new user, Windows creates a separate identity, allowing the user to keep files completely private and customize the operating system with personal preferences. The name you assign to the user appears on the Sign in screen and the Start screen. The steps to add user accounts differ, depending on whether your system is part of a domain network.

## Add an Account

1. Display the Start screen.

2. Point to the lower- or upper-right corner and up or move down (on a computer) or swipe left from the right edge of the screen (on a mobile device).

3. Click or tap the **Settings** button on the Charms bar.

4. Click or tap **Change PC settings** on the Settings panel, and then click or tap **Accounts**.

5. Click or tap **Other accounts** under Accounts.

6. Click or tap **Add a user**.

7. Enter the user's Microsoft email address or use a following link:

   ◆ **Sign up for a new email address.** Click or tap the link to sign up for a new Microsoft account.

   ◆ **Sign in without a Microsoft account.** Click or tap to create a username and local account for the device. You'll need a Microsoft account to download apps and sync across devices.

   ◆ **Add a child's account.** Click or tap the link to create a child's account with and without an email address (**New!**).

8. Click or tap **Next** and specify options as needed, and then click or tap **Finish**.

## Add an Account on a Domain Network

1. In the Start screen, click or tap the **Apps view** button, and then click or tap **Control Panel**.

2. Click or tap the **User Accounts** icon in Small icons or Large icons view..

3. Click or tap **Manage User Accounts**.

4. Click or tap the **Users** tab.

5. Click or tap **Add**.

6. Type a username and domain, and then click or tap **Next** to continue.

7. Click or tap a user access level option: **Standard user**, **Administrator**, or **Other**.

8. Click or tap **Finish**.

9. Click or tap **OK**.

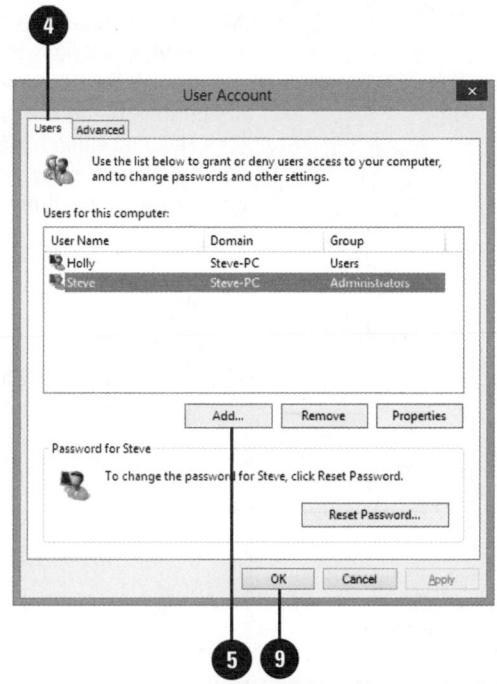

### Did You Know?

**You may need administrator access to make security changes.** If a security option displays the Action Center icon next to it, you need to enter the administrator password or provide confirmation when prompted to make a change.

**You can turn User Account Control on or off.** In the User Accounts dialog box, click or tap Turn User Account Control on or off, select or clear the User Account Control (UAC) To Help Protect Your Computer check box, click or tap OK, and then click or tap the Close button.

### For Your Information

#### Limiting an Account with Assigned Access

If you want to limit an account to use only one Windows Store app, you can make it assigned access. An account for assigned access allows you to choose an account to have access to only one Windows Store app (**New!**). Click or tap the Settings button on the Charms bar, click or tap Accounts, click or tap Other accounts, and then click or tap the Set up an account for assigned access link. To select an account,click or tap Choose an account, and then select an available accounts. To select an app that this account can access, click Choose an app, and then select an available app. To unassign access, click the account, and then click the Don't use assigned access link on the menu; you'll need to restart your PC to apply the changes. To sign out of assigned access quickly press the Windows logo key (⊞) five times.

# Deleting User Accounts

If you have an administrator account or are a member of the Administrators group, you can delete an existing one. When you delete an account, you have the choice to delete the contents of the account or keep it. When you keep the contents, Windows automatically saves the content of the User's desktop and Documents, Favorites, Music, Pictures, and video folders to a new folder (named the same as the user) on your desktop. The steps to delete user accounts differ, depending on whether your system is part of a domain network.

## Delete an Account

1. In the Start screen, click or tap the **Apps view** button, and then click or tap **Control Panel**.

2. Click or tap the **User Accounts** icon in Small icons or Large icons view.

3. Click or tap **Manage another account**.

4. Select the account you want to delete.

5. Click or tap **Delete the account**.

6. Click or tap **Delete Files** to remove all account files or **Keep Files** to save account folder (with username) to the desktop.

7. Click or tap **Delete Account**.

8. Click or tap the **Close** button.

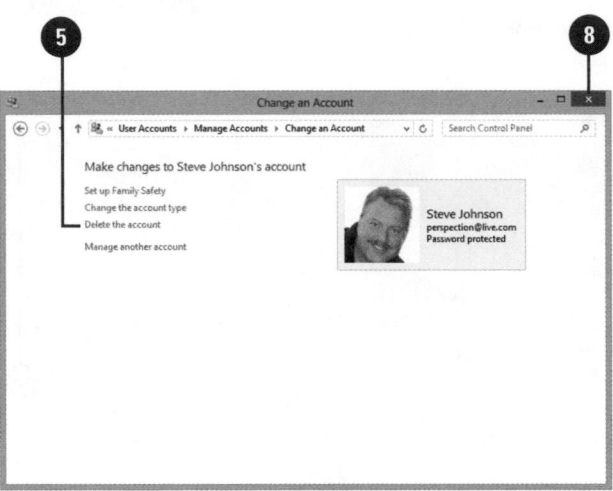

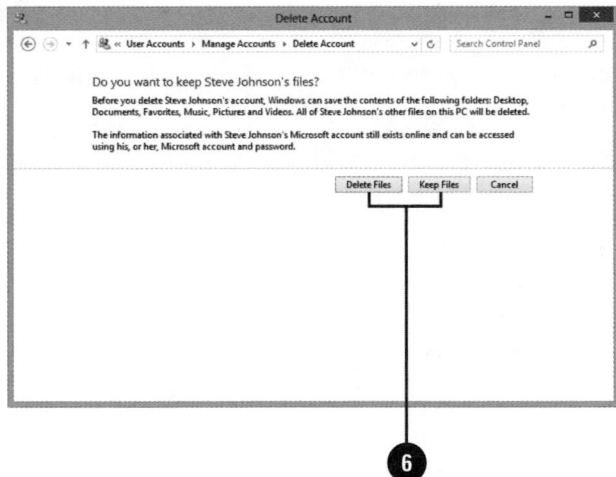

## Delete an Account on a Domain Network

1. In the Start screen, click or tap the **Apps view** button, and then click or tap **Control Panel**.

2. Click or tap the **User Accounts** icon in Small icons or Large icons view..

3. Click or tap **Manage User Accounts**.

4. Click or tap the **Users** tab.

5. Select the user you want to delete.

6. Click or tap **Remove**.

7. Click or tap **Yes** to confirm the deletion.

8. Click or tap **OK**.

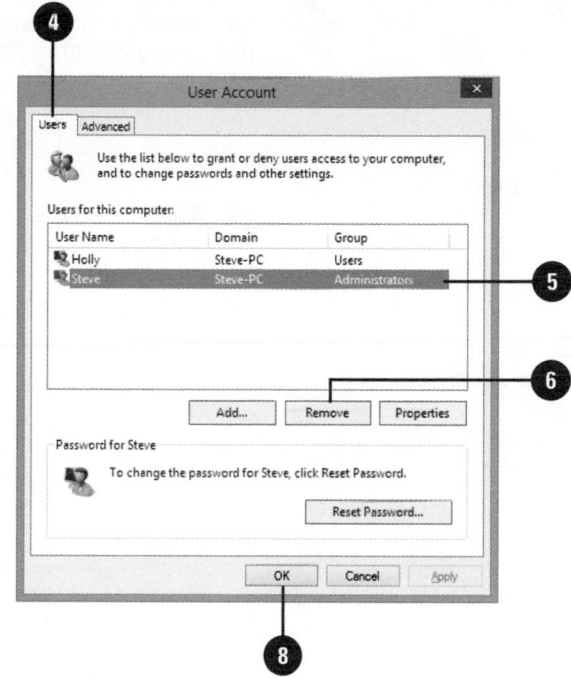

# Creating a Guest Account

If you have an administrator account or are a member of the Administrators group, you can create a guest account. A guest account provides access to a system for anyone who doesn't have a user account. The steps to create a guest account differ, depending on whether your system is part of a domain network.

## Create a Guest Account

1 In the Start screen, click or tap the **Apps view** button, and then click or tap **Control Panel**.

2 Click or tap the **User Accounts** icon in Small icons or Large icons view.

3 Click or tap **Manage another account**.

4 Click or tap the **Guest** icon.

5 Click or tap **Turn On**.

6 Click or tap the **Close** button.

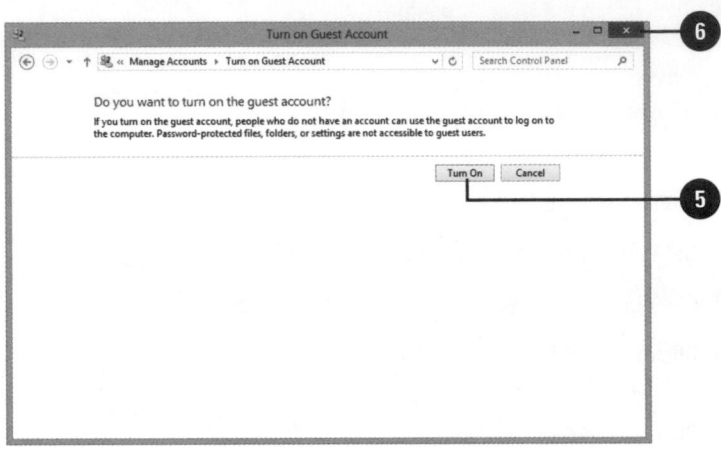

## Create a Guest Account on a Domain Network

1 In the Start screen, click or tap the **Apps view** button, and then click or tap **Control Panel**.

2 Click or tap the **User Accounts** icon in Small icons or Large icons view, and then click or tap **Manage User Accounts**.

3 Click or tap the **Advanced** tab, and then click or tap **Advanced**.

4 Click or tap **Users**.

5 Double-click or tap the **Guest** icon.

6 Clear the **Account is disabled** check box.

7 Click or tap **OK**, and then click or tap the **Close** button.

8 Click or tap **OK**.

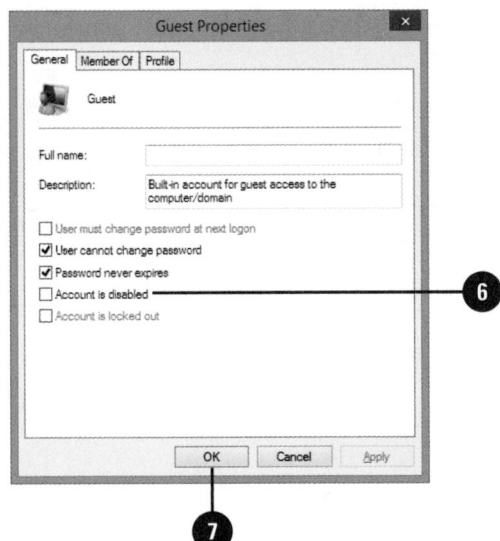

# Changing a User Account Type

If you have an administrator account or are a member of the Administrators group, you can change a user's account type (Administrator or Standard) or user group on a domain network. A user account or group grants permissions to a user to perform certain types of tasks based on the account type or user group (domain network). The steps to create a guest account differ, depending on whether your system is part of a network domain.

## Change a User Account Type

① In the Start screen, click or tap the **Apps view** button, and then click or tap **Control Panel**.

② Click or tap the **User Accounts** icon in Small icons or Large icons view.

③ If you want to change another account, click or tap **Manage another account**, and then click or tap the user's account name.

④ Click or tap **Change your account type** or **Change the account type**.

⑤ Click or tap an account type option.

⑥ Click or tap **Change Account Type**.

⑦ Click or tap the **Close** button.

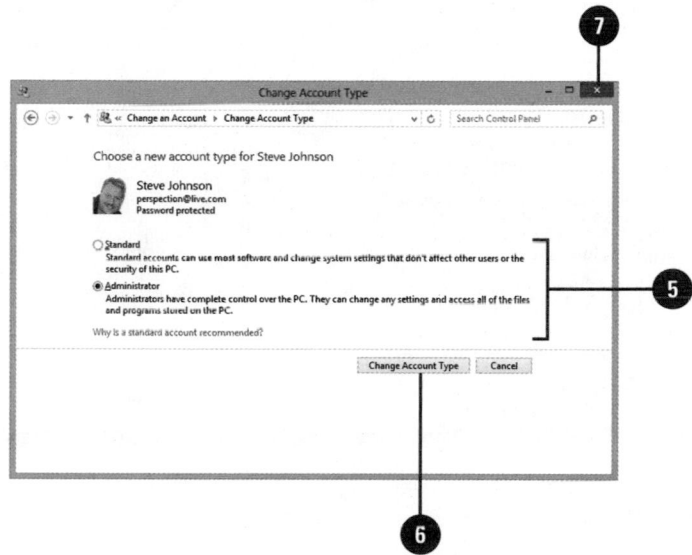

## Did You Know?

***You can change a user's group on a domain network.*** In User Accounts, click or tap Manage User Accounts, click or tap the Users tap, select a user account, click or tap Properties, click or tap the Group Membership tab, click or tap the group you want, and then click or tap OK twice.

# Changing the Start Up Screen

For added security on a domain network, you can require users to use Ctrl+Alt+Delete (or Ctrl+Alt+Del) before they can select a user account and enter a password. This prevents other programs, such as spyware or a virus, from getting your username and password as you enter it without your consent. When you lock your system or switch users, the security option also requires users to press Ctrl+Alt+Delete.

## Increase Logon Security on a Domain Network

**1** In the Start screen, click or tap the **Apps view** button, and then click or tap **Control Panel**.

**2** Click or tap the **User Accounts** icon in Small icons or Large icons view, and then click or tap **Manage User Accounts**.

**3** Click or tap the **Advanced** tab.

**4** Select the **Require users to press Ctrl+Alt+Delete** check box.

**5** Click or tap **OK**.

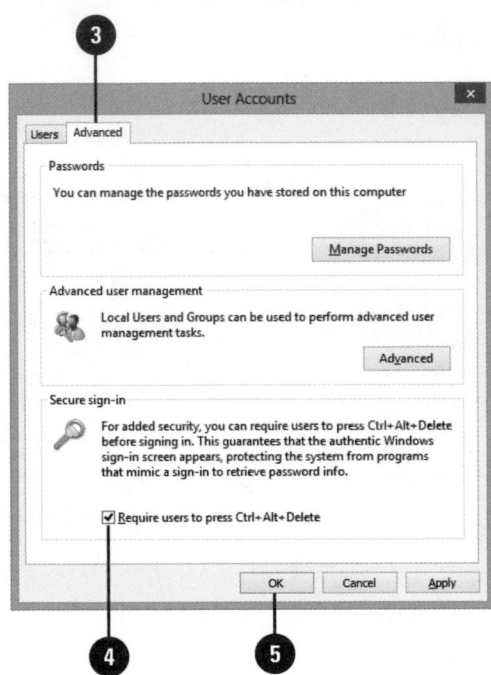

### Did You Know?

*You can also change the logon security on a workgroup network.* Open the User Accounts dialog box, click or tap the Advanced tab, select the Require Users To Press Ctrl+Alt+Delete check box, and then click or tap OK. To open the User Accounts dialog box, you can type *NetplWiz.exe* in the Run dialog box. In the Start screen, click or tap the Apps view button, and then click or tap Run. You can also press Win+R to open the Run dialog box.

# Changing an Account Picture

When you start Windows, the Sign in screen appears, displaying a list of user accounts with a picture next to each one. When you complete the sign in process, the picture associated with your account appears in the upper-right corner of the Start screen along with your username. This identifies you as the current user of the system. You can change the picture to suit your own personality using an existing file or installed camera. You can even add more than one.

## Change an Account Picture

① Display the Start screen for the account you want to change.

② Click or tap the **User Account** (username and picture).

③ Click or tap **Change account picture** on the menu.

The PC settings screen opens, displaying Your account under Accounts with an Account picture.

④ Use any of the following methods:

◆ **Use an Existing Picture.** Click or tap **Browse**, select the file, and then click or tap **Choose image**.

◆ **Use a Camera to Take a Picture.** Click or tap **Camera**. In the Camera app, click or tap the screen to take a picture, resize the crop corners, and then click or tap **OK**.

◆ **Change a Picture in People.** Click or tap **People** (**New!**). In the People app, click or tap **Take a Photo** or **Browse** on the App bar to use the Camera app or select a picture file to change the picture in People and use it in your account.

⑤ To close the app, point to the top edge of the screen (cursor changes to a hand), and then drag down to the bottom edge of the screen.

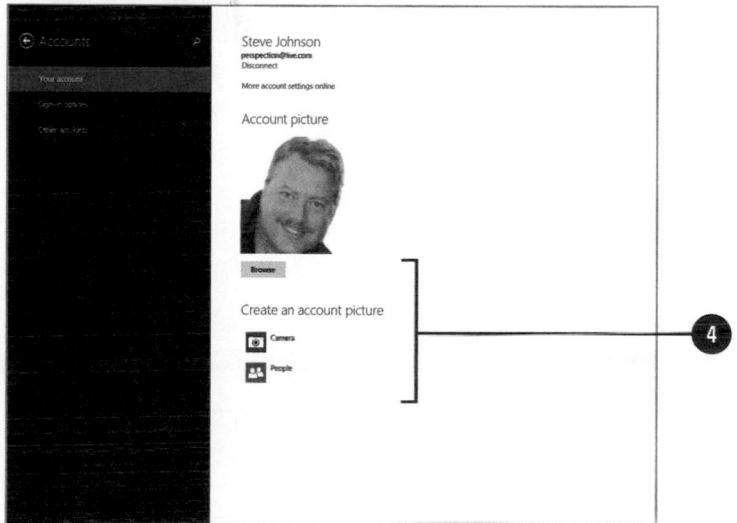

# Changing a Password

A password controls who has access to your device and all the files and information on it. When you add an account, you specify a password, however you can change it at any time. When you specify a password, enter one that is easy for you to remember, yet difficult for others to guess. Good passwords are typically at least seven characters and include letters (uppercase and lowercase), numbers, and symbols. In Windows, you can use multiple security passwords or codes, such as text or picture. In PC settings under Accounts in Sign-in option, you can change your account password, create a picture password with gestures, or create a 4-digit PIN (Personal Identification Number) code.

## Change a Password

1 Display the Start screen.

2 Point to the lower- or upper-right corner and up or move down (on a computer) or swipe left from the right edge of the screen (on a mobile device).

3 Click or tap the **Settings** button on the Charms bar.

4 Click or tap **Change PC settings** on the Settings panel, and then click or tap **Accounts**.

5 Click or tap **Sign-in options** under Accounts.

6 Specify the options you want.

♦ Password. Click or tap Change to change your password.

♦ Picture password. Click or tap **Add** to create a picture password. Click or tap **Remove** to delete it.

♦ PIN. Click or tap **Add** to create a 4-digit PIN (Personal Identification Number) code.

♦ Password Policy. Click or tap **Change** to not need a password when waking from sleep.

7 To close the app, point to the top edge of the screen (cursor changes to a hand), and then drag down to the bottom edge of the screen.

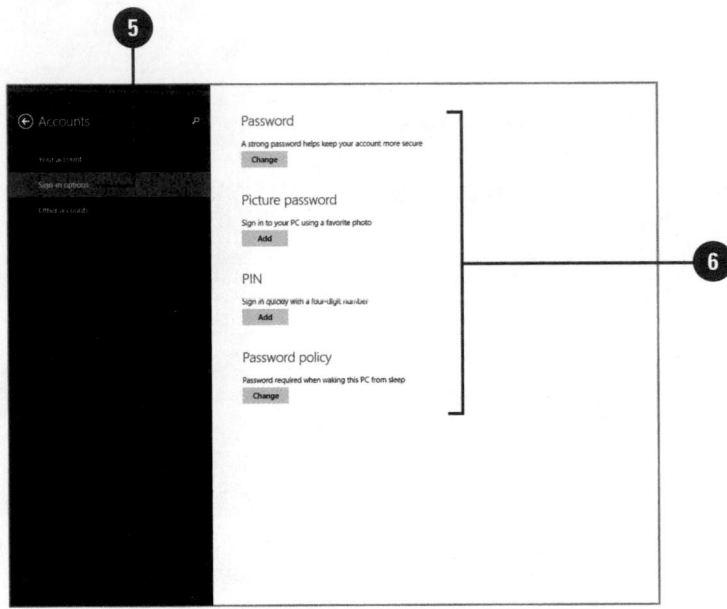

## Change an Administrator Password on a Domain Network

**1** In the Start screen, click or tap the **Apps view** button, and then click or tap **Control Panel**.

**2** Click or tap the **User Accounts** icon in Small icons or Large icons view, and then click or tap **Manage User Accounts**.

**3** Click or tap the **Users** tab.

**4** Click or tap the administrator account.

**5** Click or tap **Reset Password**.

**6** Type the new password, and then type it again.

**7** Click or tap **OK**.

**8** Click or tap **OK**.

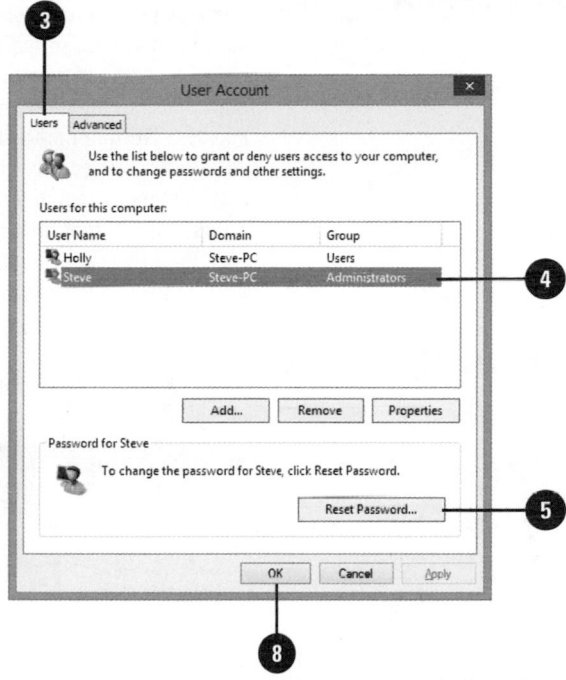

### Did You Know?

*You can change a local account password.* In User Accounts, click or tap the local account you want to change, click or tap Change The Password, type your current password, if necessary, type a new password, type it again, type a hint, and then click or tap Change Password.

*The Windows password is case-sensitive.* Windows makes a distinction between uppercase and lowercase letters. Your password should be at least seven characters, the optimal length for encryption, which logically scrambles and secures the data.

---

### Security Alert

## Working Smarter as the Administrator

If you are an administrator, it's recommended that you log out and use another account for general work to avoid harmful damage to your system by a virus or malicious user. For example, if a hacker received access to your system with administrator privileges, the attacker could reformat your hard drive, delete files, or create a new administrator account.

# Resetting a Password

If you have ever forgotten your password, you understand how important it is to write it down. However, writing down a password is not very secure. If you forget your password, you can reset it. For a Microsoft account, you can reset it online at *account.live.com/password/reset*. For a local account, you can create a Password Reset disk, either a floppy disk or USB flash drive, to help you log on and reset your password. If you have any security credentials and certificates, the Password Reset disk restores them. If you have forgotten your password and don't have a Password Reset disk, you can ask your administrator to reset it for you. Resetting your password also erases any security credentials and certificates on your system.

## Create a Password Reset Disk

**1** In the Start screen, click or tap the **Apps view** button, and then click or tap **Control Panel**.

**2** Click or tap the **User Accounts** icon in Small icons or Large icons view.

**3** Insert a blank disk in the Floppy drive or USB Flash drive.

**4** In the Tasks pane, click or tap **Create a password reset disk**.

**5** Follow the instructions in the Forgotten Password Wizard to create a password reset disk.

### Did You Know?

*You can reset a password for an online account.* Open your browser, go to *account.live.com/password/reset*, and then follow the on-screen instructions to reset your password for your Microsoft account

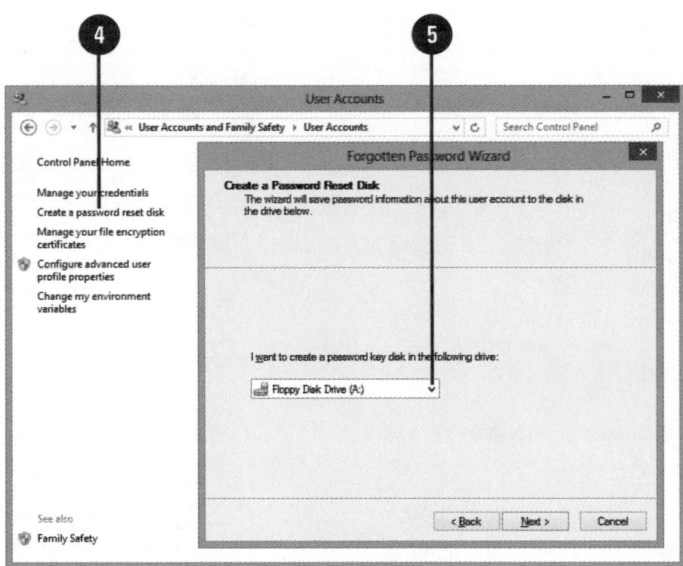

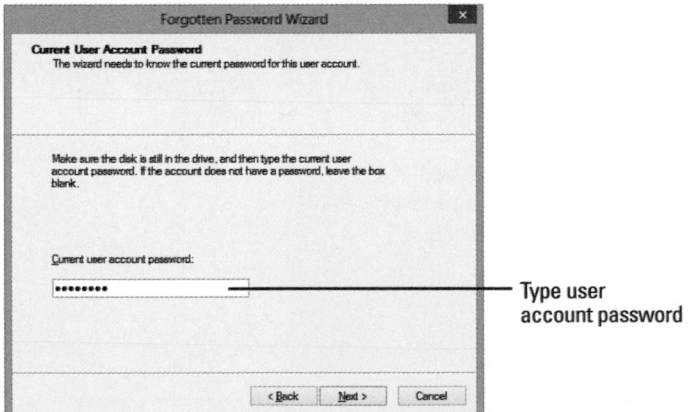

Type user account password

# Locking the Screen

If you are working on sensitive material and need to leave your PC unattended for a while, you can lock it so that no one can use it without your permission. While your PC is locked, all your programs continue to run. When you return to your PC, you can access it in the same way you started Windows, which is by selecting your account and entering your password. The Lock screen is a full screen image with the time, date and notification icons (with app status). When your screen locks, you can still access some apps without having to unlock your PC. When you display the Lock screen, you can answer Skype calls, take photos or see a slide show of your photos without having to unlock it first (**New!**). In the Start screen, click or tap the User Account, and then click or tap Lock to manually lock your PC. With a simple drag of a mouse, press of a key, or movement of your finger, you can dismiss the Lock screen to display the Sign in screen.

## Lock and Unlock the Screen

1. Display the Start screen for the account you want to change.

2. Click or tap the **User Account** (username and picture).

3. Click or tap **Lock** on the menu.

    **TIMESAVER** *Press Win+L to lock the system.*

    ◆ You can also press Ctrl+Alt+ Del, and then click or tap **Lock**.

4. When the Lock screen appears, drag your mouse anywhere on the screen, move your finger sideways from the edge, or press a key to dismiss it.

5. At the Sign in screen, click or tap your username or picture (if prompted), type your password, and then click or tap the **Submit arrow** or press Enter.

### See Also

*See "Starting Windows 8.1" on page 3 and "Switching Users" on page 20 for information on logging on to Windows 8.1.*

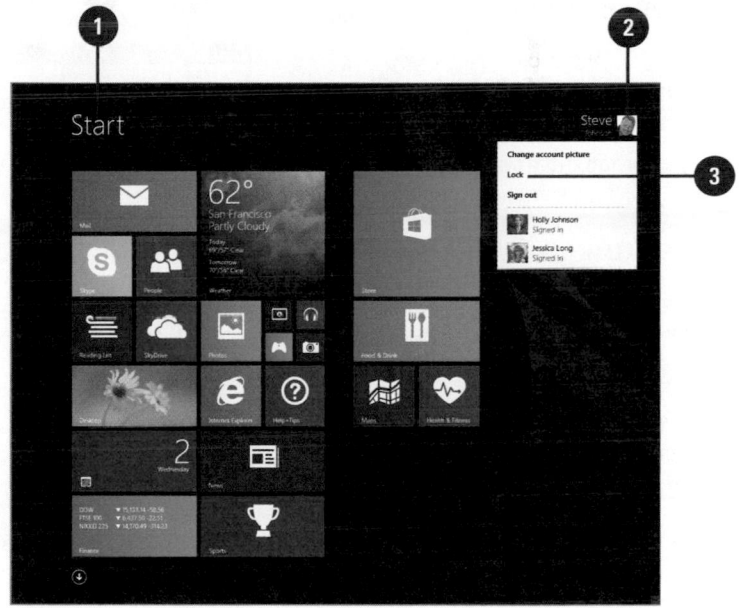

# Managing Security in One Place

The Action Center provides a single place to view alerts and take actions about security and maintenance issues with your PC. The Action Center displays important and recommended alerts that need your attention to help protect your PC and keep Windows running smoothly. It also provides links to important information about the latest virus or other security threat, or to get customer support from Microsoft for a security related issue. As you work, Windows uses security alerts and icons in the notification area on the taskbar to help you recognize potential security risks, such as a new virus, out of date antivirus software or an important security option is turned off, and choose appropriate settings. If Windows requires your attention, the Action Center icon appears in the notification area. Click or tap the Action Center icon to view alerts and suggested fixes, or open the Action Center.

## View Essential Security Settings Using the Action Center

1 In the Start screen, click or tap the **Apps view** button, and then click or tap **Control Panel**.

2 Click or tap the **Action Center** icon in Small icons or Large icons view.

   **TIMESAVER** *Click or tap the Action Center icon in the notification area (if available), and then click or tap Open Action Center.*

3 To find out information on a security area, click or tap the down arrow next to it.

4 To set Action Center settings, click or tap the **Change Action Center settings** link, select or clear check boxes to turn alert messages on or off, and then click or tap **OK**.

5 To adjust the notification setting for preventing harmful programs from making changes, click or tap the **Change User Account Control settings** link, drag the slider, and then click or tap **OK**.

6 When you're done, click or tap the **Close** button.

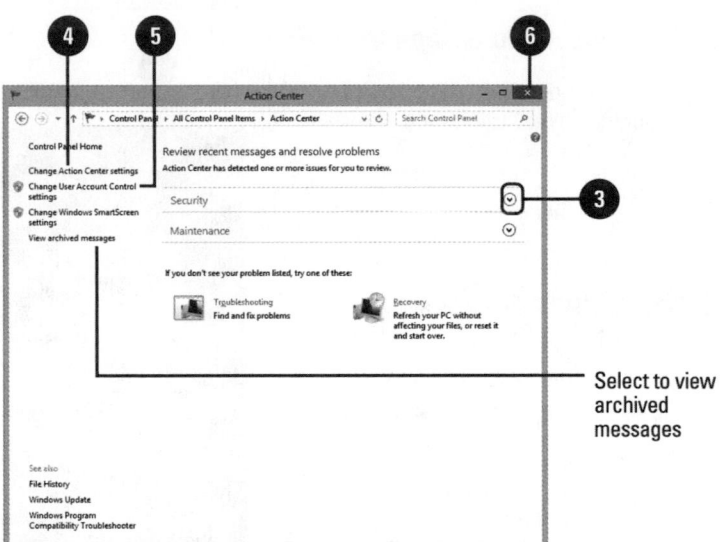

Select to view archived messages

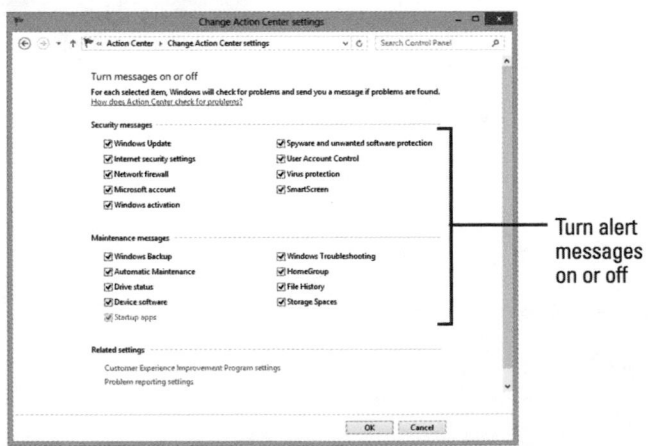

Turn alert messages on or off

## Act Upon Security Alerts

1. If Windows requires your attention, the Action Center icon appears in the notification area. Click or tap the **Actions Center** icon in the notification area, and then click or tap an issue.

   ◆ If the Action Center detects that your PC needs enhanced security, it displays an alert (if enabled) in the notification area, read the security alert, and then click or tap it..

2. To find out information on a security option, click or tap the down arrow next to it.

3. To find out how to address the problem, click or tap a link or a button, and then follow the instructions.

4. When you're done, click or tap the **Close** button.

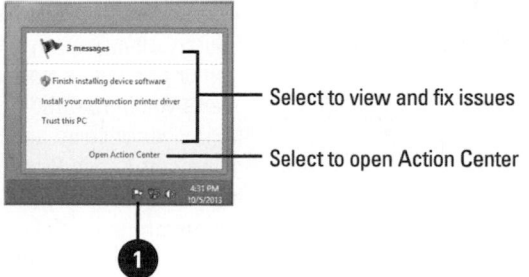

Select to view and fix issues

Select to open Action Center

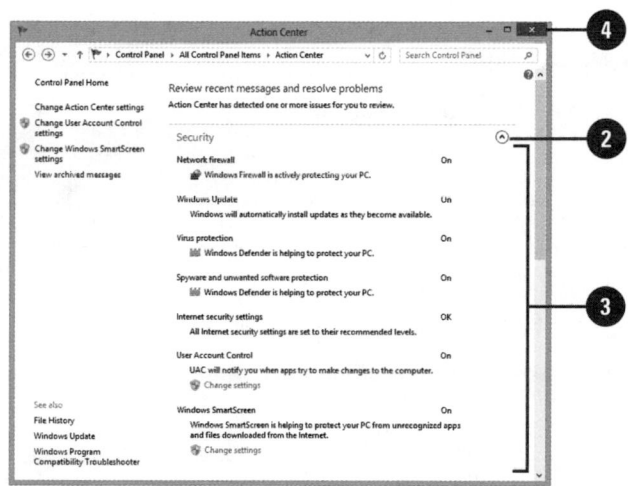

### Did You Know?

***You can change the way Automatic Updates alerts changes.*** In the Control Panel, click or tap the Windows Update icon in Small icons or Large icons view, click or tap Change Settings, select the alert option you want, click or tap OK, and then click or tap the Close button.

### See Also

*See "Troubleshooting Problems" on page 492 for more information on using the troubleshooting wizards.*

## Security Icons

| Icon | Description |
|---|---|
| | **Security Settings:** Indicates important security information and settings that are available, such as the Windows Action Center. |
| | **Potential Risk:** Indicates your system encountered a potential security risk; act upon the security alert. |
| | **No Risk:** Indicates your PC is more secure and using recommended security settings; no action needed. |
| | **Security Warning:** Indicates your PC encountered a warning alert, which is potentially harmful; consider adjusting security settings. |
| | **Security Problem:** Indicates your PC is not using recommended security settings; consider adjusting them. |

# Defending Against Malicious Software

Windows Defender helps you protect your system from spyware and other potentially harmful software that attempts to install itself or run on your system. Spyware is software that tries to collect information about you or change PC settings without your consent. Windows Defender alerts you in real-time when unwanted software tries to run on your PC. When you receive an alert of a potential problem, you can use the Microsoft Active Protection Service (MAPS) to help you determine if the software is already to run, and send information to Microsoft. Windows Defender uses definitions to determine potential problems. Since software dangers continually change, it's important to have up-to-date definitions, which you can get online.

## Use Windows Defender

1. If a real-time alert appears with an attempt to:

   ◆ **Install software.** Click or tap **Ignore**, **Quarantine**, **Remove**, or **Always Allow**.

   ◆ **Change Windows settings.** Click or tap **Permit** or **Deny**.

2. In the Start screen, click or tap the **Apps view** button, and then click or tap **Windows Defender**.

   ◆ In the Control Panel, you can also click or tap the **Windows Defender** icon in Small icons or Large icons view.

3. To get updates, click or tap the **Update** tab, and then click or tap the **Update** button.

4. To perform a scan, click or tap the **Home** tab, click or tap the **Quick Scan** or **Full Scan** option, and then click or tap **Scan now**.

5. To view or clear history, click or tap the **History** tab, select an option, click or tap **View details**, and then click or tap an item to view history. Use the **Remove all**, **Remove**, or **Restore** buttons as needed.

6. When you're done, click or tap the **Close** button.

Update tab

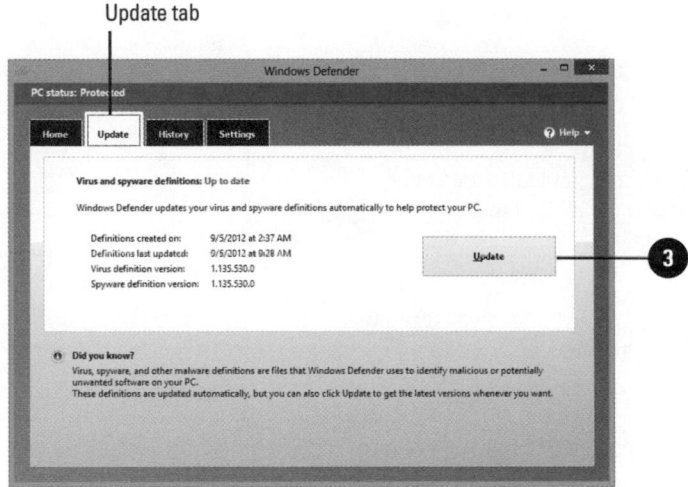

Home tab

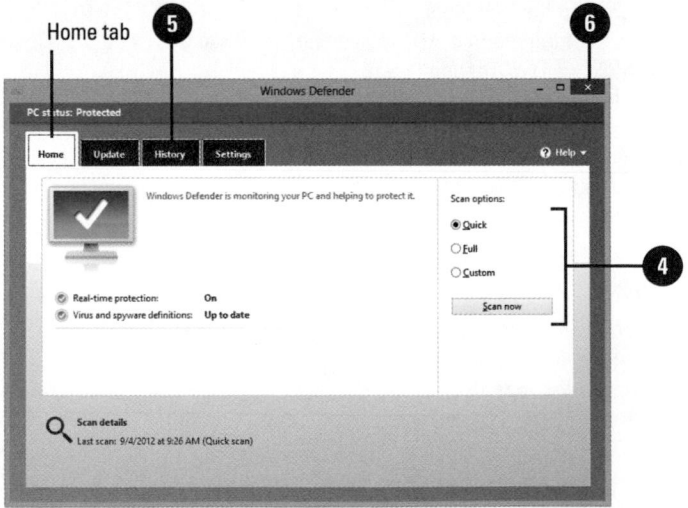

## Change Windows Defender Options

**1** In the Start screen, click or tap the **Apps view** button, and then click or tap **Windows Defender**.

◆ In the Control Panel, you can also click or tap the **Windows Defender** icon in Small icons or Large icons view.

**2** Click or tap the **Settings** tab.

**3** Click or tap a category with the options you want to change.

◆ **Real-time protection.** Set an option to get protection alerts against malicious attacks.

◆ **Exclude files and locations.** Specify files and locations to exclude to seed up the scans.

◆ **Exclude file types.** Specify file types to exclude to seed up the scans.

◆ **Exclude processes.** Specify running processes to exclude to seed up the scans.

◆ **Advanced.** Set options to scan archives or removable drives, create a restore point, view history, and remove quarantined files.

◆ **MAPS.** Microsoft Active Protection Service provides information to Microsoft when it detect intruders.

◆ **Administrator.** Set an option to enable or disable Windows Defender (default option is on).

**4** Specify the options you want for the selected category, and then click or tap **Save changes** as needed.

**5** When you're done, click or tap the **Close** button.

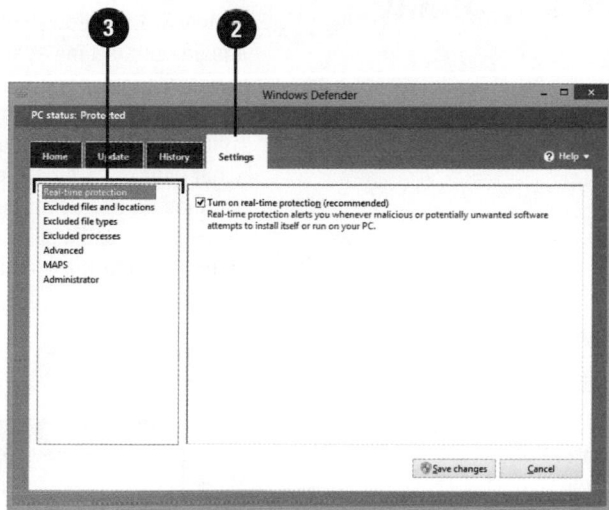

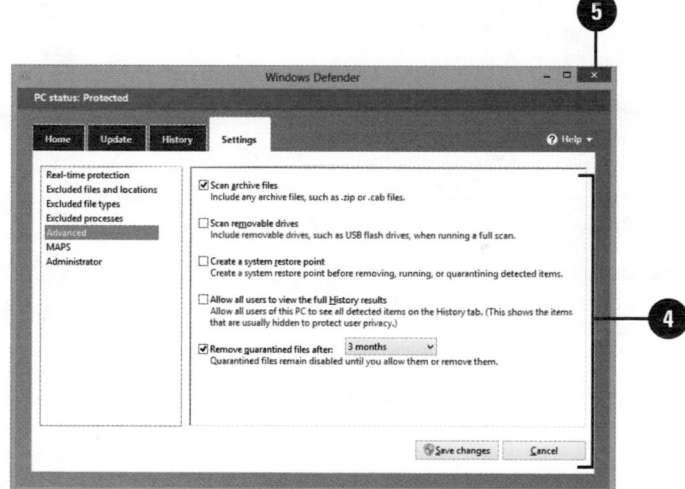

# Setting Family Safety Controls

Family Safety can help you manage how your children use the PC. Family Safety allows you to set limits on your children's web access, the amount of time spent logged on the system, and which games and programs they can use. You can set different settings for each user account on your PC, so you can adjust the level you want for each child. You can also review activity reports on a periodic basis to see what your children are doing on the PC. You can manage Family Safety settings on this device in the Control Panel or on the Family Safety web site. To turn on Family Safety (**New!**), you need to create a child's account; to turn it off, change the account to Standard or delete it.

## Enable or Disable Family Safety

1. In the Start screen, click or tap the **Apps view** button, and then click or tap **Control Panel**.

2. Click or tap the **Family Safety** icon in Small icons or Large icons view.

   ◆ **Turn on Family Safety.** Click or tap the **Account** link to create a child account (**New!**).

3. To select a rating system, click or tap **Rating Systems**, click or tap the option with the rating system you want, and then click or tap **Accounts to Monitor**.

4. Click or tap the standard user account for which you want to set controls on this device.

   ◆ **Family Safety web site.** Click or tap **Manage settings on the Family Safety website** to open your browser and make option changes for your account.

5. To enable or disable the use of Family Safety, click or tap the **On, enforce current settings** or **Off** option.

6. To enable or disable activity reports, click or tap the **On, collect information about PC usage** or **Off** option.

   ◆ Family Safety needs to be enabled to set this option.

7. Click or tap the **Close** button.

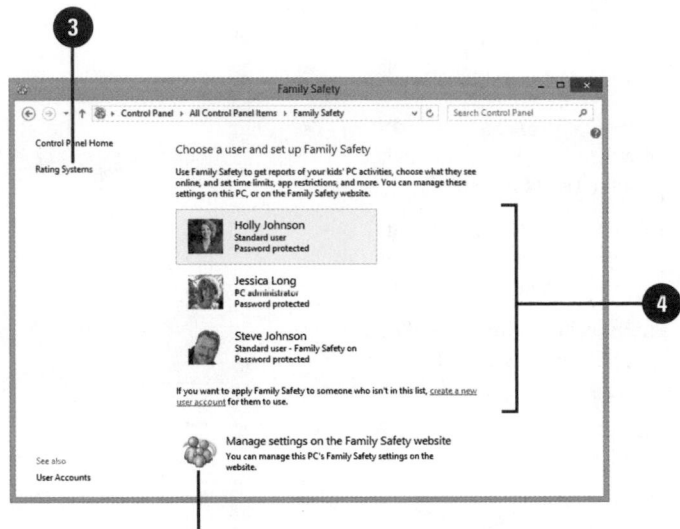

Select to manage Family Safety option online

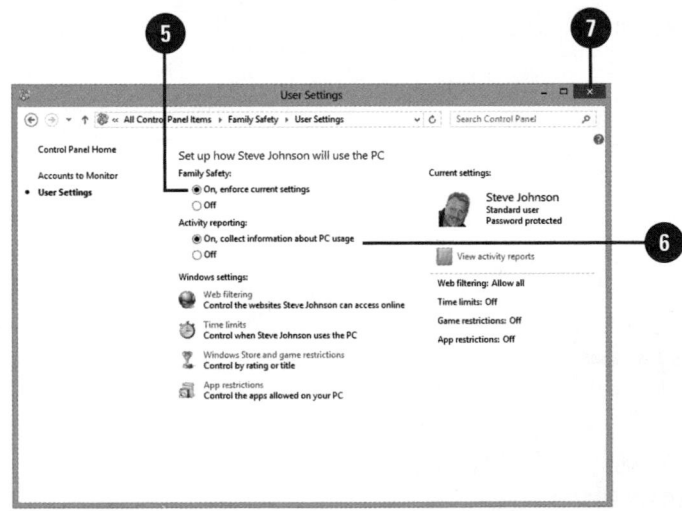

## Set Family Safety Controls

1. In the Start screen, click or tap the **Apps view** button, and then click or tap **Control Panel**.

2. Click or tap the **Family Safety** icon in Small icons or Large icons view.

   ◆ **Turn on Family Safety.** Click or tap the **Account** link to create a child account (**New!**).

3. Click or tap the standard user account for which you want to set controls.

4. Click or tap the **On, enforce current settings** option.

5. Click or tap the links to the Windows settings you want to change (use the **Back** button to go previous screens):

   ◆ **Web filtering.** Select options to block or allow web sites based on ratings and content or specific ones.

   ◆ **Time limits.** Select options to set time allowance and curfew time to set the hours you want to block or allow for device usage.

   ◆ **Windows Store and games restrictions.** Select options to block or allow Windows Store apps and games based on ratings or specific ones.

   ◆ **Apply restrictions.** Select an option to use all apps or only the apps I use.

6. Click or tap the **Close** button.

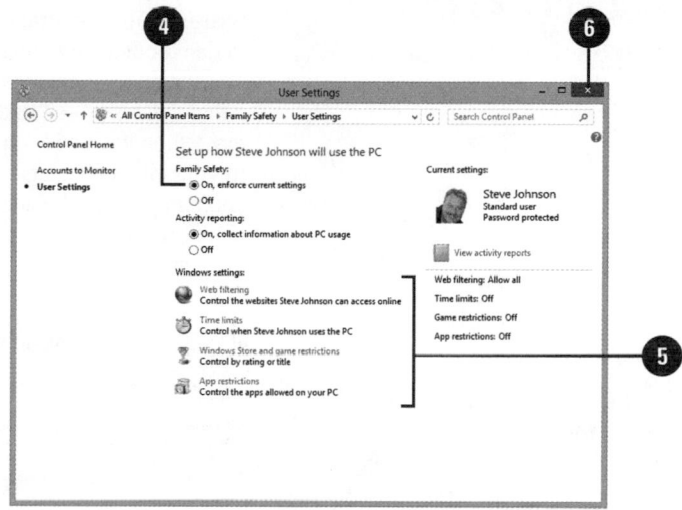

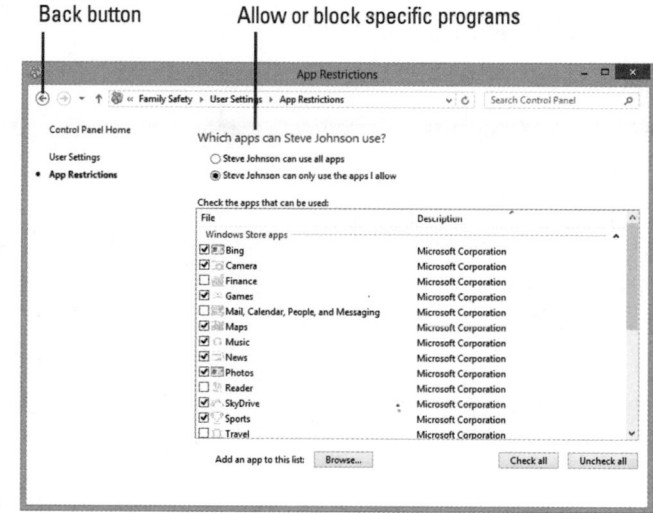

Back button    Allow or block specific programs

# Encrypting Files for Safety

If your PC uses NTFS, you can use the advanced Encrypting File System (EFS) to protect sensitive data files on your PC. If someone tries to gain access to encrypted files or a folder on your PC, a unique file encryption key prevents that person from viewing it. When you encrypt a file, you also need to decide whether you want to encrypt the folder, too. When you encrypt a folder, you need to decide whether you want to encrypt all files and subfolders within it. After you encrypt your files, you can use the Backup Wizard in the Backup and Restore Center to back them up for safe keeping.

## Encrypt or Decrypt a File or Folder

1. In File Explorer (desktop), select the file or folder you want to encrypt.

2. Click or tap the **Properties** button on the Home tab.

3. Click or tap the **General** tab.

4. Click or tap **Advanced**.

5. Select the **Encrypt contents to secure data** check box to encrypt the file or folder or clear the check box to decrypt it.

6. Click or tap **OK**.

7. Click or tap **OK**.

8. If necessary, click or tap an option to apply changes to this folder only or to this folder, subfolders, and files.

9. Click or tap **OK**.

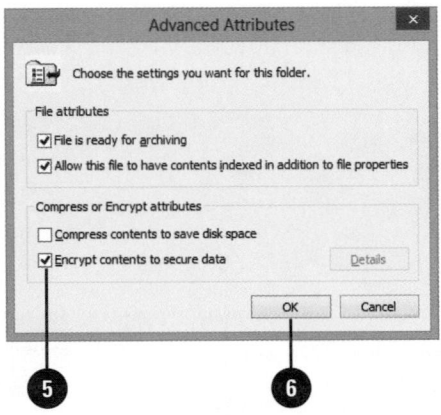

### Did You Know?

***You can compress files and folders with NTFS.*** In File Explorer (desktop), select the file or folder, click or tap the Properties button on the Home tab, click or tap the General tab, click or tap Advanced, select the Compress Contents To Save Disk Space check box, and then click or tap OK twice.

## For Your Information

### Managing and Backing Up Encryption Certificate

When you encrypt a file or folder, Windows uses information from your Encrypting File system certificate. A certificate is a digital document that verifies the identify of a person, which is issued by a trusted Certification Authority. If you lost the certificate or it becomes corrupted, you will not be able to recover an encrypted file or folder. To avoid this problem, you should back up your Encrypting File System (EFS) certificate. To manage and back up your EFS certificate, open the Control Panel (desktop), click or tap the User Accounts icon in the Small icons or Large icons view, click or tap Manage Your File Encryption Certificates, and then follow the Encrypting File System wizard.

# Encrypting Files Using BitLocker

BitLocker helps protect your system and blocks hackers from accessing sensitive information behind the scenes. For internal drives and volumes, you can use BitLocker to encrypt it. With BitLocker To Go, you can apply the same protection to portable storage devices, such as USB flash drives and external hard drives. BitLocker provides the most protection when used with a compatible Trusted Platform Module (TPM) (version 1.2) microchip and BIOS. However, it's not required. When you turn on BitLocker, it uses a password and recovery key (which gets backed up) for security. When you add files to your PC, BitLocker automatically encrypts them. When you copy files to another location, the files are decrypted. If a problem occurs at startup or someone tries to illegally access your system, Windows switches into recovery mode until you supply the recovery password.

## Use BitLocker to Encrypt Files

1. In the Start screen, click or tap the **Apps view** button, and then click or tap **Control Panel**.

2. Click or tap the **BitLocker Drive Encryption** icon in Small icons or Large icons view.

   ◆ You can also select a drive in Computers in File Explorer (desktop), and then use **BitLocker** button arrow on the Manage tab.

3. Click or tap **Turn On BitLocker** on the volume you want.

4. Follow the wizard to specify a password, recovery key, and encrypt options, click or tap **Start encrypting**, wait for BitLocker to encrypt the volume upon restart, and then click or tap **Close**.

   When your PC starts up after the encryption, you won't see any change. If a problem occurs or someone tries to illegally access the drive, your PC switches into recovery mode until you supply the recovery password.

5. To turn off BitLocker, click or tap **Turn Off BitLocker**, and then click or tap **Decrypt Drive**. To change or remove a password, save or print a recovery key, or automatically unlock a drive, click or tap a link.

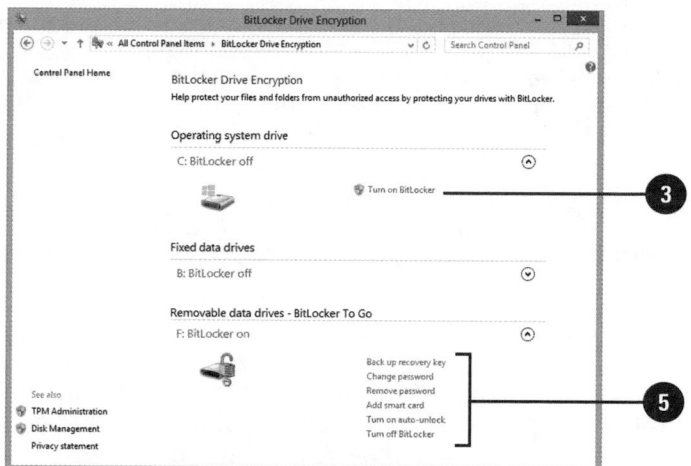

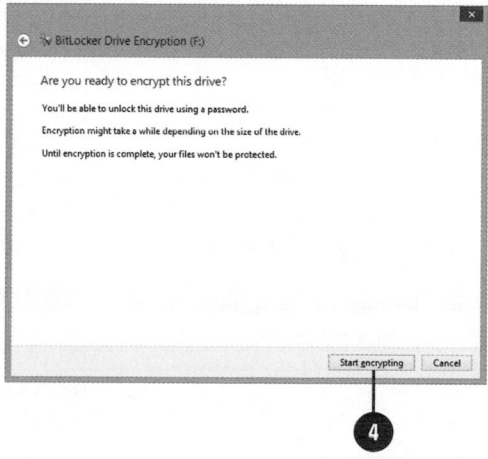

# Avoiding Viruses and Other Harmful Attacks

## Understanding Harmful Attacks

Using the Internet can expose your PC to a wide variety of harmful attacks, such as viruses, worms, and Trojan Horses. These attacks can come through email, file transferring, and even possibly through Java and ActiveX, which are both programming languages used to enhance web pages.

A **virus** is an executable program whose functions range from just being annoying to causing havoc to your PC. A virus may display an innocuous warning on a particular day, such as Friday the 13th, or it may cause a more serious problem, such as wiping out your entire hard disk. Viruses are found in executable (.exe and .com) files, along with Microsoft Word and Microsoft Excel macro files. A **worm** is like a virus, but it can spread without human action across networks. For example, a worm might send email copies of itself to everyone in your email contacts. A worm can consume memory causing your PC to stop responding or even take it over. A **Trojan Horse**, like its mythological counterpart, is a program that appears to be useful and comes from a legitimate source, but actually causes problems.

## Spreading Harmful Infections

Many viruses and other harmful attacks spread through file downloads and attachments in email messages. Virus writers capitalize on people's curiosity and willingness to accept files from people they know or work with, in order to transmit malicious files disguised as or attached to benign files. When you start downloading files to your PC, you must be aware of the potential for catching a PC virus, worm, or Trojan Horse. Typically, you can't catch one from just reading a mail message or downloading a file, but you can catch one from opening or running an infected program, such as a file attached to an email message, or one you download for free. And even though most viruses and other harmful attacks take the form of executable programs, data files that have macros or Visual Basic code attached to them, such as Word or Excel files, can also be infected with viruses.

## Avoiding Harmful Attacks

There are a few things you can do to keep your system safe from the infiltration of viruses and other harmful attacks.

**1) Make sure Windows Firewall is turned on.** Windows Firewall helps block viruses and worms from reaching your PC, but it doesn't detect or disable them if they are already on your PC or come through email. Windows Firewall doesn't block unsolicited email or stop you from opening email with harmful attachments. For more information on Windows Firewall, see "Connecting to the Internet" on page 133 and "Setting Up Windows Firewall" on page 134.

**2) Make sure Automatic Updates is turned on.** Windows Automatic Updates regularly checks the Windows Update web site for important updates that your PC needs, such as security updates, critical updates, and service packs. Each file that you download using Automatic Update has a digital signature from Microsoft to ensure its authenticity and security. For more information, see "Updating Windows" on page 458.

**3) Make sure you are using the most up-to-date antivirus software.** New viruses and more virulent strains of existing viruses are discovered every day. Unless you update your virus checking software, new viruses can easily bypass outdated virus checking software.

Companies such as McAfee and Symantec offer shareware virus checking programs available for download directly from their web sites. These programs monitor your system, checking each time a file is added to make sure it's not in some way trying to change or damage valuable system files.

**4) Be very careful of the sites from which you download files.** Major file repository sites, such as FileZ, Download.com, or TuCows, regularly check the files they receive for viruses before posting them to their web sites. Don't download files from web sites unless you are certain that the sites check their files for viruses. Internet Explorer monitors downloads and warns you about potentially harmful files and gives you the option to block them. For more information, see "Downloading Files from the Web" on page 130.

**5) Be very careful of file attachments in email you open.** As you receive email, don't open or run an attached file unless you know who sent it and what it contains. If you're not sure, you should delete it. To protect your PC from harmful attacks, see "Sending and Retrieving a File" on page 170, "Reading and Replying to Email" on page 168, and "Using Windows Live Essentials" on page 176.

**6) Make sure you activate macro virus checking protection in both Word and Excel.** To do so in Office 2010 or 2013, select the File tab, select Options, select Trust Center, select Trust Center Settings, select Macro Settings, select the Disable all macros with notification option, and then click or tap OK. And always elect not to run macros when opening a Word or Excel file that you received from someone who might not be using proper virus protection.

## Avoiding Other Intruders

**Spyware** is software that collects personal information without your knowledge or permission. Typically, spyware is downloaded and installed on your PC along with free software, such as freeware, games, or music file-sharing programs. Spyware is often associated with **Adware** software that displays advertisements, such as a pop-up ad. Examples of spyware and unauthorized adware include programs that change your home page or search page without your permission. To avoid spyware and adware, read the fine print in license agreements when you install software, scan your PC for spyware and adware with detection and removal software (such as Ad-aware from Lavasoft), and turn on Pop-up Blocker. For details, see "Blocking Pop-Up Ads" on page 369.

**Spam** is unsolicited email, which is often annoying and time-consuming to get rid of. Spammers harvest email addresses from web pages and unsolicited email. To avoid spam, use multiple email addresses (one for web forms and another for private email), opt-out and remove yourself from email lists, and turn on the Block Images And Other External Content In HTML Email option.

**Phishing** is an email scam that tries to steal your identity by sending deceptive email asking you for bank and credit card information online. Don't be fooled by spoofed web site that look like the official site. Never respond to requests for personal information via email; call the institution to investigate and report it.

# Understanding Security on the Internet

No other web browser offers as many customizable features as Internet Explorer does, particularly advanced security features that are built into the program. To understand all the Internet Explorer security features, you first have to learn about security on the Internet in general.

When you send information from your PC to another PC, the two PCs are not linked directly together. Your data may travel through multiple networks as it works its way across the Internet. Since your data is broadcast to the Internet, any PC on any of these networks could be listening in and capturing your data. (They typically aren't, but they could be.)

In addition, on the Internet it's possible to masquerade as someone else. Email addresses can be forged, domain names of sites can easily be misleading, and so on. You need some way to protect not only the data you send, but also yourself from sending data to the wrong place.

Furthermore, there is always the potential that someone (referred to as a "hacker") or something, such as a virus or worm, could infiltrate your PC systems. Once infiltrated, a hacker or virus can delete, rename, or even copy valuable information from your PC without your knowledge.

## Security Zones

Through the use of **security zones**, you can easily tell Internet Explorer which sites you trust to not damage your PC and which sites you simply don't trust. In your company's intranet you would most likely trust all the information supplied on web pages through your company's network, but on the Internet you may want to be warned first of potential dangers a site could cause your system. You can set up different levels of security based on different zones.

## Certificates

When shopping on the Internet, you want to do business with only those companies that offer a certain level of security and promise to protect your buying information. In turn, those companies want to do business with legitimate customers only. A **certificate** or **digital ID** provides both the browser and the company with a kind of guarantee confirming that you are who you say you are and that the site is secure and genuine, not a fraud or scam. When you send an email message, it also verifies your identity to your recipients.

A digital ID is made up of a public key, a private key, and a digital signature. When you digitally sign an email, email programs, like Windows Live Mail, add your public key and digital signature (the two together is the certificate) to the message. When your recipients receive the email, your digital signature verifies your identity and your public key is stored in their contacts so they can send you encrypted messages, which only you can open with your private key.

An independent company, called a **credentials agency**, issues three types of certificates: personal, authority, and publisher. A **personal certificate** identifies you so that you can access web sites that require positive identification, such as banks that allow online transactions. You can obtain a personal certificate from a credentials agency called VeriSign using the Content tab of the Internet Options dialog box. An **authority certificate** ensures that the web site you are visiting is not a fraud. Internet Explorer automatically checks site certificates to make sure that they're valid. A **publisher certificate** enables you to trust software that you download, such as ActiveX controls. Internet Explorer maintains a list of software companies whose certificates are valid and trustworthy. You can view your certificate settings on the Content tab of the Internet Options dialog box.

## Cookies

When you browse the Internet, you can access and gather information from web sites, but web sites can also gather information about you without your knowledge unless you set up Internet security on your PC. You can set Internet privacy options to protect your personal identity from unauthorized access. When you visit a web site, the site creates a **cookie** file, known as a **first-party**

**cookie**, which stores information on your PC, such as your web site preferences or personal identifiable information, including your name and email address. Not all cookies are harmful; many first-party-cookies save you time re-entering information on a return visit to a web site. However, there are also **third-party cookies**, such as advertising banners, which are created by web sites you are not currently viewing. Once a cookie is saved on your PC, only the web site that created it can read it. The privacy options allow you to block or permit cookies for web sites in the Internet zone; however, when you block cookies, you might not be able to access all the features of a web site. When a web site violates your cookie policy, a red icon appears on the Status bar.

Security zones

Certificates

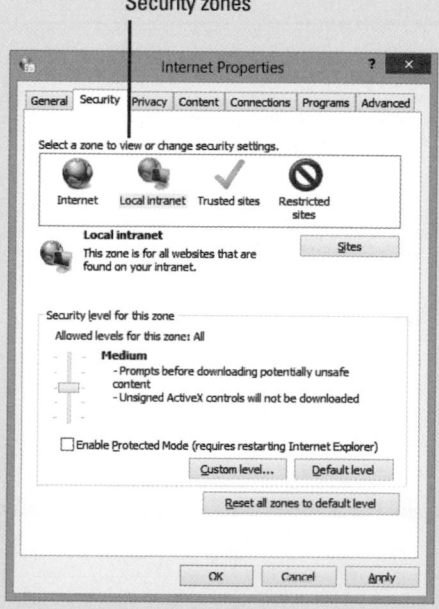

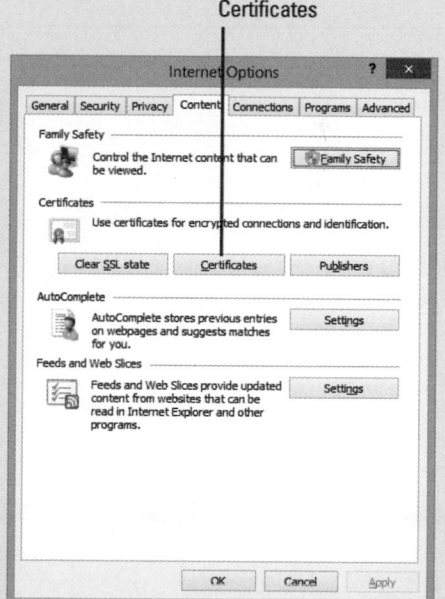

# Creating Security Zones

Internet Explorer lets you create security zones based on where information comes from. For example, you might want to restrict access to web pages that can be viewed from the Internet, but not to those sites within your company's intranet. You can specify the level of security for each of the four available security zones: Local Intranet, Trusted Sites, Restricted Sites, and Internet. When you access a web page or download content from the site, Internet Explorer checks its security settings and determines the web site's zone. Internet Explorer displays a padlock icon in the status bar to indicate the web site is secure. All Internet web sites are assigned to the Internet zone until you assign individual web sites to other zones.

## Select a Security Zone and Its Security Level

1. In the Start screen, click or tap the **Apps view** button, and then click or tap **Control Panel**.

2. Click or tap the **Internet Options** icon in Small icons or Large icons view.

3. Click or tap the **Security** tab.

4. Click or tap the zone to which you want to assign security options.

5. If you want, click or tap **Default level** to reset the settings to Microsoft's suggested level.

6. Move the slider to the level of security you want to apply.

   **TROUBLE?** *If the slider is not available, click or tap Default Level to change the security level to Medium and display the slider.*

7. If you want to specify individual security options, click or tap **Custom level**.

8. Scroll to a settings area, and then click or tap the **Enable**, **Prompt**, or **Disable** option button.

9. Click or tap **OK**.

10. Click or tap **OK**.

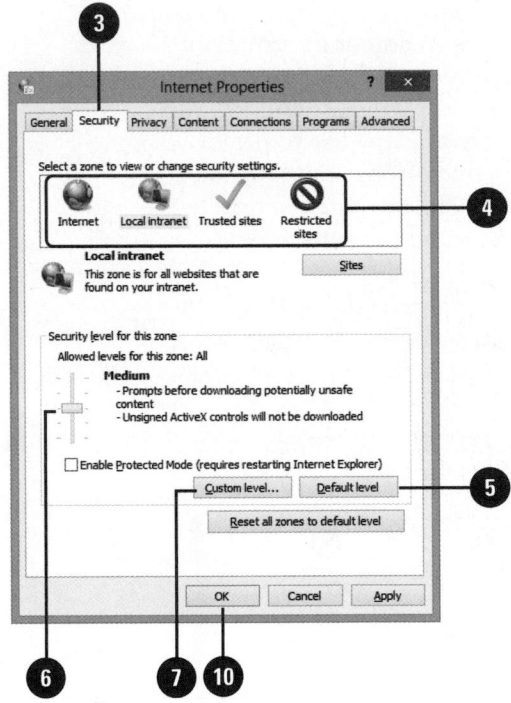

## Add Sites to Your Restricted Sites Zone

① In the Start screen, click or tap the **Apps view** button, and then click or tap **Control Panel**.

② Click or tap the **Internet Options** icon in Small icons or Large icons view.

③ Click or tap the **Security** tab.

④ Click or tap **Restricted Sites**.

⑤ Click or tap **Sites**.

⑥ Type the full URL for the site.

⑦ Click or tap **Add**.

⑧ Click or tap **Close**, and then click or tap **OK**.

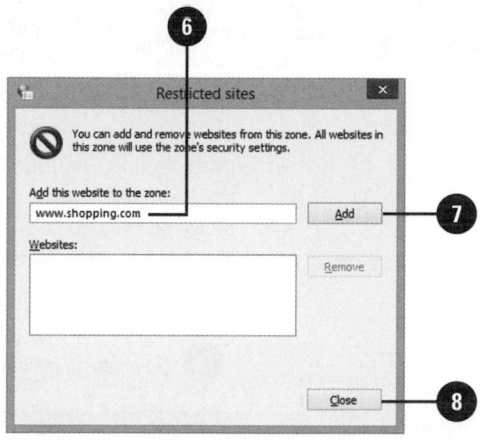

### Did You Know?

***You can reset default settings for security options.*** To return each option to its default settings for a specified security level, click or tap the Reset Custom Settings list arrow, select a level, and then click or tap Reset.

***You can remove a site from your Restricted Sites zone.*** In the Internet Properties dialog box, click or tap the Security tab, click or tap Restricted Sites, and then click or tap the Sites button. In the Web Sites box, click or tap the site you want to remove, click or tap Remove, and then click or tap OK. Click or tap OK to close the Internet Options dialog box.

***You can enable Internet Explorer protection mode in Internet Properties.*** In the Internet Properties dialog box, click or tap the Security tab, select the Enable Protected Mode (required restarting Internet Explorer) check box, and then click or tap OK.

## Security Zones

| Zone | Description |
| --- | --- |
| **Internet** | Contains all web sites that are not assigned to any other zone; default is Medium |
| **Local intranet** | Contains all web sites that are on your organization's intranet and don't require a proxy server; default is Medium |
| **Trusted sites** | Contains web sites that you trust not to threaten the security of your PC; default is Low (allows all cookies) |
| **Restricted sites** | Contains web sites that you believe threaten the security of your PC; default is High (blocks all cookies) |

# Cleaning Up Internet Files and Information

As you browse the web, Internet Explorer stores information relating to what you have provided to web sites when you log on (passwords) or fill out a form, the location of web sites you have visited (history), and preference information used by web sites (cookies). When you visit a web site, Internet Explorer saves web pages, images, media (temporary Internet files), and InPrivate filtering information for faster viewing and protection in the future. You can clean up the Internet files and information, which will also improve your PC performance. You can save web page data (cookies and temporary files) from your trusted favorites, so you don't have to restore them.

## Delete Internet Files and Information

1. In the Start screen, click or tap the **Apps view** button, and then click or tap **Control Panel**.

2. Click or tap the **Internet Options** icon in Small icons or Large icons view.

3. Click or tap the **General** tab.

4. Click or tap **Delete**.

5. Click or tap the check boxes you want to clean up your PC:

   ◆ **Preserve Favorites website data.** Keeps cookies and temporary files from your trusted favorites.

   ◆ **Temporary files.** Deletes files created while browsing.

   ◆ **Cookies.** Deletes information gathered by using web sites.

   ◆ **History.** Deletes list of web sites you have visited.

   ◆ **Form data.** Deletes saved information entered into forms.

   ◆ **Passwords.** Deletes password used for site automatic logon.

   ◆ **ActiveX Filtering and Tracking Protection Data.** Deletes saved Tracking Protection data.

6. Click or tap **Delete**.

7. Click or tap **OK**.

3 Select to delete browsing history on exit in IE

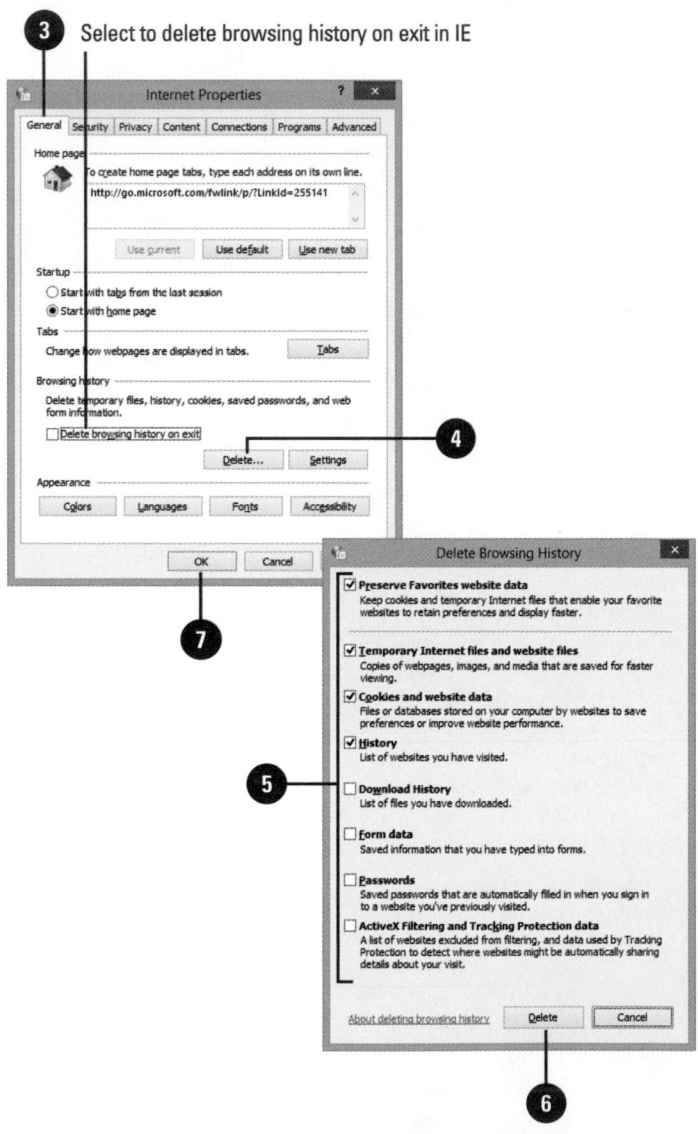

# Protecting Internet Privacy

You can set Internet privacy options to protect your personal identity from unauthorized access. The privacy options allow you to block or permit cookies for web sites in the Internet zone; however, when you block cookies, you might not be able to access all the features of a web site. When a web site violates your cookie policy, a red icon appears on the status bar. To find out if the web site you are viewing in Internet Explorer contains third-party cookies or whether any cookies have been restricted, you can get a privacy report. The privacy report lists all the web sites with content on the current Web page and shows how all the web sites handle cookies.

## Control the Use of Cookies

1. In the Start screen, click or tap the **Apps view** button, and then click or tap **Control Panel**.

2. Click or tap the **Internet Options** icon in Small icons or Large icons view.

3. Click or tap the **Privacy** tab.

4. Drag the slider to select the level of privacy you want.

5. Click or tap **OK**.

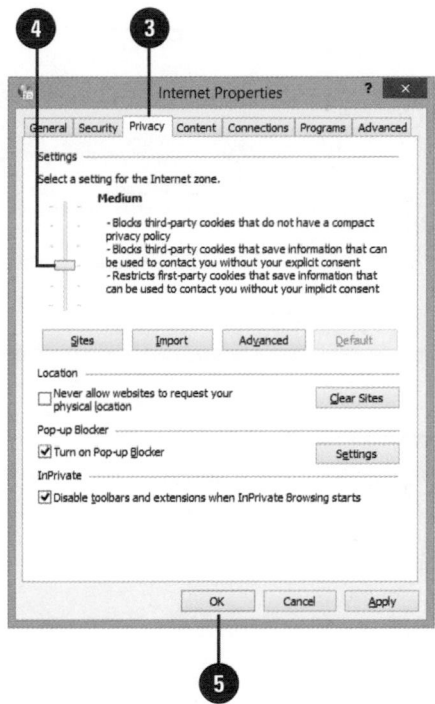

### Did You Know?

*You can delete all cookies.* In the Internet Properties dialog box, click or tap the General tab, click or tap Delete, select the Cookies check box, click or tap Delete, and then click or tap OK.

*You can get a privacy report in Internet Explorer.* Open the web page you want to view a privacy report, click or tap the Tools button on the toolbar, point to Safety, then click or tap Webpage Privacy Policy.

---

## For Your Information

### Denying Location Request from Web Sites

As you visit web sites, they can request physical location information behind the scenes. If you don't want sites to do this, you can deny their requests. In the Internet Properties dialog box, click or tap the Privacy tab, and then select the Never Allow Websites To Request Your Physical Location check box. To clear a list of sites requesting location information, click or tap Clear Sites.

# Protecting an Internet Identity

To further protect your privacy, you can use certificates to verify your identity and protect important information, such as your credit card number, on the Internet. A **certificate** is a statement verifying the identity of a person or the security of a web site. You can obtain your personal security certification from an independent Certification Authority (CA). A personal certificate verifies your identity to a secure web site that requires a certificate, while a web site certificate verifies its security to you before you send it information. When you visit a secure web site (one whose address may start with "https" instead of "http"), the site automatically sends you its certificate, and Internet Explorer displays a lock icon on the status bar. A certificate is also known as a Digital ID in other programs, such as Windows Live Mail.

## Import a Certificate

1. In the Start screen, click or tap the **Apps view** button, and then click or tap **Control Panel**.

2. Click or tap the **Internet Options** icon in Small icons or Large icons view.

3. Click or tap the **Content** tab.

4. Click or tap **Certificates**.

5. Click or tap the tab with the type of certificate you want.

6. Click or tap **Import**.

7. Follow the instructions in the Certificate Import Wizard to import a certificate.

8. Click or tap **Close**.

9. Click or tap **OK**.

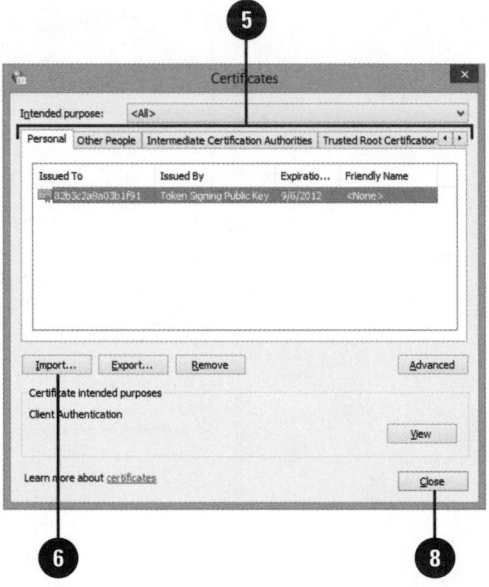

Click or tap to find out about site certificate problems

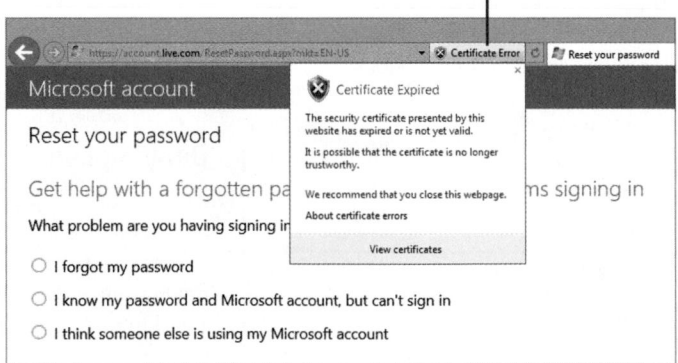

# Blocking Pop-Up Ads

The Pop-up Blocker prevents most unwanted pop-up windows from appearing. When Internet Explorer blocks an ad, a new window appears with an alert message. Blocked items are replaced in the window with a red "x". The Notification bar in Internet Explorer lets you temporarily or permanently open pop-ups, change Pop-up Blocker settings, and get help. With the Pop-up Blocker Settings dialog box, you can allow or disallow pop-ups from specific sites, play a sound or show the Notification bar when a pop-up is blocked, and set a filter level to block pop-ups.

## Set Options to Pop-Up Blocker

1. In the Start screen, click or tap the **Apps view** button, and then click or tap **Control Panel**.

2. Click or tap the **Internet Options** icon in Small icons or Large icons view.

3. Click or tap the **Privacy** tab.

4. Select the **Turn on Pop-up Blocker** check box.

   **TIMESAVER** *In Internet Explorer (desktop), click or tap the Tools menu, point to Pop-up Blocker, and then click or tap Turn off Pop-up Blocker.*

5. Click or tap **Settings**.

6. To add a pop-up exception, enter a web site address, then click or tap **Add**.

7. Select or clear check boxes to play sound or show on Notification bar when an pop-up is blocked.

8. Click or tap the **Filter level** list arrow, then click or tap a pop-up filter: **High**, **Medium**, **Low**.

9. Click or tap **Close**.

10. Click or tap **OK**.

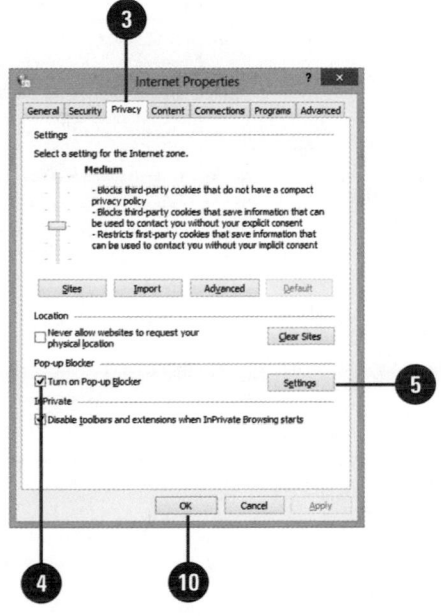

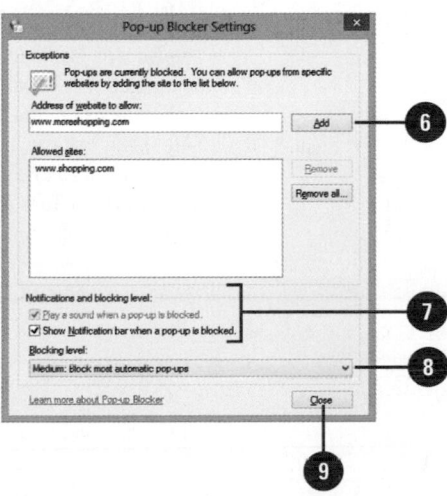

# Protecting Against Phishing

Phishing is a technique people use to trick PC users into revealing personal for financial information. Typically, a phishing scam starts with an email message that appears to come from a trusted source, such as a bank or credit card company, but actually directs recipients to provide information to a fraudulent web site. Windows and Internet Explorer provide the SmartScreen Filtering to increase security to help protect you from phishing schemes. You can set SmartScreen filtering options on the Safety menu in Internet Explorer. You can check web sites for phishing and report them to Microsoft if you think they are fraudulent.

## Protect or Unprotect Against Phishing

1. In Internet Explorer (desktop), click or tap the **Tools** button on the toolbar, and then point to **Safety**.

2. Click or tap **Turn On SmartScreen Filter** or **Turn Off SmartScreen Filter** on the menu.

3. Click or tap the **Turn on SmartScreen Filter (recommended)**, or **Turn off SmartScreen Filter** option.

4. Click or tap **OK**.

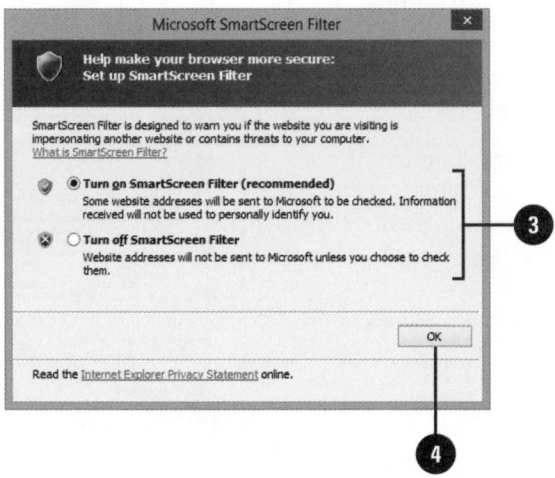

## Did You Know?

*You can browse the Internet privately.* InPrivate browsing doesn't retain or keep track of browsing history, searches, temporary Internet files, form data, cookies, and usernames and passwords. In Internet Explorer, click or tap the Tools button on the toolbar, point to Safety, and hen click or tap InPrivate Browsing. To exit InPrivate browsing, close the browser window.

*You can disable toolbar and extensions for InPrivate browsing.* In the Internet Explorer Properties dialog box, click or tap the Privacy tab, select or clear the Disable Toolbars And Extensions When InPrivate Browsing Starts check box, and then click or tap OK.

## For Your Information

### Blocking Sites with Do No Track

The Do Not Track option blocks requests from websites and advertising platforms from collecting user data. In Internet Explorer (desktop), click or tap the Tools button on the toolbar, and then point to Safety, click or tap Turn On Do Not Track Requests (**New!**) or Turn Off Do Not Track Requests (**New!**) on the menu, and then click or tap Turn On or Turn Off. You'll need to restart Internet Explorer to enable or disable Do No Track.

## Check and Report a Web Site for Phishing

**1** In Internet Explorer (desktop), click or tap the **Tools** button on the toolbar, and then point to **Safety**.

**2** Click or tap the command you want to perform:

◆ **Check This Website.** Click or tap **Check This Website**, click or tap **OK**, and then respond to the alerts as needed.

◆ **Report Unsafe Website.** Click or tap **Report Unsafe Website**, specify the website language, select the **I think this is a phishing website** check box, and then click or tap **Submit**.

### Did You Know?

***You can display security information in the Security Status bar.*** While you browse the web, Internet Explorer automatically checks for valid web site certificates and any irregularities that might indicated a possible phishing site or any unwanted or malicious programs. If Internet Explorer detects a potential problem, it displays a color warning in the Address bar with text in the Security Status bar on the right indicating the problem type. The Address bar displays red for certificate errors and known phishing sites, green for sites with high security (connected to the certificate), and yellow for suspected phishing sites. You can click or tap the security icon in the Security Status bar to find out more information and possible solutions.

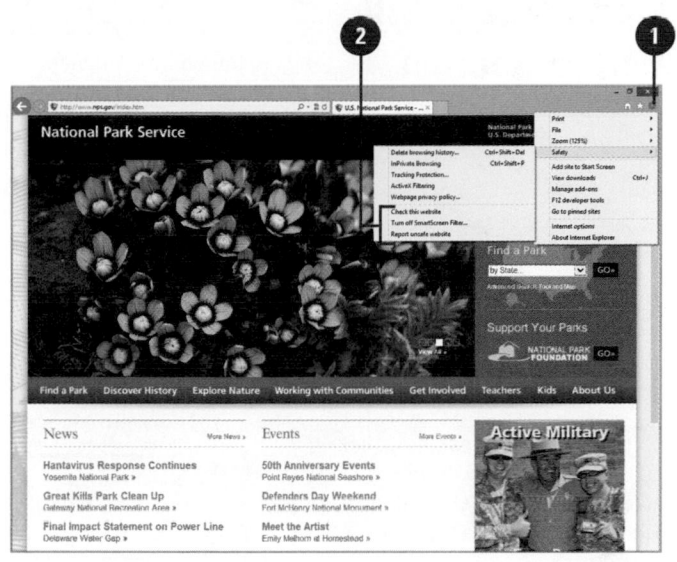

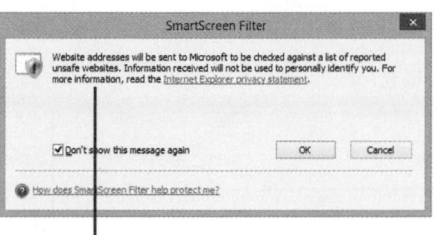

Results of check this web site

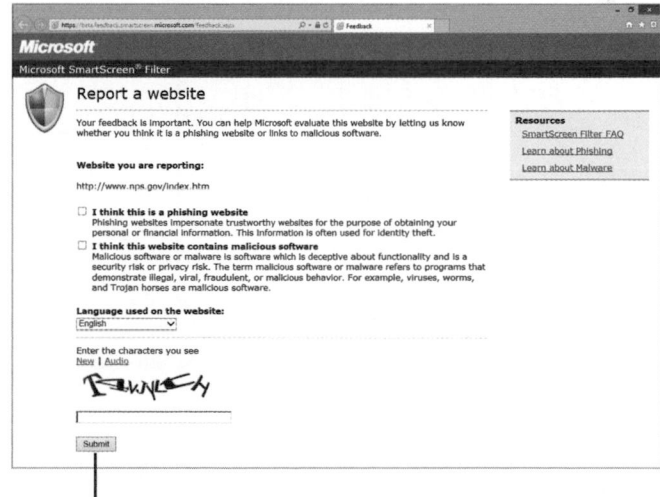

Web site to submit a possible phishing site

# Blocking Content with Tracking Protection

Tracking protection Lists (TPL) provide enhanced privacy by preventing web sites you visit from automatically sending details about your visit to the content providers. You can create a personalized list of sites to block or you can install a TPL add-on that will do it for you. When you install a TPL, a Do Not Track signal is sent to web sites and content providers not already blocked by the TPL. When Tracking Protecting is filtering content on a web site, a blue Do Not Track icon appears in the Address bar. Click or tap on the icon to turn off Tracking Protection for the current web site. If content is blocked, some portions of a web site may not be available.

## Block Content with Tracking Protection

1. In Internet Explorer (desktop), click or tap the **Tools** button on the toolbar, point to **Safety**, and then click or tap **Turn on Tracking Protection**.

2. If prompted to install a TPL, click or tap **Get a Tracking Protection List online**, click or tap **Add** for the TPL you want, and then click or tap **Add List**.

3. Click or tap **Tracking Protection**.

4. To enable or disable, or remove an installed TPL add-on, select the TPL add-on, and then click or tap **Enable**, **Disable**, or **Remove**.

5. To use your personal list, select **Your Personalized List**, do any of the following:

   ◆ **Enable** or **Disable**. Enables or disables the use of your personalized list.

   ◆ **Settings**. Allows you to select options to automatically block or choose content to block or allow. Select the options you want, and then click or tap OK.

6. Click or tap **Close**.

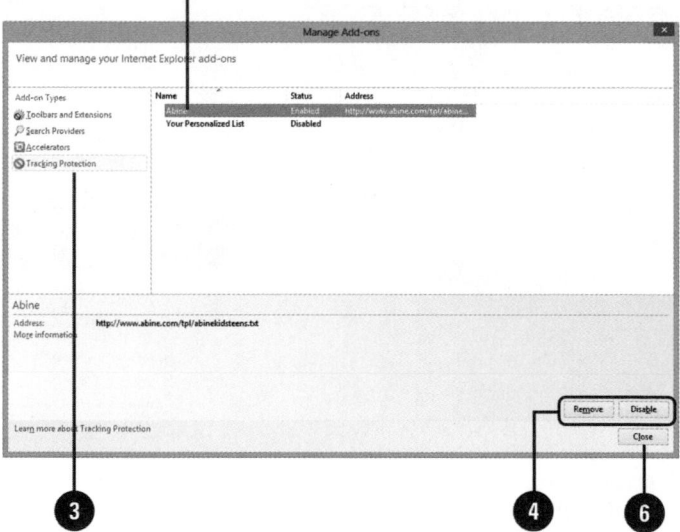

Installed and selected TPL

# Managing Add-Ons

Add-ons are programs that extend the functionality of Internet Explorer to perform a unique task, such as provide search toolbars or display Flash content. In most cases, add-ons are useful, but sometimes poorly built or old ones can slow down your PC, cause system crashes, or invade your privacy (such as Spyware or Adware that are sometimes deceptively installed). To help you work with add-ons, Internet Explorer includes the Add-on Manager, which provides a list of add-ons currently loaded or used by Internet Explorer. they are grouped into types: Toolbars and Extensions, Search Providers, Accelerators, and Tracking Protection. You can use the Add-on Manager to individually enable, disable, or update add-ons. The Add-on Manager can also detect add-ons related crashes in Internet Explorer and displays an option to disable it.

## Manage Browser Add-Ons

1. In the Start screen, click or tap the **Apps view** button, and then click or tap **Control Panel**.

2. Click or tap the **Internet Options** icon in Small icons or Large icons view.

3. Click or tap the **Programs** tab.

4. Click or tap **Manage add-ons**.

   **TIMESAVER** *In Internet Explorer (desktop), click or tap the Tools button on the toolbar, and then click or tap Manage add-ons.*

5. Click or tap the type of add-ons you want to display.

6. Click or tap the **Show** list arrow, and then click or tap the option with the type of add-ons you want to display.

7. Click or tap the add-on you want to manage.

8. Click or tap **Enable** or **Disable**.

9. Click or tap **Close**.

10. Click or tap **OK**.

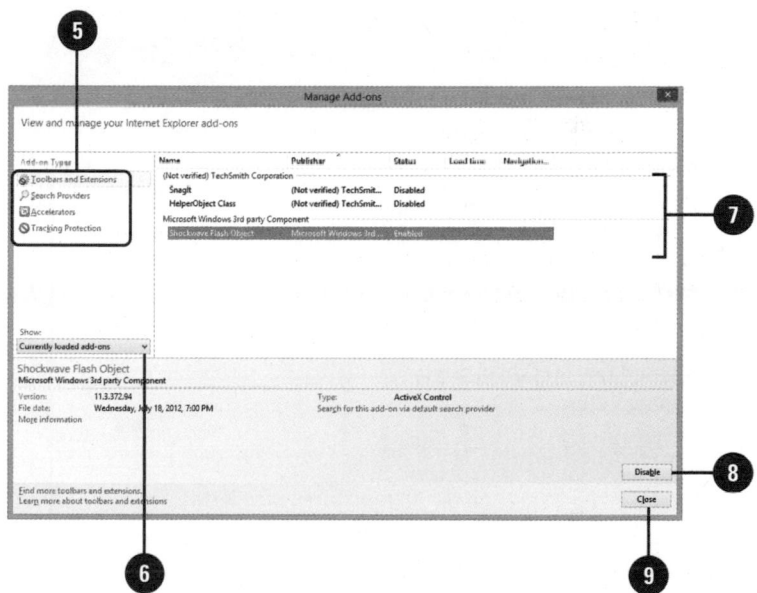

# Protecting Privacy with IE App

Before you start browsing and searching the web, you should take a look at the privacy settings and make any adjustments to make sure your personal data is protected. You set options to block content from services that could track your browsing (**New!**), send Do Not Track requests to sites (**New!**), block third-party cookies (**New!**), and let sites ask for my physical location. Web services allow you to improve your browsing experience by sharing information with Microsoft. You set options to flip ahead with page prediction (share history), suggestions as I type (**New!**), protect my PC from malware and phishing sites with SmartScreen (**New!**), and play protected media (**New!**) with downloaded licenses, identifiers, and data.

## Change IE App Privacy Settings

1. Click or tap the **Internet Explorer** tile on the Start screen.

2. Point to the lower- or upper-right corner and up or move down (on a computer) or swipe left from the right edge of the screen (on a mobile device).

3. Click or tap the **Settings** button on the Charms bar, and then click or tap **Privacy** on the Settings panel.

4. Specify any of the following options (**New!**):

   ◆ Tracking Protecting. Add protection list, and then drag the slider to turn on or off.

   ◆ Do Not Track. Drag the slider to turn on or off send requests.

   ◆ Cookies. Drag the slider to turn on or off to block cookies.

   ◆ Location. Drag the slider to turn on or off to ask for my location.

5. Under web services (**New!**), drag the slider to turn on or off the service: **Flip ahead with page prediction**, **Suggestions**, **SmartScreen**, and **Protected media playback**.

   For Protected media playback, you can delete credentials that might prevent you from accessing media.

6. Click or tap a blank area of the screen to exit the panel.

Back button to Settings panel

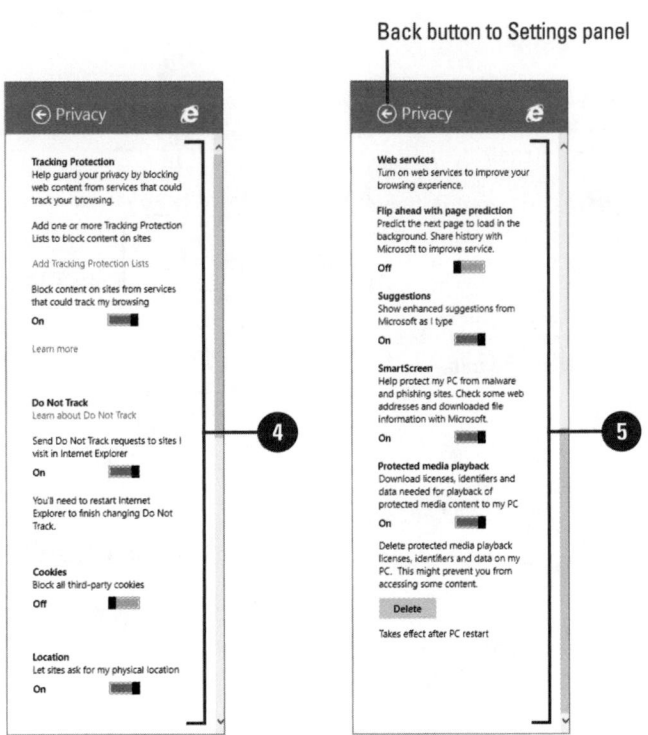

# Managing Files Using a Network

## Introduction

Windows 8.1 comes with many tools for managing files and folders across multiple PCs. One of the more powerful tools is the Network and Sharing Center. A **network** is a system of two or more PC computers and other mobile devices connected together to share resources. It consists of at least one host and one client. Using the Network folder, you can view the entire network (hosts and clients), share files and folders with people from other parts of the network, and create and manage your network connections. This chapter helps you set up your host and client PCs so they can easily share files across your network.

If you have two or more PCs connected together in a local network running Windows 8.1, you can create a homegroup, which makes it easy to share music, pictures, video, and document libraries. With a network, you can use the Share tab in a File Explorer window to easily share files and folders.

In addition, Windows provides tools for sharing files and folders with PCs that are not located in your home or in the same office (commonly referred to as remote desktops). You can connect your PC to a network in a different location via modem, or via the Internet using the Communications accessory provided. With wireless technology, such as laptop PCs or Bluetooth-enabled devices (keyboards, cell phones, and PDAs), you can seamlessly setup, discover and connect to wireless networks. You can also share and synchronize files between your laptop and your desktop PCs.

## What You'll Do

**Understand Network Services**

**View a Network**

**View the Network and Sharing Center**

**View Network Computer and Connection Properties**

**Join a Workgroup or Domain Network**

**Connect to a Network Using a Modem**

**Connect to a Network over the Internet**

**Connect to a Wireless Network**

**Set Up a Wireless Network**

**Disable or Enable a Wireless Network**

**Manage a Wireless Connection**

**Disconnect a Network**

**Map and Disconnect a Network Drive**

**Create a Shortcut to a Network**

**Share an Internet Connection**

**Set HomeGroup Sharing Options**

**Share with a Homegroup**

**Keep Files in Sync**

**Work with Offline Files**

**Control a Remote Desktop**

**Sync Files at a Workplace Network**

**Connect Devices to a Workplace Network**

# Understanding Network Services

Windows is a secure, reliable network operating system that allows people using many different PCs to share resources, such as programs, files, folders, printers, and an Internet connection. A single PC on the network, called a **server**, can be designated to store these resources. Other PCs on the network, called **clients** or **workstations**, can access the resources on the server instead of having to store them. You can share resources using two or more client PCs, or you can designate one PC to serve specifically as the server. If the workstation PCs are close together in a single building or group of buildings, the network is called a **local area network (LAN)**. If the workstation PCs are spread out in multiple buildings or throughout the entire country using dial-up or wireless connections, the network is called a **wide area network (WAN)**. To set up a network with multiple PCs, you need to install a network adapter for each PC on your network and connect each PC to a network hub using network cable or wireless technology, known as Wi-Fi. Network adapters are usually hardware cards, called **network interface cards**, or **NICs**, inserted in a slot, or **USB (Universal Serial Bus)**, port in the back of your PC that connects it to the network. A **network hub** is a hardware device that connects multiple PCs at a central location. When data arrives at one port of the network hub, it is copied to the other ports so that all connected network devices see the data. If you have two LANs or two sections of the same LAN on different floors of the same building with different network adapter types, you can connect them together with a hardware device called a **bridge**. If you have any number of LANs, you can connect them together with a hardware device called a **router**. If you want to share a printer or Internet connection with the PCs on a network, you simply connect the printer or modem to the server, a PC on the network, or directly to a network hub, router, or bridge.

## Share central resources through client/server networking

Windows offers a network configuration called **client/server networking**. Under this arrangement, a single PC is designated as a server, allowing access to resources for any qualified user. Client/server networking provides all users on a network a central location for accessing shared files. In a client/server network, individual PCs are often grouped into domains. A **domain** is a collection of PCs that the person managing the network creates in order to group together the PCs to simplify the set up and maintenance of the network. The network administrator defines the domains that exist on the network and controls access to PCs within those domains.

**Domain**

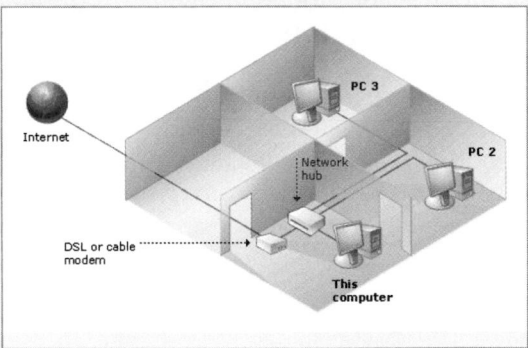

## Share resources through peer-to-peer networking

Windows also offers a network configuration called **peer-to-peer networking**. Peer-to-peer networking enables two or more PCs to link together without designating a central server. In a peer-to-peer network, individual PCs are often organized into workgroups. A **workgroup** is a group of PCs that perform common tasks or belong to users who share common duties and interests. In this configuration, any PC user can access resources stored on any other PC, as long as those resources are available for sharing. Peer-to-peer networking allows individual PC users to share files and other resources, such as a printer, with other users on the network without having to access a server. Workgroups are available on all Windows PCs.

**Workgroup**

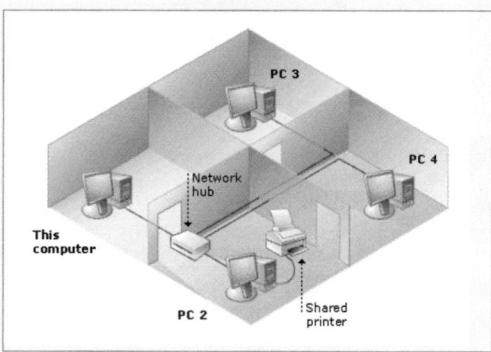

## Share resources through network connections

Windows provides connectivity between your PC and a network, another PC, or the Internet using **Network Connections**. Whether you are physically connected using a direct cable or connected remotely using a dial-up or cable modem, you can connect securely to a network over the Internet using a **Virtual Private Network (VPN)** connection or set up your PC to let other PCs connect to yours using an **incoming network connection**. VPN and incoming network connection are examples of WANs.

## Share designated files and folders on your PC with other network users

Windows provides support for security, so even though your PC is connected to a network, you can designate which resources on your PC you want to share with others. Before network users can use any resources on your PC, they must be granted the required permission.

**Wireless**

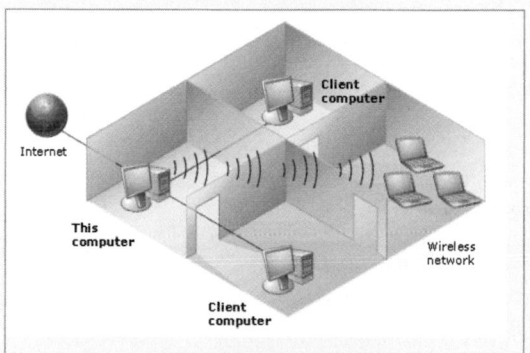

# Viewing a Network

The key to managing files and folders in a network environment is understanding the structure of your particular network. Most networks consist of multiple types of PCs and operating systems. The Network folder available in File Explorer lets you view the entire network or just your part of the network, to give you access to the servers, domains, and workgroups on the network. The Network folder also displays shared folders available on your network. If you're working on a domain network, you can use Active Search Directory to help you find network resources, such as PC and printers.

## View a Workgroup or Domain Network

1. In the Start screen, click or tap the **Apps view** button, and then click or tap **This PC**.

2. Click or tap **Network** in the Navigation pane.

3. If a Network discovery and file sharing information bar appears, click or tap the bar, and then click or tap **Turn on network discovery and file sharing**.

4. Double-click or double-tap a network icon to display the shared files, folders, and devices on the network PC.

5. When you're done, click or tap the **Close** button.

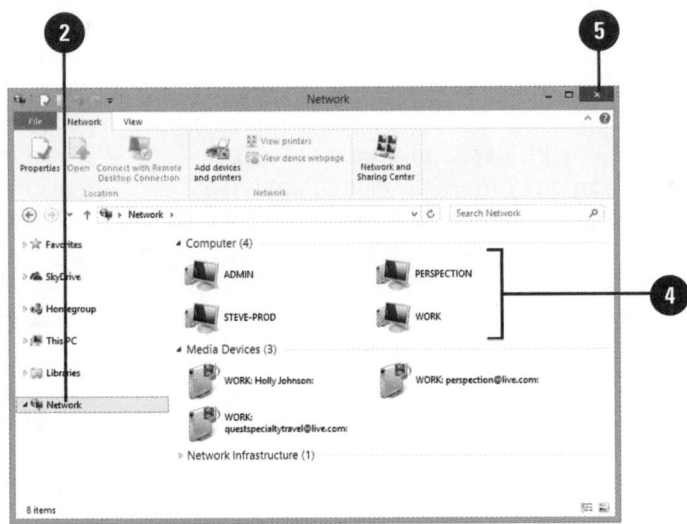

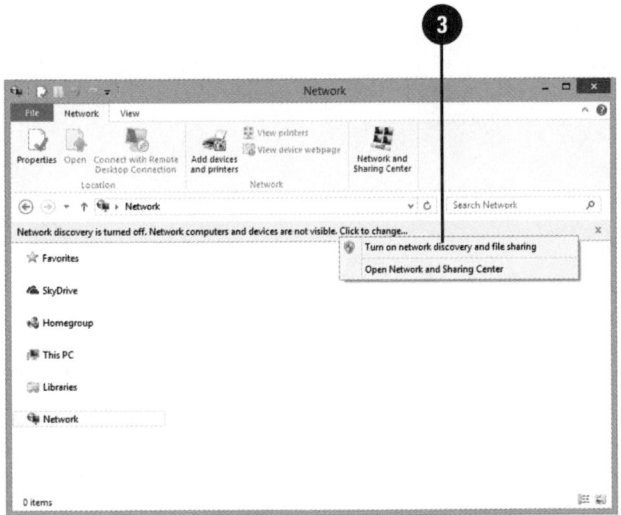

### Did You Know?

***A domain network and a workgroup are different.*** A domain network is a group of PCs connected together to share and manage resources by an administrator from a central PC called a domain controller. A workgroup is a network of PCs connected together to share resources, but each PC is maintained and shared separately.

## View a Shared Folder

1. In the Start screen, click or tap the **Apps view** button, and then click or tap **This PC**.

2. Click or tap **Network** in the Navigation pane.

3. Double-click or double-tap a network icon.

   ◆ If prompted, enter a username and password.

4. Double-click or double-tap a shared folder to display the shared files and folders in the folder.

5. When you're done, click or tap the **Close** button.

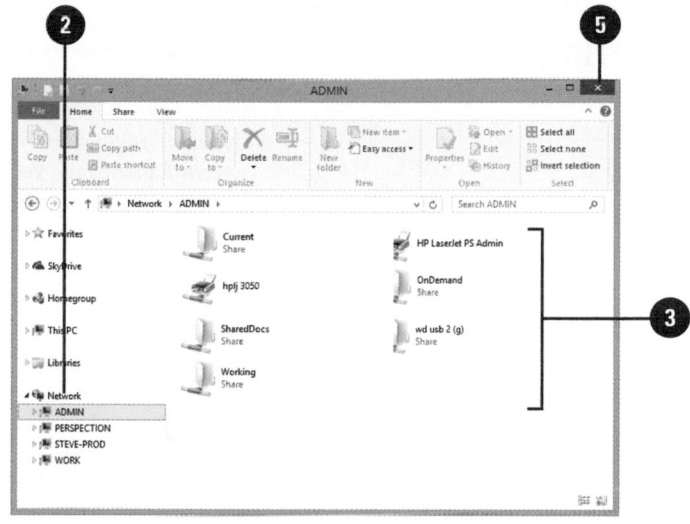

## Search a Domain Network

1. In the Start screen, click or tap the **Apps view** button, and then click or tap **This PC**.

2. Click or tap **Network** in the Navigation pane.

3. Click or tap the **Search Active Directory** button on the Computer tab, if available.

   **TIMESAVER** *Press Win+Ctrl+F to open the dialog box.*

4. Click or tap the **Find** list arrow, and then select the network resource you want to find.

5. Click or tap the **In** list arrow, and then select where you want to search.

6. Specify the criteria for the search; tabs and information vary.

7. Click or tap **Find Now**.

8. When you're done, click or tap the **Close** button.

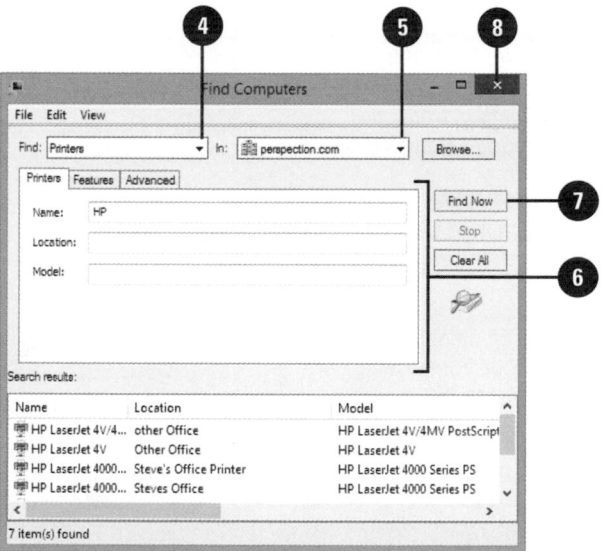

# Viewing the Network and Sharing Center

The Network and Sharing Center provides a central location where you can view and modify network and sharing options for the PC connected to a network. From a network perspective, you can view a map of the network, view network connection status information, change the network location type (either Public or Private: Work or Home), and specify whether you want others on the network to see you, known as **network discovery**. When you connect to a network for the first time, Windows automatically detects it and asks you to choose a network location. When you change the network location, Windows automatically changes firewall settings for the type of network. In addition to viewing and setting network options, you can also turn sharing options on and off.

## View Network and Choose Network a Location

1. In the Start screen, click or tap the **Apps view** button, and then click or tap **Control Panel**.

2. Click or tap the **Network and Sharing Center** icon in Small icons or Large icons view.

   **TIMESAVER** *In the desktop, right-click or tap-hold the Network icon in the notification area, and then click or tap Open Network And Sharing Center.*

3. In the left pane, click or tap **Change advanced sharing settings**.

4. Click or tap the turn on options you want for Network discovery, File and printer sharing, and Public folder sharing.

   ◆ **Expand or Collapse.** Click the arrow to expand or collapse options.

5. Click or tap **Save changes**.

6. When you're done, click or tap the **Close** button.

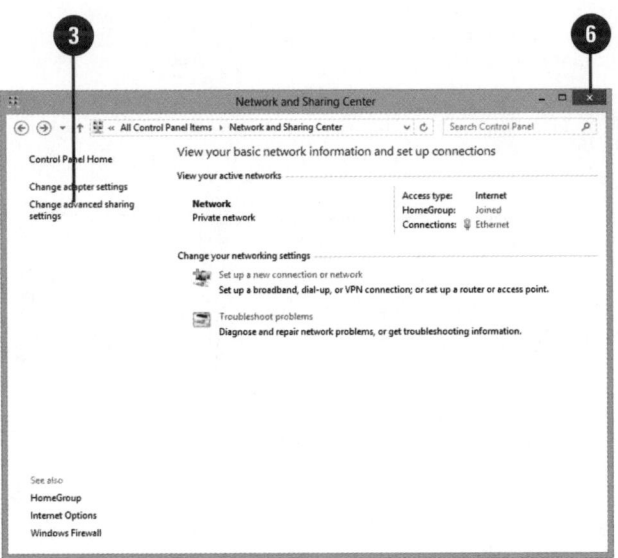

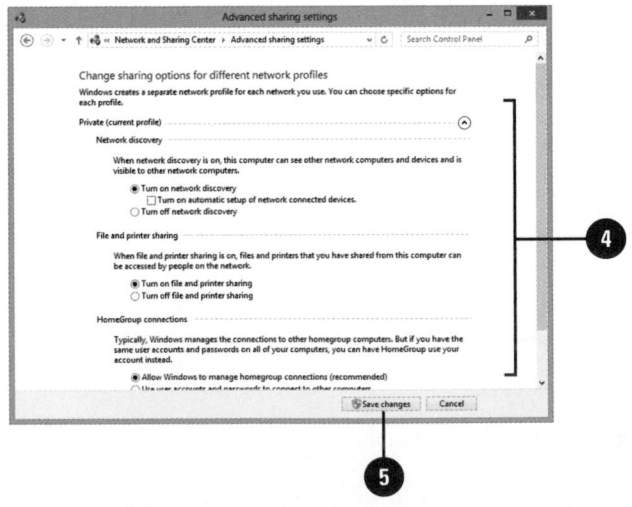

# Viewing Network Connections

You can have multiple network connections on your device. For example, with a laptop PC, you can have a wireless (Wi-Fi) connection and ethernet broadband connection with a cable. You can view all your connections by using the Network button on the Settings panel or on the taskbar (desktop) in the notifications area. The list of available networks appears on the Networks panel, where you can select one for use.

## View and Select Network Connections

1. Display the Start screen.

2. Point to the lower- or upper-right corner and move up or down (on a computer) or swipe left from the right edge of the screen (on a mobile device).

3. Click or tap the **Settings** button on the Charms bar.

4. Click or tap **Network** on the Settings panel.

   A list of available network connections appear on the Networks panel.

5. To select a network, click or tap a network connection.

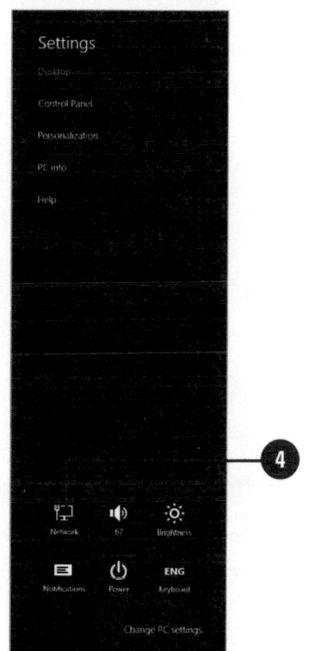 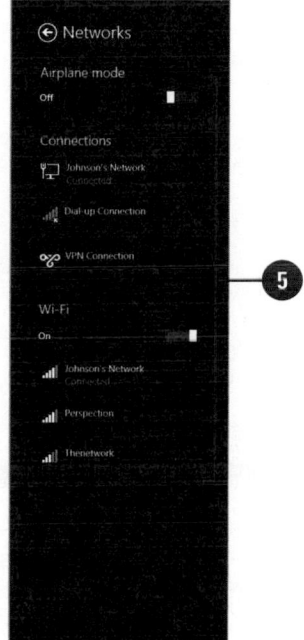

## Did You Know?

*You can use the Network icon in the notification area to access networks.* To view current networks, click or tap the Network icon on the taskbar (desktop) in the notification area.

*You can right-click or tap-hold the Network icon to troubleshoot problems.* In the desktop, right-click or tap-hold the Network icon on the taskbar in the notification area, and then click or tap Troubleshoot Problems to start the Windows Network diagnostics wizard.

## For Your Information

### Networking with Windows Firewall

For security purposes, Windows Firewall is turned on (the default setting) to protect your PC against security threats, such as viruses, worms, and Trojan Horses, spread over the Internet or a network. Windows automatically sets Windows Firewall settings to be compatible with your network. However, you might need to make adjustments for some programs, such as Internet games, to allow them to work properly. See "Setting Up Windows Firewall" on page 134 for more information.

# Viewing Network Properties

Names and locations are used to identify computers on a network. The computer's name refers to the individual machine, and the computer's location refers to how the machine is grouped together with other PCs. Computers anywhere on the network can be located easily through the naming hierarchy and can be addressed individually by name. You can find the name and workgroup or domain of a computer on the network by examining the system properties. Workgroups and domains are available on all Windows PCs.

## View Network Properties

1. In the Start screen, click or tap the **Apps view** button, and then click or tap **This PC**.

2. Click or tap the **System properties** button on the Computer tab.

   The System window opens, displaying information about Windows edition, system, PC, and Windows activation.

3. Click or tap **Change settings**.

   The System Properties dialog box opens.

4. Click or tap the **Computer Name** tab.

5. To add a computer description, type a description.

6. To change a workgroup or domain, click or tap **Change**, specify a new name, and then click or tap **OK**.

7. Click or tap **OK**.

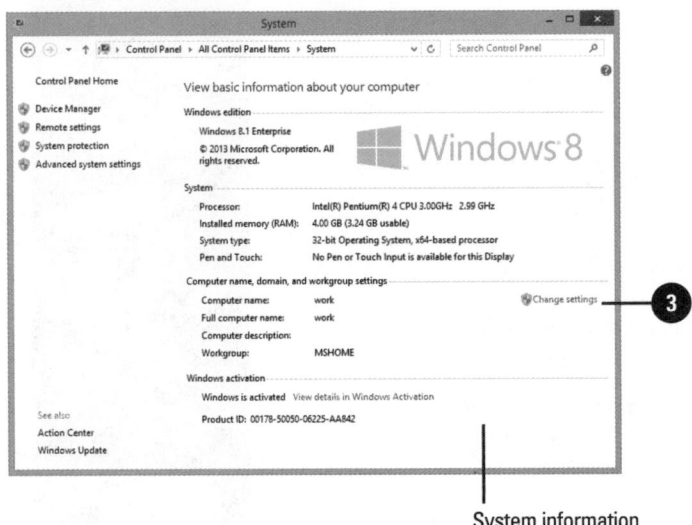

System information

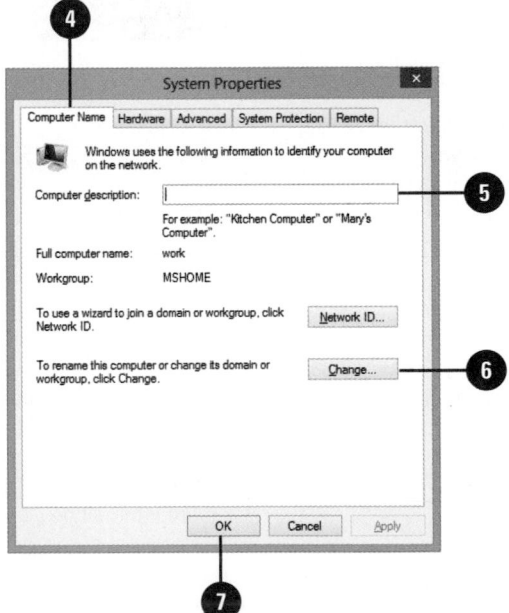

> **See Also**
>
> See "Running Commands" on page 288 for information on finding the IP configuration of a PC, and pinging another PC.

# Viewing Network Connection Properties

A PC that uses a network must be configured so that other machines on the network recognize it. Unless there is a problem, Windows handles it for you. You can view the status of the network connection and modify some of the network settings for your PC using the Network Connections window. A network connection consists of a network adapter and three types of components: client, service, and protocol. The **client** type allows you to access PCs and files on the network. The **service** type allows you to share your PC resources, such as files and printers, with other networked PCs. **Protocol** is the language that the PC uses to communicate with other PCs on the network, such as TCP/IP. Knowing which components are installed on your PC helps you understand the capabilities and limitations of your PC on the network.

## View Network Connection Properties

1. In the Start screen, click or tap the **Apps view** button, and then click or tap **Control Panel**.

2. Click or tap the **Network and Sharing Center** icon in Small icons or Large icons view.

3. In the left pane, click or tap **Change adapter settings**.

4. Double-click or double-tap the network connection you want to get status information.

    **TIMESAVER** *In the Network And Sharing Center, you can also click or tap Local Area Connection or Wireless Network Connection.*

5. If you have problems with your connection, click or tap **Diagnose**.

6. To display network components installed and enabled, click or tap **Properties**.

7. When you're done working with the components, click or tap **OK**.

8. Click or tap **Close**.

9. Click or tap the **Close** button.

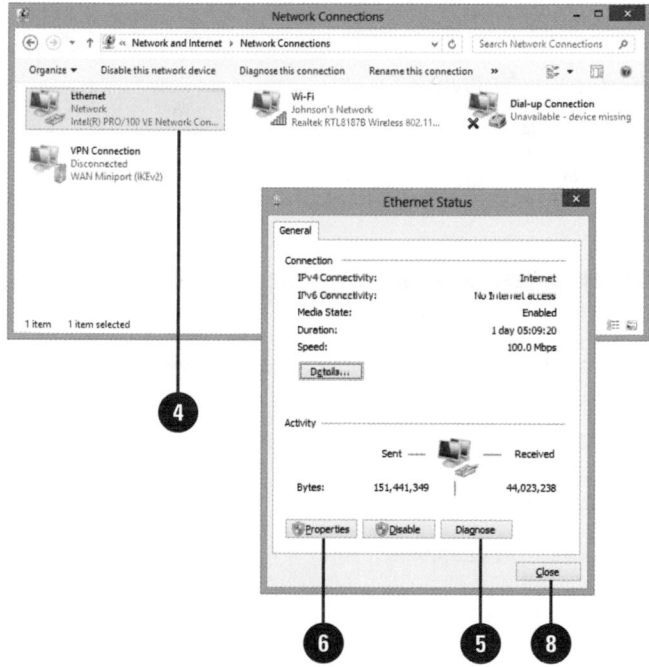

## For Your Information

### Using Network Diagnostics

If you're having problems connecting to networks or sharing files, you can use Network Diagnostics to help you identify the problem and suggest options for fixing it. Right-click or tap-hold the Network icon in the notification area on the taskbar, and then click or tap Troubleshoot Problems. Review your options, and then select the best one available. If a fix is not possible, you can report the problem to Microsoft.

# Joining a Workgroup Network

Before you can set up and configure a network at home or small office, you need to physically attach the hardware so the PCs can communicate. This includes installing the network cards in all the PCs, connecting the PCs together using cables or wireless technology, installing a modem on the host PC, turning on all PCs, printers, and external modems, and establishing a connection to the Internet. A home or small office network is typically a peer-to-peer network where individual PCs are organized into workgroups with a host and several clients. The host is a computer on the network who shares an Internet connection with the other client PCs on the network. The host computer must be turned on whenever a client PC needs to access the Internet. To join a workgroup, you can use the Join a Domain or Workgroup wizard in System Properties. After you join, you can change the workgroup name to match the other ones in your network.

## Join a Workgroup Network Using a Wizard

1. In the Start screen, click or tap the **Apps view** button, and then click or tap **This PC**.

2. Click or tap the **System properties** button on the Computer tab, and then click or tap **Change settings**.

3. Click or tap the **Computer Name** tab.

4. Click or tap **Network ID**, and then click or tap **Next** to continue.

5. Click or tap the **This is a home computer; it's not part of a business network** option, and then click or tap **Next** to continue.

6. Click or tap **Finish**, and then restart your PC.

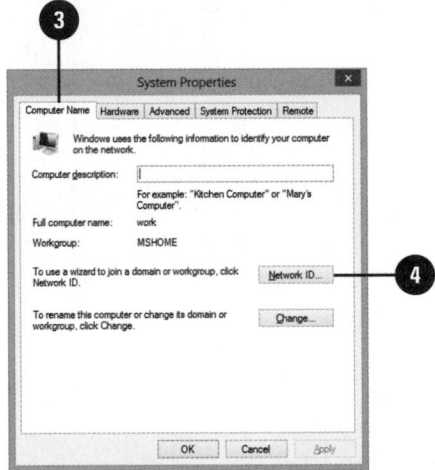

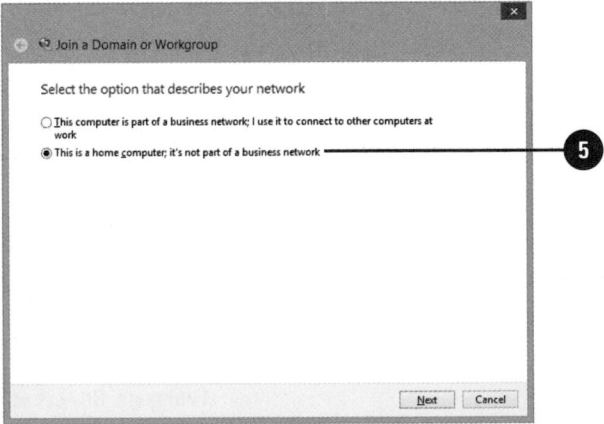

## Change a Workgroup Network Name

1. In the Start screen, click or tap the **Apps view** button, and then click or tap **This PC**.

2. Click or tap the **System properties** button on the toolbar, and then click or tap **Change settings**.

3. Click or tap the **Computer Name** tab.

4. Click or tap **Change**.

5. Click or tap the **Workgroup** option.

6. Type the workgroup name.

7. Click or tap **OK**.

8. Click or tap **OK**.

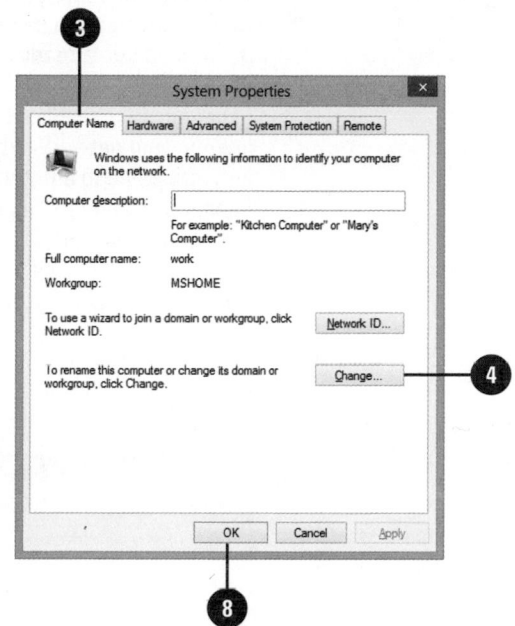

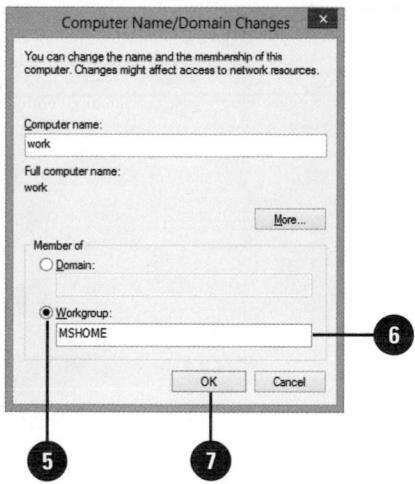

# Joining a Domain Network

If you are not connected to a domain network, you can use the Join a Domain or Workgroup wizard to join a domain and create a local user account. If you already have a user account, you can use System Properties to join a domain. Before you join a domain, you need to connect your PC computer to a client/server network using a network adapter and network cable or wireless technology. After you plug in a network cable to a network adapter, Windows detects the network connection and creates a local area connection as needed. A local area connection is the only type of network connection that Windows automatically creates. Depending on your hardware setup, your Join a Domain or Workgroup wizard options might differ.

## Join a Domain Network

1. In the Start screen, click or tap the **Apps view** button, and then click or tap **This PC**.

2. Click or tap the **System properties** button on the toolbar, and then click or tap **Change settings**.

3. Click or tap the **Computer Name** tab.

4. Click or tap **Change**.

5. Click or tap the **Domain** option.

6. Type the domain name.

7. Click or tap **OK**.

8. Click or tap **OK**.

### See Also

See *"Connecting Devices to a Workplace Network"* on page 416 for information on connecting devices to a company network.

See *"Syncing Files on a Workplace Network"* on page 414 for information on sharing files on a company network.

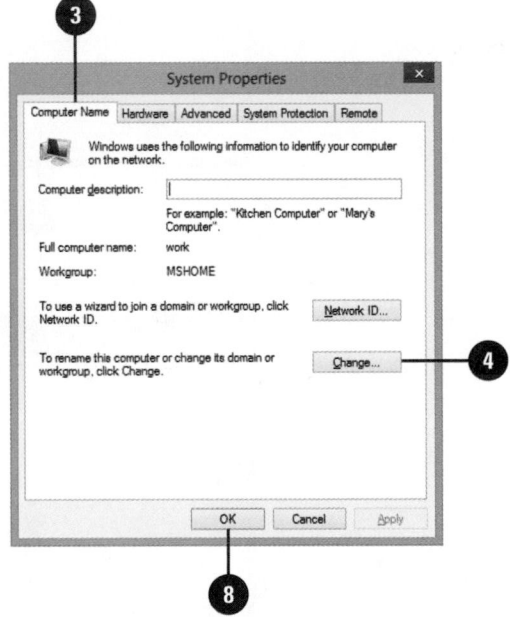

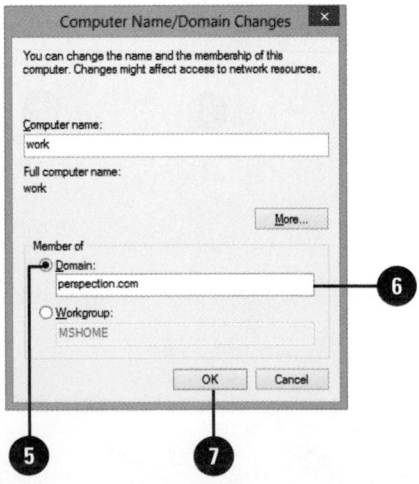

## Join a Domain Network and Create a User Account

1. In the Start screen, click or tap the **Apps view** button, and then click or tap **This PC**.

2. Click or tap the **System properties** button on the toolbar, and then click or tap **Change settings**.

3. Click or tap the **Computer Name** tab.

4. Click or tap **Network ID**, and then click or tap **Next** to continue.

5. Click or tap the **This computer is part of a business network** option, and then click or tap **Next** to continue.

6. Click or tap the **My company uses a network with a domain** option, and then click or tap **Next** to continue.

7. Read the page, and then click or tap **Next** to continue.

8. Type a username and password.

9. Type a domain name, and then click or tap **Next** to continue.

10. Type a computer name and domain name, and then click or tap **Next** to continue.

11. Click or tap the **Add the following user** option, and then click or tap **Next** to continue.

12. Click or tap an access user level, and then click or tap **Next** to continue.

13. Click or tap **Finish**, and then restart your PC.

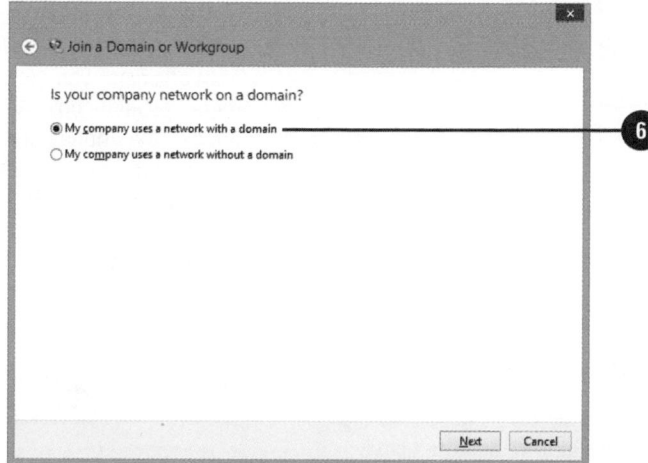

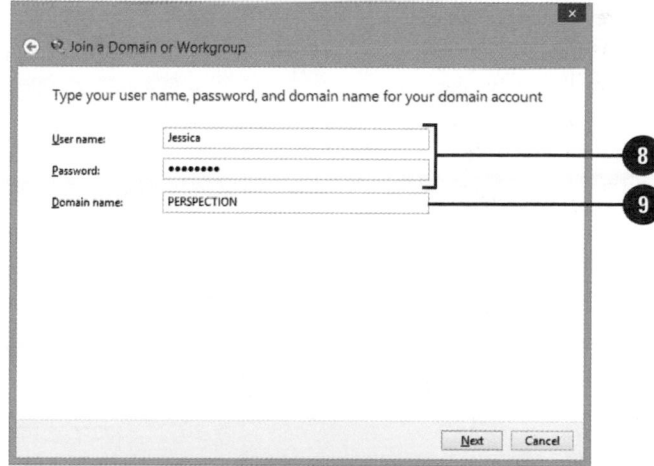

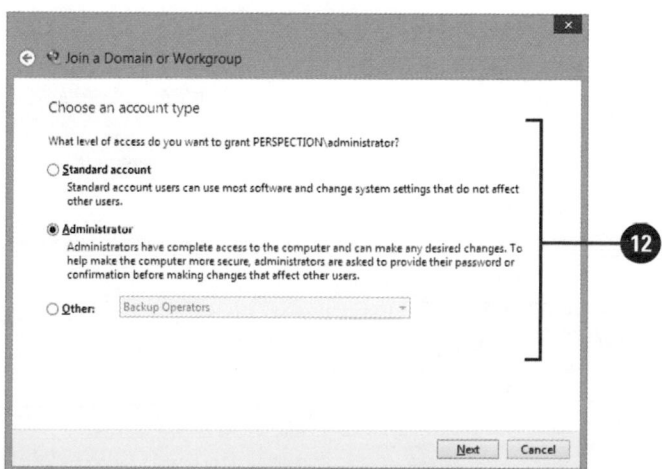

# Connecting to a Network Using a Modem

If you don't have a broadband or wireless connection and need to use a phone modem, you can use a connection wizard to set up a dial-up connection, which is slow, however it's a way to connect to the Internet or network. After you create a dial-up connection, you can change the settings to specify how Windows creates a dial-up connection. You can change the phone number, add dialing rules, and modify redial and hang up settings. You can use the Network icon in the notification area on the taskbar and on the Settings panel to select the dial-up connection to establish an Internet or network connection. You can click or tap the icon to display information available connections, and quickly connect to or disconnect from anyone of them.

## Create a Dial-Up Connection

1. In the Start screen, click or tap the **Apps view** button, and then click or tap **Control Panel**.

2. Click or tap the **Network and Sharing Center** icon in Small icons or Large icons view.

3. Click or tap **Set up a new connection or network**.

4. Click or tap **Connect to a workplace**, and then click or tap **Next** to continue.

5. Click or tap **Dial Directly**, and then click or tap **Next** to continue.

   ◆ If prompted, click or tap **Set up a connection anyway**.

6. Type the phone number for calling the network.

7. To share this network connection, select the **Allow other people to use this connection** check box.

8. Click or tap **Next** to continue.

9. Type username, password and domain name.

   ◆ To remember the password, select the **Remember this password** check box.

10. Click or tap **Create**.

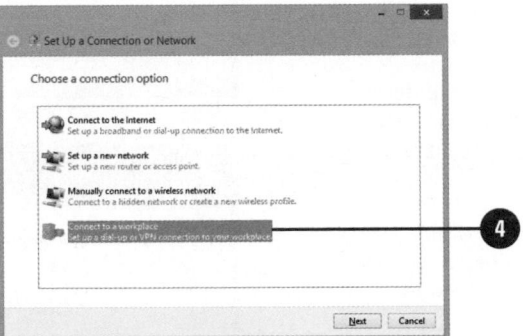

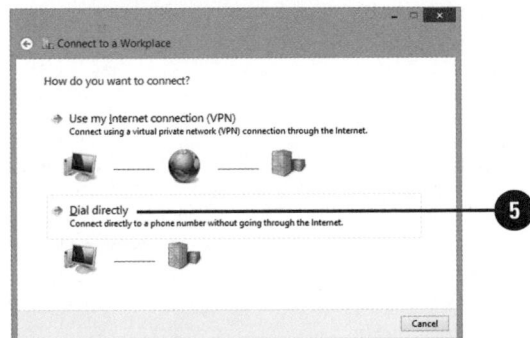

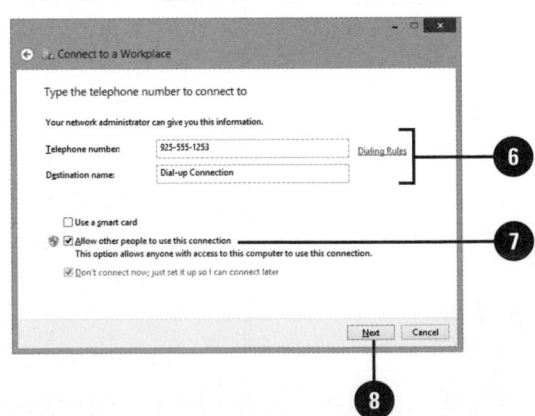

## Establish a Dial-Up Connection

1. In the Start screen, click or tap the **Settings** button on the Charms bar, and then click or tap **Network**.

   ◆ In the desktop, click or tap the **Network** icon in the notification area on the taskbar.

2. Select the dial up connection, and then click or tap **Connect**.

3. Type your assigned username and password.

4. Click or tap **OK**, and then wait for the connection.

5. When you're done, click or tap the **Network** icon, select the connection, and then click or tap **Disconnect**.

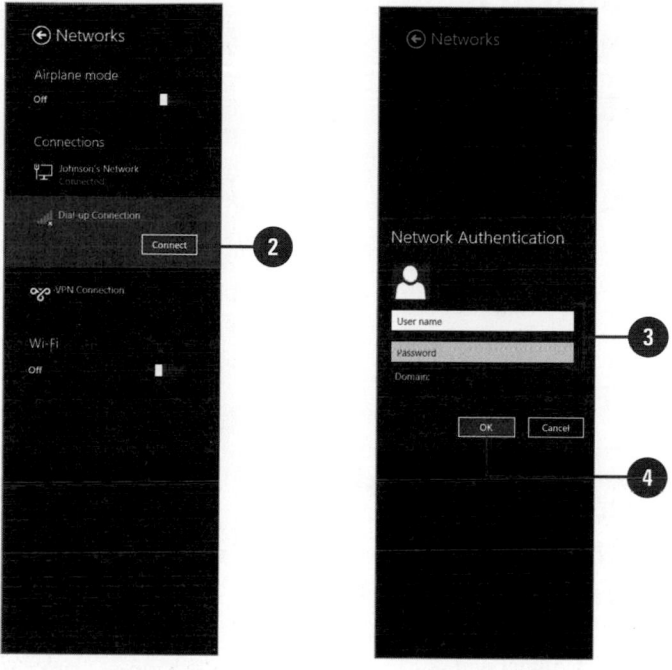

## Change a Dial-Up Connection

1. Click or tap the **Network** icon in the notification area on the taskbar, and then click or tap **Open Network and Sharing Center**.

2. In the left pane, click or tap **Change adapter settings**.

3. Right-click or tap-hold the **Dial-Up connection** icon, and then click or tap **Properties**.

4. Click or tap the **General** tab.

5. To change the number, enter a new number.

6. To use dialing rules, select the **Use dialog rules** check box, and then specify area and country codes.

7. To set redialing settings, click or tap the Options tab.

8. Click or tap **OK**.

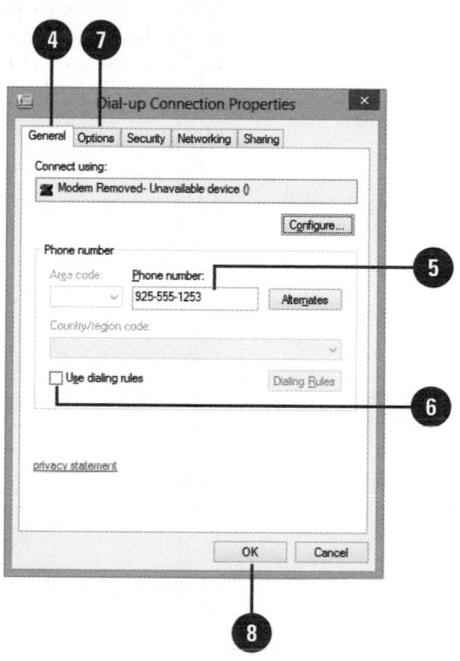

# Connecting to a Network over the Internet

You can create a VPN (Virtual Private Network) connection to connect to a network over the Internet. A VPN provides a secure connection between your PC computer and the network. The PC computer to which you want to connect must support a VPN and Internet connection. Before you create a connection, you need to have the name or IP (Internet Protocol) address of the VPN computer. You can use a connection wizard or options in PC settings (**New!**) to set up a VPN connection. You only need to set up a VPN connection to a network once. Windows displays a network icon in the notification area on the taskbar and on the Settings panel. You can click or tap the icon to display information available connections, and quickly connect to or disconnect from anyone of them.

## Create a VPN Connection

1. In the Start screen, click or tap the **Apps view** button, and then click or tap **Control Panel**.

2. Click or tap the **Network and Sharing Center** icon in Small icons or Large icons view.

3. Click or tap **Set up a new connection or network**.

4. Click or tap **Connect to a workplace**, and then click or tap **Next** to continue.

5. Click or tap **Use my Internet connection (VPN)**, and then click or tap **Next** to continue.

   ◆ If prompted, click or tap **Set up a connection anyway**.

6. Type the host name or IP address to the PC computer to which you want to connect.

7. To share this network connection, select the **Allow other people to use this connection** check box.

8. Click or tap **Create**.

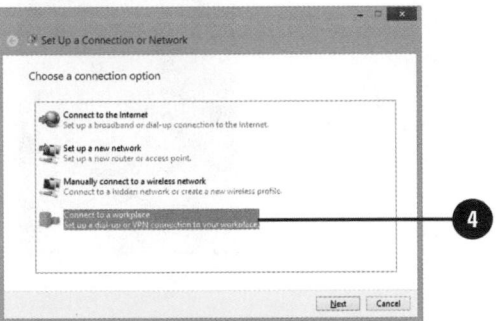

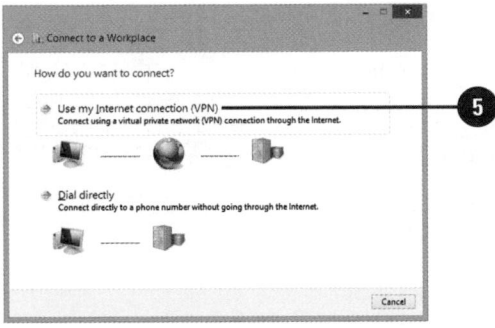

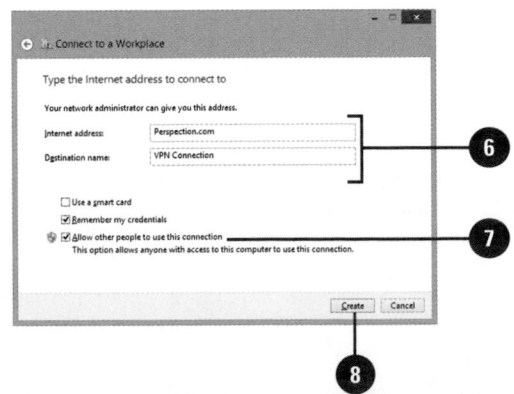

## Add a VPN Connection in PC Settings

1. Display the Start screen.

2. Point to the lower- or upper-right corner and move up or down (on a computer) or swipe left from the right edge of the screen (on a mobile device).

3. Click or tap the **Settings** button on the Charms bar.

4. Click or tap **Change PC settings** on the Settings panel, and then click or tap **Network**.

5. Click or tap **Connections** under Networks (**New!**).

6. Click or tap **Add a VPN connection** (**New!**).

7. Enter VPN connection settings, and then click or tap **Save**.

## Establish a VPN Connection

1. In the Start screen, click or tap the **Settings** button on the Charms bar, and then click or tap **Network**.

   ◆ In the desktop, click or tap the **Network** icon in the notification area on the taskbar.

2. Select the VPN connection, and then click or tap **Connect**.

3. Type your assigned username and password.

4. Click or tap **OK**, and then wait for the connection.

5. When you're done, click or tap the **Network** icon, select the connection, and then click or tap **Disconnect**.

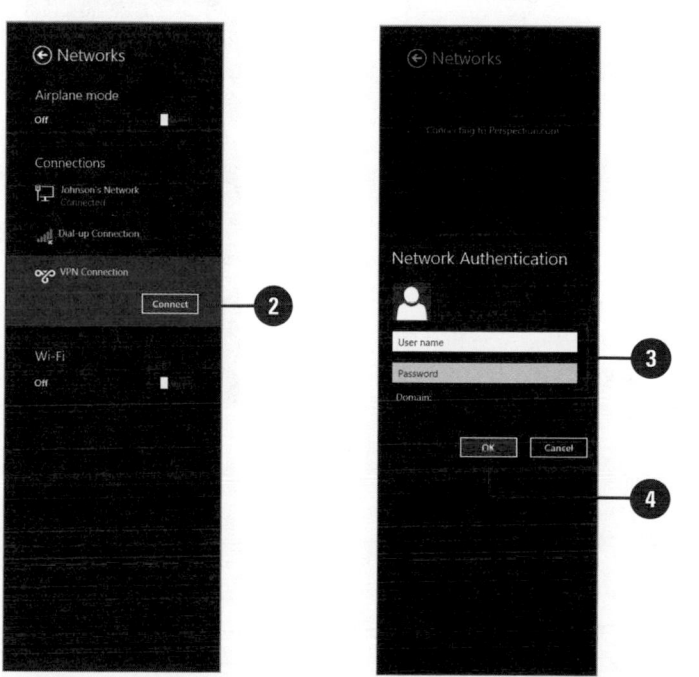

# Connecting to a Wireless Network

Windows 8.1 provides updated wireless networking, enabling you to setup and manage wireless connections with a broad range of wireless hot spots that discover and connect to wireless networks (known as Wi-Fi). The Connection wizard makes it easy to setup a Wi-Fi network. You can quickly connect to an available wireless network with a security key or manually connect to one not recognized. As you walk through the manual process, you'll specify a network name, called the SSID (Service Set Identifier). The SSID is broadcasted from your access point (AP)—typically a wireless router—to your other wireless devices. Windows also provides updated support for Bluetooth-enabled hardware devices, allowing you to take advantage of the latest wireless devices, including wireless keyboards and mice, wireless printers, and connections with cell phones and PDAs. Windows displays a Network icon in the notification area on the taskbar or on the Settings panel. You can click or tap the Network icon to display information available connections, and quickly connect to or disconnect from any one of them.

## Connect to an Available Wireless Network

1. In the Start screen, click or tap the **Settings** button on the Charms bar, and then click or tap **Network**.

   ◆ In the desktop, click or tap the **Network** icon in the notification area on the taskbar.

2. Select the wireless network to which you want to connect.

3. Select or clear the **Connect automatically** check box.

4. Click or tap **Connect**.

5. Type the security key or passphrase.

6. Click or tap **Next**, and then click or tap the option to turn On or Off sharing and connect to devices.

7. When you're done, click or tap the **Network** icon, select the connection, and then click or tap **Disconnect**.

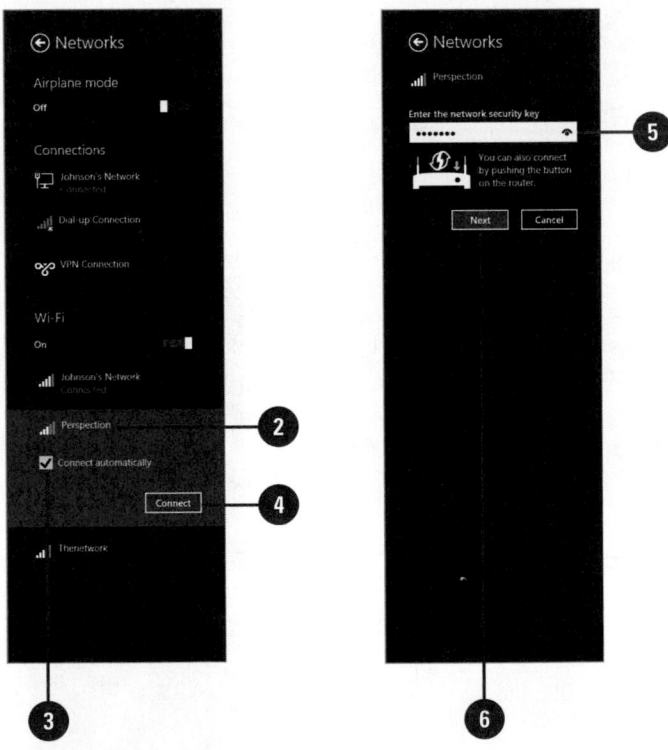

## Manually Connect to a Wireless Network

1. In the Start screen, click or tap the **Apps view** button, and then click or tap **Control Panel**.

2. Click or tap the **Network and Sharing Center** icon in Small icons or Large icons view.

3. Click or tap **Set up a new connection or network**.

4. Click or tap **Manually connect to a wireless network**, and then click or tap **Next** to continue.

5. Type the network name.

6. Specify a security type, and then specify an encryption type, if necessary.

7. To specify a security level or key (passphase), click or tap the Expand arrow.

8. Click or tap **Next** to continue.

9. Click or tap **Connect to** or **Change connection settings**.

10. If necessary, click or tap **Close**.

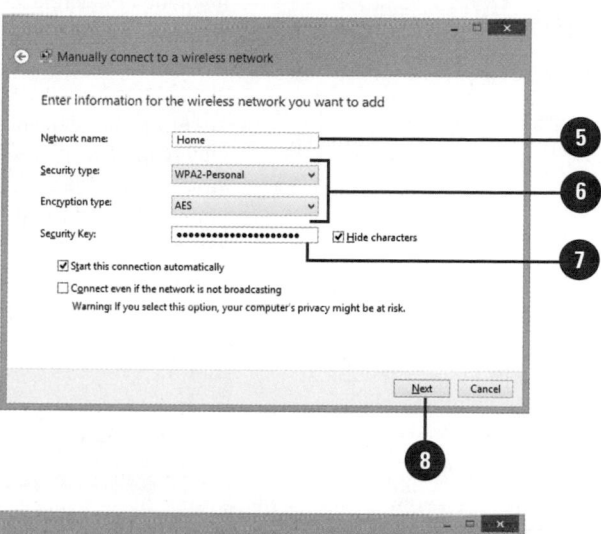

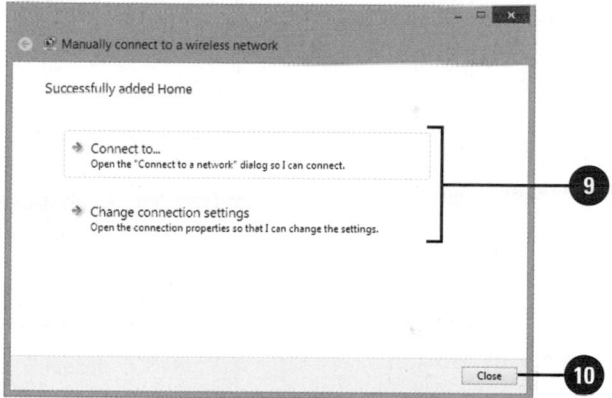

## Did You Know?

***What is Bluetooth wireless technology?*** Bluetooth technology uses radio waves to enable devices such as computers, printer, mice, or mobile phones, to communication wirelessly over a short distance. You can use Bluetooth to listen to music or use a mobile phone over wireless headphones, transfer files between mobile devices, or print to a wireless printer.

## Security Alert

### Locking Down Your Wireless Network

Wireless networks (Wi-Fi) are a popular way to network home and small office PCs. Unless you lock it down, hackers can take advantage of unsecured Wi-Fi networks. The following security techniques can keep you safe: (1) disable the SSID (Service Set Identifier) broadcast, so you no longer tell PCs near by that you have a wireless network, (2) change the password on your access point, (3) use encryption, either WEP (Wired Equivalent Privacy), which is older and less secure (uses 64- or 128-bit non-changing encryption), or WPA (Wi-Fi Protected Access), which is much more secure (uses 256-bit always changing encryption), and (4) if necessary, enable Media Access Control (MAC) filtering, which tells your access point to grant access to only MAC addresses you enter. MAC is a unique address assigned to each wireless card.

# Setting Up a Wireless Network

If you have a wireless router or access point, you can set up your own wireless network. A router directs communication traffic between two networks, such as a home or office network and the Internet. An access point provides wireless access to a wired Ethernet network. An access point plugs into a wired router and sends out a wireless signal, which other wireless PCs and devices use to connect to a wired network. During the set up process, you need to specify a network name, choose file and printer sharing options, and a security key (also known as passphrase) to provide secure access.

## Set Up a Wireless Network

1. In the Start screen, click or tap the **Apps view** button, and then click or tap **Control Panel**.

2. Click or tap the **Network and Sharing Center** icon in Small icons or Large icons view.

3. Click or tap **Set up a new connection or network**.

4. In the left pane, click or tap **Set up a new network**, and then click or tap **Next** to continue.

5. Wait for devices to show, select the wireless router or access point, and then click or tap **Next** to continue. Steps vary depending on the device installation.

6. Type the Network name (SSID), and then click or tap **Next** to continue.

7. Type a passphrase or use the one generated, and then write it down so you can use it the first time that people connect to this network.

8. Click or tap **Next** to continue.

9. Read the screen, enable the sharing options you want.

10. Click or tap **Close**.

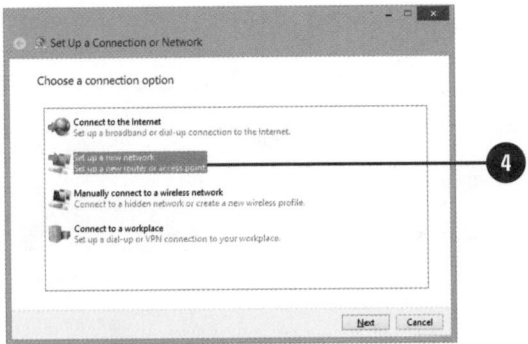

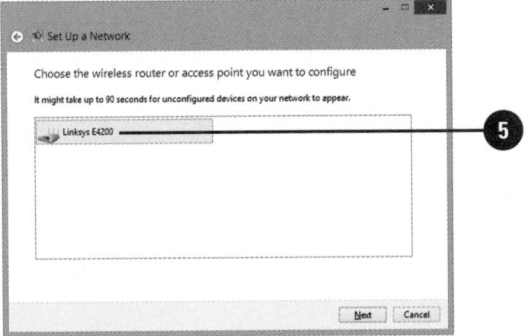

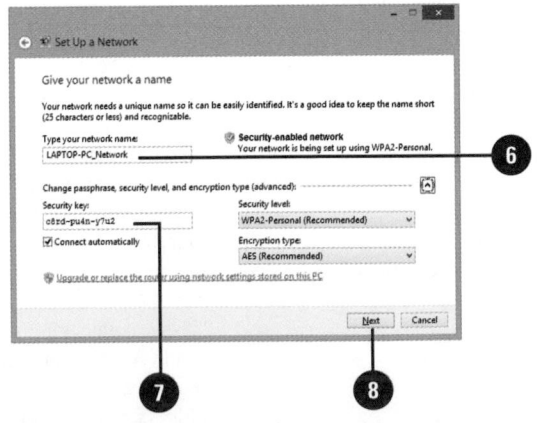

# Disabling or Enabling a Wireless Network

If you are on a airplane or other place where you need to disable a wireless network (Wi-Fi), you can quickly disable or enable it by using the Networks panel or PC settings. Airplane mode allows you to use your device on a commercial aircraft while in flight, where the operation of mobile devices that send or receive signals (search continuously for reception) is prohibited. You can not place or receive calls or text messages, however, you can typically use an FM receiver, bluetooth, wireless LAN and GPS. When you turn airplane mode on, Wi-Fi gets turned off. When you turn Wi-Fi on, airplane mode gets turned off.

## Disable or Enable a Wireless Network

1. Display the Start screen.

2. Point to the lower- or upper-right corner and move up or down (on a computer) or swipe left from the right edge of the screen (on a mobile device).

3. Click or tap the **Settings** button on the Charms bar.

   ◆ **Networks panel.** Click or tap **Network**, and then drag the Airport mode slider On or Off.

4. Click or tap **Change PC settings** on the Settings panel.

5. Click or tap **Network** under PC settings, and then click or tap **Airport mode**.

6. Specify the options you want for the category.

   ◆ **Airplane mode.** Drag the slider On or Off to enable or disable signal transmitting functions.

   ◆ **Wireless devices.** Drag the slider On or Off to enable or disable all wireless devices.

7. To close the app, point to the top edge of the screen (cursor changes to a hand), and then drag down to the bottom edge of the screen.

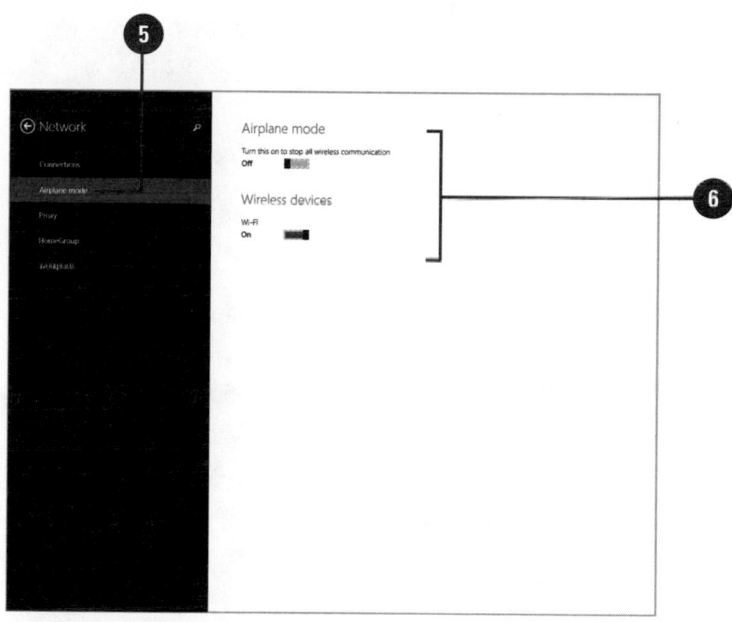

# Managing a Wireless Connection

After you setup and connect to a wireless network, you can use options on the Networks panel to work with wireless network connections. You can show or hide estimated data usage, set the connection as metered (restricts downloads and Windows updates) or non-metered, and forget (disable) a network. If you want to view or change connection and security properties for a wireless connections, you can use the Wireless Network Properties dialog box. You can view the wireless network name, SSID, type, and availability, and enable automatic or preferred connect options or change the security type and key.

## Manage a Wireless Connection

1. Display the Start screen.

2. Point to the lower- or upper-right corner and move up or down (on a computer) or swipe left from the right edge of the screen (on a mobile device).

3. Click or tap the **Settings** button on the Charms bar.

4. Click or tap **Network** on the Settings panel.

5. Right-click or tap-hold an active wireless connection.

6. On the menu, select an option:

   ◆ **Show or Hide estimated data usage.** Shows or hides the amount of network data usage.

   ◆ **Set as metered or non-metered connection.** A metered connection restricts downloads to lower wireless connect time.

   ◆ **Forget this network.** Disables a wireless network.

   ◆ **Turn sharing on or off.** Enables or disables file sharing.

   ◆ **View connection properties.** Open the connection properties dialog box (see next page).

7. To close the app, point to the top edge of the screen (cursor changes to a hand), and then drag down to the bottom edge of the screen.

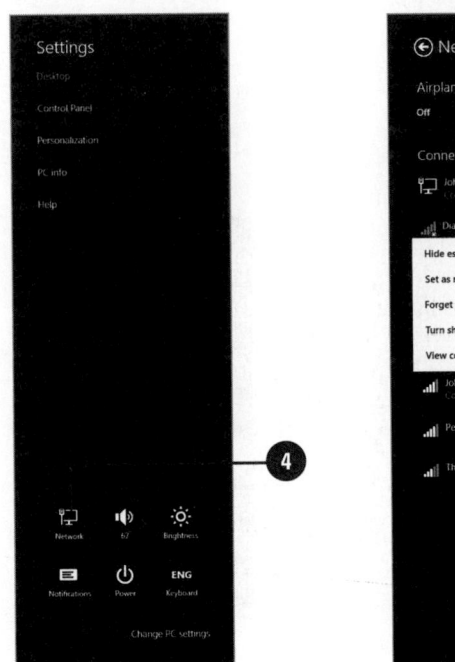

## For Your Information

### Troubleshooting Connection Problems

If you are having trouble connecting to an ethernet or wireless network, you can specify proxy setup options to create a manual connection. In PC settings, click or tap Network, and then click or tap Proxy (**New!**). Automatic proxy setup is turned on by default to help create network connections, however, if there is a problem, you can manually specify options. You can get the proxy information from your network administrator.

## Display Wireless Connection and Security Properties

① In the Start screen, click or tap the **Apps view** button, and then click or tap **Control Panel**.

② Click or tap the **Network and Sharing Center** icon in Small icons or Large icons view.

③ Click or tap the Wi-Fi connection link.

④ Click or tap **Wireless Properties**.

⑤ Click or tap the **Connection** tab.

⑥ Select or clear the following connection check boxes:

◆ **Connect automatically when this network is in range.**

◆ **Connect to a more preferred network if available.**

◆ **Connect even if the networks is not broadcasting.**

⑦ Click or tap the **Security** tab.

⑧ To change the security type, click or tap the list arrow, and then select the type you want.

When you change the security type, the other options change, which you can then modify.

⑨ Click or tap **OK**, and then click or tap the **Close** button.

### Did You Know?

***Windows 8.1 supports 802.11n wireless connections.*** In addition to current support for 802.11g, Windows 8.1 adds support for 802.11n by which a user can plug in an 802.11n Draft 2.0 compatible wireless adapter and connect to an 802.11n Draft 2.0 network.

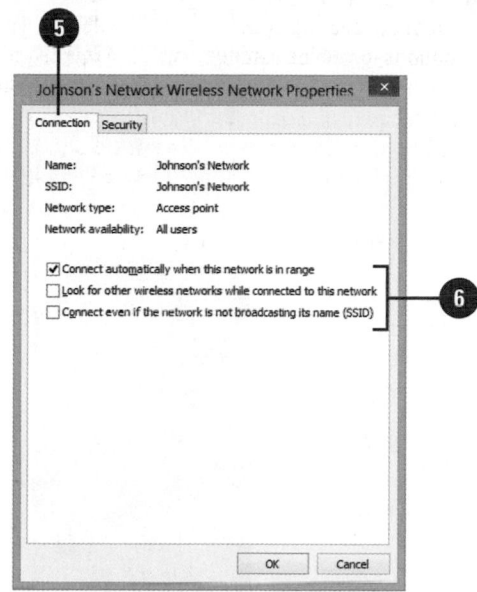

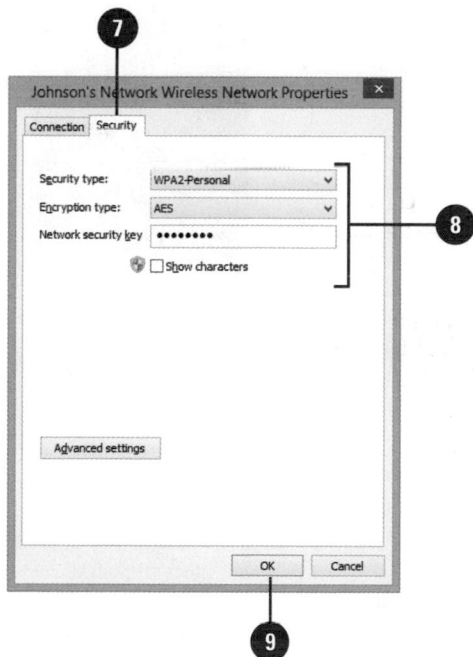

# Disconnecting a Network

When you are no longer using a connection to a wireless, dial-up, or VPN (Virtual Private network) network, you can use the disconnect from the network. You can disconnect from a network connection by using the Network icon in the notification area on the taskbar or on the Settings panel. Just, select the network on the panel, and then click or tap Disconnect. If you no longer want to use a LAN (Local Area Network), you need to disable it.

## Disconnect a Wireless Network

1. In the Start screen, click or tap the **Settings** button on the Charms bar, and then click or tap **Network**.

    ◆ In the desktop, click or tap the **Network** icon in the notification area on the taskbar.

2. Select the connection you want to disconnect.

3. Click or tap **Disconnect**.

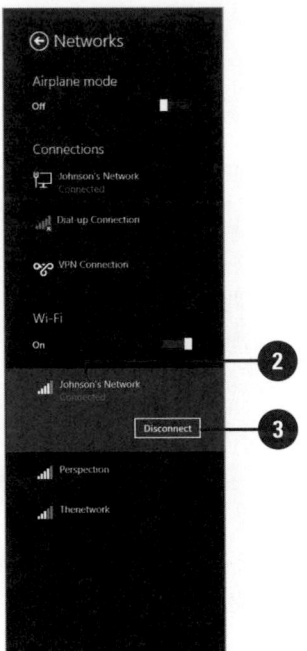

### Did You Know?

***Disable or enable a network connection.*** You can disable or enable a network connection by turning the network adapter for the connection off or on. To make this change, open the Network And Sharing Center from the Control Panel (desktop), click or tap Change Adapter Settings in the left pane, right-click or tap-hold the connection you want to change, and then click or tap Disable or Enable.

***You can delete a connection.*** In the Network and Share Center, click or tap Change Adapter Settings, right-click or tap-hold the connection you want to delete, and then click or tap Delete.

***You can perform a security check on your wireless network.*** Install the free program NetStumbler available at *www.netstumber.com* onto a laptop, mobile device, smart phone, or PDA.

## For Your Information

### Multihoming

Multihoming refers to a PC or a device that has connectivity to one or more networks via two or more methods, either wired or wireless. Multihoming is becoming more common, especially with the wide use of wireless devices, such as Pocket PCs and wireless connectivity on laptops. Multihoming automatically selects the route with best performance for a particular data transfer. Each route has a corresponding interface, therefore the selection of the best route also implies an interface selection for an outgoing connection.

# Mapping and Disconnecting a Network Drive

Windows networking enables you to connect your PC to other PCs on the network quite easily. If you connect to a network location frequently, you might want to designate a drive letter on your PC as a direct connection to a shared drive or folder on another PC. Instead of spending unnecessary time opening the Network folder and the shared drive or folder each time you want to access it, you can create a direct connection, called **mapping** a drive, to the network location for quick and easy access. If you no longer use a mapped drive, you can right-click or tap-hold the mapped drive in the Computer folder and then click or tap Disconnect.

## Map a Network Drive

1. In the Start screen, click or tap the **Apps view** button, and then click or tap **This PC**.

2. In File Explorer, navigate to and select the drive or folder you want to map.

3. Click or tap the **Easy access** button on the Home tab, and then click or tap **Map as drive**.

   ◆ You can also select a drive from the Computer folder, and then click or tap the **Map network drive** button.

4. Click or tap the **Drive** list arrow, and then select a drive letter.

5. Click or tap **Browse**.

6. Select the folder you want to connect to.

7. Click or tap **OK**.

8. To reconnect each time you log on to your PC, select the **Reconnect at logon** check box.

9. Click or tap **Finish**.

10. To disconnect from a mapped drive, select the drive in the Computer folder, click or tap the **Map network drive** button arrow, on the Computer tab and then click or tap **Disconnect network drive**.

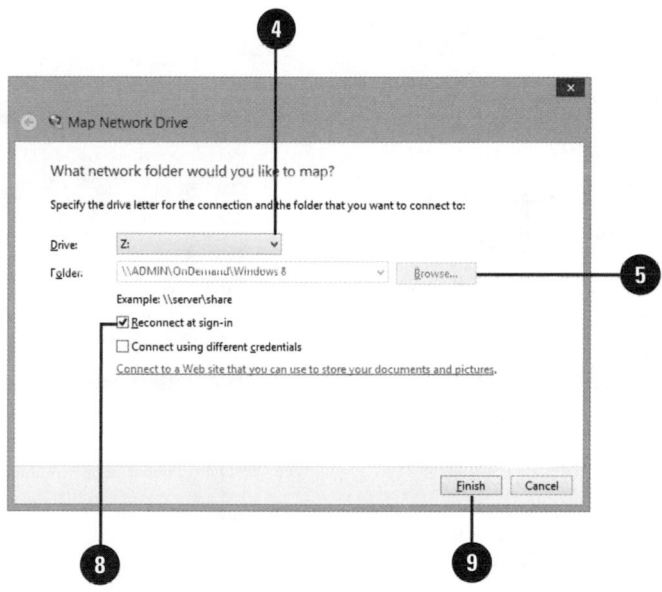

# Creating a Shortcut to a Network

Instead of clicking or tapping numerous icons in the Network folder to access a network location, you can create a shortcut to the network location to provide easy access. A **shortcut** is a link that you can place in any location to gain instant access to a particular file, folder, or program on your hard disk or on a network just by double-clicking or double-tapping. The actual file, folder, or program remains stored in its original location, and you place an icon representing the shortcut in a convenient location, such as in a folder or on the desktop. If you want to create a shortcut to a web site, an FTP (File Transfer Protocol) site, or other network location, you can use the Add Network Location wizard to help you step through the process.

## Create a Shortcut to a Network

1. In the Start screen, click or tap the **Apps view** button, and then click or tap **This PC**.

2. Click or tap **Network** in the Navigation pane.

3. Right-click or tap-hold a network icon or a folder on a network, and then click or tap **Create Shortcut**.

   The shortcut appears on the desktop or in the folder.

4. Drag the shortcut icon to a convenient location.

Shortcut to a network

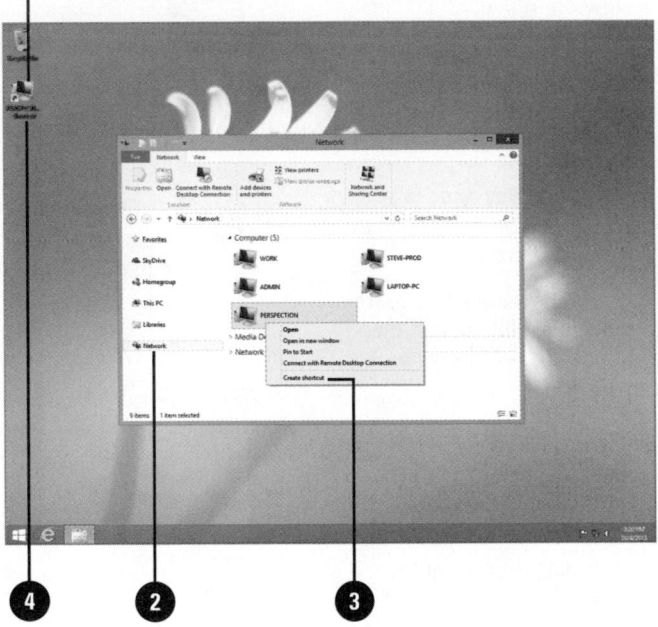

## Create a Shortcut to a Network Location

1. In the Start screen, click or tap the **Apps view** button, and then click or tap **This PC**.

2. Click or tap the **Add a network location** button on the Computer tab.

   The Add Network Location wizard opens.

3. Read the introduction screen, and then click or tap **Next**.

4. Click or tap **Choose a custom network location**, and then click or tap **Next**.

5. Enter the address of the web site, FTP site, or network location, and then click or tap **Next**.

   ◆ **Examples.** \\server\share
   http://webserver/share
   ftp://ftp.perspection.com

6. Select or clear the **Log on anonymously** check box, enter a username if cleared, and then click or tap **Next**.

7. Type a name or use the existing one, and then click or tap **Next**.

8. Select or clear the **Open this network location when I click Finish** check box, and then click or tap **Finish**.

   The shortcut icon appears in the Computer folder.

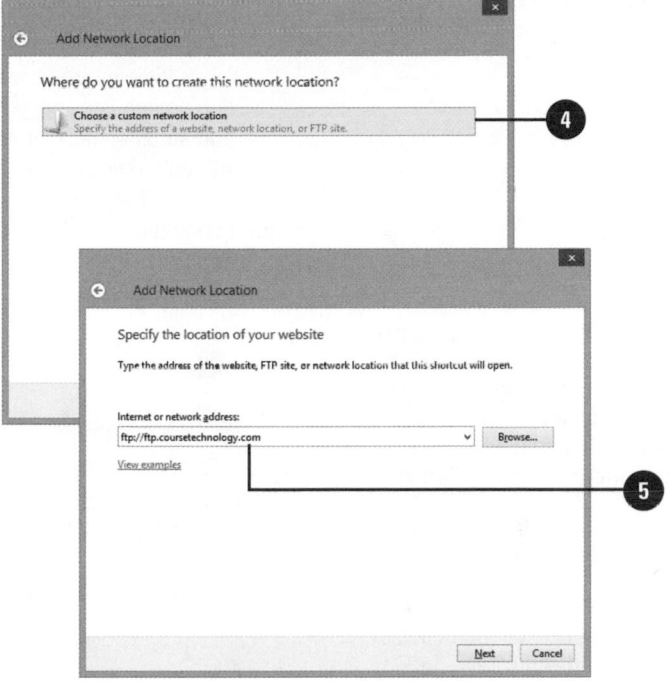

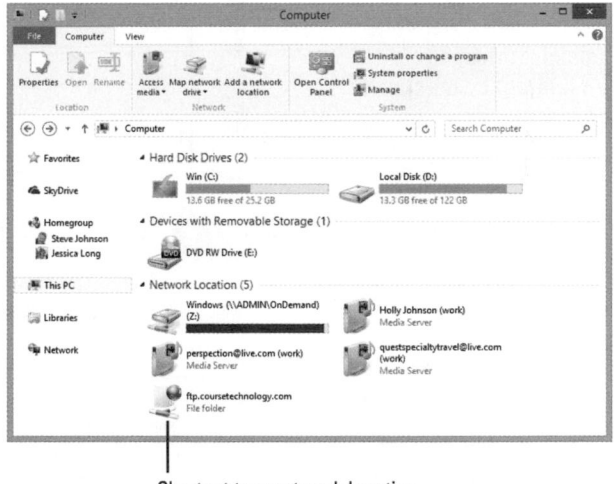

Shortcut to a network location

# Sharing an Internet Connection

If you have a home or small office network using Windows 8.1, you can use Internet Connection Sharing (ICS) to connect all the PCs on the network to the Internet with one connection, which saves you money on multiple connections. If you have a shared dial-up Internet connection no one is using, you can change settings to have the connection end automatically, or you can manually end the connection from your PC. Windows displays a network icon in the notification area on the taskbar. You can click or tap the icon to display information available connections, and quickly connect to or disconnect from anyone of them.

## Share an Internet Connection

1. Click or tap the **Network** icon in the notification area on the taskbar, and then click or tap **Open Network and Sharing Center**.

2. In the left pane, click or tap **Change adapter settings**.

3. Right-click or tap-hold the Internet Network icon, and then click or tap **Properties**.

4. Click or tap the **Sharing** tab.

5. Select the **Allow other network users to connect through this computer's Internet connection** check box.

6. For a home network, if available, select the adapter that connects to other networked PCs.

7. If you want this connection to dial automatically, select the **Establish a dial-up connection whenever a computer on my network attempts to access the Internet** check box.

8. Select or clear the **Allow other network users to control or disable the shared Internet connection** check box.

9. To select specific services to share, click or tap **Settings**, select the services you want, and then click or tap **OK**.

10. Click or tap **OK**.

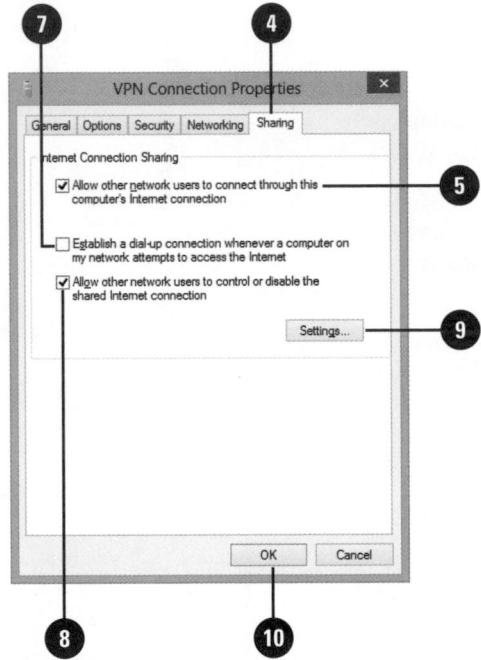

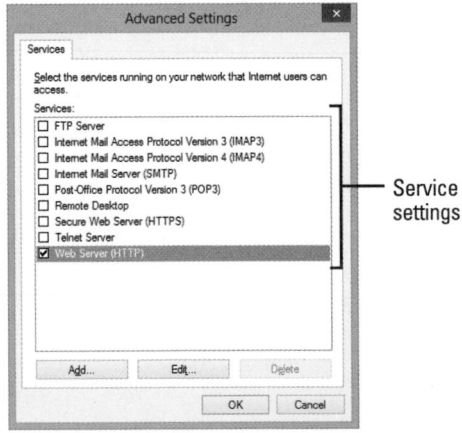

Service settings

# Setting Network Sharing Options

In the Network and Sharing Center you can set options to share files, printers, public folders, and media on the network. Sharing files, public folders, and printers provides a convenient way to share information and resources over a network. The sharing options allow you to share materials on a workgroup, domain, or homegroup network. After you turn on sharing options for file or public folders, you can use the Share tab in File Explorer to share your files with others on the homegroup or other networks using permissions.

## Set File or Public Folder Sharing Options

1. In the Start screen, click or tap the **Apps view** button, and then click or tap **Control Panel**.

2. Click or tap the **Network and Sharing Center** icon in Small icons or Large icons view.

3. In the left pane, click or tap **Change advanced sharing settings**.

4. Click or tap the Current Profile expand arrow, as needed, click or tap the **Turn on file and printer sharing** or **Turn off file and printer sharing** option.

5. Click or tap the All Networks expand arrow as needed, and then select the Public folder sharing option you want.

   ◆ **Turn on sharing so anyone with network access can read and write files in the Public folders.**

   ◆ **Turn off Public folder sharing (people logged on to this computer can still access these folders).**

6. Click or tap **Save changes**.

7. Click or tap the **Close** button.

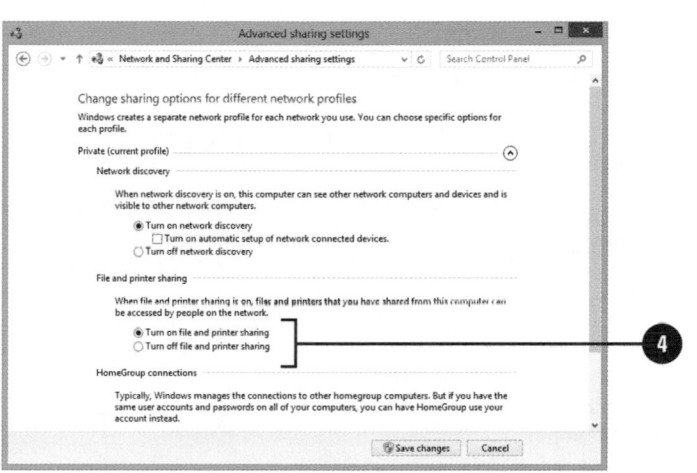

Expand or collapse arrows

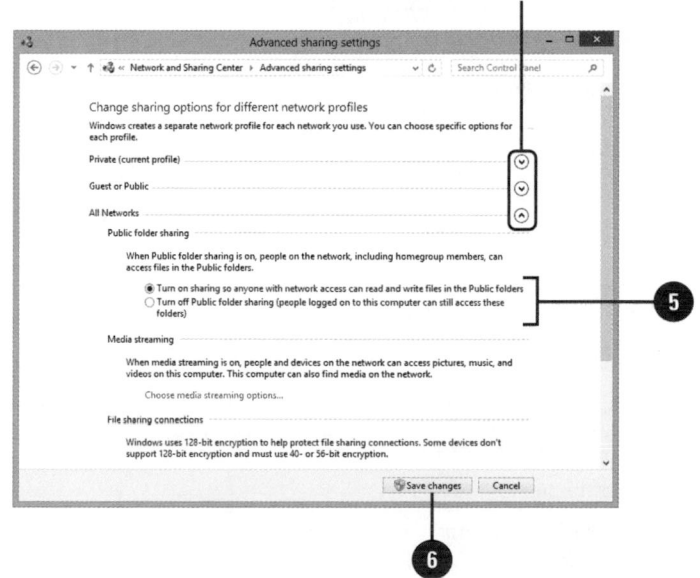

# Setting Homegroup Sharing Options

If you have two or more PCs running Windows 8 or 7 on the Home network type, you can set up and join in a homegroup to share files, printers, and media. You can even play music streamed from another person's PC on a homegroup using Windows Media Player. Before you can use a homegroup, you need to create one first (only workgroups; one per network). During the setup process Windows creates a password, which you can view, print, and change later, for everyone to use on individual PCs to join the homegroup. If you no longer want to be a part of the homegroup, you can leave it.

## Create and Set Homegroup Options in File Explorer

1. In the Start screen, click or tap the **Apps view** button, and then click or tap **This PC**.

2. Click or tap **Homegroup** in the Navigation pane.

3. To create a new homegroup, click or tap **Create a homegroup**, click or tap **Next**, select the items you want to share, click or tap **Next**, write down the join password, and then click or tap **Finish**.

4. To change shared items, click or tap the **Share libraries and devices** button to use the wizard.

5. Click or tap the **Change homegroup settings** button.

6. To share media, select the **Allow all devices ... to play my shared content** link, click or tap **Allow All**, **Block All**, or select individual settings, click or tap **Next**, and then finish the wizard.

7. Perform any homegroup actions:

   ◆ **View or print the homegroup password.**

   ◆ **Change the password.**

   ◆ **Leave the homegroup.**

   ◆ **Start the HomeGroup troubleshooter.**

8. Click or tap the **Close** button.

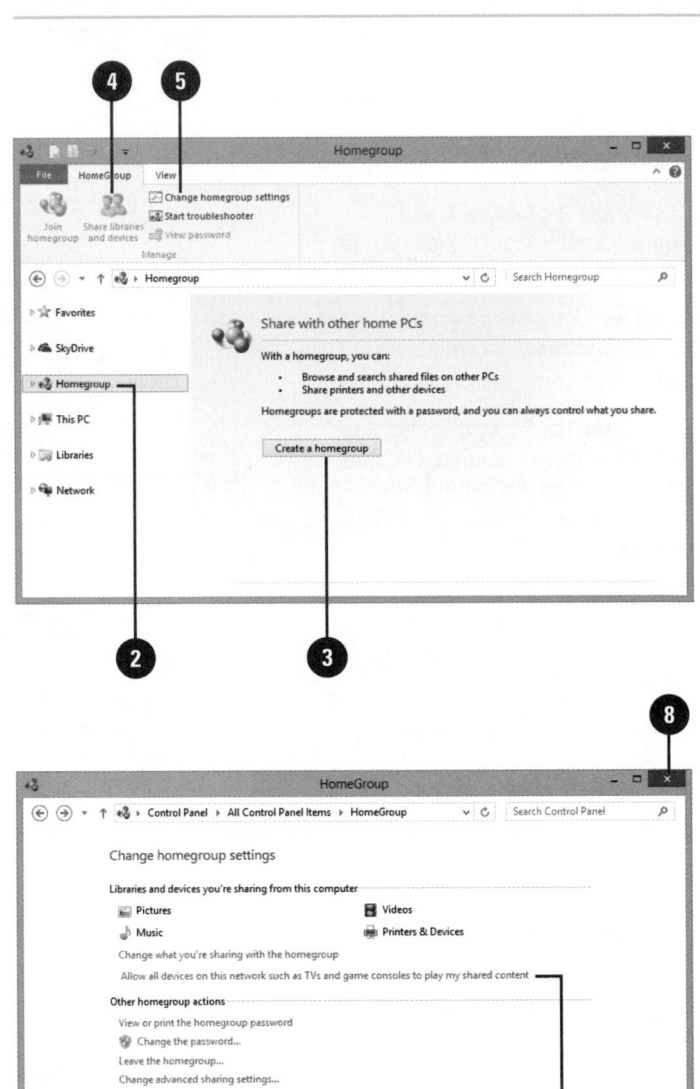

## Create and Set Homegroup Options from PC Settings

1. Display the Start screen.

2. Point to the lower- or upper-right corner and move up or down (on a computer) or swipe left from the right edge of the screen (on a mobile device).

3. Click or tap the **Settings** button on the Charms bar.

4. Click or tap **Change PC settings** on the Settings panel, and then click or tap **Network**.

5. Click or tap **HomeGroup** under Networks.

6. Select an option to create or join a homegroup:

   ◆ **Create a homegroup.** If not available, click or tap **Create**.

   ◆ **Join a homegroup.** Type the password from the user who created the homegroup, click or tap **Join**.

7. Drag the sliders to On or Off to enable or disable sharing for individual libraries (Music, Pictures, and Videos) and devices (Printers, etc.), and all media devices.

8. To disconnect from the homegroup, click or tap **Leave**.

9. To close the app, point to the top edge of the screen (cursor changes to a hand), and then drag down to the bottom edge of the screen.

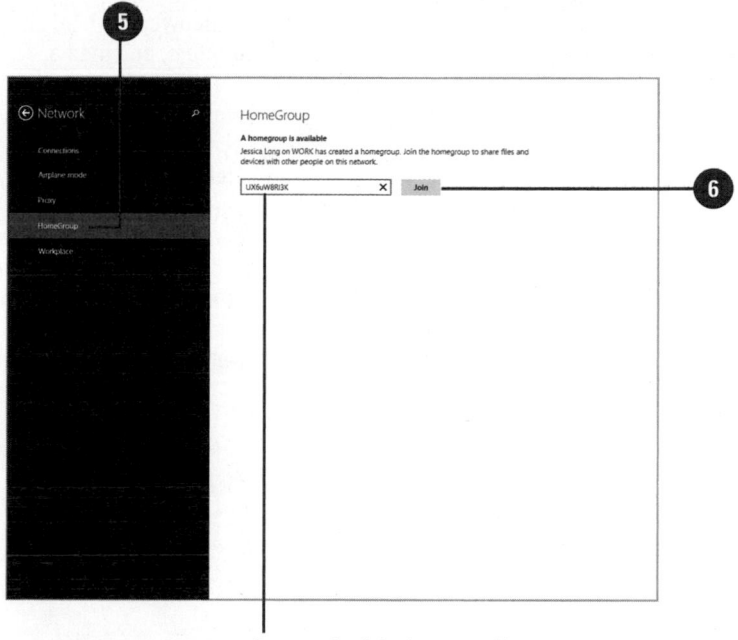

Password to join the created homegroup

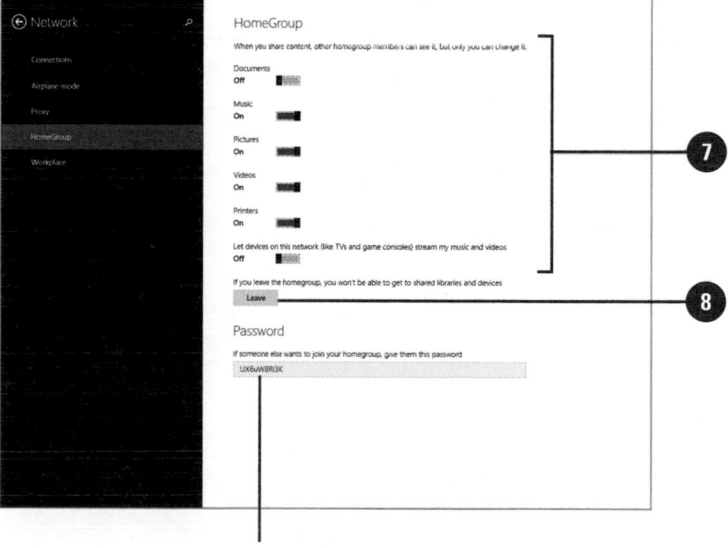

Password for others to join

# Sharing with a Homegroup

A homegroup is a sharing home network with two or more PCs running Windows 8 or 7. You can create or join a homegroup to share files, printers, and media. You can play music streamed from another person's PC on a homegroup using Windows Media Player or other networked digital media player/receiver, such as Xbox 360; you can access the media from a shared media folder that appears in the Network folder. Before you can view and use files from other people on your network, you need to join the homegroup. To join the homegroup, you'll need the password generated during the homegroup set up process. After you join in, you can use the Share tab in File Explorer to share your files with others on the homegroup or other network. It's important to note that any PCs turned off or sleeping do not appear in the homegroup.

## Join a Homegroup

1. In the Start screen, click or tap the **Apps view** button, and then click or tap **This PC**.

2. Click or tap **Homegroup** in the Navigation pane.

   ◆ If prompted to create a homegroup, see previous page for details.

3. Click or tap **Join now** or click or tap **Join homegroup** button on the HomeGroup tab.

4. Type the password (generated during setup) from the user who created the homegroup, click or tap **Next**, and then follow the remaining steps to complete the process.

   ◆ **Get password from homegroup creator.** In the File Explorer, click or tap Homegroup in the Navigation pane, click or tap the **View password** button on the HomeGroup tab.

5. To view files in a homegroup, click or tap **Homegroup** in the Navigation pane.

   ◆ Any PCs turned off or a sleep do not show up in the homegroup.

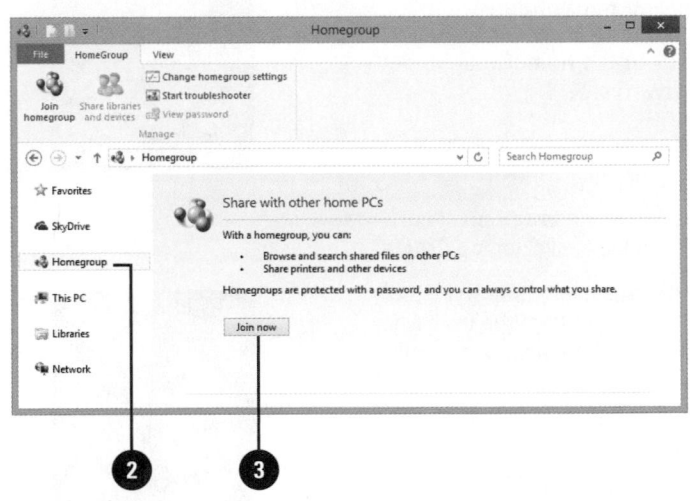

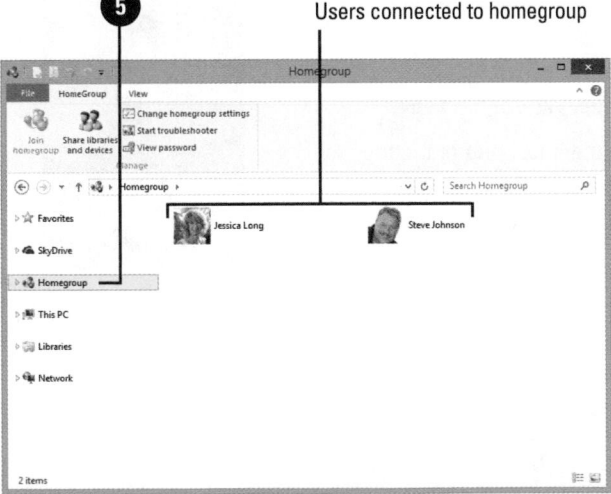

Users connected to homegroup

## Share Files and Folders

1. In the Start screen, click or tap the **Apps view** button, and then click or tap **This PC**.

2. In File Explorer, navigate to the folder with the files or folders you want to share.

3. Click or tap the **Share** tab, and then select a share option:

   ◆ **Homegroup (view) or Homegroup (view and edit).** Select to share with a homegroup using permissions.

   ◆ **Specific people.** Select to share with a specific person.

   ◆ **Stop sharing.** Click or tap to stop sharing selected items.

4. Click or tap **Homegroup** in the Navigation pane to work with shared files from other people.

5. When you're done, click or tap the **Close** button.

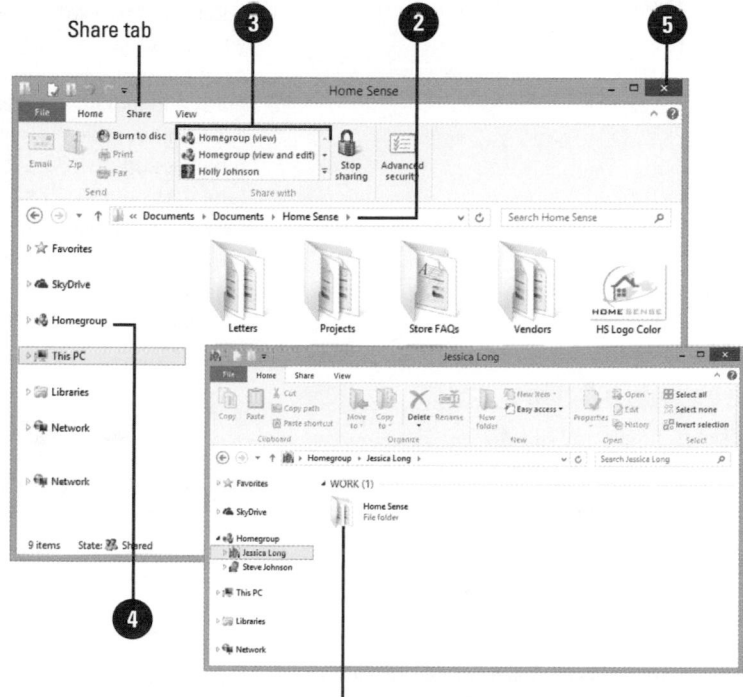

Shared homegroup folder used on another networked PC

## Play Shared Media

1. In the Start screen, click or tap the **Apps view** button, and then click or tap **This PC**.

2. Click or tap **Network** in the Navigation pane.

3. Double-click or double-tap a shared media folder icon.

   Windows Media Player opens.

3. Use Windows Media Player to play the shared media files.

   ◆ When you're done playing music, exit Windows Media Player.

4. When you're done, click or tap the **Close** button.

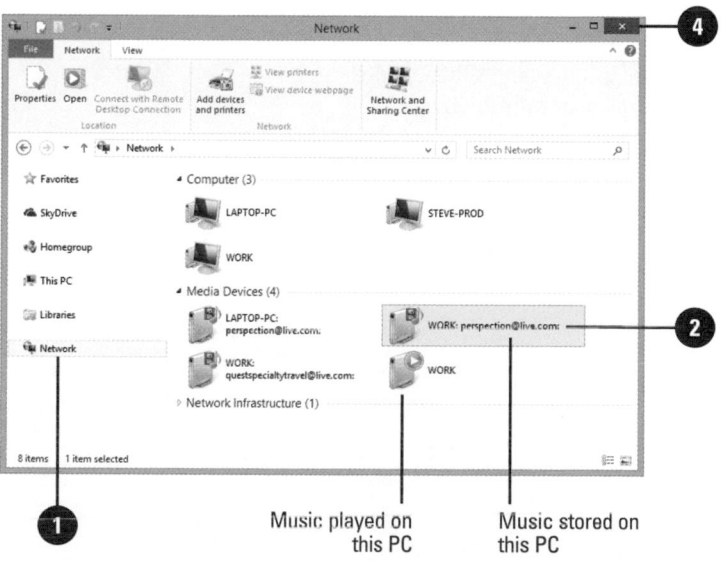

Music played on this PC

Music stored on this PC

# Keeping Files in Sync

Keeping track of the latest versions of all your files on your PC computer and mobile devices can become a problem. With the Sync Center, you can keep files (including documents, music, photos, and in some case contacts) and other information up-to-date between your PC computer and mobile devices, network folders, and compatible programs. You can keep files in sync (short for *synchronization*) in one direction (changes on one PC get changed on the other) or in both directions (changes on both PCs get changed on both). The Sync Center compares files between the two PCs and then copies the latest version in the appropriate place. If the same files get changed on both PCs, the Sync Center asks you to resolve it. The Sync Center also works with offline files and keeps them in sync.

## Sync with a Device

1. Establish a connection between your computer and the mobile device, network folder, or program.

2. In the Control Panel (desktop), click or tap the **Sync Center** icon in Small icons or Large icons view.

3. In the left pane, click or tap **Set up new sync partnerships**.

4. Click or tap the name of the device in the list of partnerships.

5. Click or tap the **Set Up** button on the toolbar.

6. Follow the wizard instructions to select the settings and sync schedule you want. When you're done, click or tap **Finish**.

7. To start syncing now, click or tap the **Sync** button on the toolbar.

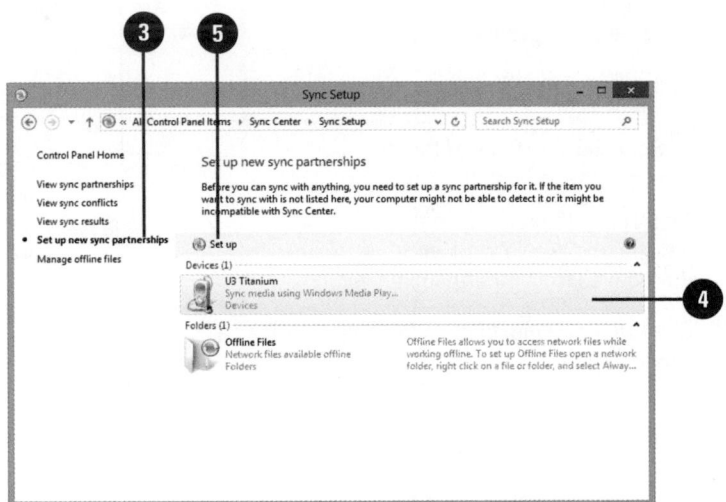

## Sync All Offline Files

1. In the Control Panel (desktop), click or tap the **Sync Center** icon in Small icons or Large icons view.

2. Click or tap the **Offline Files** sync partnership.

3. If you want to sync the contents of a folder, open it up.

4. Click or tap the **Sync All** button on the toolbar.

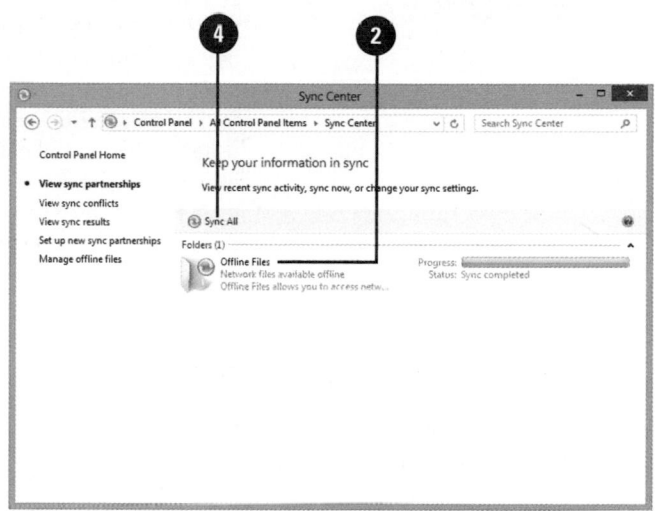

## Sync Individual Offline Files

1. In the Control Panel (desktop), click or tap the **Sync Center** icon in Small icons or Large icons view.

2. Click or tap the **Offline Files** sync partnership.

3. Select the folder you want to sync.

4. To open the folder to view its contents, click or tap the **Browse** button on the toolbar. When you're done, click or tap the **Close** button.

5. Click or tap the **Sync** button on the toolbar.

    **TIMESAVER** *Select the file or folder, click or tap the Easy access button on the Home tab, and then click or tap Sync.*

6. To schedule the time you want to sync this folder, click or tap the **Schedule** button on the toolbar, and then follow the wizard instructions.

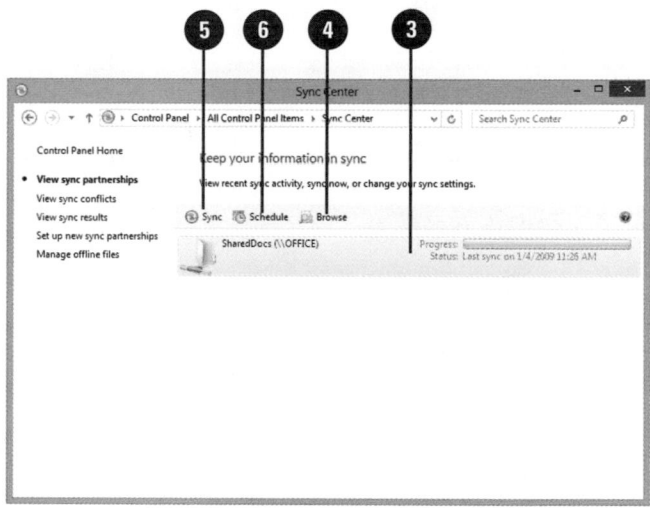

# Working with Offline Files

The Sync Center works with offline files and keeps them in sync. An offline file is a copy of a network file that is stored on your local PC for use when the network connection is not available. Before you can make a network file available offline, you need to enable offline files in the Sync Center utility in the Control Panel, where you can also set disk usage, security, and network options. When you make a network file available offline, the Windows automatically creates a copy on your local PC. Whenever the network versions are not available, the Sync Center opens the offline copy and then syncs it back with the network version when the connection becomes available again.

## Change Offline Files Settings

1. In the Control Panel (desktop), click or tap the **Sync Center** icon in Small icons or Large icons view.

2. Click or tap **Manage offline files**.

3. To disable or enable offline files, click or tap the **Disable Offline Files** or **Enable Offline Files**.

4. Click or tap **OK**.

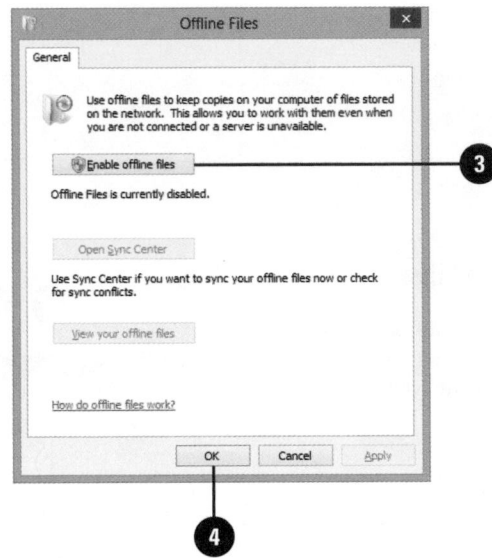

## Make Files Available Offline

① In File Explorer, open the network file or folder you want to make available offline.

② Select the file or folder you want to make available offline.

③ Click or tap the **Easy access** button on the Home tab, and then click or tap **Always available offline**.

> **TIMESAVER** *Select the file or folder, click or tap the Easy access button on the Home tab, and then click or tap Work offline.*

④ To check if you're working offline or not, open the network folder with the offline files, and check the Details pane for offline status information.

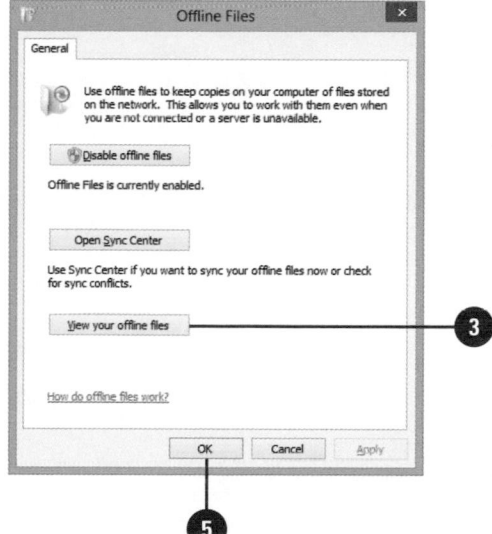

## View Offline Files

① In the Control Panel (desktop), click or tap the **Sync Center** icon in Small icons or Large icons view.

② Click or tap **Manage offline files**.

③ Click or tap the **View your offline files** button.

④ When you're done, click or tap the **Close** button on the window with the offline files.

⑤ Click or tap **OK** to close the Offline Files dialog box.

# Controlling a Remote Desktop

You can use Remote Desktop Connection to connect to a remote PC on your network or the Internet and use the remote desktop as if you were working on it. Before you can connect to a remote desktop, you need to turn on the Windows PC (version 8, 7, Vista, or XP) and set the option to allow users to connect remotely to the desktop. Doing this provides security for the remote desktop. You can allow anyone to connect to the remote desktop, or you can specify users with a password. You also need to have the name or IP (Internet Protocol) address of the remote desktop and the username and password you use to log on to the PC. You can also customize settings for the remote connection, which include the display size and color depth, when to use local or remote resources, and what programs to use and options to allow. Once you connect to the remote PC, the remote desktop appears on your screen. You can use the remote desktop as if you were working at the PC.

## Set Up a Remote Computer

1. In the Start screen, click or tap the **Apps view** button, and then click or tap **This PC**.

2. Click or tap the **System properties** button on the Computer tab, and then click or tap **Change settings**.

3. Click or tap the **Remote** tab.

4. Select the **Allow Remote Assistance connections to this computer** check box.

5. Click or tap **Advanced**.

6. Specify whether you want others to remotely control this PC, and how long a remote invitation is available, and then click or tap **OK**.

7. Select the remote desktop connection option you want.

8. Click or tap **Select Users**.

9. Click or tap **Add**, type usernames, and then click or tap **OK**.

   **TROUBLE?** *Click or tap Examples for help with usernames.*

10. Click or tap **OK**.

11. Click or tap **OK**.

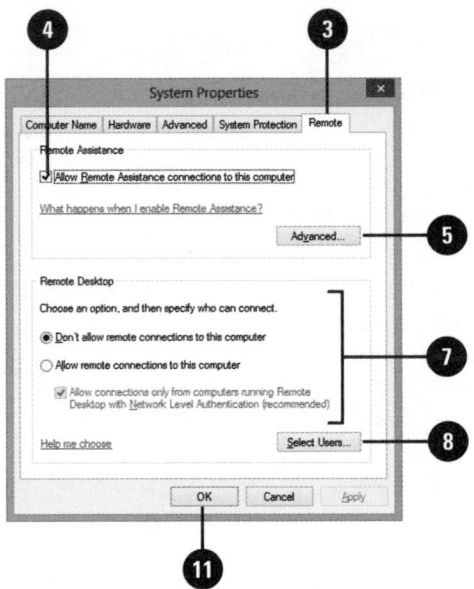

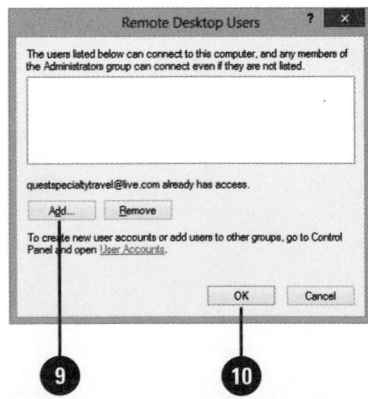

## Connect to and Control a Remote Desktop

① Establish a connection to your network.

② In the Start screen, click or tap the **Apps view** button, and then click or tap **Remote Desktop Connection**.

③ Type the name or IP address of the remote PC.

④ If available, type a username.

⑤ Click or tap **Connect**.

⑥ If prompted, enter the needed connection credentials.

⑦ Use the remote desktop as if you were sitting in front of the remote PC.

⑧ Click or tap the **Minimize** or **Restore Down** button to resize the remote desktop and to display the local desktop.

⑨ Use the local desktop.

⑩ When you're done, click or tap the **Close** button, and then click or tap

### Did You Know?

*You can quickly connect with Remote Desktop Connection.* The remote desktop needs to be turned on, available on the network, and set up to allow remote assistance. In File Explorer (desktop), click Network in the Navigation pane, select a networked PC, and then click the Connect With Remote Desktop Connection button on the Network tab.

**Yes** to disconnect.

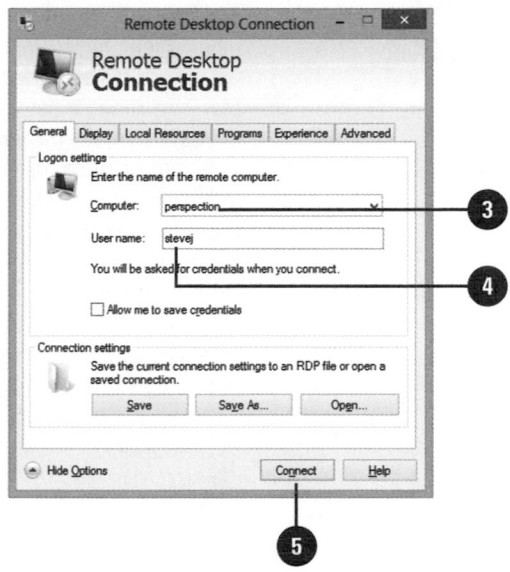

### For Your Information

#### Using RemoteApp and Desktop Connection

You can use a wizard to setup a remote application or desktop connection. You can use your PC to open and use apps and desktops on another PC. In the Control Panel (desktop), click or tap the RemoteApp and Desktop Connection icon in Small icons or Large icons view, click or tap Access RemoteApp And Desktop Connections, click or tap Access RemoteApp And Desktops, and then follow the on-screen wizard instructions. To disconnect from a connection, right-click or tap-hold the RemoteApp and Desktop Connections icons in the notification area on the taskbar (desktop), and then click or tap Disconnect. To remove a connection, open Access RemoteApp And Desktop Connections, select the connection, and then click or tap Remove.

# Syncing Files at a Workplace Network

Works Folders (**New!**) allow you to make your files available on devices with Win 8.1, RT, and Win 7 or iPad (with additional software)—you use, even when offline, from a file server. Work Folders syncs files from devices to file servers using Windows Server 2012 R2 or later. For example, if you bring a device from home to work, you can access files from the server on the device. You can work on documents on company computers or on personal devices, and have the documents synced automatically between them, similar to SkyDrive. The difference between the too is that Work Folders use a company controlled local network server, while SkyDrive uses a Microsoft controlled online network server. During set up, you'll need to enter a work email address or URL provided by your network administrator. You can access the Work Folder from the local network or over the Internet, which requires a server certificate and a registered domain name and public DNS record.

## Set Up Work Folders

1. In the Start screen, click or tap the **Apps view** button, and then click or tap **Control Panel**.

2. Click or tap the **Work Folders** icon (**New!**) in Small icons or Large icons view.

3. Click or tap the **Set up Work Folders** link.

4. Enter a work email address or click the **Enter a work Folders URL instead** link, and then click **Next**.

   ◆ **Example.** *https://workfolders. perspection.com.*

5. If prompted, enter your user name and password to your domain, and then click **OK**.

   A work folder is created on your device, such as C:\stevejohnson\ WorkFolders.

6. Click **Next**, and read the security policies to use Work Folders.

7. Select the **I accept these policies on my PC** check box, and then click **Set up Work Folders**.

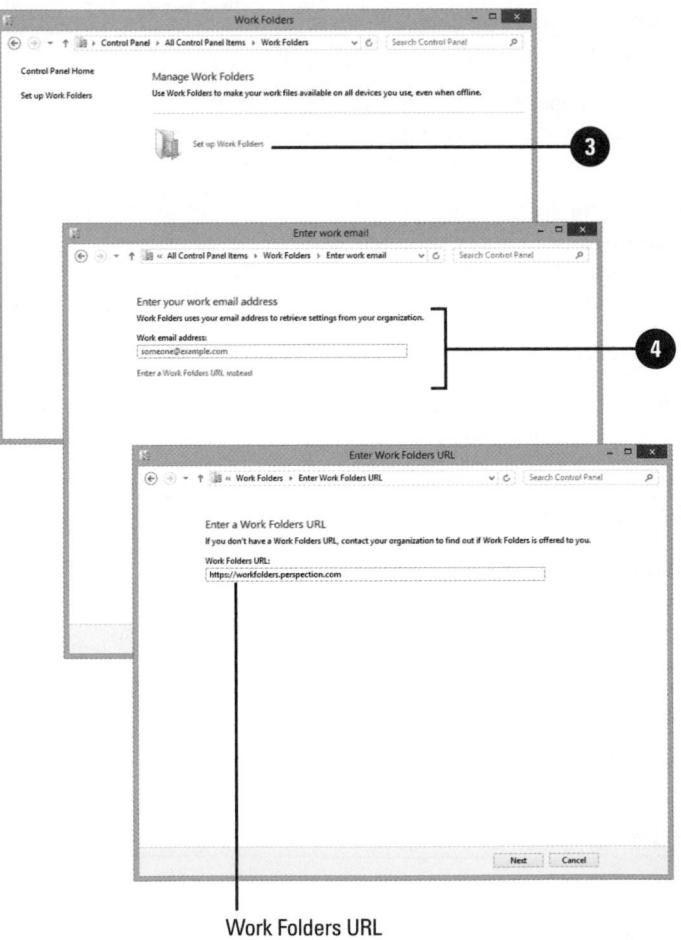

Work Folders URL

## Use Work Folders

- **Clients.** You can access Work Folders from the following clients:

  - **Windows 8.1 Domain Joined.** If you're at work, you can access Work Folders.

  - **Windows 8.1 Non-Domain Joined.** If you're at home, you can access Work Folders.

  - **Windows 8.1 RT.** If you're on the device, you can access Work Folders.

  - **Windows 7 or Apple iPad.** With downloaded software, you can access Work Folders.

- **Open Work Folders.** In File Explorer (desktop), click or tap **This PC** in the Navigation pane, and then click or tap **Work Folders** (**New!**).

- **Add Files to Work Folders.** In File Explorer (desktop), click or tap **This PC** in the Navigation pane, open the folder with the files you want, and then drag them to the **Work Folders** folder (**New!**) in the Navigation pane.

  Files in the Work Folders get synced to the file server. Synced files are in green.

- **Remove Files from Work Folders.** In File Explorer (desktop), click or tap **This PC** in the Navigation pane, click or tap **Work Folders**, select the files, and then drag the files out of the Work Folders folder (**New!**) to keep it or press Delete to remove it. If prompted, accept the change.

- **Stop Using Work Folders.** In the Control Panel, click or tap the **Work Folders** icon in Small icons or Large icons view, and then click or tap **Stop using Work Folders** link (**New!**).

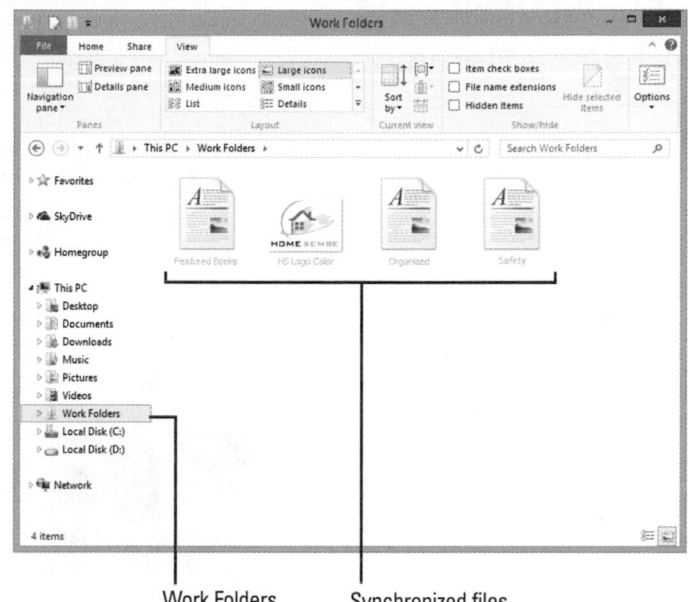

Work Folders          Synchronized files

# Connecting Devices to a Workplace Network

If you want to connect a device—such as a laptop, tablet, or smart-phone—to a workplace network, you can use the Workplace options (**New!**) in PC settings. This allows you to join and register the device on your company network using a Windows Server 2012 R2 or later. In order to join a company network, you'll need to enter a work email address provided by your network administrator in PC settings. If you would like to your network administrator to set up apps and services for you, you can turn on device management. When you join a company network, group policy controls access company assets, however, it doesn't affect your personal assets.

## Join a Workplace Network

1. Display the Start screen.

2. Point to the lower- or upper-right corner and move up or down (on a computer) or swipe left from the right edge of the screen (on a mobile device).

3. Click or tap the **Settings** button on the Charms bar.

4. Click or tap **Change PC settings** on the Settings panel, and then click or tap **Network**.

5. Click or tap **Workspace** under Networks.

6. Enter a work email address.

7. To join a workplace network, click or tap **Join**. If prompted, enter your username and password and any other requested credentials.

8. To enable device management, click or tap **Turn on**.

   ◆ If you want to turn it off, click or tap **Turn off**.

9. To close the app, point to the top edge of the screen (cursor changes to a hand), and then drag down to the bottom edge of the screen.

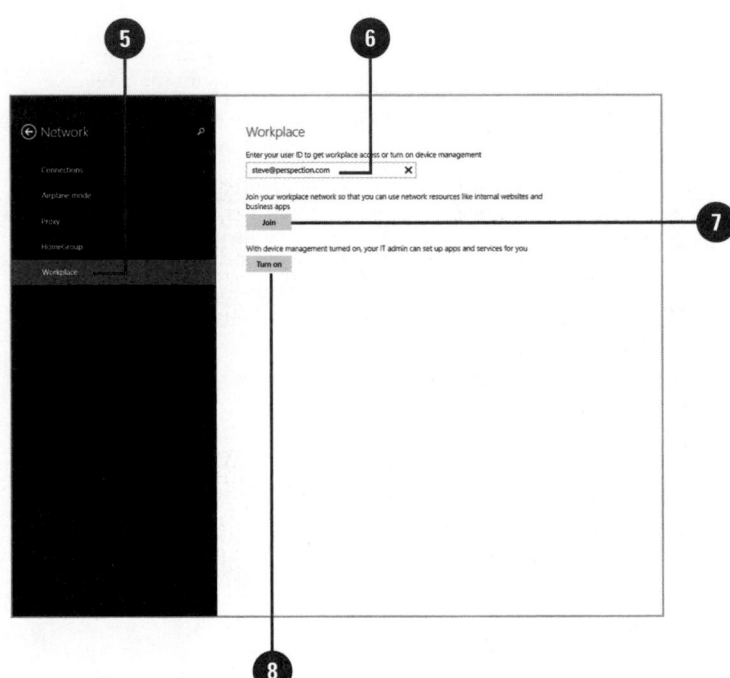

# Printing, Faxing, and Scanning

## Introduction

After you create a document or picture, or open a web page or an e-mail, you can use Windows printing options to create a hard copy. You can print files from a folder window or within a program. The Add a Printer wizard makes it easy to install a printer directly attached to your PC computer or connected to a network. After you send a print job to the printer, you can check the status, pause and resume the print job, or cancel it. If a printer is not working the way you want, you can change printer properties, such as a printer's connection or network location, sharing options, related software drivers, color management options, graphics settings, installed fonts, and other advanced settings. To customize your print jobs, you can also change printer preferences, such as orientation, page order, pages per sheet, paper size, paper tray selection, copy count, print quality, and color.

Windows also provides you with complete fax facilities from your PC computer. After the fax is set up, you can configure fax settings, send and receive faxes, track and monitor fax activity, and view faxes. Using Windows Fax and Scan, you can send and receive faxes, fax or e-mail scanned documents, and forward faxes as e-mail attachments from your PC computer. You can also change the send and receive properties for the fax to work with your phone line. In addition to faxes, you can also use Windows Fax and Scan to scan a document or picture. Beside Windows Fax and Scan, you can use the Scan app to quickly create a scan.

## What You'll Do

**Understand Printers**

**View Printers**

**Install a Printer**

**Specify a Default Printer**

**Rename or Delete a Printer**

**Print Documents**

**Manage Printers and Print Jobs**

**Change Printer Properties and Preferences**

**Share a Printer**

**Create an XPS Document**

**Understand Faxes**

**Set Up a Fax**

**Create a Fax Cover Page**

**Send a Fax**

**Manage Outgoing Faxes**

**Receive and Review a Fax**

**Change Fax Properties**

**Scan a Document**

# Understanding Printers

Although there are many different kinds of printers, there are two main categories: ink-jet, laser and 3D (**New!**). An **ink-jet printer** works by spraying ionized ink on a sheet of paper. Ink-jet printers are less expensive and considerably slower than laser printers, but they still produce a good quality output. A **laser printer** utilizes a laser beam to produce an image on a drum, which is rolled through a reservoir of toner and transferred to the paper through a combination of heat and pressure. Laser printers are faster and produce a higher quality output than ink-jets, but they are also more expensive.

Ink-jet and laser printers are combined with other hardware devices, such as a copier and scanner, into a multi-function device. A **multi-function device** provides common device functionality at a lower cost than purchasing each device separately. Printers are classified by two main characteristics: resolution and speed. Printer resolution refers to the sharpness and clarity of a printed page. For printers, the resolution indicates the number of dots per inch (dpi). For example, a 300-dpi printer is one that is capable of printing 300 distinct dots in a line one-inch long, or 90,000 dots per square inch. The higher the dpi, the sharper the print quality. Printer speed is measured in pages per minute (ppm). The speed of printers varies widely. In general, ink-jet printers range from about 4 to 10 ppm, while laser printers range from about 10 to 30 ppm. The speed depends on the amount of printer memory (the more the better) and the page's contents: if there is just text or the page has only one color, the ppm is in the high range, but when a page contains graphics and/or has multiple colors, the ppm rate falls to the low range.

Ink-jet and laser printers are 2D printers that print documents on paper. In Windows 8.1, you can also print to 3D printers (**New!**). A **3D printer** builds physical objects from digital 3D models that you can actually hold, which is useful for rapidly creating prototypes for products and creating art projects. It allows you to model a 3D object on a computer using a CAD (Computer Aided Design) or 3D modeling app and then print it using a variety of materials from plastic, ceramics to metal. Many consumer 3D printers, such as Cubify CubeX and LulzBot AO-101, use a plastic filament to build a 3D object a layer at a time.

Ink-jet printer

Laser printer

Multi-function device

# Viewing Printers

After you install a printer, the printer appears in the Devices and Printers window (from Control Panel) and on the Devices panel (from Settings panel)—a centralized place to check and manage all your devices—and in a program's Print dialog box, where you can view and change printer properties and preferences. Every installed printer is represented by an icon in the Devices and Printers window. When you select a printer icon, status information for that printer appears in the Details pane, such as number of documents to be printed, and whether the printer is ready to print. A printer icon appears in the window without a cable indicates a **local printer**, while a printer icon with a cable (not all instances) indicates a **network printer**. A local printer is a printer connected directly to your PC, and a network printer is one connected to a network to which you have access. A printer icon that appears with two heads indicates that other network users share the printer directly connected to your PC, known as a **shared printer**.

## View Printer Properties

1. In the Start screen, click or tap the **Apps view** button, and then click or tap **Control Panel**.

2. Click or tap the **Devices and Printers** icon in Small icons or Large icons view.

3. Click or tap a printer icon.

   Printer properties appears in the Details pane.

4. Click or tap the **Close** button.

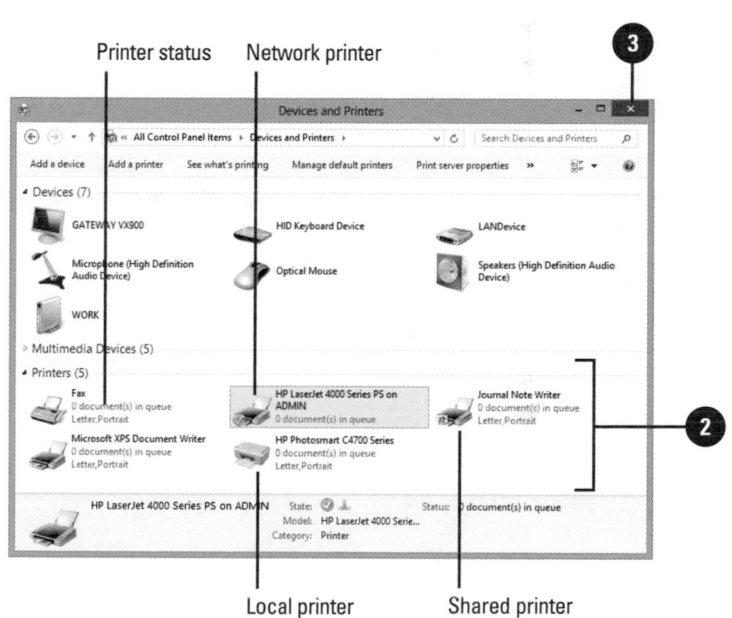

Printer status    Network printer

Local printer    Shared printer

## Did You Know?

*You can access additional buttons on the toolbar in the Devices and Printers window.* In the Devices and Printers window, if a double arrow (>>) appears on the toolbar when you select a device, you can click or tap it to show additional commands.

*You can display printer status by displaying views in the Devices and Printers window.* In the Devices and Printers window, click or tap the Views button on the toolbar, and then click or tap Tiles or Details. Printer status appears along with the printer name.

# Installing a Printer

To install a printer, you do not need to shut down your system. Simply attach the printer cable to the appropriate connector on your PC, according to the manufacturer's instructions. If you connect your printer—either 2D or 3D (**New!**)—to your PC through a USB port, Windows detects the new hardware device and installs the printer, and you are ready to print. Otherwise, you can use the Add a printer wizard in the Control Panel or Devices panel in PC settings to detect and install the printer. The Add a printer wizard asks you a series of questions to help you install a printer—either a shared printer by name, printer using a TCP/IP address, Bluetooth printer, local printer, or network printer—establish a connection, and print a test page.

## Set Up a Detected Printer

1. In the Start screen, click or tap the **Apps view** button, and then click or tap **Control Panel**.

2. Click or tap the **Devices and Printers** icon in Small icons or Large icons view.

3. Click or tap the **Add a printer** button on the toolbar.

4. Select the printer you want to install, and then click or tap **Next** to continue.

5. If necessary, click or tap **Install driver** to install the printer driver.

6. Type a printer name, and then click or tap **Next** to continue.

7. Select or clear the **Set as the default printer** check box.

8. To test the printer, click or tap **Print a test page**.

9. Click or tap **Finish**.

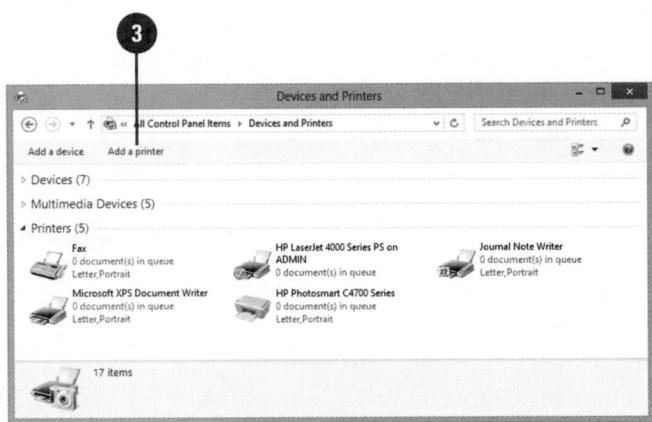

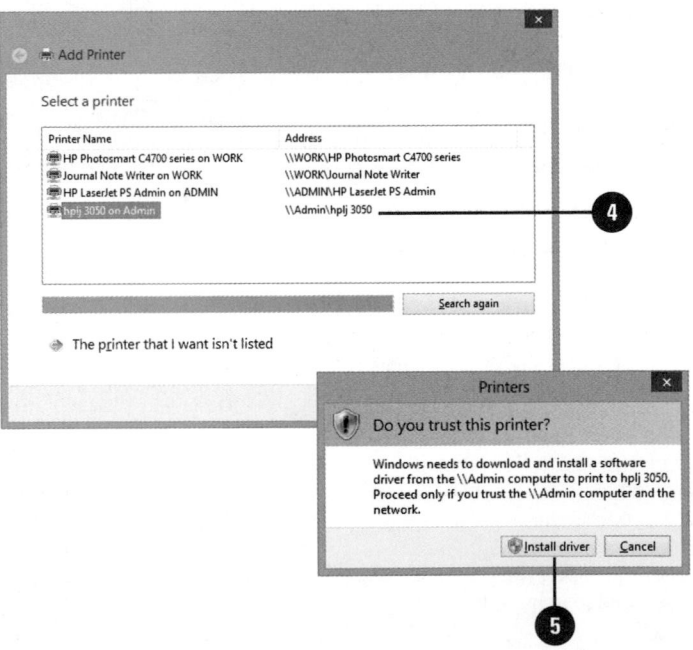

## Did You Know?

*You can display printer and communication ports.* In the Devices and Printers window, select a printer, click or tap the Print Server Properties button on the toolbar, and then click or tap the Ports tab.

## Set Up a Non Detected Printer

1. In the Start screen, click or tap the **Apps view** button, and then click or tap **Control Panel**.

2. Click or tap the **Devices and Printers** icon in Small icons or Large icons view.

3. Click or tap the **Add a printer** button on the toolbar.

4. Click or tap **The printer that I want isn't listed**.

5. Select an option with the type of printer you want to install: Shared printer by name, printer using a TCP/IP address, Bluetooth printer, or local or network printer.

6. Click or tap **Next** to continue.

   Options vary depending on the selected printer; steps provided for a local or network printer.

7. Select the **Use an existing port** or **Create a new port** option, and then click or tap **Next** to continue.

8. Select the printer manufacturer and model, and then click or tap **Next** to continue.

9. Type a printer name, and then click or tap **Next** to continue.

10. Click or tap the **Do not share this printer** or **Share this printer so that others on your network can find and use it** option, and then click or tap **Next** to continue.

11. Select or clear the **Set as the default printer** check box.

12. To test the printer, click or tap **Print a test page**.

13. Click or tap **Finish**.

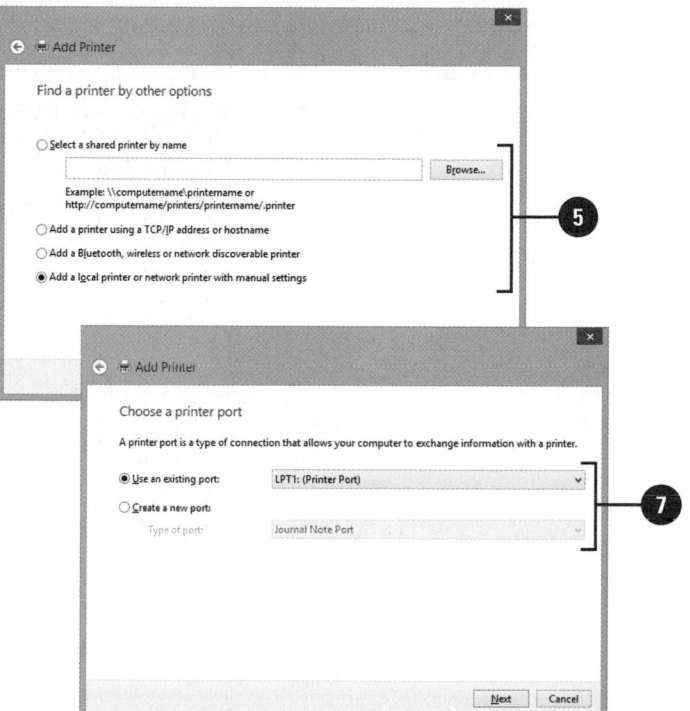

## For Your Information

### Understanding USB Ports

A **port** is the location on the back of your PC where you connect the printer cable. You can connect the cable to either a printer port, which is labeled LPT1 or LPT2, to a communications port, which is labeled COM1 or COM2, or to a Universal Serial Bus port, which is labeled USB. A printer port is called a **parallel port**, which sends more than one byte simultaneously. A communications port is called a **serial port**, which sends information one byte at a time. The USB port is a new technology that is expected to replace parallel and serial ports. A **USB (Universal Serial Bus) port** is an external hardware interface on the PC that allows you to connect a USB device. A single USB port can be used to connect up to 127 peripheral devices, such as mice, modems, and keyboards, and supports data transfer rates of 480 Mbs (480 million bits per second). USB also supports plug and play installation and **hot plugging**, which is the ability to add and remove devices to a PC while it's running and have the operating system automatically recognize the change.

# Specifying a Default Printer

If your PC is connected to more than one printer, you can choose the default printer. The default printer is typically the printer that you use most often. However, if you use different default printers based on your location, you can set them and let Windows use location-aware printing to automatically select the right one, which is great for laptops. When you start a print job without specifying a printer, the job is sent to the default printer. You can select a default printer in the Devices and Printers window or when you set up a new printer. The default printer displays a green circle with a check mark in the printer icon.

## Select a Default Printer

1. In the Start screen, click or tap the **Apps view** button, and then click or tap **Control Panel**.

2. Click or tap the **Devices and Printers** icon in Small icons or Large icons view.

3. Right-click or tap-hold the printer icon you want to set as the default, and then click or tap **Set as default printer**.

4. Click or tap the **Close** button.

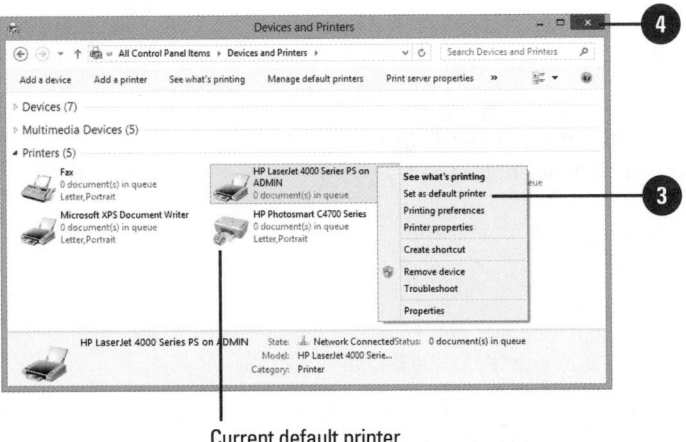

Current default printer

## Manage Default Printers

1. In the Devices and Printers window, click or tap the **Manage default printers** button on the toolbar.

2. Click or tap the **Always use the same printer as my default printer** or **Change my default printer when I change networks** option.

3. Select a network, select a printer, and then click or tap **Add**.

4. To change a printer, select and change it, and then click or tap **Update**.

5. To remove a printer, select it, and then click or tap **Remove**.

6. Click or tap **OK**.

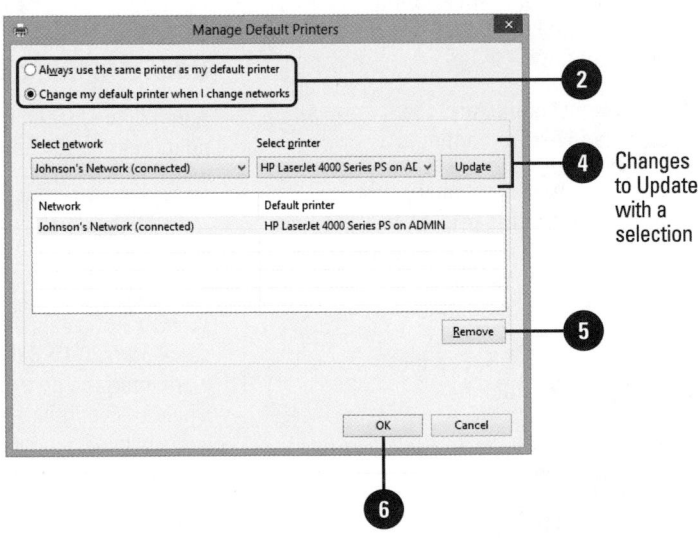

Changes to Update with a selection

# Renaming or Deleting a Printer

If you have trouble identifying a printer, or if you just want to change the name, you can rename it. You rename the same way you rename a file or folder. When you rename a printer, the new name appears in the Print dialog box for all your programs. If you no longer use a printer, you can delete it. When you delete the default printer, Windows displays a warning and changes the default printer to another available printer.

## Rename a Printer

1. In the Start screen, click or tap the **Apps view** button, and then click or tap **Control Panel**.

2. Click or tap the **Devices and Printers** icon in Small icons or Large icons view.

3. Right-click or tap-hold the printer icon you want to rename, and then click or tap **Printer properties**.

4. Type a new name for the printer on the General tab.

5. Click or tap **OK**.

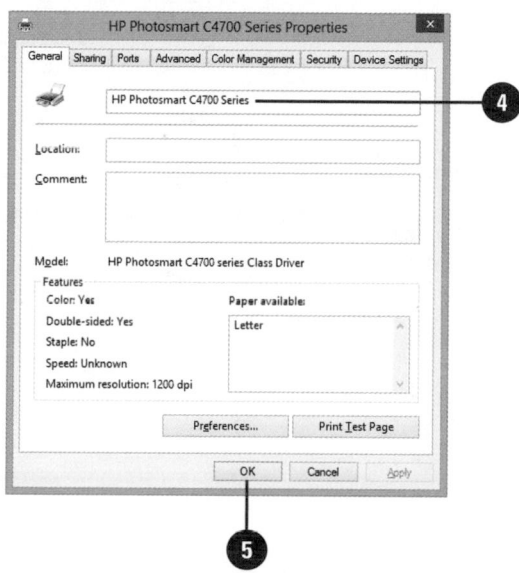

## Delete a Printer

1. In the Devices and Printers window, select the printer icon you want to delete.

2. Click or tap the **Remove Device** button on the toolbar (click or tap >> to access, if necessary) or press the Delete key.

   **TIMESAVER** *You can also right-click or tap-hold the printer icon you want to delete, and then click or tap Remove device.*

3. Click or tap **Yes** to confirm the deletion.

4. Click or tap the **Close** button.

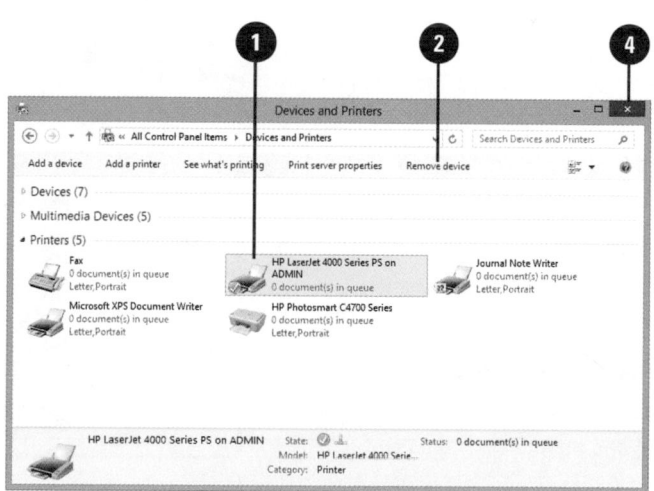

# Printing Documents

With an installed 2D or 3D (**New!**) printer, you can print documents and 3D models from a desktop or metro app. The process is the same. If you want to print multiple documents, you can print them all directly from a folder window from the desktop without having to open each one in its app. The app needs to be installed on your PC to complete the job. If you are using a metro app, you can print documents or selected content with the Devices button on the Charms bar.

## Print a Document in Desktop Apps

1. In File Explorer (desktop), open the app and the document that you want to print.

2. Click or tap the **File** tab or menu, and then click or tap **Print**.

3. Select the printer you want to use.

4. Select the options you want.

   Options vary depending on the type of documents you select.

5. Click or tap **Print**.

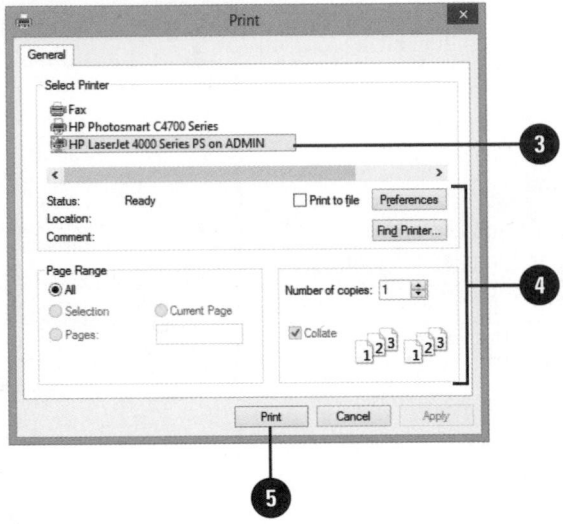

## Print Multiple Documents from the Desktop

1. In File Explorer (desktop), open the folder that contains the documents you want to print.

2. Select the documents.

3. Click or tap the **Print** button on the Share tab.

   ◆ You can also click or tap the **Open** button arrow on the Home tab, and then click or tap **Windows Photo Viewer**.

4. If prompted, select the options you want, and then click or tap **Print**.

   Options vary depending on the type of documents you select.

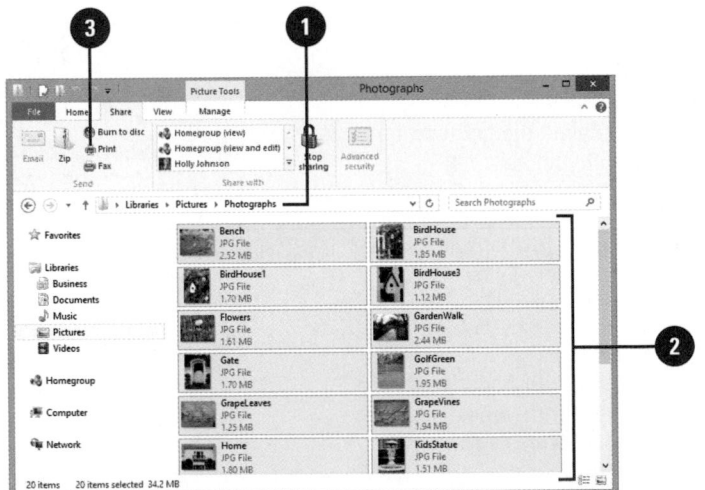

## Print a Document in Metro Apps

1. In a metro app, open a document, and then select or display the content or document you want to print.

2. Click or tap the **Devices** button on the Charms bar.

3. Click or tap **Print** on the Devices panel.

   ◆ **Add a printer.** Click or tap the **Add a printer** link to open the Devices panel in PC settings, click or tap **Add a device**, and then select an attached printer.

4. Click or tap the printer you want to use on the Print panel

5. Select the print options you want. for additional option, click or tap **More settings**.

   Options vary depending on the printer you select.

6. Click or tap **Print**.

### Did You Know?

*You can add a printer from PC settings.* Click or tap the Settings button on the Charms bar, click or tap PC settings, click or tap PC and devices, click or tap Devices, click or tap Add a device, and then select an attached printer.

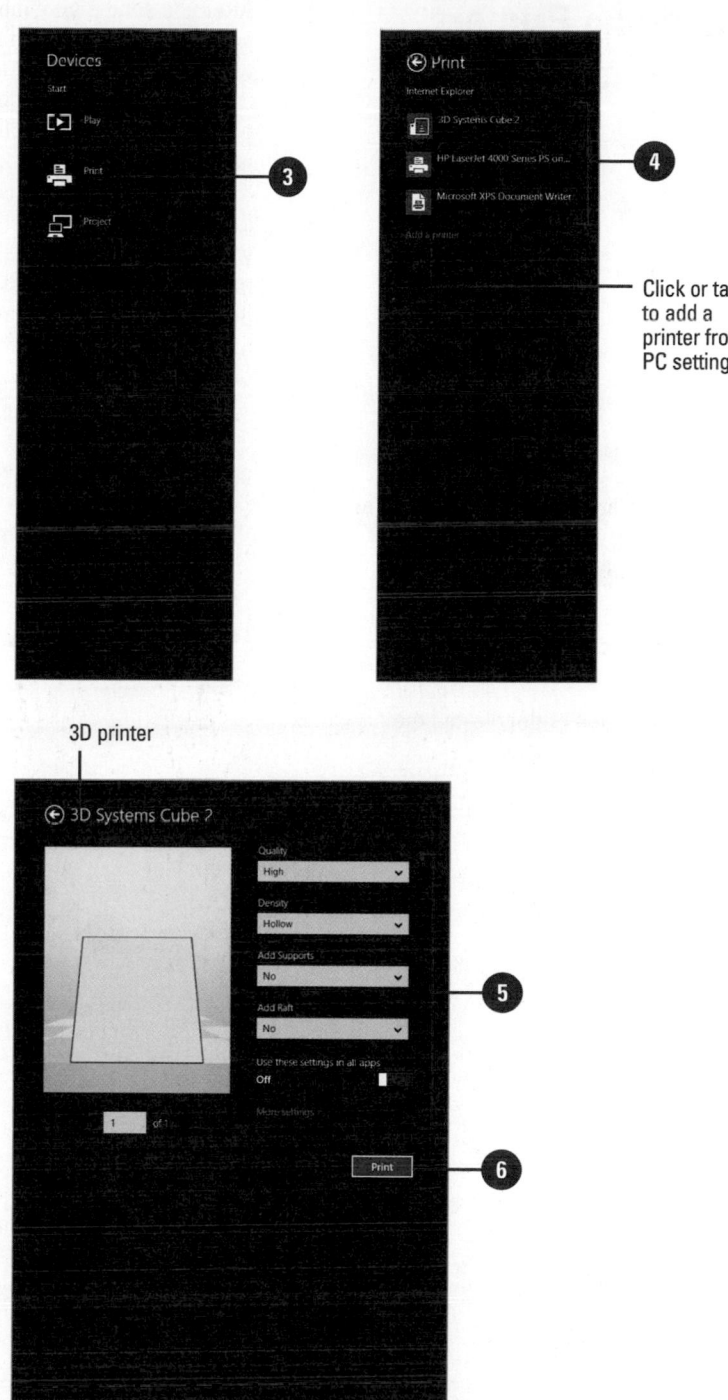

Click or tap to add a printer from PC settings

3D printer

# Managing Printers and Print Jobs

After you send a print job to the printer from the Print dialog box in a program, or drag files to the Printer icon in the Devices and Printers window, you can check the status. To check the status of a printer or manage multiple print jobs, you can double-click or tap the appropriate printer icon in the Devices and Printers window or on the taskbar in the notification area. A window opens showing the **print queue**, which is the list of files to be printed. You can use this window to cancel print jobs, temporarily pause print jobs, view printer properties, and so on. If you are having problems with a printer or print job, you can **defer**, or halt, the printing process to avoid getting error messages. With deferred printing, you can send a job to be printed even if your PC is not connected to a printer. To do this, you pause printing, and the file waits in the print queue until you turn off pause printing.

## Pause and Resume Printing

**1** In the Start screen, click or tap the **Apps view** button, and then click or tap **Control Panel**.

**2** Click or tap the **Devices and Printers** icon in Small icons or Large icons view.

**3** Double-click or double-tap the printer icon.

**4** If a printer window opens, click or tap the **Printer** link at the top.

**5** Click or tap the **Printer** menu, and then click or tap **Pause Printing**.

**6** To resume printing, click or tap the **Printer** menu, and then click or tap **Resume Printing**.

**7** Click or tap the **Close** button.

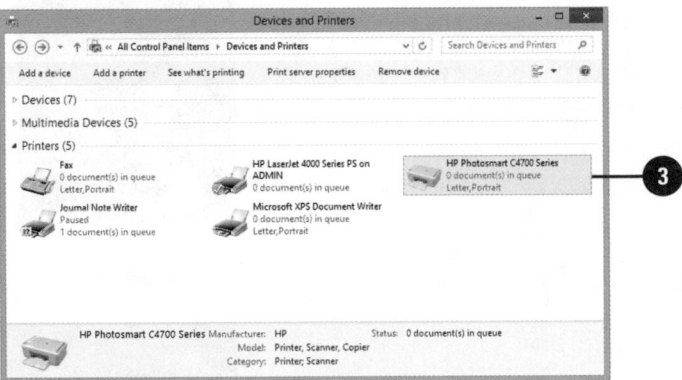

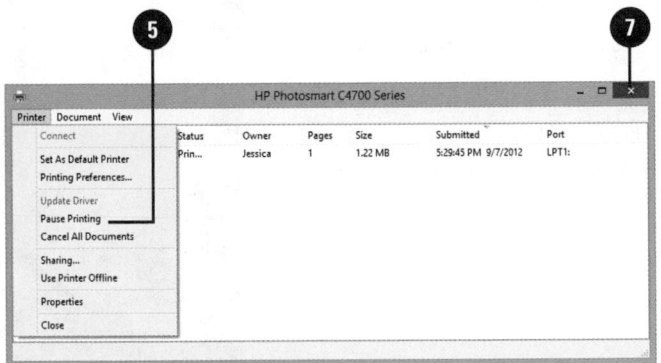

## Pause a Print Job

1 In the Devices and Printers window, double-click or double-tap the printer icon.

2 If a printer window opens, click or tap the **Printer** link at the top.

3 Right-click or tap-hold the document you want to pause, and then click or tap **Pause**.

4 To resume the document printing, right-click or tap-hold the document you want to resume, and then click or tap **Restart**.

5 Click or tap the **Close** button.

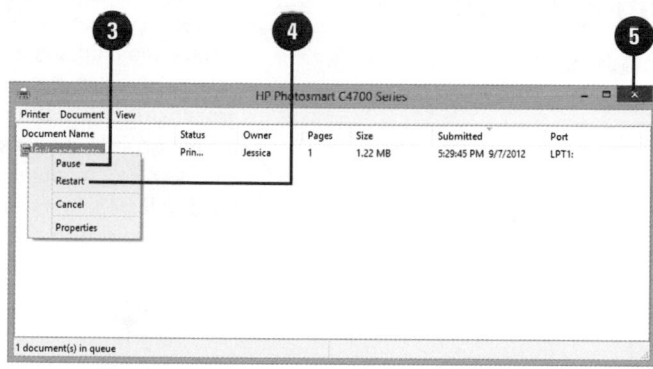

## Cancel a Print Job

1 In the Devices and Printers window, double-click or double-tap the printer icon.

2 If a printer window opens, click or tap the **Printer** link at the top.

3 Right-click or tap-hold the document you want to stop, and then click or tap **Cancel**.

4 To cancel all documents, click or tap the **Printer** menu, click or tap **Cancel All Documents**, and then click or tap **Yes** to confirm the cancelation.

5 Click or tap the **Close** button.

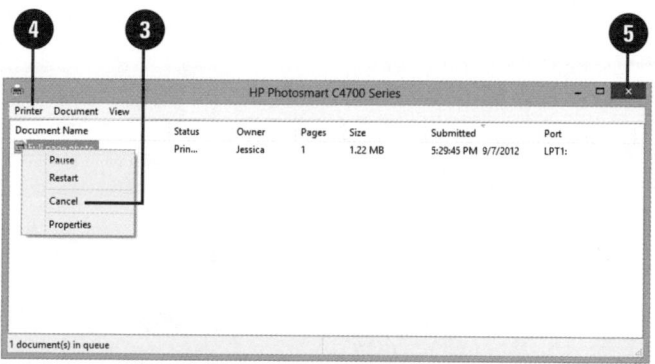

---

### Security Alert

## Displaying Printer Notification

For security purposes, if Windows Firewall is turned on (the default setting), printer notification information, such as "Ready" or "Paused," in the Devices and Printers folder is slightly delayed and your PC no longer receives other printer notifications, such as "Print job completed" or "Printer out of paper".

# Changing Printer Properties

Viewing printer properties gives you information about a printer's connection or network location, sharing options, related software drivers, color management options, graphics settings, installed fonts, and other advanced settings, such as **spooling**. Spooling, also known as **background printing**, is the process of storing a temporary copy of a file on the hard disk and then sending the file to the print device. Spooling allows you to continue working with the file as soon as it is stored on the disk instead of having to wait until the file is finished printing.

## Change Printer Device and Spooling Properties

1. In the Start screen, click or tap the **Apps view** button, and then click or tap **Control Panel**.

2. Click or tap the **Devices and Printers** icon in Small icons or Large icons view.

3. Right-click or tap-hold the printer icon you want to change, and then click or tap **Printer properties**.

4. Click or tap the **Device Settings** tab.

5. Click or tap an option link.

6. Click or tap an option list arrow, and then select a setting.

7. Click or tap the **Advanced** tab.

8. Click or tap the **Spool print documents so program finishes printing faster** option.

9. Click or tap a spooling option to specify when you want the printer to start printing your documents.

10. To keep documents in the spooler after printing, select the **Keep printed documents** check box.

11. To print documents that have completed spooling before others, select the **Print spooled documents first** check box.

12. Click or tap **OK**.

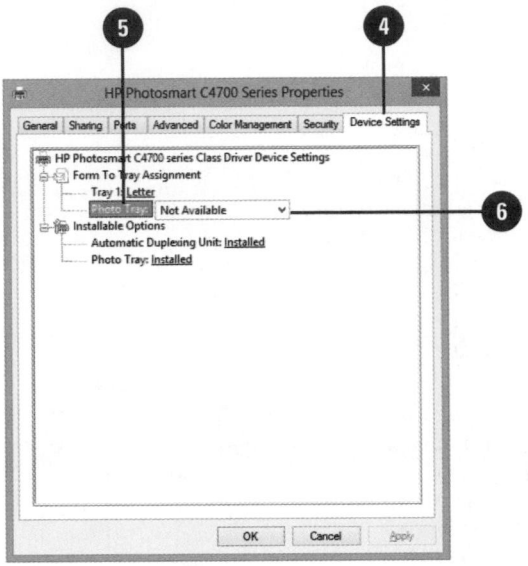

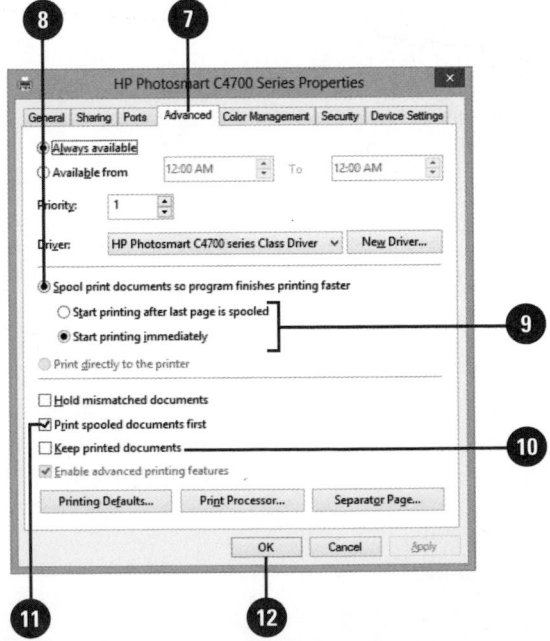

# Changing Printer Preferences

In addition to printer properties, you can also view and change personal printer preferences, such as orientation, page order, pages per sheet, paper size, paper tray selection, copy count, and print quality and color. When you change personal printing preferences from the Devices and Printers folder, the default settings are changed for all documents you print to that printer. When you change personal preferences from the Print or Page Setup dialog boxes within a program, the settings are changed for individual documents. The available printing preferences depend on the printer.

## Change Printer Preferences

1 In the Start screen, click or tap the **Apps view** button, and then click or tap **Control Panel**.

2 Click or tap the **Devices and Printers** icon in Small icons or Large icons view.

3 Right-click or tap-hold the the printer icon you want to change, and then click or tap **Printing preferences**.

4 Click or tap the tab with the option you want to change; tabs and options vary depending on the printer.

5 Change the printer preferences you want to modify.

6 Click or tap **OK**.

7 Click or tap the **Close** button.

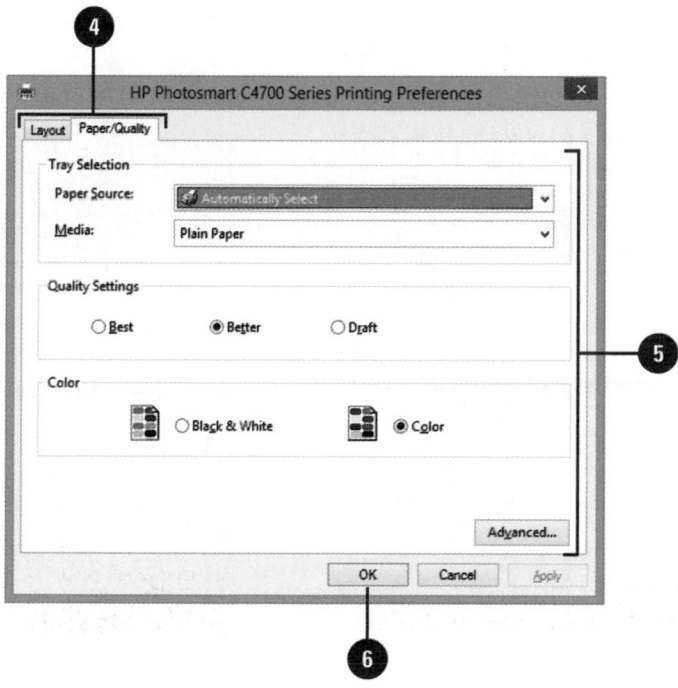

# Sharing a Printer

If you have a printer connected to your PC computer and it's connected to a network, you can share your printer with other network users. Before you can share a printer, you need to turn on printer sharing in the Network and Sharing Center window, which you can accomplish by using the Sharing tab in the Printer Properties dialog box. After you share a printer, the printer icon appears with two heads in the Devices and Printers window. For security purposes, if Windows Firewall is enabled (the default setting) on the system with the shared PC computer, then you need to select the File and Printer Sharing check box on the Exceptions tab in Windows Firewall for others to use the shared printer.

## Share a Printer

1. In the Start screen, click or tap the **Apps view** button, and then click or tap **Control Panel**.

2. Click or tap the **Devices and Printers** icon in Small icons or Large icons view.

3. Right-click or tap-hold the printer you want to share, and then click or tap **Printer properties**.

4. Click or tap the **Sharing** tab.

5. Select the **Share this printer** check box.

6. Type a name for the printer (eight characters recommended), or use the suggested one.

7. If other PCs on the network are using different versions of Windows, click or tap **Additional Drivers** to install other drivers for other PCs, select the check boxes for the operating systems you want, and then click or tap **OK**.

8. If prompted to install drivers, click or tap **Install** or **OK**.

9. Click or tap **OK**.

10. Click or tap the **Close** button.

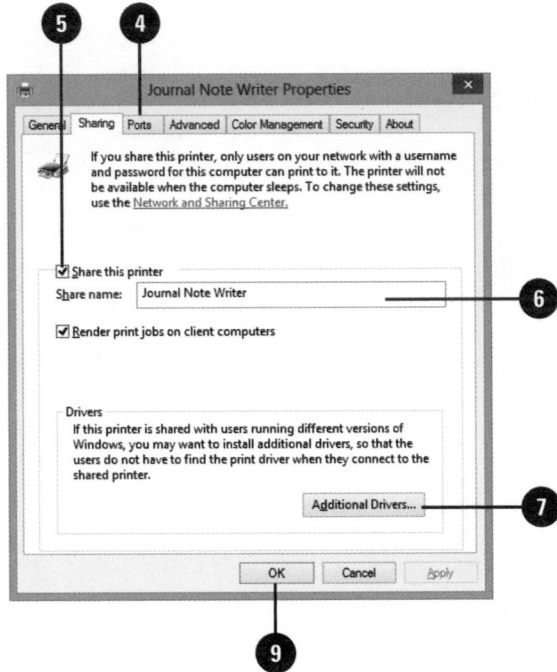

# Creating an XPS Document

Have you ever used Adobe Reader to view a document or created a PDF document? Well, now you can do the same type of thing with Microsoft's XPS (XML Paper Specification). An XPS file looks the same on the destination as it does on the source, so you can share it with others who don't have the source software. You create an XPS document, either XPS Document (.xps) or OpenXPS Document (.oxps), by printing it with the Microsoft XPS Document Writer printer. The XPS Viewer or the Reader app allows you to open any XPS document. The OpenXPS Document format is only supported by Windows 8.1. In the XPS Viewer, you can set permissions to take notes or fill in forms and add digital signatures to protect the document from unauthorized viewing or printing.

## Create and View an XPS File

1. Open the program and document you want to create as an XPS document.

2. Click or tap the **File** tab or menu, and then click or tap **Print**.

3. Select **Microsoft XPS Document Writer** as your printer.

4. Click or tap **Print**.

5. Specify a location, name the XPS document, select a file format (XPS or OXPS), and then click or tap **Save**.

6. In the Start screen, click or tap the **Apps view** button, and then click or tap **XPS Viewer**.

   ◆ You can also click or tap **Reader** to open and view the document in a metro app.

7. Click or tap the **File** button, and then click or tap **Open**.

8. Navigate to and select the XPS document you want to view, and then click or tap **Open**.

9. Use the buttons on the toolbar to set and remove permissions, add digital signatures, print the document, and change the view percentage.

10. When you're done, click or tap the **Close** button.

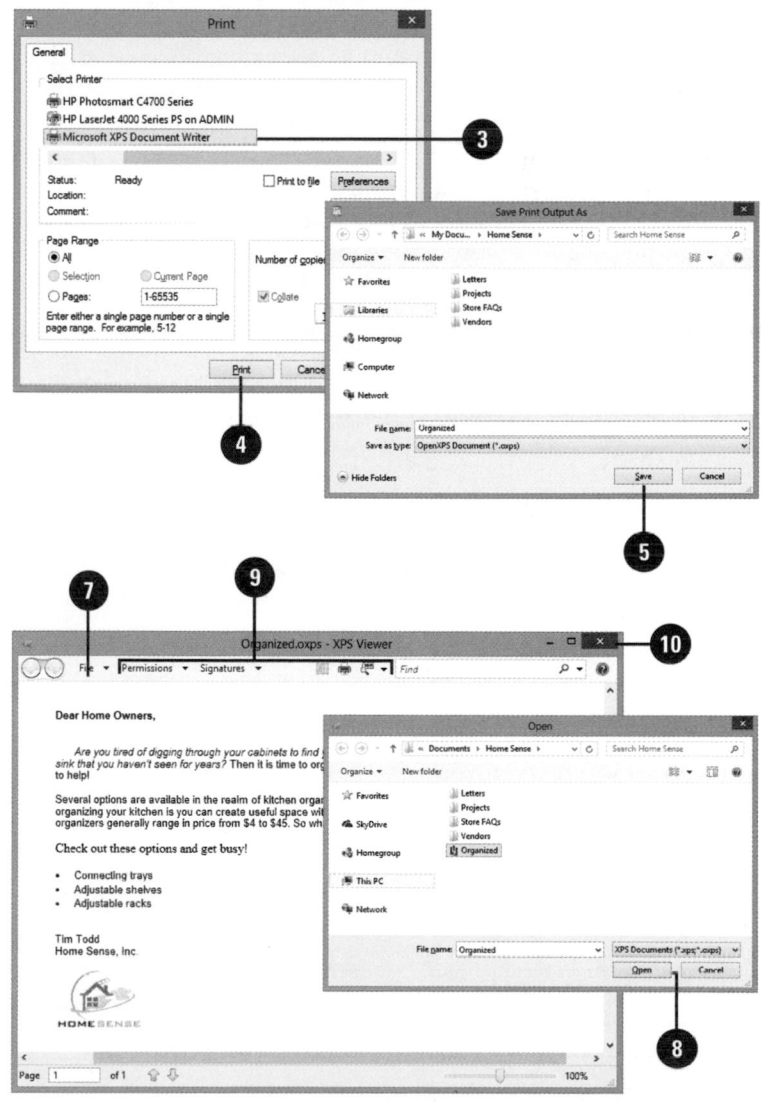

# Understanding Faxes

Windows Fax and Scan is a program that allows you to send and receive faxes, fax or e-mail scanned documents, and forward faxes as e-mail attachments from your PC. From Windows Fax and Scan, you can monitor the progress of incoming and outgoing fax activity.

Before you can use Windows Fax and Scan, you need a fax device for sending and receiving faxes. The fax device can be directly attached to your PC, known as a **local fax**, or located on a network, known as a **fax server**. Windows Fax and Scan makes it easy to setup a fax device with the Fax Setup wizard. You can only connect to one local fax, however you can connect to multiple fax servers or devices on a network. To start the Fax Setup wizard and set up a fax, click or tap Windows Fax and Scan on the Apps screen, click or tap Fax in the left pane, click or tap the Tools menu, click or tap Fax Accounts, and then click or tap Add. In the wizard, click or tap Connect To A Fax server On My Network, and then follow the on-screen instructions.

Once your fax is installed, you can use Windows Fax and Scan to send and receive faxes, manage incoming and outgoing faxes, and change fax device properties. You can also send faxes from a folder window or the Print dialog box in a program. When you print using a fax printer, Windows Fax and Scan starts and opens the New Fax window, where you can send a fax just like you send an e-mail message.

With the Fax Cover Page Editor, you can create and edit cover pages to use when you send a fax. The Fax Cover Page Editor is a full page editor that makes it easy to insert common fax page items, such as recipient, subject, number of pages, and message, and to format the page to create a professional look. You can also customize a few samples that come with the program.

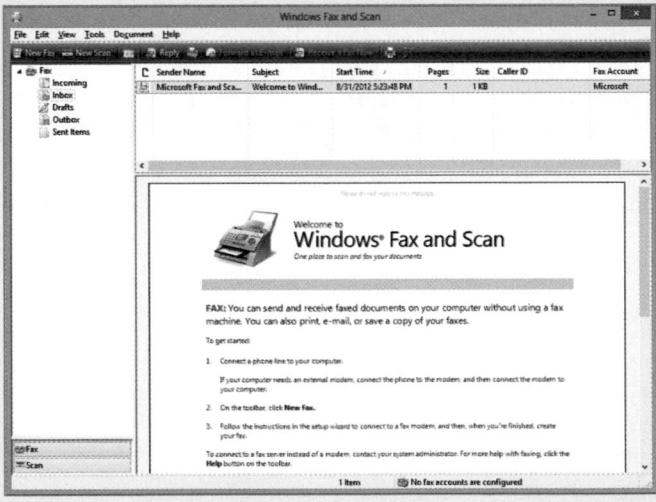

# Setting Up a Fax

If your PC or printer has a fax modem installed, you can send and receive faxes through your device. If you are not sure, you can use the Devices and Printers window to check if you have one installed. If not, you can use Add a device to install one. Using Windows Fax and Scan, you can send and receive faxes, fax or e-mail scanned documents, and forward faxes as e-mail attachments from your PC. The Fax Setup wizard helps you set up the Fax Service using a modem or a fax server. Afterwards, you can enter some personal information for the fax cover page, a phone number, and some options for the way you want to send and receive faxes.

## Set Up for Faxing

1. In the Start screen, click or tap the **Apps view** button, and then click or tap **Windows Fax and Scan**.

2. In the left pane, click or tap **Fax**.

   If you're connecting to a fax device for the first time, the New Fax button starts the Fax Setup wizard.

3. Click or tap the **New Fax** button on the toolbar.

   If the wizard doesn't start, click or tap the **Tools** menu, click or tap **Fax Accounts**, and then click or tap **Add**.

4. Click or tap **Connect to a fax modem** or **Connect to a fax server on my network**.

5. Follow the wizard instructions to complete the set up; options vary depending on the fax modem.

6. Click or tap the **Close** button on the New Fax window.

7. Click or tap the **Tools** menu, and then click or tap **Sender Information**.

8. Enter the information you want cover pages to display.

9. Click or tap **OK**.

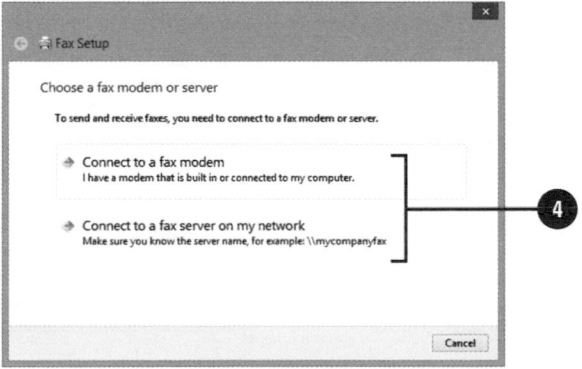

# Creating a Fax Cover Page

A cover page is typically a one page cover memo sent along with a fax containing the fax sender, a recipient, number of pages, a short message, and the transmission date and time. You can use the Fax Cover Page Editor to create your own cover pages or to customize cover page templates, known as common cover pages, that come with the program. You can copy and modify common cover pages without affecting the original templates. You can also edit existing cover pages and rename or delete personal cover pages as needed.

## Create a New Cover Page

1. In the Start screen, click or tap the **Apps view** button, and then click or tap **Windows Fax and Scan**.

2. Click or tap the **Fax** tab.

3. Click or tap the **Tools** menu, click or tap **Cover Pages**, and then click or tap **New**.

4. Click or tap the **View** menu, and then click or tap **Grid Lines**.

5. Click or tap the **Insert** menu, point to **Recipient**, **Sender**, or **Message**, and then click or tap an item.

6. Press and hold Ctrl, and then click or tap the items you want to select.

7. Drag the items to a new location, or use the alignment buttons on the toolbar.

8. Use the formatting buttons on the toolbar to format the text.

9. Use the drawing tools on the toolbar to add shapes and lines.

10. Click or tap the **File** menu, and then click or tap **Save As**.

11. Type a name for the cover page.

12. Click or tap **Save**.

13. Click or tap the **Close** button on the Fax Cover Page Editor.

14. Click or tap **Close**.

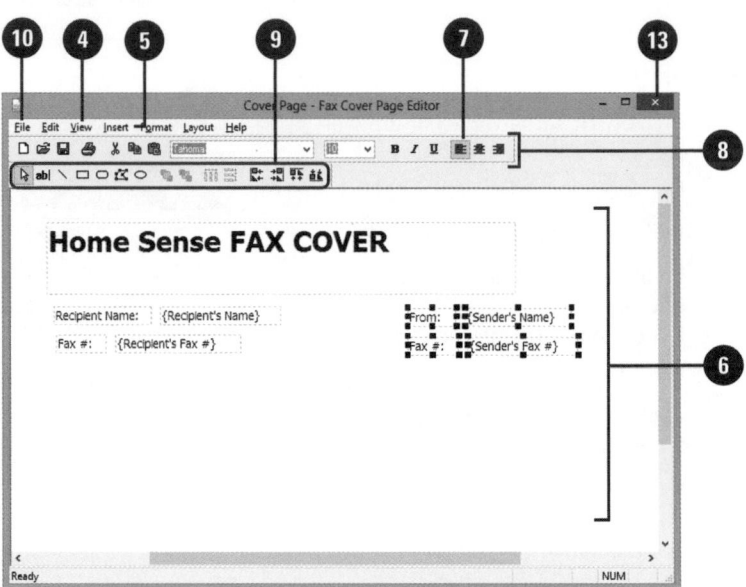

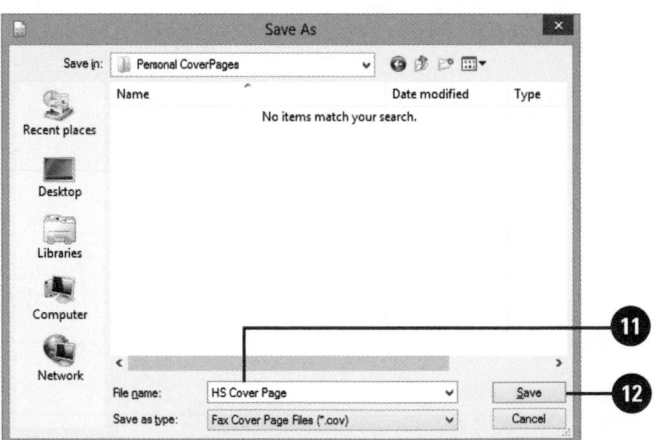

## Copy a Cover Page Template

1. In the Start screen, click or tap the **Apps view** button, and then click or tap **Windows Fax and Scan**.

2. Click or tap the **Fax** tab.

3. Click or tap the **Tools** menu, and then click or tap **Cover Pages**.

4. Click or tap **Copy**.

5. Select a common fax cover page.

6. Click or tap **Open**.

7. Click or tap **Close**.

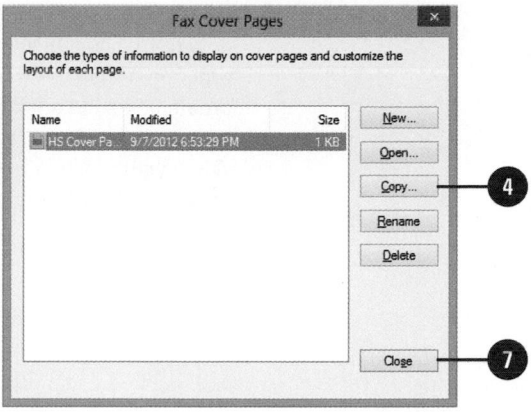

## Rename or Delete a Cover Page

1. In the Start screen, click or tap the **Apps view** button, and then click or tap **Windows Fax and Scan**.

2. Click or tap the **Fax** tab.

3. Click or tap the **Tools** menu, and then click or tap **Cover Pages**.

4. Click or tap a cover page.

5. To rename the cover page, click or tap **Rename**, type a new name (include the extension .cov), and then press Enter.

6. To delete the cover page, click or tap **Delete**, and then click or tap **Yes** to confirm it.

7. Click or tap **Close**.

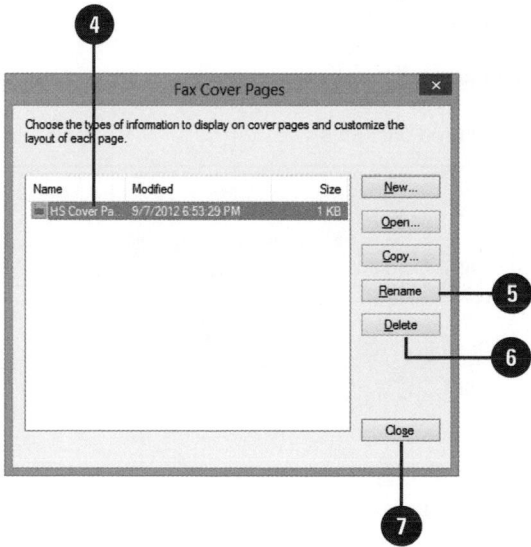

# Sending a Fax

After you install and configure your fax, you can send a fax using the New Fax window. You can send a cover page fax from the Printer window or from within Windows Fax and Scan, or a document fax from a program. When you send a fax, the New Fax window opens to help you create and send a fax. When you send a document fax, the program in which you open or create the document prints it to the fax device. When you print to a fax device, Windows Fax and Scan starts and opens the New Fax window where you can send the fax. Once a fax is sent successfully, it is moved to the Sent Items folder.

## Send a Fax

1 In the Start screen, click or tap the **Apps view** button, and then click or tap **Windows Fax and Scan**.

2 Click or tap the **Fax** tab.

3 Click or tap the **New Fax** button.

4 Click or tap the **Cover Page** list arrow, and then select a cover page.

5 Click or tap the **To** button, select the recipients you want, click or tap the **To** button, and then click or tap **OK**.

6 Type a subject.

7 Click or tap the **Dialing rule** list arrow, and then select a rule.

8 Type the message you want.

9 Click or tap the **Send** button on the toolbar.

10 To view the sent fax, click or tap the **Sent Items** icon, click or tap the fax you want to view, and then review the fax information.

11 When you're done, click or tap the **Close** button.

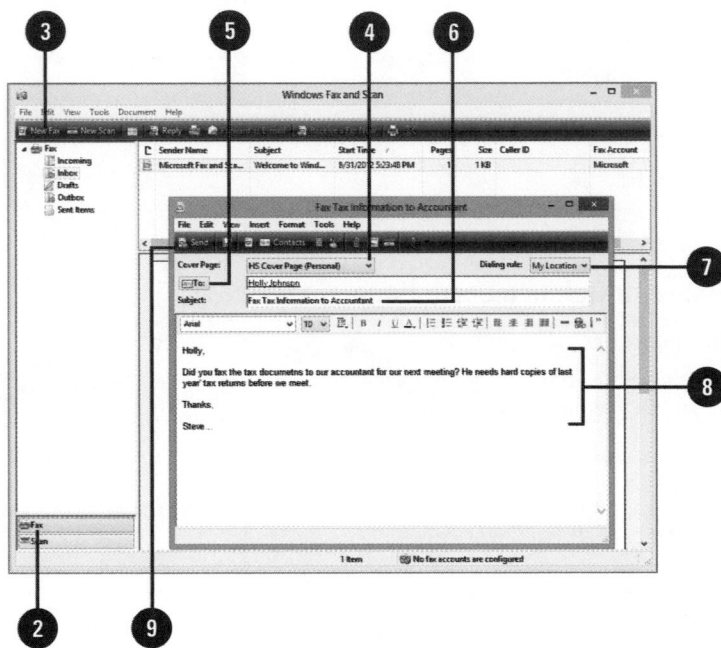

## Send a Fax from a Document

1. Start the program and open or create the document you want to send as a fax.

2. Click or tap the **File** tab or menu, and then click or tap **Print**.

   ◆ For a Microsoft Office 2013 program, click or tap the **File** tab, point to **Print**, and then click or tap **Print**.

3. Click or tap the Fax printer as your printer.

4. Click or tap **Print** or **OK**.

   Windows Fax and Scan opens and starts a new fax.

5. Click or tap the **Cover Page** list arrow, and then select a cover page.

6. Click or tap the **To** button, select a recipients you want, click or tap the **To** button, and then click or tap **OK**.

7. Type a subject, and any cover page notes you want.

8. Click or tap the **Dialing rule** list arrow, and then select a rule.

9. Type the message you want.

10. Click or tap the **Send** button on the toolbar.

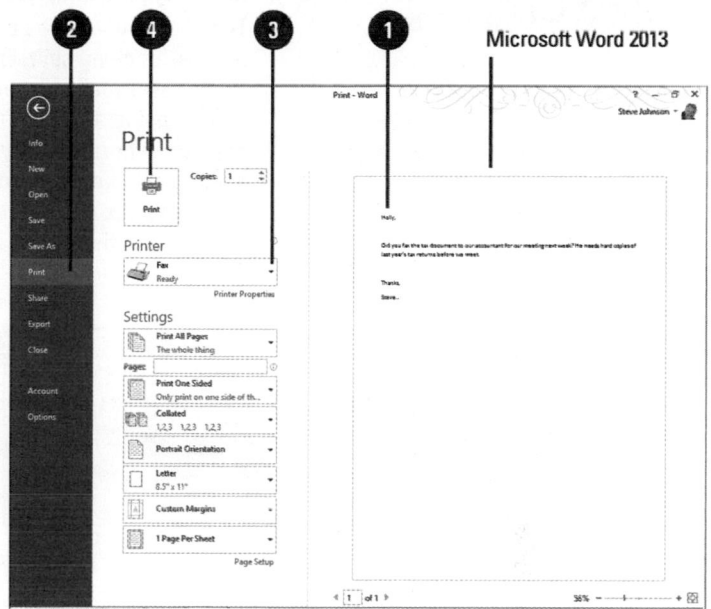

Microsoft Word 2013

### Did You Know?

*You can scan and fax a document.* Scan the document using a scanner, open the scanned document in a program, and then print it to the fax directly from the program.

# Managing Outgoing Faxes

After you send a fax, it's sent to the Outbox folder of the Fax Console. The Outbox is a storage area for all faxes waiting to be sent, or in the process of being sent. From the Outbox, you can pause and resume faxes, restart failed faxes, and remove individual faxes as necessary. If a fax is being sent to multiple recipients, the fax for each recipient appears separately, so you can pause or delete a fax to one of the multiple recipients without affecting the others. When you change the status of a fax in the Outbox, the Status column changes to indicate the new state of the fax.

## Cancel, Restart, Pause, or Resume an Outgoing Fax

1 In the Start screen, click or tap the **Apps view** button, and then click or tap **Windows Fax and Scan**.

2 Click or tap the **Fax** tab.

3 Click or tap the **Outbox** icon.

4 To cancel a fax, click or tap the fax, and then click or tap the **Delete** button.

5 To restart a failed fax, click or tap the fax, click or tap the **Document** menu, and then click or tap **Restart**.

6 To pause or resume a fax, click or tap the fax, click or tap the **Document** menu, and then click or tap **Pause** or **Resume**.

7 When you're done, click or tap the **Close** button.

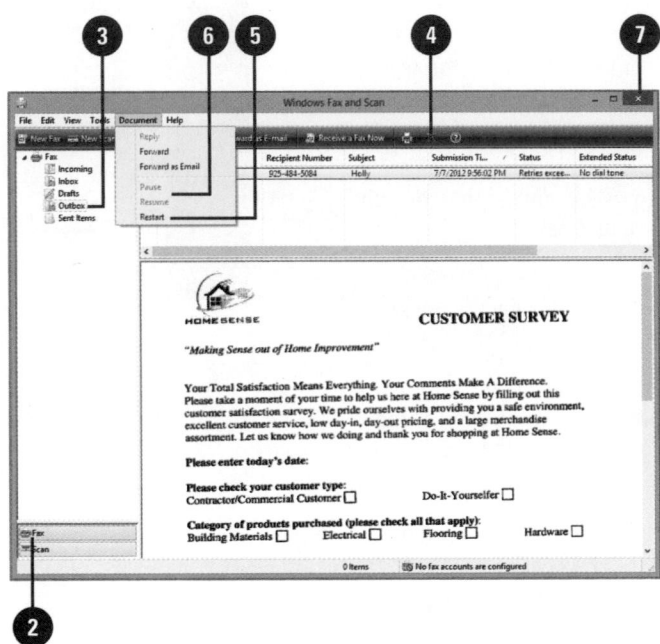

### Did You Know?

*You can't remove a fax from a remote fax printer without deleting the fax printer.* In the Devices and Printers window, click or tap the remote fax printer icon, and then click or tap the Delete Device button on the toolbar.

# Receiving a Fax

If you have a phone line attached to your PC, you can set up Windows Fax and Scan to receive faxes automatically or manually. If the phone line is a dedicated fax line and set to receive faxes automatically, Windows Fax and Scan automatically stores the fax in your Inbox, just like an e-mail in your e-mail program. If the phone line is used for voice and fax calls, Windows Fax and Scan waits for you to answer the call before it receives the fax.

## Receive a Fax Manually

1. When you receive a call for a fax, click or tap to receive the call to open the Fax Status Monitor dialog box.

2. Click or tap **Answer call**, if necessary.

3. Click or tap **View details** to see details about the call.

4. If there are problems with the fax or if you don't want to receive it, click or tap **Disconnect**.

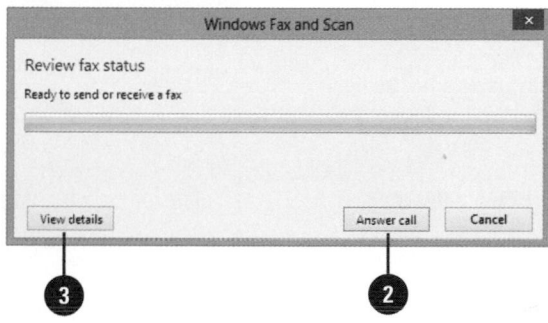

## Change Receive Answer Mode

1. In the Start screen, click or tap the **Apps view** button, and then click or tap **Windows Fax and Scan**.

2. Click or tap the **Fax** tab.

3. Click or tap the **Tools** menu, and then click or tap **Fax Settings**.

4. Click or tap the **General** tab.

5. Select the **Allow the device to receive fax calls** check box.

6. Click or tap the **Manually answer** or **Automatically answer after X rings** option.

7. Click or tap the **Tracking** tab, and then select the **Received** check box.

8. Click or tap **OK**.

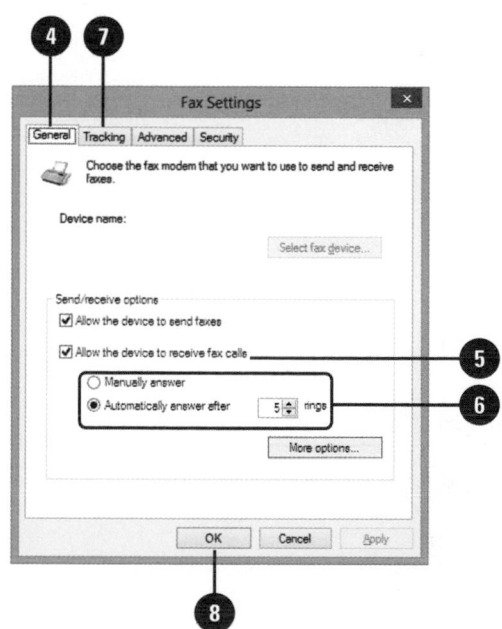

# Reviewing a Fax

After you receive a fax, you can use Fax Console to view, print, save, or e-mail the fax. Windows Fax and Scan informs you when a fax arrived, who sent it, how many pages were received, and the status of the job.

## Review a Received Fax

1. In the Start screen, click or tap the **Apps view** button, and then click or tap **Windows Fax and Scan**.

2. Click or tap the **Fax** tab.

3. To review the status of a fax being received, click or tap the **Incoming** icon.

4. Click or tap the **Inbox** icon.

5. Click or tap the fax to view.

6. Use the buttons on the toolbar to do the following:

    ◆ **Reply to the fax as another fax.**

    ◆ **Forward the fax as another fax.**

    ◆ **E-mail the fax as an attachment to a message.**

    ◆ **Print the fax to your printer.**

    ◆ **Delete the fax.**

7. To save the fax as a TIF file, click or tap the **File** menu, click or tap **Save As**, specify a name and location, and then click or tap **Save**.

8. When you're done, click or tap the **Close** button.

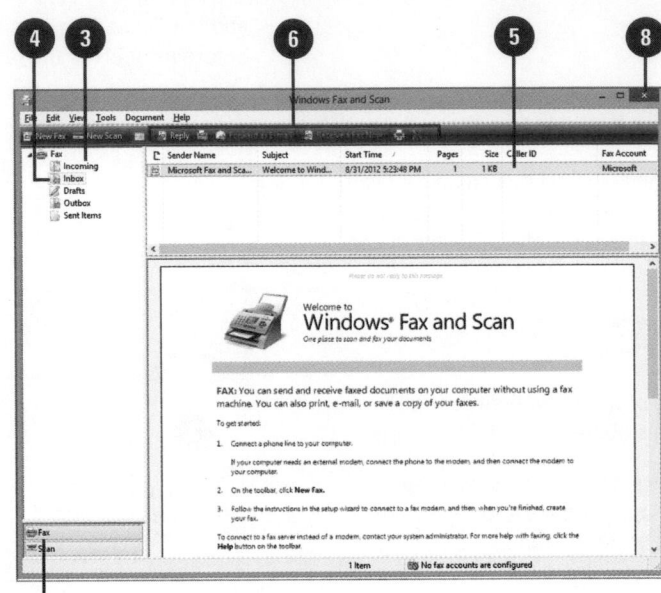

## Did You Know?

*You can sort faxes by a variety of different categories.* In Windows Fax and Scan, click or tap the View menu, point to Arrange By, and then select the way you want to sort. You can arrange by Fax Account, Caller ID, Subject, and Number of Pages, etc.

# Changing Fax Properties

You can change the send and receive properties for a fax device to effectively work with your phone line. You can change the number of times the the fax device tries to resend a fax and track and notify you when events take place. You can also change where to store a fax when you receive it. If you need to specify the use of a Transmitting Station Identifier (TSID), which is an identification sent along with a fax to identify the source, and a Called Subscriber Identifier (CSID), which is an identification sent back to the sending fax device to confirm the source identity, you can specify those settings as well.

## Change Fax Properties

1. In the Start screen, click or tap the **Apps view** button, and then click or tap **Windows Fax and Scan**.

2. Click or tap the **Fax** tab.

3. Click or tap the **Tools** menu, and then click or tap **Fax Settings**.

4. Click or tap the **General** tab.

5. Select the **Allow the device to send faxes** check box.

6. Select the **Allow the device to receive fax calls** check box, and then click or tap the **Manually answer** or **Automatically answer after X rings** option.

7. To change TSID or CSID, click or tap **More options**, enter fax numbers, and then click or tap **OK**.

8. To monitor fax events and send notifications, click or tap the **Tracking** tab, and then select the check boxes you want.

9. Click or tap the **Advanced** tab.

10. Type the number of redialing attempts and type the number of minutes to dial again for a redial.

11. To send faxes at a specific time when discount phone charges apply, specify a start and end time.

12. Click or tap **OK**.

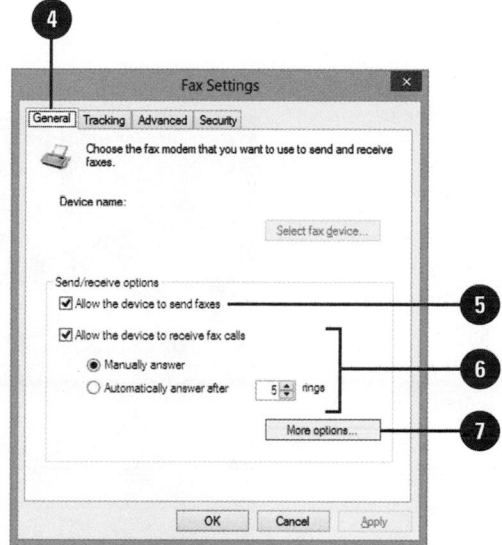

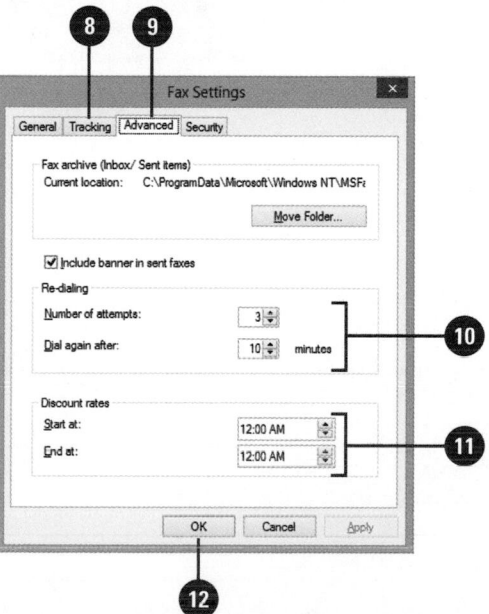

# Scanning a Document

After you connect and install a scanner, you can use the device in the Devices and Printer window in the Control Panel or start the Scan app (**New!**) on the Apps screen to scan documents. In the Scan app, you can specify easy to use scan settings (File Type, Color mode, Resolution (DPI), and Save folder), and then quickly preview or scan a document or picture. The Preview button previews the scan (doesn't save), while the Scan button scans and automatically save it. After the scan, you can choose to view your scan. If you saved it as an image file, it automatically opens in the Photos app in a split window. If you want to edit the scan, you can use the Rotate, Crop, or Edit buttons on the App bar.

## Scan a Document or Picture

**1** In the Start screen, click or tap the **Apps view** button, and then click or tap **Scan**.

**2** Place the document or picture on the scanner.

**3** Click or tap the **Expand/Collapse** arrow to display and set the following scan settings:

◆ **Source.** Select the scanner.

◆ **File Type.** Select a file type, such as PNG.

◆ **Color mode.** Select a color mode.

◆ **Resolution (DPI).** Select the number of dots per inch.

◆ **Save file to.** Select a location to save the file

**4** Click or tap the **Preview** button to preview the scan.

**5** Drag adjustment handles around what you want to scan.

**6** Click or tap the **Scan** button to final scan and save, and then click or tap **View** to display it in a side by side window.

### See Also

*See "Understanding Picture File Formats" on page 214 for information on the scanning settings.*

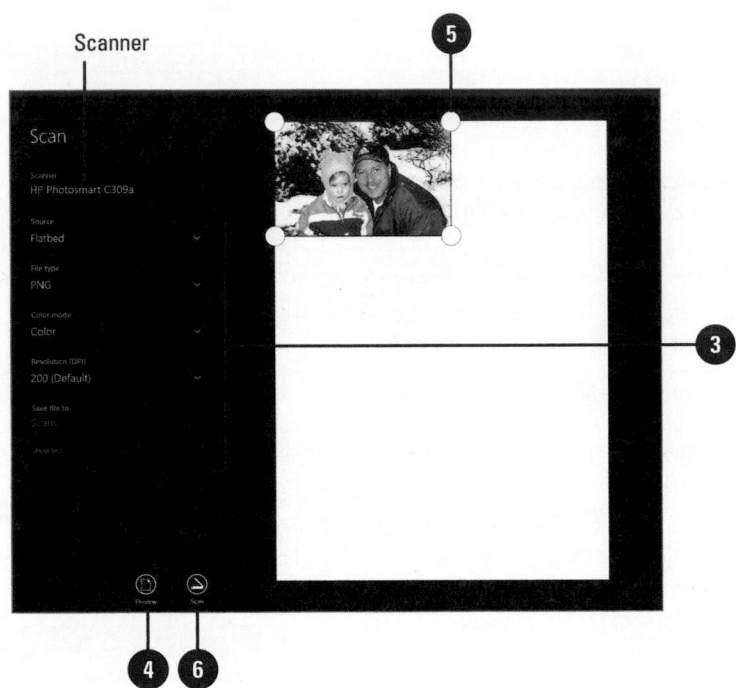

# Maintaining Your Computer

## Introduction

Windows 8.1 offers a number of useful tools for managing and maintaining routine tasks on your personal computer, such as installing and removing programs, and formatting, copying, and repairing disks. Windows also provides tools to find and fix disk problems, speed up disk access, and clean up disk space. By periodically finding and repairing disk errors, you can keep your files in good working condition and prevent disk problems that might cause you to lose your work. You can also schedule these tasks to run on a regular basis. If you find Windows performing sluggishly even after performing routine maintenance, you can adjust system processing and memory settings to improve performance.

Keeping your PC up-to-date is another way to keep your PC in good working condition and protect it against new and ongoing attacks over the Internet. Windows Update scans your PC for any software components or fixes (including security and high priority updates) that need to be installed and automatically or manually downloads them from the Internet. Each file that you download using Windows Update has a digital signature from Microsoft to ensure it's authenticity and security.

Windows 8.1 comes with File History that allows you to back up and restore drives and files on your system. The File History options process walks you through the steps of backing up or restoring files. If your system crashes and Windows cannot start, you can use a Startup Recovery drive and other recovery options to repair the problem or restore data from a backup. You can also use one of several startup options to help you start Windows in a safe environment with basic files and drivers where you can restore settings and fix the problems.

## What You'll Do

**Understand Disk File Systems**

**Format a Disk**

**Display Disk and Folder Information**

**Set Disk Quota for Users**

**Detect and Repair Disk Errors**

**Encrypt a Disk**

**Optimize and Clean Up a Disk**

**Boost Speed with a Removable Disk**

**Add or Remove Windows Components**

**Install or Uninstall a Program**

**Update Windows**

**Update and Refresh Windows**

**Keep a File History**

**Restore a File History**

**Create a System Image**

**Restore System Settings**

**Create a System Recovery Drive**

**Set Startup and Recovery Options**

**Start Windows When Problems Occur**

# Understanding Disk File Systems

A disk must be formatted with a **file system** that allows it to work with the operating system to store, manage, and access data. Two of the most common file systems are FAT (or FAT32, which is an improvement on FAT technology) and NTFS. Disks on DOS and pre-Windows XP PCs use the FAT file system, while disks on PCs running Windows XP and later can use either the NTFS or FAT system. NTFS is a newer file system that improves on some of the shortcomings of FAT disks that make them less desirable on a network. NTFS is the preferred file system for Windows 8.1.

There are important differences between FAT and NTFS file systems:

## FAT

When you format a disk with the FAT file system, a formatting program divides the disk into storage compartments. First it creates a series of rings, called **tracks**, around the circumference of the disk. Then it divides the tracks into equal parts, like pieces of a pie, to form sectors. The number of sectors and tracks depends on the size of the disk.

Although the physical surface of a disk is made of tracks and sectors, a file is stored in clusters. A cluster, also called an **allocation unit**, is one or more sectors of storage space. It represents the minimum amount of space that an operating system reserves when saving the contents of a file to a disk. Thus, a file might be stored in more than one cluster. Each cluster is identified by a unique number. The first two clusters are reserved by the operating system. The operating system maintains a file allocation table (or FAT) on each disk that lists the clusters on the disk and records the status of each cluster, whether it is occupied (and by which file), available, or defective. Each cluster in a file "remembers" its order in the chain of clusters—and each cluster points to the next one until the last cluster, which marks the end of the file. The FAT and FAT32 formats provide compatibility with other operating systems on your PC, which means you can configure your PC for a dual-boot or multi-boot setup and you can backup a previous operating system.

## exFAT

The exFAT file system is the next generation file system in the FAT (FAT12/16, FAT32) family. While retaining the simplicity advantages of FAT32, exFAT overcomes FAT32's 4 GB file size limit and scales up past FAT32's 32 GB formatter limit. This means you can copy files greater than 4 GB in size to an exFAT file system and format removable storage (Flash or hard disk) greater than 32 GB in capacity. In addition, exFAT is designed to enable cross operating system and cross-device (such as cameras and phones) interoperation, which will be possible as manufacturers build support for exFAT into their devices.

## NTFS

NTFS features a built-in security system that does not allow users to access the disk unless they have a user account and password with the necessary rights and permissions. NTFS protects disks from damage by automatically redirecting data from a bad sector to a good sector without requiring you to run a disk-checking utility. Given the reliability and the built-in repair mechanisms of NTFS disks, only rarely do they require maintenance. This is an example of **fault tolerance**, the ability of a disk to resist damage, which is a critical issue with disks on a network.

## Selecting a file system

NTFS supports removable Flash media, but not floppy disks, so they are formatted with a FAT. If you are running Windows on a stand-alone PC, you can choose either a FAT or NTFS, but in most cases, the file system has already been determined either by the person who originally set up the PC or by the manufacturer from whom you purchased the PC. If your PC is a client on a Windows network, it is likely that your hard disk uses NTFS. Because

NTFS is more suited to network demands, such as a high level of security and resistance to system failure, network administrators format network disks with NTFS whenever possible. Sometimes, however, users on a network want or need to use a non-Windows operating system. Also, a user might need a PC that is capable of running an earlier version of Windows. The disks on that PC would then be formatted with a FAT.

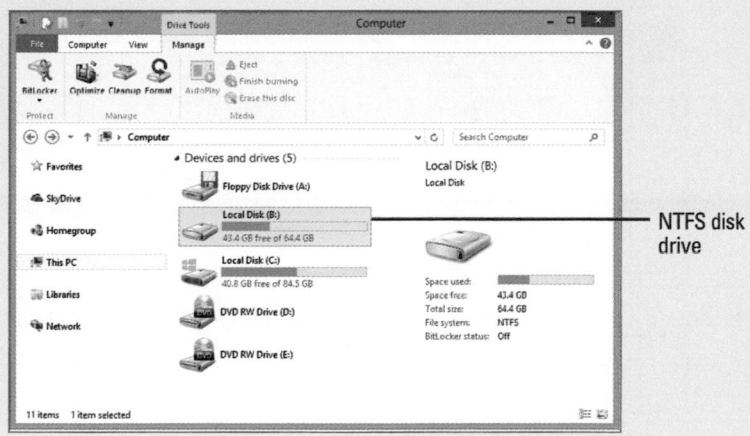

NTFS disk drive

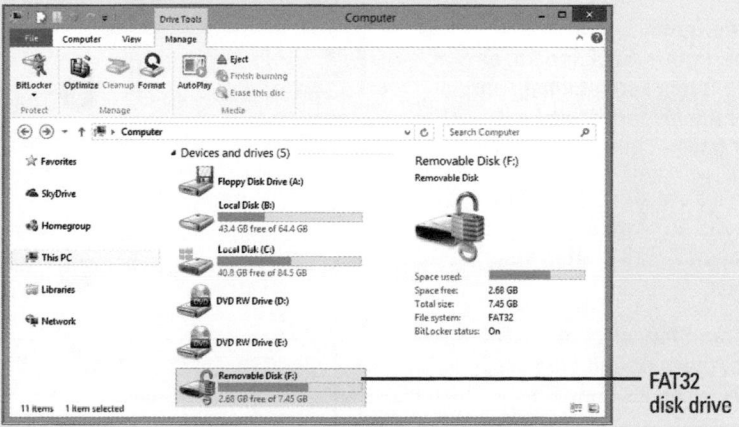

FAT32 disk drive

# Formatting a Disk

Formatting a disk—including hard disks, USB flash drives and flash memory cards—prepares it so that you can store information on it. Formatting removes all information from the disk, so you should never format a disk that has files you want to keep. When you format a disk, you need to specify the certain settings; Windows has default settings recommended. Capacity is how much data the disk or partition can hold, such as the physical size, storage size, and sector size. A file system is the overall structure in which files are named, stored, and organized. NTFS, FAT, FAT32, and exFAT are types of file systems. Disk allocation unit size, or cluster size, is a group of sectors on a disk. The operating system assigns a unique number to each cluster, and then keeps track of files according to which clusters they use. If your hard disk uses a FAT file system, you can convert it to the NTFS format.

## Format a Disk

1. Insert the disk or drive you want to format in the appropriate drive or USB port.

2. In the Start screen, click or tap the **Apps view** button, and then click or tap **This PC**.

3. Select the disk or drive you want to format.

4. Click or tap the **Manage** tab under Drive Tools the drive.

5. Click or tap the **Format** button.

6. Specify the Capacity, File system (**NTFS, FAT (Default), FAT32** or **exFAT**), and Allocation unit size.

7. Select the **Quick Format** check box to perform a quick format, or clear the **Quick Format** check box to perform a full format and disk scan for bad sectors.

8. To use a disk to start up your PC and run MS-DOS, select the **Create an MS-DOS startup disk** check box.

9. Click or tap **Start**, click or tap **OK** to format the disk, and then click or tap **OK** when it's done.

10. Click or tap **Close**.

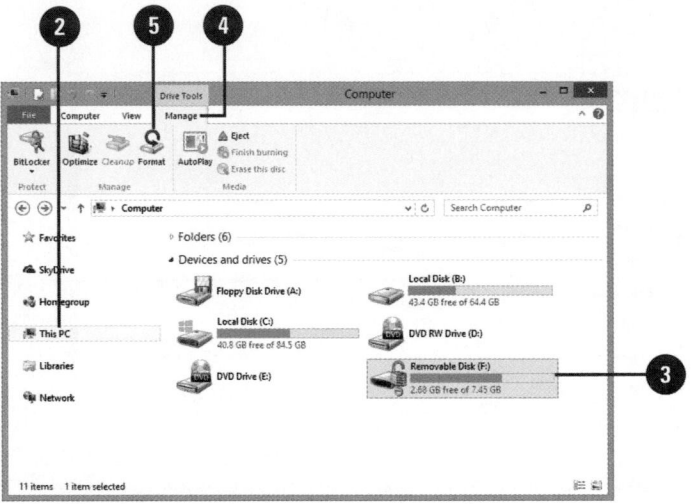

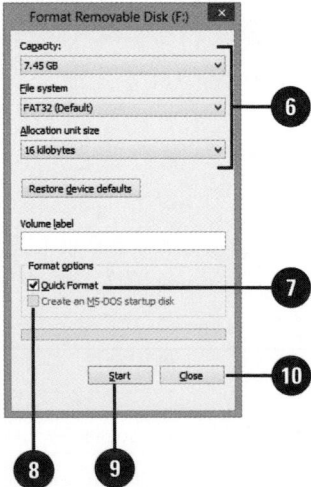

## Convert a Disk

①  In the Start screen, click or tap the **Apps view** button, and then click or tap **Command Prompt**.

②  Type **convert** *drive* **: /fs:ntfs /v**, and then press Enter.

Where *drive* is the drive letter of the drive you wanted converted to NTFS.

③  If you upgraded your PC, type **Y**, and then press Enter to delete the backup, or type **N,** and then press Enter to cancel the procedure.

④  If you're asked to force a dismount, type **N**, and then press Enter.

⑤  If you need to restart the system to complete the conversion, type **Y**, and then press Enter.

⑥  Click or tap the **Close** button.

⑦  Click or tap the **Settings** button on the Charms bar, click or tap the **Power** button, and then click or tap **Shut Down**, and then wait for the PC to restart and convert the drive.

### See Also

*See "Detecting and Repairing Disk Errors" on page 450 for information on bad sectors.*

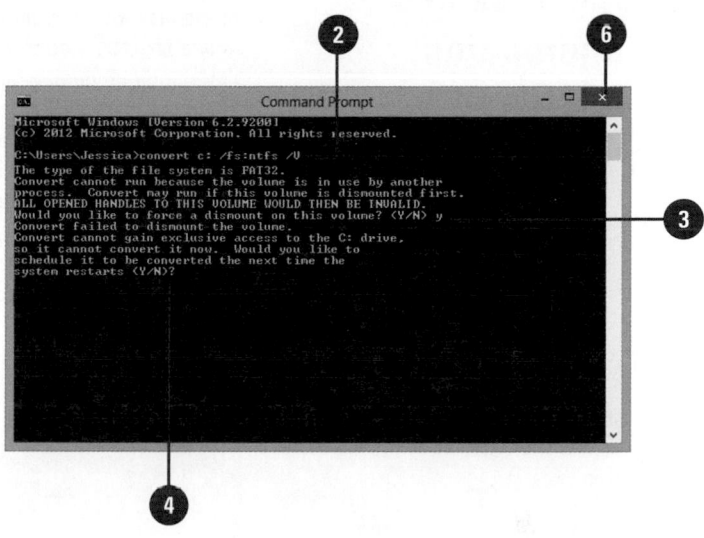

## For Your Information

### Erasing a Rewritable Disc

A rewritable disc is a CD or DVD that you can read, write, and erase multiple times. It functions like a hard or removable drive. A rewritable disc is labeled as CD-RW and DVD-RW, where RW stands for ReadWrite. When you select a rewritable disc in File Explorer under Computer, you can use the Erase This Disc button on the Manage tab under Drive Tools to erase the entire disc.

# Displaying Disk and Folder Information

As you work with files, folders, and programs, you should know the size of the disk and how much space remains available. A disk can store only a limited amount of data. Hard disks can store large amounts of data (in gigabytes), while removable disks, such as a USB flash drive or flash memory card, store smaller amounts. You can use the Properties command on a disk to display the disk size or the amount of used and free space, and to change a disk label, which is a name you can assign to a hard or removable disk. Besides checking hard disk drive or floppy disk information, you can also use the Properties command on a folder to find out the size of its contents. This can be helpful when you want to copy or move a folder to a removable disk or CD/DVD.

## Determine Free Space on a Disk

1. In the Start screen, click or tap the **Apps view** button, and then click or tap **This PC**.

2. Select the disk or drive, and then click or tap the **Properties** button on the Computer tab.

3. On the **General** tab, identify the amount of free space on the disk.

4. Click or tap **OK**.

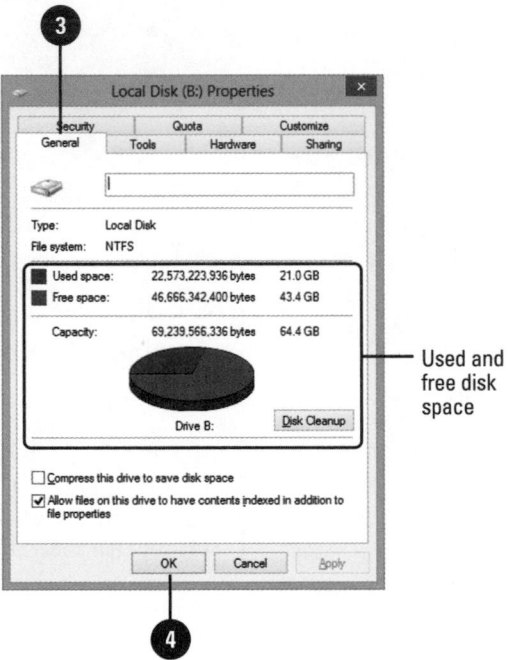

Used and free disk space

### Did You Know?

***You can see how much space your apps are using.*** In the Start screen, click or tap the Settings button on the Charms bar, click or tap Change PC settings, click or tap General, and then click or tap View app sizes.

***You can display basic system information.*** In the Start screen, click or tap the Apps view button, click or tap This PC, and then click or tap the System Properties button on the Computer tab. The basic information about your PC includes system rating, processor, memory (RAM), system type, network information, and Windows activation.

---

## For Your Information

### Understanding File Sizes

When you create a file, it takes up space on a disk. Files with text are smaller than files with graphics. The size of a file is measured in bytes. A byte is a unit of storage capable of holding a single character or pixel. It's the base measurement for all incremental units, which are kilobyte, megabyte, and gigabyte. A kilobyte (KB) is 1,024 bytes of information while a megabyte (MB) is 1,048,576 bytes, which is equal to 1,024 kilobytes. A gigabyte (GB) is equal to 1,024 megabytes.

# Setting Disk Quotas for Users

If you are using a PC with multiple users, you can set up disk quotas, so a single user cannot fill the entire disk. Disk quotas are not enabled by default, so you need to turn this feature on before you can use it. You can enable and set different disk quotas for individual users. If a user exceeds the quota, you can specify whether to allow or deny disk space. If you're not sure what to set, you can create quota logs to monitor disk usage and then decide what you want to do.

## Set Disk Quotas

1. In the Start screen, click or tap the **Apps view** button, and then click or tap **This PC**.

2. Select the disk or drive, and then click or tap the **Properties** button on the Computer tab.

3. Click or tap the **Quota** tab.

4. Click or tap **Show Quota Settings**.

5. Select the **Enable quota management** check box.

6. Select the **Deny disk space to users exceeding quota limit** check box.

7. Click or tap the **Do not limit disk usage** option or click or tap the **Limit disk space to** option and specify the disk space limit.

8. Select either of the log event check boxes to create a record of disk usage.

9. To set specific limits for individual users, click or tap **Quota Entries**.

   ◆ In the Quota Entries window, click or tap the **Quota** menu, click or tap **New Quota Entry**, and then select a user and fill in property information.

10. Click or tap **OK**.

11. Click or tap **OK**.

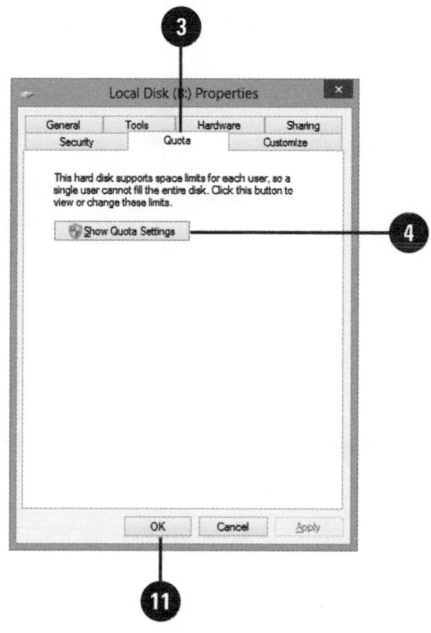

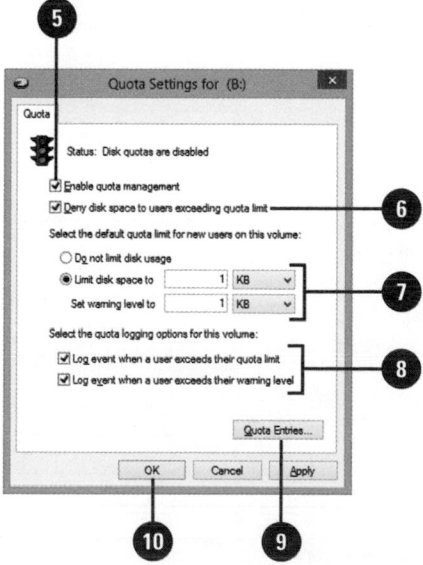

# Detecting and Repairing Disk Errors

Sometimes an unexpected power loss or program error can create inaccessible file segments that take up space on a disk. The Check Disk program that comes with Windows helps you find and repair damaged sections of a disk. Check Disk can also be used to find physical disk errors or **bad sectors**. The program doesn't physically repair your media, but it moves data away from any bad sectors it finds. To keep your hard disk drive working properly, you should run Check Disk from time to time. When you run Check Disk, all files must be closed for the process to run. While the Check Disk process is running, your hard disk will not be available to perform any other task.

## Check a Disk for Errors

1 In the Start screen, click or tap the **Apps view** button, and then click or tap **This PC**.

2 Select the disk or drive, and then click or tap the **Properties** button on the Computer tab.

3 Click or tap the **Tools** tab.

4 Click or tap **Check**.

5 Click or tap **Scan and repair drive**.

Wait while error checking takes place. This might take a while (depends on the size of the drive), and you might need to restart your PC.

6 When it's done, click or tap **Close**.

7 Click or tap **OK**.

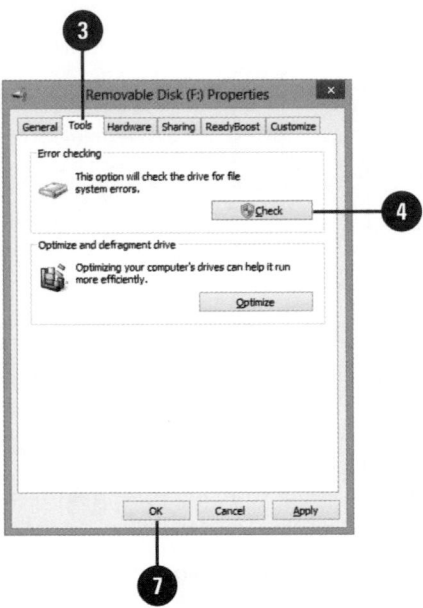

### Did You Know?

*You should run Check Disk before the Disk Defragmenter.* For best results, run Check Disk to check for errors on your disk before you start the disk defragmentation process.

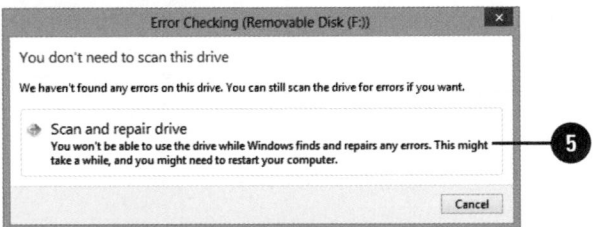

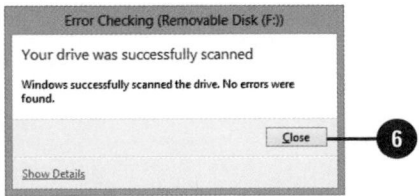

# Encrypting a Disk

BitLocker helps protect your drives—either internal or external (including USB)—and blocks hackers from accessing them. When you turn on BitLocker, it uses encryption and a recovery key (which gets backed up) for security. When your PC starts up after the encryption, you won't see any change. The encrypted volume automatically unlocks when the system boots into the operating system drive. When you add files to your PC, BitLocker automatically encrypts them. When you copy files to another location, the files are decrypted. If a problem occurs or someone tries to illegally access your system, Windows switches into recovery mode until you supply the recovery password.

## Encrypt a Disk with BitLocker

1. In the Start screen, click or tap the **Apps view** button, and then click or tap **This PC**.

2. Select the disk or drive, and then click or tap the **Manage** tab under Drive Tools.

3. To turn on encryption for the selected drive, click or tap the **BitLocker** button, and then click or tap **Turn on BitLocker**.

   Follow the wizard to specify a password, recovery key, and encrypt options, click or tap **Start encrypting**, wait for BitLocker to encrypt the volume upon restart, and then click or tap **Close**.

4. To manage the BitLocker drive, click or tap the **BitLocker** button, and then click or tap an option:

   ◆ **Manage BitLocker.** Use to change options, and turn off BitLocker.

   ◆ **Change password/PIN.** Use to change the recovery password.

### See Also

See "Encrypting Files Using BitLocker" on page 359 for more information on using BitLocker options.

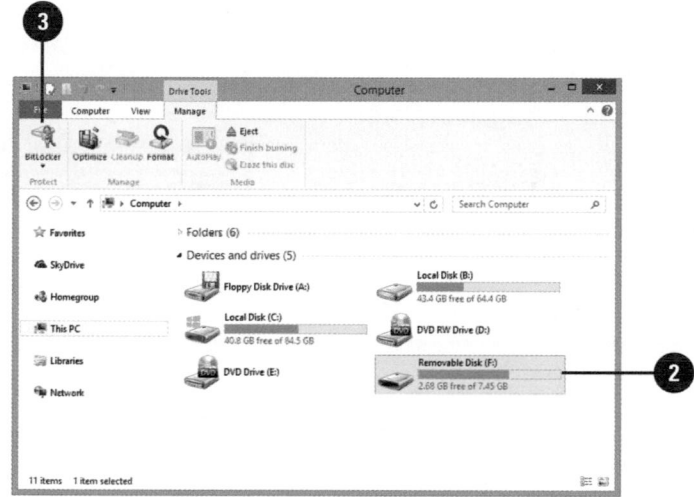

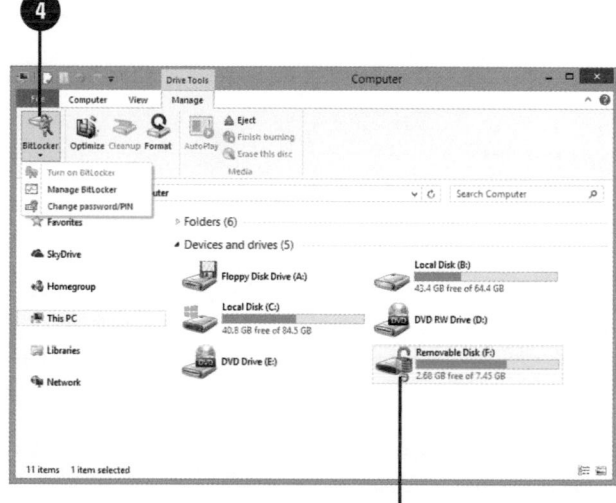

BitLocker on USB disk

# Optimizing a Disk

When you delete files from a disk, you create empty spaces that might be fragmented over different areas of the disk. When you create a new file on a fragmented disk, parts of the file are stored in these empty spaces, resulting in a single file that is broken into many parts, which takes longer to retrieve or store when you open or save the file. A file broken up in this way is called a **fragmented file**, which is undetectable to the user. You can use Disk Defragmenter to place all of the parts of a file in one **contiguous**, or adjacent, location. This procedure, which efficiently rearranges all of the files and unused space, is called **optimization**. Optimization makes your programs run faster and your files open more quickly. You can select disk volumes, analyze them, and set a schedule to run Disk Defragmenter on a regular basis. While the Disk Defragmenter works, you can use your PC to carry out other tasks; however, your PC will operate more slowly.

## Schedule and Defragment Disks

1. In the Start screen, click or tap the **Apps view** button, and then click or tap **This PC**.

2. Select the disk or drive, and then click or tap the **Optimize** button on the Manage tab.

3. Click or tap **Change settings**.

4. Select the **Run on a schedule (recommended)** check box.

5. Click or tap the list arrow, and then select the schedule frequency.

6. Click or tap **Choose**, select the drives you want, and then click or tap **OK**.

7. Click or tap **OK**.

8. To defragment disks, select the drives you want. Press and hold Ctrl to select more than one drive.

9. To analyze your disks to determine if you need defragmenting, click or tap **Analyze**.

10. Click or tap **Optimize**.

11. To stop the process, click or tap **Cancel Defragment**.

12. Click or tap **Close**.

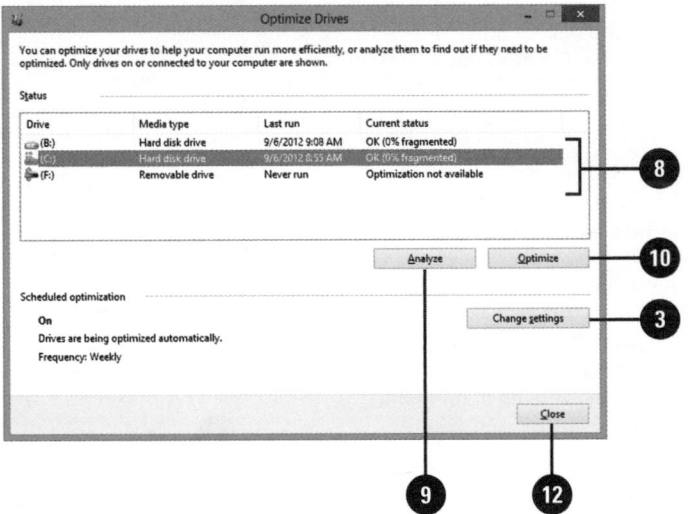

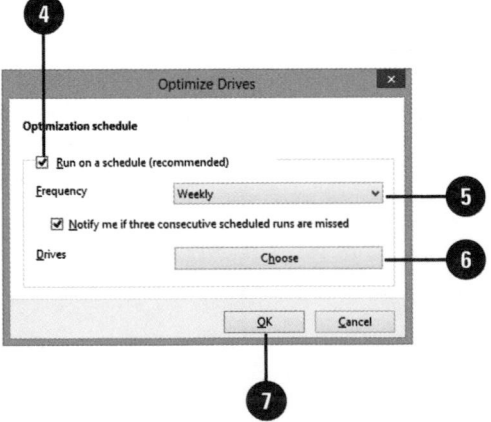

# Cleaning Up a Disk

Cleaning up a disk involves removing unneeded files to make room for other files on your PC, which can be difficult if you don't know the significance of each file. You can use a Windows program called Disk Cleanup to clean up your hard disk drive safely and effectively. Disk Cleanup searches your drive, then lists temporary files, Internet cache files, the Recycle Bin, system files, game related files, and unnecessary program files that you can safely delete. Disk Cleanup also gives you the option to remove Windows components and installed programs that you no longer use. You can select the types of files you want Disk Cleanup to delete. Before you select and delete files, make sure you will not need them in the future. If you have multiple users on your PC, you can specify whether to clean up only your files or all the files on the PC.

## Clean Up a Disk

1. In the Start screen, click or tap the **Apps view** button, and then click or tap **This PC**.

2. Select the disk or drive, and then click or tap the **Cleanup** button on the Manage tab.

   Wait while Disk Cleanup calculates how much space it can free up.

3. Select the check boxes for the folders and files you want to delete.

4. To clean up only system files, click or tap **Clean up system files**.

   Wait while Disk Cleanup calculates how much space it can free up.

5. To view the contents of a folder, click or tap **View Files**, and then click or tap the **Close** button.

6. Click or tap **OK**, and then click or tap **Yes**.

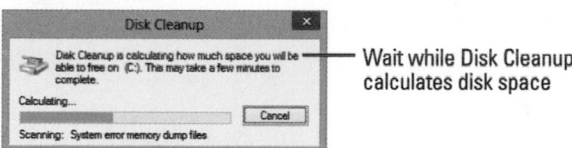

Wait while Disk Cleanup calculates disk space

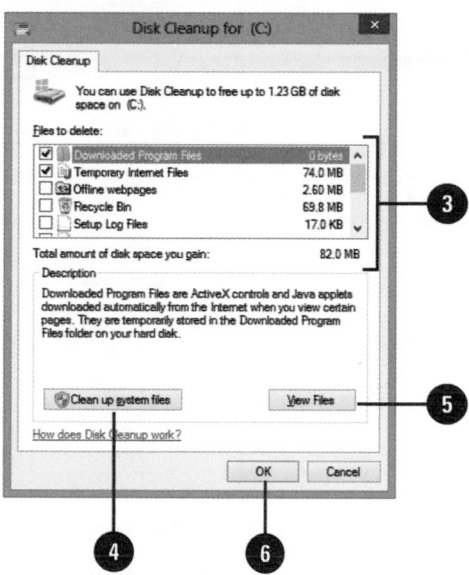

# Boosting Speed with a Removable Disk

You can use Windows ReadyBoost to speed up your PC by using disk space on certain removable media devices, such as USB flash drives. When you insert a compatible removable media device (one that uses fast flash memory), the AutoPlay pop-up opens and provides the option to use Windows ReadyBoost as a dedicated or non dedicated device. Before you can use it, you need to turn it on and specify the amount of space you want to allocate. Windows provides a recommended space amount. In general, ReadyBoost recommends one to three times the amount of random access memory (RAM) installed on your PC for the best performance results.

## Use Windows ReadyBoost

**1** In the Start screen, click or tap the **Apps view** button, and then click or tap **This PC**.

**2** Select the removable media drive, and then click or tap the **Properties** button on the Computer tab.

**3** Click or tap the **ReadyBoost** tab.

**4** Click or tap the **Use this device** or **Dedicate this device to ReadyBoost** option.

**5** If you want, drag the slider to specify the space to reserve for system speed.

**6** Click or tap **OK**.

**7** To use ReadyBoost, remove the device, re-insert it, and then use the AutoPlay pop-up to start it.

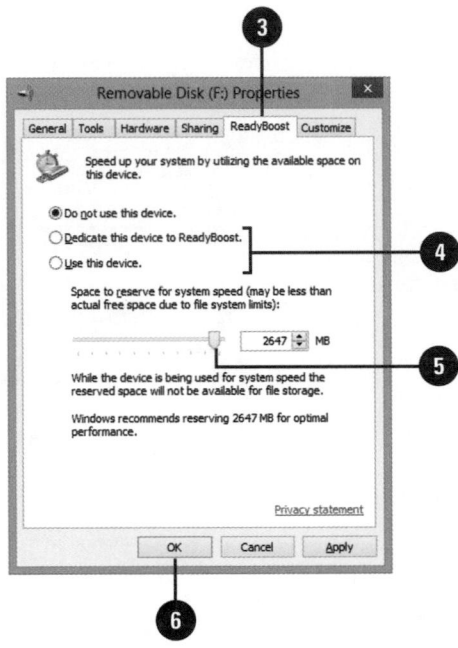

---

**For Your Information**

### Changing the Size of Virtual Memory

If you are running out of virtual memory (using hard disk space as RAM), you can increase the minimum size of the paging file (**a virtual memory**). The Initial size is set to installed RAM plus 300 MB and the Maximum size is set to 3 times installed RAM. To increase the size, double-click or double-tap the System icon in the Control Panel, click or tap Advanced System settings in the left pane, click or tap the Advanced tab, click or tap Settings (under Performance), clear the Automatically Manage Paging File Size For All Drives check box, click or tap the drive you want, click or tap Custom size, type a new size in the Initial or Maximum Size, click or tap Set, and then click or tap OK.

# Adding or Removing Windows Components

Windows 8.1 comes with a collection of components, such as Internet Explorer, Windows Media Player, or Solitaire, you can use to get work done and have fun on your PC. When you install Windows 8.1, not all the components on the installation disc are installed on your PC. You can use the the Programs and Features utility in the Control Panel to install additional components. If you are no longer using a Windows component, you can remove it to save disk space.

## Add or Remove a Windows Component

1. In the Start screen, click or tap the **Apps view** button, and then click or tap **Control Panel**.

2. Click or tap the **Programs and Features** icon in Small icons or Large icons view.

3. In the left pane, click or tap **Turn Windows features on or off**.

4. Click or tap the plus sign (+) to expand a category or click or tap the minus sign (-) to collapse a category.

   A blue check box indicates that only some of the items in a component group are installed.

5. Select a check box to add the item, or clear a check box to remove an item.

6. When you're done, click or tap **OK**.

7. If prompted, insert the Windows 8.1 DVD into the drive.

8. Click or tap **OK** if prompted to restart your PC.

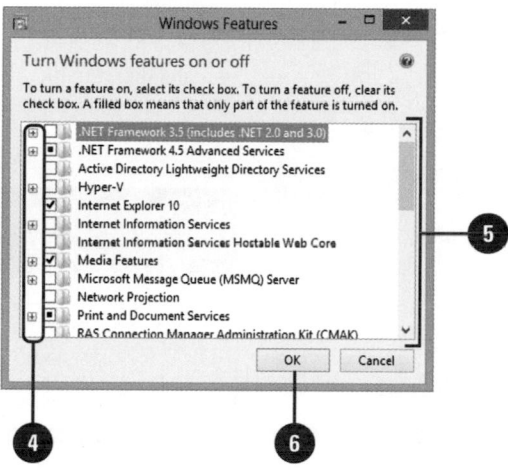

# Installing or Uninstalling a Program

Windows comes with a collection of accessory programs with simple functionality. If you need more functionality, software programs are available for purchase. Before you can use a software program, you need to install it using a separate installer program. Most software programs come with their own installation program, which copies the program files to different places on your PC, some in a program folder and others in the Windows folder. If you no longer use a program or a Windows update, you can remove it from your PC, which saves hard disk space. Programs and Features in the Control Panel provides a faster display and shows you all the programs and/or software updates installed on your PC. Windows keeps track of all the files you install, so you should uninstall a program or system update, instead of deleting folders and files to remove it.

## Install a Software Program

① Close all running programs, and then insert the program installation disc into the drive.

♦ **Download.** You can also download the software program from the Internet to your hard drive.

If the disc starts, the AutoPlay pop-up opens. Click or tap the pop-up, and then start the setup and follow the instructions provided to install the software.

**IMPORTANT** *Only users with administrator privileges can add or remove programs.*

② If the disc doesn't start or you're installing from a network or different drive, display the Start screen, click or tap the **Apps view** button, and then click or tap **This PC**.

③ Double-click or double-tap the CD or DVD icon or the folder with the installation set up.

④ Double-click or double-tap the set up file, and then follow the installation instructions.

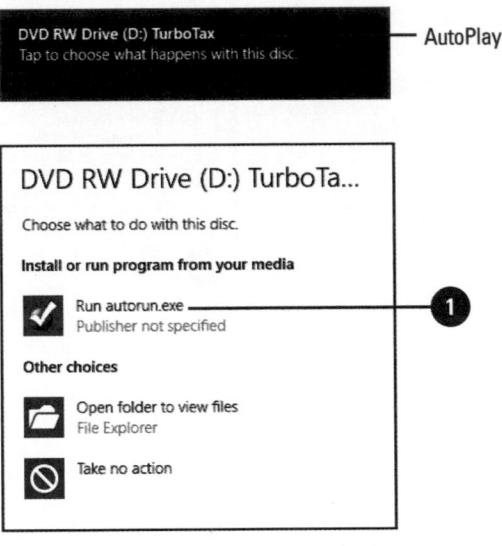

AutoPlay pop-up

① (label pointing to image)

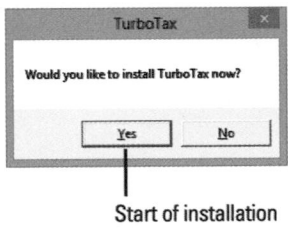

Start of installation

## Uninstall, Change, or Repair a Software Program

1 In the Start screen, click or tap the **Apps view** button, and then click or tap **Control Panel**.

2 Click or tap the **Programs and Features** icon in Small icons or Large icons view.

3 In the left pane, click or tap **View installed updates** or **Uninstall a program** to display the software you want.

4 Click or tap the program you want to uninstall or change.

5 Click or tap the **Uninstall, Change,** or **Repair** button on the toolbar; availability varies depending on the program.

6 If prompted, click or tap **Yes** to confirm the removal. If an uninstall program starts, follow the instructions.

7 When it's done, click or tap **OK**, and then click or tap the **Close** button.

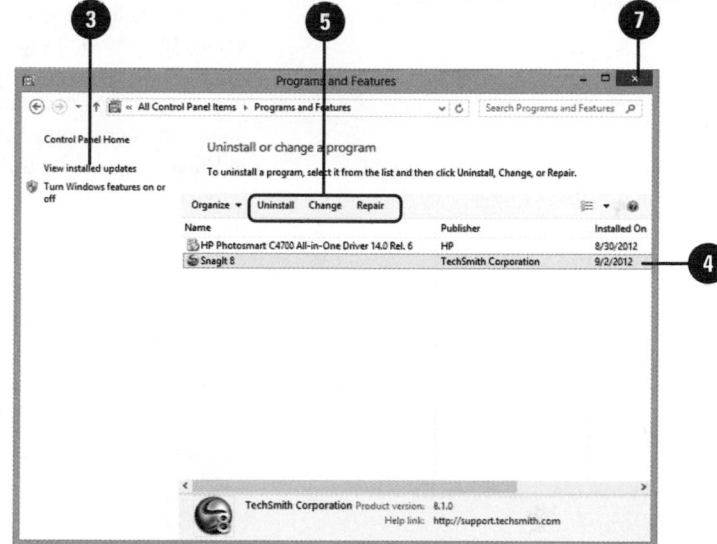

# Updating Windows

Microsoft continues to improve Windows 8.1 with new features or security fixes, known as updates. Windows Update allows you to keep your PC up-to-date with the latest system software and security updates over the Internet. You can choose to have Windows regularly check for critical updates and download them in the background or you can manually select the ones you want to install. You can manually check for updates in PC settings or Control Panel. Automatic updates occur at scheduled times or by notification acceptance. If you're busy, you can ignore/hide the update to install it later. Windows Update confidentially scans your PC for updates that need to be installed. Updates are identified as important or optional. Important updates are critical for your system to run properly, while optional updates are for personal preference. If your PC is turned off or in hibernate or sleep mode during a scheduled update, updates are installed the next time you start your PC. If you lose an Internet connection, Windows Update resumes where it left off.

## Update Windows Manually in Control Panel

1. In the Start screen, click or tap the **Apps view** button, and then click or tap **Control Panel**.

2. Click or tap the **Windows Update** icon in Small icons or Large icons view.

3. Click or tap **Check for updates**.

4. If you need to install any important or optional updates, click or tap the link, select the check boxes next to the items you want to install, and then click or tap **OK**.

5. To view update history, click or tap **View update history**.

6. Click or tap **Install updates**.

7. If prompted, restart your PC.

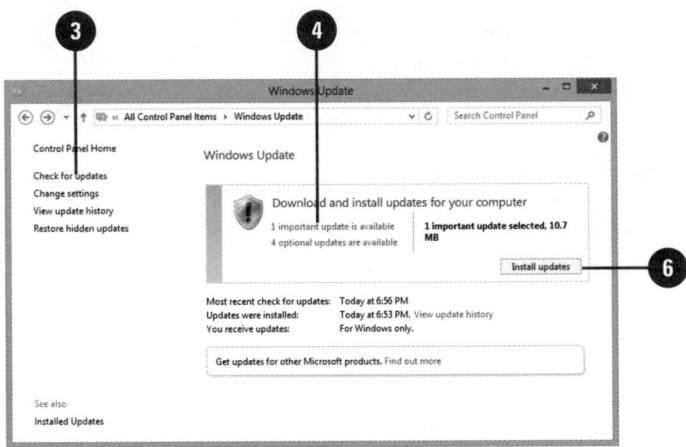

> ### See Also
>
> See "Updating and Refreshing Windows" on page 460 for more information on updating or reinstalling Windows using PC settings.

## Update Windows Automatically

1. In the Start screen, click or tap the **Apps view** button, and then click or tap **Control Panel**.

2. Click or tap the **Windows Update** icon in Small icons or Large icons view.

3. In the left pane, click or tap **Change settings**.

4. Click or tap the **Important updates** list arrow, and then select an option:

   ◆ **Install updates automatically (recommended),** and then specify a time.

   ◆ **Download updates, but let me choose whether to install them.**

   ◆ **Check for updates but let me choose whether to download and install them.**

   ◆ **Never check for updates (not recommended).**

5. Click or tap to select or clear the following check boxes:

   ◆ **Give me recommended updates the same way I receive important updates.**

   ◆ **Give me updates for other Microsoft products when I update Windows (New!).**

6. Click or tap **OK**, and then click or tap the **Close** button.

7. If a Windows Update icon appears in the notification area, click or tap the alert or icon, and then follow any instructions as needed.

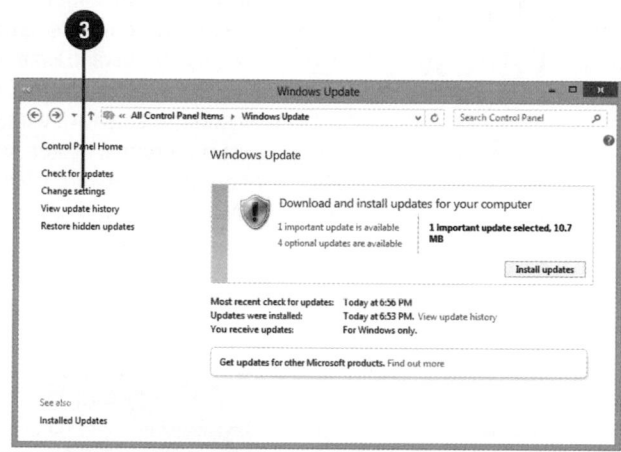

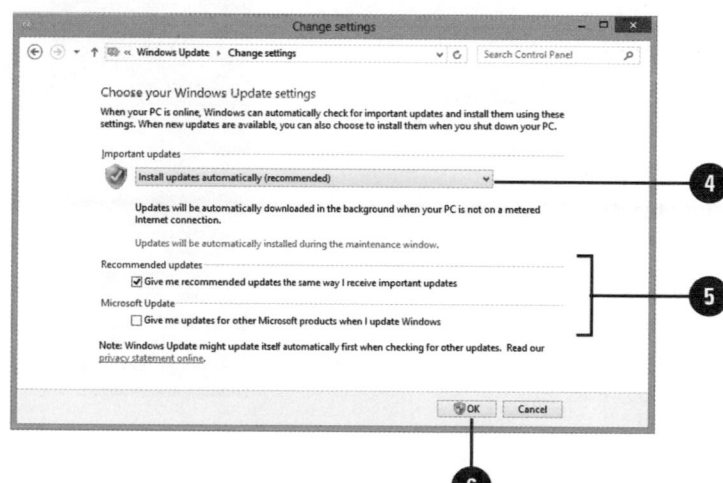

# Updating and Refreshing Windows

In PC settings under Updates and recovery, you can set options to update windows (**New!**) with the latest fixes and patches as well as refresh (reinstall), reset (new install), or restart the Windows 8.1 operating system. If your system is not running very well, you can refresh the Windows software without affecting your personal files. If you want to start up from a device such as a USB or DVD, change Windows startup settings, or restore Windows from a system image (.iso), you can restart Windows from a Restart screen.

## Update Windows Manually in PC Settings

1. Display the Start screen.

2. Point to the upper-right corner and move down (on a computer) or swipe left from the right edge of the screen (on a mobile device).

3. Click or tap the **Settings** button on the Charms bar.

4. Click or tap **Change PC settings** on the Settings panel, and then click or tap **Update and recovery**.

5. Click or tap **Windows Update** under Update and recovery.

6. To set update options, click the **Choose how updates get installed** link, specify the options, and then click or tap **Apply**.

    ◆ **Important updates.** Select a method for updates: Install, Download, Check, or Never.

    ◆ **Recommended updates.** Get updates with important ones.

    ◆ **Microsoft updates.** Get updates from other Microsoft products.

7. Click or tap **Check now**; if available, click or tap the **View details** link (**New!**), and then click or tap **Install (New!)**.

8. To close the app, point to the top edge of the screen (cursor changes to a hand), and then drag down to the bottom edge of the screen.

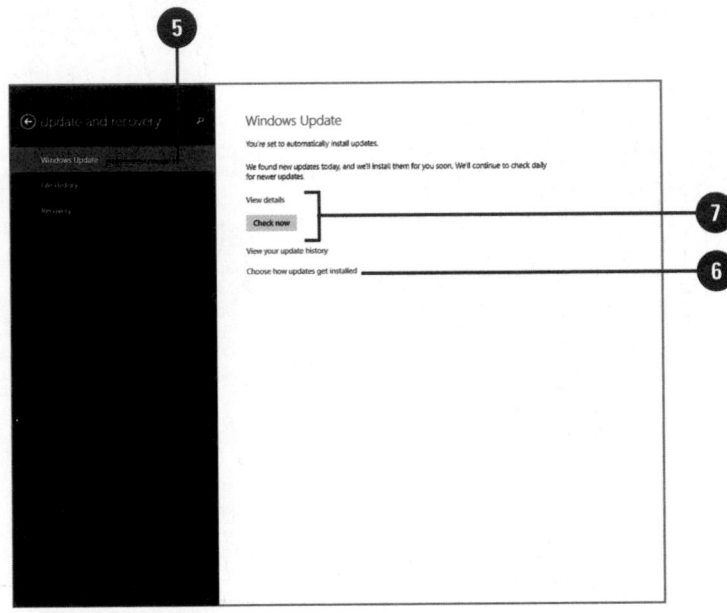

Windows update options

## Refresh, Remove, or Startup Windows in PC Settings

1. Display the Start screen.

2. Point to the upper-right corner and move down (on a computer) or swipe left from the right edge of the screen (on a mobile device).

3. Click or tap the **Settings** button on the Charms bar.

4. Click or tap **Change PC settings** on the Settings panel, and then click or tap **Update and recovery**.

5. Click or tap **Windows Update** under Update and recovery.

6. Specify the options you want:

   ◆ **Refresh your PC without affecting your files.** Click or tap **Get started**, and then follow the wizard instructions to reinstall Windows (keeps your files).

   ◆ **Remove everything and reinstall Windows.** Click or tap **Get started**, and then follow the wizard instructions to reinstall Windows (deletes your files).

   ◆ **Advanced startup.** Click or tap **Restart now** to restart up from a device or disc. Choose an option from the Restart screen: **Continue**, **Troubleshoot**, or **Turn off your PC**.

      ◆ For Troubleshoot, choose an option: **Refresh your PC**, **Reset your PC**, or **Advanced options**.

      ◆ For Advanced options, choose an option: **System Restore**, **System Image Recovery**, **Startup Repair**, **Command Prompt**, or **Startup Settings**.

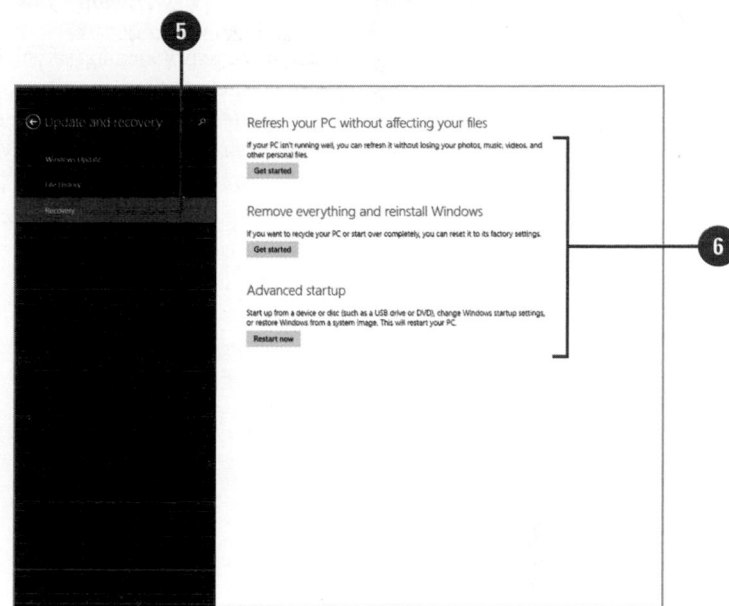

# Keeping a File History

File History allows you to make back up copies of files that are in your libraries, favorites, SkyDrive, and your desktop to an external drive or network location. If you have files or folders in other locations, you can include them in an existing library or create a new one. In PC settings (**New!**) or the Control Panel, you can specify advanced settings to specify how often to save copies and how long to keep them. You can quickly restore a folder or individual file to the version you want.

## Set Up File History

1. In the Start screen, click or tap the **Apps view** button, and then click or tap **Control Panel**.

2. Click or tap the **File History** icon in Small icons or Large icons view.

3. To select a back up location, click or tap **Select drive**, select a drive (add a network location if needed), and then click or tap **OK**.

4. To exclude a folder, click or tap **Exclude folders**, click or tap **Add**, select a folder, click or tap **Select Folder**, and then click or tap **Save changes**.

5. To set save and version options, click or tap **Advanced settings**, specify options, and then click or tap **Save changes**.

   ◆ **Save copies of files.** Specify a time interval.

   ◆ **Size of offline cache.** Specify a disk percentage of disk space.

   ◆ **Keep saved versions.** Specify an option or time interval.

   ◆ **Clean up versions.** Deletes older versions of files and folders.

6. To enable File History, click or tap **Turn on**.

7. To disable File History, click or tap **Turn off**.

8. Click or tap the **Close** button.

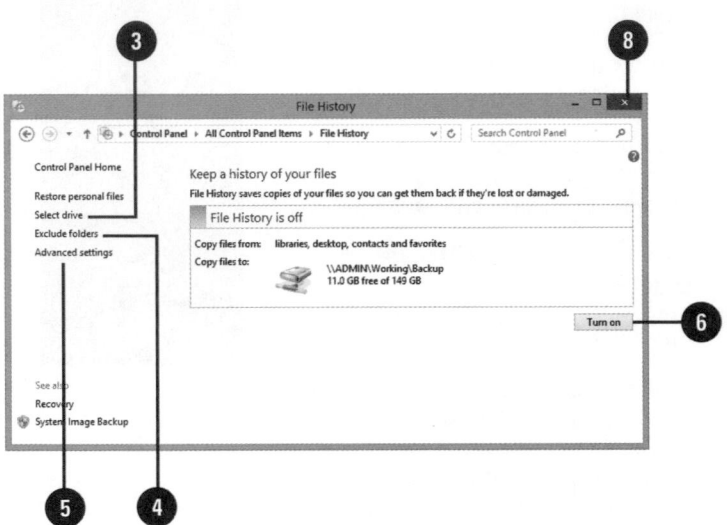

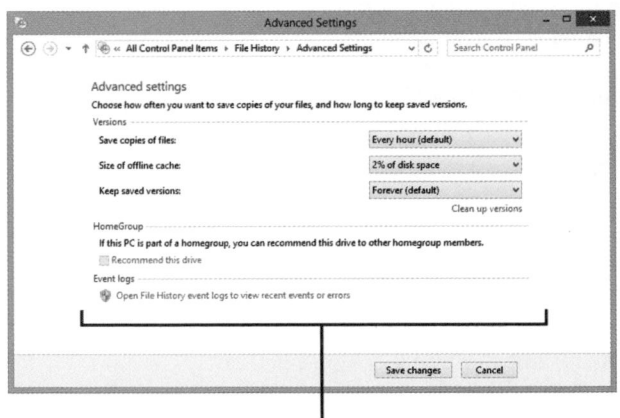

Advanced settings for File History

## Restore a File or Folder Using File History

① Display the Start screen.

② Point to the upper-right corner and move down (on a computer) or swipe left from the right edge of the screen (on a mobile device).

③ Click or tap the **Settings** button on the Charms bar.

④ Click or tap **Change PC settings** on the Settings panel, and then click or tap **PC and devices**.

⑤ Click or tap **Update and recovery**, and then click or tap **File History (New!)**.

⑥ Drag the slider on or off to enable or disable File History.

⑦ To select a drive to store file back ups, click or tap the **Select a different drive** link, and then select a drive.

⑧ To perform a manual back up, click or tap **Back up now**.

⑨ To close the app, point to the top edge of the screen (cursor changes to a hand), and then drag down to the bottom edge of the screen.

# Restoring a File History

When you use File History to make back up copies of files that are in your libraries, favorites, SkyDrive, and your desktop to an external drive or network location, you can quickly restore a folder or individual file to the version you want. If you have files or folders in other locations, you can include them in an existing library or create a new one. You can specify advanced settings to specify how often to save copies and how long to keep them. When you restore files, you can replace the original in the same location or keep both versions. If you not sure about a file version, you can open it directly in File History to view it.

## Restore a File or Folder Using File History

1. In the Start screen, click or tap the **Apps view** button, and then click or tap **Control Panel**.

2. Click or tap the **File History** icon in Small icons or Large icons view.

3. To run a manual copy of File History, click or tap the **Run now** link.

4. In the left pane, click or tap **Restore personal files**.

5. Navigate to the file or folder that you want to restore.

6. To open a file, double-click or double-tap the file icon.

   ◆ Use the **Back** and **Forward** buttons to move back and forth between folders and files.

   A preview of the document appears, where you can review versions.

7. Click or tap the **Previous version** or **Next version** button to view them.

8. To restore a version, click or tap the **Restore to original location** button.

9. Click or tap **Replace the file in the destination**, **Skip this file**, or **Compare info for both files**.

10. Click or tap the **Close** button.

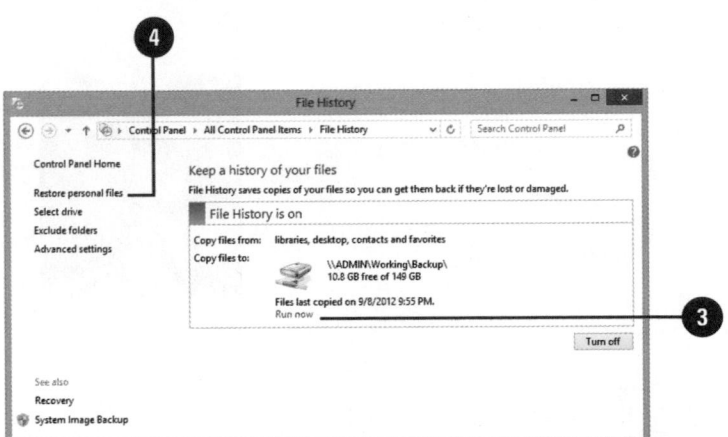

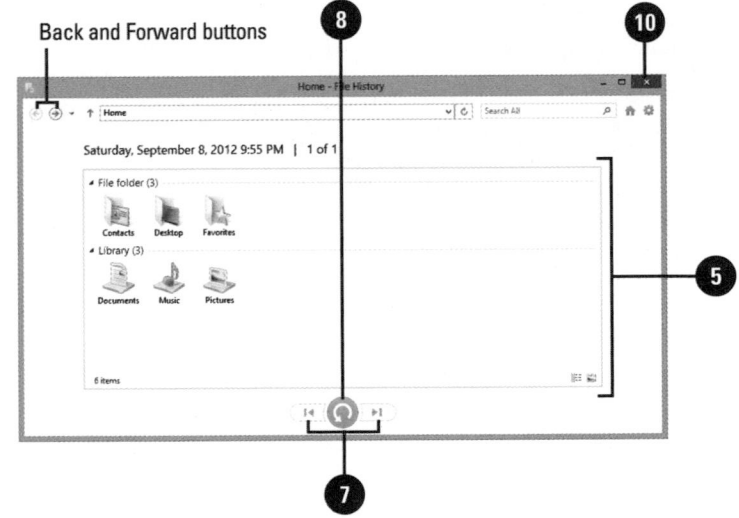

Back and Forward buttons

# Creating a System Image

A system image is an exact copy of a drive, including Windows system files, program files, and your personal files. If you have problems with your hard drive, you can use the system image to restore it. You can create your own system image or let Windows create one for you. If your backup drive is formatted using NTFS, has enough space, and you let Windows choose the files to backup, Windows automatically backs up your files and creates a system image of your programs, Windows, and all drivers and registry settings.

## Create a System Image

1. In the Start screen, click or tap the **Apps view** button, and then click or tap **Control Panel**.

2. Click or tap the **File History** icon in Small icons or Large icons view.

3. In the left pane, click or tap **System Image Backup**.

4. Select the location where you want to back up your PC.

5. To select a network location, if available, click or tap **Select** to select a network, type a user-name and password, and then click or tap **OK**.

6. Click or tap **Next** to continue.

7. Click or tap **Start backup**.

8. If prompted to insert a disc, insert a CD or DVD, and then click or tap **OK**.

9. If prompted to format the disc, click or tap **Format**.

   The backup starts, displaying back up status.

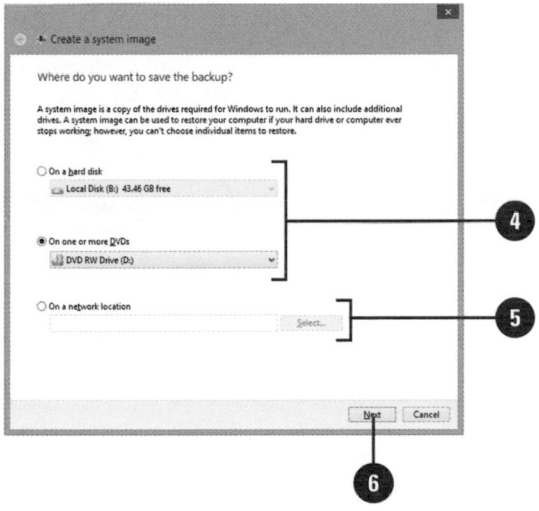

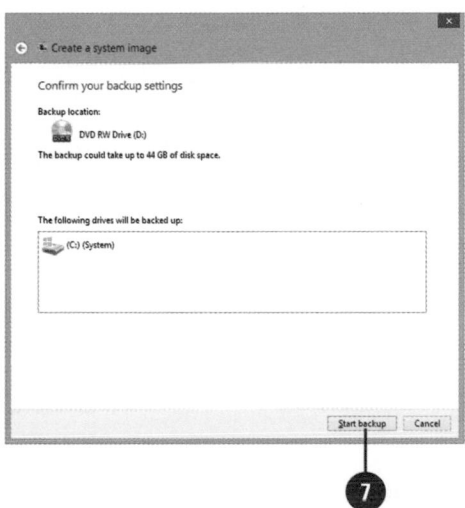

> ## See Also
>
> See "Reinstalling Windows 8.1" on page 518 for more information on restarting your system from a system image.

# Restoring System Settings

Windows 8.1 is a reliable operating system, but any time you make changes to your PC, such as adding or removing software and hardware, you run the risk of causing problems with your operating system. To alleviate potential problems, you can use System Restore to undo harmful changes to your PC and restore its settings. System Restore returns your system, but not your personal files, to an earlier time, before the changes were made, called a **restore point**. As you work, System Restore monitors your changes and creates restore points on a daily basis or at important system events, but you can also create your own restore point at any time. If you have recently performed a system restoration, you can use System Restore to undo your most recent restoration. System Restore is turned on by default, but you can turn it off or change System Restore options for individual drives. However, you need at least 300 MB of free space on each hard disk.

## Set System Protection

1. In the Start screen, click or tap the **Apps view** button, and then click or tap **Control Panel**.

2. Click or tap the **Recovery** icon in Small icons or Large icons view.

3. Click or tap **Configure System Restore**.

4. Select the drive you want to protect.

5. Click or tap **Configure**.

6. Click or tap the system protection option you want:

   ◆ **Turn on system protection.**

   ◆ **Disable system protection.**

7. To adjust the maximum disk space used for system protection, drag the slider.

8. To delete all restore points (this includes system settings and previous versions of files), click or tap **Delete**.

9. Click or tap **OK**, click or tap **OK**, and then click or tap the **Close** button.

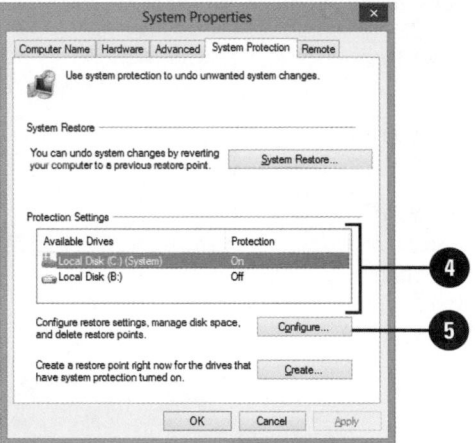

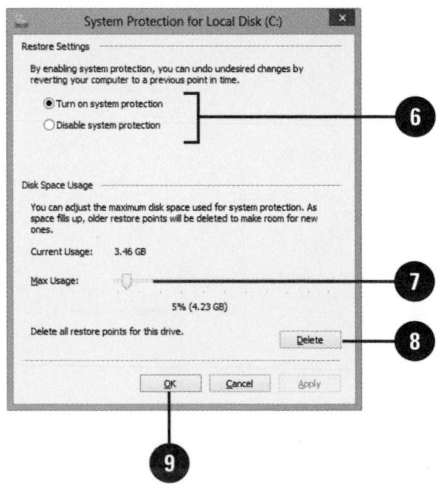

## Restore the System

1. Close all programs and make sure no one else is logged on to the PC.

2. In the Start screen, click or tap the **Apps view** button, and then click or tap **Control Panel**.

3. Click or tap the **Recovery** icon in Small icons or Large icons view.

4. Click or tap **Open System Restore**.

5. Click or tap **Next** to continue.

6. Select a restore point, and then click or tap **Next** to continue.

7. Review the information, click or tap **Finish**, and then click or tap **Yes** to confirm the restore.

8. Wait for the system to be restored, and log on when prompted.

9. When it's done, click or tap **OK** if necessary, and then click or tap the **Close** button.

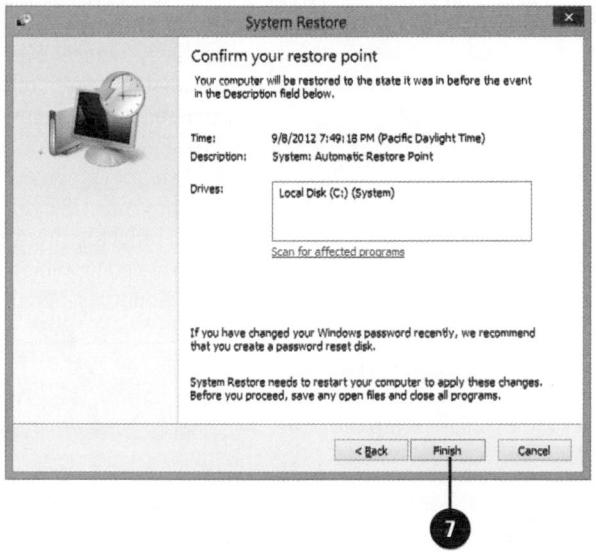

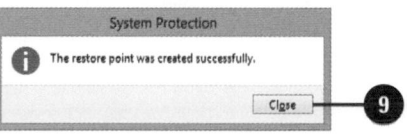

## Create a Restore Point

1. In the Start screen, click or tap the **Apps view** button, and then click or tap **Control Panel**.

2. Click or tap the **Recovery** icon in Small icons or Large icons view.

3. Click or tap **Configure System Restore**.

4. Click or tap **Create**.

5. Type a restore point name.

6. Click or tap **Create**.

7. When it's done, click or tap **OK**, and then click or tap the **Close** button.

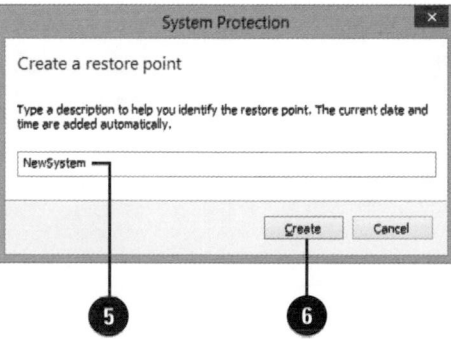

# Creating a System Recovery Drive

Before you start making changes to your PC, you should create a system recovery USB drive. If a serious error occurs with your system, you can use the system recovery USB drive with at least 256 MB to boot your PC and provide system recovery tools to help you restore your PC. You may also need your Windows 8.1 installation disc. After you create a recovery USB drive, store it along with your Windows 8.1 installation disc for safe keeping. If you ever have a problem, insert the system recovery drive into your USB drive, restart your PC, press a key to boot from the system recovery drive, select a language setting, and then select a recovery option, which includes Startup Repair, System Restore, System Image Recovery, Windows Memory Diagnostic, and Command Prompt.

## Create a System Recovery Drive

**1** In the Start screen, click or tap the **Apps view** button, and then click or tap **Control Panel**.

**2** Click or tap the **Recovery** icon in Small icons or Large icons view.

**3** Click or tap **Create a recovery drive**.

**4** Connect a USB drive with at least 256 MB of disk space.

**5** Click or tap **Next**.

**6** Select the USB flash drive, if necessary, and then click or tap **Next**.

**7** Read the warning that all contents will be deleted, and then click or tap **Create**.

Wait while Windows formats the drive and copies the recovery files.

**8** Upon completion, click or tap **Finish**.

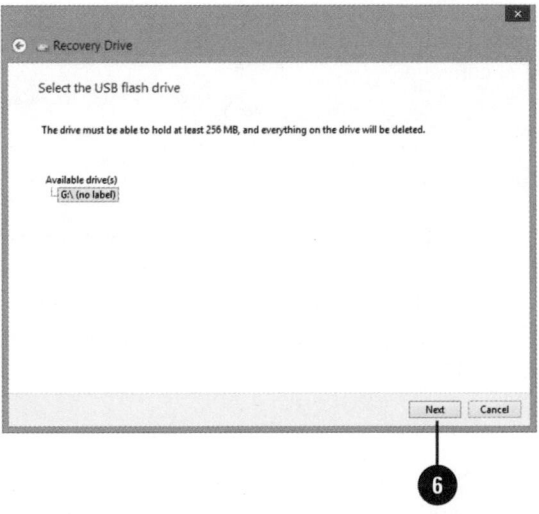

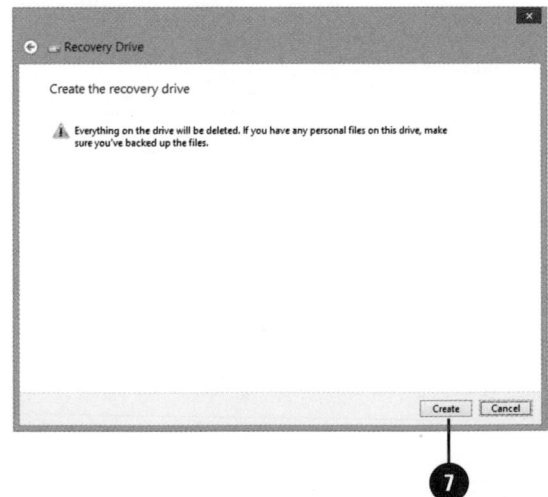

# Setting Startup and Recovery Options

If you installed more than one operating system on your PC (known as a **dual-boot**), such as Windows Vista/7 and Windows 8.1, you can select the default operating system you want to use when you start up your PC. You can also specify how much time to display the list of operating systems for a dual boot before the default starts. If you have problems starting Windows, you can set options to instruct Windows what to do. You can set options to automatically restart and create a system log of events to track where the problem occurs.

## Set Windows Startup and Recovery Options

1. In the Start screen, click or tap the **Apps view** button, and then click or tap **This PC**.

2. Click or tap the **System properties** button on the Computer tab.

3. In the left pane, click or tap **Advanced system settings**.

4. Click or tap **Settings** (under Startup and Recovery).

5. Click or tap the **Default operating system** list arrow, and then select the operating system you want to start as default.

6. Select the system startup check boxes you want to use and specify the time you want to wait to select the operating system or recovery options.

7. Select the system failure check boxes you want to use.

8. Click or tap **OK**.

9. Click or tap **OK**.

10. Click or tap the **Close** button.

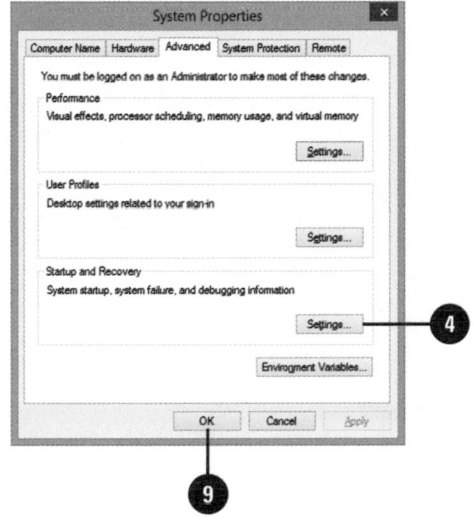

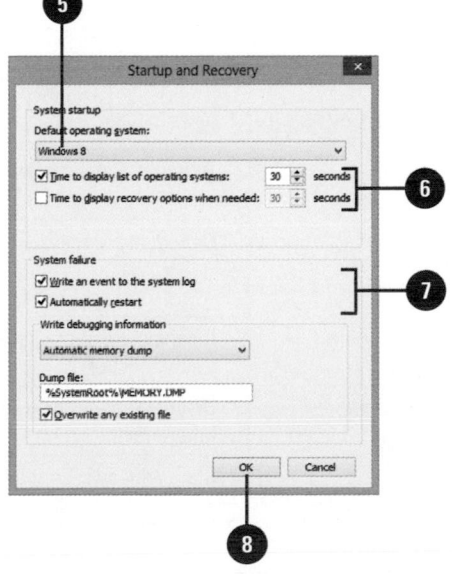

# Starting Windows When Problems Occur

If you have a problem starting Windows, you can use one of several startup options to help you start Windows in a safe environment or use the System Recovery Options menu to restore settings and repair your PC. Safe Mode is a good place to start. If a problem does not occur when you start in Safe Mode, you can eliminate basic Windows files and drivers as possible causes of the problem. If you added a device or changed driver, you can use Safe Mode to remove the device or restore the changed driver. You can also use Choosing Last Known Good Configuration to restore settings saved when your PC was last shut down properly. Lastly, you can use Repair Your PC.

## Start Windows When Problems Occur

1. Restart your PC.

2. As your PC boots, press and hold F8.

3. Use the arrow keys to select a startup or repair option, and then press Enter.

4. If you have a dual-boot system, select the operating system you want, and then press Enter.

5. Restore any recent system changes, or remove any newly installed software that might be causing the problem.

6. Shut down your PC.

7. Start your PC to see if it works properly.

8. If problems persist, try a different startup option, or seek assistance from a support technician.

## Did You Know?

*You can use Startup Repair to fix Windows 8.1 problems.* Restart your PC with the Windows installation disc in the drive, click or tap Repair Your PC, select your system, click or tap Next, and then click or tap Startup Repair.

## Computer Startup Options

| Option | Description |
|---|---|
| Repair Your Computer | Provides access to the System Recovery Options menu |
| Safe Mode | Starts with basic files and drivers and without a network connection |
| Safe Mode With Networking | Starts with basic files and drivers and a network connection |
| Safe Mode With Command Prompt | Starts with basic files and drivers and without a network connection to the command prompt |
| Enable Boot Logging | Starts and logs startup information in the *ntbtlog.txt* file |
| Enable low-resolution video | Starts using the basic VGA driver |
| Last Known Good Configuration | Starts using Registry settings saved at the last properly done shutdown |
| Directory Services Restore Mode | Restores active directory services |
| Debugging Mode | Starts and sends debugging information to another PC using a serial cable |
| Disable automatic restart on system failure | Prevents automatic reboot after a crash |
| Disable Driver Signature Enforcement | Allows drivers containing improper signatures to be loaded |
| Start Windows Normally | Starts the PC normally |

# Managing Hardware

## Introduction

A **hardware device** is any physical device that you plug into and is controlled by your personal computer or mobile device. This device can be a network or modem card that you install inside your system. It can be a printer or a scanner that you plug into the outside of the system. When you plug or insert a hardware device into the appropriate port or expansion slot, Windows attempts to recognize the device and configure it for you using plug-and-play technology. Plug-and-play automatically tells the device drivers (software that operates the hardware and comes with Windows 8.1) where to find the hardware device. After a hardware device is installed, you can change settings and options to customize the way the device works. Plug-and-play technology will recognize most any kind of hardware device, such as a mouse, modem, keyboard, game controller, laptop battery, or secondary monitor just to name a few.

All hardware devices can be managed or removed from the Control Panel. Most hardware devices are managed under the Devices and Printers folder or in the Device Manager, but some have their own program for managing them (for example, Mouse or Keyboard are located in the Control Panel).

## What You'll Do

**Understand Plug and Play Hardware**

**View Hardware Devices**

**Install Hardware Devices**

**View System Hardware Settings**

**Change Windows Update Driver Settings**

**Change Keyboard Settings**

**Change Mouse Settings**

**Change Phone and Modem Options**

**Mange Storage Spaces**

**Manage Color**

**Use the Windows Mobility Center**

**Add a Secondary Monitor**

**Control Power Options**

**Remove Hardware Devices**

**Remove Plug and Play Hardware**

**Troubleshoot Problems**

# Understanding Plug and Play Hardware

Windows includes **plug and play** support for hardware, making it easy to install and uninstall devices quickly. With plug and play support, you simply plug the device in, and Windows sets the device to work with your existing hardware and resolves any system conflicts. When you install a hardware device, Windows installs related software, known as a **driver**, that allows the hardware to communicate with Windows and other software applications. Plug and play tells the device drivers where to find the hardware devices. Plug and play matches up physical hardware devices with the software device drivers that operate them and establish channels of communication between each physical device and its driver. With plug and play, you can be confident that any new device will work properly and that your device will restart correctly after you install or uninstall hardware. Microsoft recommends that you use only device drivers with the Designed for Microsoft Windows 8.1 logo, which have a digital signature from Microsoft, indicating that the product was tested for compatibility with Windows 8.1. You might need to be logged on as an administrator or a member of the Administrators group in order to install a hardware device. In order to install a plug and play device, you need to do the following:

**1) Gather your original Windows 8.1 installation disc**, the hardware device that you want to install, and the discs that come with the device, if available.

**2) Turn off your system before you physically install a hardware device**, such as a network card or a sound card, inside your system. To install a hardware device that plugs into the outside of your system, such as a scanner, printer or other USB (universal serial bus) device, you can plug it in without turning off your system. If your USB device uses a power cord, you need to connect the device to the power cord and turn it on before you connect the USB device to your system.

**3) Follow the manufacturer's instructions to plug the new device into your system.**

**4) Turn on your system, or start the Add Hardware utility program in the Control Panel.** Windows tries to detect the new device and install the device drivers. If Windows doesn't recognize the new hardware device, the device might not be plug and play compatible or installed correctly. Turn off your system, check the device documentation and installation carefully, and then turn on your system again. If the device driver is not available on your system, Windows asks you to insert into the appropriate drive the Windows 8.1 installation disc or the disc that comes with the device from the manufacturer. After the driver software is installed, you can disconnect and reconnect the device without taking any further action.

**5) Follow the instructions on the screen until a message indicates that you are finished.** Windows notifies all other devices of the new device so there are no conflicts and manages the power requirements of your hardware and peripherals by shutting them down or conserving power when you are not using them. If you are working in another program when you install or uninstall a device, plug and play lets you know that it is about to change your system configuration and warns you to save your work.

**6) Use the Safely Remove Hardware and Media Eject icon in the notification area** to safely unplug or eject plug and play hardware. The Safely Remove Hardware dialog box helps you stop the device, so it's safe to remove.

Plug and play finds new hardware

The Found New Hardware wizard installs the new hardware

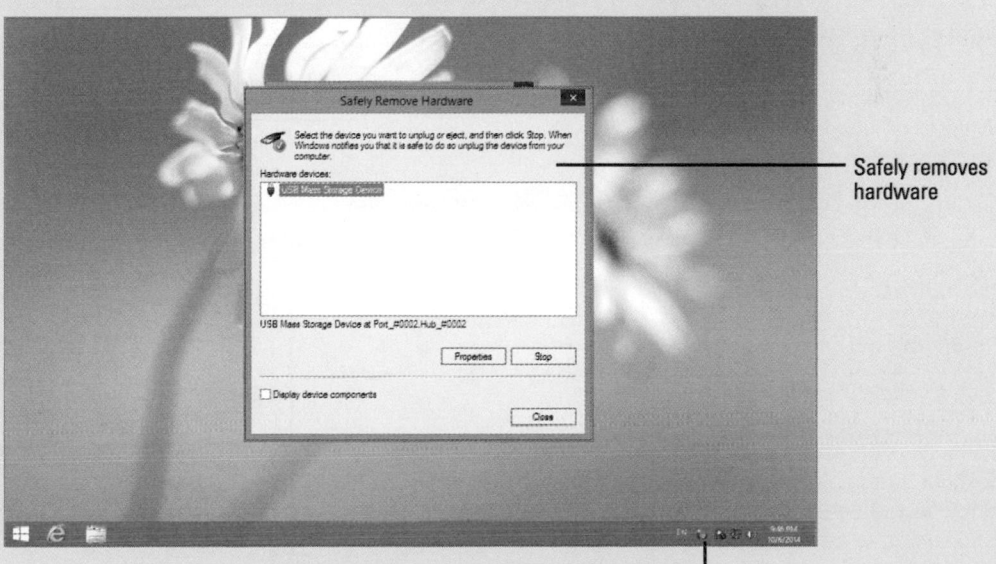

Safely removes hardware

Safely Remove Hardware and Eject Media icon

# Viewing Hardware Devices

If you connect an external device—typically those you plug into a USB port or add wirelessly—to your system, Windows 8.1 detects and installs it using plug and play. After a device is installed, it appears in the Devices and Printers folder, Devices panel and in PC Settings. The Devices and Printers folder and PC Settings are two places where you can check and manage all devices connected to your system—such as a USB hard drives, flash drives, webcams, Bluetooth, scanners, keyboards, or mice. Devices installed inside your system—such as internal hard drives, disc drives, sound cards, video cards, RAM, and older devices—do not appear in the Devices and Printers folder; you can find these devices in the Device Manager. In the Devices and Printers folder, you can add a new wireless or network device or printer to your system. If there is a problem with a device (indicated by a yellow warning icon), you can also start the troubleshooter to help you detect and fix the problem.

## View Hardware Devices

1. In the Start screen, click or tap the **Apps view** button, and then click or tap **Control Panel**.

2. Click or tap the **Devices and Printers** icon in Small icons or Large icons view.

3. Click or tap the **down** or **up** arrow to expand or collapse the Devices or Printers and Faxes section.

4. Click or tap a hardware device.

5. View hardware details in the Details pane.

6. For more information about a hardware device, double-click or double-tap the device icon.

7. View the hardware properties.

8. Click or tap **OK**.

9. If you see a yellow warning icon for a hardware device, click or tap the device, click or tap the **Troubleshoot** button on the toolbar, and then follow the on-screen instructions to detect and fix the problem.

10. Click or tap the **Close** button.

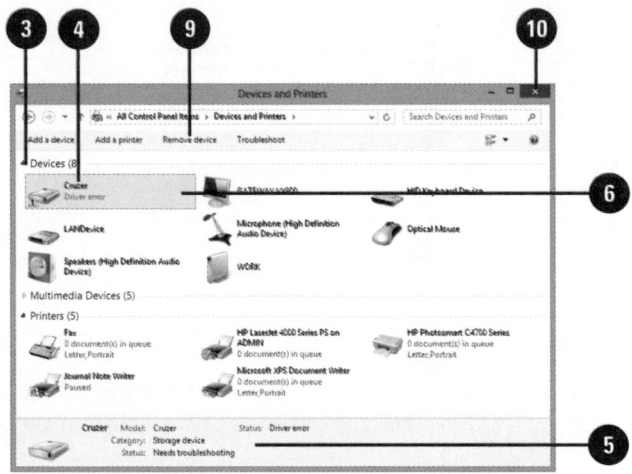

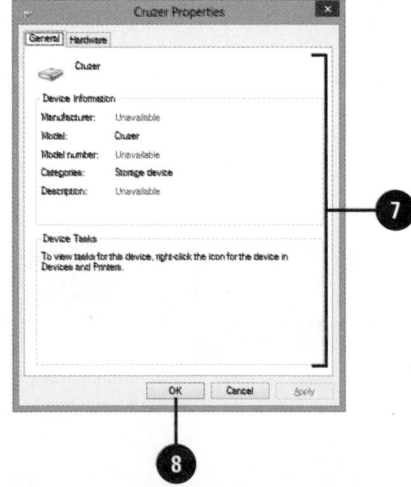

## Work with Devices in PC Settings and Devices Panel

**1** Display the Start screen.

**2** Point to the lower- or upper-right corner and move up or down (on a computer) or swipe left from the right edge of the screen (on a mobile device).

**3** Click or tap the **Settings** button on the Charms bar.

**4** Click or tap **Change PC settings** on the Settings panel.

**5** Click or tap **PC and devices** under PC settings, and then click **Devices** on the panel.

**6** Specify the options you want for the category.

◆ **Add a device.** Click or tap the **Add** button (+), select the device, and then follow the on-screen instructions.

◆ **Remove a device.** Select the device, and then click or tap the **Remove device** button.

**7** To close the app, point to the top edge of the screen (cursor changes to a hand), and then drag down to the bottom edge of the screen.

**8** To use a device with an open app, click or tap the **Devices** button on the Charms bar, click or tap a device type, such as a Play, Print, or Project, on the Devices panel, and then select an option.

### See Also

*See "Using Devices with Apps" on page 266 for more information on using the Devices button to use attached devices.*

Add button         Remove device button

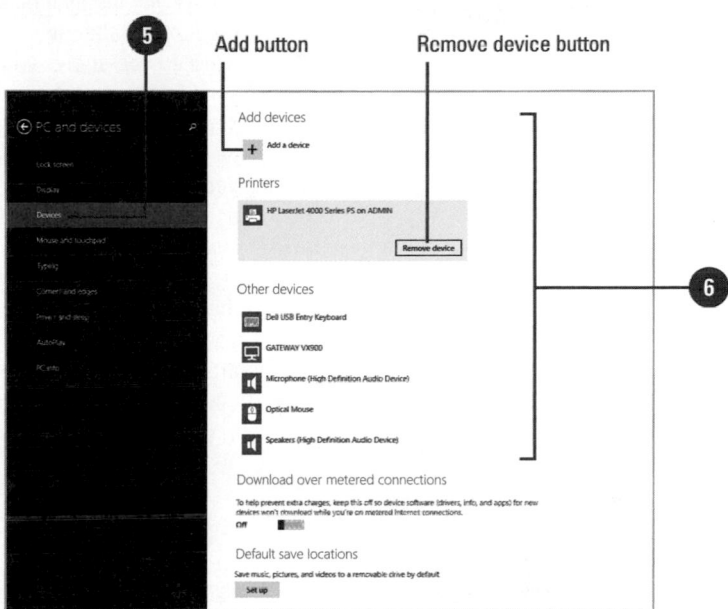

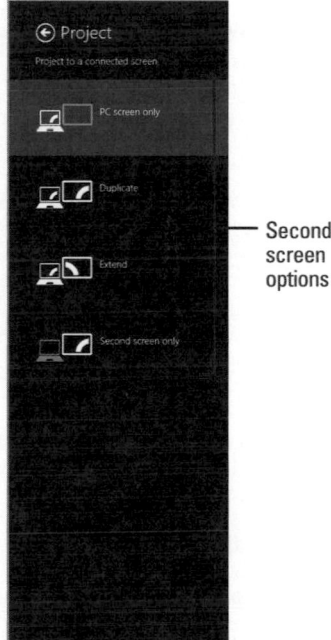

Second screen options

# Installing Hardware Devices

Before you install a new hardware device, be sure to carefully read the product installation guide provided by the manufacturer. If the hardware device comes with an installation disc, it is recommended that you use the manufacturer's disc and related instructions to install the hardware. If the product documentation instructs you to perform a typical plug and play installation, turn off your system, physically connect your hardware to your system, and then turn on your system again. In most cases, Windows detects your new hardware device and installs it or starts the Add a device wizard. The Add a device wizard installs hardware devices by asking you a series of questions to set up the necessary software for the new hardware device. If Windows doesn't detect the new hardware, you can start the Add a device wizard in the Devices and Printers folder and select the new hardware device to install it. You might need to be logged on as an administrator in order to install a hardware device.

## Install a Hardware Device Using the Add a Device Wizard

1. If necessary, attach the hardware device you want to install according the manufacturers directions.

   If Windows doesn't detect and install it, use the Add a device wizard to complete the installation.

2. In the Start screen, click or tap the **Apps view** button, and then click or tap **Control Panel**.

3. Click or tap the **Devices and Printers** icon in Small icons or Large icons view.

4. Click or tap the **Add a device** button on the toolbar.

5. Select the discovered device you want to install.

6. Click or tap **Next** to continue.

7. Follow the Add a device wizard instructions to complete the installation; steps vary depending on the hardware device.

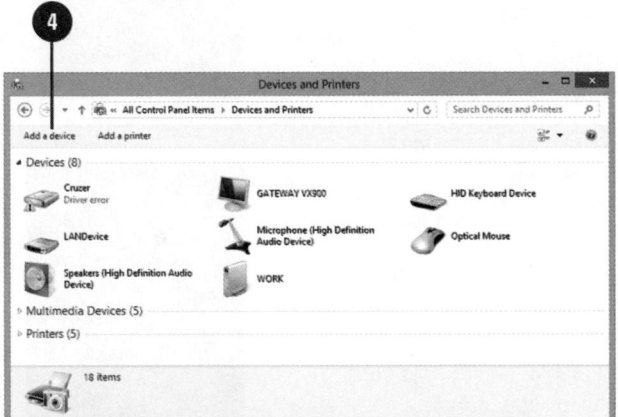

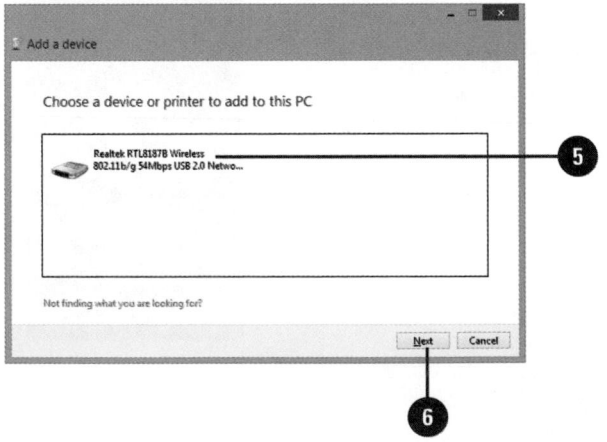

# Viewing System Hardware Settings

When you install a new operating system, such as Windows 8.1, it is important to make sure that you are using the latest software drivers with your system hardware. If you are not using the latest software drivers, your hardware devices might not work to full capacity. You can view your system hardware using a Windows utility called the Device Manager. Device Manager provides you with a list of the hardware types, also known as **hardware classes**, which are attached to your system. With the Device Manager, you can determine the software driver versions being used with your system hardware, update the software driver with a newer version, roll back to a previous driver version if the device fails with the new one, or uninstall a driver. After viewing your software driver version numbers, you can contact the manufacturer or visit their web site to determine the latest versions. Most manufacturers allow you to download drivers from their web sites for free. You will need to be logged on as an administrator in order to work with hardware devices in the Device Manager.

## View System Hardware Settings Using the Device Manager

1. In the Start screen, click or tap the **Apps view** button, and then click or tap **Control Panel**.

2. Click or tap the **Device Manager** icon in Small icons or Large icons view.

3. Click or tap the white arrow next to a category to expand it.

4. Select the device you want to view.

5. Click or tap the **Properties** button on the toolbar.

6. To work with drivers, click or tap the Driver tab. You can choose any of the following buttons:

   ◆ **Driver Details**. View details.

   ◆ **Update Driver**. Update driver.

   ◆ **Roll Back Driver**. Roll back to a previously installed driver.

   ◆ **Disable**. Disable the device.

   ◆ **Uninstall**. Remove the driver.

7. Click or tap **OK**.

8. Click or tap the **Close** button.

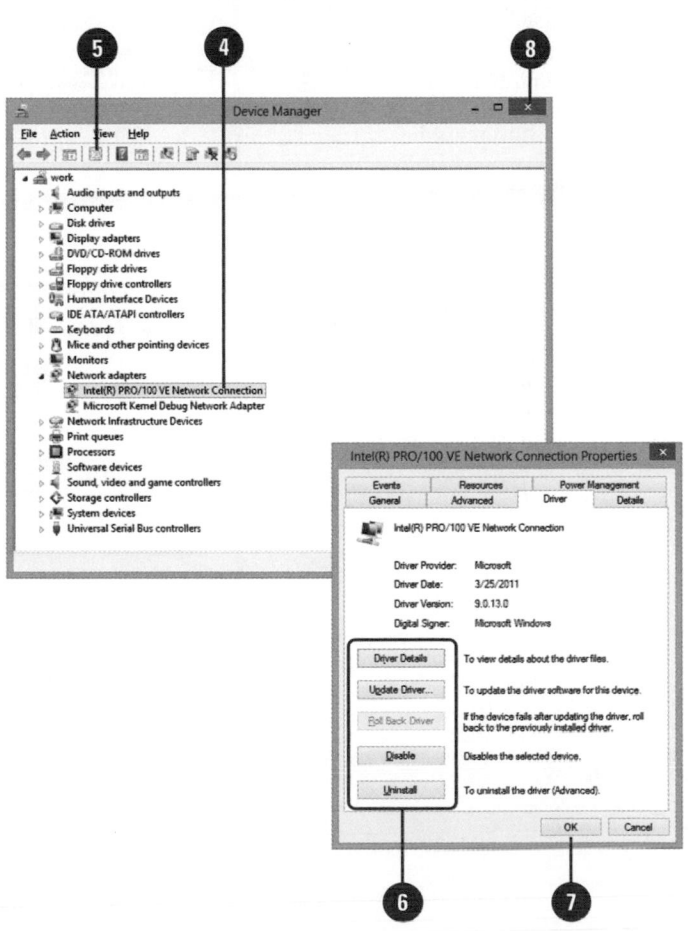

# Changing Windows Update Driver Settings

When you connect a new device to your system, you can specify how you want Windows Update to find a software driver for the device. The default setting is to automatically check for a driver on your system or online from the Microsoft Windows Update web site. However, if you want more control over the process, you can change it to have Windows ask you each time you connect a new device before to check for drivers or never check for drivers. You can use System Properties to specify the option you want.

## Change Windows Update Driver Settings

1. In the Start screen, click or tap the **Apps view** button, and then click or tap **This PC**.

2. Click or tap the **System properties** button on the Computer tab.

3. In the left pane, click or tap **Advanced system settings**.

4. Click or tap the **Hardware** tab.

5. Click or tap **Device Installation Settings**.

6. Select the option you want to use.

   ◆ **Yes, do this automatically (recommended).**

   ◆ **No, let me choose what to do.**

      ◆ Always install the best driver software from Windows Update.

      ◆ Install driver software from Windows Update if it is not found on your system.

      ◆ Never install driver software from Windows Update.

7. Click or tap **Save Changes**.

8. Click or tap **OK**.

9. Click or tap the **Close** button.

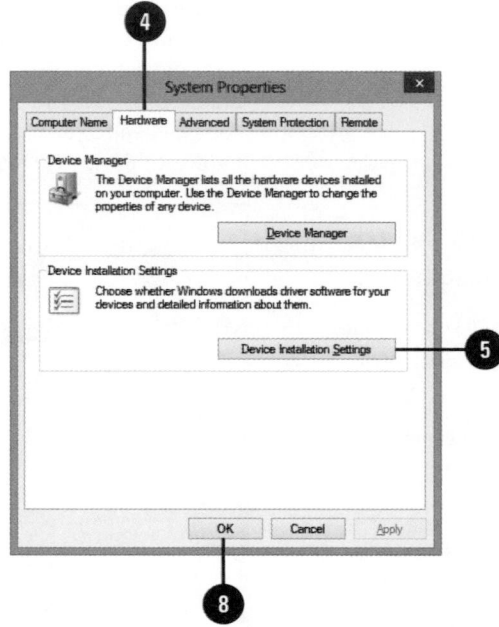

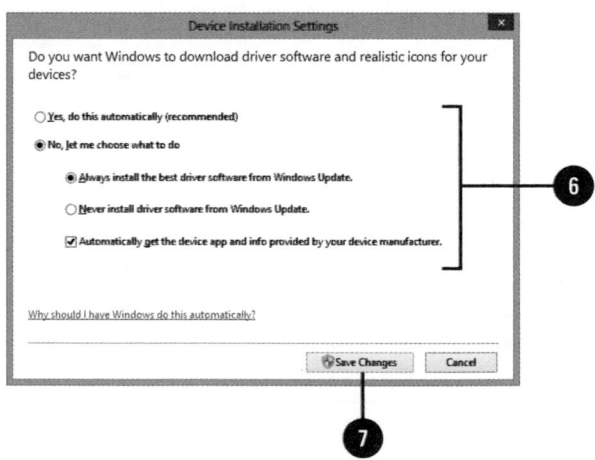

# Changing Keyboard Settings

While your keyboard should just work when you start up your system, you can use Keyboard properties in the Control Panel to adjust the rate at which a character is repeated when you hold down a key, and the time delay before it starts repeating. You can also adjust the blink rate of the insertion point.

## Change Keyboard Settings

① In the Start screen, click or tap the **Apps view** button, and then click or tap **Control Panel**.

② Click or tap the **Keyboard** icon in Small icons or Large icons view.

③ Click or tap the **Speed** tab.

④ To adjust the character repeat delay, drag the slider.

⑤ To adjust the character repeat rate, drag the slider.

⑥ Click or tap **OK**.

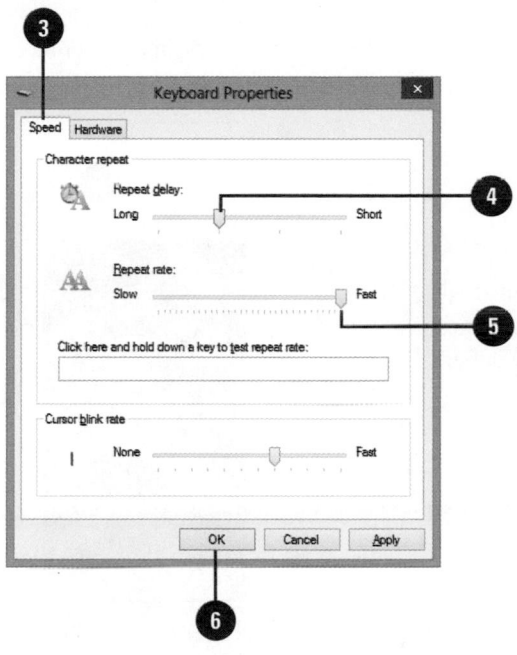

### See Also

*See "Changing Language Options" on page 316 for information on changing languages and keyboard layouts.*

# Changing Mouse Settings

A mouse does not require adjustments after you plug it in and start Windows. However, you can use Mouse and touchpad options in PC settings (**New!**) or Mouse properties in the Control Panel to change the way your mouse works and the way the pointer looks and behaves. For the mouse, you can switch the role of the buttons, or you can change the double-click or taping speed. For the mouse pointer, you can modify its appearance using a pointer scheme, increase or decrease its speed, improve its visibility with a pointer trail, or set it to be hidden when you are typing. If your button has a wheel, roll the wheel with your forefinger to move up or down in a document or on a web page.

## Change Button and Scroll Options

1. Display the Start screen.

2. Point to the lower- or upper-right corner and move up or down (on a computer) or swipe left from the right edge of the screen (on a mobile device).

3. Click or tap the **Settings** button on the Charms bar.

4. Click or tap **Change PC settings** on the Settings panel.

5. Click or tap **PC and devices** under PC settings, and then click **Mouse and touchpad (New!)** on the panel.

   ◆ **Same Options in the Control Panel.** You can also change the following options on the Buttons and Wheel tabs in the Mouse Properties dialog box.

6. Specify the following options:

   ◆ **Select your primary button.** Select Left or Right.

   ◆ **Roll the mouse wheel to scroll.** Select Multiple lines at a time or One screen at a time.

   ◆ **Choose how many lines to scroll each time.** Drag to set the number of lines.

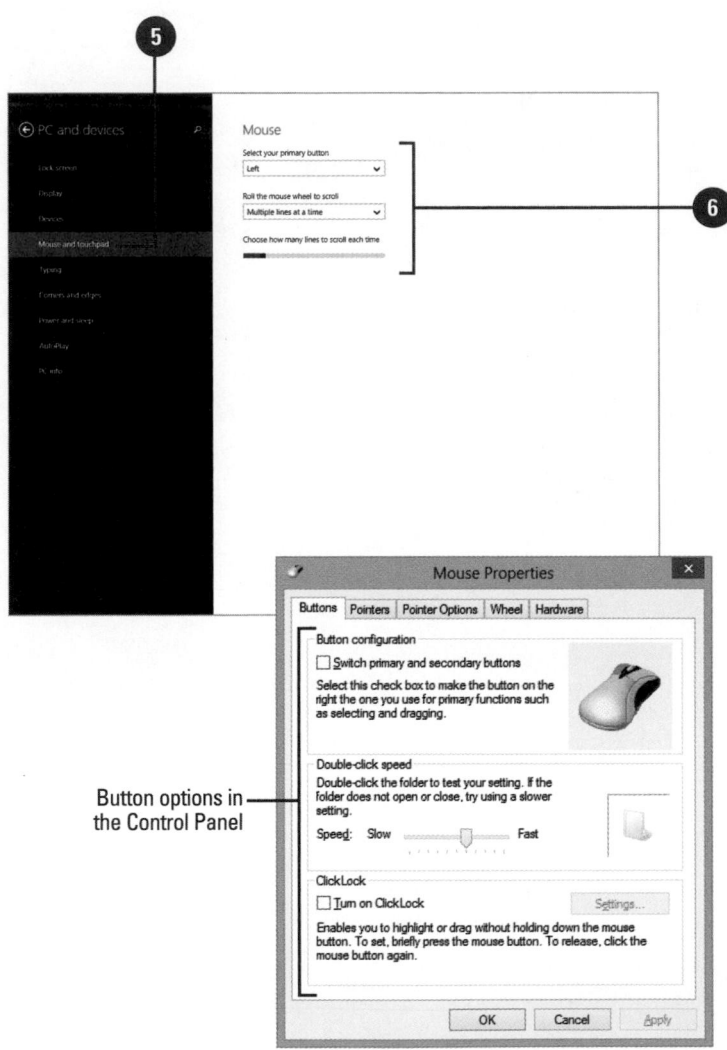

Button options in the Control Panel

## Change Pointer Appearance

**1** In the Start screen, click or tap the **Apps view** button, and then click or tap **Control Panel**.

**2** Click or tap the **Mouse** icon in Small icons or Large icons view.

**3** Click or tap the **Pointers** tab.

**4** Click or tap the **Scheme** list arrow, and then select a pointer scheme.

**5** Click or tap **OK**.

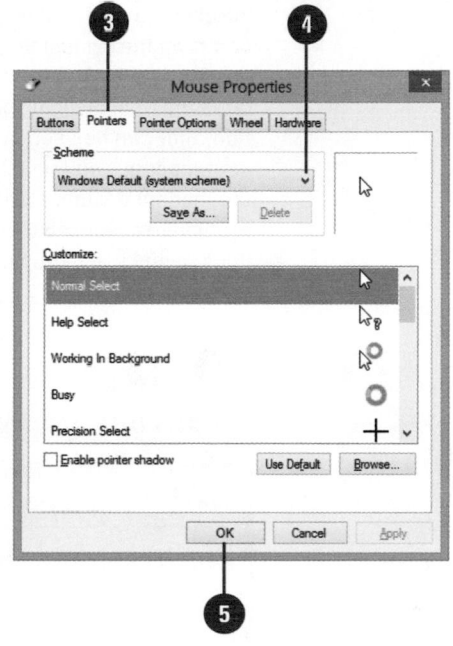

## Change Pointer Options

**1** In the Start screen, click or tap the **Apps view** button, and then click or tap **Control Panel**.

**2** Click or tap the **Mouse** icon in Small icons or Large icons view.

**3** Click or tap the **Pointer Options** tab.

**4** To adjust the pointer speed, drag the **Motion** slider.

**5** To snap the pointer to a button, select the **Automatically move pointer to the default button in a dialog box** check box.

**6** To display a trail after the pointer, hide the pointer while you type, or show the pointer location, select the visibility check box you want.

**7** Click or tap **OK**.

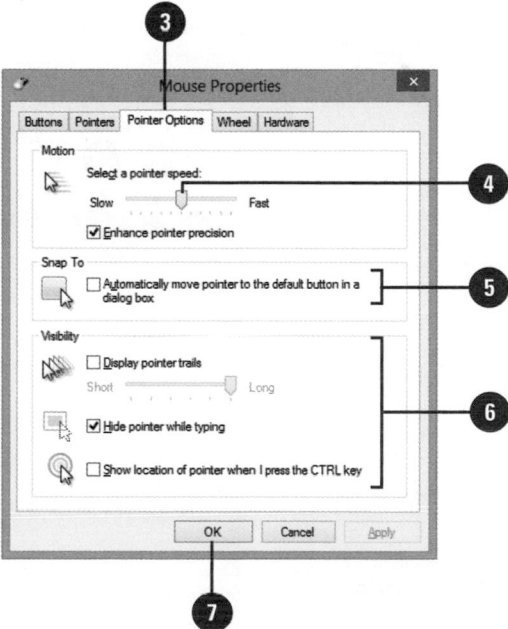

# Changing Phone and Modem Options

A **modem** is a hardware device that allows two systems to transmit information over a phone line. A modem translates the binary information from the system to an analog signal (known as modulation) that can pass over the phone line. At the receiving end, another modem translates the analog signal back to binary information (known as demodulation) that can be used by the system. If you are having problems with your modem, you can test it. With the results of the test you can consult the modem documentation or a support technician to help you fix the problem. You can also update the phone dialing options your modem uses to make a dial-up connection for one or more locations.

## Change Phone and Modem Hardware Settings

1. In the Start screen, click or tap the **Apps view** button, and then click or tap **Control Panel**.

2. Click or tap the **Phone and Modem** icon in Small icons or Large icons view.

3. Click or tap the **Dialing Rules** tab.

4. Click or tap click or tap a dialing location, click or tap **Edit**, and then click or tap the **General** tab.

5. Change the country or area code, and then specify dialing rules. To set area code dialing rules, use the **Area Code Rules** tab.

6. If you want, select the **To disable call waiting** check box.

7. Click or tap the **Modems** tab.

8. Click or tap the modem you want to change, and then click or tap **Properties**.

9. Click or tap the **Modem** tab.

10. Change the maximum port speed and speaker volume.

11. To test the modem, click or tap the **Diagnostics** tab, and then click or tap **Query Modem**.

12. Click or tap **OK**, and then click or tap **OK** again.

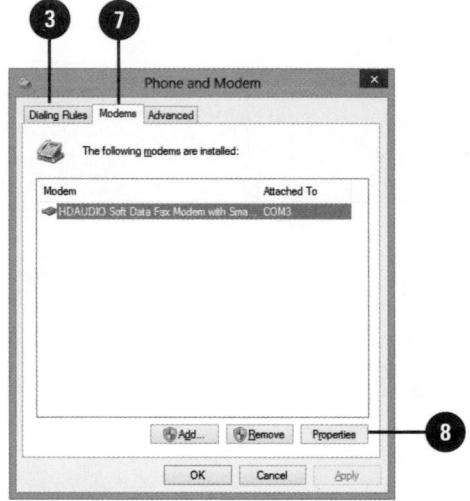

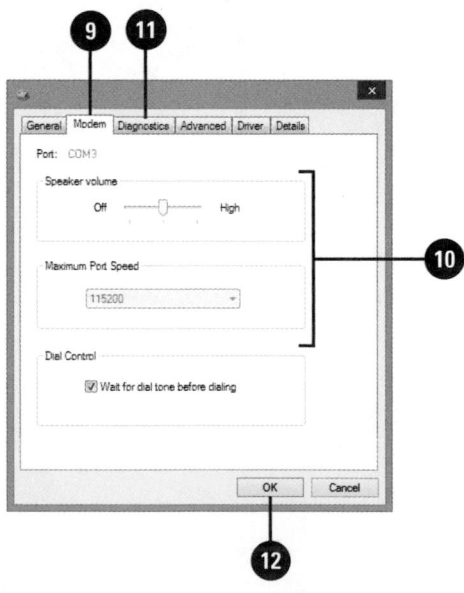

# Managing Storage Spaces

If you have more than one drive attached to your system, you can use Storage Spaces to group drives together in a storage pool. This allows Windows to save files on multiple drives. If there is a failure with a drive, your files are still protected. If you add more drives later, you can include them in the pool. You can use different types of internal and external drives, including USB, SATA, and SAS drives. Storage spaces are virtual drives that you can use in File Explorer.

## Manage Storage Spaces

1. Connect all the drives that you want to group together.

2. In the Start screen, click or tap the **Apps view** button, and then click or tap **Control Panel**.

3. Click or tap the **Storage Spaces** icon in Small icons or Large icons view.

4. To set Storage Spaces, click or tap **Create a new pool and storage space**, select the drives, click or tap **Create pool**, enter a name and letter, select a layout, enter the max size, and then click or tap **Create storage space**.

5. To manage Storage Spaces, select from the following options.

   ◆ **Rename pool.** Renames the storage pool of drives.

   ◆ **Create a space.** Creates a new space.

   ◆ **Add drives.** Adds one or more drives to the pool.

   ◆ **View files.** View files in the pool.

   ◆ **Rename or Delete space.** Rename or delete a space.

   ◆ **Rename drive.** Renames a drive in the pool.

6. Click or tap the **Close** button.

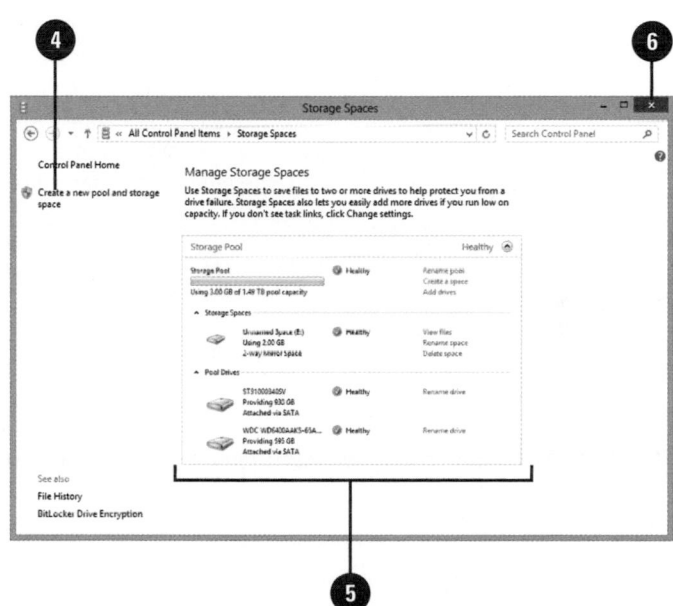

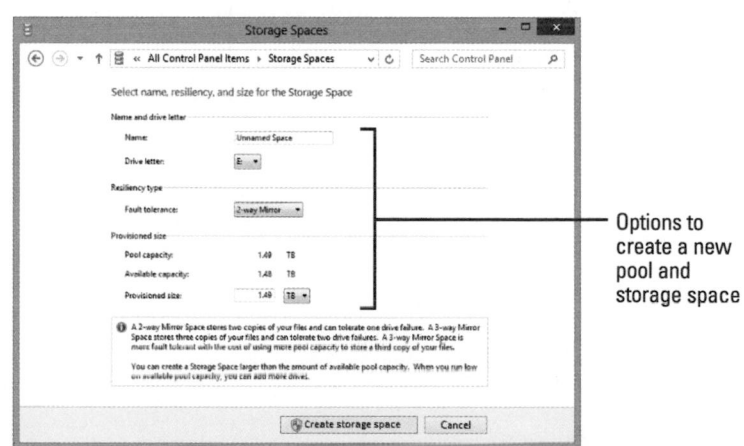

Options to create a new pool and storage space

# Managing Color

Color management is a system that makes sure the color you see on your display or printer is the color you want. Not all hardware displays color in the same way; each hardware device uses different characteristics, or methods, when rendering and processing color on a specific device. Even programs don't all render and process color the same way. Color Management controls the relationship between the device characteristics and the display conditions to produce the most accurate results. A color profile describes the color characteristics of a specific device. With the Color Management properties in the Control Panel, you can add or remove a color profile, associate a different color profile with a device, change the default profile, and change the color options, such as rendering intent and color space. Color profiles are typically added when you install a hardware device or software program that requires it. Windows 8.1 supports the standard ICC color standard and can add to it with Windows Color System.

## View Color Profiles

1. In the Start screen, click or tap the **Apps view** button, and then click or tap **Control Panel**.

2. Click or tap the **Color Management** icon in Small icons or Large icons view.

3. Click or tap the **Devices** tab.

4. Click or tap the **Device** list arrow, and then click or tap the device you want to view.

   If a device uses a color profile, it appears in the list.

5. If you want to change the color profile, select the **Use my settings for this device** check box.

6. Use the **Add**, **Remove**, and **Profiles** buttons to modify profile associations.

7. To view all profiles on your system or add a profile, click or tap the **All Profiles** tab.

8. To change specific attributes and characteristics of a profile, click or tap the **Advanced** tab.

9. Click or tap **Close**.

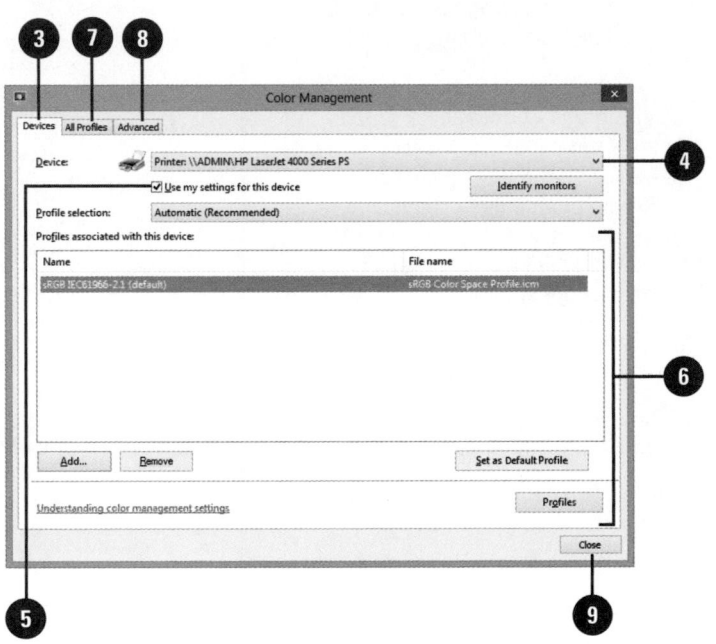

# Using the Windows Mobility Center

With the Windows Mobility Center, you can change or access mobile PC related options all in one place. You no longer have to change mobile PC related options in different places. In the Windows Mobility Center, you can adjust volume level and power options, check your network connectivity, connect to an external display, enable presentation settings, and access the Sync Center, which helps you keep files up-to-date when you're working on different devices, such as a desktop computer and a laptop or tablet. You can make an option change in Windows Mobility Center, or click or tap the icon on a tile to open the utility in the Control Panel, where you can make additional changes.

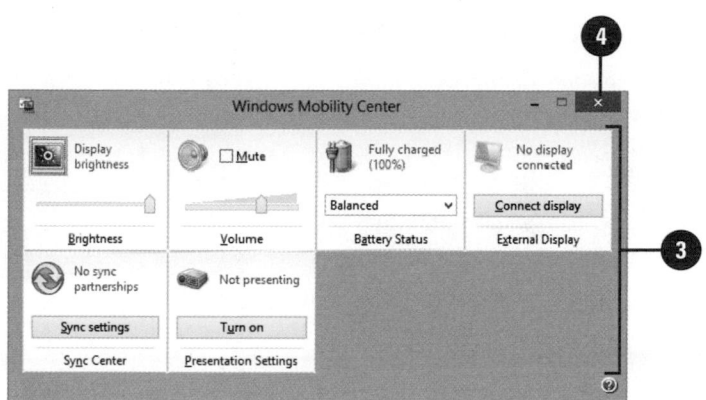

## Use Windows Mobility Center

1. In the Start screen, click or tap the **Apps view** button, and then click or tap **Control Panel**.

2. Click or tap the **Windows Mobility Center** icon in Small icons or Large icons view.

   **IMPORTANT** *The Windows Mobility Center is only available on laptop and mobile devices.*

3. Click or tap a button or change an option for any of the following settings (options vary depending on your system):

   ◆ **Brightness** for the display.

   ◆ **Volume** for the speakers.

   ◆ **Battery Status** for power usage.

   ◆ **Wireless Network** on and off.

   ◆ **Screen Rotation** for a Tablet PC.

   ◆ **External Display** add or remove.

   ◆ **Sync Center** to keep files up-to-date.

   ◆ **Presentation Settings** on and off for giving a presentation; turn on or off the screen saver, set the volume, and set a background.

4. When you're done, click or tap the **Close** button.

# Adding a Secondary Monitor

If you need more space on your desktop to work, you can add a secondary monitor to your system. This allows you to view and work with more than one full size window on the screen at the same time. Before you can use more than one monitor, you need another **display adapter**—a hardware device that allows a system to communicate with its monitor—on your system, or use a built-in one that supports multiple monitor ports. One monitor serves as the primary display while the other serves as the secondary display. You can set the multiple displays to duplicate the displays on both monitors, extend the displays over two monitors, and show desktop only on one or the other. In addition, you can set different screen resolutions and orientation settings for each monitor.

## Set Secondary Monitor Options

1. In the desktop, right-click or tap-hold a blank area of the desktop, and then click or tap **Screen resolution**.

2. If the secondary monitor doesn't appear, click or tap **Detect**.

3. Click or tap the **Multiple displays** list arrow, and then select an option:

   ◆ **Duplicate these displays.**

   ◆ **Extend these displays.**

   ◆ **Show desktop only on 1.**

   ◆ **Show desktop only on 2.**

4. Select a monitor icon or drag an icon to represent how you want to move items from one monitor to another.

5. Select any of the following monitor options:

   ◆ **Display.** Changes the display driver.

   ◆ **Resolution.** Changes the screen resolution; drag the slider.

   ◆ **Orientation.** Changes the screen to landscape or portrait.

6. To change the primary display, select a non primary monitor, and then select the **Make this my main display** check box.

7. Click or tap **OK**.

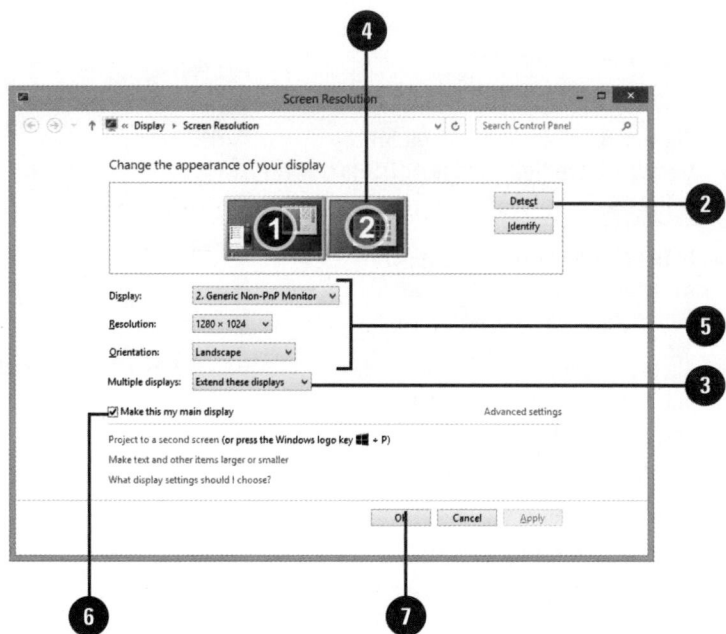

## Select Secondary Screen Options in the Devices Panel

**1** Connect the monitor or projector device you want to use to your system.

◆ You can use **Connect to a Second Screen** in the Screen Resolution dialog box to select secondary monitor options in the Devices panel.

**2** In the Start screen, select the content or open the app you want to use.

**3** Point to the upper-right corner and move down (on a computer) or swipe left from the right edge of the screen (on a mobile device).

**4** Click or tap the **Devices** button on the Charms bar.

**TIMESAVER** *Press Win+K to display the Devices panel.*

**5** Click or tap **Project** on the Devices panel.

**TIMESAVER** *Press Win+P to display the Project panel.*

**6** Click or tap an option: **PC screen only**, **Duplicate**, **Extend**, or **Second screen only**.

**7** To go back to the previous panel, click or tap the **Back** button.

### See Also

*See "Using Devices with Apps" on page 266 for more information on using the Devices button to use devices.*

*See "Viewing Hardware Devices" on page 474 for more information on installing hardware devices.*

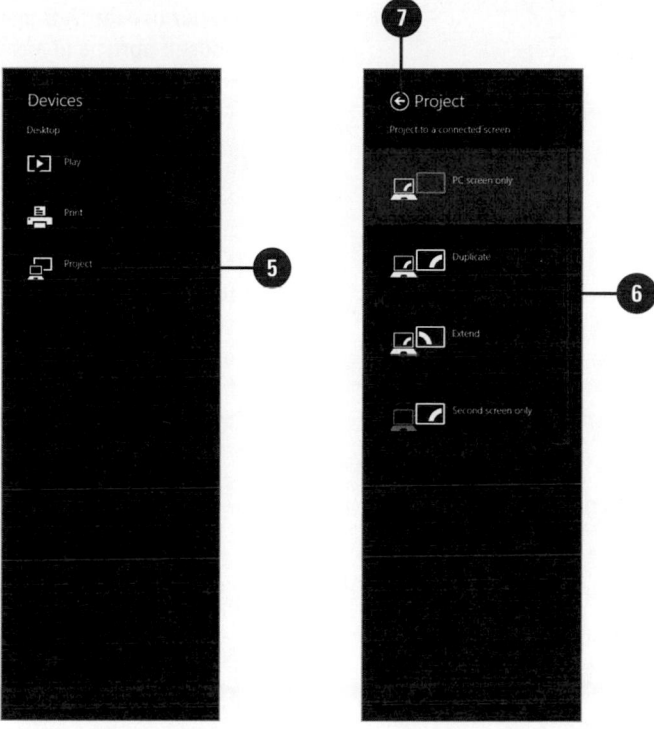

# Controlling Power Options

Windows 8.1 works more efficiently for longer battery life including less power use for DVD playback, automatic screen dimming, power off unused ports, and more accurate battery life. You can change power options properties for a laptop, notebook, or tablet to reduce power consumption and maximize battery life. For example, if you often leave your system for a short time while working, you can set your system to go into **sleep**, a state in which your system saves everything in memory and turns off your monitor and hard disks after being idle for a set time. If you are often away from your system for an extended time, you can set it to go into **hibernate**, a state in which your system saves everything in memory and to your hard disk, and then shuts down. To help you set power options, you can choose one of the power plans, modify one to suit your needs, or create your own. A **power plan** is a predefined collection of power usage settings (dim display, turn off display, put to sleep, and adjust brightness). If you want more options, you can set advanced options to define the power button (sleep, hibernate, or shut down) or other settings, such as **hybrid sleep**, which adds saving to your hard disk to sleep mode.

## Select and Modify a Power Plan

**1** In the desktop, click or tap the **Power** icon in the notification area, and then click or tap **More power options**.

◆ In the Control Panel, you can also click or tap the **Power Options** icon in the Small or Large icons view.

**2** To adjust screen brightness, drag the slider.

**3** Click or tap the power plan option you want: **Balanced**, or **Power saver**, **High performance**.

**4** Click or tap **Change plan settings** below the selected option.

**5** Select an amount of time to:

◆ **Dim the display.**

◆ **Turn off the display.**

◆ **Put the computer to sleep.**

◆ **Adjust plan brightness.**

**6** To restore defaults, click or tap **Restore default settings for this plan**, and then click or tap **Yes**.

**7** Click or tap **Save changes.**

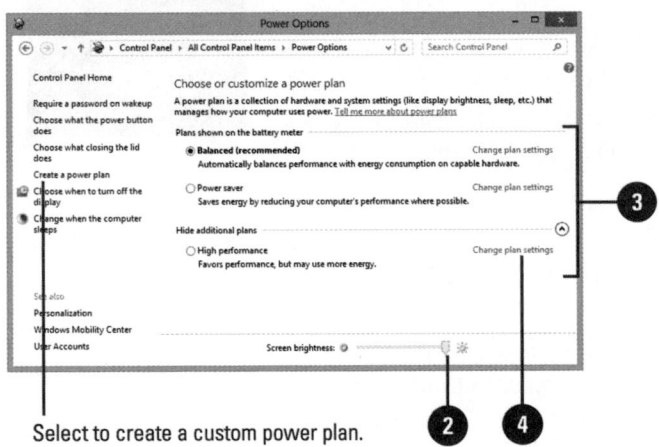

Select to create a custom power plan.

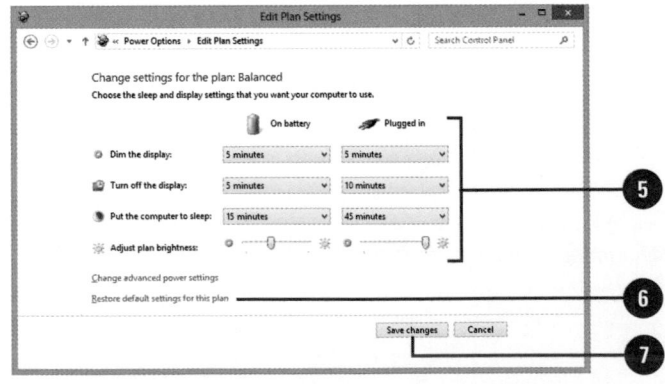

## Define Power Button and Set Password Protection

1. In the desktop, click or tap the **Power** icon in the notification area, and then click or tap **More power options**.

   ◆ In the Control Panel, you can also click or tap the **Power Options** icon in the Small or Large icons view.

2. Click or tap **Choose what the power buttons does**.

3. Specify the options you want when you press the power or sleep button, or when you close the lid.

4. Select the **Require a password (recommended)** or **Don't require a password** option.

5. Click or tap **Save changes**.

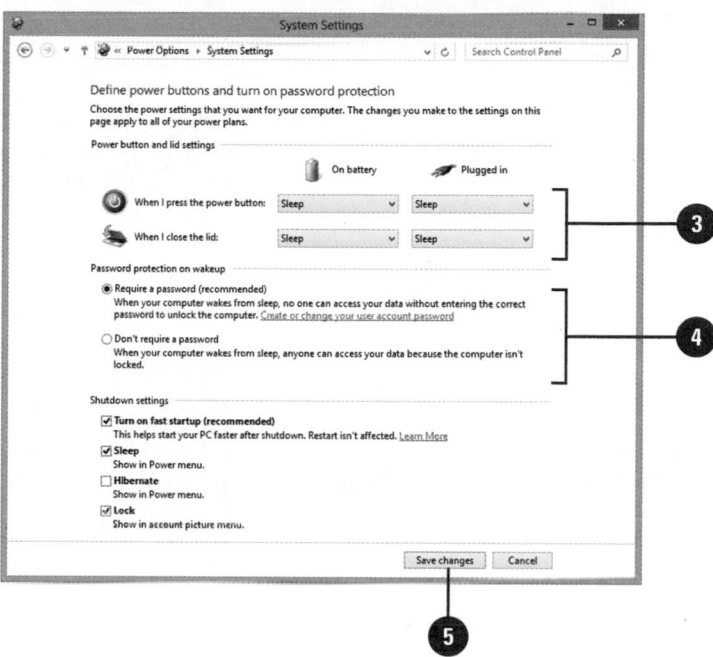

## Set Advanced Options

1. In the desktop, click or tap the **Power** icon in the notification area, and then click or tap **More power options**.

   ◆ In the Control Panel, you can also click or tap the **Power Options** icon in the Small or Large icons view.

2. Click or tap **Change plan settings** below the selected power plan.

3. Click or tap **Change advanced power settings**.

4. Click or tap the plus sign (+) and minus sign (-) icons to display the option you want to change.

5. Click or tap the option list arrow, and then select a setting.

6. When you're done, click or tap **OK**.

7. Click or tap **Save changes**.

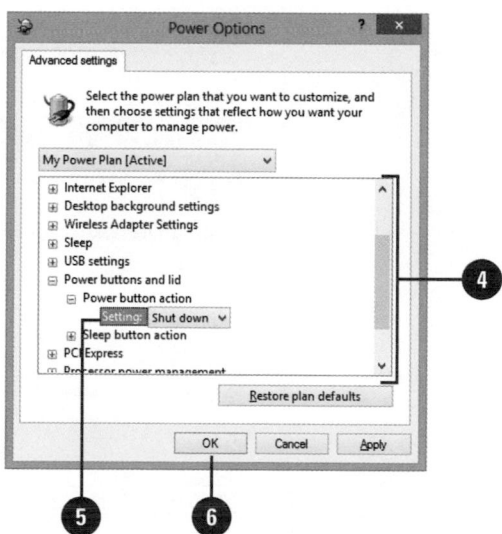

# Removing Hardware Devices

If you no longer use a hardware device (not plug and play), such as a sound or modem card, or if you have an older hardware device that you want to upgrade, you need to remove the hardware device drivers and related software before you remove the physical hardware device from your system. With the Device Manager, you can remove hardware devices and any related device drivers. Before you remove a legacy device, printing the device settings is a good idea in case you need to reinstall the device later.

## Remove a Hardware Device

**1** In the Start screen, click or tap the **Apps view** button, and then click or tap **Control Panel**.

**2** Click or tap the **Device Manager** icon in Small icons or Large icons view.

**3** Click or tap the white arrow next to the hardware category you want to expand.

**4** Click or tap the device you want to remove.

**5** Click or tap the **Uninstall** button.

**6** Click or tap **OK**.

**7** Click or tap the **Close** button.

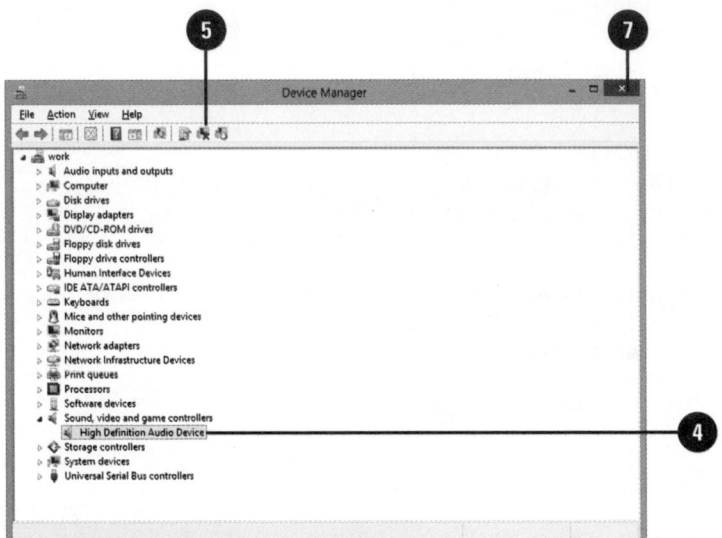

### Did You Know?

*You can quickly delete a printer.* In the Devices and Printers window, select the printer icon you want to delete, and then click or tap Remove Device, and then click or tap Yes.

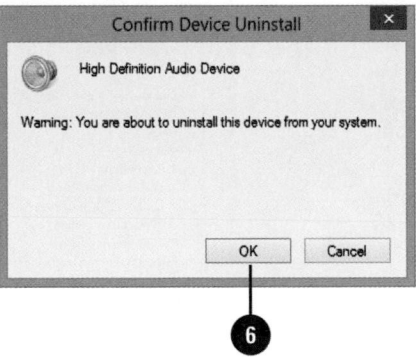

# Removing Plug and Play Hardware

Most plug and play hardware devices, such as a USB Flash or external drive, can be removed and unplugged at anytime as long as the system is not using it. However, it's not easy to know if the system is done with it. If the Safely Remove Hardware icon appears in the notification area on the taskbar, you can use it to quickly and safely remove the hardware.

## Remove or Eject a Plug and Play Hardware Device Safely

① In the desktop, click or tap the **Safely Remove Hardware and Eject Media** icon in the notification area on the taskbar, and then select a device.

> **TIMESAVER** *Right-click or tap-hold the device in the Computer window, and then click or tap Safely Remove.*

② If prompted, click or tap **OK** to confirm the removal.

③ Unplug or eject the device.

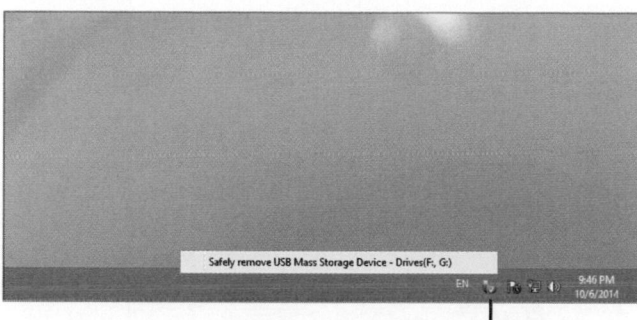

Safely remove hardware

Eject media

# Troubleshooting Problems

If you're having problems with your system, you can use a troubleshooting wizard to help you diagnosis and fix the problem. You can access Troubleshooting in the Control Panel. From the Troubleshooting window, you can run troubleshooters to fix programs made for previous versions of Windows, reconfigure a hardware device, establish an Internet connection, access shared files, fix Windows Update, maintenance, and performance issues, and improve power usage. If you need further help, you can also access and use Remote Assistance to contact someone you trust for help.

## Troubleshoot Problems

1. In the Start screen, click or tap the **Apps view** button, and then click or tap **Control Panel**.

2. Click or tap the **Troubleshooting** icon in Small icons or Large icons view.

3. To set troubleshooting options, click or tap **Change settings** in the left pane, set the options you want, and then click or tap **OK**.

4. Click or tap a link for the area you want to troubleshoot.

   ◆ **Programs.** Use to run programs made for previous versions of Windows.

   ◆ **Hardware and Sound.** Use to reconfigure a hardware device.

   ◆ **Network and Internet.** Use to fix a connect to the Internet and file sharing.

   ◆ **System and Security.** Use to fix Windows Update, maintenance, and performance issues.

5. Follow the on-screen troubleshooting wizard.

6. To use Remote Assistance to contact someone you trust for help, click or tap **Get help from a friend** in the left pane.

7. Click or tap the **Close** button.

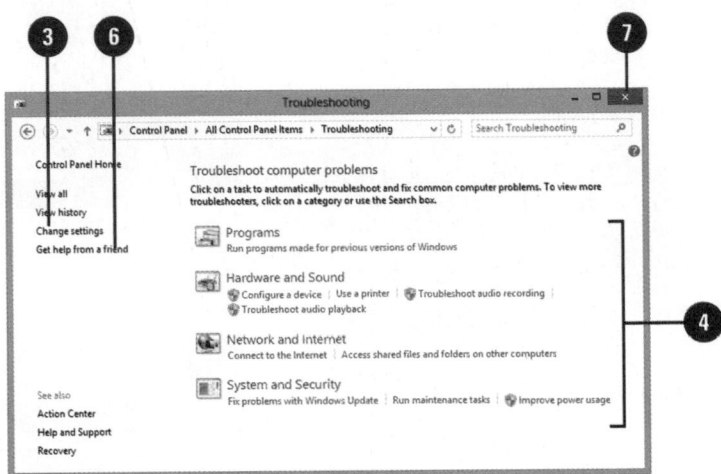

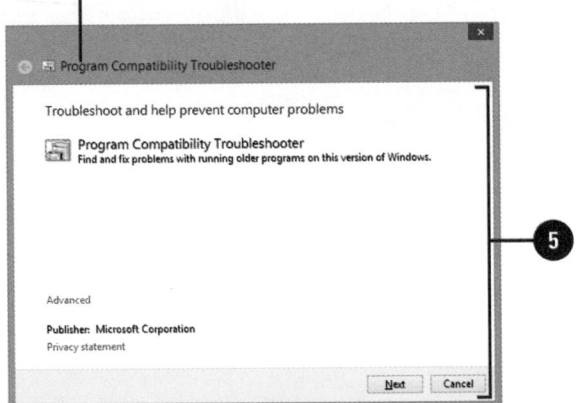

Program Compatibility troubleshooting wizard

# Administering Your Computer

## Introduction

If you have purchased a personal computer and set it up in your home, you are that PC's administrator. Computers on a network in a company or an institution, such as at a university, are called clients. The clients are managed by one or more system or network administrators, who have the task of ensuring that the network and its services are reliable, fast, and secure. Although most network administration takes place on the server (host, as described in earlier chapters), clients must also be administered. Windows 8.1 includes administrative tools that make it easy to ensure that client PCs are operating as they should.

You can use the administrative tools to track and view the activity on your PC. You can set up criteria for gathering event information, and then Windows automatically gathers that information for you. In the event of a problem, you can view that data to help you find and fix the problem.

When you open an administrative tool, Windows uses a two-pane view that is similar to File Explorer. The hierarchy of tools in the left pane of the window is called a **console tree**, and each main category of tools is called a **node**. The nodes in the console tree allow you to manage and monitor system events and performance, and make adjustments as necessary.

## What You'll Do

**Explore Windows Administrative Tools**

**Schedule Tasks**

**Monitor Activity with Event Viewer**

**Manage an Event Log**

**Manage All Printers**

**Check Memory for Problems**

**View and Create Performance Charts**

**Monitor Local Security Settings**

**View Computer Management Tools**

**Manage Disks**

**Manage Local Users and Groups**

**View and Save System Information**

**Set System Configuration Options**

# Exploring Windows Administrative Tools

Windows 8.1 offers a set of tools that helps you administer your PC and ensure it operates smoothly. Administrative Tools, available from the Control Panel or App screen (**New!**) (when a Tiles setting is enabled), provide utilities that allow you to configure administrative settings for local and remote PCs. If you are working on a shared or network PC, you might need to be logged on as a PC administrator or as a member of the Administrators group in order to view or modify some properties or perform some tasks with the administrative tools. You can open User Accounts in the Control Panel to check which account is currently in use or to check with your system administrator to determine whether you have the necessary access privileges. Many Windows users won't ever have to use Administrative Tools, but PCs on a network will probably require administrative support.

## View Administrative Tools from the Control Panel

1. In the Start screen, click or tap the **Apps view** button, and then click or tap **Control Panel**.

2. Click or tap the **Administrative Tools** icon in Small icons or Large icons view.

3. When you're done, click or tap the **Close** button.

Administrative tools

### Did You Know?

*You can access many Administrative Tools using a shortcut key.* Press Win+X or right-click or tap-hold the lower left corner of the screen to display a context menu. On the menu, you can select Event Viewer, System, Device Manager, Disk Management, Command Prompt, and Command Prompt (Admin).

## View Administrative Tools from the App Screen

① In the Start screen, click or tap the **Apps view** button to display the App screen.

② Point to the lower- or upper-right corner and move up or down (on a computer) or swipe left from the right edge of the screen (on a mobile device).

③ Click or tap the **Settings** button on the Charms bar.

④ Click or tap **Tiles** on the Settings panel.

⑤ Drag the Show administrative tools slider to **Yes**.

⑥ Click or tap in a blank area off the panel or press Esc to close the panel.

The administrative tools appear on the Apps screen.

⑦ In the App screen, click or tap the tile for the administrative tool that you want to open

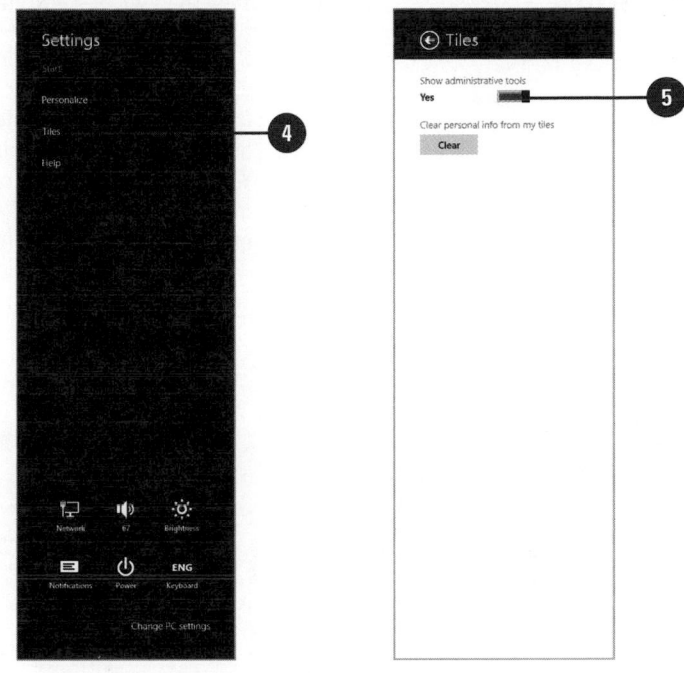

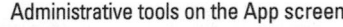

Administrative tools on the App screen

# Scheduling Tasks

Task Scheduler is a program that enables you to schedule tasks to run regularly, such as Disk Cleanup, at a time convenient for you. Task Scheduler starts each time you start Windows. With Task Scheduler, you can schedule a task to run daily, weekly, monthly, or at certain times (such as when the PC starts or idles), change the schedule for or turn off an existing task, or customize how a task runs at its scheduled time. You can create a basic task using the Create Basic Task wizard or a more complex task using the Create Task dialog box. Before you schedule a task, be sure that the system date and time on your PC are accurate, as Task Scheduler relies on this information to run.

## Scheduled a Basic Task

1. In the App screen, click or tap the **Task Scheduler** tile.

   ◆ With Show administrative tools enabled on the Tiles panel.

2. In the Actions pane, click or tap **Create Basic Task**.

3. Type a name and description for the scheduled task, and then click or tap **Next** to continue.

4. Click or tap a scheduled task time interval option, and then click or tap **Next** to continue.

5. Specify a start time and a recurring interval, and then click or tap **Next** to continue.

6. Select an action option, and then click or tap **Next** to continue.

7. Specify the information or options related with the selected action, and then click or tap **Next** to continue.

8. Click or tap **Finish**.

9. To run, end, disable, or delete a task, click or tap the **Task Scheduler Library**, select the task in the console window, and then click or tap the command you want at the bottom of the Actions pane. To edit a task, select it, and then make changes at the bottom of the console window.

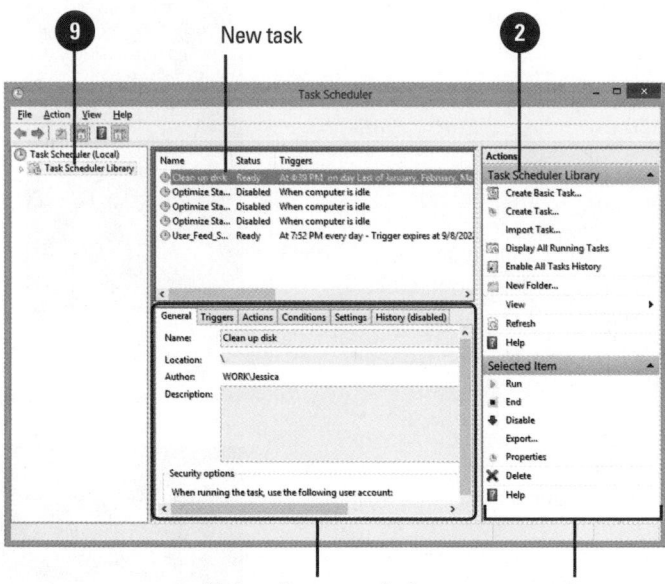

New task

Task attributes     Action pane commands

Summary of task attributes

# Monitoring Activity with Event Viewer

Every time you start Windows, an event-logging service notes any unusual event that occurs, such as a failed logon, the installation of a new driver for a hardware device, the failure of a device or service to start, or a network interruption. For some critical events, such as when your disk is full, a warning message appears on your screen. Most events, however, don't require immediate attention, so Windows logs them in an event log file that you can view using the Event Viewer tool. Event Viewer maintains several logs in two categories: Windows Logs and Applications and Services Logs. Windows Logs maintains three logs: System, for events logged by Windows operating system components; Security, for security and audit events (such as who logged on); and Application, for Windows program events. Applications and Services Logs maintains individual program and service logs. When you are troubleshooting problems on your PC, you can use the Event Viewer logs to monitor what activity took place.

## Monitor Activities

1. In the App screen, click or tap the **Event Viewer** tile.

   ◆ With Show administrative tools enabled on the Tiles panel.

   ◆ You can also double-click or double-tap the **Event Viewer** icon in the Administrative Tools window (Control Panel).

2. Click or tap arrow next to the log category to expand it, and then click or tap the log in which you want to monitor events.

3. Double-click or double-tap an event.

4. Click or tap the **Up Arrow** button or the **Down Arrow** button to display other events.

5. Click or tap **Close**.

6. When you're done, click or tap the **Close** button.

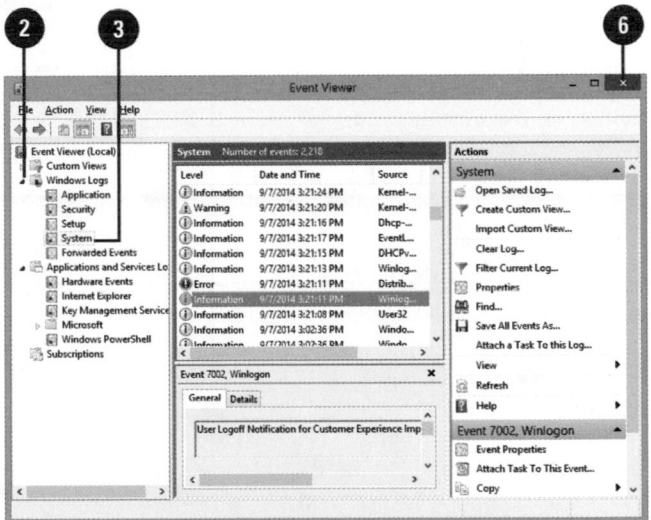

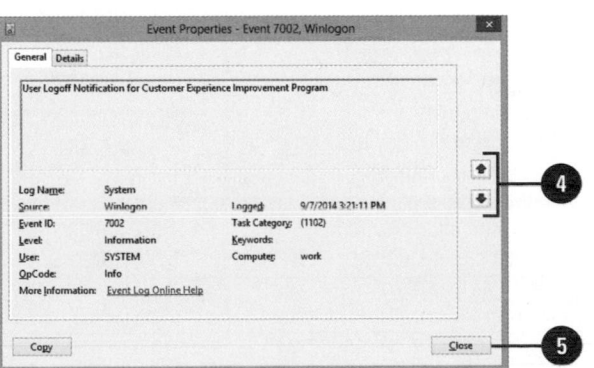

# Managing an Event Log

Event logs grow in size as you work on your PC, but Event Viewer provides tools that help you view just the information you need and store the information you want to save for later. For example, you can apply a **filter** that allows you to view only events matching specified criteria, such as all events associated with a certain user. You can also search for a specific event using similar criteria. You probably don't want your active log to include events that happened long ago. With Event Viewer, you can **archive**, or save, your log periodically and then clear the archived events. Most administrators archive event logs on a regular schedule.

## Sort and Filter an Event Log

① In the App screen, click or tap the **Event Viewer** tile.

   ◆ With Show administrative tools enabled on the Tiles panel.

② Select the event log you want to sort or filter events.

③ Click or tap the **View** menu, point to **Sort By**, and then click or tap the sort method you want.

④ In the Actions pane, click or tap **Filter Current Log**.

⑤ Select the Event Level check boxes in which you want to filter.

⑥ Specify filter information by specific value.

⑦ Click or tap **OK**.

⑧ When you're done, click or tap the **Close** button.

### Did You Know?

*You can find information in the Event Viewer.* In the Event Viewer, click or tap Find in the Actions pane, type what you want to find, and then click or tap Find Next. When you're done, click or tap Close.

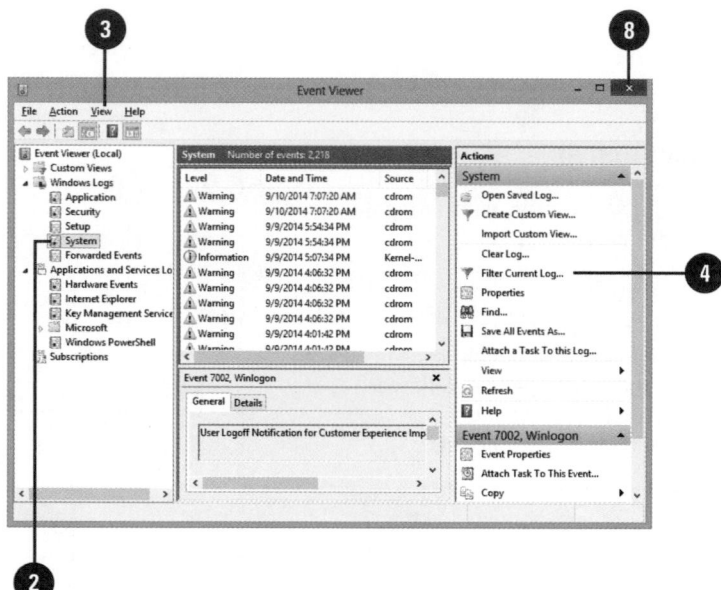

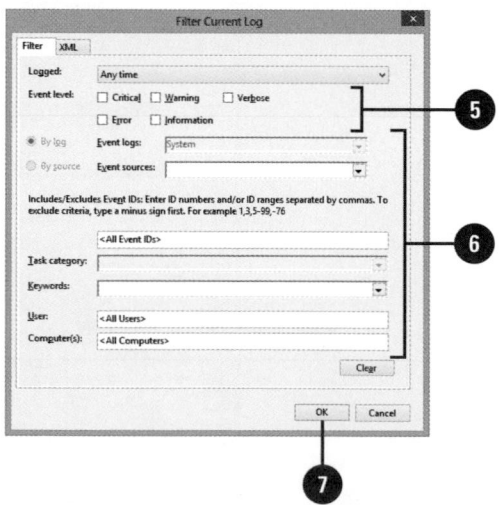

## Save an Event Log

1. In the App screen, click or tap the **Event Viewer** tile.
   - With Show administrative tools enabled on the Tiles panel.

2. Select the event log you want to save.

3. In the Actions pane, click or tap **Save Log File As** or **Save All Events As**.

4. Select a location for the log file.

5. Type a name for the log file.

6. Click or tap **Save**.

7. When you're done, click or tap the **Close** button.

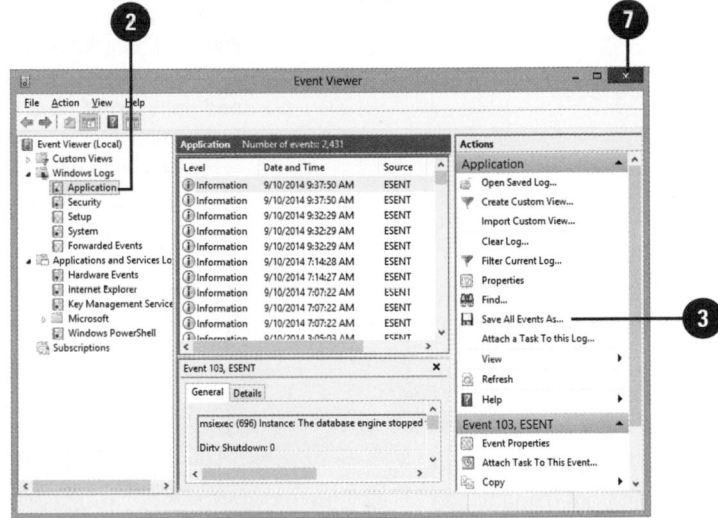

### Did You Know?

**You can open the log file from the Event Viewer.** In the Event Viewer, click or tap Open Saved Log in the Action pane, select the log file, and then click or tap Open.

**You can change log settings.** You can control how any log in the Event Viewer collects data by defining a maximum log size (the default is 512K) and instructing Event Viewer how to handle an event log that has reached its maximum size. In the Event Viewer, select the log you want to change, click or tap Properties in the Actions pane, click or tap the General tab, specify the maximum log size, select an option when the maximum size is reached, click or tap OK, and then click or tap the Close button.

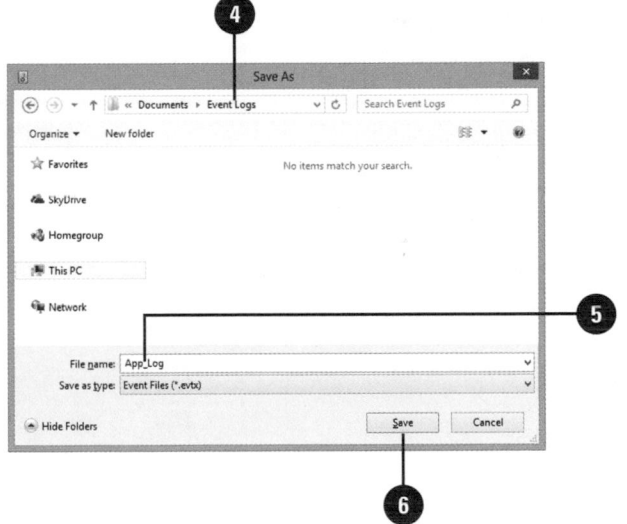

# Managing All Printers

For PCs on a network running Windows 8.1 and Windows Server 2010 or later, you can use Print Management to monitor print queues and get alerts when print queues stop processing print jobs. The Print Management tool allows you to work with shared printers on a network and print server from a central location. You can get status information for printers and print servers on a network and find printers that have an error by using filters. When a printer or print server needs attention, Print Management can send e-mail messages or run scripts.

## Manage All Printers

1. In the App screen, click or tap the **Print Management** tile.

   ◆ With Show administrative tools enabled on the Tiles panel.

2. Click or tap the white arrow to expand Print Management.

3. To monitor printers, expand **Custom Filters**, and then click or tap **All Printers**, **All Drivers**, **Printers Not Ready**, or **Printers With Jobs**.

4. To work with printers, select a printer, click or tap **More Actions**, and then click or tap a command.

5. To work with print servers, expand **Print Servers**, select a print server, click or tap **More Actions**, and then click or tap a command: **Add Printer**, **Set Notifications**, or **Properties**.

6. When you're done, click or tap the **Close** button.

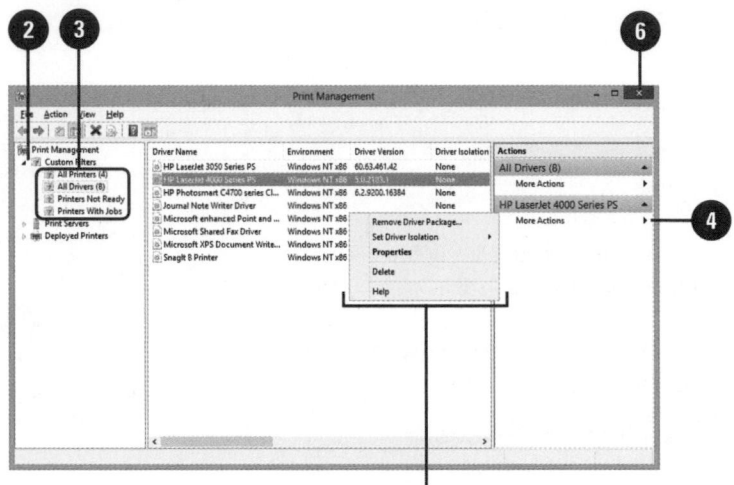

Printer related commands

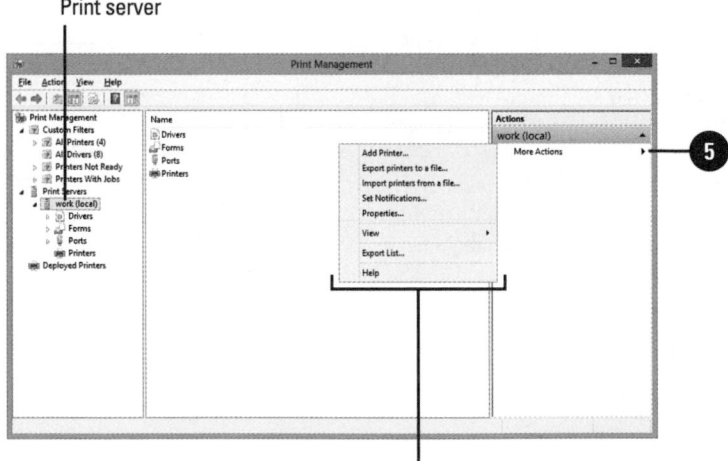

Print server

Print server related commands

# Checking Memory for Problems

If a problem arises related to the memory on your PC, Windows automatically tries to detect it and displays an alert message, which allows you to run the Windows Memory Diagnostic. If you also suspect a memory problem, you can run the Windows Memory Diagnostic from Administrator Tools. When the memory tool starts, you can have the program restart your PC and run the memory tool immediately or run it later. While the memory tool runs, a progress bar indicates the status of the test. When the test is done, Windows restarts again. If the results indicate a problem, you should contact your PC or memory manufacturer for information about fixing the problem.

## Check for Memory Problems

1. In the App screen, click or tap the **Windows Memory Diagnostics** tile.

   ◆ With Show administrative tools enabled on the Tiles panel.

2. Click or tap **Restart now and check for problems** or **Check for problems the next time I start my computer** option.

3. Follow the on-screen instructions to complete the test.

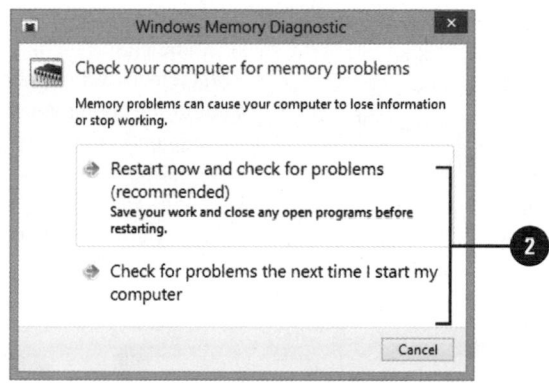

## Did You Know?

**You can change registry settings.** Windows manages all its internal settings with a database called the **Registry**. If you are an administrator or seasoned veteran of Windows and know what you want to change in the Registry, you can fix a problem with your system or a program, or you can enhance the functionality of Windows. In the App screen, click or tap click or tap Run, type **regedt32**, click or tap OK, open the folder and double-click or tap the item you want to change, and then click or tap OK. When you're done, click or tap the Close button.

# Viewing and Creating Performance Charts

On a daily basis, your system generates a variety of performance data, such as your device memory or processor use, or the amount of congestion on a device. As the system administrator, you can use the Performance tool to create charts from the data that enable you to observe how a device processor behaves over time. The types of performance data you monitor and record are called **performance objects**. Each performance object has a set of counters associated with it that provides numeric information. The Performance tool charts the numeric data gathered from the counters and provides graphical tools to make it easier to analyze and track the performance of your device. Performance charts include statistics about each counter you select, but unless you know how your system should perform, these statistics might not be very meaningful. For this reason, administrators create baseline charts—charts made when the PC or network is running at a normal level. When there are problems, the administrator can create another performance chart that can be compared to the baseline chart. In addition to the Performance Monitor, you can also view performance information in the Task Manager. The Performance tab in the Task Manager displays performance information for the CPU, Memory, Disks, and network connections, while the Processes tab displays performance information for individual apps and the Windows operating system.

## View or Create a Performance Chart

1. In the App screen, click or tap the **Performance Monitor** tile.

   ◆ With Show administrative tools enabled on the Tiles panel.

2. In the left pane, click or tap the arrow next to **Monitoring Tools**, and then click or tap **Performance Monitor**.

3. To add counts and create a chart, click or tap the **Add** button on the System Monitor toolbar.

4. Click or tap the counter you want, and then click or tap **Add**. You can continue to add other counters.

5. When you're done, click or tap **OK**.

6. Click or tap the **Close** button.

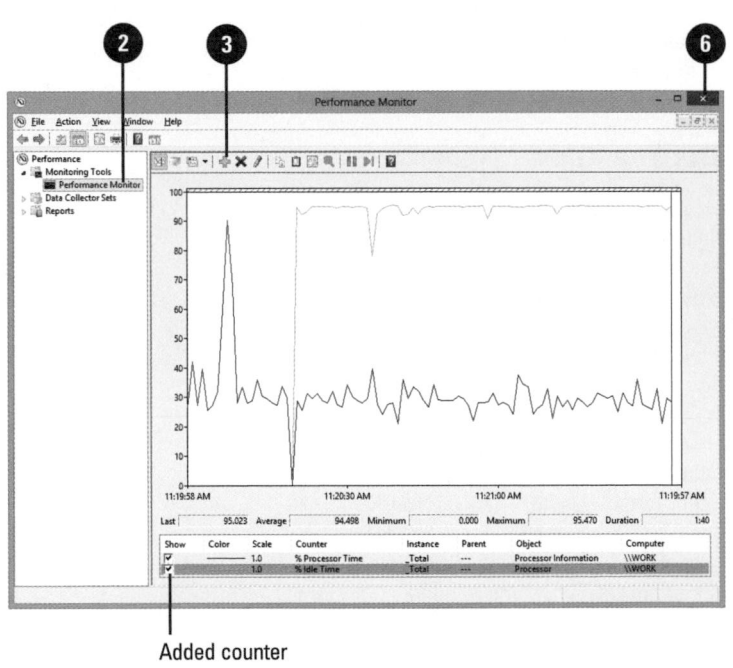

Added counter

## View Resource Performance Charts

1. In the App screen, click or tap the **Performance Monitor** tile.

   ◆ With Show administrative tools enabled on the Tiles panel.

2. In the left pane, click or tap **Performance**.

3. Click **Open Resource Monitor**.

4. Click or tap a tab or bar (**CPU, Disk, Network,** or **Memory**) to display program specific information.

5. Click the bar again to hide the specific programs.

6. Click or tap the **Close** button.

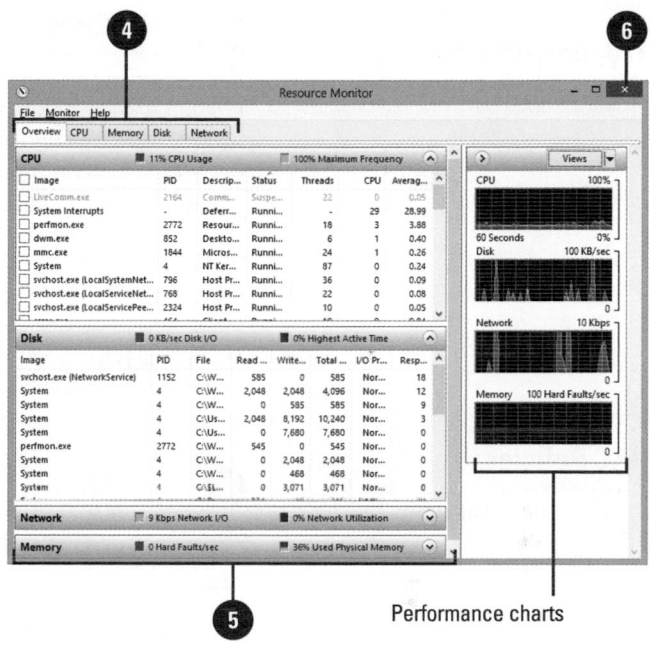

Performance charts

## View Windows Task Manager Performance Charts

1. In the desktop, right-click or tap-hold the taskbar, and then click or tap **Task Manager**.

   **TIMESAVER** *You can also press Ctrl+Shift+Esc or press Ctrl+Alt+Del, and then click or tap Task Manager.*

2. Click or tap **More details**, if necessary, and then click or tap the **Performance** tab.

3. To open the Resource Monitor, click or tap **Open Resource Monitor**.

4. To view individual process performance, click or tap the **Processes** tab.

5. When you're done, click or tap the **Close** button.

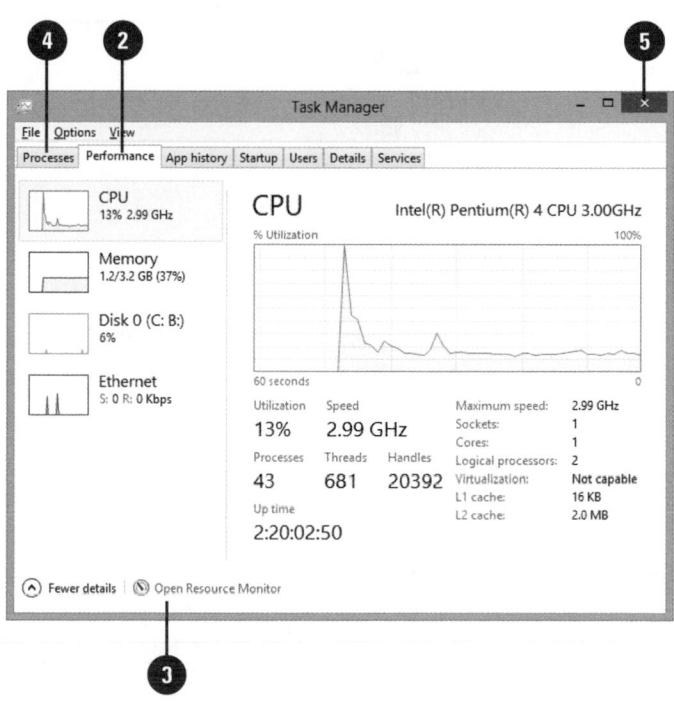

# Monitoring Local Security Settings

Using Windows, you can monitor local security settings with the Local Security Settings tool to ensure that PC users are adhering to the organization's security policies. For example, you can change the way the **User Account Control (UAC)** works, including how and when Windows prompts administrators and standard users for permission to make system changes. You can also set user account and password options to require PC users to create complex passwords of a specific length and change them on a regular basis. A **complex password** contains characters from at least three of the four following categories: uppercase (A - Z), lowercase (a - z), numbers (0 - 9), and nonalphanumeric (!, $, *, etc.). In addition to setting security options, you can also **monitor**, or **audit**, the success or failure of security related events, such as account logon and logoff activities, and user account changes, which appear in the Event Viewer in the Security node.

## Change UAC Policies

1. In the App screen, click or tap the **Local Security Policy** tile.

   ◆ With Show administrative tools enabled on the Tiles panel.

2. Click or tap the arrow next to **Local Policies**.

3. Click or tap the **Security Options** folder.

4. Scroll down the list, and then double-click or double-tap the User Account Control policy you want to change; two common ones include:

   ◆ **Behavior of the elevation prompt for administrators.**

   ◆ **Behavior of the elevation prompt for standard users.**

5. Change the policy setting.

6. Click or tap **OK**.

7. When you're done, click or tap the **Close** button.

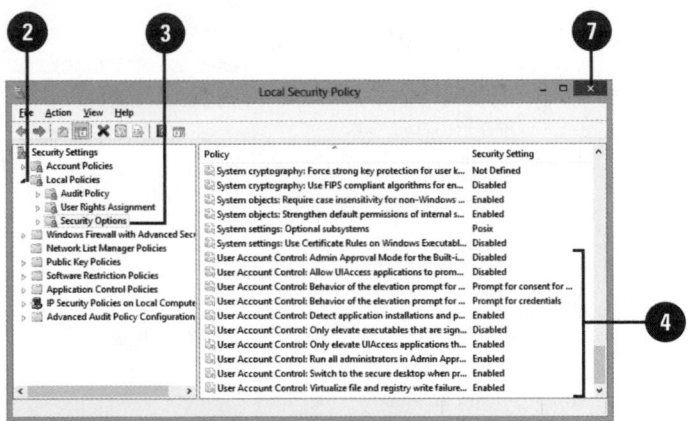

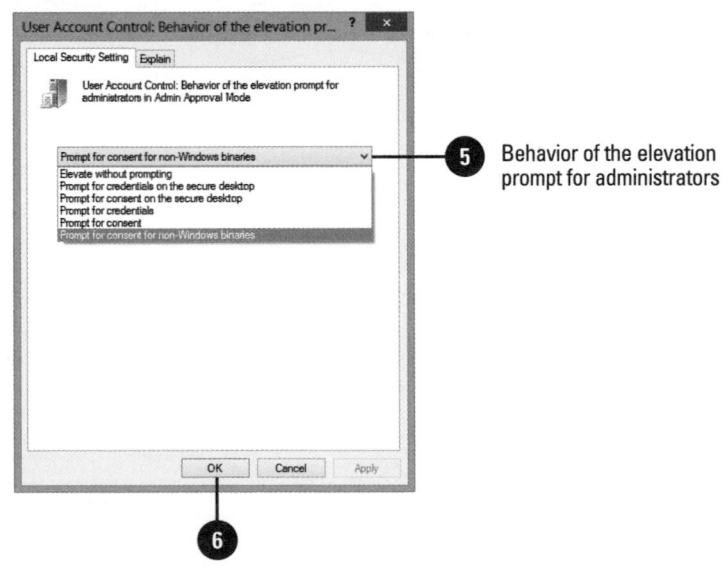

Behavior of the elevation prompt for administrators

## Change Password Policies

1. In the App screen, click or tap the **Local Security Policy** tile.

   ◆ With Show administrative tools enabled on the Tiles panel.

2. Click or tap the arrow next to **Account Policies**.

3. Click or tap the **Password Policy** folder.

4. Double-click or double-tap the policy you want to change.

5. Change the policy setting.

6. Click or tap **OK**.

7. When you're done, click or tap the **Close** button.

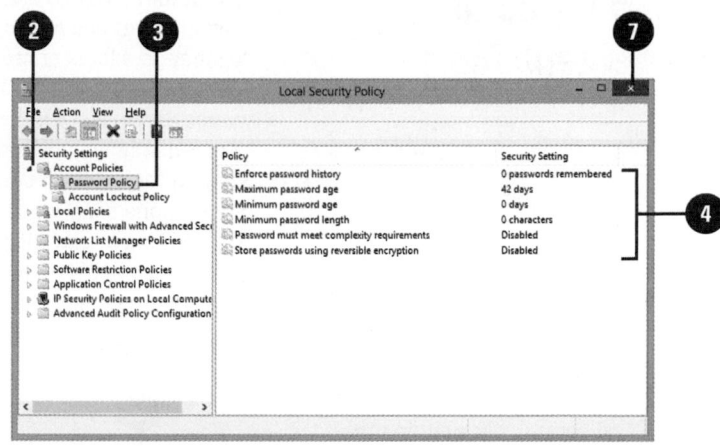

## Change Audit Policies

1. In the App screen, click or tap the **Local Security Policy** tile.

   ◆ With Show administrative tools enabled on the Tiles panel.

2. Click or tap the arrow next to **Local Policies**.

3. Click or tap the **Audit Policy** folder.

4. Double-click or double-tap the audit policy you want to change.

5. Select the **Success** and/or **Failure** check box.

6. Click or tap **OK**.

7. When you're done, click or tap the **Close** button.

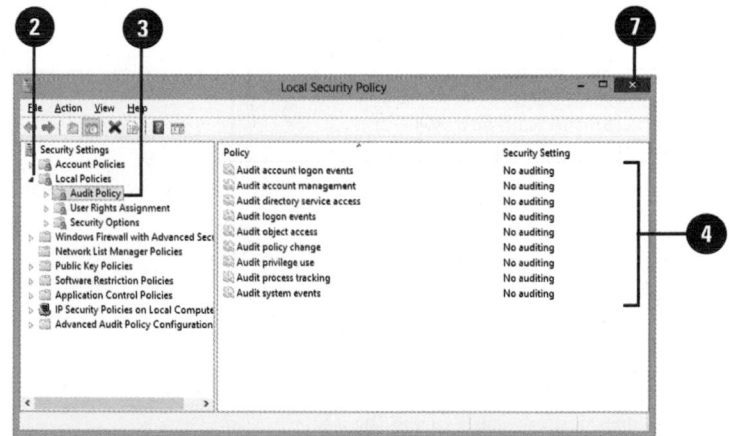

# Viewing Computer Management Tools

**Computer Management** consolidates administrative tools, such as Event Viewer and Performance, into a single window that you can use to manage a local or remote PC. The three nodes in the Computer Management window (System Tools, Storage, and Services and Applications) allow you to manage and monitor system events and performance and to perform disk-related tasks. Each node contains **snap-in tools**, which come in two types: stand-alone or extension. Stand-alone snap-ins are independent tools, while extension snap-ins are add-ons to current snap-ins. The selected tool appears in the right pane, and you can use the toolbars and menus that appear to take appropriate action with the tool.

## View Management Tools

1. In the App screen, click or tap the **Computer Management** tile.

   ◆ With Show administrative tools enabled on the Tiles panel.

   **TIMESAVER** *To open Computer Management, right-click or tap-hold the lower left-corner of the screen, and then click or tap Computer Management.*

2. Click or tap the arrow next to the category you want to view.

3. Click or tap the item you want to view.

4. Double-click or double-tap the item you want to change, adjust the setting, and then click or tap **OK**.

   You can continue to change other items.

5. When you're done, click or tap the **Close** button.

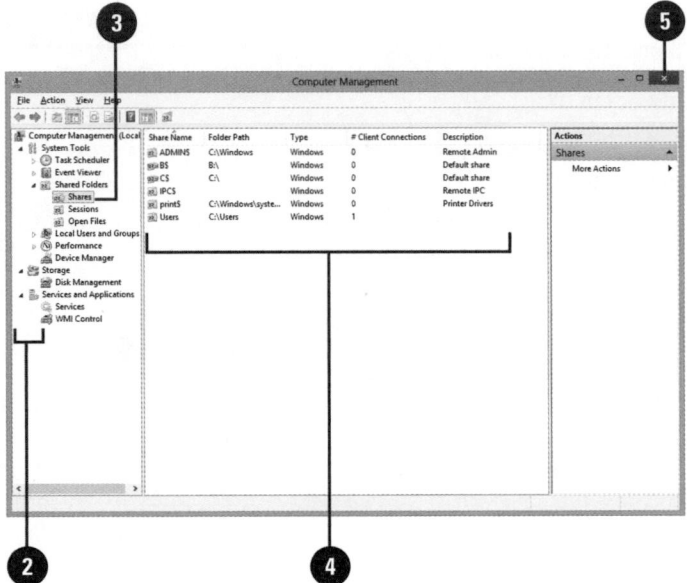

# Managing Disks

The Storage node in the Computer Management window provides you with tools, such as Disk Defragmenter and Disk Management, to help you manage your disks. The Disk Management tool is a graphical tool for managing disks that allows you to partition unallocated portions of your disks into volumes. A **volume** is a fixed amount of storage on a disk. A single disk can contain more than one volume, or a volume can span part of one or more disks. Each volume on a disk is assigned its own drive letter, which is why the term volume is often synonymous with the term drive. Thus, the same physical disk might contain two volumes. Each volume can use a different file system, so you might have a single disk partitioned into two volumes, each with its own file system. You might partition a single hard disk in two different ways: first, with a single NTFS volume, and second, with one NTFS volume and one FAT volume, which can be helpful if you have a PC with two operating systems, Windows 98/Me on the FAT volume and Windows 8.1 on the NTFS volume.

## View Disk Settings

① In the App screen, click or tap the **Computer Management** tile.

◆ With Show administrative tools enabled on the Tiles panel.

② Click or tap the arrow next to **Storage**.

③ Click or tap **Disk Management**.

**TIMESAVER** *To open Disk Management, right-click or tap-hold the lower left-corner of the screen, and then click or tap Disk Management.*

The volumes on your computer display in the right pane.

④ Click or tap the drive you want to modify.

⑤ Click or tap the **Action** menu, point to **All Tasks**, and then click or tap a command, such as **Format**, **Change Drive Letter and Paths**, **Mark Partition as Active**, or **Delete Volume**.

⑥ When you're done, click or tap the **Close** button.

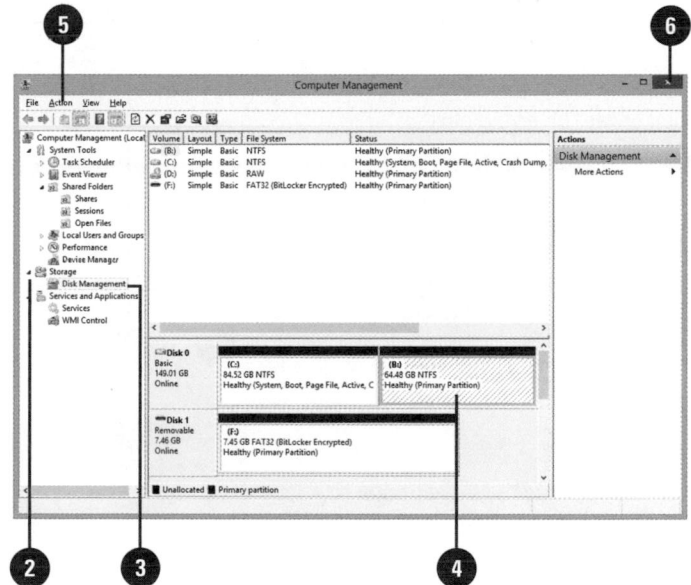

# Managing Local Users and Groups

In Windows, you can manage the access privileges and permissions of local user and group accounts. A local user account is an individual account with a unique set of permissions, while a group account is a collection of individual accounts with the same set of permissions. You can change local user and group accounts in the Computer Management window using the Local Users And Groups tool. This security feature limits individual users and groups from accessing and deleting files, using programs such as Backup, or making accidental or intentional system-wide changes. You can create or modify a user account, disable or activate a user account, identify members of groups, and add or delete members to and from groups.

## Manage Local Users and Groups

1. In the App screen, click or tap the **Computer Management** tile.

   ◆ With Show administrative tools enabled on the Tiles panel.

2. Click or tap the arrow next to **System Tools**.

3. Click or tap the arrow next to **Local Users and Groups**.

4. Click or tap the **Users** or **Groups** folder.

5. Double-click or double-tap the account you want to change.

6. Change the settings you want; add members if requested.

7. Click or tap **OK**.

   You can continue to change other settings.

8. When you're done, click or tap the **Close** button.

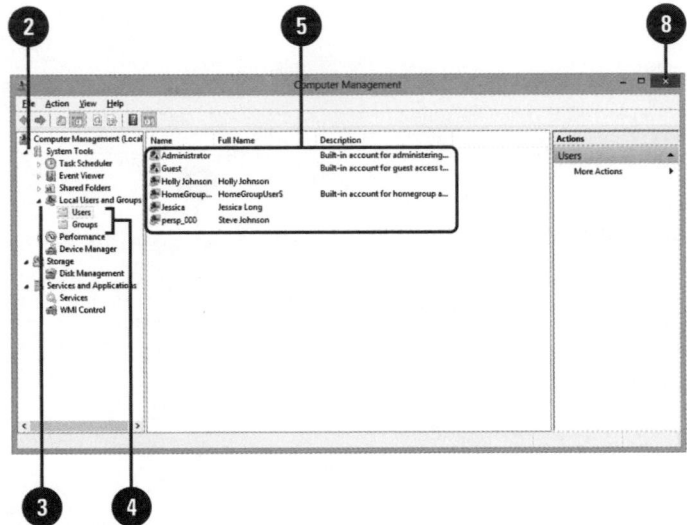

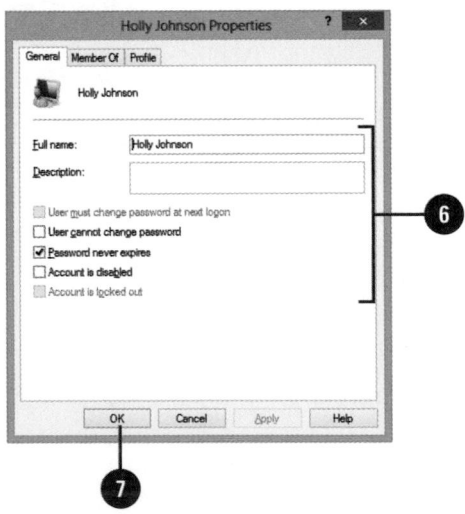

# Viewing and Saving System Information

If you are having problems with Windows 8.1 or a program installed on your PC and can't figure out what to do, you can use System Information to locate valuable information for a support technician. For most people, the information in System Information is difficult to understand. However, if a support technician asks you for information about your system, you know where to find it. After you find the information, you can save and send it to the support technician.

## View and Save System Information

1. In the App screen, click or tap the **System Information** tile.
   - With Show administrative tools enabled on the Tiles panel.

2. Click or tap **System Summary** to view the main information about your system.

3. Click or tap a plus sign (+) to view a system area.

4. Click or tap the item you want to view.

5. Click or tap the **File** menu, and then click or tap **Save**.

6. Select a folder.

7. Type a name for the file.

8. Click or tap **Save**.

9. When you're done, click or tap the **Close** button.

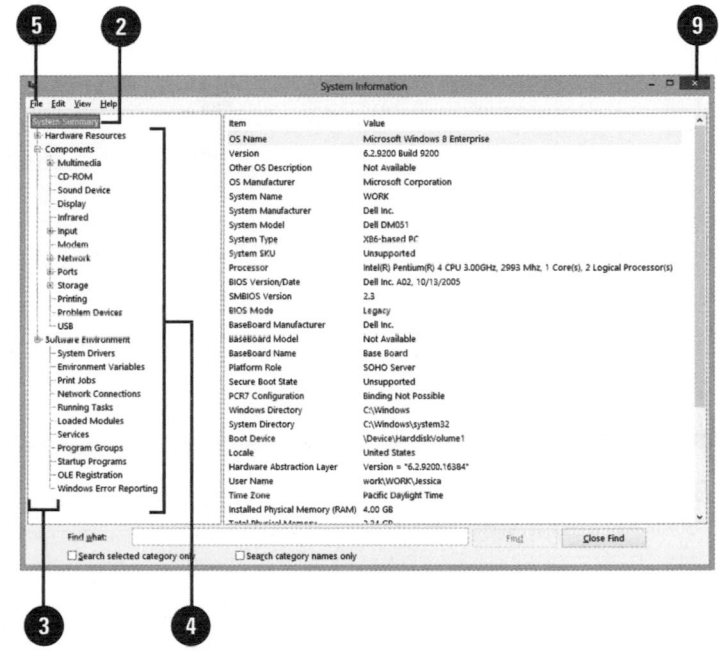

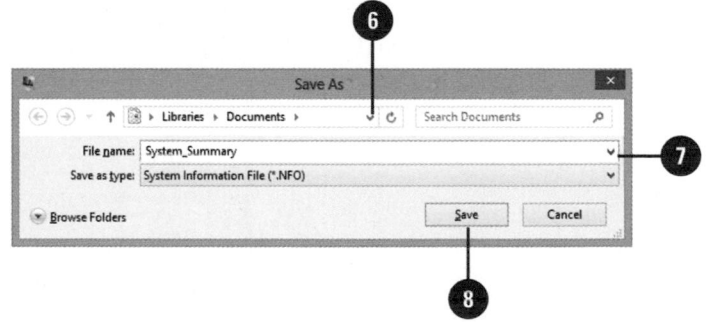

### Did You Know?

*You can display basic system information.* In the App screen, click or tap This PC, and then click or tap the System Properties button on the Computer tab. The basic information about your PC includes system rating, processor, memory (RAM), system type, network information, and Windows activation.

# Setting System Configuration Options

If you're experiencing problems with your system, you can use the System Configuration tool from Administrator Tools to help you troubleshoot and configure your PC. To help you troubleshoot your system, you can select an option to start Windows 8.1 with a minimal set of resources, which can help you successfully boot and narrow down the problem. After you reboot successfully, you can start to select services and startup items to add them into the equation and determine what works and what doesn't. If you need to launch an administrator tool during the process, you can do it from the Tools tab.

## Change System Configuration Options

1. In the App screen, click or tap the **System Configuration** tile.

   ◆ With Show administrative tools enabled on the Tiles panel.

2. Click or tap the **General** tab.

3. To change the way Windows starts up, click or tap the option you want: Normal, Diagnostic, or Selective.

4. Click or tap the tab with the options you want to change:

   ◆ **Boot.** Select options to perform a safe boot.

   ◆ **Services.** Select what services (code segments) start up.

   ◆ **Startup.** Select what programs start when Windows starts.

   ◆ **Tools.** Launch an administrator related tool.

5. When you're done, click or tap the **OK** button.

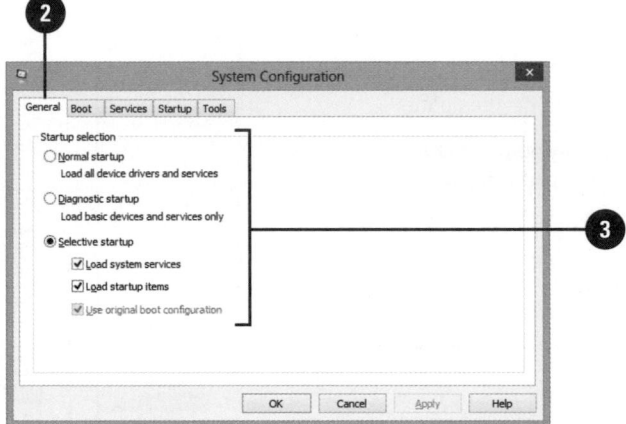

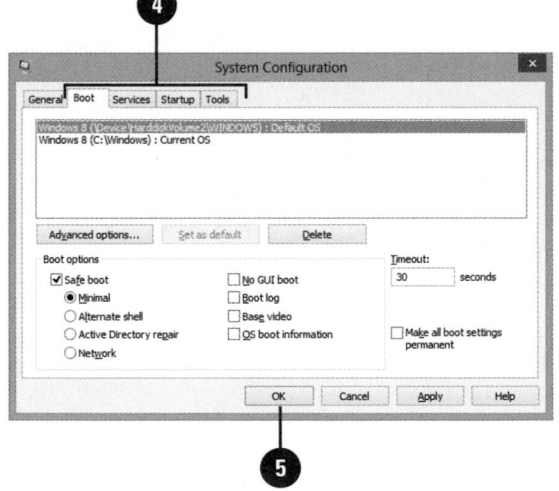

# Appendix: Installing Windows 8.1

**A**

## Introduction

If you're upgrading to Windows 8.1 from a previous version of Windows, this appendix describes how to prepare and install Windows 8.1. The temptation is to insert the Windows 8.1 install disc or download the software and start the installation, but you can avoid problems by making sure your system is ready for Windows 8.1. Before you install Windows 8.1 for the first time, you need to check your system hardware and software and make several setup decisions that relate to your system. The Windows 8.1 Setup wizard walks you through the installation process.

Microsoft is continually updating and enhancing Windows 8. Instead of releasing multiple updates individually, periodically Microsoft releases an update, known as a Service Pack (SP), which provides all-in-one access to the most up-to-date drivers, tools, enhancements, and other critical updates. Service packs, as well as, individual updates are available free for download and installation over the Internet using Windows Update. Windows 8.1 is a free service pack release for Windows 8 users.

If you purchased a new computer or mobile device that came with Windows 8.1 already installed on it, you can use the Windows Easy Transfer wizard to transfer the files and customized settings from your old system to your new one.

After you install or upgrade to Windows 8.1, you can use the Help+Tips app on the Start screen to help you get started with Windows 8.1 as well as describe what's new.

## What You'll Do

**Prepare to Install Windows 8.1**

**Install Windows 8.1**

**Update Windows 8.1**

**Reinstall Windows 8.1**

**Use Windows to Go**

**Transfer Files and Settings from Another PC**

**Get Help+Tips for Windows 8.1**

# Preparing to Install Windows 8.1

The Windows 8.1 Setup wizard guides you through many of the choices you need to make, but there are some decisions and actions you need to make before you start the wizard. To ensure a successful installation, do the following:

**Make sure your hardware components meet the minimum requirements.** Your system hardware needs to meet the following minimum hardware requirements to be Windows 8.1 PC Capability Ready:

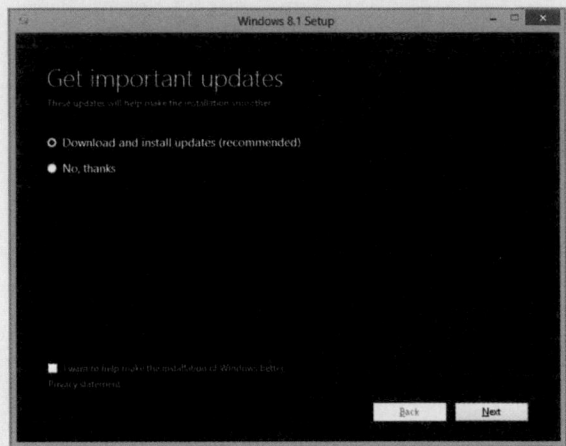

- 1 GHz 32-bit (x86) or 64-bit (x64) processor.

- 1 GB for 32-bit or 2 GB for 64-bit of system memory.

- 16 GB for 32-bit or 20 GB for 64-bit available hard disk space.

- DirectX 9 graphics device with WDDM 1.0 or later.

- For touch, a tablet or a monitor that support multitouch.

- For Windows Store, active Internet connection and a screen resolution of at least 1024 x 768.

- For snap apps, a screen resolution of at least 1366 x 768.

- For Windows Media Center, download from Microsoft as an separate file or as part of Windows 8.1 Pro Pack.

Beyond the basic requirements, some software and hardware services, such as networking, voice and video, and sound playback, call for you to meet additional requirements; see Windows 8.1 documentation for specific details.

**Make sure your hardware and software are compatible using the Windows 8.1 Upgrade Assistant.** If you are running a Windows 7-based system, you can run the Windows 8.1 Upgrade Assistant, which scans your system and creates an easy-to-understand report of all known system, device, and program compatibility issues, and recommends ways to resolve them. Upgrade Assistant can also help you choose the edition of Windows 8.1 that best fits the way you want to use your system. The Upgrade Assistant software is available on the Microsoft web site at *www.microsoft.com*, and then search for *Windows 8.1 Upgrade Assistant.*

**Make sure you have the required product key information.** On the back of the Windows 8.1 DVD packaging is a unique 25-character product key, such as KFEPC-12345-MHORY-12345-IROFE, that you need after installation to activate and use Windows 8.1. Keep the product key in a safe place, and do not share it with others. Product activation and product registration are not the same. Product activation is required and ensures that each Windows product is not installed on more than the limited number of systems allowed in the software's end user license agreement. Activation is completely anonymous and requires no personal identification information to complete. When Windows needs activation, it displays "Activate Windows. Go to

PC settings to activate windows." in the lower-right corner of the screen. To complete the activation process, you enter your unique 25-character product key in PC settings under Activate Windows after you complete the Windows 8.1 installation process. You have a 30-day grace period in which to activate your Windows product installation. If the grace period expires and you have not completed activation, all features will stop working except the product activation feature. After activation, if you need to change the product key, you can do so in PC settings under PC and devices and PC info (**New!**), where you can also view information about your PC, such as product ID, processor, installed RAM, system type, pen and touch device, and Windows edition.

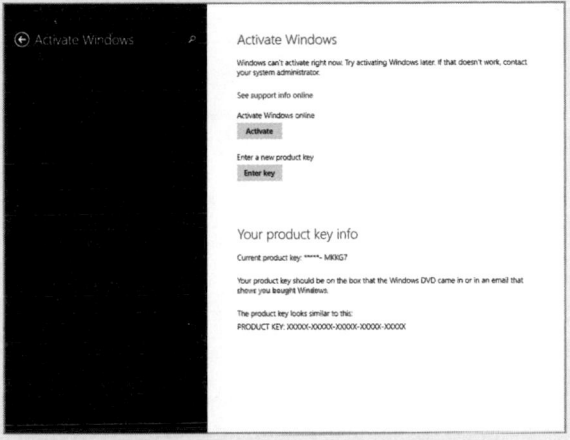

**Determine whether you want to perform an in-place upgrade or install a new copy of Windows 8.1.** After you start the Windows 8.1 Setup wizard, you need to decide whether to upgrade your current operating system or to perform an entirely new installation, known as a **clean install**. A clean install includes completely erasing your hard drive and reformatting it with a new file system, which eliminates incompatibilities and makes your system run better. Before you perform a clean install, you need to backup your files and settings on a CD or DVD, removable, or network drive before you begin. After a clean install you still need to re-install all of your programs. Windows 8 or Windows 7 provides the best upgrade path and brings everything with it, including Windows settings, personal files, and apps. For Windows 8, you can simply use Windows Update to install Windows 8.1. For Windows 7, you need to use the Windows 8.1 Setup wizard. Earlier Windows operating systems, such as Windows XP and Windows

Vista, are not supported for upgrading, so those users will need to perform a clean install.

**Back up your files in case you need to restore your current operating system.** If you're upgrading from an earlier version of Windows or performing a clean install, you should back up your current files so you can correct any problems that might arise during the installation. You can back up files to a removable disk, a DVD-R or DVD-RW drive, a USB drive, or another system on your network. See Chapter 16, *"Maintaining Your Computer,"* starting on page 443 for more information.

**Make sure you have the required network information.** If you are connecting to a network, you need the following information from your network administrator: name of your system, name of the workgroup or domain, and a TCP/IP address if your network doesn't use a DHCP (Dynamic Host Configuration Protocol) server. If you are not sure whether you are connecting to a workgroup or a domain, select the workgroup option. You can always connect to a domain after you install Windows 8.1 Professional.

# Installing Windows 8.1

The Windows 8.1 Setup wizard guides you step-by-step through the process of installing Windows 8.1. When the installation is finished, you are ready to log on to Windows 8.1. Be aware that your system restarts several times during the installation process. There are two main types of installations: upgrade (keep settings and files) or clean (nothing). If you perform an upgrade or clean install on a Windows version, you simply start your system and insert the Windows 8.1 installation DVD or use a downloaded version to start the Windows 8.1 Setup wizard. However, if you perform a clean install on a nonsupported operating system or a blank hard disk, you need to start your system by inserting the Windows 8.1 installation DVD into the DVD drive, which starts the Windows 8.1 Setup wizard. A clean install requires you to select additional options as you step through the wizard, but the steps are basically the same.

## Install Windows 8.1

1. Insert the Windows 8.1 installation disc into your DVD drive, and then start your system, if necessary.

   ◆ If you downloaded the Windows setup file from the web, double-click or double-tap the file to start the installation.

2. Click or tap an option whether to go online to get important updates for the installation.

3. Click or tap the **I accept the license terms** check box, and then click or tap **Accept** to continue.

4. Click or tap an option (**New!**) to **Keep Windows settings, personal files, and apps**, **Keep personal files only**, or **Nothing**, and then click **Next**.

5. Click or tap **Install**.

6. Wait while Setup copies and installs Windows 8.1 on your system. Your system might reboot several times during this process.

7. As prompted, select the initial Windows options (**New!**) you want; options vary depending on the installation type.

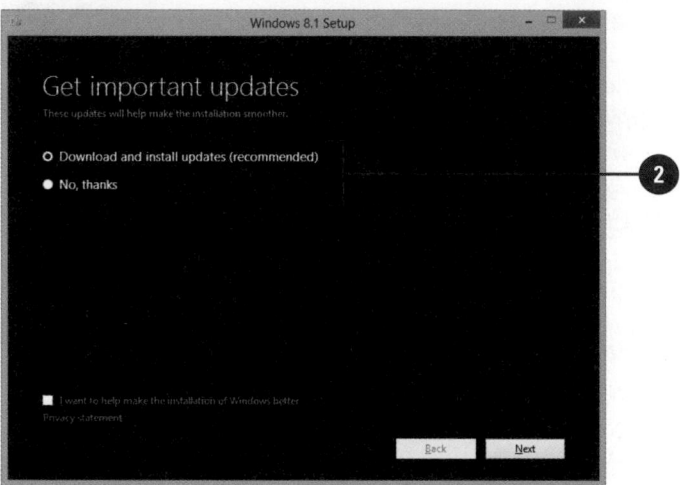

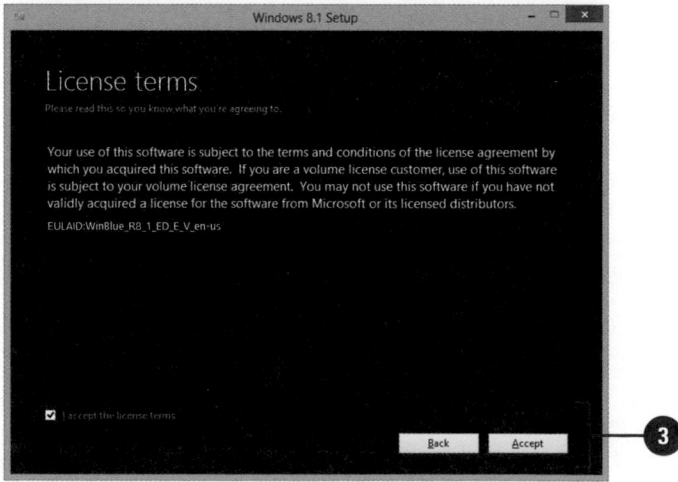

- ◆ **Region and Language.** Select country or region, app language, keyboard, and time zone, and then click or tap **Next**.

- ◆ **Personalize.** Select color scheme, enter a name for your PC, and then click or tap **Next**.

- ◆ **Wireless.** Click or tap a wireless connection, select the **Connect automatic-ally** check box, click or tap **Connect**, enter a password, and then click or tap **Connect**.

- ◆ **Settings.** Click or tap **Use express settings** (recommended) or **Customize**.

- ◆ **Sign in to your PC.** Enter your Microsoft account email, click or tap **Next**, enter a password, and then click or tap **Next**.

- ◆ **Add security info.** Specify a phone number and alternate email, and then click or tap **Next**.

- ◆ **Security code.** Specify an email address, click or tap **Next**, enter the security code (**New!**), and then click or tap **Next**.

- ◆ **Sync settings.** If prompted, set options to sync/copy from another PC, and then click or tap **Next**.

8 Wait while Setup configures and prepares Windows 8.1.

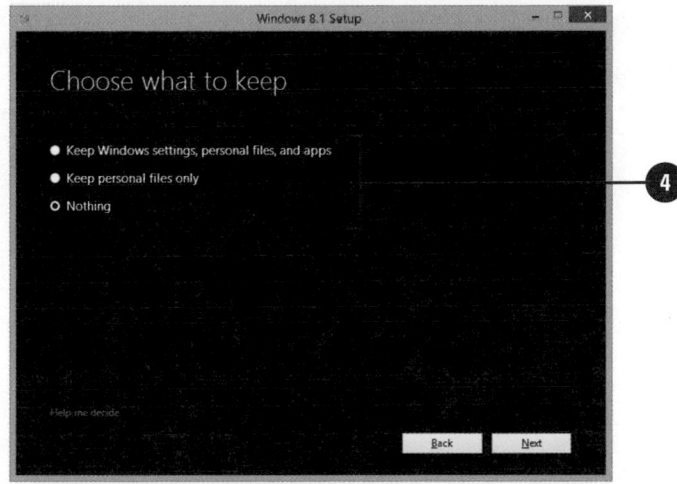

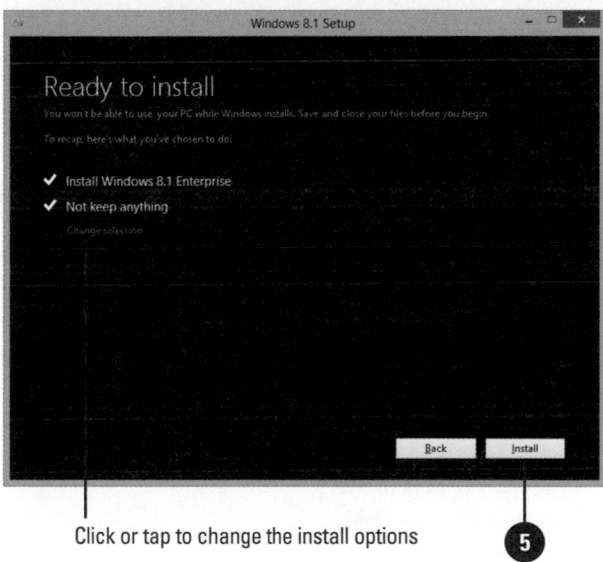

Click or tap to change the install options

## Did You Know?

***You can check the compatibility of your system for Windows 8.1.***
The Upgrade Assistant software is available at *www.microsoft.com*. Search for Windows 8 Upgrade Assistant. You can also go to the Compatibility Center for Window 8 to check for your apps and devices.

# Updating Windows 8.1

Microsoft is continually updating and enhancing Windows 8. Instead of releasing multiple updates individually, periodically Microsoft releases an update, known as a Service Pack (SP), which provides all-in-one access to the most up-to-date drivers, tools, enhancements, and other critical updates. Windows 8.1 is a free service pack (**New!**) release for Windows 8 users. Service packs as well as individual updates are available free for download and installation over the Internet using Windows Update. With Windows Update, Microsoft makes it easy to securely download and install this important update over the Internet. You can check for and install updates in PC settings (**New!**) or Control Panel. After you complete the installation, turn on Automatic Updates to help you keep your system up-to-date and secure. If you're experiencing problems with the service pack and need to reinstall it again, you can uninstall (or remove) it from your system using Programs and Features in the Control Panel.

## Install Updates in Control Panel

1. In the Start screen, click or tap the **Apps view** button, and then click or tap **Control Panel**.

2. Click or tap the **Windows Update** icon in Small icons or Large icons view.

3. In the left pane, click or tap **Check for updates**, and then wait for the update scan to complete.

4. If you need to install any important or optional updates, click or tap the link.

5. Select the check boxes next to the service pack or any other updates you want to install.

6. Click or tap **OK**.

7. Click or tap **Install updates**.

8. If prompted, review the End User License Agreement, click or tap **I accept the license terms** option, and then click or tap **Finish**.

   Wait for the updates to be installed on your system.

9. If prompted, follow any further instructions and restart your system as needed.

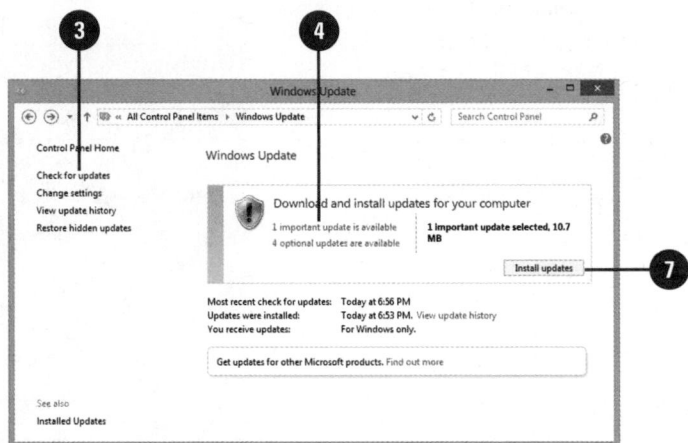

## Install Updates in PC Settings

1. Display the Start screen.

2. Point to the lower- or upper-right corner and move up or down (on a computer) or swipe left from the right edge of the screen (on a mobile device).

3. Click or tap the **Settings** button on the Charms bar.

4. Click or tap **Change PC settings** on the Settings panel, and then click or tap **Update and recovery**.

5. Click or tap **Windows Update** under Update and recovery.

6. Click or tap **Check now**; if available, click or tap the **View details** link (**New!**), and then click or tap **Install** (**New!**).

7. To close the app, point to the top edge of the screen (cursor changes to a hand), and then drag down to the bottom edge of the screen.

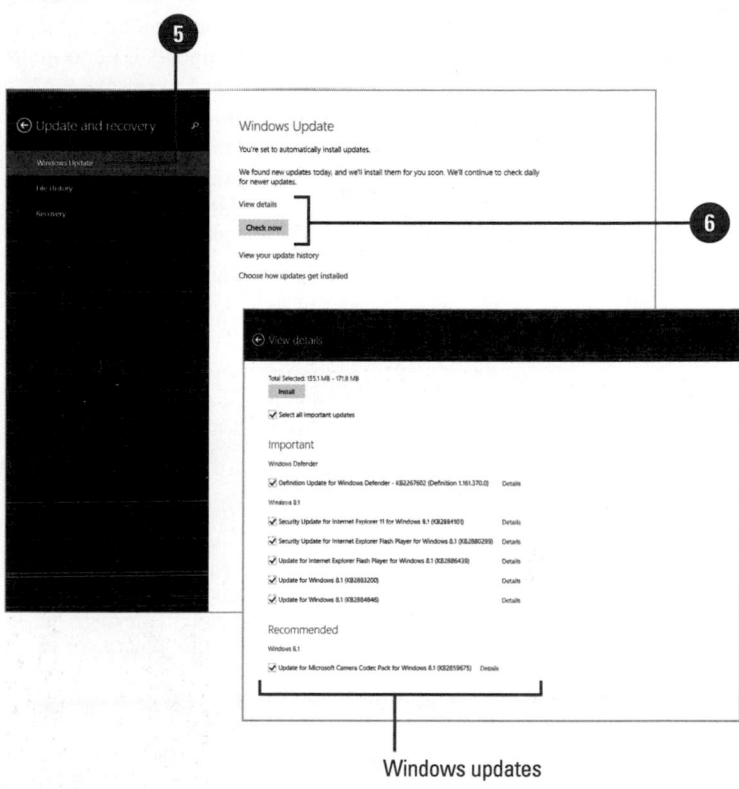

Windows updates

## Uninstall Updates

1. In the Start screen, click or tap the **Apps view** button, and then click or tap **Control Panel**.

2. Click or tap the **Programs and Features** icon in Small icons or Large icons view.

3. In the left pane, click or tap **View installed updates**.

4. Select the service pack or update you want to uninstall.

5. Click or tap **Uninstall**.

6. Click or tap **Yes** to confirm the removal, follow the instructions, and then click or tap **OK**.

7. Click or tap the **Close** button.

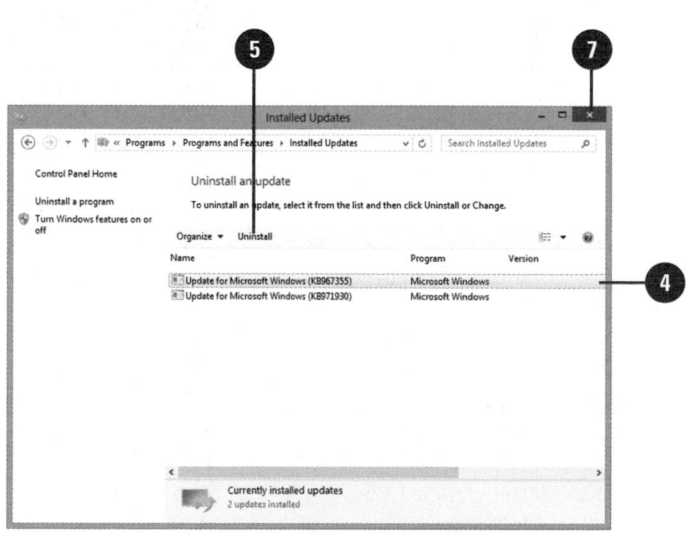

# Reinstalling Windows 8.1

In PC settings under PC and devices in Updates and recovery, you can set options to refresh (reinstall), reset (new install), or restart the Windows 8.1 operating system. If your system is not running very well, you can refresh the Windows software without affecting your personal files. If you want to start over from scratch with a new Windows installation, you can reset your system to the factory settings. If you want to start up from a device such as a USB or DVD, change Windows startup settings, or restore Windows from a system image (.iso), you can restart Windows from a Restart screen.

## Reinstall, Reset, or Restart Windows 8.1

1. Display the Start screen.

2. Point to the lower- or upper-right corner and move up or down (on a computer) or swipe left from the right edge of the screen (on a mobile device).

3. Click or tap the **Settings** button on the Charms bar.

4. Click or tap **Change PC settings** on the Settings panel, and then click or tap **Update and recovery**.

5. Click or tap **Recovery** under Update and recovery.

6. Specify the options you want:

   ◆ **Refresh your PC without affecting your files.** Click or tap **Get started**, and then follow the wizard instructions to reinstall Windows (keeps your files).

   ◆ **Remove everything and reinstall Windows.** Click or tap **Get started**, and then follow the wizard instructions to reinstall Windows (deletes your files).

   ◆ **Advanced startup.** Click or tap **Restart now** to restart up from a device or disc, change Windows startup settings, or restore a system image (ISO); choose an option from the Restart screen.

# Using Windows To Go

If you are using Windows 8.1 Enterprise Edition, you can create a Windows To Go workspace that allows you to install Windows 8.1 on a USB 3.0 or compatible device with 32 GB or more of space and then use it on a system when you need it. In order to create a Windows To go workspace, you need a Windows 8.1 image file (with the .wim extension; built with Microsoft Deployment Toolkit or extract *install.wim* from a Windows DVD install disc), which Windows To Go will typically find for you. You can insert and use the USB drive with Windows To Go on a system with Windows 7 or 8.1. Windows To Go consists of the Windows 8.1 operating system and all the files, folders, and apps that are copied to the USB drive. When you're done, shut down the Windows To Go workspace, remove the drive (after the shut down is complete), and then restart.

## Install Windows on a USB Drive

1. Insert a USB 3.0 drive with at least 32 GB into a USB port.

2. In the Start screen, click or tap the **Apps view** button, and then click or tap **Control Panel**.

3. Click or tap the **Windows To Go** icon in Small icons or Large icons view.

4. Select the USB drive, and then click or tab **Next** to continue.

5. Select the Windows image file (.wim) drive, and then click or tab **Next** to continue.

6. Click or tap **Skip**, or select the **Use BitLocker with my Windows To Go workspace** check box, specify passwords, and then click or tab **Next** to continue.

   The USB drive will be reformatted; any data on the USB drive will be deleted.

7. Click or tap **Create**.

8. Select a **Yes** or **No** option to automatically reboot from the USB drive.

9. Click or tap **Save and restart** or **Save and close**.

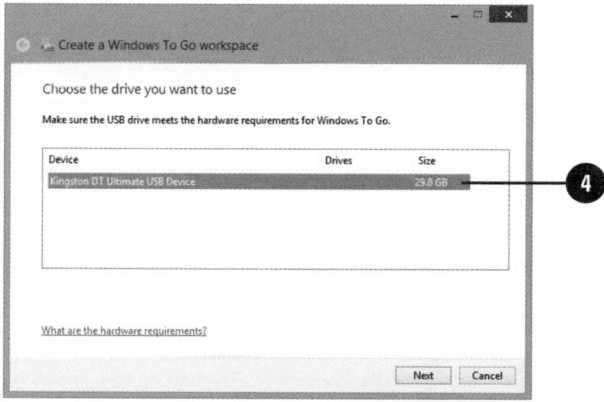

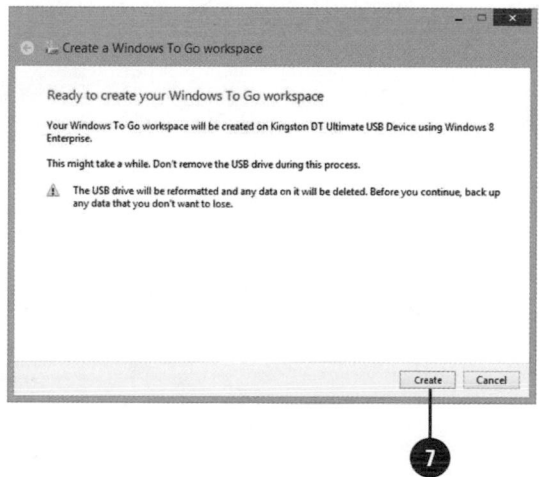

# Transferring Files and Settings from Another PC

Instead of trying to re-create Windows settings manually from an old PC (running Windows 7, 8, or RT) on a new Windows 8.1 PC, you can use Windows Easy Transfer. If you have a removable hard drive, such as an external hard disk or USB flash drive, you can use Windows Easy Transfer to transfer files and settings for Windows 7 or 8, such as user accounts, desktop and display properties, and browser and e-mail setup options. It transfers only files for Windows RT. Windows Easy Transfer is not meant for transferring your programs. It's important to note that you can't transfer files from a Windows 64-bit version to a 32-bit version. The options to use an Easy Transfer Cable (a direct connect cable) or network with a transfer key found in earlier versions are no longer supported in Windows 8.1; you can only transfer to Windows 8.1, not from it to another PC (it's only a one-way street).

## Prepare the Old PC

1. Start Windows Easy Transfer on the old PC:
   - ◆ **Windows 8/RT.** Click or tap the **Windows Easy Transfer** tile on the Apps screen.
   - ◆ **Windows 7.** Click or tap the **Start** button, point to **All Programs**, click or tap **Accessories**, click or tap **System Tools**, and then click or tap **Windows Easy Transfer**.

2. Read the welcome screen, and then click or tap **Next** to continue.

3. Click or tap **An external hard disk or USB flash drive**.

4. Click or tap **This is my old PC**.

5. Follow the on-screen instructions to select files and settings to transfer, specify a password, and then save the transfer file.

6. Click or tap **Next** to complete it, and then click or tap **Close**.

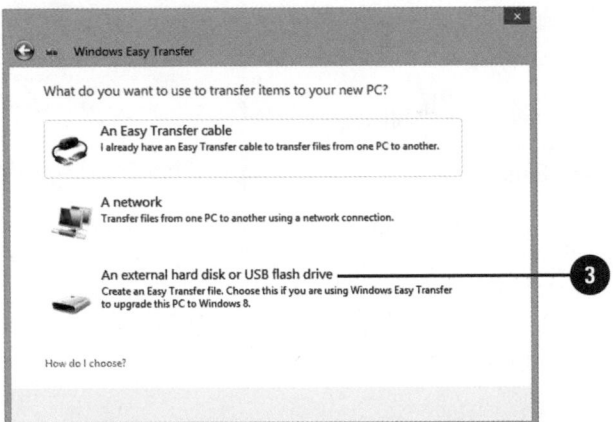

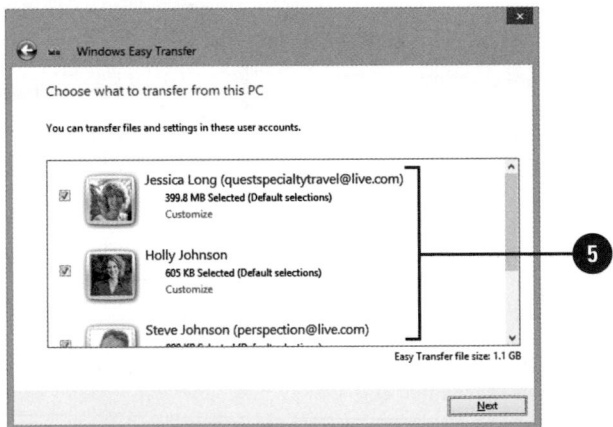

## Transfer Files and Settings to the New System

**1** On the new Windows 8.1 system, display the Start screen, click or tap the **Apps view** button, and then click or tap **Windows Easy Transfer**.

**2** Read the welcome screen, and then click or tap **Next** to continue.

**3** Click or tap **Yes** to select the file with your saved files from your old PC.

**4** Navigate to and select the transfer file (with the .mig extension), and then click or tap **Open**.

**5** Enter your protection password for the file, and then click or tap **Next**.

**6** Click or tap **Transfer** to start the transfer process.

**7** Follow any additional on-screen instructions to complete the process. to view transfer reports, click or tap any of the following:

- **See What was Transferred.**

- **See a List of Apps You Might Want to Install on Your New PC.**

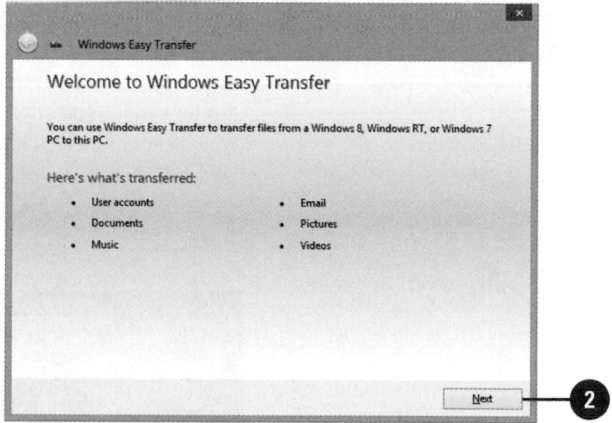

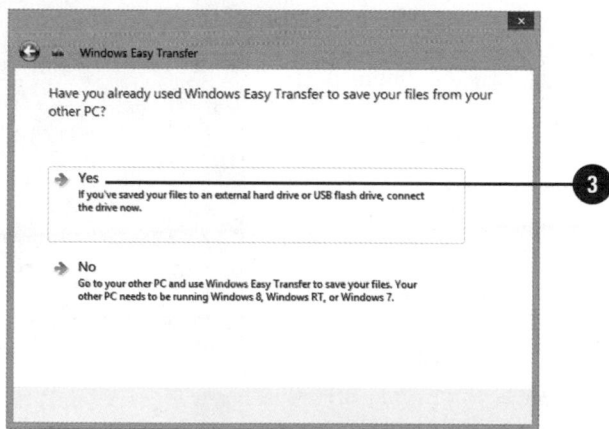

# Getting Help+Tips for Windows 8.1

If you're upgrading to Windows 8.1 from Windows 7 or earlier, the user interface is very different and navigating can be a little confusing for first timers until you get the hang of it. To help you get started, you can use the Help+Tips app (**New!**) on the Start screen. You can view any of the following topics (**New!**): Start and apps, Get around, Basic actions, Your account and files, settings, and What's new. Along with the topics, you can also click or tap links or perform a search to access more info on Windows.com.

## Get Help+Tips for Windows 8.1

1. Click or tap the **Help+Tips** tile on the Start screen.

2. Click or tap a tile for any of the Help+Tips topics.

   ◆ **Start and apps.** Find out about the Start screen and getting apps from the Windows Store.

   ◆ **Get around.** Find out about navigating in Windows 8.1.

   ◆ **Basic actions.** Find out about search, share, print, and more.

   ◆ **Your account and files.** Find out about Microsoft accounts and files on This PC and SkyDrive.

   ◆ **Settings.** Find out about PC settings.

   ◆ **What's new.** Find out about what's new in Windows 8.1

3. Read the information on the topic; scroll as needed.

   ◆ **Windows.com.** Click or tap links or use the Search box to find out more online using your default browser.

4. To go back to the Home screen, click or tap the **Back** button.

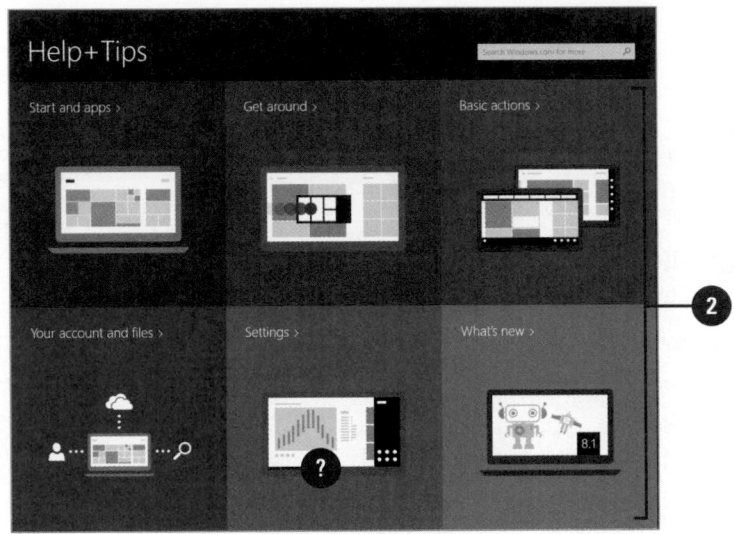

Search box for Windows.com

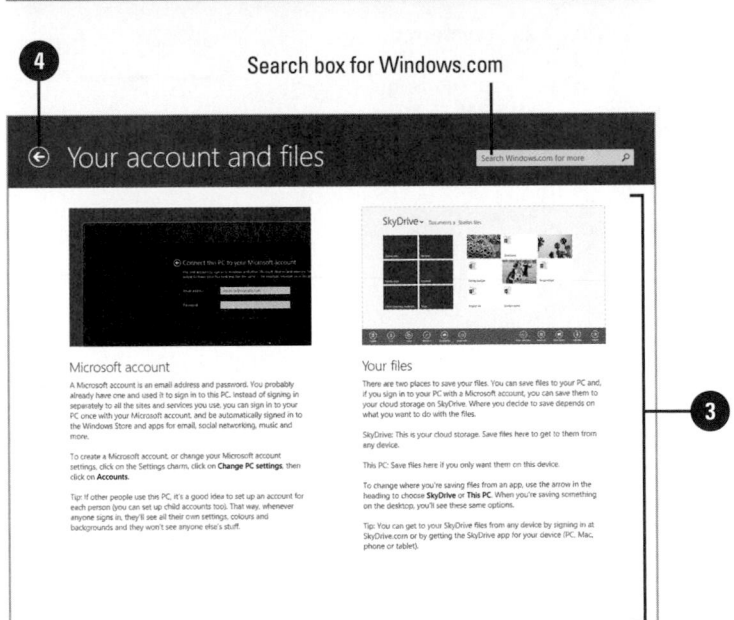

> ## See Also
>
> *See "Using Windows Help and Support" on page 18 for information on getting more online and local help and support information from Microsoft.*

# New! Features

## Microsoft Windows 8.1

Microsoft Windows 8.1 comes with new features that make your PC computer or mobile device significantly easier and faster to use than earlier versions of Windows. Windows 8.1 makes it easier to use the Start screen, open files and programs, find information, and accomplish other common tasks, such as browse the Internet, scan and view pictures, play music and videos, and change settings. Windows 8.1 enhances the metro user experience with new apps, including Alarms, Calculator, Food & Drink, Health & Fitness, Help+Tips, Reading List, Scan, and Skype.

## Only New Features

If you're already familiar with Microsoft Windows 8, you can access and download all the tasks in this book with Microsoft Windows 8.1 New Features to help make your transition to the new version simple and smooth. The Microsoft Windows 8.1 New Features, as well as other Windows 8 to 8 transition helpers, are available on the web at *www.perspection.com*.

## What's New

If you're searching for what's new in Windows 8.1, just look for the icon: **New!**. The new icon appears in the table of contents and throughout this book so you can quickly and easily identify a new or improved feature in Windows 8.1. The following is a brief description of each new feature, and it's location in this book.

## Windows 8.1

- ◆ **Windows8.1 N Editions (p. 2, 215)** If you live in an European Economic Area, the above editions have an N, which doesn't include media apps—Windows Media Player, Camera, Music, and Video; you need to download them from the Microsoft web site or other ones from a third-party.

- ◆ **Apps View (p. 6-7, 24-27, 268)** The Apps view button allows you to view all your apps on the Apps screen and return to the Start screen. In the Apps screen, you can sort your apps by name, date installed, most used, or category, and use the Search box or simply typing text from the Start screen to find apps.

- ◆ **Start Screen Options (p. 6-7)** You can customize the Start screen by changing options in the Taskbar and Navigation properties dialog box.

◆ **Corner Navigation Options (p. 6-7, 302)** In PC settings under Corner and edges, you can enable or disable pointing to the upper-right corner to show charms or clicking the upper-left corner to switch between my recent apps.

◆ **Start Button (p. 8, 10-12)** The Start button appears at the bottom of the Start bar and on the left side of the Taskbar desktop) to switch to the Start screen.

◆ **Touch Keyboard (p. 13)** When you type on the touch keyboard, it shows suggestions above the keyboard you can quickly select. You can also quickly insert numbers with a swipe on the top row of the touch keyboard. In addition, emoji character symbols are in color for easier viewing.

◆ **Lock Screen (p. 21, 299, 351)** In the Lock screen, you can answer Skype calls, take photos or see a slide show of your photos without having to unlock it first. You can customize the Lock screen by changing it's picture, displaying status, showing alarms, playing a slide show, or using a camera.

◆ **Power User Menu (p. 21)** When you right-click the Start button, a power user menu appears with computer options. You can use it to shutdown or sign out.

◆ **Power and Sleep Options (p. 22)** In PC settings under Power and sleep, you can specify how long your screen waits before it turns off or goes to sleep to save power.

◆ **New Metro Apps (p. 28, 177-190, 209, 248, 249, 252, 259, 286, 442, 522)** Windows 8.1 comes with new metro apps, including Alarms, Calculator, Food & Drink, Health & Fitness, Help+Tips, Reading List, Scan, and Skype.

◆ **Start Multiple Apps (p. 29)** Some metro apps allow you to start multiple instances.

◆ **Close Apps (p. 29)** When you close an app, it's no longer active; however it's put to sleep, or tombstoned, to run in the background. When you reopen a tombstoned app, you can start where you left off.

◆ **Minimized App Bar (p. 30)** Some apps, such as Calendar, display a minimized App bar with three dots, which you can click or tap to expand and display it.

◆ **Side by Side Apps (p. 33)** The snap feature enables you to display up to four apps side by side. The number of apps you can use depends on your display resolution; four apps need a large screen resolution of 2,560 x 1,600.

◆ **PC Settings (p. 35, 298, 313, 326, 334)** PC settings has been reorganized and more options (many from the Control Panel) have been added to change Windows settings. When you open PC settings, the Personalize screen appears with links to access personalization options and recently used settings.

◆ **Windows Store (p. 36-37)** The redesigned Windows Store organizes apps by categories to make apps easy to find and discover. If you're looking for a specific app, you can use Search box. If you have a gift card or promotional code you can redeem it in Settings under Accounts.

◆ **Customize Start Screen (p. 40-41, 300)** When you install an app, it appears on the Apps screen, which allows you to customize the Start screen with the apps you want. You can use options on the Personalize panel (instead of PC settings) to use the same background on the Start screen as your desktop screen.

- **Resize Tiles on Start Screen** (p. 42-43)  On the Start screen, you can resize tiles to large, wide, medium, or small at any time. After you organize your apps into a group, you can name each group for easy identification.

- **Notification Options** (p. 44)  In Notification settings, you can specify a quiet time to stop notifications and calls when you're away.

- **Search Options** (p. 45)  In Search settings, you can set options to use Bing to search online, get personalized results from Bing, filter search results, get search suggestions for metered connections.

- **Privacy Settings** (p. 46)  In Privacy settings, you can set options for apps, such as Maps, to use privacy information from Windows, such as my name and account picture, my location, my webcam, my microphone, and other devices.

- **Navigation Pane** (p. 48, 60)  The Navigation pane in File Explorer includes SkyDrive to access your online Microsoft SkyDrive cloud drive and This PC (used to be Computer) to access your local PC.

- **This PC Window** (p. 52)  The This PC window (formally Computer) displays local folders and several types of local, removable, and network drives.

- **Libraries** (p. 56-57)  The Documents library, for example, includes files and folders from your Documents—This PC and SkyDrive—folders, which are actually stored in your Users folder.

- **Personal Folder** (p. 58)  The Personal folder includes a SkyDrive folder.

- **SkyDrive in File Explorer** (p. 58, 60, 86, 256)  You can use SkyDrive in File Explorer to share files in a Public folder.

- **File Explorer Layout** (p. 61)  The Panes group on the View tab provides options to show or hide the File Explorer windows layout elements. You can show or hide Libraries in the Navigation pane.

- **View Downloads in IE App** (p. 94)  In the Internet Explorer app, you can view downloads.

- **Reading List in IE App** (p. 96)  If a web page contains article, you can switch to Reading view, which displays the page article for easy reading.

- **Tabs Bar in IE App** (p. 98)  The improved Tab bar allows you to reopen the most recently closed tab. You can also access the Tab bar from the Favorites bar.

- **Share Web Pages in IE App** (p. 100)  From the Favorites bar, you can quickly share web pages using the Share panel from Windows.

- **Search for Web Pages in IE App** (p. 100-101)  The improved Search panel in Windows provides more options to narrow down the search.

- **IE App Options** (p. 102)  You can set options to always show the address bar and tabs, specify a default zoom, set home pages, customize reading view, delete browsing data types, manage passwords, detect phone numbers, and select site font usage and language encoding, and reading direction.

- **Accounts for People App** (p. 136, 138, 146)  You can add contacts to the People app from Sina Weibo. When you delete contacts, you can specify the account.

◆ **Contacts in People App** (p. 140-141)  You can view all contacts or only the ones organized by A to Z. If you can't find it, you can use the Search box.

◆ **Favorites in People App** (p. 143)  Favorites appear on the People app Home screen for easy access along with the Add a Favorites (with Star icon) button to quickly add one or more favorites.

◆ **What's Next in Calendar App** (p. 149, 156)  In the Calendar app, you can adjust the Calendar app Home screen to show events using the What's next. You can customize the background in What's next view with a picture of your choice.

◆ **5-Day Work Week in Calendar App** (p. 149)  You can use the calendar with the Work Week (5-days instead of seven) view.

◆ **View Arrow in Calendar App** (p. 149)  You can use the View list arrow to navigate the calendar.

◆ **Options in Calendar App** (p. 156)  In Calendar options, you can show or hide Forward and Back buttons.

◆ **Folders Pane in Mail App** (p. 159, 162-163, 165)  The Folders pane provides easy access to folders, including Favorites, Flagged messages, Newsletters, and Social Updates (such as Facebook, Twitter, and Linkedin).

◆ **Select Messages in Mail App** (p. 159, 168)  You can use the check boxes (Selection Mode) in the Messages pane to select one or more messages and use the App bar—which automatically appears—to work with messages.

◆ **Draft Messages in Mail App** (p. 164-165)  When you create a new message, Mail designates it as a draft (which you can save) until you send it.

◆ **Formatting Options in Mail App** (p. 166)  You can use added formatting options on the App bar, including Highlight and Hyperlink.

◆ **Open in a Window in Mail App** (p. 166)  If you want to multitask, you can open a message in a side by side window.

◆ **Options in Mail App** (p. 166, 170)  You can set options in the Mail app for the default message text, and whether to group messages by conversation or show messages from sent items in conversations.

◆ **Sweep in Mail App** (p. 174)  If you want to delete messages from a specific person, you can sweep them out (only available for Outlook.com).

◆ **Favorite Contact or Folder in Mail App** (p. 172-173)  If you receive email messages from the same person, you can make them a favorite so you can easily view them from the Folders pane. You can also do the same for folders.

◆ **Skype App** (p. 177-190)  The Skype app replaces the Messaging app. It allows you to make phone call and exchange instant messages over the Internet.

◆ **Navigation in Photos App** (p. 193)  You can use the Location list arrow to navigate to locations, such as Pictures Library or SkyDrive, in the Photos App.

◆ **Edit Images in Photos App** (p. 196-197)  You can use the Photos app to edit and enhance a photo. You can use options to automatically fix images or apply enhancements like rotate, crop, remove red eye, or retouch.

- **Scan App  (p. 209)**   After you connect and install a scanner, you can use the Scanner device in the Devices and Printer window in the Control Panel or start the Scan app in Apps view to scan documents.

- **Get Started Panel  (p. 240-241, 244-245, 246-247, 249)**   In some apps, such as News, Sports, Weather, and Health & Fitness, it comes with a Get Started panel with options, such as take a tour, customize the app, and dismiss the panel.

- **Food & Drink App  (p. 248)**   You can find and view recipes, even using hands-free mode by waving your hand in front of a camera. You can add your own recipe to a collection for easy future reference or add it to your meal planning for the week. If you need ingredients, you can add them to a shopping list.

- **Health & Fitness App  (p. 249)**   You can find and track information on nutrition and calories, exercise, and health, including symptoms, drugs, and conditions.

- **Maps App  (p. 250-251)**   The improved Maps app allows you to add pin points, and search for points of interest, such as places to eat, see, shop, bank, or park.

- **Reading List App  (p. 252)**   If you don't have time to read an article in an app or on the web, you can add it to your Reading List so you can read it later. The Reading List app helps you keep track of and share your articles.

- **Manage Files in SkyDrive  (p. 256-257)**   If you have files on a SkyDrive and not on your PC, you can make them available offline. If you don't want to have SkyDrive files on your PC, you can make them online-only.

- **SkyDrive Settings  (p. 258, 301)**   In PC settings, you can set SkyDrive options to customize the way files and settings are synced to your SkyDrive and devices. In addition, you can turn on or off access to all files offline by opening the SkyDrive app, and displaying Options from the Settings panel.

- **Music App  (p. 264-265)**   The redesigned Music app allows you to create music collections on your PC or in the cloud, and add and play Xbox Music radio stations. You can also personalize your music by creating or importing playlists.

- **Display Options  (p. 309)**   You can change the text size on the display to extra large 200% to go along with the others or let Windows choose the best size.

- **Child Account  (p. 336, 340,356-357)**   The child account is for a person that you want to manage and limit PC use with Family Safety. When you add a child account, it turns on Family Safety, which you can manage in the Control Panel.

- **Local and Online Accounts  (p. 338-339)**   You can switch (disconnect and connect) between local and online accounts by using links in Your account under Accounts in PC settings.

- **Limit Accounts  (p. 341)**   You can limit an account to use only one Windows Store app with by using the assigned access option.

- **Account Picture  (p. 347)**   In PC settings, you change an account picture in the People app.

- **Privacy Options  (p. 370, 374)**   In Internet Explorer, you set options to block content from services that could track your browsing, send Do Not Track requests to sites, block third-party cookies, let sites ask for my physical location, and protect my PC from malware and phishing sites with SmartScreen.

- ◆ **VPN Connection (p. 390-391)** In PC settings, you can set up a VPN (Virtual Private Network) connection.

- ◆ **Proxy Network Settings (p. 396)** Automatic proxy setup is turned on by default to help create network connections, however, if there is a problem, you can manually specify options.

- ◆ **Work Folders (p. 414-415)** Works Folders allow you to make your files available on devices with Win 8.1, RT, and Win 7 or iPad (with additional software)—you use, even when offline, from a file server. Work Folders syncs files from devices to file servers using Windows Server 2012 R2 or later.

- ◆ **Workplace Join (p. 416)** If you want to connect a device—such as a laptop, tablet, or smartphone— to a workplace network, you can use the Workplace options in PC settings. This allows you to join and register the device on your company network using a Windows Server 2012 R2 or later.

- ◆ **3D Printer (p. 418, 420, 424-425)** You can print to 3D printers, which builds physical objects from digital 3D models that you can actually hold.

- ◆ **Windows Update (p. 459)** You can select an option to get updates for other Microsoft products when I update Windows.

- ◆ **File History (p. 462-463)** In PC settings, you can specify advanced settings for File History to specify how often to save copies and how long to keep them.

- ◆ **Mouse and Touchpad Options (p. 480)** In PC settings, you can use Mouse and touchpad options to change the way your mouse works and the way the pointer looks and behaves.

- ◆ **Administrative Tools (p. 494-495)** You can set a Tiles option on the Settings panel to show or hide Administrative Tools on the App screen.

## What Happen To ...

- ◆ **Windows 7 File Recovery** The Windows 7 File Recovery utility in the Control panel has been removed.

- ◆ **Windows Experience Index** The Windows Experience Index in the System utility in the Control panel has been removed.

- ◆ **System Repair Disc** The option to create a system repair disc in the Windows 7 File Recovery utility has been removed. However, you can use the Recovery utility in the Control panel to create a recovery drive with a USB drive.

- ◆ **Performance Information and Tools** The Performance Information and Tools utility in the Control panel has been removed.

- ◆ **Messaging App** The Messaging app has been replaced by the Skype app.

- ◆ **Facebook and Flickr in the Photos App** The integration of Facebook and Flickr photos in the Photos app has been removed.

- ◆ **Windows Easy Transfer** The options to use an Easy Transfer Cable or network with a transfer key are no longer supported in Windows 8.1.

# Index

## X-Z